T0335345

Intelligent and Knowledge-Based Computing for Business and Organizational Advancements

Hideyasu Sasaki
Ritsumeikan University, Japan

Dickson K. W. Chiu
Dickson Computer Systems, Hong Kong

Epaminondas Kapetanios
University of Westminster, UK

Patrick C. K. Hung
University of Ontario Institute of Technology (UOIT), Canada & University of Waterloo, Canada

Frederic Andres
National Institute of Informatics, Japan

Ho-Fung Leung
Chinese University of Hong Kong, China

Richard Chbeir
University of Bourgogne, France

Information Science
REFERENCE

Managing Director:	Lindsay Johnston
Senior Editorial Director:	Heather A. Probst
Book Production Manager:	Sean Woznicki
Development Manager:	Joel Gamon
Development Editor:	Development Editor
Acquisitions Editor:	Erika Gallagher
Typesetter:	Russell A. Spangler
Cover Design:	Nick Newcomer, Lisandro Gonzalez

Published in the United States of America by
   Information Science Reference (an imprint of IGI Global)
   701 E. Chocolate Avenue
   Hershey PA 17033
   Tel: 717-533-8845
   Fax: 717-533-8661
   E-mail: cust@igi-global.com
   Web site: http://www.igi-global.com

Library of Congress Cataloging-in-Publication Data

Intelligent and knowledge-based computing for business and organizational advancements / Hideyasu Sasaki ... [et al.], editors.
     p. cm.
   Includes bibliographical references and index.
   Summary: "This book examines the emerging computing paradigm of Collective Intelligence (CI) and offers the computer and information science communities as it continue to move toward a new period of fully technology-integrated businesses"--Provided by publisher.
     ISBN 978-1-4666-1577-9 (hbk.) -- ISBN 978-1-4666-1578-6 (ebook) -- ISBN 978-1-4666-1579-3 (print & perpetual access) 1. Management information systems. 2. Expert systems (Computer science) 3. Swarm intelligence. I. Sasaki, Hideyasu.
   T58.6.I5779 2012
   658.4'038011--dc23
                              2012002103

British Cataloguing in Publication Data
A Cataloguing in Publication record for this book is available from the British Library.

The views expressed in this book are those of the authors, but not necessarily of the publisher.

Table of Contents

Detailed Table of Contents

Chapter 1

    Epaminondas Kapetanios, University of Westminster, UK

In this article, the author explores the notion of Collective Intelligence (CI) as an emerging computing paradigm. The article is meant to provide a historical and contextual view of CI through the lenses of as many related disciplines as possible (biology, sociology, natural and environmental sciences, physics) in conjunction with the computer science point of view. During this explorative journey, the article also aims at pinpointing the current strengths and weaknesses of CI-related computational and system engineering design and implementation methodologies of CI-based systems. A non-exhaustive list of case studies set up the stage for CI applications as well as challenging research questions. These can be particularly directed towards the Social Web, as a very prominent example of synergistic interactions of a group of people with diverse cultural and professional backgrounds and its potential to become a platform for the emergence of truly CI-based systems.

Chapter 2

    Dickson K.W. Chiu, Dickson Computer Systems, Hong Kong

    Shing-Chi Cheung, Hong Kong University of Science and Technology, Hong Kong

    Sven Till, Hong Kong University of Science and Technology, Hong Kong

    Lalita Narupiyakul, University of Ontario Institute of Technology, Canada

    Patrick C. K. Hung, University of Ontario Institute of Technology, Canada

In a business-to-business (B2B) e-service environment, cross-organizational collaboration is important for attaining the interoperability of business processes and their proper enactment. The authors find that B2B collaboration can be divided into multiple layers and perspectives, which has not been adequately addressed in the literature. Besides regular e-service process enactment, robust collaboration requires enforcement, while quality collaboration involves relationship management. These problems are challenging, as they require the enactment of business processes and their monitoring in counter parties outside an organization's boundary. This paper presents a framework for B2B process collaboration with three layers, namely, collaboration requirements layer, business rule layer, and system implementation layer. The collaboration requirements layer specifies the cross-organizational requirements of e-service processes. In the business rule layer, detailed knowledge of these three types of process collaboration requirements is defined as business rules in a unified Event-Condition-Action (ECA) form. In the system implementation layer, event collaboration interfaces are supported by contemporary Enterprise JavaBeans and Web Services. Based on this architecture, a methodology is presented for the engineering of e-service process collaboration from high-level business requirements down to system implementation details. As a result, B2B process collaboration can be seamlessly defined, enacted, and enforced. Conceptual models of various layers are given in the Unified Modeling Language (UML). We illustrate the applicability of our framework with a running example based on a supply-chain process and evaluate our approach from the perspective of three main stakeholders of e-collaboration, namely users, management, and systems developers.

Chapter 3

The authors are finding rising demands for sensing values in existing/new events and items in the real life. Chance discovery, focusing on new events significant for human decision making, can be positioned extensively as an approach to value sensing. This extension enables the innovation of various artificial systems, where human's talent of analogical thinking comes to be the basic engine. Games for training and activating this talent are introduced, and it is clarified that these games train the an essential talent of human for chance discovery, by discussing the experimental results of these games on the logical framework of analogical abductive reasoning.

Science and technology are expected to support actual service provision and to create new services to promote service industries' productivity. However, those problems might not be solved solely in a certain research area. This paper describes that it is necessary to establish transdisciplinary approaches to service design in consideration of consumers' values and decision making. Recent research trends of services are overviewed. Then a research framework is proposed to integrate computer sciences, human sciences, and economic sciences. Three study examples of services are then presented. The first study is a multi-agent simulation of a cellular telephone market based on results of a psychological survey. The second presents a cognitive model constructed through integration of questionnaire data of a retail business and Bayesian network modeling. The third presents a pricing mechanism design for service facilities—movie theaters—using an economic experiment and agent-based simulation.

In recent years, we witness the formation of social spaces in computers and networks where children, youths and young adults learn, play, socialize and participate in civic life. The question we want to ask is: if this participatory culture of user-generated content in which socially constructed and collective intelligence is to be harnessed, what are the critical success factors that determine the acceptance of this participatory culture in the learning environments? As an illustration, the paper describes two studies focused on tertiary students' perceptions of acceptance of social tools such as Weblogs and instant messaging in facilitating collaborative and collective learning with the aim of tapping onto the collective intelligence of user communities. Congruent to other studies, findings from these two preliminary studies have shown that factors influencing the acceptance of social tools such as Weblogs and instant messaging for learning are dependent on learners' perceptions of usefulness, followed by usability of the social tools. The paper concludes with design implications for socially constructed, learning environments.

Khouloud Boukadi, Ecole des Mines, Saint-Etienne, France
Lucien Vincent, Ecole des Mines, Saint-Etienne, France
Chirine Ghedira, University Lyon 1, France
Zakaria Maamar, Zayed University, UAE

Since the beginning of the Service-Oriented Architecture (SOA) paradigm, with its various implementation technologies such as Web services, the focus of industrial communities has been on providing tools that would allow seamless and flexible application integration within and across enterprises' boundaries. In this paper, the authors present a Context-based, Service-oriented Modeling and Analysis (CSMA) method that guides service engineers in their choices of identifying, defining, and analyzing adaptable business services. The proposed method is business centric and comprises a set of structured steps grouped in two phases. Besides, the CSMA embraces Model-Driven Architecture (MDA) principles to model and refine adaptable business services models in the PIM level. The results from a pilot validation of CSMA for SOA enablement of a realistic enterprise training solutions are also presented.

Weiliang Zhao, Macquarie University, Australia
Jian Yang, Macquarie University, Australia

Existing identity metasystems provide enabling tools to manage, select, and control of digital identities but they have not provided the support of trust management that should cover how trust requirements associated with digital identities are modeled, how runtime conditions for trust are evaluated, and how the results of trust evaluation are consumed by systems/applications. In this paper, the authors propose an approach toward a trust management enabled identity metasystem that covers the analysis of trust requirements and the development of trust management system in a consistent manner. The proposed trust management architecture extends the existing identity metasystems by introducing computing components for carrying out typical trust management tasks associated with digital identities. The computing components in proposed architecture provide intelligent services for these tasks. The proposed high level architecture targets the automation of the development of the trust management layer for digital identities.

Chapter 8

Jian Li, Hong Kong Baptist University, China

William K. Cheung, Hong Kong Baptist University, China

Semantic Web technologies allow on-line resources to be semantically annotated to support more effective and intelligent online services. However, ontologies sometimes may contain sensitive information. Providing access to them requires proper control to ensure the data protection requirement. Yet, the protection should not be too restrictive to make the access management inflexible. While there has been recent work on policy-based access control, in this paper, the authors present a policy representation specifically for access control on ontology-based data and explain how issues like policy propagation and policy conflict resolution are addressed. The authors present bucket-based query rewriting algorithms for realizing the access control policies to avoid sensitive resources leakage in the context of the Semantic Web. The authors validate the correctness of the proposed mechanisms by going through some illustrative examples in detail.

Chapter 9

An Liu, University of Science & Technology of China, China

Liu Wenyin, City University of Hong Kong, China

Liusheng Huang, University of Science & Technology of China, China

Qing Li, City University of Hong Kong, China

Mingjun Xiao, University of Science & Technology of China, China

As more web services that implement core functions of business are delivered to customers with service charges, an open and competitive business web services market must be established. However, the qualities of these business web services are unknown without real experiences and users are unable to make decisions on service selection. To address this problem, the authors adopt insurance into business web services composition. In this paper, the authors propose three insurance models for business web services. Based on the insurance models, the authors propose an approach to compute the expected profit of composite business web services, which can be used as a criterion for business web services composition. The insurance of business web services and the criterion for business web services composition will help service competition and boost the development of more business web services and the software industry.

Chapter 10

Jeff J.S. Huang, National Central University, Taiwan

Stephen J.H. Yang, National Central University, Taiwan

Jeng C.C Chen, National Central University, Taiwan

Irene Y.S. Li, National Central University, Taiwan

Indy Y.T. Hsiao, National Central University, Taiwan

The emergence of Web 2.0 has brought along the trend of community. It is also the trend that contributes to socialization of the Internet. The essence of Web 2.0 is creation and sharing which give rise to social networking communities such as Blog, Wikipedia and Facebook. Through Wikipedia, Blogs, Facebook and other kinds of social networking websites, interactive relationship and bridge of knowledge sharing have been built up successfully. This paper attempts to propose an effective way to locate people with shared interests. By using Internet resources bookmarked by the users, the similarity of interests between them can be analyzed. Based on this relationship, people could build communities. Also, through community activities, the innovation and exchange of collective intelligence are accomplished.

Sietse Overbeek, Delft University of Technology, The Netherlands
Yiwei Gong, Delft University of Technology, The Netherlands
Marijn Janssen, Delft University of Technology, The Netherlands

For decades, information systems have been designed for controlling and managing business processes. In the past, these systems were often monolithic in nature and not made for interacting and communicating with other systems. Today, departments and organizations must collaborate, which requires distributed Web-based systems to support the enactment of flexible business processes. In this paper, four architectures of process management systems are investigated by studying the components and the relationships with the tasks that make up the business processes. These different architectures support automation of non-repetitive, customized processes, and are compared based on dimensions of flexibility. This evaluation showed that the process orchestration architecture scored best, but still has its shortcomings. The results from the comparison are used for developing a research agenda that includes the suggestion to develop reference architecture for connecting individual architectural components.

Ting Yu, University of Sydney, Australia

This paper presents an integrated and distributed intelligent system being capable of automatically estimating and updating large-size economic models. The input-output model of economics uses a matrix representation of a nation's (or a region's) economy to predict the effect of changes in one industry on others and by consumers, government, and foreign suppliers on the economy (Miller & Blair, 1985). To construct the model reflecting the underlying industry structure faithfully, multiple sources of data are collected and integrated together. The system in this paper facilitates this estimation process by integrating a series of components with the purposes of data retrieval, data integration, machine learning, and quality checking. More importantly, the complexity of national economy leads to extremely large-size models to represent every detail of an economy, which requires the system to have the capacity for processing large amounts of data. This paper demonstrates that the major bottleneck is the memory allocation, and to include more memory, the machine learning component is built on a distributed platform and constructs the matrix by analyzing historical and spatial data simultaneously. This system is the first distributed matrix estimation package for such a large-size economic matrix.

Krissada Maleewong, Shinawatra University, Thailand
Chutiporn Anutariya, Shinawatra University, Thailand
Vilas Wuwongse, Asian Institute of Technology, Thailand

This paper presents a novel approach to harnessing collective intelligence that will allow a community to create, collaborate, and share knowledge based on the Semantic Argumentation Model (SAM). It encourages multiple users to express ideas or positions on complex issues, and to submit arguments that support or oppose the ideas of the other members. In principle, ideas considered possible solutions to an issue are those that contain high content quality and achieve great community agreement. Therefore, the authors define several useful measures to analyze the deliberation for determining the content quality, community preference, and achieving quality-assured consensual knowledge. Finally, a web-based prototype system founded on the proposed approach is developed and made available for public use. A preliminary study on the system usability shows that the system is practical and can enhance the collaborative knowledge creation and sharing process.

Chapter 14

Takeshi Shimmura, National Institute of Advanced Industrial Science and Technology, Japan
Takeshi Takenaka, National Institute of Advanced Industrial Science and Technology, Japan
Motoyuki Akamatsu, National Institute of Advanced Industrial Science and Technology, Japan

In full-service restaurants, it is important to share customer information among staff members in real time in order to perform complicated operations. Conventional point of sale (POS) systems in restaurants was developed to improve the verification and transmission of order information passed from the dining hall to the kitchen. However, POS systems have remained insufficient to share customers' order information among many staff members in different positions. This paper introduces an information sharing system for full-service restaurants using an advanced POS system with which staff members can share order information in real time. Using this system, kitchen staff members can grasp the total number of orders and the elapsed time for preparation of each order. Moreover, service staff members can grasp the status of each customer quickly. Using this system in a large-scale restaurant, preparation processes can be made more efficient and reduce customer complaints.

Chapter 15

Gerard Briscoe, London School of Economics and Political Science, UK
Philippe De Wilde, Heriot-Watt University, UK

A primary motivation this research in digital ecosystems is the desire to exploit the self-organising properties of biological ecosystems. Ecosystems are thought to be robust, scalable architectures that can automatically solve complex and dynamic problems. However, the computing technologies that contribute to these properties have not been made explicit in digital ecosystems research. In this paper, the authors discuss how different computing technologies can contribute to providing the necessary self-organising features, including Multi-Agent Systems (MASs), Service-Oriented Architectures (SOAs), and distributed evolutionary computing (DEC). The potential for exploiting these properties in digital ecosystems is considered, suggesting how several key features of biological ecosystems can be exploited in Digital Ecosystems, and discussing how mimicking these features may assist in developing robust, scalable self-organising architectures. An example architecture, the Digital Ecosystem, is considered in detail. The Digital Ecosystem is then measured experimentally through simulations, which consider the self-organised diversity of its evolving agent populations relative to the user request behaviour.

Chapter 16

Saikat Mukherjee, International Institute of Information Technology, India
Srinath Srinivasa, International Institute of Information Technology, India
Krithi Ramamritham, Indian Institute of Technology, India

Stream grids are wide-area grid computing environments that are fed by a set of stream data sources, and Queries arrive at the grid from users and applications external to the system. The kind of queries considered in this work is long-running continuous (LRC) queries, which are neither short-lived nor infinitely long lived. The queries are "open" from the grid perspective as the grid cannot control or predict the arrival of a query with time, location, required data and query revocations. Query optimization in such an environment has two major challenges, i.e., optimizing in a multi-query environment and continuous optimization, due to new query arrivals and revocations. As generating a globally optimal query plan is an intractable problem, this work explores the idea of emergent optimization where globally optimal query plans emerge as a result of local autonomous decisions taken by the grid nodes. Drawing concepts from evolutionary game theory, grid nodes are modeled as autonomous agents that seek to maximize a self-interest function using one of a set of different strategies. Grid nodes change strategies in response to variations in query arrival and revocation patterns, which is also autonomously decided by each grid node.

Chapter 17

Stefano Montanelli, Università degli Studi di Milano, Italy
Silvana Castano, Università degli Studi di Milano, Italy
Alfio Ferrara, Università degli Studi di Milano, Italy
Gaia Varese, Università degli Studi di Milano, Italy

In this paper, the authors present a reference P2P architecture based on autonomous, self-emerging semantic communities of interest (CoIs) for collective intelligence creation and management. An approach for enabling knowledge organization and management at the level of a single peer is presented in the paper, as well as techniques for supporting a peer to participate to the construction of a shared community vocabulary, according to the terminological preferences automatically extracted from its personal knowledge. Furthermore, an application example in the e-health domain is presented in the framework of the iCoord system for P2P semantic coordination to show the use of a manifesto-based collective intelligence for enforcing effective collaboration in a real case study.

Chapter 18

Ahmed Mostefaoui, University of Franche-Comte (LIFC), France
Benoit Piranda, LASELDI, France

Multimedia sensor networks have emerged due to the tremendous technological advances in multimedia hardware miniaturization and the application potential they present. However, the time sensitive nature of multimedia data makes them very problematic to handle, especially within constrained environments. In this paper, the authors present a novel approach based on continuous 3D real time reconstruction of the monitored area dedicated for video surveillance applications. Real-time 3D reconstruction allows an important network bandwidth reduction in context to sensor nodes sending descriptive information to the fusion server instead heavy video streams. Each node has to support additional processing in order to extract this descriptive information in real-time, which results in video sensors capturing tasks, data analysis, and extraction of features needed for 3D reconstruction. In this paper, the authors focus on the design and implementation of such sensor node and validate their approach through real experimentations conducted on a real video sensor.

In this paper, the authors present a time-efficient approach to index objects moving on the plane in order to answer range queries about their future positions. Each object is moving with non small velocity u, meaning that the velocity value distribution is skewed (Zipf) towards u_{min} in some range $[u_{min}, u_{max}]$, where u_{min} is a positive lower threshold. This algorithm enhances a previously described solution (Sioutas, Tsakalidis, Tsichlas, Makris, & Manolopoulos, 2007) by accommodating the ISB-tree access method as presented in Kaporis et al. (2005). Experimental evaluation shows the improved performance, scalability, and efficiency of the new algorithm.

Preface

This book is an anthology of articles that were published in the inaugural volume of the *International Journal of Organizational and Collective Intelligence,* which provide researchers and practitioners in the communities of computer and information sciences with a forum to advance the practice and understanding of computing theories and empirical analyses as sound technical solutions for realizing "intelligent organizations," i.e., intelligent computing for organizational information from not only technical but also institutional and social aspects. Collective Intelligence (CI) is discussed in many related disciplines including biology, sociology, natural and environmental sciences, physics, etc. in conjunction with computer science. CI-related computational and system engineering design and implementation methodologies of CI-based systems gives a variety of case studies which are directed towards the Social Web, as a very prominent example of synergistic interactions of a group of people as a platform for the emergence of truly CI-based systems of diverse applications in cultural and professional backgrounds.

Collective intelligence is a cross-disciplinary subject of challenge-based research of modern computer science. The current environments and resources surrounding global enterprises and dynamic organizations demand rational theories and reliable applications, which allow technically sound solutions and uniformly implement proper functions to their managerial issues. Those issues on organizational management need trans-disciplinary solutions not given by any single theory or application, like Information and Knowledge Computing, Knowledge Management, Knowledge Bases, Decision Science, Semantic Web, Organizational Systems, Middleware, Applications and Experiences, Enterprise Security, Global Enterprise Systems, Artificial Intelligence, Robotics, *etc.* We should have a uniformed theory and its applications for intelligent organizations by integrating and implementing those individual solutions. The first volume comprises various topics, which include knowledge computing, knowledge management, decision science, semantic Web, organizational systems, security, enterprise systems, AI, and robotics, and discuss those subjects only from the technical aspects. The Journal makes great advances as a forum of practical and theoretical discussions on those technologies and solutions from the trans-disciplinary or cross-disciplinary aspects of science and technology with respect to social dynamics and institutional analysis including global solutions of intelligent organizations practicing knowledge management, implementing decision support systems, collaborative applications with other technical areas, and so on.

This book spins off the success of the journal, and its wide range of topics from computing theories to empirical analyses of intelligent organizations reflect current technical achievements in a variety of solutions in knowledge computing, knowledge management, decision science, semantic Web, organizational systems, security, enterprise systems, AI, and robotics from both technical and managerial aspects. The research of *collective intelligence* is a hot issue in the twenty-first century, because the recent expansion of network connectivity to the Internet, known as ubiquitous environment, allows people in enterprises and organizations to enjoy a number of contents and programs stored in the digital forms, which wait for dynamic and intelligent organization and analysis by technical solutions automatically. The advent of new technical solutions in those individual areas discussed above begs one to question whether their applications to enterprises and organizations are proper solutions from not only a technical but also an institutional perspective, in the context of organizational information from managerial aspects. Facing that issue, one needs proper technical solutions in social and organizational dynamics, those in the technical fields have been aware of a necessity of a specific forum to offer an interdisciplinary or trans-disciplinary journal for leading researchers and practitioners with both technical backgrounds and managerial experiences to tackle the research of collective intelligence. In this book, practical and theoretical contributions on various topics are discussed from the latest aspects, while they are focusing on the technological, social, and global dynamics of intelligent organizations practicing knowledge management, implementing decision support systems, collaborative applications, and so on.

This book is designed to give insights of collective intelligence and its practical solutions in computer science to researchers and practitioners including graduate students who study computer science, information engineering, system engineering, information studies, and management of information technology in the fields of Information and Knowledge Computing, Knowledge Management, Knowledge Bases, Decision Science, Semantic Web, Organizational Systems, Middleware, Applications and Experiences, Enterprise Security, Global Enterprise Systems, Artificial Intelligence, Robotics, etc. Another target is researchers and students who work for professional degrees in business schools, management schools, public policy schools, or their equivalents. The book helps its audience in the above technical fields to learn which technical solution has sound reasoning and proper application to their current demands, which is not available in any other books. Meanwhile, for an audience in managerial fields, it is easy to access and understand individual technical solutions from their familiar words of management.

The book focuses on computing theories and empirical analyses of organizational intelligence and collective intelligence. The mission of its publication is to provide researchers and practitioners in the communities of computer and information sciences with a forum to advance the research on collective intelligence, i.e., intelligent computing for organizational and collective information. The book reflects the current technical achievements in a variety of solutions, which question whether their applications to enterprises and organizations are proper solutions from not only a technical but also from institutional aspects. The organizational intelligence and collective intelligence are cross-disciplinary subjects of challenge-based research on modern computer science, which demand trans-disciplinary solutions given by not any single theory or application but by the integration and implementation of the individual solutions discussed below as exemplary but not exhausted:

- Soft Computing in Organizations
- Game Theoretic and Information Economic Analysis
- Data Mining and Knowledge Bases for Organizational Management
- Classification and Clustering
- Optimization
- Machine Learning
- Neural Networks, Bayesian Networks, Fuzzy Techniques and Systems
- Genetic Algorithms and Evolutionary Computing
- Self-organizing and Complex Systems
- Knowledge Discovery
- Service Computing
- Organizational Systems, Middleware, Applications and Experiences
- Semantic Web Architecture and Applications
- Intelligent Web-Based Systems
- Intelligent Agents and Multi-Agent Systems
- Decision Science, Decision Making Theory and Modeling

- Decision Support Systems and Crisis Management Systems
- Collaboration and Communication Systems
- Artificial Intelligence for Organizational Management
- Security and Access Control
- Machine and Computer Vision
- Robotics for Intelligent Organizations
- Information and Knowledge Computing (including applications)
- Soft Computing in Organizations
- Collective Intelligence for Organizational Management
- Game Theoretic and Information Economic Analysis
- Monitoring and Planning
- Industrial Control
- Fault Diagnosis
- Traffic and Communication Optimization
- Financial and Stock Market Monitoring and Prediction
- Digital Ecosystems
- Intelligent Web-Based Systems
- Pervasive Computing
- Intelligent Web Personalization
- Mobile Computing and Systems
- Business Intelligence Systems
- Medical and Diagnostic Systems
- Context-Aware and Affective (Emotional) Computing
- User Profiling
- Knowledge Management for Organizational Management
- Classification and Clustering
- Optimization
- Statistical Approaches for Large Scale Date
- Data Mining
- Visual and Audio Data Mining
- Web Mining
- Link and Graph Mining
- Knowledge Synthesis and Visualization
- Information Extraction
- Information Filtering
- Information Integration
- Recommender Systems
- Knowledge Bases for Organizational Management
- Machine Learning
- Neural Networks
- Bayesian Networks
- Artificial Immune Systems
- Fuzzy Techniques and Systems
- Genetic Algorithms and Evolutionary Computing

- Self-Organizing and Complex Systems
- Intelligent Agents and Multi-Agent Systems
- Virtual Reality and Multi-Media Intelligent Information Systems
- Knowledge Discovery
- Data Analysis and Pattern Recognition
- Knowledge Representation and Management
- Knowledge Acquisition
- Computational Neuroscience
- Intelligent Web Mining and Applications
- Decision Science
- Decision Making Theory and Modeling
- Collaborative Solutions
- Fairness Solutions
- Decision Support Systems
- e-Auction Systems and e-Negotiation Systems
- Decision Support and Visualization
- Semantic Web for Organizational Management
- Organizational Systems, Middleware, Applications and Experiences
- Collaboration and Communication Systems
- E-commerce Systems
- Enterprise Resource Planning
- Supply Chain Management
- Web Conferencing
- Enterprise Security
- Intelligent and Secure Information Systems
- Security and Access Control
- Data Privacy
- Cryptography
- Machine and Computer Vision
- Visualization and Virtual Technologies for Intelligent Organizations
- Visualization and Virtual Reality on Medical and Health Care Organizations
- Visualization and Virtual Reality on Financial Services
- Service Computing
- Artificial Intelligence for Organizational Management
- Intelligent Agent-based Systems
- Cognitive and Reactive Distributed Management Systems
- Mobile, Ad Hoc, and Sensor Network Management
- Skill Sciences
- Robotics for Intelligent Organizations
- Biology and Medicine
- Business and Management
- Artificial Societies
- Chemicals, Pharmaceuticals and Materials
- Environment Engineering

Collective intelligence has its promising fields of applications as solutions. This book dedicates two specific fields of solutions: service computing and knowledge management.

Service-oriented solutions are appreciated in collective intelligence that is built in enterprise information systems. Many research works on services provision involve cross-disciplinary approaches. Its typical framework is found in business-to-business process collaboration with three layers: collaboration requirements layer, business rule layer, and system implementation layer. Those layers allow users to specify the cross-organizational requirements of e-service processes and define detailed knowledge of process collaboration requirements as business rules in a unified Event-Condition-Action (ECA) and from with technical support of event collaboration interfaces by contemporary Enterprise JavaBeans and Web Services. This approach gives a seamless definition to enact and enforce B2B process collaboration with conceptual models of various layers in the Unified Modeling Language (UML) and a running example based on a supply-chain process. We evaluate our approach from the perspective of three main stakeholders of e-collaboration, namely users, management, and system developers.

Beyond the Services Oriented Architecture (SOA), intelligent computing is essential to achieve excellent services for requirements in computation environments. This phenomenon demands knowledge integration from various disciplines such as computer science, industrial and systems engineering, management science, operations research, and so on. Since the beginning of SOA paradigms, with its various implementation technologies such as Web services, the focus of industrial communities has been on providing tools that would allow seamless and flexible application integration within and across enterprise boundaries. A new paradigm demands a method, which is to guide service engineers in their choices of identifying, defining, and analyzing adaptable business services. Such method is business-centric and comprises a set of structured steps grouped in two phases, embracing model-driven architecture principles to model and refining adaptable business services models.

Some chapters in this book discuss challenges and solutions to service-oriented intelligent computing. So-called killer applications are required to drive Web services and systems in the field of intelligent service computing. A fundamental system for service computing is Web-based solutions, which go forward and elevate to the stages of Web 2.0, Web 3.0, and so on. Web 2.0 refers to the second-generation platform, facilitating communications, information sharing, interoperability, and collaboration. Virtual systems and virtual communities work together with autonomous or peer-to-peer systems of communications under this direction. A wide range of intelligent services and analyses are applicable to many solutions as hot issues from the aspects of collective intelligence. The emergence of Web 2.0 has brought along the trend of community. It is also the trend that contributes to socialization of the Internet. The essence of Web 2.0 is creation and sharing, which give rise to social networking communities such as Blogs, Wikipedia, and Facebook. Through Wikipedia, Blogs, Facebook, and other kinds of social networking websites, interactive relationships and bridges of knowledge sharing have been built up successfully. This book attempts to propose an effective way to locate people with shared interests. By using Internet resources bookmarked by the users, the similarity of interests between them can be analyzed. Based on this relationship, people can build communities. Also, through community activities, the innovation and exchange of collective intelligence are accomplished.

Those emerging systems and architectures have brought intelligent services into various domains, such as context-aware services. They also increase complexities of system design. For example, existing identity meta-systems provide enabling tools to manage, select, and control digital identities but they have not provided the support of trust management that should cover how trust requirements associated with digital identities are modeled, how runtime conditions for trust are evaluated, and how the results of trust evaluation are consumed by systems/applications. A new approach toward trust management is to enable such identity meta-systems that cover analysis of trust requirements and development of trust management systems in a consistent manner. Trust management architectures extend the existing identity meta-systems by introducing computing components for carrying out typical trust management tasks associated with digital identities. The computing components in such architectures provide intelligent services for these tasks and realize automation of the development of trust management layer for digital identities.

Agent-based technologies are one of the most promising solutions for integration of systems and services in intelligent computing. Agents built in communication systems are autonomous and independent to each other. Various technologies from artificial intelligence are introduced to service computing under the diversity of solutions such as computational intelligence, soft computing, game theory, genetic algorithms, evolutionary computing, logics, machine learning, optimization, and so on. Such solutions are vital for excellence in service computing. Mobile networks are a promising field of application and integration between collective intelligence and service computing. As mobile devices become more powerful and widespread, demand for adaptive solution in mobile computing increases and engineering requirements and design constraints become challenging. For example, grid computing is a high-potential technology for its solution. One of those solutions, which are software as a service, utility computing, and meta-services, is introduced into cloud computing. Cloud computing emphasizes a large collection of services rather than a single product, as shared resources. In cloud computing, there are many open issues to which collective intelligence can provide a solution. In particular, how traditional information systems can be migrated to new cloud platforms is a key issue of its adoption. To empower service computing in systems and services, intelligent computing contributes to various technical problems in collective intelligence. An exemplary solution is decision support systems. Other examples are found in context-based modeling in software available to enterprise systems, which provide intelligent service-oriented systems, trust management, access control on semantic Web using ontologies, insurance modeling to improve trust and service qualities, and knowledge management in community-oriented services. Semantic Web technologies allow on-line resources to be semantically annotated to support more effective and intelligent online services. However, ontologies sometimes may contain sensitive information. Providing access to them requires proper control to ensure the data protection requirement. Yet, the protection should not be too restrictive to make the access management inflexible. While there has been recent work on policy-based access control, a solution to this problem is to provide a policy representation specifically designed for access control on ontology-based data and to explain how issues like policy propagation and policy conflict resolution are addressed. An exemplary measure is found in bucket-based query rewriting algorithms, which realize the access control policies to avoid sensitive resources leakage in the context of semantic Web.

Research in service computing raises concerns of solutions originating from collective intelligence that provides technical solutions to high-level requirements in modeling and designs. Inter-discourse between collective intelligence and service computing brings various insights into a wide range of challenges and opportunities. Trans-disciplinary approaches for implementation of service design and reflection on consumers' values and decision-making are very productive in the real world with the recent research trends of services and propose a research framework to integrate computer sciences, human sciences, and economics. In a typical way, service computing and collective intelligence are integrated in the context of multi-agent simulation with the advent of a psychological survey on a cognitive model constructed by integration of questionnaire data from retailers using Bayesian networks modeling and price mechanisms design. An integrated and distributed intelligent system is another approach that enables automatic estimation and updates of large-sized economic models based on input-output modeling using a matrix representation of national or regional economy. Its unique distribution in memory allocation allows accurate implementation of large-size models.

Knowledge management is a well-appreciated field in the long-standing tradition of Computer Science and Artificial Intelligence. Information processing and management as well as knowledge engineering principles and techniques have been envisioned and practiced claiming some kind of intelligence in organization, processing, and behavior. Effective memory models and organization have always attracted research and development efforts in an attempt to address the challenges of intelligent behavior in humans and machines. Among the oldest examples are nature-inspired models such as cellular automaton conceived by Ulam and von Neumann in the 1940s, which has been investigated as a framework for the understanding of the behavior of complex systems.

In spite of the controversial opinions about the degrees of success for understanding and applying intelligence, today's computer impacted culture is characterized by the production and consumption of knowledge and information in an assembly of smaller universes of entities, i.e., people, machines, software, data, computational models, rather than truly intelligent systems. In order to adhere to the evolutionary and cultural impact of computer science in society and organizations, we need to re-visit memory and organizational models within a universe of discourse where entity participation and connectionism are of paramount importance. Data, information, and knowledge management principles and techniques need to be conceived as contributing to the creation of a huge associative memory, which could enable a collectively, eventually truly, intelligent society and organization. Within such a Collective Intelligence (CI) Universe of Discourse, coping with and harnessing complexity and diversity remains a key challenge, which can be met by conceiving data and knowledge engineering and management as an ecosystem underlying synergy and natural selection processes.

For example, data and knowledge engineering principles and techniques are often discussed in a CI Universe of Discourse. Particular emphasis has been given to principles and techniques underpinning all processes from ergonomics, conceptualization, and conceptual modeling to querying, retrieval, and storage of data and knowledge as integral parts of a larger associative memory. Especially, Digital Ecosystems, inspired by natural ecosystems, are a good field for integrating knowledge and data from the aspect of collective intelligence in the contexts of self-organization, scalability, and sustainability, which are of paramount importance for harnessing complexity in large-scale systems, in open social-technical systems. Digital ecosystems give a critical overview of digital counterparts for the behavior and constructs of biological ecosystems, instead of simulating or emulating such behavior or constructs. In this critical view, what parallels can be drawn from bio-aspects in digital systems? For instance, Multi-Agent Systems are discussed in order to explore the references to agents and migration. This is followed by evolutionary computing and Service Oriented Architectures for the references to evolution and self-organization in computing and computational environments rather than natural and environmental ones.

Not only are digital counterparts of self-organization, sustainability, and scalability desirable properties of an ecosystem but also autonomous agent approaches are promising in collective intelligence that is introduced into knowledge management. A way of optimization queries in stream grids is a good exemplary technique for bridging gaps between collective intelligence and knowledge management. Nodes in a grid act as local agents, which try to optimize stream grid queries based on their local interests. In such an ecosystem, it becomes apparent that there cannot be any global optimization strategy, but one emerging out of local optima and choices among alternative strategies. Stream grids are grid-computing environments that are fed with streaming data sources from instrumentation devices like cameras, RFID (Radio-Frequency Identification) sensors, network monitoring, or other applications. Queries by users or applications seek to tap into one or more such streams. The main costs for such queries include bandwidth costs and bookkeeping costs at each grid node. In such scenarios, there are conflicting optimization requirements.

In the context of Peer-to-Peer (P2P) system architectures, management of collective intelligence in semantic communities is a key solution in knowledge management. How queries can be supported once Semantic CoIs form a community level CI with this design architecture that departs from traditional P2P approaches in that there is a shift from a network of units to a network of coalitions where the community itself (and not the peers on their own) has the role to support effective query execution and data availability. This approach also involves creation and maintenance of a community-level collective intelligence in order to push attention to the critical aspects of distributed knowledge management in P2P environments, where the goal of establishing a shared agreement among a set of peers conflicts with the intrinsic P2P nature that pursues peer autonomy, communication scalability, and rapid change propagation.

The discussion of how to improve information management and querying is taken further in a collective setting of multimedia sensor networks, where the handling of a voluminous amount of multimedia sensor data is of paramount importance. Such an approach is to handle the huge and voluminous data generated by an ecosystem of multimedia sensors in a video surveillance context (e.g., super market environment). The key idea behind it is to "continuously" construct a 3D representation of the monitored area, in which video streams originating from the video sensors are fused. In other words, the "views" of the sensor nodes are merged in the 3D scene of the monitored region. This approach presents many interesting advantages, in particular for resources limited environments like those of sensor networks. Another advantage of this kind of approach is its ability to answer some spatio-temporal requests that are very hard to handle with raw video data.

Finally, another promising approach is found in challenges and problems for indexing and querying objects on the move with particular interest on predictively querying their future position. In an ecosystem of data, information and knowledge where data or queries are being migrated or moved across networks of communication for the sake of query optimization and effectiveness of information provision, new indexing, and querying techniques are requested.

IJOCI BEST PAPER OF THE YEAR

This is our honor and pleasure to announce the first IJOCI annual best paper award, which goes to Sietse Overbeek, Yiwei Gong, and Marijn Janssen's "Architectures for Enabling Flexible Business Processes: A Research Agenda." Their article discusses a brand new architecture of process management for business requirements with a brilliant idea that realizes flexibility originating from collective intelligence in organizations. We quote their abstract here.

For decades, information systems have been designed for controlling and managing business processes. In the past, these systems were often monolithic in nature and not made for interacting and communicating with other systems. Today, departments and organizations must collaborate, which requires distributed Web-based systems to support the enactment of flexible business processes. In this chapter, four architectures of process management systems are investigated by studying the components and the relationships with the tasks that make up the business processes. These different architectures support automation of non-repetitive, customized processes, and are compared based on dimensions of flexibility. This evaluation showed that the process orchestration architecture scored best, but still has its shortcomings. The results from the comparison are used for developing a research agenda that includes the suggestion to develop reference architecture for connecting individual architectural components.

We particularly appreciate contributors who have made great commitments with research in collective intelligence. Without their devotion to this field, this book does not exist. In concluding to this preface, we extend appreciation to our friends and colleagues who are involved in this project from review to edition: Akinori Abe, Hisao Ishibuchi, Hiroshi Ishikawa, Ivan Jordanov, Eleanna Kafeza, Shiguo Lian, Yasuo Matsuyama, Tomonobu Ozaki, Shigeo Sugimoto, Takeshi Takenaka, Yuzuru Tanaka, Yin Leng Theng, Ajith Abraham, Tieyan Li, Nikolaos Nikolaidis, Husrev Taha Sencar, Shuiming Ye, Yinghua Ma, Youakim Badr, Fernando Ferri, Agma Traina, Caetano Traina, Maria Luisa Sapino, Mario Koeppen, Shengfeng Qin, Frank Stowell, Antoniya Georgieva, Sanaz Mostaghim, Toshiharu Hatanaka, Edwin Lughofer, Ferrante Neri, Hisashi Handa, Kevin Kok Wai Wong, Liya Ding, Wenyin Liu, Huiye Ma, Wendy W. Y. Hui, Yi Zhuang, Chi Keong Goh, Xiaohui Zhao, Maggie M. Wang, Markus Schaal, Sietse Overbeek, Yuqing Sun, Farid Meziane, Zongwei Luo, Chutiporn Anutariya, Kouzou Ohara, Doina Tatar, Jin-Cheon Na, Takehsi Yamakawa, Fu-ren Lin, Zbigniew Galias, Pierre Levy, Nariaki Nishino, Susan Elias, Chi-hung Chi, G.R. Gangadharan, Koichi Moriyama, Chei Sian Lee, Lei Chen, Yoichi Motomura, Hiroshi Igaki, Raymond Y. K. Lau, Naoki Fukuta, Penny Hart, Yasufumi Takama, Nariaki Nishino, Hsueh-hua Chen, Akira Maeda, Tsukasa Ishigaki, Carmen Ka Man Lam, Kengo Katayama, Yoshiko Hanada, Haiyang Hu, Sally Jo Cunningham, Nobutada Fujii, Mitsunori Matsushita, Hideaki Takeda, Tetsuo Sakaguchi, Keiichi Horio, Paulo Pinheiro da Silva, Vilas Wuwongse, Hiroshi Igaki, Jim Dimarogonas, P. Radha Krishna, Atsuyuki Morishima, Xi Chen, Ting Yu, Ichiro Kobayashi, Yusuke Nojima, Tomoya Takenaka, and Yu Suzuki. Actually, this is not an exhaustive list, but instead, just a list of people who have come to mind. Nothing could be done without your support. Thank you so much!

Hideyasu Sasaki
Ritsumeikan University, Japan

Dickson K. W. Chiu
Dickson Computer Systems, Hong Kong

Epaminondas Kapetanios
University of Westminster, UK

Patrick C. K. Hung
University of Ontario Institute of Technology (UOIT), Canada & University of Waterloo, Canada

Frederic Andres
National Institute of Informatics, Japan

Ho-Fung Leung
Chinese University of Hong Kong, China

Richard Chbeir
University of Bourgogne, France

January 30, 2012

Chapter 1
On the Notion of Collective Intelligence:
Opportunity or Challenge?

Epaminondas Kapetanios
University of Westminster, UK

ABSTRACT

In this article, the author explores the notion of Collective Intelligence (CI) as an emerging computing paradigm. The article is meant to provide a historical and contextual view of CI through the lenses of as many related disciplines as possible (biology, sociology, natural and environmental sciences, physics) in conjunction with the computer science point of view. During this explorative journey, the article also aims at pinpointing the current strengths and weaknesses of CI-related computational and system engineering design and implementation methodologies of CI-based systems. A non-exhaustive list of case studies set up the stage for CI applications as well as challenging research questions. These can be particularly directed towards the Social Web, as a very prominent example of synergistic interactions of a group of people with diverse cultural and professional backgrounds and its potential to become a platform for the emergence of truly CI-based systems.

INTRODUCTION

At the dawn of the 21st century, we are witnessing an ever increasing transition from personal computers to personalization of data, knowledge and contents in computing and computer science.

DOI: 10.4018/978-1-4666-1577-9.ch001

The emergence of the Social Web phenomenon as a realm of "linked people" and the vision of the Semantic Web as a realm of "linked data" already paved the way towards considerations of new forms of intelligence, which emerges from the "interaction of minds" paradigm. In this context, the role of humans as contributors to knowledge creation and collectively problem solving in a networked society is being emphasized. The emphasis is also put on the role of computers as facilitators of learning and knowledge sharing in collaborative environments via multimedia enriched contents or games.

The transition, however, from personalized data, knowledge and contents towards collectively intelligent forms of synergies in an amalgamation of humans and machines, as a new paradigm of *Intelligence*, is at its infancy and raises many questions varying from the very notion of Collective Intelligence to the methodologies and principles for computations and engineering of CI-based systems.

In this article, an explorative journey through memories and approaches has been attempted in order to give some hints for finding some answers to the many questions ahead. In particular, an exploration of the definition of the term *Collective Intelligence* has been provided by first section. This section gives some overview of what is in the essence of this term to be coined as an umbrella of an intelligence paradigm through synergistic efforts.

Section 2 crosses the boundaries of computing and computer science and attempts to get to know the understanding and approaches of other disciplines such as biology, sociology, natural and environmental sciences, physics, towards the notion of collective systems and

(super-) organisms, in a hope that this interaction will shed more light into the dark side of the definition of Collective Intelligence.

Section 3, in turn, explores computational and mathematical underpinnings of Collective Intelligence in an attempt to highlight the impact and reflection of lessons learned from other disciplines with particular emphasis on natural, biological and sociological approaches to the CI-phenomenon. In addition, section 4 discusses and illustrates the lack of commonly agreed upon methodologies for the design and development of CI-based systems. Therefore, an attempt has been taken to set up a framework for the development of a CI

enabling methodology, which may depart from many conventional information systems design methodologies as known and practiced so far.

Section 5 embarks on the description of an indicative list of case studies and application areas with a twofold purpose: to highlight the many contributions CI-enabling systems may have in society and technology and to point at particular areas for investigation and validation of research questions in applied CI. Finally, section 6 summarizes in terms of interesting and open research questions.

1. ON THE DEFINITION OF COLLECTIVE INTELLIGENCE

According to a definition in Wikipedia *"Collective intelligence is a shared or group intelligence that emerges from the collaboration and competition of many individuals. Collective intelligence appears in a wide variety of forms of consensus decision making in bacteria, animals, humans, and computer networks - a field that studies collective behaviour from the level of quarks to the level of bacterial, plant, animal, and human societies."*

Occasionally, the term Collective Intelligence appears to be a synonym of *Swarm Intelligence, Group IQ, Symbiotic Intelligence*. Our quest in Oxford English Dictionary, however, returns no entry for the term *Collective Intelligence*. Instead, terms like Central Intelligence Agency, Military Intelligence, Artificial Intelligence, SETI, Secret Intelligence Service, Nous and Intelligent Quotient are prompted as potential candidates of an answer to our quest.

However, if one attempts to reconstruct the meaning of Collective Intelligence from its compound terms *Collective* and *Intelligence* separately, then we would be tempted to adhere to *"understanding (from the Latin Intelligere) which belongs to or operated cooperatively by all members of a group as a whole or aggregate"*. Further meanings adhered to the adjective *Collective* such as *"a joint identity", "a collective mind" and the "corporate good"* are given by WordNet 3.0 linguistic Ontology. In a different context, the term explanation of *Collective* is set up on the principle of *collectivism or ownership and production by the workers involved usually under the supervision of a government) "collective farms"*.

According to key theorists, Collective Intelligence is attributed the *capacity of human communities to evolve towards higher order complexity and harmony, through such innovation mechanisms as differentiation and integration, competition and collaboration* (George Pór). Furthermore, it is also attributed *achieving a single focus of attention and standard of metrics which provide an appropriate threshold of action* (Tom Atlee and George Pór).

The latter is rooted to the *Scientific Community Metaphor*, which in Computer Science states one way of understanding scientific communities (Kornfeld & Hewitt, 1981; Kornfeld, 1981; Kornfeld, 1982). The first publications on the Scientific Community Metaphor involved the development of a programming language named *Ether* that invoked procedural plans to process goals and assertions concurrently by dynamically creating new rules during program execution. *Ether* also addressed issues of conflict and contradiction with multiple sources of knowledge and multiple viewpoints.

With the emergence of new media technologies and from an Information and Communication Tools (ICT) perspective, *Collective Intelligence can be attributed to media convergence and participatory culture. Collective intelligence is not merely a quantitative contribution of information from all cultures, it is also qualitative.* Also, according to Flew (2008), Collective Intelligence is interpreted as *the ability of networked ICT's to enhance the community knowledge pool. These communications tools enable humans to interact and to share and collaborate with both ease and speed.* Moreover, *computer networks give participating users the opportunity to store and to retrieve knowledge through the collective access* to these databases and allow them to *"harness the hive"* (Flew, 2008).

It is obvious that from an ICT point of view Collective Intelligence becomes a synonym for *Mass Collaboration.* In order for this concept to happen, four principles need to exist: openness, peering, sharing and acting globally. It is characteristic the view and perspective holding among bloggers about Collective Intelligence as *combining social and electronic technologies for large-scale, collaborative meaning making* (http://www.community-intelligence.com/blogs/public/). Also, Collective intelligence is viewed as *the capacity of human communities to evolve towards higher order complexity and harmony, through such innovation mechanisms as differentiation and integration, competition and collaboration.*

Through the political economy lens, Collective Intelligence is perceived as the "General intellect embodied in the collective knowing of the society, embedded in all the ways of its knowing, has always been a force that shaped the creative capacities and daily life of people and organizations." *Through the cognitive lens, Collective Intelligence is adhered to* "describing human communities, organizations and cultures exhibiting 'mind-like' properties, such as learning, perceiving, acting, thinking, problem-solving, and so on... Intelligence refers to the main cognitive powers: perception, action planning and coordination, memory, imagination and hypothesis generation, inquisitiveness and learning abilities. The expression 'collective intelligence' designates the cognitive powers of a group." *The latter definition and view is attributed to Pierre Lévy. To this extent, we should lay back and make some general observations so far:*

- There are few concepts, theories or data on intelligence as something collective
- There are a few intriguing texts that are ostensibly about Collective Intelligence, but none that really integrates different disciplines.

- It seems to be something about knowledge how large groups think or decide (the wisdom or folly of crowds).
- We know much less about how these fit together, and there is no meta-theory of Collective Intelligence.

There are also many viewpoints in regards with

- How groups can work on developing software
- Tapping the good sense of the public for advocates of democracy
- Advocates of markets to aggregate the intelligence of consumers and entrepreneurs
- Advocates of civil society as the best way to spot new needs or demands and innovate solutions.
- Advocates of permanent civil services as good ways to identify and solve collective problems

Despite the divergent aspects and many viewpoints of the concept of Collective Intelligence, there are many initiatives and centres addressing this concept. For instance, the MIT Centre for Collective Intelligence *and the* Presencing Institute at Cambridge, Massachusetts *as well as manifestation in social practices such as citizen journalism, bar camps, inter- and multi-generational movement, un-conferences, a term which is primarily used in a geek community and refers to* a facilitated, participant-driven conference centered around a theme or purpose.

Moreover, definitions and perspectives of Collective Intelligence are bound with the wisdom of crowd (Surowiecki, 2005), mass productivity (Leadbeater, 2008), new media and Wikinomics (2008), mankind's emerging world in cyberspace (Levy, 1999).

2. ON THE CROSS-DISCIPLINARY CONTEXT OF COLLECTIVE INTELLIGENCE

Despite the strong social and human perspective attributed to Collective intelligence, the concept appears to be older than humankind itself. A broader definition is given as *any intelligence that arises from -- or is a capacity or characteristic of -- groups and other collective living systems.*

Primal forms of Collective Intelligence manifest in the synergies and resilience of natural ecosystems. This is often referred to as "the wisdom of nature", which "learns from its experience" through the interactive create-and-test dynamics of evolution. Collective intelligence becomes more obvious in groups of social animals like ants, bees, certain fishes and birds, and many mammals, including wolves and primates. Also, members of the first human groups shared with those evolutionary ancestors the instinct to combine their respective information and expertise to meet survival tasks they could not possibly meet separately. Those early forms of collective intelligence also gave rise to language and tools which, in turn, enabled new forms of collective intelligence to evolve that were capable of absorbing more complexity.

Having a closer look, however, approaches and studies for understanding the phenomenon of Collective Intelligence have been carried out by other disciplines quite a few decades ago. In a biological context, for instance, W. M. Wheeler (Parker, 1938), a Professor at Harvard, saw this collaborative process at work in ants, who acted like the cells of a single beast with a collective mind. He called the larger creature that the colony seemed to form a "*super organism*".

In the same biological context and particularly in the context of cellular robotic systems, Swarm Intelligence (SI) was introduced by Gerardo Beni and Jing Wang in 1989 (Beni & Wang, 1989). A thorough overview of Swarm Intelligence is given by Engelbrecht (2005). It is based on the collective behaviour of decentralized, self-organized systems.

The idea has been primarily exploited in global optimization problems through observations of particle swarm optimization (Psaropoulos & Vrahatis, 2002).

Generally speaking, the definition of a *super-organism* in biology relies on the following principles: (a) an organism may be unicellular or made up, as in humans, of many billions of cells grouped into specialized tissues and organs, (b) an organism is a living thing (such as animal, plant, fungus, or micro-organism), (c) in at least some form, all organisms are capable of reacting to stimuli, reproduction, growth and maintenance as a stable whole. This view, however, triggers the question of the extent to which an *ant colony* or *viruses* should be considered as a super-organism. For instance, *viruses* could not, typically, considered to be organisms because they are incapable of "independent" reproduction or metabolism.

In a sociological context, the definition of a super-organism has been brought Durkheim, a French sociologist, into connection with the society or a social structure, which is being viewed as a living organism. This organism manifests itself with three core activities: culture, politics, economics, whereas, health of such a social organism can be thought of a function of the interaction of culture, politics, and economics. In this context, society constitutes a higher intelligence because it transcends the individual over space and time (Durkheim, 1912).

A distinction, however, between a *social* and *organic* structure as a super-organism has been drawn by evolutionists such as Herbert Spencer (Elwick, 2003). He explored the holistic nature of society as a social organism while distinguishing *the ways in which society did not behave like an organism*. The super-organic was an emergent property of interacting organisms, that is, human beings. Putting in parallel the two contexts, sociological and biological, it is hard to see a difference or a similarity. In order for a social unit to be considered an organism by itself, the individuals should be in permanent physical connection to each other, and its evolution should be governed by selection to the whole society instead of individuals.

The notion of a super-organism is also defined in an ecological context via the Gaia hypothesis. According to this hypothesis, a super-organism is set identical to *a complex entity involving the Earth's biosphere, atmosphere, oceans, and soil; the totality constituting a feedback or cybernetic system which seeks an optimal physical and chemical environment for life on this planet.* This hypothesis has been attributed to James Lovelock (2000), an independent research scientist, who first formulated this hypothesis in the 1960s as a consequence of his work for NASA on methods of detecting life on Mars. In this context, *the Earth survival hypothesis in a Universe full of asteroids and threats* is collective protection mechanism by the surrounding planets and solar system not to be hit, or burnt, or frozen.

All these aspects and approaches raise, instead of settling down, more questions about "what is collectively intelligent". Can we set equal this question to the question of what is the "unit of natural selection"? Is it the selfish gene (Dawkins, 1989) or a pool of genes? Or is it the whole genome of an organism? Can ant-colonies and social insects as a breeding entity be selected (Wilson, 1971)? Can we assume that biological selection occurs at multiple levels simultaneously? Do individual human beings qualify as *super-organisms*? Does only one super-organism exist on Earth that of the DNA? Do social organisms underlie natural selection processes? Can we define Collective Intelligence as *a set of conditions to be fulfilled in order to form a super organism?* Can we define Collective Intelligence as *a set of evolutionary processes for the formed "super-organism" to go through?*

3. COMPUTATIONAL UNDERPINNINGS OF COLLECTIVE INTELLIGENCE

Having reflected upon the major views and attempts to define Collective Intelligence under the perspectives of, e.g., biology, social and environmental sciences, we embark in this section on the computational aspects of CI. These rely, as one may have expected, on socially and biologically inspired systems. To this extent, building and engineering of computational systems rely on two major principles: (a) complex behaviour at the global level emerges in a nonlinear manner from large numbers of low-level component interactions, (b) behaviour is more than the sum of its parts. This could be metaphorically explained by *'flock of birds'*, where the flock is a dynamic entity consisting of hundreds (or thousands) of entities (individuals, machines). The flock constantly changes shape and direction but maintains overall cohesion. Could this metaphor be the one for a new computing paradigm?

If this metaphor is meant to hold for a new computing paradigm, then one could rely on the definition of cellular automata and treat each bird in the flock as an autonomous agent. This is also sometimes called *cellular computing* or *in vivo computing*. Another point of view has been that the entire genomic regulatory system can be thought of as a computational system, the "genomic computer". On the other side, it is believed that one of the possible contributions of computer science to biology could be *the development of a suitable language to accurately and succinctly describe and reason about biological concepts and phenomena.*

However, in addition to the autonomous cells of evolution, it is of paramount importance to adhere to the characteristics of computational CI by defining local rules controlling agent behaviour relative to closest neighboring birds as well as to aim at constructing a system the *overall behaviour of which is determined by the collective agents reflecting the behaviour of the real flock.* For instance, using a "flocks of birds" similar component methodology promises to offer many advantages for solving complex problems. In addition, algorithmic complexity is achieved through software that is simple and flexible compared to conventional software development techniques.

Though, there is no clear answer yet, at least to the author's knowledge, of what are the computational and mathematical techniques of Collective Intelligence as a computational model, it appears that one could answer the question of what it is *not*. To this extent, it is not a Turing Computational Model due to multi-thread inference processes, human-centred computing and other characteristics. Additionally, it is not only simulating the behavioural patterns of swarming bees, flocking birds and schools of fish and it is not only complex dynamic systems problems such as scheduling, optimisation and space exploration. Similarly, in the realm of methodologies, Collective Intelligence appears to borrow from a variety of topics such as classifier systems, neural networks, biological immune systems, autocatalytic networks, adaptive game theory, chaos theory, general nonlinear systems and artificial life.

Attempts and approaches, however, to adhere to a more CI specific computational model and theory led to formalization, analysis and modeling based on a quasi-chaotic model of computation of the global behavior of beings in structured environments. A typical case has been the expression of higher-level logical structures (e.g., facts, rules, goals) as enclosed by membranes e.g., Clause molecules (CMs in PROLOG), which move quasi-randomly in a structured computational space. To this extent, an inference process can occur if and only if the logical conditions are fulfilled.

In parallel with these sophisticated and, eventually, highly complex computational models, a more systemic and simplified approach has been provided by research question such as *measuring the IQ of a social structure.* In this context, a CI activity is being monitored in terms of displacements and actions of beings as well as exchange of information among beings. Means of communication and exchange of information are considered to be human language, ant's pheromone communication system, dance of honeybees to direct toward a source of honey, the crossover of genes between bacteria resulting in spreading specific resistance.

In all these explorations of mind in regards with the theoretical underpinnings of CI, it turns out that the major challenge, from an engineering and methodological point of view, is creating systems, which truly enable CI rather than simulating behavior of social and biological structures and organisms with computational models. The main premises are: (a) the "network" as a cluster of humans and machines, (b) involvement of human beings as creators and consumers in problem solving and learning tasks, (c) formation of Social Groups and Networks follows the same principles of social behaviour, (d) synergy between humans and machines as the key of Collective IQ.

In line with the questions as posed in the previous section, some more research questions can be posed in respect with (a) engineering methodologies and techniques for building up CI-based systems (b) the software ingredients for "cooking" a CI promoting cluster of humans and machines and, therefore, a "super organism", (c) definition of "units of natural selection", (d) definition of conditions for survival of human-machine clusters, (e) measurement principles of Collective IQ.

With the rise of the Social Web, two more important research questions turn up as a consequence of the thoughts made previously: (a) are current systems for Social Networking such as *MySpace, Del.icio.us, Facebook, Second Life* as well as the *Social Web* in general, really CI based or CI promoting systems? (b) Can we advance existing or build new Social Networking systems with embedded CI?

4. ON DESIGN AND IMPLEMENTATION METHODOLOGIES OF CI BASED SYSTEMS

The lessons learned so far in respect with any engineering methodologies for the design and implementation of CI-based systems point at a new system design thinking with no boxes and layers as well as no formal foundation but addressing an empirical part. This is anchored in the definition of the properties *self-organisation* and *emergence* themselves, which cannot be understood and analysed in an only-formal fashion. Simulation, instead, could take up the role of empirical part in the methodology. The design methodology, if any, should rely more on creating conditions and constraint satisfaction frameworks to reach equilibrium.

The expecting properties of such an emergent CI-based system (Bonabeau et al, 1999) could possibly be those of *social insects* (Bonabeau et al, 1999), i.e., feedback (amplification), negative feedback, amplification of fluctuations (e.g., random walks or errors), multiple interactions. According to Holland (1995), the properties of *aggregation, tagging, nonlinearity, flows, diversity, internal models, building blocks,* could be attributed to a CI-based system as well, whereas the properties *robustness, flexibility, scalability, performance* express more the view of Mondada et al (2004).

Therefore, the bottom-line premise for the design of a CI-based system is the quest for *some kind of engine that takes in some collective task description and outputs a solution that prescribes the (adaptive) behavior of the involved individuals.* Metaphorically speaking, if the design objective for a flock of birds would have been *looking for an appropriate parameter setting to get the flock moving in a straight line, square or circle,* three behavior steering parameters need to be considered: *separation, alignment, cohesion.* Flocking as observed in the real-world can be simulated by specific settings of these three parameters.

According to some other views, however, the ultimate goal of designing collective systems, has been robustness against selfish behavior. It is being claimed that methodologies for the design of collective systems should be based on the analogous assumption that *individuals are selfish optimizers and their behavior and their*

7

selfish behavior should not degrade the system performance (Namatame, 2006). Given that it is important to investigate the loss of collective welfare due to selfish and uncoordinated behavior, recent research efforts have focused on quantifying this loss for specific environments and the resulting degree of efficiency loss known as "price of anarchy".

Methodologies could also adhere to other theories such as those exposed by Darwinian dynamics on mutation and selection, which form the core of models for evolution in nature. Evolution through natural selection is frequently understood to imply improvement and progress. On the other side, however, if multiple populations of species continuously adapt to each other in a co-evolutionary process and in more and more specialized ways, then this race will never stabilize in a desirable outcome. On the contrary, importance of a biodiversity has been explained by the Rock-Scissors-Paper game, where it is shown that diversity resulting from proper dispersal by achieving Nash equilibrium is not efficient and the involved agents may benefit from achieving a better relationship. In this context, a potential methodology does not refer to general rules but to coupling rules only with which agents in a population are engaged in the nearest neighborhood. These rules are adapted, optimized and converge into some more general rules after lots of interactions.

In a much broader context, the design approaches for engineering CI-based systems can be roughly categorized into two main categories: *numerical* and *conceptual*. Numerical approaches include, for example, utility-based reinforcement learning methods, and have a more theoretical nature, whereas conceptual approaches have a more practical nature. For instance, Yamins (2208) presents a formal model to systematically describe and analyze a variety of problems within the context of self-organization.

From a more conceptual and practical point of view as the one provided by the *Technical Fo-*

rum Group Self-Organisation, self-organisation mechanisms are incorporated in the design of, e.g., cellular radio networks, traffic simulation, etc. *The main* mechanisms leading to self-organization are considered to be *direct interaction (e.g., broadcast, localisation), indirect interaction (e.g., stigmergy), reinforcement (e.g., behavioral rewards), cooperation, generic architectures (e.g., holarchies)*. From an Agent-Oriented Software Engineering (AOSE) point of view, there should be an ignorance of requirements analysis and the focus should be put on *architectural components, actors, roles, interactions*.

4.1 Generic Research Methodology into the Design and Analysis of CI-Based Systems

Crystallization of the very essence of CI-based systems may lead to the re-thinking of methodologies for the development of CI-based systems at all stages as depicted by Figure 1. In the following, we only set up the stage for the development of a commonly agreed upon, if possible, methodology for the development of a CI-based system. We only scratch the surface of an iceberg in terms of some key ingredients.

In particular, *identification of performance measure, description of input data and expected results* and *identification of involved entities* are the key ingredients for the problem assessment and requirements engineering phase of the potential methodology. Taking this further onto the next stage of modelling and implementation of the system, the involved entities should be given "eyes" and "hands" for observations and actions, respectively. At the next stage, simulation or emulation of the interacting entities could give an idea of how the system will potentially evolve. Finally, analysis and validation focus on adapting or correcting the steering parameters of the behaviour of the intended system towards the objectives.

Some more specific design modelling techniques can be summarised by the following generic algorithm:

Figure 1. A tabular representation of main areas for development of CI-based systems methodology

Problem Assessment
System (Model + Implementation)
Analytical Solution - Simulation - Emulation
Analysis
Validation

```
Initialise Individuals
Initialise World
For each Individual
Observe the World
Perform an Action
World: Determine new Observations
World: Process Costs and Benefits for
All Individuals
```

In this context, application and problem definition are based on conceptual distinction between *World* (Environment) and *Individuals* to inhabit the World. Challenges to be met are bound with (a) diversity (not all individuals have same action set, observation set, policy methods), (b) not every state of affairs is the inevitable consequence of antecedent state of affairs (*non-determinism*). Some existing models, however, like cellular automata, particle based methods, game and decision theory can instantiate the design model.

More specific considerations in regards with the simulation-emulation phase lead to the following diversifications: (a) "emergent" performance resulting from many interactions between the system parts is too complex, (b) alternatively, define functionality and behaviour by observation (simulation as an intuition aid rather than deduction and induction in science), (c) emulation goes one step further by replacing (function wise) parts of the system.

For the analysis and validation phases, some more specific issues to be taken into consideration are the *rigorous* analysis of obtained (output) results and determine whether the model and solution fit reality. It could be stated that *no validation methods for CI-based systems currently exist.*

5. CASE STUDIES AND APPLICATIONS

Collective Intelligence and systems have been brought into connection with many

subject and application areas. We refer to those areas in the following as an attempt to pinpoint the potential of contribution of CI-based systems and techniques. Though scattered across many application areas and with no reference to any common design methodologies, CI-based techniques or those, which could be classified as such, can be found in a wide variety of applications as follows. This is by no means an exhaustive list of applications but only an indicative one where CI could act as a problem solver.

In the context of Information Retrieval, text understanding and natural language processing still pose a big challenge, since there has been no efficient solution on a large-scale (Allan, 2003). Same holds with the classification and relevance calculation, the so-called "Web-clustering" problem. It has always been an ultimate goal to hit a compromise between the "fast and meaningful" search and efficient indexing for the whole Internet. Besides, the amount of human labor and effort required to create and maintain such an index, e.g., via a taxonomy, grows in progression with the growth of the corpus This process is also bound with high possibility of human errors and slow updating.

To this extent, solutions have been suggested, which carry on the label "collaborative" or "hybrid" such as systems combining browsing with automated indexing IR and Data Mining 'mash ups', IR and DB amalgamation of search and querying aspects, or even a multi-agent collaborative Web mining system, i.e., collaborative functionality allowing users to re-use the results of other users (Chau et al, 2003). In our approach (Tanase & Kapetanios, 2008), personalized dictionaries are being constructed for a healthy and sustainable growth of query term translation knowledge bases for Cross-Lingual Information Retrieval.

In the context of Ontology Engineering, it has been proved difficult and time-consuming to create acceptable concept ontology manually for a large domain. In addition, it might be rough and incomprehensive if the concept structure is created by one expert/administrator. Instead, collaborative ontology engineering tools (Auer et al, 2006, Bao et al, 2006, Farquhar et al, 1997), where ontology creation is based on a social agreement degree, have been suggested in order to integrate a number of experts' knowledge. This, however, introduced the *"Ontology Crystallization Problem"* where conflict detection, resolution and ontology convergence turned out to be a challenge.

Normally, consensus in collaborative ontology engineering is reached by applying the *Delphi* method for group decision making. Accordingly, discussion group is formed firstly with several discussion members and one communication leader. Discussion and conflict resolution processes are performed with several rounds until the social

agreement is achieved. There are three stages in each round which are (a) the brainstorming stage to allow the users contribute their opinions in the initial round, (b) the responds compiling stage to let the communication leader classify the opinions and list the conflict points, (c) the conflict resolution stage to allow the group members evaluate the opinions by questionnaire or revise their opinions to achieve the agreement.

The most prominent example of collaborative ontology engineering in its very simplistic, however, effective recently has been the emergence of *folksonomies* and collaborative tagging for the Social Web (Halpin et al, 2007, Golder & Huberman, 2006, Begelman et al, 2006). According to this paradigm, (a) no fixed hierarchy is required when annotating, (b) previously resolved hierarchies do not need to be considered, (c) it is much easier to annotate in a tagging system than on a classification system, i.e., from a small number of specialists to a large number of non-specialists. Despite the simplicity and effectiveness, there are also drawbacks such as the selection of tags as mostly based on frequencies, where most frequent terms appear with worst discrimination values and most popular one or two tags and their related ones dominate most of the tag-cloud. In addition, spam tags for commercial purposes are very often the case.

In the context of Intelligent Transportation Systems, they are traditionally based on site (AVI), sensor or probing vehicles schemes. Some coverage, cost and real-time issues have remained unsolved due to one way broadcasting system. Real-time traffic information is important for *Advanced Traffic Management Systems (ATMS)*, *Advanced Traveller Information Systems (ATIS)*, *Commercial Vehicle Operation (CVO)* as well as *Emergency Management System (EMS)*. However, several drawbacks have been reported.

For instance, site-based and sensor based methods have the spatial coverage problem due to the fixed and limited sensors. Vehicle-based scheme has cost, spatial and temporal coverage problems due to the very high cost for maintaining a dedicated fleet of urban network traffic probing vehicles. Finally, cost of real-time transmission for the whole traffic network in each data collection scheme is considered very high. On the other side, mobile personal (Mobile Phones, PDA's) as well as personal navigation devices (PND's, UMPC's) are equipped with location capability connecting to a GPS module. With such a technology available, does it make sense to envision a collaborative, two-way broadcasting, real-time traffic information collection, fusion and distribution?

In the context of Law Enforcement, mapping crimes collaboratively has been suggested and, to some extent, practiced where more transparency and publicity to criminal information has been viewed as potential reduction of the phenomena of under-reporting. For example, this has been on the political agenda of several countries, e.g., Brazil, with high rates of violence and low trust in law enforcement authorities.

Challenge, however, is finding the equilibrium between people's participation and information credibility. Open and participatory cultures are susceptible to abuses and fraud attempts. An envisioned CI-based system within the law enforcement context could comprise agents playing system roles (institutional, monitor, reputation agents), agents playing context roles (agents keeping the social network formed), domain ontology (here identified as Crime Ontology), system ontology reputation, set of interaction protocols, etc.

In the context of Artificial Intelligence, there has been a growing consensus that natural intelligence is likely to be composed of multiple diverse algorithms and knowledge representation formats. To this extent, it has been viewed that hundreds of specialised subsystems collaborate in some network or 'Society of Mind'. This is in contrast to the 'one size fits all' approach of many popular algorithms in Artificial Intelligence. If such diverse, extremely hybrid artificial agents are to be built, many authors will need to be involved, each with a different area of specialization. And if the future of AI is one of multiple authors and

multiple laboratories building vast collaborative systems, how is this work to be organized?

A response to this question has been the World-Wide-Mind project (w2mind.org), which proposes that AI research should be organized online, using an agreed, stripped-down and simplified protocol for communication between different subcomponents of the artificial minds. This is related to large online 'open source' collaborative projects, but differs from them in that it is not proposed that the components actually have to be open source. The Society of Mind Mark-up Language (SOML) is the protocol of the World-Wide-Mind (WWM), in much the same way as HTTP is the protocol of the World-Wide-Web. The WWM defines three types of entities, each of which interacts with the others using this protocol.

In the context of Software Engineering, a natural extension of the modular approach has been the distributed modular approach. Middleware standards such as CORBA and Web Services have provided developers with the means to connect modules over the Internet without knowing anything about remote modules apart from their URL and interface. However, though middleware platforms such as JADE (Java Agent Development Environment) provide support for multiple interacting autonomous agents, there has been little or no attention to how the integration of independent remote components can further our understanding of the diversity required for artificially intelligent agents.

In the same context with particular emphasis on of Search Based Software Engineering (Harman, 2007), it has been stated that the static nature of the search problems studied in the existing literature on SBSE has tended to delimit the choice of algorithms and the methodology within which the use of search is applied. It is also stated that *Particle Swarm Optimization and Ant Colony Optimization techniques have not been used in the SBSE literature*, due to the fact that these techniques work well in situations where the problem is rapidly changing and the current best solution must be continually adapted. However, it seems likely that the ever changing and dynamic nature of many software engineering problems would suggest possible application areas for Ant Colony Optimization and Particle Swarm Optimization techniques. It is somewhat surprising that highly adaptive search techniques like Ant Colony Optimization have yet to be applied in SBSE. However, these highly dynamic software engineering application areas have yet to be identified. Perhaps Service Oriented and Agent Oriented Software Engineering paradigms will provide candidate application areas for ant colony and particle swarm optimization.

In the context of Space Exploration, new approaches to exploration missions such as ANTS (Autonomous Nano Technology Swarm) augur great potential, but simultaneously pose many challenges. The missions will be unmanned and necessarily highly autonomous. They will also exhibit the properties of autonomic systems of being self-protecting, self-healing, self-configuring, and self-optimizing in order to assist in the survivability of the mission. Many of these missions will be sent to parts of the solar system where manned missions are simply not possible, and to where the round roundtrip delay for communications to spacecraft exceeds 40 minutes, meaning that the decisions on responses to problems and undesirable situations must be made in situ rather than from ground control on Earth.

Further application areas have been reported in the literature, which cannot be described in this paper due to lack of space. For instance, building and modelling of a computational digital economy as based on algorithmic game theory, modelling multilateral cooperative behaviour, management of modern dynamic networks, development models for robust, fault-tolerant systems, the study of the human immune response to HIV infection, self-organized routing in mobile ad-hoc networks.

6. CONCLUSION AND FUTURE OUTLOOK

In this article, we explored the many facets of Collective Intelligence as a form of Intelligence in society and technology through synergistic efforts, in both collaborative and competitive terms. We have drawn upon conceptions and perceptions of how we should design and implement CI-based systems. It also turned out that open research questions need to be answered in order to scientifically and methodologically underpin the notion of Collective Intelligence. For instance, research towards design and analysis of information systems as being different from conventional top-down design as well as conventional (numerical) analytical approaches. The investigated methodology should rely primarily on the specification of *World* and a *Domain of Discourse* in terms of interacting entities and constraints thereto, as currently targeted by the Semantic Web, e.g., a Web of Entities instead of documents.

This is also bound with research into harnessing complexity of self-organizing and emergence digital ecosystems such that global system behaviour is predictable and not a candidate of chaotic behaviour. To some extent, this is related with the current global financial crisis as a result of how much one regulates or deregulates. In addition, in order to monitor sustainability of growth in such digital ecosystems, research into harnessing qualitative indicators complements the picture. For instance, questions like "which quality measurement methodologies and techniques should we apply for CI-based and collective IQ".

In addition, investigation onto the strong relationship with *nature inspired computing* as well as *sociology*, *biology* and *physics* may unleash the potential of computational and methodological underpinnings with theoretical and practical merits. Particularly interesting is the investigation of the compliance with the notion of Collective Intelligence of currently available social networking portals, e.g., *Twine, Facebook, LinkedIn, MySpace, Second Life, Twitter*, with truly CI-enabling systems as well as their transition towards CI-enabling systems.

REFERENCES

Allan, J. (2003). Challenges in information retrieval and language modeling. Report of a workshop held at the Center for Intelligent information retrieval. *ACM SIGIR Forum, 37*(1), 31–47. doi:10.1145/945546.945549

Auer, S., Dietzold, S., & Riechert, T. (2006). *OntoWiki - A tool for social, semantic collaboration*. (*. Lecture Notes in Computer Science, 4273*, 736–749. doi:10.1007/11926078_53

Bao, J., Hu, Z., Caragea, D., Reecy, J., & Honavar, V. G. (2006). A tool for collaborative construction of large biological ontologies, In *Proceedings of the 17th International Conference on Database and Expert Systems Applications.*

Begelman, G., Keller, P., & Smadja, F. (2006). Automated tag clustering: Improving search and exploration in the tag space. *In WWW 2006*, Edinburgh, UK.

Beni, G., & Wang, J. (1989). Swarm intelligence in cellular robotic systems. In *Proceedings of NATO Advanced Workshop on Robots and Biological Systems,* Tuscany, Italy.

Bonabeau, E., Dorigo, M., & Theraulaz, G. (1999). *Swarm intelligence: From natural to artificial system.* UK: Oxford University Press.

Cernuzzi, L., Cossentino, M., & Zambonell, F. (2000). Process models for agent-based development. *Journal of Engineering Applications of Artificial Intelligence, 18*(2), 205–222. doi:10.1016/j.engappai.2004.11.015

Chau, M., Zeng, D., Chen, H., Huang, M., & Hendriawan, D. (2003). Design and evaluation of a multi-agent collaborative Web mining system. *Decision Support Systems: Web Retrieval and Mining, 35*(1), 167–183. doi:10.1016/S0167-9236(02)00103-3

Dawkins, R. (1989). *The selfish gene* (2nd edition). UK: Oxford University Press

Durkheim, É. (1912). *The elementary forms of religious life.*

Elwick, J. (2003). Herbert Spencer and the disunity of the social organism. *History of Science, 41*, 35–72.

Engelbrecht, A. P. (2005). *Fundamentals of computational swarm intelligence.* Hoboken, NJ: Wiley.

Farquhar, A., Fikes, R., & Rice, J. (1997). The Ontolingua server: A tool for collaborative ontology construction. *International Journal of Human-Computer Studies, 46*(6), 707. doi:10.1006/ijhc.1996.0121

Flew, T. (2008). *New media: An introduction.* Melbourne, Australia: Oxford University Press

Golder, S. A., & Huberman, B. A. (2006). Usage patterns of collaborative tagging systems. *Journal of Information Science, 32*(2), 198. doi:10.1177/0165551506062337

Halpin, H., Robu, V., & Shepherd, H. (2007). The complex dynamics of collaborative tagging, In *Proceedings of the 16th International Conference on World Wide Web,* (pp. 211-220).

Harman, M. (2007). The current state and future of search based software engineering. In L. Briand & A. Wolf, (Eds.), *Future of software engineering 2007,* (pp 342-357).

Holland, J. (1995). *Hidden order: How adaptation builds complexity.* Cambridge, MA: Perseus Books.

Kari, L., & Rozenberg, G. (2008). The many facets of natural computing. *Communications of the ACM, 51*(10), 72–83. doi:10.1145/1400181.1400200

Leadbeater, C. (2008). *We-think: The power of mass creativity*: London: Profile.

Levy, P. (1999). *Collective intelligence: Mankind's emerging world in cyberspace*. Cambridge, MA: Basic Books

Lovelock, J. (2000). *Gaia: A new look at life on Earth* (3rd edition). Oxford University Press

Mondada, G., Pettinaro, A., Guignard, I., Kwee, D., Floreano, J.-L., & Deneubourg, S. (2004). Swarm-bot: A new distributed robotic concept. *Autonomous Robots, 17*(2-3), 193–221. doi:10.1023/B:AURO.0000033972.50769.1c

Namatame, A. (2006). Collective intelligence and evolution. *ERCIM News, 64.*

Parker, G. H. (1938). Biographical memoir of William Morton Wheeler, 1865-1937. *National Academy of Sciences Biographical Memoirs, 19,* 201–241.

Parsopoulos, K. E., & Vrahatis, M. N. (2002). recent approaches to global optimization problems through particle swarm optimization. *Natural Computing, 1*(2-3), 235–306. doi:10.1023/A:1016568309421

Surowiecki, J. (2005). *The wisdom of crowds.* New York: Anchor Books.

Tanase, D., & Kapetanios, E. (2008). Evaluating the impact of personal dictionaries for cross-language information retrieval of socially annotated images. *iCLEF Workshop, ECDL 2008,* Aarhus, Denmark.

Wilson, E. O. (1971). *The insect societies*. Cambridge, MA: Harvard University Press.

Yamins, D. *(2007).* A theory of local-to-global algorithms for one-dimensional spatial multiagent systems. *Doctoral thesis, Harvard School of Engineering and Applied Sciences.*

This work was previously published in International Journal of Organizational and Collective Intelligence, Volume 1, Issue 1, edited by Hideyasu Sasaki, pp. 1-14, copyright 2010 by IGI Publishing (an imprint of IGI Global).

Chapter 2
Enhancing E–Service Collaboration with Enforcement and Relationship Management:
A Methodology from Requirements to Event Driven Realization

Dickson K.W. Chiu
Dickson Computer Systems, Hong Kong

Sven Till
Hong Kong University of Science and Technology, Hong Kong

Shing-Chi Cheung
Hong Kong University of Science and Technology, Hong Kong

Lalita Narupiyakul
University of Ontario Institute of Technology, Canada

Patrick C. K. Hung
University of Ontario Institute of Technology, Canada

ABSTRACT

In a business-to-business (B2B) e-service environment, cross-organizational collaboration is important for attaining the interoperability of business processes and their proper enactment. The authors find that B2B collaboration can be divided into multiple layers and perspectives, which has not been adequately addressed in the literature. Besides regular e-service process enactment, robust collaboration requires enforcement, while quality collaboration involves relationship management. These problems are challenging, as they require the enactment of business processes and their monitoring in counter parties outside an organization's boundary. This paper presents a framework for B2B process collaboration with three layers, namely, collaboration requirements layer, business rule layer, and system implementation layer. The collaboration requirements layer specifies the cross-organizational requirements of e-service processes. In the business rule layer, detailed knowledge of these three types of process collaboration requirements is defined as business rules in a unified Event-Condition-Action (ECA) form. In the system implementation layer, event collaboration interfaces are supported by contemporary Enterprise JavaBeans and Web Services. Based on this architecture, a methodology is presented for the

DOI: 10.4018/978-1-4666-1577-9.ch002

engineering of e-service process collaboration from high-level business requirements down to system implementation details. As a result, B2B process collaboration can be seamlessly defined, enacted, and enforced. Conceptual models of various layers are given in the Unified Modeling Language (UML). We illustrate the applicability of our framework with a running example based on a supply-chain process and evaluate our approach from the perspective of three main stakeholders of e-collaboration, namely users, management, and systems developers.

INTRODUCTION

The Internet has recently become a global common platform on which organizations and individuals communicate among each other to carry out various commercial activities and to provide value-added services. The term *e-service* generally refers to service provided over the Internet. Organizations that offer such services are known as *e-service providers*. The adoption of e-services in business-to-business (B2B) environment, however, arouses the need for a more in depth study on process collaboration across organizations. Most existing research and practice are still focusing on *regular* e-service process enactment, which represents only the basic knowledge (Chiu et al., 2003b). Effective collaboration requires robustness and quality. More robust B2B process collaboration requires the capturing and dissemination to business partners of the knowledge for correct and effective exception detection and handling, i.e., *enforcement. Exception detection* in particular has not been adequately addressed in the literature. We distinguish exception detection from *exception handling* (Chiu et al. 1999; 2001). The former concerns the knowledge of "what" has been deviated from an agreed collaboration process while the latter concerns "how" deviations can be controlled or compensated. Besides these mandatory actions, *quality* collaboration involves also optional actions that relate to business relationship management. Yet, most work on relationship management focuses on customer relationship management (Tiwana 2001) in the B2C context, instead of B2B. Thus, the problem of process collaboration is challenging because

a generally accepted infrastructure for controlling or monitoring the business processes of an organization's counter-parties is not available.

The study in this paper is motivated by our previous work on the feasibility of modeling e-Contracts based on cross-organization workflows with workflow views (Chiu et al., 2002). We have also studied the engineering of e-Contracts for its enactment (Cheung et al. 2002) and enforcement (Chiu et al., 2003b). Based on these foundation studies together with our recent work on collaborative workflow (Chiu et al., 2009; Wong & Chiu, 2007), we identified the difficulties in modeling e-Contracts (Krishna et al., 2004) and the limitations towards quality collaboration. In particular, requirements solely based on e-Contracts are inadequate because of their incompleteness and ambiguities (Chiu et al., 2003b). Although research on e-service has been steadily progressing, requirement engineering for e-service collaboration beyond basic enactment is almost unexplored.

In this paper, we propose a methodology to structure B2B process collaboration in multiple layers, namely, collaboration requirements layer, business rule layer, and system implementation layer, as well as from multiple perspectives of process enactment, enforcement, and relationship management. Based on our experience on event-driven process execution and exception handling from the ADvanced Object Modeling Environment (ADOME) Workflow Management System (WFMS) (Chiu et al., 1999; 2001), we further utilize event-condition-action (ECA) rules from the active database paradigm (Dayal, 1988) as a unified foundation artifact for eliciting various requirements for cross-organizational e-service process collaboration. In this paper, we do not require the use of a WFMS so that light weight collaborating systems as well as large distributed and scalable systems can be developed. Conceptual models of the three layers can be expressed in the Unified Modeling Language (UML), a widely accepted notation in object-oriented modeling (Lunn, 2002). We believe that B2B process collaboration should be subject to a life cycle similar to that of a software system, i.e., definition, analysis, and realization (Chiu et al., 2003b). This approach facilitates a more thorough understanding of B2B process collaboration from its fundamentals to system implementation, which has been demonstrated in our earlier work on basic cross-organizational process enactment (Cheung et al., 2002) and related applications (Chiu et al., 2005; 2009).

The contribution and coverage of this paper are: (i) a three-layer framework for B2B process collaboration that supports process enactment, enforcement, and relationship management, (ii) a methodology for requirement elicitation of B2B e-service process collaboration based on this multiple layered architecture, (iii) formulation of these three different types of requirement into a unified artifact of ECA rules, (iv) a feasible implementation framework for flexible B2B process collaboration with standard Web Services and Enterprise JavaBeans (EJB) (Hansen, 2007), and (v) an evaluation of our approach with respect to the perspective of the main stakeholders.

The rest of our paper is organized as follows. Section 2 introduces a motivating example. Section 3 related work. Section 4 presents our meta-model and framework for B2B process collaboration based on ECA rules. Section 5 details the elicitation and transformation of requirements specification in the collaboration requirements layer to ECA rules in the business rule layer. Section 6 outlines the system implementation layer based on Web Services and EJB. Section 7 evaluates the applicability of our methodology in response to different stakeholders' perspective. We conclude the paper with ongoing research work in Section 8.

MOTIVATING CASE AND RESEARCH APPROACH

In this section, we introduce our motivating case of a typical supply-chain business process to illustrate various B2B process collaboration requirements beyond basic enactment. Our case is based on the management and operation experience of the first author in Dickson Computer Systems as well as our case study in Dell (Chiu et al., 2001, 2002; 2003b).

Figure 1 depicts a motivating example of cross-organizational workflow process based on a supply chain e-commerce application (Chiu et al., 2001; 2003b). The diagram represents the basic *enactment requirements* that involve three organization roles, namely, end-users, system integrators, and parts vendors. While each individual process is simple, the cross-organizational interactions are interesting and complicated as explained in the following.

Suppose an end-user undergoes a requisition process to acquire an advanced server system. First, quotation enquiries are sent to a number of system integrators. The received quotations with product information are evaluated. A purchase order is then issued to the selected system integrator. Afterwards, the server system is received and checked. Finally, payment is arranged.

A system integrator's process starts when an enquiry is received. The first step is to check from its parts vendors the lead-time and updated price of major parts, especially for those with a large price fluctuation (say, CPU and memory). After evaluation, a quotation is sent to the end-user. While the end-user evaluates the quotation, the system integrators may need to provide additional or updated information for the bid. After a purchase order is received, the successful system integrator then orders necessary missing parts that are not in stock, and estimates a delivery schedule. When all the parts are ready, the system integrator assembles, tests the server, and then delivers it. Finally, after receiving the payment, the workflow ends.

Figure 1. A workflow process of a B2B supply chain application

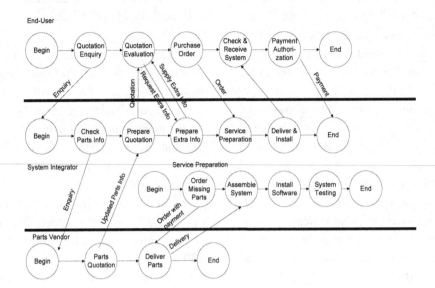

A parts vendor's process also starts when an enquiry is received. It updates system integrators with revised parts information and delivers parts upon receives an order. Assuming that orders of parts are made together with payment, the workflow of parts vendor ends after the delivery of ordered parts.

Now let us consider how we can make these processes more robust beyond its basic enactment. *Enforcement requirements* concern with exceptions arisen from the workflow process specified in the enactment requirements. The detection of exceptions performed by business partners in B2B collaboration involves information exchanged across organization boundaries, which indicates the occurrences of anomalous situations in the enactment workflow process. Once exceptions have been detected, actions are performed to control or compensate for the consequences of these exceptions. Some example enforcement requirements for the supply chain application are as follows.

- When there are changes in delivery requirements or payment arrangement, the end user should notify the affected system integrator so that it may react timely.

- When a vendor changes the lead-time but the delivery schedule can still be met within the end user's deadline, the change can be tolerated. Otherwise, another source for the part causing the problem is sought for, or an alternative part is used subject to the end user's approval.

- When there are changes in delivery date, the system integrator should notify the affected end user. The system integrator should present a revised delivery schedule to the end user according to the parts vendor's reported lead-time.

- When the price for a certain part rises to an extent that there are no more profits, the system integrator may wish to revise the product price, to use an alternate cheaper part, to postpone the delivery until price drops, or to cancel the order. If a prohibition policy of non-delivery is stated in the enforcement requirements, the end user has the rights to enforce the contract.

- When a certain part is stopped from production, the system integrator may request the end user's approval of using an alternative part. Further details of the process "service preparation" are available to the end user so that the user can further monitor the progress of the job and estimate the delivery date.

- When there is a significant aggregated price change in parts during the end user's evaluation, a revised quotation (price) is sent to the end user through an event-triggering mechanism.

It should be noted that the collaboration process could be affected by exceptions (or messages) from organizations external to the collaboration parties. An example is a message from a news channel about the damage of a major semi-conductor factory in Taiwan in an earthquake. This message is critical to the decision making of a computer manufacturer because the prices of hardware, in particular memory chips and motherboards, may shortly surge. In that case, the manufacturer may decide to abort or reject large orders based on an old price. In this paper, we limit our scope to the detection and handling of exceptions within collaboration parties.

Further, business partners often want to improve the quality of collaboration and thereby their mutual relationships. *Relationship management requirements* concern with these extra or optional actions. Some of them have to be carried out in response to certain situation and at appropriate time, while some others are provided as gratitude services. Such requirements, now in a B2B context, are often similar to those for business-to-customer (B2C) relationship management (Chiu et al., 2003; Kwok & Chiu, 2004; Wong & Chiu, 2007; Tiwana 2000). Some examples are as follows:

- Any involved organization wants to be able to inquire the progress of business processes at other business partners' side such as order processing, and payment.
- A service provider wants to relay relevant information to business partners from other sources or upon enquiry, such as techni-

cal information, drivers update, and product news.
- Effective measures for handling complaints and feedbacks from business partners are essential to help rescue threatened relationship and reduce attrition.

Traditionally, all these three types of requirements are typically supported either by "hardcoded" information systems or partially with a WFMS). Two problems arise when these systems are extended beyond individual organizational boundaries. Firstly, cross-organizational interactions (such as quotation enquiry or order placement) are not handled with full automation, which generally requires the provision of well-defined programming interfaces. Secondly, process collaboration cannot be effectively maintained without a distributed event-triggering support system.

Our research approach follows the design research approach for information systems (Hevner et al. 2004). First, our *awareness of the problem* is motivated by these extended requirements in enforcement and relationship management based on our business and consultation experiences. We start off our study by gathering and organizing such objectives and requirements. We notice that recent advances in information technology, especially Web service and SOA, can be deployed to facilitate their realization in information systems. Actually, we have concentrated on these advanced aspects in a number of other projects in various application domains and have some success on them (Chiu et al., 2003; Kwok & Chiu, 2004; Lau et al., 2006; Lam & Chiu, 2006; Ng et al., 2007; Cheong et al., 2007). So, our more ambitious objective is to summarize on *how* this can be accomplished, that is, the development methodology.

Second, our *suggested model* is a B2B collaboration conceptual model based on the ECA-rule mechanism, which acts a core to a three-layered conceptual architecture (requirements, rules, implementation), as presented in Section 4. The essence of ECA-rules is to provide a unified artifact for capturing the requirements of enactment, enforcement, and relationship management in order to facilitate the overall B2B processes and workflows.

Third, the *development* (see Section 5) follows our conceptual architecture by first developing a detailed methodology for eliciting these requirements into rules, discussing how to address typical problems and difficulties in such process, like ambiguities, monitorability, and timeliness. Next, we develop a design and implementation framework based on standard web service and widely adopted EJB technologies (see Section 6). We show how such ECA-rules can be supported by our event support system framework as well as typical publish-and-subscribe web services can be built to facilitate the communication for B2B process collaboration. We stress on the importance of exception handling and monitoring mechanisms.

Fourth, we present the *evaluation* of our approach with the discussion on the benefits with major system stakeholders (see Section 7).

RELATED WORK

There are three main approaches to e-service collaboration for B2B applications. A more traditional approach is the application of WFMS across organizations. This approach based on cross-organizational workflow models, which focuses on processes and actions. The second approach is based on e-Contracts, which aims at transforming requirements from formal contracts to its realization. This approach focuses more on requirements. The third more recent approach is based on the service-oriented architecture (SOA), which focuses on service composition and collaboration. Our methodology attempts to integrate all these three approaches to achieve the multiple perspectives as required in robust and flexible cross-organizational e-service collaboration.

Although there are many web-enabled WFMS research prototypes and commercial products, few of them addresses problems in e-service process collaboration beyond normal enactment comprehensively. For example, Casati and Shan (2001) presented a framework for dynamic and adaptive composition of e-services based on the Hewlett-Packard's eFlow system. The framework focuses on service discovery and run-time process modification but not on exception detection or handling. Casati et al. (2002) further presented a methodology for engineering the requirement for workflow applications. The methodology mainly deals with the basic process enactment and does not focus on cross-organizational collaboration. Crossflow (Grefen et al. 2000) models virtual enterprises based on a service provider-consumer paradigm, in which organizations (service consumers) can delegate tasks in their workflows to other organizations (service providers). High-level support is obtained by abstracting services and offering advanced cooperation support. Virtual organizations are dynamically formed by contract-based matchmaking between service providers and consumers. Although Crossflow presents a detailed discussion on contracts, it has not studied exceptions and other sophisticated control between workflows of different organizations. We have proposed a novel concept of workflow view for cross-organizational workflow interoperability in the E-ADOME framework, as motivated by views in object-oriented data models (Chiu et al., 2002). The architecture supporting e-Contract development with workflow views is equipped with ECA-rules mechanisms driven by cross-organizational events. However, the study on requirements engineering for event-driven asynchronous processes, especially on exception handling, has not been explored. So, most approaches based on cross-organizational workflow mainly focus on basic e-service enactment. The issues in both enforcement and relationship management have not been adequately studied.

The study of e-contracts is originated from the work of Contract Net Protocol (1980). However, the protocol only concentrates on low-level transaction aspects. The research in e-contracts revives with the wide adoption of e-business activities. For example, Grosof (1999) introduced a declarative approach to business rules in e-commerce contracts by combining Courteous Logic Program and XML. Grisler et al. (2000) presented an architecture for legal e-Contracts, but not a mechanism for modeling e-Contracts. Marjanovic and Milosevic (2001) proposed a contract model based on contract clauses including obligation, permission, and prohibition. However, the detail requirement for achieving the obligations (that is, enactment of the main business process or *how*) involves domain knowledge and are often mostly not covered in the contract. Krishna et al. (2004) proposed a meta-model for e-Contracts with entity-relationship diagrams, but not an overall e-Contract development process or a possible system design and implementation methodology. Our methodology presents a more detailed and general approach, not just transforming contract clauses into workflows and rules. Recently, Angelov and Grefen (2008) have reviewed principles of the e-Contracting for B2B and proposed a reference architecture with the necessary system functionalities and qualities to be addressed in the implementation of an e-contracting system. Neither are the issues of enforcement and relationship management explicitly addressed.

On the other hand, recent researches for e-service collaboration focus on the Service-Oriented Architecture (SOA) and Web services. In recognition of the need to streamline cross-organizational services or processes by creating an open and distributed system environment, a number of studies have shown increased interest in the field of Web services, which enable flexible service selection and composition for cross-organizational processes (Zhao et al., 2005; van der Aalst et al., 2007; Herrero et al., 2008). Service-Oriented Architecture (SOA) is essentially a collection of services which communicate with each other (Erl, 2006). SOA is a logical way of designing a software system to provide services to either end-user applications or other services distributed in a network through published and discoverable interfaces (Papazoglou & Georgakopoulos, 2003).

The adoption of Web Services on SOA is mainly driven by its interoperability for Internet applications. Web Services typically offer self-contained and self-describing services that can be published, located, and invoked across the Internet. Web services perform functions that can be anything from simple requests to complicated processing of business data. Once a Web service is deployed, other applications as well as Web services can discover it via Universal Description, Discovery and Integration (UDDI) registries (Erl, 2006), and invoke the Web service based on the technologies that it supports. Web services are described through their interface definitions in the Web Service Description Language (WSDL) (Erl, 2006), which is an eXtensible Markup Language (XML) based language. Based on the SOA, the Web Services Business Process Execution Language (BPEL) is a representation system to describe both executable and abstract business processes (Weerawarana et al., 2005). Another related example is the Web Services Choreography Description Language (WS-CDL). The WS-CDL is an XML-based language that describes peer-to-peer collaborations of Web Services participants by defining, from a global viewpoint, their common and complementary observable behavior; where ordered message exchanges result in accomplishing a common business goal (Mending & Hafner, 2005). Wohed et al. (2003) present an excellent comparison between BPEL and other composition languages, which use workflow patterns and communication patterns as the evaluating criteria.

As for methodologies, Yang et al. (2002) approached service composition in three steps: planning, definition, and implementation, which is in line with ours. Kuo et al. (2006) proposed the XML interaction service as a generic Web service for use by human tasks that provides HTML form-based Web interfaces for users to interact with and update schema-compliant XML data for a workflow application. Wutke et al. (2008) proposed a model for decentralized workflow enactment based on a variant of Petri nets. The model supports the SOA and is designed for flexible and adaptable distributed processes as orchestrations of a set of self-coordinating components, without the need for central coordination. Huemer et al. (2008) introduced a three level approach for an e-Business registry meta-model, introducing the economics layers on top of the traditional the process choreography and the service implementation layers.

Facilitation of the relationship management using information systems is traditionally discussed in the context of B2C instead of B2B. Customer relationship management (CRM) is the strategy for optimizing the lifetime value of customers. Tiwana (2001) provided a detailed guide to CRM applications in e-business environment with a knowledge management approach. Romano and Fjermestad (2002) presented an extensive survey on electronic commerce customer relationship management (ECCRM), but there have been relatively few published studies on the details of building CRM systems for e-business environments, as compared with other marketing or data-mining papers. However, the work does not provide any detailed case study in system architecture or technical implementation details. We have recently proposed an event driven approach and system architecture for supporting customer relationship management in e-Brokerage environment (Chiu et al., 2003; Kwok and Chiu, 2004) as well as collaborative customer support (Wong and Chiu, 2007). We discovered that several techniques developed for B2C can be adapted for B2B collaboration with appropriate automation as discussed in later sections.

In summary, previous work address either only specific portions of B2B e-service collaboration (mainly process enactment) or just part of the supporting facilities. In particular, neither enforcement and relationship management aspects nor their requirement elicitation has been addressed adequately.

A FRAMEWORK FOR B2B PROCESS COLLABORATION

In the section, we first present a three-layer architecture for B2B process collaboration and then highlight how a meta-model of business rules can facilitate this in a unified way.

A Three-Layered Conceptual Architecture for B2B Process Collaboration

To streamline the B2B process collaboration in an e-commerce environment, involved organizations should clearly define their roles and the requirements of business processes (Chiu et al., 2002b; 2003b). This definition is subjected to further analysis that aims to: (i) identify the relations between the involved data entities, (ii) the events or actions that take place in different parts of the business processes, and (iii) the exceptions that may arise. Finally, B2B process collaboration is realized and enacted using standard Internet technologies, such as Web Services and EJB (Hansen, 2007).

Depending on their job responsibilities, users across an organization may have different perspectives on the collaboration. For example, a system implementation model that contains details of system implementation in Web Services may not provide the middle management with information at the right level of abstraction. Instead, a business rule layer with knowledge expressed in rules and actions is more appropriate. On the other hand, the system implementation model is more relevant to a system analyst who needs to refine the required B2B process collaboration into system design and implementation for subsequent enforcement. To address this issue, a

Figure 2. A three-layered conceptual architecture for B2B collaboration

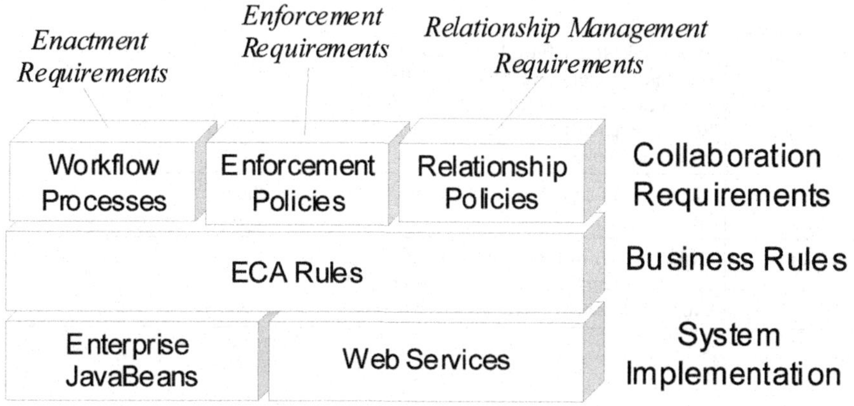

three-layered architecture, as shown in Figure 2, is proposed to provide multiple perspectives of the business process. The architecture is formulated in an object-oriented model using UML to allow for reusability and extensibility.

The *collaboration requirements layer* consists of three types of requirements: enactment, enforcement, and relationship management. Enactment requirements refer to the execution of an agreed collaboration workflow process, such as the one given by Figure 1 in a supply chain example. Enforcement requirement refers to the intolerable or alarming deviations from the agreed workflow process. These deviations are modeled as *exceptions*. Realization of enforcement requirements typically involves (i) the detection of exceptions and (ii) the subsequent actions taken to handle those exceptions. Enforcement requirements can be represented by a set of policy clauses, which typical includes *obligation, permission,* or *prohibition* (Marjanovic and Milosevic, 2001). Relationship management requirements are optional or extra actions that facilitates quality collaboration, and are usually not covered by the above two categories.

The *business rule layer* elicits B2B collaboration requirements and related domain knowledge from the viewpoint of business rules. *Business*

rules specify all three types of requirements in a unified paradigm of *Event-Condition-Action* rules (Dayal, 1989; Chiu et al. 1999), which originate from active databases. When a business rule is triggered by some business *events* under pre-specified *conditions*, business *actions* required for collaboration are carried out, which may lead to the generation of other business events. The following presents an ECA rule that raises a delivery exception should the delivery of some items has not occurred by deadline.

Event: onDay(deadline(DELIVER))
Condition: NOT occurred(DELIVER)
Action: raise(exception(DELIVER))

The *system implementation layer* refines business rules into two parts, the exchange of *events* across organizations through Web Services interfaces and the realization of business *actions* based on Enterprise JavaBeans (EJB) technologies (Hansen, 2007). We choose business actions to be realized in EJB components because it is component based and supports high interoperability across platforms. For the cross-organizational event interface, we employ Web Services Description Language (WSDL) to define the required interactions, in which XML schemas

Table 1. Artifacts of an architecture for B2B collaboration

Layer	Artifacts
Collaboration requirements	Meta-model for B2B Collaboration: Enactment requirements (Workflow Processes) Enforcement requirements (Enforcement Polices) Relationship management requirements (Relationship Management Polices) Parties and Roles
Business rules	Meta-model for process enactment and exception handling: Business events, Business rules, Business actions and Business entities
System implementation	Task system (Enterprise JavaBeans components) Process system (WSFL or workflow engine) Cross-organizational interface (Web Services XML schemas)

of business entities are specified for this purpose (Erl 2006). The advantage of using Web Services is to establish cross-organizational collaboration via existing Internet standards, supporting both human web-based interactions and automatic programmed interactions. Table 1 summarizes the artifacts used in our three-layered architecture.

A Meta-Model of B2B Process Collaboration

Figure 3 presents our meta-model for B2B process collaboration in the class diagram of the UML, as explained in the following. A collaboration requirement is modeled as an aggregation of a set of enactment, enforcement, and relationship management requirements. An enforcement requirement is specified using a policy clause while an enactment requirement is specified by a workflow process. Both policy clauses and workflow processes can be realized by a set of business rules in the ECA format. In subsequent discussions, a business *action* refers to a workflow process that performed by a *single* business party. Complex actions are recursively decomposed into simpler actions. For example, an action Check System Configuration that performed by the system integrator consists of two simpler actions: (i) to receive quotation request from end user and (ii) to validate the system configuration required in the request.

An *event* is the happening of something interesting to the system itself or to user applications (Chiu et al., 1999). When an event occurs, it triggers some business rules and the *condition* parts of these rules will be evaluated. *Conditions* are logical expressions defined on the states of some business data, such as the status of an order. Only if the *condition* is satisfied, the *action* part, which can be itself a workflow process, is executed and may lead to other events. The semantics of ECA rules for contract enforcement can be summarized by the following: *On* event *if* condition *then* action. There are several types of events. For example, *business events* are events due to successful executions of some business actions. Examples of business events include the receipt of a request for quotation or purchase order. *Temporal events* are events due to the expiration of some deadlines. *Exceptions* are events due to violations of enforcement requirements or unsuccessful executions of business actions. Each event is published by some business party and subscribed by others. It should be noted that event subscription could be implicit. For example, the placement of an order implies a subscription to the event of change in delivery date, as this is an obligation of the supplier.

ELICITATION AND TRANSFORMATION OF PROCESS COLLABORATION REQUIREMENTS

We now proceed to discuss how each type of B2B process collaboration requirements can be elicited

Figure 3. A Meta-model of B2B process collaboration in UML

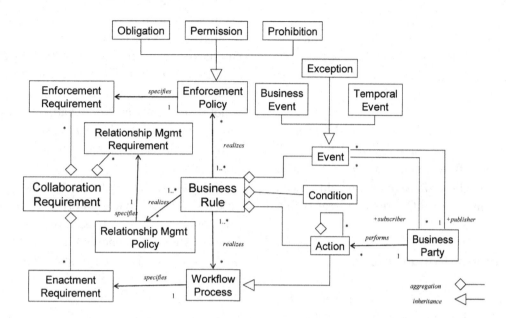

and transformed into ECA rules in the business rule layer, based on our experience in event-driven workflow management and exception handling (Chiu et al., 1999; 2001; 2003).

Enactment Requirements

Enactment requirements concern with the basic requirements of the business processes for collaboration. It should be noted that these requirements may not be covered adequately or completely in a contract or other documentary communications among the participating organizations. This is because most of these requirements may involve common sense, specific domain knowledge, experiences, laws, and regulations. The source of information for elicitation of these enactment requirements is basically similar to those of requirement engineering for standard business processes (Casati et al., 2002, Chiu et al., 1999) and is therefore not the focus of this paper.

However, we still advocate an event driven activity execution (that is, ECA rule based) model to provide a unified approach for B2B

process collaboration (Chiu et al., 1999; 2001). Moreover, this is necessary for cross-organization business processes because business partners have to trigger the corresponding start-events (say, quotation enquiry) to start B2B process collaboration. Upon a start-event, if the process is a composite one, the *collaboration process enactor* will raise a *start-event* for the first sub-process. This will continue recursively downward the composition hierarchy until a leaf sub-process or *task* is reached. The *collaboration process enactor* sends a start-event to the task to initiate it. After the task is finished successfully, the task replies to the *collaboration process enactor* by raising a finish-event with the results (if any). The *collaboration process enactor* then carries on with the next step according to the returned result. Upon failures or timeouts, an appropriate *exception event* will also be raised accordingly. Further details of expressing process execution in ECA rules can be found in our previous work (Chiu et al. 1999, 2001). For example, the system integrator's process can be facilitated by the following ECA rules:

E: received (QUOTATION_ENQUIRY), C: true,
A: perform (CHECK_PART_INFO)

E: finish (CHECK_PART_INFO), C: true, A:
perform (PREPARE_QUOTATION)

E: finish (PREPARE_QUOTATION), C: true, A:
perform (PREPARE_EXTRA_INFO)

As such, a collaboration process designed in the form of an UML Activity Diagram (Lunnl, 2002) or workflow specification in accordance with the Workflow Management Coalition can be transformed into ECA rules systematically (Chiu et al. 1999).

Enforcement Requirements

Motivated by the notion of contract modeling based on deontic logic (Marjanovic and Milosevic, 2001), we focus the elicitation on the enforcement requirements of a collaboration process on the following three types of *policy clauses*: *obligations* (what a party have to do), *prohibitions* (what a party must not to do) and *permissions* (what a party can do but is not obliged to do). Though contracts and agreements may not be available or complete, we may follow this classification to analyze requirement statements in all available relevant documents. These policy clauses are used to cross check and to enforce the mutual agreement made by multiple business parties in process collaboration. In order to enforce a policy clause, various variables such as status of the delivery, including confidential information, such as bank accounts,, have to be monitored. One approach is to launch an enforcement service checking the validity of all these variables (according to the policy clauses) constantly. However, this incurs tremendous overheads to a system, and this mechanism is not practical to extend across organizational boundaries. Alternatively, motivated by well-accepted active database paradigms (Dayal 1989), the transformation of policy clauses into ECA-rules can systematically reduce the monitoring effort. Now the monitor becomes only active when an interesting event occurs. Interesting events are to be raised by each party or some information sources. The demand of resources for enforcement is greatly reduced by using ECA-rules because the amount of surveyed variables at one time is much less and the monitoring software is not permanently active. In particular, we shall discuss how *temporal events* are heavily used to model various temporal constraints of these policy clauses.

To facilitate exception detection and handling, collaboration requirements are analyzed and then transformed to a set of ECA rules formulated based on the meta-model in Figure 3. This set of ECA rules collectively formulates an operational model of the requirements of exception detection and handling. Because exception handling is specific to different situations and different application, we concentrate on discussing the analysis for exception detection across organizations in this section. Our methodology can help systematically specify ECA rules for exception detection from collaboration requirements. When an exception is detected, it will trigger, in turn, ECA rules specified for exception handling. From our experience (Chiu et al. 1999; 2001), once we can identify and specify an exception, formulating an exception-handling rule reduced to specifying the condition and action parts of the ECA-rule, and is therefore much more straightforward then exception detection.

With reference to the example depicted in Figure 1, we made a study based on a related service agreement referred to as the "Terms and Conditions of Sale, Service and Technical Support" at the official website of Dell, Hong Kong (2007), in which *Dell* also plays the role of system integrator and *customers* play the role of end user as in our motivating example. Table 2 summarizes our methodology to map different types of clauses into ECA rules for exception detection and handling, which will be detailed in the following subsections. *BAO* stands for an object that encapsulates a business action whose

Table 2. Basic mapping of requirements clauses into ECA rules

Enforcement rule Clause type	Event	Condition	Action
Obligation	*onDay(deadline(BAO))*	*NOT occurred(BAO)*	*raise (exception(BAO))*
Prohibition	*onOccurred(BAO)*	*prohibitionCondition (BAO)*	
Permission		*NOT permitted(BAO)*	

execution triggers the object creation. Our methodology helps discover some typical problems that arise from the ambiguity of natural languages in requirements specification and the autonomous nature of individual organizations. We also suggest some measures to overcome them during the discussion.

After the involved parties have agreed the collaboration requirements, an analysis is conducted. The analysis is driven by a methodology mapping the three policy types of requirements clauses, namely, *obligations*, *prohibitions*, and *permissions* into ECA rules. Common wordings may provide an additional hint in the analysis to classify the policy type of the clauses. For example, the term "shall" tends to imply an obligation, "may" a permission, and "shall not" a prohibition or a permission (a non-obligation). Since natural language formulations (particularly in contracts) can be multifarious, further analysis in the clause structures is often necessary.

An alternative is to map these rules into a set of logical expressions in deontic logic, a class of formal logic (Marjanovic and Milosevic, 2001). A rule of deontic logic has the following formal structure:

Rule #: <role> [is] (obligated | forbidden| permitted) [to] [do] (<action> [before <condition>] | satisfy <condition>) [, if <condition>][, where <condition>] [, otherwise see Rule <#>]

Unlike ECA rules, deontic logic was not designed to be executable and therefore not associated with a well-defined operational semantics.

For instance, the triggering event for an action is often omitted, making it difficult to determine the execution of logical expressions. In addition, the deadline of an action or a task is often not stated. However, this is important for the enforcement of obligations; otherwise a party may defer the obliged action indefinitely. An obligation without stating a deadline or an event before which the obliged action must have taken place may even imply enforcement is inapplicable. Sometimes, the deadline is implied due to standard practices of the business, governmental regulation, etc., and must be added explicitly by the analyst. All these kinds of ambiguities, once found, should be clarified and confirmed by both parties to avoid confusion or later unnecessary disputes, and should not simply left in a rule.

Enforcing Obligations

Consider an ECA rule R_{obl} that formulates an obligation where a business action A_{obl} must be performed by a deadline T_{obl}. The obligation can be enforced using the following mechanism. Upon reaching the deadline T_{obl}, a temporal event is generated by the *Timer*. This triggers the *exception detector* to fire rule R_{obl} and executes the enforcement action checking if the obliged party has performed the required business action A_{obl}. This checking can be achieved by, as for example, searching the log file for invoked actions or occurrence of related events. In the case of payment obligations, suitable events could be the acceptance of a payment receipt or a change in the bank account balance. If the obligation has not been fulfilled, the *exception detector* raises an exception. Based on this mechanism, ECA rules for obligation enforcement can be formatted using the following predicates. Here, *BAO* is an object encapsulating the required business action with a deadline of *deadline(BAO)*. A temporal event is generated on the date of deadline, denoted as *onDay(deadline(BAO))*. The predicate *occurred(BAO)* holds if the business action has occurred. An exception, denoted as *exception(BAO)*, is raised as a result of the rule execution.

$$
\left.
\begin{array}{l}
E : onDay\left(deadline\left(BAO \right) \right) \\
C : NOT\ occurred\left(BAO \right) \\
A : raise\left(exception\left(BAO \right) \right)
\end{array}
\right\} \textit{An ECA Rule for Obligation Enforcement}
$$

For example, the clause: "*7.1 Dell shall deliver the Products to the place of delivery designated by Customer and agreed to by Dell as evidenced in Customer's invoice ("Place of Delivery")*" can be formulated by the following enforcement ECA rule.

E: onDay(deadline(DELIVER))
C: NOT occurred(DELIVER)
A: raise(exception(DELIVER))

The customer could monitor this obligation by checking the list of products delivered before and on the delivery date, denoted as *deadline(DELIVER)* in the rule. However, problems may arise if Dell has sent the products but due to certain circumstances, they have not reached the customer. In this case, Dell could prove the product delivery, as for example, by providing the tracking number of the dispatched package. In fact, this should be done as soon as the package is dispatched, in order to improve customer relationship.

As mentioned above, there are two sets of ECA rules necessary to implement B2B process collaboration - for the *enforcement* and for the *enactment*. Enactment rules are triggered to invoke necessary actions on time, while enforcement rules are triggered on deadline of obligations. Since an obliged action may need some time to complete, the action must be triggered early enough, as for example, six days before the deadline. The following enactment ECA rule for the same clause illustrates this difference:

E: onDay(before(deadline(DELIVER), 6))
C: valid(place(DELIVER)) & ready(DELIVER)
A: perform(DELIVER)

We conclude this subsection by discussing a general problem of the impreciseness of natural languages. Phrases like "as soon as practicable" or "as soon as possible" are imprecise, lacking a concrete deadline. The handling of such ambiguity generally requires human attentions. The analyst has to substitute these with concrete deadline in the formulation of ECA rules. For instance, consider the clause "*10.7 ...Dell shall respond to a request for such Emergency Service as soon as practicable after its receipt of such request. ...*" The corresponding enforcement ECA rule can be formulated in the following. Here, *N* is a chosen time allowance.

E: onDay(after(receiptDate(EMERGENCY_RE-
       QUEST), N)))
C: NOT responded(EMERGENCY_REQUEST))
A: raise(exception(EMERGENCY_REQUEST))

Enforcing Prohibitions

The occurrence of a prohibited action (or prohibition) should be treated as an exception by the *exception detector*. Our meta-model in Figure 5 supports this scenario without any extension. One problem of the observation of prohibitions is that if a party performs a prohibited action, the party will probably try to hide or distract this fact as long as possible (unless the party does this by mistake or misunderstandings). Thus, in general, it will be quite difficult to observe or to recognize a

Figure 5. Implementation of cross-organizational interfaces using Web services

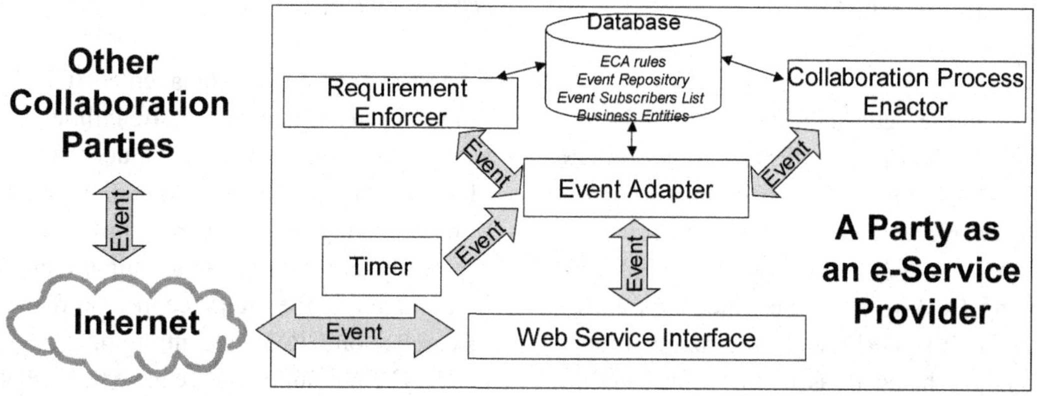

prohibited action. Should it be easy to detect such an event of a prohibited action, the party probably would not invoke this specific action. This is a problem due to the autonomous nature of different organizations rather than that of our architecture or our model. A general ECA rule for prohibition enforcement can be described as follows:

E: onOccurred(BAO)
C: prohibitionCondition(BAO)
A: raise(exception(BAO))

For example, the clause: "*14. Each party shall treat as confidential all information obtained from the other pursuant to a Contract which as marked "confidential" or the equivalent or has the necessary quality of confidence about it and shall not divulge such information to any persons without the other party's prior written consent provided that this clauses shall not extend to information which was rightfully in the possession of such party prior to the commencement of the negotiations leading to the Contract, ...*" can be formulated by the following enforcement ECA-rule.

E: onOccurred(INFO)
C: confidential(INFO)
A: raise(exception(INFO))

If a party really passes confidential information to a third party, this is almost impossible to detect. Thus, the event "*onOccurred(INFO)*" is *non-monitorable*. Dell encounters a similar problem. For instance, there is another clause stating that the customer warrants buying the products only for its own internal use and not for re-sale. But Dell may not easily check if the end-user buys the product for itself or for resell to a third-party.

Enforcing Permissions

A permission is a temporary allowance to perform an otherwise prohibited action, i.e., a specific action may only be carried out only within a certain allowed time period. Some actions may be permitted under specific *situations* (i.e., events plus conditions). Note that a party is not obliged to carry out a permitted business action. After the message of the invocation of permitted action is received, the *exception detector* checks whether the conditions for the permission are met. If the permission situations are not met, the *exception detector* raises an exception. Whether the actual action invocation will be interrupted or not depends on the exception handler. A general ECA rule for permission enforcement can be formulated as follows:

E: onOccurred(BOA)
C: NOT permitted(BOA)
A: raise(exception(BOA))

For example, consider the clause "*2.1 ... Dell shall be entitled to refuse to accept orders placed by the Customer if the Customer breaches or Dell, on reasonable grounds, suspects that the Customer will breach this warranty.*" A corresponding ECA-rule can be stated as follows where REFUSE_ORDER is the action object encapsulating the business action "refuse order".

E: onOccurred(REFUSE_ORDER)
C: NOT badlisted(customer(REFUSE_ORDER))
A: raise(exception(REFUSE_ORDER))

The event *onOccurred(REFUSE_ORDER)* can be observed by the customer upon the receipt of a order cancellation message. But the customer may have problems in understanding the applicability of the condition, as the internal criteria of Dell for trustable customer is not disclosed to the public.

Consider another clause "*3.1 Dell may, at its sole discretion, allow a Customer to cancel its order after acceptance at no charge, if written notice of such cancellation is received by Dell before commencement of manufacture of the Products. If Dell allows a Customer to cancel its order after manufacture but before shipment of the Product, Dell shall be entitled to levy a cancellation charge equal to 20% of the price of the Products.*" The clause may be formulated by the following ECA rule. The business action "levy cancellation charge" is encapsulated by an action object LEVY.

E: onOccurred(LEVY)
C: NOT (dateOfCancellation(order(LEVY)) > dateOfManufacture(order(LEVY)) & cancellationApproved(order(LEVY)))
A: raise(exception(LEVY))

Relationship Management Requirements

Customer Relationship Management (CRM) solutions help an organization to streamline customer services and maximize the value of customers (Tiwana, 2001). The move to deploy CRM solutions is getting popular across industry sectors, especially as a measure to sustain the growth of e-commerce in the digital economy. While most researches on CRM concentrate on data mining and B2C e-commerce, there have been relatively few published research papers on the detailed system architectures and implementation methodologies for CRM activities enactment. To our knowledge, the study of relationship management in the context of B2B process collaboration is new. In this context, the main objectives include: (i) provision of quality service (ii) monitoring of collaborating processes, (iii) better dissemination of information, and (iv) effective handling of complaints. As these objectives likely require appropriate actions to be carried out effectively and efficiently in response to different situations, causes, and information sources, we propose to employ also an event driven approach to address these issues. Comparing with our study on event driven approach to CRM in a B2C environment (Chiu et al. 2003; 2008), we find out that automation is even more essential for a B2B environment. This is because the desired degree of automation among business process is much higher, while human intervention is required to handle exceptions and complaints.

We suggest the elicitation of relationship management requirements to be concentrated on business rule designs for asynchronous event driven rather than procedural knowledge of enactment. This is because an event can be used to trigger the enactment of a relevant process that has already been designed or to be designed later. Such a top-down approach facilitates the management to capture precious knowledge of relationship management and turn it into business actions.

One key issue is to capture business rules are often in *if-then* form, which is different from the ECA-rule (*on-if-then*) format. Therefore, we need to isolate the relevant events from the conditions by analyzing the *if*-part from these business rules (Chiu et al., 1999), as illustrated in the previous sub-section. Furthermore, during requirement elicitation, we should record the objectives of each rule in order to determine its usefulness and hence its priority of implementation in a phased approach. This also helps the management to understand and validate their functions.

Quality of service is often not explicitly enforced in a contract, i.e., optional in this sense. However, the management may decide to do better than required or specified in consideration of relationship management. For example, though some obliged actions may have a distant deadline, the management may decide to perform it as soon as feasible after knowing that the action is necessary. The following modified ECA rule illustrates that delivery is made immediately upon order if the product is ready instead of several days before deadline:

E: received (ORDER)
C: valid(place(DELIVER)) & ready(DELIVER)
A: perform(DELIVER)

Monitoring of collaborating processes helps business partners to plan ahead and reduce uncertainties. Further to the example in the previous sub-section, a customer can hardly tell whether the manufacture process of the product has already commenced when the order is cancelled. It is almost non-monitorable because a customer normally does not have access to such kind of internal information. However, Dell may improve the situation by informing the customer when the manufacturing process has commenced through its enactment system. As such, the monitorability / enforceability of this specific permission would change from non-monitorable to monitorable. Active notification, when correctly employed,

is even better than handling enquiries passively as this can reduce the need for human enquiries and thus operating costs. The following ECA rule illustrates that the customer is notified upon the product is dispatched:

E: start (DELIVERY)
C: true
A: notify (customer (DELIVER))

Dissemination of useful information to customers has been widely in practice for B2C relationship management. For example, financial institutions often provide market information to their customers as extra services. There is no reason why such services should not be extended to B2B environment. These value-added services facilitate the customer to make decision and in turn may help effective collaboration. For example, upon receiving technical information or software updates, etc., .the system integrator would like to notify the relevant customers to prevent problems from occurring. This also improves the service quality and may reduce the cost of support. The following ECA rule illustrates such a deed:

E: received (INFO)
C: relevant (INFO, customer)
A: notify (customer (INFO))

Effective handling of complaints avoids attrition and is essential to help rescue threatened relationship and reduce attrition. Often complaints involve exception conditions and need to be handled by trained personnel or even the management manually. In addition, this should be performed as soon as possible to reduce customer grievance. The following ECA rule illustrates such arrangement:

E: received (COMPLAINT)
C: true
A: notify (handling_personnel (customer (COM-
    LAINT)))

Figure 4. System design of an event support system for B2B process collaboration

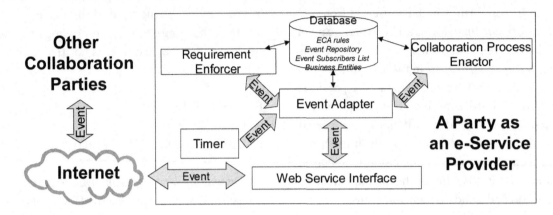

A WEB SERVICES BASED IMPLEMENTATION FRAMEWORK FOR B2B PROCESS COLLABORATION

Web Services can be used to interface different process enactment systems, exception detectors and exception handlers within and across organizations by supporting the appropriate cross-organizational communication and collaboration. In this section, we present a system design of an event support system for B2B process collaboration together with its implementation of cross-organizational interfaces based on Web Services.

Event Support System

Figure 4 depicts the system design of an event support system for B2B process collaboration. Each collaboration party is an e-service provider, which hosts a *collaboration process enactor* subsystem and a *requirement enforcer* subsystem. The *collaboration process enactor* carries out the enactment requirements. The *requirement enforcer* detects and handles exceptions. Events involved in both subsystems are published and subscribed through an *event adapter*. The event adapter collects internal events from the collabo-

ration process enactor and external events from the *Web Service interface.* Events collected are filtered and transformed to a structure accepted by the requirement enforcer. Temporal events are generated by a *timer* subsystem. In addition, each party maintains a database, which stores the ECA rules, business entities (that is, data), event repository (event log) and event subscriber lists. The advantage of this system is its support of a flexible peer-to-peer model. It does not require a central facilitator or moderator.

Based on the functional and data requirements of the *event adaptor*, three Web services, namely, for publishing events, receiving events, and subscribing events, are identified as shown in Figure 5. The examples of these Web services are summarized in Table 3.

The *publish* Web Service will be invoked by the *event adaptor*. The input parameter is the occurred event or exception. Based on this, the Web Service checks the subscribers list and the security policies, and notifies the subscribers. Notification can be performed via different kinds of protocols like e-mail, fax, ICQ message, or even an invocation of another Web Service. The subscribers have to specify how they are notified in the subscription process via the *subscribe* Web Service. The *publish* Web Service can be

Table 3. Sample Web service specifications for B2B process collaboration

Publish Web Service	*Subscribe* Web service	*Receive* Web Service

Input: EventReceivingAcknowledge
• EventReceivingAcknowledge
Output: EventMessage
• Date
• Sender
• Receiver
• Event
  ◦ Event name
  ◦ Event type
  ◦ Event subject
  ◦ Event message body
  ◦ Prio
	Input: SubscriptionRequest
	• Eventprovider
	  ◦ Name
	  ◦ Address
	  ◦ E-Mail
	• SubscribedEvent
	• NotificationParameter
	  ◦ transmissionPort
	  ◦ TransmissionParameter
	  (like email | fax | icq number |...)
	Output: SubscriptionResponse
	• SubscriptionResult
		Input: EventNotification
		• Date
		• Sender
		• Receiver
		• Event
		  ◦ Event name
		  ◦ Event type
		  ◦ Event subject
		  ◦ Event message body
		• Prio
		Output: EventReceivingResponse
		• EventReceivingAcknowledge

a composite Web Service, which uses different Web services for the various ways of transmission.

The *subscribe* Web Service registers the requests for an event subscription including several parameters such as the requester, the subscribed event, and how the requester wants to receive the event notification. In a real application scenario, one non-dedicated *subscribe* Web Service is sufficient. However, it is also possible to provide a Web Service for each subscribable event. This is also true for the *receive* Web Service. A non-dedicated Web Service can parse the incoming message and invoke other Web services or components based on the message sender, event type or event name. Dedicated event receiving Web Services may be invoked directly by the event publishing party or by a message queue handler after receiving an e-mail message.

In addition, a system integrator can offer more specific Web Services like *takeOrder* or *trackOrder* as shown in Table 4. In order to provide a better service and to increase the trust between the involved parties, the *trackOrder* Web Service can be composed with another *trackDelivery* service, so that customers may acquire all necessary information from one provider.

External Exception Reception

It should be noted that the Web Services listed in Table 4 involve external events from counter

Table 4. Some possible Web services for B2B process collaboration

takeOrder Web Service	*trackOrder* Web Service

Input: OrderRequest
• Buyer
  ◦ Name
  ◦ Address
  ◦ E-Mail
• ProductList
  ◦ Product
  • Product ID
  • Product Name
  • Quantity
  • Price
Output: OrderResponse
• OrderResult
  ◦ OrderNr
  ◦ Password
  ◦ Estimated Delivery Date
	Input: OrderStatusRequest
	• OrderNr
	• Password
	Output: OrderStatus
	• Progress
	• Estimated Delivery Date
	• Optional: DeliveryNr

Table 5. Web service for change order request

Name: ChangeOrderRequest
Input:
• ChangeContractDataRequest
  ◦ ChangeRequestID
  ◦ Customer Id
  ◦ OrderNumber
  ◦ ToChangeContractData [which contract parameter should be changed]
    ◦ OldValue
    ◦ NewValue
    ◦ ReasonOfChange
	Output:
	• ChangeContractDataResponse
	  ◦ ChangeRequestID
	  ◦ Approved (Yes/No)
	  ◦ AuthorizedBy
	  ◦ AdditionalComment
	  ◦ ToChangeContractData
	  ◦ NewValue

parties (i.e., business partners) for collaboration process enactment. In addition, a robust business process should be able to handle various exception scenarios. External events can be due to exceptions caught from or thrown to external parties. We call them *external exception events*. External exception events due to the End User include Cancel Order Request, Change Order Request, Delay Payment Request and Return Unsatisfied System Request, etc. In addition, Change Order Request can be further refined to include Change Delivery Date Request and Change Delivery Location Request, etc. Example exception events issued by the Part Vendor include: Price List Update, Part Recall Notification, Part Obsolescence Notification and Driver Update, etc. Price List Update includes Price Update and New Parts Update, etc.

Besides capturing an event itself with a Web Service, it is much more convenient and efficient to capture also the data required for the process of the event handler (i.e., the condition and/or the action parts of the ECA-rules) with the same Web Service. Some researchers treat these as event parameters [39], [6]. For example, in the Change Delivery Date Request, the New Delivery Date and the reasons for change are extra parameters in the Web Service.

Events generally form an inheritance hierarchy. Where appropriate, we can design a Web Service to capture events in a whole class hierarchy such as capturing Change Order Request as one service (as illustrated in Table 5). This is because once the event is captured to the internal system, the

different ECA rules can be triggered according to the semantics of these rule, which is independent of the event detection method.

As a *catch-all* precaution for unexpected events, it is generally advisable to set up a generic handler to capture all undefined events, especially if they are from important sources, such as regular business partners. An additional action to avoid receiving undefined events is to instruct these business partners (either manually or through their Web Services) that they should only send events through defined Web Services; otherwise unexpected exceptions or events should be sent by emails in a verbose manner.

Alternatively, we may consider a Change Order Request to be another separate workflow, especially if the handling of this business sub-process is complicated enough. We conceptually model all the data items related to a Change Order Request as contained in a "Change Order Request Form", which is the first required item in this process (analogous to the data item *enquiry* in the main System Integrator's workflow).

Sending Events to Business Partners

The main objectives of sending events to business partners include: (a) to request for partner's services, and (b) to supply event feed as requested by the business partners (subscribed events). In addition to regular events, the same mechanism can be used to request for exception handling services and passing exception events.

If the partner has a relevant Web Service, we can simply invoke it accordingly to its specification, passing additional data items (parameters) as required. However, if a party does not support Web Service or does not have a definition for a particular Web Service, these events (together with the relevant data) can be sent by email or ICQ for notification purpose. In this case, the partner may need to manually process this event or set up a mail message automatic handler to process it.

For example, the system integrator can invoke the Web Service of a part vendor to cancel an order, if that is supported. However, without a Web Service, the cancel order request can only be sent via emails or processed with manual procedures.

Event Subscription Services

When both business partners support Web Services, a more efficient and preferred way for event passing is to use the publish-and-subscribe paradigm. Each party publishes a list of subscribe-able events at a Universal Description, Discovery, and Integration (UDDI) directory (Erl, 2006). This allows business partners subscribe to events that are relevant or interesting to them, through the event subscription service of the event-publisher. The event receiver should have a corresponding Web Service to receive and process the subscribed event; otherwise event delivery via emails or ICQ may need human intervention.

Subscription to regular business events, such as price updates, is useful for *asynchronous* cross-organizational information alert, which can trigger automatic processing with ECA-rule mechanisms upon the event. Apart from regular events for normal processing, a party may subscribe to exception events (such as order cancellation, delivery delayed, etc.) in order to trigger ECA-rules for automatic exception handling.

Event Chaining

With automated receipt and sending of events, a party can relay an event and distribute it to other business partners, together with other useful or processed information. This *event chaining* mechanism enables the provision efficient and effective knowledge dissemination.

For example, the system integrator can subscribe to all the parts vendors on drive update alerts, and in turn, provide driver update alert subscription services to the end users. When the system integrator receives a drive update alert from a part vendor, it can check which end users have bought a system with such parts. Then, a driver update alert is sent to all these end users. This process can be modeled and executed automatically with an ECA-rule triggering mechanism. Similarly, a part upgrade order cancellation request from the end user may trigger a part order cancellation request to the part vendor via the system integrator's event driven execution of an order cancellation workflow.

Process Monitoring and Directory Services

Furthermore, it is useful to provide additional information about the progress of a process of a business partner. For example, the system integrator updates the customer of the progress of the

Table 6. Partial listing of Web service for process monitoring

Name: GetProcessStatus
Input: ProcessStatusRequest
 • CustomerId
 • OrderNumber
Output: ProcessStatusResponse
 • CustomerID
 • OrderNumber
 • StatusReport (content depend on the customer, status, etc.)
 • ContactPersonInfo (for further information)

subscribed e-service or the end user provides the system integrator with information about the status of the quotation evaluation. A monitor service (cf. Table 6) provides a specific snapshot of a view of an internal workflow. Since the relationships between different business parties are different, it is useful to personalize the monitoring service. The information to be monitored for each party depends on its unique role in the business process. Additional definitions of Web Services are required for exception handling and personalized monitoring.

The BPEL (Erl, 2006) is a standard XML language for the description of Web Service compositions. The language distinguishes between two different types of compositions. In the first type, the execution order of a business process is specified by the flow of control and the flow of data between the involved Web Services. The second type has a more decentralized or distrib-

uted nature. It considers the interactions between Web Services. In contrast to the previous flow model, this model describes how Web Services interact with each other. Each link corresponds to the interaction of a Web Service with an operation of another Web Service's interface. Basic composition operators like sequences, forks and joins can be defined in WSFL so that they may use to describe successions, parallelisms, and synchronizations in cross-organizational workflows.

DISCUSSIONS

Before concluding our paper, we evaluate the applicability of our implementation framework and methodology with respect to the major stakeholders, including users, management, and system developers (as summarized in Table 7).

Table 7. Concerns of different stakeholders in e-service collaboration

	General Concerns	Enactment	Enforcement	Relationship Management
User's Perspective	**Assist their work** Interoperability and connectivity System / information availability Convenience and ease of use	Workflow automation Reliability – retries, search alternatives	Reduce tedious manual checking Timeliness of services	Improved service call-center or web page More transparent business processes
Management's Perspective	**Cost vs. Benefit** Improve productivity Scalability Security Reduction in total development cost Communications cost	Increase business opportunities Convergence of disparate business functionalities	Business process monitorability Compliance to contracts / trade standard / regulations / laws Exception and crisis management Knowledge management	Improve customer relationships Improved services Knowledge management
System Developer's Perspective	**Development / Maintenance effort & cost** Requirement elicitation Reusability Scalability Uncertainty in the use of new technologies Overall system complexity Integration with existing systems	Phase approach that accommodate existing basic enactment information systems	Event monitorability Difficulties in programming captured knowledge	Difficulties in programming captured knowledge

As mentioned, our proposed methodology for e-service collaboration involves the following three dimensions: enactment, enforcement, and relationship management. We compare each of the three dimensions with respect to the stakeholders' general concerns.

User's Perspective

Users benefit from e-service collaboration in streamlining their work through improved inter-organizational interoperability and connectivity. The systems and information from other partner organizations once not available can now be easily accessed through Web services clients or webpage front-ends. Traditional information request through email or telephone conversion can therefore be speeded up through direct information system queries. Regular information exchange can be further automated through publish and subscribe mechanisms.

Cross-organizational workflow enactment no longer requires manual interactions with cross-organizational e-services interfaces. This is not only eliminates waiting time for human attention but also increase reliability through automation. Furthermore, the reliability is increased through retries, search of alternatives, and the provision for enforcement mechanisms. In particular, enforcement mechanisms reduce the need for tedious regular manual checking unless exception events are raised to draw human attention. Deadlines are also observed or anticipated in this way to ensure timeliness of services.

Through improved quality of services under the rational for relationship management, users benefit from expanded and improved services. Users can convey exceptions and complaints, which are not handled with regular enactment or enforcement, through web pages, call centers, or other automated channels. Through various channels for service monitoring, more transparent business process can be archived, thereby increasing users' confidence of the services.

Management's Perspective

A major concern of the management is the cost against the benefits of e-service collaboration. In particular, if any improvements to the organization's members as discussed in the previous sub-section can significantly help to improve their productivities, the cost is justified. The e-service collaboration provides tangible benefit for organizations by allowing information sharing between partners and participants. Reducing the need for human-based communication also implies a significant reduce of traditional communication (such as phone and fax) costs.

Next, incorporation of e-service collaboration increases business opportunities. It also helps to improve relationships due to improved communications. In particular, through standardized technologies such as Web Services, the challenges in converging and interfacing different businesses across the different organizations can be tackled in a proper approach. Web services provide a standard means to support interoperable service-to-service interaction over a network in conjunction with other Web-related standards. The disparity of heterogeneous organizational applications has created inflexible boundaries for communicating and sharing information and services among different organizations. Therefore, Web services technologies provide a standardized way to share the information and services among various heterogeneous applications, and also the standardized Web services interfaces among business operations can be established to take the convergent benefits of all the organizational applications.

Problems arise from the autonomous nature of individual organizations. Events that need to be monitored often come from counter parties in other organizations, and might not be monitorable. Thus, cooperation and trust should be developed among trade partners to alleviate this problem. In general, this improves the transparency of operations, services, and in turn, customer (or partner) relationships, and is therefore vital in contemporary e-service providers with strong competitions. Moreover, such events may be made monitorable by specifying additional requirements for the provision of such events and knowledge among the parties where appropriate. As a long term solution, trade standards or e-services standards should be established accordingly to minimize such efforts and to streamline fair and effective monitoring of e-service provision in the digital economy. Such standardization also helps reduce costs of development and deployment of the required software through reusable components and systems.

In order to balance trust and security, a service provider would like to provide information on only the relevant part of its internal workflow to customers. This kind of partial workflows is known as workflow views (Chiu et al., 2002). It helps to convey the information in a fully controlled and understandable manner. In addition, by offering different views to different information requesters, the service provider only needs minor or even no modification to its own workflow, but can systematically arrive at a customized interface. The components of a workflow view include the process flow graph, input/output parameters, objects, rules, events, exceptions and exception handlers derived from the original workflow. Chiu et al. (2002) provides a detailed description of these components. We are working on providing workflow views for e-services to different types of customers via directory services, such as UDDI.

Further benefits arrive from the pre-programming of business processes and their enforcements. This helps improve the quality and consistency of decision results, as well as flexibility and adaptation. As such, costs to program the operation and even management knowledge into the enactment and enforcement of business processes as well as the relationship management are well justified. Also, expertise to handle practical problems can be incorporated into exception handling mechanisms. As for cost factors, our approach is suitable for adaptation of *existing* systems and extension of system functionality with a phased approach.

Through software reuse, a reduction in not only the total development cost but also training and support cost can be achieved.

System Developer's Perspective

System developers often concern about system development cost and subsequent maintenance efforts. These concerns can be addressed by systematic fine-grained requirement elicitation. Analysis of contract is only one of the important issues in the study, which highlights obligations, permissions, and prohibitions. Often, contracts do not specify how the collaboration should be done in details and sometimes contracts or other formal documents may not be available. Other sources of requirement for process collaboration include laws, regulations, standard trade practices, etc. However, to avoid unnecessary disputes, the parties involved should discuss and clarify the matter, and if necessary, amend existing or forthcoming collaborations accordingly. Capturing requirements from domain specific knowledge and expertise is ultimately important in designing detail business processes and asynchronous event-triggered rules for exception handling and relationship management. An event driven approach allows human intervention for handling exceptions and complaints to be integrated smoothly with automated collaboration processes. Further problems in analyzing requirements and contracts arise from ambiguity and impreciseness of natural languages. We believe our continuing research in formal analysis of contracts and other documents with semantic web technologies will further help.

Recent advances in technologies have resulted in fast evolving Web standards. The e-service collaboration systems require much greater extents of adaptations to keep up with such blooming technologies. Service based interface is more readily to be adapted to cope with new technologies and to allow for more comprehensive unit testing. Therefore, our approach further helps reduce uncertainties through adequate testing and experimentations of new technologies. This can significantly shorten the system development time, meeting management expectation in competitive edges.

Our methodology is also suitable for the phased system development. Often, many organizations already have information systems that can satisfy the enactment requirements. Our methodology help proceed to implement cross-organization collaboration, and in particular, enhancements in enforcement and relationship management, on top of existing systems. Thus, such enhancements can be incrementally implemented according to their relative importance and urgencies. Overall, this can also reduce the time to software delivery and costs incurred as well as cope with changes in requirements.

For legacy systems, developers can build wrappers around them to enable compatibility with Web Services, with our WebXcript approach (Chiu et al., 2005b)[REMOVED REF FIELD]. As such, the existing business process can be gradually extended to collaborate with business partners with adequate testing and streamlining the switch-over, which may otherwise cause a great impact for a major enterprise-wide system. In order to further streamline interactions among enterprises, application layer semantics (such as content taxonomy and category definitions), protocols for interaction, and service-level standards are called for. Trade unions and regulatory bodies may help in such standardizations and service grids (Gentzsch, 2002) can be formed for seamless and large-scale effective B2B process collaboration in the future.

CONCLUSION

This paper has presented a pragmatic three-layer architecture for B2B e-service process collaboration, supporting enactment, enforcement, and relationship management. The three layers are collaboration requirement layer, business rule layer, and system design layer. We have also presented a meta-model for B2B collaboration based on a unified artifact of ECA rules. To demonstrate the feasibility of our architecture, we have presented a methodology for eliciting knowledge of collaboration requirements into business rules in ECA format in an e-service environment, using a supplier chain example. We have also highlighted typical problems that can be discovered by our methodology, together with some measures of overcoming them. We finish our discussion with an outline of the *system design layer*, which is facilitated by contemporary standard software technologies of EJB and Web Services. As such, the development of a system for B2B process collaboration can be streamlined in the context of e-service providers and consumers.

At the same time, we are working on further details e-service negotiation, methodologies for preventive measures avoiding contract breaches, and formal semantics. Relationship management in B2B context is an area that worth extensive research efforts with the emergence and acceptance of B2B process collaboration. On the other hand, we are interested in the application of B2B collaboration in various advanced real-life e-service environments, such as supply-chain, procurement, finance, stock trading and insurance.

ACKNOWLEDGMENT

This work was partially supported by the Hong Kong Research Grant Council with an Earmarked Research Grant (HKUST6170/03E).

REFERENCES

Aalst, W. M. P., Benatallah, B., Casati, F., Curbera, F., & Verbeek, E. (2007). Business process management: Where business processes and web services meet. *Data & Knowledge Engineering*, *61*(1), 1–5. doi:10.1016/j.datak.2006.04.005

Angelov, S., & Grefen, P. (2008). An e-contracting reference architecture. *Journal of Systems and Software, 81*(11), 1816–1844. doi:10.1016/j.jss.2008.02.023

Casati, F., Fugini, M. G., Mirbel, I., & Pernici, B. (2002). WIRES: A methodology for developing workflow applications. *Requirements Engineering, 7*(2), 73–106. doi:10.1007/s007660200006

Casati, F., & Shan, M. C. (2001). Dynamic and adaptive composition of e-services. *Information Systems, 26*(3), 143–163. doi:10.1016/S0306-4379(01)00014-X

Cheong, F. K. W., Chiu, D. K. W., Cheung, S. C., & Hung, P. C. K. (2007). Developing a distributed e-monitoring system for enterprise Website and Web services: An experience report with free libraries and tools. In *Proceedings of the IEEE 2007 International Conference on Web Services (ICWS 2007)*, Salt Lake City, Utah (pp. 1008-1015).

Cheung, S. C., Chiu, D. K. W., & Till, S. (2002). A three-layer architecture for cross-organization e-contract enactment. In *Proceedings of Web Services, E-Business and Semantic Web Workshop*, Toronto, Ontario, Canada, (pp. 78-92).

Chiu, D. K. W., Chan, W. C. W., Lam, K. W. G., Cheung, S. C., & Luk, T. F. (2003). An event driven approach to customer relationship management in an e-brokerage environment. In *Proceedings of the 36th Hawaii International Conference on System Sciences (HICSS36)*, Big Island, Hawaii, IEEE Computer Society Press, CDROM, 10 pages.

Chiu, D. K. W., Cheung, S. C., Hung, P. C. K., Chiu, S. Y. Y., & Chung, A. K. K. (2005). Developing e-Negotiation support with a meta-modeling approach in a Web services environment. *Decision Support Systems, 40*(1), 51–69. doi:10.1016/j.dss.2004.04.004

Chiu, D. K. W., Cheung, S. C., Kafeza, E., & Leung, H.-F. (2003c). A three-tier view methodology for adapting m-services. *IEEE Transactions on Man, Systems and Cybernetics. Part A, 33*(6), 725–741.

Chiu, D. K. W., Cheung, S. C., Kok, D., & Lee, A. (2003). Integrating heterogeneous Web services with WebXcript. In *Proceedings of the 27th Annual International Computer System and Applications Conference (COMPSAC 2003)*, Dallas, Texas (pp. 272-277).

Chiu, D. K. W., Cheung, S. C., & Till, S. (2003b) An architecture for e-contract enforcement in an e-service environment. In *Proceedings of the 36th Hawaii International Conference on System Sciences (HICSS36)*, Big Island, Hawaii, IEEE Computer Society Press, CDROM, 10 pages.

Chiu, D. K. W., Kafeza, M., Cheung, S. C., Kafeza, E., & Hung, P. C. K. (2009). Alerts in healthcare applications: process and data integration. *International Journal of Healthcare Information Systems and Informatics, 4*(2), 36–56.

Chiu, D. K. W., Karlapalem, K., Li, Q., & Kafeza, E. (2002). Workflow views based e-contracts in a cross-organization e-service environment. *Distributed and Parallel Databases, 12*(2-3), 193–216. doi:10.1023/A:1016503218569

Chiu, D. K. W., Kok, D., Lee, A., & Cheung, S. C. (2005b). Integrating legacy sites into Web services with WebXcript. *International Journal of Cooperative Information Systems, 14*(1), 25–44. doi:10.1142/S0218843005001006

Chiu, D. K. W., Li, Q., & Karlapalem, K. (1999). A meta modeling approach for workflow management system supporting exception handling. *Information Systems, 24*(2), 159–184. doi:10.1016/S0306-4379(99)00010-1

Chiu, D. K. W., Li, Q., & Karlapalem, K. (2001). Web interface-Driven cooperative exception handling in ADOME workflow management system. *Information Systems, 26*(2), 93–120. doi:10.1016/S0306-4379(01)00012-6

Dayal, U. (1988). Active database management systems. In *Proceedings of the 3rd International Conference on Data and Knowledge Bases,* (pp. 150-169).

Dell Corp. (2007) *Dell's Online policies*. Retrieved March 31, 2009 from http://www.ap.dell.com/ap/hk/en/gen/local/legal_terms.htm

Erl, T. (2006). *Service-oriented architecture: Concepts, technology, and design*. Prentice-Hall.

Gentzsch, W. (2002). Grid computing: a new technology for the advanced Web. In *Proceedings of the NATO Advanced Research Workshop on Advanced Environments, Tools, and Applications for Cluster Computing*, (Lecture Notes in Computer Science, 2326, pp. 1-15).

Grefen, P., Aberer, K., Hoffner, Y., & Ludwig, H. (2000). CrossFlow: Cross-organizational workflow management in dynamic virtual enterprises. *International Journal of Computer Systems Science & Engineering*, *15*(5), 277–290.

Hansen, M. D. (2007) *SOA using Java*(TM) *Web services*. NJ: Prentice Hall PTR.

Herrero, P., Bosque, J. L., Salvadores, M., & Pérez, M. S. (2008). WE-AMBLE: A workflow engine to manage awareness in collaborative grid environments. *International Journal of High Performance Computing Applications*, *22*(3), 250–267. doi:10.1177/1094342007086225

Hevner, A. R., March, S. T., Park, J., & Ram, S. (2004). Design science in information systems research. *MIS Quarterly*, *28*(1), 75–105.

Huemer, C., Liegl, P., Schuster, R., & Zapletal, M. (2008). A 3-level e-business registry meta model. In *Proceedings of the 2008 IEEE International Conference on Services Computing*, Washington, DC, USA (pp. 441-450).

Krishna, P. R., Karlapalem, K., Dani, A. R., & Chiu, D. K. W. (2004). An ER^EC framework for e-contract modeling, enactment and monitoring. *Data & Knowledge Engineering*, *51*(1), 31–58. doi:10.1016/j.datak.2004.03.006

Kuo, Y. S., Tseng, L., Hu, H., & Shih, N. C. (2006). An XML interaction service for workflow applications. In *Proceedings of the 2006 ACM Symposium on Document Engineering*, (pp. 53-55). New York.

Kwok, K., & Chiu, D. K. W. (2004). An integrated Web services architecture for financial content management. In *Proceedings of the 37th Hawaii International Conference on System Sciences (HICSS37)*, Big Island, Hawaii, Jan 2004, IEEE Computer Society Press, CDROM, 10 pages

Lam, A. C. Y., & Chiu, D. K. W. (2006). Co-operative brokerage integration for transaction capacity sharing: A case study in Hong Kong. In *Proceedings of the 39th Hawaii International Conference on System Sciences (HICSS39)*, IEEE Press, CDROM.

Lau, G. K. T., Chiu, D. K. W., & Hung, P. C. K. (2006). Web-service based information integration for decision support: A case study on e-mortgage contract matchmaking service. In *Proceedings of the 39th Hawaii International Conference on System Sciences (HICSS39)*, IEEE Press, CDROM.

Lunn, K. (2002). *Software development with UML*. Houndmills, Basingstoke, Hampshire: Palgrave Macmillan. ISBN 0-333-98595-8.

Marjanovic, O., & Milosevic, Z. (2001). Towards formal modeling of e-contracts. In *Proceedings of the 5th IEEE International Enterprise Distributed Object Computing Conference* (pp. 59-68).

Mendling, J., & Hafner, M. (2005). From inter-organizational workflows to process execution: Generating BPEL from WS-CDL. In *Proceedings of the On the Move to Meaningful Internet Systems: OTM Workshops* (pp. 506-515).

Ng, N. L. L., Chiu, D. K. W., & Hung, P. C. K. (2007). Tendering process model (TPM) implementation for B2B integration in a Web services environment. In *Proceedings of the 40ᵗʰ Hawaii International Conference on System Sciences (HICSS39)*, CDROM, IEEE Press.

Papazoglou, M. P., & Heuvel, W.-J. d. (2007). Service-oriented computing: concepts, characteristics and directions. *The VLDB Journal, 16*(3), 389–415. doi:10.1007/s00778-007-0044-3

Romano, N. C., & Fjermestad, J. (2002). Electronic commerce customer relationship management: an assessment of the research. *International Journal of Electronic Commerce, 6*(2), 61–113.

Smith, R. G. (1980). The contract net protocol: high level communication and control in a distributed problem solve. *IEEE Transactions on Computers, 12*(29), 104–1113.

Tiwana, A. (2001). *The Essential Guide to Knowledge Management – E-Business and CRM Applications.*: Prentice Hall.

Weerawarana, S., Curbera, F., Leymann, F., Storey, T., & Ferguson, D. F. (2005). *Web services platform architecture: SOAP, WSDL, WS-policy, WS-addressing, WS-BPEL, WS-reliable messaging, and more.* Prentice Hall.

Wohed, P., Aalst, W. M. P. d., Dumas, M., & Ter Hofstede, A. H. M. (2003). Analysis of Web services composition languages: The case of BPEL4WS. In *Proceedings of the 22ⁿᵈ International Conference on Conceptual Modeling (ER 2003)* (pp. 200-215).

Wong, D. S. F., & Chiu, D. K. W. (2007). Collaborative workflow management with alerts: An integrated retailing system for garments brands. In *Proceedings of the 2007 IEEE International Conference on e-Business Engineering (ICEBE)*, Hong Kong IEEE Press (pp. 433-438).

Wutke, D., Martin, D., & Leymann, F. (2008). Facilitating complex Web Service interactions through a tuplespace binding. In *Proceedings of the 8ᵗʰ IFIP WG 6.1 International Conference on Distributed Applications and Interoperable Systems*, LNCS 5053, Springer (pp. 275-280).

Yang, J., Papazoglou, M. P., & Heuvel, W. J. d. (2002). Tackling the challenges of service composition in e-marketplaces. In *Proceedings of the 12ᵗʰ International Workshop on Research Issues in Data Engineering: Engineering E-Commerce/E-Business Systems* (pp. 125-133).

Zhao, J. L., & Cheng, H. K. (2005). Web services and process management: a union of convenience or a new area of research? *Decision Support Systems, 40*(1), 1–8. doi:10.1016/j.dss.2004.04.002

This work was previously published in International Journal of Organizational and Collective Intelligence, Volume 1, Issue 1, edited by Hideyasu Sasaki, pp. 15-43, copyright 2010 by IGI Publishing (an imprint of IGI Global).

Chapter 3
Chance Discovery as Analogy Based Value Sensing

Yukio Ohsawa
The University of Tokyo, Tokyo

Akinori Abe
ATR Knowledge Science Laboratories, Japan

Jun Nakamura
The University of Tokyo, Tokyo

ABSTRACT

The authors are finding rising demands for sensing values in existing/new events and items in the real life. Chance discovery, focusing on new events significant for human decision making, can be positioned extensively as an approach to value sensing. This extension enables the innovation of various artificial systems, where human's talent of analogical thinking comes to be the basic engine. Games for training and activating this talent are introduced, and it is clarified that these games train the an essential talent of human for chance discovery, by discussing the experimental results of these games on the logical framework of analogical abductive reasoning.

INTRODUCTION: CHANCE DISCOVERY AS VALUE SENSING

Value sensing, to feel associated with the something in one's environment, has been defined as a dimension of human's sensitivity in the literature of developmental psychology (Donaldson, 1992, p.143). It is meaningful to extend this concept to the creation of business strategies based on real data. The "value" here can be dealt with as a relation to the social environment, which business workers and customers create from their interaction via products and services, to redesign the market sustainably. For example, data mining may be regarded as a method for showing objectively useful knowledge, if we read the application results of data mining superficially, because data are collected from the real world via sensing systems such as POS (position of sales) registers, RFID tags, etc. However, the relational

DOI: 10.4018/978-1-4666-1577-9.ch003

patterns among items obtained by those tools mean no useful knowledge if the user does not sense the value of commercial items from the visualized result.

Since year 2000, we started studies on Chance Discovery under the definition of "chance" as an event significant for human's decision, and edited books and special issues of journal. In these publications, we have been standing on the principle that a decision is to choose one from multiple scenarios of actions and events to be taken in the future. Based on this principle, a chance defined above can be regarded as an event at the cross point of scenarios, which forces humans to choose one from multiple scenarios. Events/items bridging multiple clusters of strongly co-related frequent items, which a tool such as C4.5, Correspondence Analysis, KeyGraph, etc may show, have been regarded as the candidates of "chances" that are rare events meaningful for making a decision. This way of looking at the result of data visualization has been proven to be more useful than the diagrams themselves, according our case studies involving users who are marketers and designers in real business sites. In this paper, we focus on the thought of these users, and present two games for activating and training the thinking skills for chance discovery. The behaviors of players are discussed, borrowing the concept of analogical abduction developed in artificial intelligence, to point out the essence of the games' effect on human's power for chance discovery.

CASES USING SCENARIO MAPS AS BASIS OF CHANCE DISCOVERY AND VALUE SENSING

In projects we conducted with companies, the marketing teams acquired novel awareness of valuable parts of their market they had not taken into consideration so far. For acquiring this awareness, KeyGraph assisted business people by showing a diagram as a map of the market having (1) clusters of items frequently bought as a set, i.e., at the same time together, and (2) items bridging the clusters in (1), which may embrace a latent market coming up in the near future.

From the original algorithm (Ohsawa et al., 1998), we improved and extended KeyGraph in response to opinions of users working in real business. For example, let us show an example where a diagram obtained by KeyGraph assisted textile marketers seeking new hit products (Ohsawa & Usui, 2006). Although they already had popular products, they also desired to develop new markets from a niche product, i.e., a product which may be rare for the time being but may expand the company's opportunity. For this purpose, they started from data which had been collected in exhibition events, where pieces of textile samples had been arranged on shelves for customers representing apparel companies to pick preferable samples. Previously, the list of picked-up samples had been used as an order card on which to send samples to customers. However, once the marketers came to aim at hit sales, the same list was put into an electronic dataset. In comparison with data on past sales, the exhibition data were expected to include customers' preferences of products not yet displayed in stores.

They visualized the data using decision trees (Quinlan, 1993), correspondence analysis (Greenacre, 2007) etc, but not even one expected niche has been discovered. After all, they reached KeyGraph, which showed (1) clusters of frequent items in the data, i.e., popular item-sets which tend to be ordered by the same customer, and (2) items which appear rarely but appear in the same baskets as items in multiple clusters. The diagram obtained was as in Figure 2, where the black nodes linked by black lines show the clusters corresponding to (1) above, and the red nodes and the red lines show the items corresponding to (2) above and their co-occurrence with items in clusters respectively. Note: The nodes are not colored in black and red in this paper, but the distinction is not necessary here.

This figure was still difficult for marketers to understand, due to the complexity of the graph and the long names of product items. The marketers, in order to overcome this problem, attached the product samples as in Figure 1, to sense the smoothness, colors, etc with eyes and fingers simply. The meeting of 10 marketers, looking at the figure and touching the textile items on it, ran as follows:

1. First, they noticed the clusters corresponding to popular item sets mentioned in (1) above. Here, 3 experts of women's blouse noticed the cluster at the top of Figure1 (b), i.e., of "*dense textile for neat clothes, e.g., clothes for blouse*" and 3 others noticed the cluster in the right corresponding to business suits. 2 others noticed the popular item, not linked to any clusters of (1) via black lines, in the left, corresponding to materials of casual clothes. These clusters corresponded to established submarkets of the company, according to the marketers in the experiment room.

2. During the period in (1), a marketer who had been working for the company for 10 years paid attention to the relations between the other marketers' opinions about the clusters above. Then he pointed out women daily wearing business clothes (suits and blouse) may dislike to continue in the same cloth, but desire to change into casual cloth made of the textile in the left of Figure 1(b).

3. Based on the scenario found in (2) above, i.e., the marketers paid attention to the item between the item in the left and the large cluster which is the combination of the cluster at the top and the right. These *between* nodes appeared as red nodes (the one of "New Corduroy" in the dotted circle in Figure 1(b)), i.e., rare *niche* items lying between popular clusters, on which a marketer of the richest experience came up with a scenario to design a new semi-casual cloth in which women can go both to workplaces and to light dinner after working. As a result, the new corduroy marked a hit – 13th highest sales among their 800 products (previously, the sales of new products had been normally lower than the 100th).

All the time, the marketers were also visualizing their own thoughts to themselves, during the meetings, by writing on a white board.

In another case, where we applied KeyGraph to a machine manufacturer, the co-occurrences

Figure 1. Marketing as value sensing (Left: KeyGraph's result for exhibition data Right: The topic flow in the marketing team)

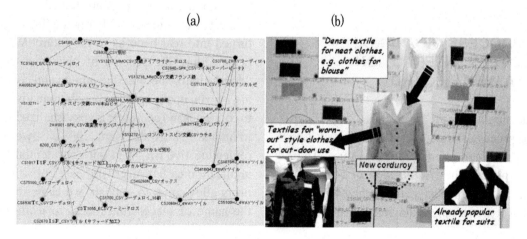

Figure 2. The White Board Model: The spiral process for chance discovery: Data as objective evidences are the results of subjective interests, and vice versa. Data on both are visualized to the user(s).

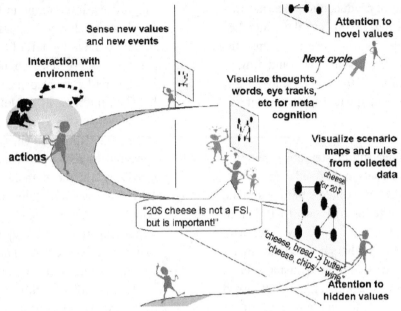

of words in customers' claims were visualized, and machine designers referred to the diagram all the time of meeting. At the same time, they also visualized their communication on the co-occurrences of words in the same utterances (Horie & Ohsawa, 2006) by KeyGraph. The two graphs, i.e., of customers' claims and designers' utterances, have been presented in the meeting room all time. As a result, the team successfully designed a new machine to occupy the largest share in the market.

THE PROCESS OF CHANCE DISCOVERY: INTERACTION WITH A WHITE BOARD

We can summarize the cases above as in Figure 2. The process started from *collection of data*, based on a keen interest in new values. Then, they introduced the *visualization of data* using suitable tools, which happened to be KeyGraph. Looking at the visualized diagram, regarding it as

a map of the market, they discussed the scenarios for developing and selling products. Through this discussion, the marketers and designers obtained novel scenarios which lead them to successful business.

In each case, objective data from the real world and subjective data presenting the ideas of participants, who are creators of scenarios, have been visualized on the white board to themselves. Thus, participants were always aware of the target of their own current and previous attentions, and understood which targets are linked to the core interest of teammates, and how the links may be turned into real benefits in the future. We have been calling the process of chance discovery "double helix" because the human and computer always run up the spiral, where human gives data to computer and computer gives visualized results to human (Ohsawa & Nara, 2003). However, by reviewing five (of 38 in our confidential list of application cases) successful cases of which the users allowed us to publish, we came to revise the name of successful process to *white board* process, because users in four cases referred to multiple results of visualization (the graph of KeyGraph's output for the business data, plus for ideas written on a white board or diagrams obtained by applying KeyGraph to the text of communication) in parallel. On the other hand, among five failure cases, where no meaningful niche has been detected, the users of three cases looked at only one KeyGraph obtained from the target data on business.

ANALOGICAL THINKING: THE KEY TALENT FOR CHANCE DISCOVERY

Analogy is a cognitive process of transferring information from a particular subject (the base) to another particular subject (the target) (Gentner, 1983, 1989). For instance, if we know about the water flow system where water flows from a place of high pressure to a place of low pressure, we may infer the heat flows from a place of high temperature to of low temperature. Thus, if we know the original (base) system, we can infer about the target system by an analogical reasoning (mapping). Thus analogical reasoning is useful if we know the source domain and relationships between the source and the target domains. The human's talent of analogical thinking can be positioned as the basis of chance discovery regarded as a way to value sensing, by discussing the four human roles in the white board process as:

1. **Sensing external events:** Feel the possibility that a part of the real life may embrace a chance, to be motivated to collect data on events latently relevant to oneself. For example, data from the exhibition of products may be felt to embrace hints for creating a product, in the case of a textile company. This enables to collect objective data from the environment.

2. **Recollection:** Be enabled to explain situations underlying observed events from the real-world experiences. This enables to collect subjective data on human's thought, so that the thoughts can be visualized as an itemized list of sentences or a graph of words describing the thoughts.

3. **Scenarization:** Explain not only about the past, but also about plans and predictions of the future. These explanations are presented as a sequence of situations, events, or actions occurring in a coherent context, which is why we call such a presentation a *scenario*.

4. **Co-evolution of scenarios:** Exchange explained scenarios with colleagues. Scenarios may be combined like in a cross-over of genes, to make a new scenario satisfactory to multiple participants. Participants need to embody a new value criterion sharable with colleagues. The cross points of scenarios are identified, and presented as a strong candidate of a chance because one should make a decision to choose a scenario on meeting such a cross point.

All in all, human(s) needs to activate analogical reasoning during the process. That is, the latent value of daily events, i.e., their possibility to be chances, are to be sensed in (1) above, by feeing the similarity between the confronted event and some in the past. The past event plays a role of basis, and the present event a target. In the recollection phase (2), utterances by users are the evidence of their analogical reasoning. For example, a marketer said "the Indian textile reminded me of a lady wearing a cloth of a similar touch feeling on a hot day in summer" where his past experience worked as the basis for solving the target problem, i.e., what the Indian textile means for consumers. In (3), a scenario may come out from the analogy with the past experience of events similar to the connection of nodes in the visualized graph. These steps can be regarded as business applications of analogical problem solving (Gick & Holyoak, 1980, p.346). For example, a marketer said the corduroy textile in the center of Figure 1 can be improved to a material of soft suits, on the basis of his experience to design a suit of a textile (basis) of which the smoothness and strength is similar to corduroy (target). On the other hand, another marketer said the corduroy is more useful for lady's one-piece casual cloth, on the basis of his experience to observe students of women's university wearing a cloth of the similar thickness and color (basis) to the corduroy (target). And, finally, phase (4) has much of analogical reasoning as the marketer of the richest experience worked in the textile case. That is, he said "the desire of business people, who wear suits daily, is to change to easier and softer cloth on the way home and in the weekend. This desire can be satisfied by applying the corduroy to making a semi-business (semi-casual in other words) jacket, which is casual but does not look bad after working time." Here we find an analogical reasoning to apply multiple bases (casual cloth possibly made of the corduroy, a semi-business jacket he dealt with in the past, etc) to the target (the virtual business people currently discussed who likes softer cloth than suits). In other words, he noticed the similarity among three items, i.e., what business people desire, what young ladies desire to live in, and what the corduroy is like, and externalized the latent value "soft and natural for wearing both at and after working time."

GAMES FOR TRAINING AND ACTIVATING THINKING SKILLS FOR CHANCE DISCOVERY

In this section, we introduce two games for training and activating the thinking skills of which analogical thinking is at the center, and findings from experiments are summarized.

Analogy Game: Vacillation Accelerates Analogical Thinking

As in Figure 3, the player is initially presented with 20 random words put in small square nodes.

The words are placed at random positions initially. The player's goal is to categorize all words into at most 5 groups, none of which is allowed to include only one card nor be labeled by the concept "no meaning." Then, players relocate the words on the screen, categorizing the words into common-concept clusters by coloring word-nodes of the same concept with the same color. For example, "car" and "rocket" can be classified into the same category of the concept "vehicle," whereas "elephant" and "cat" can be in the same category of "animals" based on the player's subjective awareness of similarities. In this case, the two clusters can be colored by red and green, for example.

Note that we do not mean similarity and analogy are equivalent, but we assume an awareness of similarities is in the basis of analogical reasoning as we found in textile marketers' awareness of similarities between "corduroy" and "a material for suit" by common concepts (e.g. smoothness, strength, etc. of the textile), to achieve an analogy-based invention of a new selling strategy.

When a player notices the emergence of a new meaning of a word, he/she can click on the card to have a balloon emerge, to enter (write in the balloon) the concept. If the player discovers a common concept to a group of words, he enters the name in one of the rectangles at the bottom of the screen, of the same color as he assigned to the words in the group, hence a cluster. If there are words unable to be categorized into any cluster, it is encouraged to reconstruct clusters. Such an item is called a *vacillating item*. The player continues to play until all words get categorized into five or less clusters. The following data are collected automatically from player's actions:

- The location of words after each time it is dragged on the screen (X,Y axis: 800 x 600 px)
- The color the used for identifying a cluster, at each time

Figure 3. The screen image of the developed environment

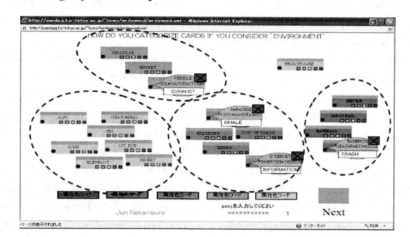

- Each word's meaning that user entered,
- The concept for each cluster that user entered,
- Time in seconds for the above-mentioned user's actions.

Experiment on Analogy Game: We prepared 20-word card set such as: Strawberry, Baseball, University of Tokyo, Japanese, Sea, Rocket, Barbecue, Edison, Alps, Service, Mobile, Internet, Japan-Rail, Sushi, Elephant, Mount Fuji, Statistics, Automobile, Desert, Medical-Care. 100 participants, including 60 students, performed the experiment so far.

Results: In Figure 4, we show the average number of actions for coloring (i.e. clustering) of items and entering concepts for items/clusters. The data have been taken from four players who took longer than 30 minutes for the game. The number of such careful players is small, but we can believe such players' actions during the game reflect their real thinking process.

As in Figure 4 (a) and (b), the clustering actions increased before the increase in the wording actions. After this, we find a period of time where the wording remains at a high level, whereas the clustering activity fades. Players

Figure 4. Actions related to the cognition of clusters and meanings: We do not show bars of standard deviation, because they disturb the comparison of two curves

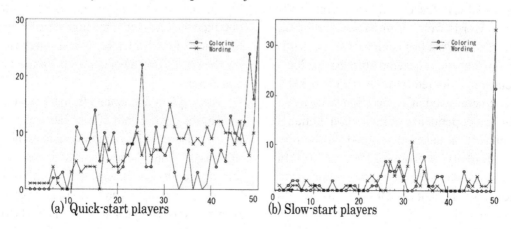

hardly found meaningful new categories at this period, but wrote words for the meanings of items and concepts for clusters. Meanwhile, the players orally uttered thoughts about how to categorize uncolored items (the vacillating items above) and how new clusters should be named, by moving but not coloring words. In this period of time, we can say players created new concepts. Let us call this period a *vacillation period*. According to our observation of words entered during the game, in the vacillation period, players concentrated in assigning a consistent meaning to words within each cluster, until finalizing the composition. Thus, the vacillation period can be considered an exploratory cognitive process (Finke, 1995, p.274, Finke & Ward, 1992, p18).

Especially, the trend in Figure 4 (a) shows this tendency, whereas the trend of slow-starting players as in Figure 4 (b) does not show it outstandingly. The difference of (a) and (b) is that the players in (a) moved the cards more frequently on the display in the early half of the gaming time, whereas the players in (b) did in the later half. This means the players in (a) tried to make major decisions of item categorization quickly, whereas the players in (b) made it slowly and carefully until the end of the game.

As a result, the players in (a) came to be forced to restructure the clusters so that all vacillating items shall be categorized into some clusters, and this induced insight to reconstructing all the words from an impasse state being at a loss. The insight has been said to be originated from individual mental process reflecting social environment (Mead, 1934, p.311), which can be viewed in association with value sensing. The dependence of insight on human's social interaction has been studied profoundly (Csikszentmihalyi & Sawyer, 1995, p.358). In this regard, an Analogy Game urges human to activate player's talent of value sensing, which works via insight.

Innovation Game: Empathy Accelerate Innovative Thinking

Innovation Game is an environment for communication we invented, where combinatorial creativity, i.e., creating a new idea from combination of ideas, is activated. The game starts with 50 basic cards, on each of which the title and the summary of some existing knowledge for business is written. The core players are called innovators (like innovative leaders of companies), who starts with the capital of $10. The innovator's main operation is to (1) buy a preferable number of basic cards for $1 per card, (2) combine the cards of one's own or with cards bought/borrowed from other players, and present with an idea of his new business by the combination. Other innovators may propose the presenter to start collaboration, or borrow/buy the new idea, with negotiating the dealing price. At the halting time after 2 hours after starting, the richest player, i.e., the player having the largest amount of money wins.

There are investors and consumers around innovators who all start from $10 capital. Each investor buys stocks from innovators who seem to be promisingly excellent, according to the investor's own subjective sense of ideas' values, or from other investors. The investor having obtained stocks of the highest amount of total price at the halting time comes to be the winning investor. And, each consumer buys ideas one likes to add to his/her own lifestyle, on the prices determined by negotiation with innovators. The consumer who obtained the idea-set of the highest total price (on the price of each idea at its last purchase time) for the same cost ($10) comes to be the winning consumer.

The KeyGraph obtained from the idea-cards is used as the game-board of Innovation Game, as in Figure 5. Here the KeyGraph visualizes the market of ideas, showing the positions of not only existing knowledge but also of latent ideas which has not been written on any basic cards but may be created by combinations. This visualization came to be enabled by an extension of KeyGraph, called Data Crystallization (Ohsawa, 2005; Maeno & Ohsawa, 2007), which shows *the black nodes and links*, showing basic cards organizing clusters, where each cluster embraces a common-sense context, i.e., a set of cards which share words in the summary sentence, and nodes (in red in the original output) connecting the clusters via dotted lines. For example, a node starting from "DE" (e.g. DE25 and DE61) in Figure 5 mean a new idea may emerge at the position by combining ideas in the connected (black) clusters. On this graph, the Innovation Game goes on with the activities of innovators as:

1.   Put basic cards on corresponding black nodes, when combining the cards for creating an idea, or
2.   Put a "wild" card which is a white paper on which the player can write his own created idea, on some space on the graph. Putting on a "DE" node is recommended, but not forced.

The quality of created ideas is evaluated after the game, by investors and consumers on criteria such as "orginality" "cost" "utility" and "reality." For example, the idea cards on black nodes in Figure 5, are:

Customized education: A customized program for computer-aided education

Room of time: A room the resident can experience a longer time than the really passed time

Note that the exemplified game here was an imaginary one, i.e., where the basic ideas and innovators represented those of 2050 when these technologies may appear, and the investors evaluated the utility, reality, etc of ideas in buying stocks.

An idea obtained by combining the two above was "ultra-efficient education system," a system to enable students to study efficiently in the room of time on the well coordinated schedule supported by the customized education. Although the room of time may seem unrealistic, the expected utility of the new idea was supported by investors. The players of games we conducted (we organized 47 games so far) mention they feel their skills of communication and thought for creating socially useful knowledge in business has been elevated during the game. The effect for their talent acquisition after the game is being evaluated currently.

Figure 6 shows the changes in the number of empathetic utterances exchanged between innovators, after each new idea was proposed, from the beginning to the end of two games. An empathetic utterance is one with which a participant expresses his/her value evaluation (positive or negative) of

Figure 5. Innovation game on the game board, made of KeyGraph with data crystallization

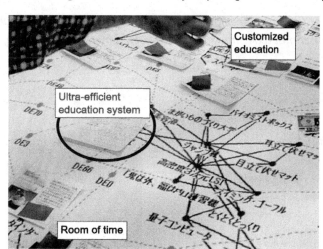

a presented idea with respect to the use scene. For example, a positive utterance such as "your idea is useful when I ..." and a negative "when I apply your idea, a problem is..." are classified as empathetic, whereas "let us hear the next idea" or "I buy your idea for $10" is not. As a result, Figure 6 presents the originality of ideas increase shortly after the empathetic utterances of investors/consumers. Among five games we investigated all the utterances, four games showed the correspondence (co-occurrence within two sequentially presented ideas) between the fastest increase in the number of empathetic utterances and in the score of originality, where the originality of each idea (A, B, C, ...) was scored between 0 and 3 by all investors after the game and the average score was plotted in Figure 6.

Analogical Abduction as Logical Framework for Chance Discovery

In the previous section, we showed a part of results of experimental Analogy Game and Innovation Game. In both games, ideas have been generated with relating pieces of knowledge. This is a typical manner in creating technologies to provide the society with sustainable progress, because a novel idea going too far beyond the existing knowledge is hard to be accepted by the daily life of human.

Thus, humans usually refer to known concepts in generating a new concept. This generation may be inspired simply by mimesis. For instance, a young artist begins his/her study from copying an old masters' painting. After copying several, he/she obtains an original new style based on the lessons from the mimesis. Even Picasso, regarded as one of the most innovative painters, showed an influence from Lautrec in his early days. Hurley and Chater pointed out that mimesis is a capacity related to fundamental to human mentality (Hurley & Chater, 2005).

For creativity-directed applications of extended mimesis, a semi-automatic catch-phrase generation system has been proposed (Abe, 2002). Based on an existing phrase, this software generates a phrase containing a new message. In the generation, mimesis on the similarity of words and sounds plays a significant role. For instance, by generating a phrase which has a similar sound to the original one but has a different meaning, a high impact can be acquired. For example, "Register, Free Male!" means single men are invited to register for a community to search a spouse, and the viewer can guess the original phrase "Register, Free Mail!" Thus, the new phrase comes to carry the impression that the registration can be easily done via the Web.

Several methods for creative thinking can be positioned in the extension of mimesis. In the busi-

Figure 6. The correlation of changes in empathetic utterances and originality scores, in two (the left and the right) games. The horizontal axis shows the ideas sorted by time from the left to the right.

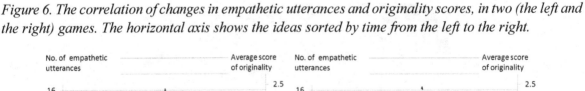
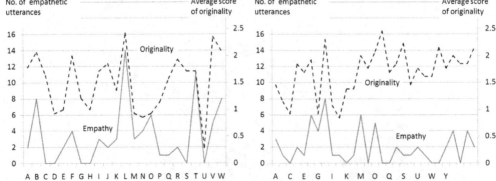

ness fields, mind maps (Buzan, 1996) have been introduced for creating rich amount of ideas with considering the relevance to the central keyword corresponding to the main goal of the user. To generate a map, words are step-wisely attached starting from the central keyword, and linked to relevant words already existing in the graph. The created mind map functions for a goal-directed brainstorming. For instance, when something like ``1 - 1 (one minus one)'' is observed on a wall and the user is demanded to infer what it really means, the user might add ``zero'' and ``H,'' whose shape is similar to ``1-1,'' to different branches of the graph. By putting "Here" at the branch of "H," the user may notice the observed letters may mean a part of "Here," which comes to be supported by paying a keen attention to the near-by part of the wall and finding "ere" in a weaker color than "H." Thus, trying to obtain an explanation of an ambiguous observation on similarity might inspire the user to generate novel concepts, which finally reaches an analogy (base: knowledge of the word "Here," target: "1-1" like letters) to solve the problem.

Several studies on analogical reasoning such as (Russell, 1988; Turney, 2008) have been conducted on computational and psychological viewpoints, and extracted essential hurdles to go over for realizing analogical reasoning. In (Sowa & Majumdar, 2003), logical reasoning and analogical reasoning have been viewed as incompatible alternatives. The two approaches should work sequentially rather than in parallel together. Before the target problem comes to be formalized so that logical reasoning can be applied, analogies should derive an abstract (i.e. logical) representation from a mass of details. After the formalization is complete, each logical step of deduction, induction, or abduction involves some analogy. On the other hand, Poole and Goebel has also shown that analogical reasoning (mapping) can be explained by the Theorist's framework of hypothetical reasoning i.e., of abduction (Poole et al. 1987, Goebel 1989). Abe proposed Abductive

Analogical Reasoning (AAR) (Abe, 2000) where unknown hypotheses are justified with respect to the explanation of an observation or to the achievement of a goal, by analogical mapping from facts (trustworthy knowledge). We can formalize AAR by describing as to derive some goal G' from the background knowledge S0 and additional uncertain knowledge S1', when a goal G in the past has been derived successfully from the background knowledge S0 and additional uncertain knowledge S1 acquired in the past. The projection rule, i.e., the analogical relationship from the past (base) and the present (target) justifies S1'.

And, here is the hurdle. The projection rule should be chosen from a large number of human's experiences. For example, let G in AAR be a goal in the target "make a useful catch phrase." Suppose a researcher had base knowledge S1 "natural language analysis (NLA) is useful for extracting keywords" which enabled to achieve a previous goal G to extract keywords from newspapers for making a search engine by being combined with background knowledge S0 including concrete methods of NLA. One day, he encounters a marketer who requests the researcher to invent a good catch phrase of a product. Let this request be a new goal G'. The researcher creates a new but uncertain hypothesis S1' "natural language analysis (NLA) might be useful for finding catch phrases by applying NLA methods to Web pages about the product" and combines this with his background knowledge S0. This researcher here needed a projection rule M: "If the style of data (input and output) to be dealt with for achieving a new goal G' is similar to the style of data for past goal G, the data mentioned in knowledge S1 can be replaced by the data for G'." Here, a hard work is involved: Telling "catch phrase" is similar to "keywords," and "newspapers" to "Web pages" by retrieving human's common senses. This is the difficulty in defining the projection rule, i.e., the rule for mapping the base to the target.

In face of this weakness, we require analogy for chance discovery where a chance (an event significant for human's decision) should be taken advantage of. In the real world, a huge number of candidates of analogical relationships may exist, and we should take one link between the confronted novel event and some in the knowledge (Dietrich et al., 2003). Some studies on computational natural language processing presents a hint for coping with the problem of projection rule. According to (Kasahara, 1996), the similarities between words in the target document of search and words in the search-key entered by the user can be activated by taking account of contextual information. For example, if the user enters "horse" in the context of animals, then a number of animal hospitals are retrieved due to the activated rule to map from "domestic animal" to "hospital for animals" which is active in the context of animals. On the other hand, if the user chooses the context of sports, then documents about horse races are retrieved due to a mapping rule in the context of sports. Different dictionaries are prepared for different domains, and switched reflecting the context of user's interest in such a computational approach. However, a switching rule cannot be given among the huge number of contexts in the case of human's analogical thinking in the real world.

The Analogy Game and the Innovation Game can be regarded as games for training and activating the skills of efficiently choosing useful analogical mapping rules, via the discovery of the common context between the target and the base. In the Analogy Game, the common contexts between words are assigned by the user's mind, from his/her tacit knowledge where a huge number of contexts in the real world experiences are waiting for being the base of thought. The chosen context is entered by the user's hand, accounting for the similarity between words in a cluster. Thus, although Analogy Game does not always involve directional reasoning (i.e. projection from/ to base to/from target), the user's thinking skill for analogical reasoning is trained. And, in the Innovation Game, players search good contexts in two-fold (1) In combining basic cards, the common

context between card A and card B means a latent market of the idea to be created by combining A and B. (2) In presenting a new combination, the knowledge in card C is mapped to some goal G spoken as an investor's demand. The innovator must tell a scenario for applying C to achieving G, by creating a new idea C' which comes from the combination of card C and some other card D.

CONCLUSION AND FUTURE WORK

In this paper, we introduced chance discovery as one aspect of value sensing. According to the real cases of chance discovery in business, a new value is created by combining pieces of basic knowledge, via human's interaction with other people and with real social events. Then, we showed analogical reasoning is essential for chance discovery, and that the finding of projection rule is the critical hurdle for analogical reasoning, by referring to the literature on logical analogical reasoning. We pointed out the awareness and the choice of suitable context is the key for coping with this difficulty, the human's talent for which can be trained and activated by the two games presented in this paper. Our future work is addressed to the validation of our hypothesis that these games really elevate the human's talent of value sensing, which will lead to innovations in the real human society.

REFERENCES

Abe, A. (2000). Abductive analogical reasoning. *Systems and Computers in Japan*, *31*(1), 11–19. doi:10.1002/(SICI)1520-684X(200001)31:1<11::AID-SCJ2>3.0.CO;2-E

Abe, A. (2002). Computational generation of affective phrase. In *Proceedings of the World Multi Conference on Systemics, Cybernetics and Informatics*, (SCI 2002, Vol. 16, pp. 261-266). Orlando, FL: International Institute of Informatics and Systemics.

Buzan, T. (1996). *The mind map book*. London: Penguin Books.

Csikszentmihalyi, M., & Sawyer, K. (1995). Creative insight: The social dimension of a solitary moment. In R. J. Sterngerg & J. E. Davidson (Eds.), *The nature of insight*, (pp. 329-364). Cambridge, MA: MIT Press.

Dietrich, E., Markman, A. B., Stilwell, H., & Winkley, M. (2003). The prepared mind: The role of representational change in chance discovery. In Y. Ohsawa & P. McBurney, (Eds.), *Chance discovery*, (pp. 208-230). Heidelberg, Germany: Springer.

Donaldson, M. (1992). *Human minds: An exploration*. London: Penguin Books.

Finke, R. A. (1995). Creative insight and pre-inventive forms. In R.J. Sternberg & J.E. Davidson (Eds.), *The nature of insight*, (pp. 255-280). Cambridge, MA: MIT Press.

Finke, R. A., Ward, T. B., & Smith, S. M. (1992). *Creative cognition*. Cambridge, MA: MIT Press.

Gentner, D. (1983). Structure mapping: A theoretical framework for analogy. *Cognitive Science, 7*(2), 155–170.

Gentner, D. (1989). The mechanisms of analogical learning. *Similarity and Analogical Reasoning*, (pp. 199-241). Cambridge, UK: University Press.

Gick, M. L., & Holyoak, K. J. (1980). Analogical problem solving. *Cognitive Psychology, 12*, 306–355. doi:10.1016/0010-0285(80)90013-4

Goebel, R. (1989). A sketch of analogy as reasoning with equality hypotheses. In *Proceedings of the International Workshop Analogical and Inductive Inference, LNAI-397*, 243–253.

Greenacre, M. J. (2007). *Correspondence analysis in practice (Interdisciplinary statistics)*. London: Chapman & Hall.

Horie, K., & Ohsawa, Y. (2006). Product designed on scenario maps using pictorial keygraph. *WSEAS Transaction on Information Science and Application, 3*(7), 1324–1331.

Hurley, S., & Chater, N. (2005). *Perspectives on imitation -from neuroscience to social science*. Cambridge, MA: MIT Press.

Kasahara, K., et al. (1996). Viewpoint-based measurement of semantic similarity between words. In *Proceedings of the 5th Workshop on Artificial Intelligence & Statistics*, (LNS112, pp. 433-442). New York: Springer.

Maeno, Y., & Ohsawa, Y. (2007). Human-computer interactive annealing for discovering invisible dark events. *IEEE Transactions on Industrial Electronics, 54*(2), 1184–1192. doi:10.1109/TIE.2007.891661

Mead, G. H. (1934). *Mind, self, and society*. IL: University of Chicago Press.

Ohsawa, Y. (2005). Data crystallization: Chance discovery extended for dealing with unobservable events. *New Mathematics and Natural Computation, 1*(3), 373–392. doi:10.1142/S1793005705000226

Ohsawa, Y., Benson, N. E., & Yachida, M. (1998). KeyGraph: Automatic indexing by co-occurrence graph based on building construction metaphor. In *Proceedings of the Advanced Digital Library Conference* (pp. 12-18). Los Alamitos, CA: IEEE Press.

Ohsawa, Y., & Nara, Y. (2003). Understanding Internet users on double helical model of chance-discovery process. *New Generation Computing, 21*(2), 109–122. doi:10.1007/BF03037629

Ohsawa, Y., & Usui, M. (2006). Creative marketing as application of chance discovery. In Y. Ohsawa & S. Tsumoto (Eds.), *Chance discoveries in real world decision making* (pp. 253-272). Heidelberg, Germany: Springer

Poole, D., Goebel, R., & Aleliunas, R. (1987). Theorist: A logical reasoning system for defaults and diagnosis. In N. J. Cercone & G. McCalla (Eds.), *The knowledge frontier: Essays in the representation of knowledge* (pp.331-352). Heidelberg, Germany: Springer.

Quinlan, J. R. (1993). *C4.5: Programs for machine learning*. San Mateo, CA: Morgan Kaufmann.

Russell, S. J. (1988). *The use of knowledge in analogy and induction*. London: Pitman.

Sowa, J. F., & Majumdar, A. K. (2003). Analogical reasoning. In *Proceedings of the International Conference on Conceptual Structures,* (LNAI 2746, pp.16-36). Heidelberg, Germany: Springer.

Turney, P. D. (2008). The latent relation mapping engine: Algorithm and experiments. *Artificial Intelligence Review, 33*, 615–655.

This work was previously published in International Journal of Organizational and Collective Intelligence, Volume 1, Issue 1, edited by Hideyasu Sasaki, pp. 44-57, copyright 2010 by IGI Publishing (an imprint of IGI Global).

Chapter 4
Transdisciplinary Approach to Service Design Based on Consumer's Value and Decision Making

Takeshi Takenaka
National Institute of Advanced Industrial Science and Technology, Japan

Nariaki Nishino
The University of Tokyo, Japan

Tsukasa Ishigaki
National Institute of Advanced Industrial Science and Technology, Japan

Kousuke Fujita
The University of Tokyo, Japan

Yoichi Motomura
National Institute of Advanced Industrial Science and Technology, Japan

ABSTRACT

Science and technology are expected to support actual service provision and to create new services to promote service industries' productivity. However, those problems might not be solved solely in a certain research area. This paper describes that it is necessary to establish transdisciplinary approaches to service design in consideration of consumers' values and decision making. Recent research trends of services are overviewed. Then a research framework is proposed to integrate computer sciences, human sciences, and economic sciences. Three study examples of services are then presented. The first study is a multi-agent simulation of a cellular telephone market based on results of a psychological survey. The second presents a cognitive model constructed through integration of questionnaire data of a retail business and Bayesian network modeling. The third presents a pricing mechanism design for service facilities—movie theaters—using an economic experiment and agent-based simulation.

DOI: 10.4018/978-1-4666-1577-9.ch004

INTRODUCTION

Recently, scientific studies of services have gained considerable attention from government, industry, and academia. The promotion of service productivity is a crucial issue in both developed and developing countries in response to changes in industrial structures and rapid globalization of business activities (Spohrer & Maglio, 2008). Many governments have initiated national projects for the promotion of service productivity and service innovation in the past several years. For example, the Japanese Ministry of Economy, Trade and Industry (Japanese Ministry, 2007) started a commission for academic–industrial cooperation in 2007 with a view to increasing service industry productivity. In Japan, a research center—the Center for Service Research—was established at the National Institute of Advanced Industrial Science and Technology in 2008 based on the discussion of that commission. Especially, in Japan, it has been noted that the growth rate of service industry productivity is lower than that of manufacturing industries. One reason for this phenomenon is that many existing services are thought to be provided less efficiently than manufactured products because actual service businesses include many human factors of service providers and consumers. Consequently, efficiency and optimization are salient issues addressed in recent studies of services. At the same time, it is necessary to elucidate how we can enhance the value of services in the market. From this viewpoint, human-related factors such as consumers' behaviors, cognition, value judgments, and social interactions are receiving greater attention for the improvement of actual services and design of new services. Nevertheless, those problems might not be solved through certain traditional disciplines such as engineering, psychology, and economics because they entail multiple aspects: technological, psychological, social, and economical aspects. Instead, science and technology are expected to support actual service provision by integrating some different research areas.

This paper advocates the importance of a transdisciplinary approach to service studies by presenting discussion related to the research trends in studies of services and by presenting some study examples of the authors. The subsequent section portrays an overview of research trends in service studies, particularly addressing academic fields and key technologies.

RESEARCH TRENDS OF SERVICE STUDIES

Targets of service studies have varied over time. Using an academic database, the authors examined 150,000 articles describing studies of services, particularly addressing historical trends and key technologies (Takenaka & Ueda, 2008). Historically, studies of services are considered to have started with examinations of problems of public and social services. Until the 1970s, service studies were mostly undertaken in the fields of medical science, public administration, and library sciences. Public service infrastructure, for instance, was a main research topic during that period (Weinerman et al., 1965). In the 1980s, although displaying main concerns that were apparently the same as those of previous periods, discussions elemental technologies in the fields of telecommunications engineering gradually entered the relevant literature. During the 1990s, two changes of research targets occurred in service studies. Engineering (electrical, telecommunications, and computer sciences) rose to prominence among research fields related to service studies. That phenomenon corresponds with the worldwide adoption of the internet after 1996. Moreover, management science and management engineering assumed an important role in service studies. Those two important changes suggest that not only public or social services but also service businesses had become important research targets. After the late 1990s, growing interest is apparent in actual service processes, especially those related to internet services and mobile services.

Figure 1 depicts the number of articles including keywords that closely co-occurred with "service" during 2000–2007, according to the Web of Science database, March 2009. For this study, keywords were selected from among hundreds of keywords related to technologies, research fields and academic problems by trial-and-error so that growing research interests became apparent. As the figure shows, human characteristic related words such as *satisfaction*, *cognitive*, and *personality* might express concerns about the diversity of consumers' (or patients') preferences. It is interesting to note that those keywords are found in various research fields. For example, articles co-occurring with *satisfaction* (articles of 2000–2007 were 2570) are classified as those of computer sciences, healthcare sciences, medical sciences, management sciences, telecommunications, and so on. Sensing-technology related keywords such as Global Positioning System (GPS), IC Card, Radio Frequency IDentification (RFID), and wearable sensors are garnering attention in recent service studies. Human characteristic related words and

sensing-technology related keywords suggest that researchers target the assessment of consumers' behaviors and value judgments. Nevertheless, based on those keywords, it is not easy to establish a service design methodology that enhances the values of services to service diverse consumers. Because the amount of available data grows in services, managing that information becomes increasingly difficult. *Complexity* and *optimization* therefore characterize recent academic interest related to services. Moreover, *agent* and *adaptation* suggest that researchers explore not only static optimized solutions but also dynamic and adaptive solutions using agent-based approaches or optimization techniques.

Finally, *innovation* and *sustainability* are increasingly popular keywords in recent service studies. Those keywords suggest that researchers have started studies not only for business objectives but also for social or environmental objectives. The authors believe that sustainability is a good research target for service studies because individual happiness and the overall purpose

Figure 1. Articles including some technical keywords co-occurring with "service"

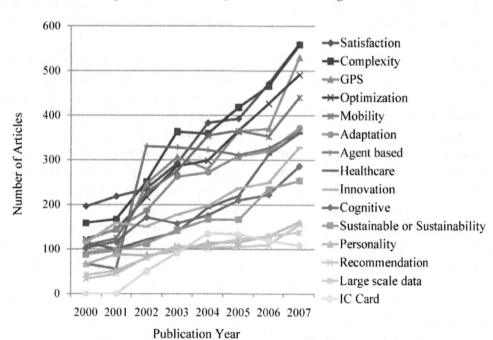

(environmental and social sustainability) must be solved simultaneously.

The next section presents a description of further difficulties in service studies and proposes a research framework that aims to establish transdisciplinary studies of services.

TRANSDISCIPLINARY FRAMEWORK FOR SERVICE STUDIES

As discussed above, we must consider many aspects of actual services for the improvement of service productivities and for the promotion of service innovations in the society. Takenaka & Ueda (2008) classified recent research problems of services into the following three types.

A. Optimization or streamlining of complex service systems
B. Assessment of human behavior, values, and lifestyles to create new services
C. Elucidation of service innovations in society and search for service design principles

With respect to A, the process modeling of actual services and data collection techniques is necessary for the streamlining of services. However, actual service businesses have various provision processes. For that reason, we cannot always have access to the necessary data for computations. Moreover, data of different kinds such as data related to operation systems, sales, behaviors of providers and consumers, and questionnaire data should be integrated for the investigation of overall service processes. For our investigation, process modeling methodologies have been developed in computer sciences mainly for web-based systems (Li et al., 2008). On the other hand, management sciences have analyzed the best practices in the actual service businesses (Morimoto, 2008). However, those methodologies of process modeling differ from each other. The authors assume that comprehensive methodolo-

gies of process modeling of actual services are needed for integration of computer sciences and management sciences. Optimization techniques such as genetic algorithms (GAs), neural networks, and multi-agent systems used in recent service studies are thought to have been developed in other research areas such as computer science and manufacturing engineering. For future studies of services, multi-objective and heterogeneous optimization methodologies will be sought to treat the complexity of actual services.

Regarding B above, psychological approaches are strongly anticipated to clarify consumers' value and behaviors. However, such problems might present difficulty for psychologists because they cannot always control experimental environments in the real world. Moreover, values for consumers should be understood from various viewpoints such as behavioral, cognitive, emotional, social, and economical viewpoints. Recently, studies of lifestyles have received attention in service and product design studies (Pattabhiraman et al., 2007). A lifestyle seems to have holistic characteristics because lifestyle components are not mutually independent. Moreover, individual lifestyles are not independent of those of others in a community or society. Therefore, the authors believe there will be good opportunities to create new values of services by synthesizing some different components of lifestyles. To this end, collaboration among cognitive and social psychology, computer science, management science, and actual businesses must be encouraged.

Furthermore, economic approaches are necessary to understand the values of consumers as well as psychological approaches. An important issue in service design is the economic mechanism of service. Economic studies that adopt the experimental method are established as experimental economics (Smith, 1976; Friedman & Sunder, 1994). Just as engineers and scientists do in other fields, an experimenter can design an economic experiment to examine a particular theory or an economic system. A remarkable point is that subjects who are recruited for experiments are promised a monetary reward according to their performance in experiments. By the monetary reward, economic incentives are given to subjects; then the experimenter observes their actions in the experiment to verify whether those actions reflect the theory as it was hypothesized.

Finally, regarding C, value creation mechanisms through interactions among various stakeholders are also important topics for services. The network externality is defined as an externality by which a consumer's utility depends on the number of users who consume the same product (Katz & Shapiro, 1992). Consequently, it is often observed that a certain product or service becomes dominant in the market in a short period. Therefore, for elucidation of innovation mechanisms, we must devote greater attention to social interactions among consumers, providers, and services. Institutional designs for a sustainable society can be done only through active integration of various disciplines such as economic sciences, social sciences, and computer sciences.

Figure 2 portrays a transdisciplinary research framework for services. Scientific approaches must be based on objective data. The problems confronting service industries today are how to improve actual services and how to design new services based on available data. Even a great deal of data is useless if no good methodology is established for the modeling and design of services. Therefore, we must integrate disciplines to achieve some sub-goals of service studies.

The following sections introduce examples of three studies that employ transdisciplinary approaches. The first integrates psychological survey and multi-agent simulation. The second introduces an effective mining methodology using Bayesian networks to elucidate consumers' valuations of a service. The third study combines economic experiments and multi-agent simulation to design price mechanisms of services in movie theaters.

Figure 2. Transdisciplinary research framework for services: Integration of available data and disciplines for the achievement of objectives

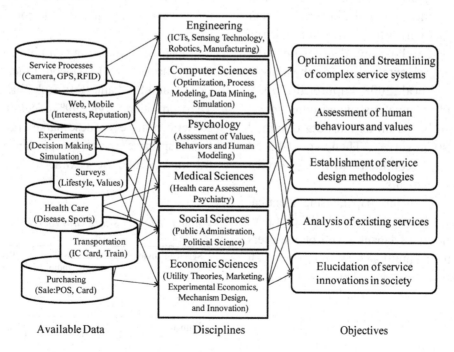

STUDY EXAMPLE 1: AGENT BASED MODELING OF A CELL PHONE MARKET BASED ON CONSUMER PREFERENCES

This study is intended to clarify the mechanism of service diffusion in a market. With rapid networking and market globalization, it has become increasingly difficult to predict the diffusion of products and services. To understand its mechanism, we must devote attention to consumers' values and decision-making. Moreover, we must consider social interaction among consumers because they make decisions depending not only on subjective valuations but also on social factors such as network externalities (Ueda et al., 2008).

Agent-based modeling is effective to clarify the process of service diffusion because it can readily include heterogeneity in individual preferences and its interactions (Takenaka & Ueda, 2008; Rahmandad & Sterman, 2008). Janssen & Jager (2003), for instance, demonstrated the dynamics of various markets considering product characteristics and the structure of interactions among agents. Beck et al. (2008) demonstrated the impact of direct and indirect network effects on the adoption of technology. The authors have demonstrated the impact of network externalities on the market diffusion (Ueda et al., 2008; Fujita et al., 2008). In those studies, we constructed consumers' agent models based on actual data obtained from a lifestyle survey. Then, agent-based simulations were conducted to verify service diffusion mechanisms.

As described in this paper, using identical methodology, we introduce the results of a psychological survey of Japanese cell phone users and demonstrate a multi-agent simulation of cell phone market considering changeover costs of providers and network externalities.

Survey of Cell Phone Services in Japan

This section introduces results of a survey of cell phone services. The survey was designed to elucidate the multiple demands for cell phone services and to reveal meaningful factors affecting users' decision-making. For this purpose, the survey involves not only questions related to cell phone services but also questions about everyday buying behaviors. Through analyses, we construct an agent model for the computer simulation and set parameters of agents considering the diversity of consumers' preferences and decision making in the real world.

The survey was conducted during three days in August 2008 using a membership questionnaire system on a mobile-phone network. A mobile research company (Point-On Inc., Tokyo, Japan) produced the system. In this system, participants' information about age, sex, job, and living area were available.

In all, 6121 (3286 female and 2835 male) people participated in the survey. We adopted the random sampling method to each generation and to each sex. We administered 200 questions to subjects of each generation, from teenagers to users in their fifties.

Japan has three main cell phone service providers: docomo (NTT Docomo Inc.), au (KDDI Corp.), and Softbank (Softbank Telecom Corp.). These providers service 99% of cellular telephone subscribers in the Japanese market. Table 1 presents their respective market shares in Japan and the distribution of 1000 users extracted from the survey.

Table 1. Market share and distribution of users

Service Provider	Market Share (July, 2008)	Distribution of 1000 Users
docomo	51.6%	50.1%
au	29.1%	42.4%
Softbank	18.6%	7.5%

We asked 25 questions related to everyday purchasing behavior (7 questions), the use of cell phone services (10 questions), the choice of cell phone services (7 questions), and other attributes (1 question). Table 2 presents a list of questions.

To elucidate important factors affecting the use of cell phone services, an exploratory factor analysis is conducted of 13 questions (Q1–Q10, Q21–Q23). Three factors are extracted using maximum likelihood estimation: Promax method is used for the rotation of factor loadings.

Figure 3 shows three-dimensional scatter plots of factor loadings. As shown there, Q2, Q3, Q4, and Q5 contribute to the first factor, which might be related to sensitivity to trends. Because Q21 and Q22 contribute to the second factor, it might be related to interests in functionality. It is also

Table 2. List of questions

No.	Question
Q1	Are you careless with money?
Q2	Are you sensitive to trends?
Q3	Do you often try new products?
Q4	Are you interested in what your friends have?
Q5	Do you select a popular thing through word-of-mouth?
Q6	Do you put priority on price when you select things?
Q7	Do you compare similar things when you buy goods?
Q8	How much do you spend monthly in cell phone charges?
Q9	How often do you make calls with your cell phone?
Q10	How often do you send or receive E-mails using your cell phone?
Q11	Which cell phone functions do you use?
:	
Q13	Do you want to change your cell phone service provider?
:	
Q21	I do not care about anything other than basic functions (communication services).
Q22	I check the details of functions when buying a cell phone.
Q23	I am sensitive to the cell phone design.

apparent that Q8, Q9, and Q10 contribute to the third factor, which might be related to communication services.

Using those data, we conduct one-way analysis of variance tests of some questions which contribute to three factors to clarify the characteristics of consumers in each provider. The answers of Q10, Q11, and Q22 show significant differences among users of each service provider. Regarding Q10, Softbank users tend to use mail services less frequently than other users. On the other hand, as for Q22, Softbank users tend to check the details of cell phone functions more than docomo users. No difference was observed in Q10 and Q11 between docomo users and au users.

With regard to Q11, we asked about the use frequency of five functions: Camera, One-segment broadcasting, Mobile wallet, GPS, and Music player. We found significant differences in the use frequency of mobile wallet and music player among users: docomo users use the music player less frequently than other users; au users use the mobile wallet less frequently than other users do.

Through these analyses, we sought to find meaningful factors in the selection of cell phone services and the difference of each user's values and behaviors.

Model Construction

Based on the survey, we construct an agent-based market model comprising 1000 consumer agents and 3 service provider agents. A consumer agent corresponds to those who answer the questionnaire. Provider agents are described as providers serving the Japanese market, which are "*A*", "*B*", and "*C*". Figure 4 portrays this model of the cell phone market. In this model, each provider is assumed to be able to provide one service. Therefore, three services exist in the market.

The decision-making process of consumer agents and service provider agents is the following. First, provider agents determine which service

Figure 3. Scatter plots of factor loadings

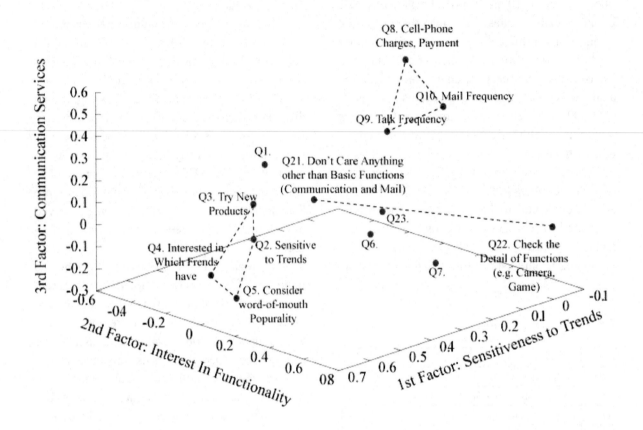

Figure 4. Schematic model of the cell phone market

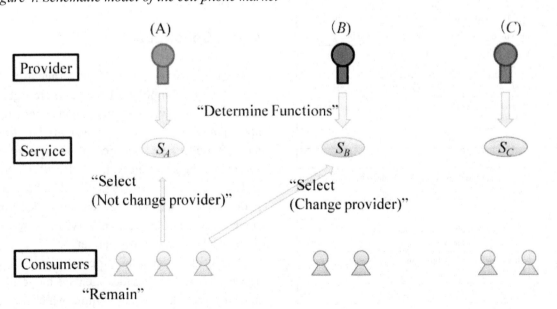

they provide in the market. In other words, they set the functions of their services. Then, consumers evaluate the expected value of each service. They make a decision to select the service if their expected surplus becomes greater than their threshold. When some services surpass their threshold, they select the best service, which is the one having the highest expected value.

For these analyses, we define s_j as the service provided by provider j; it consists of functions of two kinds: $f_{j1} \in F_1$ and $f_{j2} \in F_2$. In addition, $F_1 = \{f \mid \underline{f_1} \leq f \leq \overline{f_1}\}$ and $F_2 = \{f \mid \underline{f_2} \leq f \leq \overline{f_2}\}$ respectively represent sets of the functions. In addition, f is a natural number and $\underline{f}$ and $\overline{f}$ respectively signify a lower bound and upper bound. The first function f_{j1} stands for an additional function such as a camera, GPS or music player; the second function f_{j2} is a basic function such as telecommunication or text messaging. For example, considering the case in which the first function is a camera, then F_1 is a set of a feasible resolutions of the camera and f_{j1} is the specific value of the resolution. With respect to the second function, it is fundamentally similar to the example of the first function. Accordingly, in this model, we assume that a service is described as a combination of two functions.

The three provider agents are indexed by $j \in \{A, B, C\}$. A provider determines what service is provided. In other words, as the service is described as $s_j = (f_{j1}, f_{j2})$, provider j selects f_{j1} and f_{j2} from sets of F_1 and F_2. In this model, the function of a service is addressed and service price is not dealt with explicitly.

There are 1000 consumer agents, who are indexed as $i \in \{1, 2, ..., 1000\}$. Consumer i is assumed to use a service $s_j \in \{s_A, s_B, s_C\}$ in the initial state and has his/her own demand $D_i = (d_{i1}, d_{i2})$, where $d_{i1} \in D_1 \equiv \{d \mid \underline{d_1} \leq d \leq \overline{d_1}\}$ and $d_{i2} \in D_2 \equiv \{d \mid \underline{d_2} \leq d \leq \overline{d_2}\}$ respectively represent an amount demanded of the first func-

tion and an amount demanded of the second function. Consumer i's expected value function is defined as

$$E_i(s_j) = \alpha \left[w_1(1 - |f_{j1} - d_{i1}|) + w_2(1 - |f_{j2} - d_{i2}|) + w_3 m(s_j)/1000 \right] - K,$$

where signifies a constant, and w_1, w_2, and w_3 respectively denote weight parameters and satisfy $w_1 + w_2 + w_3 = 1$. In addition, $m(s_j)$ represents the number of consumers who use service s_j. In function $1 - |f_{jn} - d_{in}|$, $(n=1,2)$ shows how well the functions of a service match the individual demands of consumer i. These demands show the consumer's preferences. Preferences of two different kinds were distinguishable (Thurstone, 1931). First, an individual preference is proportional to a function. The second type of an individual preference implies an ideal point type of preference. The second kind of a preference is adopted in this model, which Jager (2007) formalized as the equation presented above. Furthermore, $m(s_j)/1000$ represents the network effect. In the market model, consumer agents know the market share of provider j. They evaluate the network effect related to the market share.

Parameter K signifies the changeover cost. When consumers change their service provider, they must pay a switching fee, which decreases their expected value.

$$K = \begin{cases} 0 & s_j = s_i \\ b(const.) & s_j \neq s_i \end{cases}.$$

The weights of respective attributes w_i $(i=1,2,3)$ represent the type of the market and consumer decision-making processes. All attributes are weighted and summed up; the changeover cost (K) is considered. Finally, Consumer i's utility is determined.

Consumers evaluate the expected value of all services; then they select the service and obtain utility U_i.

Figure 5. Distribution of consumer agents

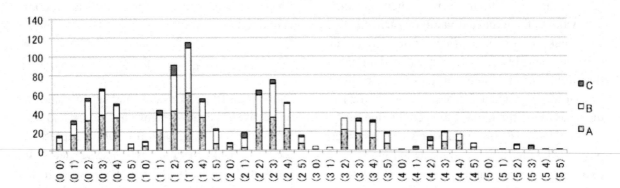

$$U_i = \begin{cases} E_i^{MAX} & E_i^{MAX} \geq T_i \\ T_i & E_i^{MAX} < T_i \end{cases}.$$

In that equation, E_i^{MAX} is the highest value among the expected values; T_i is the threshold, which is the utility of the use of the service in the initial state. When the expected value (E_i^{MAX}) exceeds the threshold (T_i), then consumer i makes a decision to use service s_j. When Utility (E_i^{MAX}) does not exceed the threshold (T_i), she continues her service s_i. This state is "*remain*" in Figure 4.

The consumer's parameters (D_i and T_i) are set by the questionnaires. We apply the questionnaires to the parameters consumer agents have. To set d_{i1}, we use question Q11. The number of functions the participants selected is set as the parameter d_{i1}, which are 0–5. To set d_{i2}, we use two questions: Q9 and Q10. The answers of these two questions are summed up, then consumers are ranked according to this value. The levels of d_{i2} are set as six levels of 0–5.

The functions of services (F_1 and F_2) are related to consumers' demands. Consequently, f_{m1} and f_{m2} are ranged as follows.

$$F_1 = \{f \mid 0 \leq f \leq 5\}$$

$$F_2 = \{f \mid 0 \leq f \leq 5\}$$

To set the value of T_i, we use question Q13. When the answer is "yes", parameter T_i is set low ($T_i = 0.42$). When the answer is "no", T_i is set high ($T_i = 0.62$). There are 176 agents set low; the others are set high. Consumer agents are assumed to use service s_j in the initial state. This service provider j is the same as that elicited in the answer of Q25. Figure 5 depicts the distribution of consumers by provider. The horizontal axis shows the consumer demand (D_i). The vertical axis is the number of consumers.

The distribution factor (α) is set as a constant value ($\alpha = 0.7$). The weights (W_i) and the additional cost (K) are processed as variables. In the next section, we examine network effects and the effect of the changeover costs.

Simulation Experiment

To verify the diffusion mechanism, we examine the network effect and the effect of the changeover costs. We first run the simulation, considering neither the network effect nor the effect of the changeover cost (in case (1)). Then, we separately consider the network effect and the changeover cost (in case (2) and (3)). Finally, we consider both the network effect and the changeover cost (in case (4)). Table 3 shows the simulation setting. The parameters are as presented below.

Table 3. Simulation Setting

		Network effect	
		Not considered	**Considered**
Changeover cost	Not considered	(1) $w_1=w_2=0.5$, $w_3=0$, $b=0$	(2) $w_1=w_2=0.475$, $w_3=0.05$, $b=0$
	Considered	(3) $w_1=w_2=0.5$, $w_3=0$, $b=0.04$	(4) $w_1=w_2=0.475$, $w_3=0.05$, $b=0.04$

We explored the all combinations of services and selected the combination which maximizes the sum of the consumers' utilities. Figure 6 portrays the number of users by provider in each case. In case (1), there is not so much difference in the market share among providers. This result is far from the real market share. Cases (2) and (3) show similar results. In these cases, the users of provider *C* are twice as numerous as those in the initial state. When both the network effect and the changeover cost are considered (in case (4)), the market share in the simulation result is more closely resembles that of the real market than the other cases. Table 4 presents the selected services and the sum of the consumers' utilities. Specifically examining the functions of the selected services, in case (4), provider *C* selected the service with the lower functions (0 1). These results suggest that, as in the real world, in the market model, two providers provide similar services; the other provider provides services with lower functions.

On the other hand, the sum of consumers' utilities is the lowest in case (4) (Table 4), but highest in case (1), which suggests that when consumers select the most satisfying service, the network effect and the changeover cost can be disincentives hindering consumers from selecting a service.

These simulation results suggest that the market share of each provider approximates the real cell phone market in Japan when both changeover costs and network effects are considered. However, those factors might present obstacles to enhancement of the total benefit of consumers. Providers might need to balance business structures, such as changeover costs, in consideration of the network effect in the market.

Figure 6. Number of users by providers

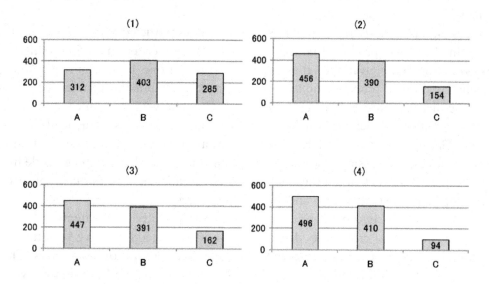

Table 4. Selected services and consumers' utilities

Case (1)			Case (2)		
644.535			631.353		
A (0 3)	B (1 3)	C (2 3)	A (2 3)	B (1 3)	C (1 2)
Case (3)			Case (4)		
631.925			622.032		
A (1 3)	B (2 3)	C (1 2)	A (1 3)	B (2 3)	C (0 1)

(Upper row) Total of consumers' utilities
(Lower row) Selected services (f_{j1} f_{j2})

STUDY EXAMPLE 2: PROBABILISTIC COGNITIVE STRUCTURE MODELING USING A BAYESIAN NETWORK IN A RETAIL SERVICE

Concomitantly with the rapid development of information technologies, a large-scale data about consumers' preferences and behaviors are obtainable in actual businesses. To understand consumers' satisfaction or values, we require effective modeling methods of consumers based on such data. This section introduces a method of constructing a customer's cognitive model to understand customer satisfaction and decision making in a retail service using statistical graphical modeling (Ishigaki, 2009). The presented method constructs a cognitive model through integration of questionnaire data and a Bayesian network.

The Bayesian network (Korb, 2004) is a modeling method that produces network structures as relations among variables that are realized using conditional probabilistic tables or probabilistic distributions. It is difficult for conventional statistical modeling, which assume linear or Gaussian models, to address the nonlinearity or the non-Gaussian distribution in variables. Figure 7 shows that the Bayesian network can cope with the nonlinearity and the interaction of the relation between the variables in the form of a conditional probability distribution. The model structure can be constructed automatically based on information criteria.

Additionally we can embed some experiences of the model designer and/or physical or social rules in advance. The probabilities of each variable are calculable using efficient probabilistic computational algorithms such as the belief propagation or the Loopy BP (Murphy, 1999; Bishop, 2006).

Herein, we present an example of the probabilistic cognitive model constructed through integration of the Bayesian network and the questionnaire data. The questionnaire data used for this study were obtained in 2008 from 311 consumers who had bought shoe inserts in 2007. The questions are designed to elicit information related to demographic information (5 variables), reasons for purchase (12 variables), evaluation after use (3 variables), expectations before use (1 variable), and the intention of continuing use (1 variable).

The constructed model is based on the Akaike information criterion (AIC) (Akaike, 1974) in Figure 7. Links between the variables show a strong probabilistic relation according to the AIC. It shows, for instance, that the intention of continuing use is influenced by the reasonability of price and total satisfaction of it. On the other hand, demographics aside from being married and having children might affect other attributes.

Additionally, we evaluated the validity of the constructed cognitive structure using the classification rate of consumers. The classification rate of the Bayesian network model

Figure 7. Schematic model of Bayesian network

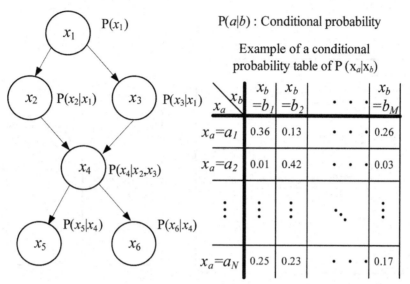

is comparable to the classification rate of the naïve Bayes classifier, discriminant analysis for categorical data (qualification theory), and the support vector machine (Bishop, 2006). The results of classification experiments showed that the Bayesian network model has a higher performance than other methods. In the experiment using the Bayesian network model (Figure 8), the intention of continuing use is calculable according to the reasons for purchase at approximately 75%. Furthermore, we conducted a sensitivity analysis with respect to customers' behavior. Although we sufficiently explain the details here, results show that the advertising statement for the shoe insert seems not to contribute to its functional characteristics.

Although results presented in this section are limited, the presented method is useful for many other services using variety of data. Furthermore, it is useful for the recommendation for each consumer. The authors now explore the customer relation management and constructing recommendation systems using Bayesian network methodologies.

STUDY EXAMPLE 3: SERVICE OF MOVIE THEATERS - DESIGN OF A PRICING MECHANISM USING EXPERIMENTAL ECONOMICS AND AGENT BASED SIMULATION

Movies are now known worldwide as a popular leisure activity. Movies are also a good example of a service. Most movies are generally available at a fixed price. Both popular movies and boring movies are usually provided at the same price. In addition, especially in the case of Japan, the price is high. Therefore, it is doubtful whether the value of movies is reflected appropriately in the movie price. In general, according to market mechanisms, prices should be high if goods or services are in high demand, while prices should be low in the case of unpopular ones. The problem of price setting is a central issue of service design.

This study proposes a new movie service pricing mechanism by introducing auction theory, using methodology of experimental economics, and agent-based simulation.

Figure 8. Cognitive model constructed by questionnaire data in the framework of Bayesian network

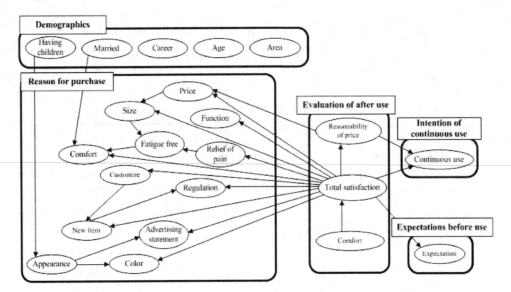

Model of a Movie Theater and Consumers

In this model, *n* consumers and a movie theater exist. The movie theater provides movies of one kind; *M* seats exist in the theater. Each consumer has a reservation price for the movie and believes that it is acceptable to pay the amount of the reservation price at most. The payoff function of a consumer is defined as $\pi = Rp - P$, where Rp represents the reservation price and P stands for the movie price. The movie theater's profit function is $\Pi = mP$, where m represents the number of consumers who watch the movie; for simplicity, costs are not considered. In addition, *m* does not exceed *M* even if many consumers want to watch the movie because the number of seats provided by the theater is *M*.

Pricing Mechanism and Seat Matching

We adopt auction theory to determine the movie price. Each consumer decides a bid price and simultaneously requests favorite seats. Consumers who bid higher than the *M*+1th highest price

win tickets for the movie at the *M*+1th highest price. Moreover, seats are arranged in order of bid price ranking. Therefore, a bid price that a consumer chooses is not the actual contract price, but a high bid price is appropriate for obtaining the favored seat.

This pricing and seat-matching mechanism is based on two famous mechanisms in the field of mechanism design: the Vickrey–Clarke–Groves (VCG) mechanism (Vickrey, 1961; Clarke, 1971; Groves, 1973) and the Gale–Shapley mechanism (Gale & Shapley, 1962). In our model, the VCG mechanism is applied to the pricing process and the Gale–Shapley mechanism is applied to a seat-matching process.

Experiments with Human Subjects

To examine the behavior of actual humans, experiments with human subjects are conducted based on the methodology of experimental economics. In experiments, each subject is given different reservation prices that are predetermined randomly in advance. Based on the reservation prices, subjects decide their own bidding price. If subjects win a bid, they obtain the payoff *Rp-P*, where *P* stands

Figure 9. Examples of experimental results

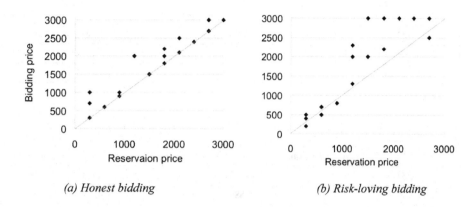

(a) Honest bidding   *(b) Risk-loving bidding*

for contract price. After experiments are finished, subjects are paid a monetary reward depending on the payoff obtained in experiments.

Figure 9 presents an example of experimental results. In the figure, the vertical axis shows the bidding prices, the horizontal axis shows reservation prices; a point in the graph represents a decision by a subject. Figure 9(a) depicts all decisions by a certain subject. Many points are on the 45° line. Consequently, the subject often honestly makes bids at reservation prices. On the other hand, Figure 9(b) shows that the subject makes maximum bids when the reservation price is high. The subject pursues a good seat with the risk of a negative payoff because the subject considers that if the reservation price is high, he can win a bid at a lower price than the reservation price.

Agent-Based Simulation

Subjects' behaviors of some types, including those described for the cases above, are observed in the experiments. We construct agents that make such decisions as outputs observed in experiments. For example, in the case of honest bidding presented above, the agents make a bid at their own reservation price. Agents of several types, including honest-bidding agents and risk-loving agents, participate in this movie theater auction. Subsequently, we examine how the profit of the

movie theater and consumers' surplus (sum of all consumers' payoffs) are formed in agent-based simulation, comparing some cases using a fixed price.

In simulation, parameters are set as follows: $n=50$ and $M=24$. Moreover, movies of three types are prepared: basic, popular, and niche. Differences of three movies are described by the distribution of reservation prices that each consumer agent is given in advance. For example, the average of reservation prices in the case of a popular movie is set higher than that in the case of a basic movie.

Tables 5–7 present simulation results. The tables respectively present the movie theater's surplus, consumers' surplus, and total surplus. Bold face symbols in the tables signify the highest surplus of the three pricing mechanisms. From Table 5, results show that the proposed mechanism increases the theater's surplus over that of other cases of fixed price. On the other hand, with respect to consumers' surplus, the low price case shows good performance (Table 6). Increasing the consumer's payoff is very natural if they can watch movies at low prices. However, the proposed mechanism can increase consumers' surplus in cases of a niche movie. Therefore, niche demand is properly extracted. In Table 7, the total surplus (sum of movie theater's surplus and consumers' surplus) is shown. The proposed

Table 5. Movie theater's surplus

	Proposed mechanism	Low fixed price	High fixed price
Basic movie	**35422**	14400	25492
Popular movie	**47446**	14400	32166
Niche movie	**17526**	14336	14638

Table 6. Consumers' surplus

	Proposed mechanism	Low fixed price	High fixed price
Basic movie	5147	**19360**	3936
Popular movie	-1547	**27889**	4577
Niche movie	**12250**	5436	3380

Table 7. Total surplus

	Proposed mechanism	Low fixed price	High fixed price
Basic movie	**40568**	33760	29428
Popular movie	**45899**	42289	36743
Niche movie	**29776**	25923	18018

mechanism outweighs other fixed price cases. Therefore, the result implies that the proposed mechanism might increase the efficiency of movie theater services.

CONCLUSION

This paper presents a proposal of a multidisciplinary research framework for studies of services and introduces three study examples integrating some disciplines to solve problems associated with actual services. For improvement of service productivity, both streamlining of service processes and enhancement of service values are important. The values of services for consumers and service providers must be understood from various viewpoints: psychological, economical, and social. Although resent information technologies bring us a large scale data on consumers' behaviors and values,

there is no well-established methodology to create a new service using such data. Science and technologies, therefore, are expected to combine the analytic and synthetic approaches to solve the problems in the real world. To this end, multidisciplinary approaches should be more encouraged.

Additional studies should be undertaken to explore the mechanism of service innovations in society. Value co-creation is an important keyword to verify mechanisms affecting interactions among various stakeholders in the networked society.

ACKNOWLEDGMENT

This study is partially supported by the project for the promotion of Service Research Center from Japanese Ministry of Economy, Trade and Industry (METI) in 2008.

REFERENCES

Akaike, H. (1974). A new look at the statistical model identification. *IEEE Transactions on Automatic Control, 19*(6), 716–723. doi:10.1109/TAC.1974.1100705

Beck, R., Beimborn, D., Weitzel, T., & Konig, W. (2008). Network effects as drivers of individual technology adoption: Analyzing adoption and diffusion of mobile communication services. *Information Systems Frontiers, 10*(4), 415–429. doi:10.1007/s10796-008-9100-9

Bishop, C. M. (2006). *Pattern recognition and machine learning.* London: Springer.

Clarke, E. H. (1971). Multipart pricing of public goods. *Public Choice, 11,* 17–33. doi:10.1007/BF01726210

Friedman, D., & Sunder, S. (1994). *Experimental methods: A primer for economics.* UK: Cambridge University Press.

Fujita, K., Takenaka, T., & Ueda, K. (2008). *Service diffusion in the market considering consumers' subjective value.* Paper presented at the 5th International Conference on Soft Computing as Transdisciplinary Science and Technology, Pontoise, France.

Gale, D., & Shapley, L. S. (1962). College admissions and the stability of marriage. *The American Mathematical Monthly, 69*(1), 9–15. doi:10.2307/2312726

Groves, T. (1973). Incentives in teams. *Econometrica, 41,* 617–631. doi:10.2307/1914085

Ishigaki, T., & Motomura, T. Dohi, Masako, & Mochimaru, M. (2009, June 17-19). *Analysis of continuous use by a Bayesian network modeling based on a questionnaire data.* Paper presented at the Annual Conference of JSAI, Kagawa, Japan.

Jager, W. (2007). The four P's in social simulation, A perspective on how marketing could benefit from the use of social simulation. *Journal of Business Research, 60*(8), 868–875. doi:10.1016/j.jbusres.2007.02.003

Janssen, M. A., & Jager, W. (2003). Simulating market dynamics: Interactions between consumer psychology and social networks. *Artificial Life, 9*(4), 343–356. doi:10.1162/106454603322694807

Japanese Ministry of Economy. Trade and Industry (2007). *Towards innovation and productivity, improvement in service industries.* Retrieved March 27, 2009, from http://www.meti.go.jp/english/report/downloadfiles/0707ServiceIndustries.pdf

Katz, M. L., & Shapiro, C. (1992). Network effects, software provision, and standardization. *The Journal of Industrial Economics, 40*(1), 85–103. doi:10.2307/2950627

Korb, K. B., & Nicholson, A. E. (2004). *Bayesian artificial intelligence.* Boca Raton, FL: Chapman & Hall/CRC.

Li, Y. S., Shen, J. P., Shi, J. S., Shen, W. M., Huang, Y., & Xu, Y. X. (2006, May 03-05). *Multi-model driven collaborative development platform for service-oriented e-business systems.* Paper presented at the 10th International Conference on Computer Supported Cooperative Work in Design, Nanjing, PRC.

Morimoto, S. (2008, June 23-25). *A survey of formal verification for business process modeling.* Paper presented at the 8th International Conference on Computational Science, Cracow, Poland.

Murphy, K., Weiss, Y., & Jordan, M. I. (1999, July 30 – August 1). *Loopy belief propagation for approximate inference: An empirical study.* Paper presented at Uncertainty in Artificial Intelligence, London, UK.

Pattabhiraman, R., Unmehopa, M., & Vemuri, K. (2007). Enhanced active phone book services: Blended lifestyle services made real! *Bell Labs Technical Journal, 11*(4), 315–326. doi:10.1002/bltj.20211

Rahmandad, H., & Sterman, J. (2008). Heterogeneity and network structure in the dynamics of diffusion: Comparing agent-based and differential equation models. *Management Science*, *54*(5), 998–1014. doi:10.1287/mnsc.1070.0787

Smith, V. L. (1976). Experimental economics – Induced value theory. *The American Economic Review*, *66*(2), 274–279.

Spohrer, J., & Maglio, P. P. (2008). The emergence of service science: Toward systematic service innovations to accelerate co-creation of value. *Production and Operations Management*, *17*(3), 238–246. doi:10.3401/poms.1080.0027

Takenaka, T., & Ueda, K. (2008). An analysis of service studies toward sustainable value creation. *International Journal of Sustainable Manufacturing*, *1*(1-2), 168–179.

Ueda, K., Takenaka, T., & Fujita, K. (2008). Toward value co-creation in manufacturing and servicing. *CIRP Journal of Manufacturing Science and Technology*, *1*(1), 53–58. doi:10.1016/j.cirpj.2008.06.007

Vickrey, W. (1961). Counterspeculation, auctions and competitive sealed tenders. *The Journal of Finance*, *16*, 8–37. doi:10.2307/2977633

Weinerman, E. R., Rutzen, S. R., & Pearson, D. A. (1965). Effects of medical triage in hospital emergency service. *Public Health Reports*, *80*(5), 389–399.

This work was previously published in International Journal of Organizational and Collective Intelligence, Volume 1, Issue 1, edited by Hideyasu Sasaki, pp. 58-75, copyright 2010 by IGI Publishing (an imprint of IGI Global).

Chapter 5
Students' Perceptions and Acceptance:
Lessons from Two Studies on Social Tools on Collaborative and Collective Learning

Yin-Leng Theng
Nanyang Technological University, Singapore

Jimmy Chong Jeah Leong
Nanyang Technological University, Singapore

Elaine Lew Yee Wen
Nanyang Technological University, Singapore

Stanley See Boon Yeow
Nanyang Technological University, Singapore

Ding Hong Yan
Nanyang Technological University, Singapore

ABSTRACT

In recent years, we witness the formation of social spaces in computers and networks where children, youths and young adults learn, play, socialize and participate in civic life. The question we want to ask is: if this participatory culture of user-generated content in which socially constructed and collective intelligence is to be harnessed, what are the critical success factors that determine the acceptance of this participatory culture in the learning environments? As an illustration, the paper describes two studies focused on tertiary students' perceptions of acceptance of social tools such as Weblogs and instant messaging in facilitating collaborative and collective learning with the aim of tapping onto the collective intelligence of user communities. Congruent to other studies, findings from these two preliminary studies have shown that factors influencing the acceptance of social tools such as Weblogs and instant messaging for learning are dependent on learners' perceptions of usefulness, followed by usability of the social tools. The paper concludes with design implications for socially constructed, learning environments.

DOI: 10.4018/978-1-4666-1577-9.ch005

1. INTRODUCTION

The biggest revolution engendered by the Web is happening right before our eyes, due to the evolution of the Web from a one-way information warehouse focusing on access to information by users to a distributed platform for collaboration in which content is created and shared for free among users. Social networks layered on top of digital networks are transforming business models and our very lifestyles. With new digital technologies on the Web leading to new communication practices, Jenkins et al (2006) called this new phenomenon where barriers to artistic expression and civic engagement are bypassed "participatory culture".

In recent years, we witness the formation of social spaces in computers and networks where children, youths and young adults learn, play, socialize and participate in civic life. In these spaces, people present themselves, meet with other people, exchange news, play games together, do business, or jointly look for information. Examples of such social networking spaces include blogs (e.g. Blogger), wikis (e.g. Wikipedia), social networking (e.g. MySpace), media sharing (e.g. YouTube) and social tagging (e.g. del.icio.us), among many others. Hoschka (1998) introduced the term "Social Web" to describe the shift from using computers and the Web as simple cooperation tools to using the computer as a social medium.

With the development of the Internet and its widespread use, the opportunity to contribute to community-based knowledge spaces on the Web, such as Wikipedia, is greater than ever before. These new forms of space for action and interaction could not have been predicted by conventional economics because the content is generated by users voluntarily. Such spaces create real economic value and form new kinds of habitats resulting in "social production" or "commons-based peer production" (Benkler, 2006).

Information technology (IT) and the Internet have made inroads into teaching and learning in higher education. Students accustomed to a high degree of IT and Internet penetration in daily life have themselves come to expect schools to use IT and the Internet to deliver education. Further, the current trend in education away from instructor-centred teaching and towards to student-centred learning (Wrede, 2003) has necessitated corresponding changes to delivery modes and instructional design, and have prompted instructors to look towards IT- and Web-based tools for solutions.

For example, there is an increasing focus on developing adaptive environments in which socially constructed, collaborative and peer learning are investigated. Current information technology tools (ICTs) of communication tools are getting more sophisticated and powerful, enabling humans to interact, share and collaborate with ease and speed. To respond to the need that human interactions are equally important in the virtual space as it is in traditional classroom setting, a variety of social software has been developed to facilitate student-teacher and peer-to-peer interactions. Connell (2004) and Boyd (2003) contend that generally accepted definitions of social software are those that address the desire of individuals to be pulled into groups to achieve goals and feature support for conversational interaction between individuals or groups, support for social feedback, and/or support for social networks. Kaplan-Leiserson (2003) argues that while the initial focus of e-learning was on the technology that drove it, these new social software tools are being adapted from those used by teens and business people to keep in touch, collaborate and learn from each other.

The question we want to ask is: if this participatory culture of user-generated content in which socially constructed and collective intelligence is to be harnessed, what are the critical success factors that determine the acceptance of this participatory culture in the learning environments?

As an illustration, the two studies were focused on tertiary students to answer the question on identifying factors that might influence the ac-

Figure 1. Original technology acceptance model (TAM)

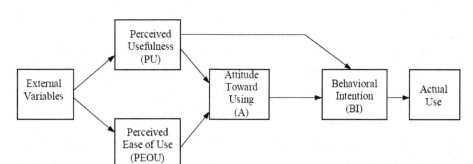

ceptance of this participatory culture via social tools on the Internet for the purpose of facilitating learning. Tertiary students, between 18 – 35 years old, were selected as they belonged to the most prolific and Internet-savvy age group in Singapore that may embrace and benefit from engaging in this participatory culture. In the studies, popular social tools such as Weblogs, essentially online journals, were investigated in Study I and instant messaging tools, examples of Internet-based synchronous text messaging software, were examined in Study II.

The remainder of this paper discusses the well-established Technology Acceptance Model (TAM) adapted as the underlying research model to investigate the constructs and factors that influence the acceptance of social tools in learning. Next, the findings and analyses of the two studies are briefly discussed. The chapter concludes with a discussion on implications of social tools for collaborative and collective learning in education.

2. UNDERLYING RESEARCH MODEL

Over the years, a significant body of research has focused on identifying various factors that influence of user acceptance behaviour in IT. Davis' Technology Acceptance Model (TAM) has received considerable attention (e.g., Burton-Jones & Hubona, 2005; etc.) in the study of user

acceptance. TAM, as originally conceived by Davis (1989), aims to provide an explanation of the determinants of computer acceptance from perspectives of user behaviour across a broad range of end-user computing technologies and user populations, while at the same time being both parsimonious and theoretically justified. It is a model that links constructs of perceived usefulness (PU) of the technology, users' perceived ease of use (PEOU) of such technology, attitude towards using, behavioural intention (BI) and actual use of the technology. In TAM, PU and PEOU are main independent constructs while BI and actual use are main dependent constructs. PU is defined as user's personal belief that using a particular technology will enhance his or her performance at the job, and PEOU refers to the extent to which the user anticipates the specific technology he or she is using is free of difficulty. There are external variables that control PU and PEOU in determining attitudes toward using the technology, that is, user's willingness to use the technology.

TAM has been applied in various types of technology and software, such as computers (Igbaria, Guimaraes & Davis, 1995); groupware (Lou, Luo & Strong, 2000), email (Karahanna & Straub, 1999) and facsimile (Straub, 1994), mostly in the organizational environment. There have also been a number of studies that have examined students' acceptance of Web-based learning systems (Stoel & Lee, 2003), use of the Internet in university (Cheung, & Huang, 2005), course Websites (Selim, 2003) and digital libraries (Hong, Thong, Wong & Tam, 2002).

However, to the best of our knowledge at the point of the two studies, there have been no known studies using TAM to model students' acceptance of social tools in high institutes of learning in Singapore, and hence the motivation to conduct the two studies proposed in this paper.

3. STUDY I ON WEBLOGS

3.1 Background

Weblogs are one of the latest and most quickly expanding forms of communication and Web publishing. The blogosphere – or world of Weblogs – appears to be growing in size by the day. A census conducted in 2003 by the United States' NITLE (National Institute of Technology and Liberal Education) reported over 1.3 million sites calling themselves "blogs", of which about 870,000 were considered "active" (Nardi, Schiano & Gumbrecht, 2004). Technorati, a real-time Weblog search engine, reports that as of the end of July 2005, it was tracking over 14.2 million Weblogs, or nearly double the 7.8 million Weblogs tracked in March 2005 and 4 times the number of Weblogs tracked in October 2004. The blogosphere appeared to double about every five months. These numbers indicated 80,000 Weblogs created each day, and new Weblog created almost every second (Sifry, 2005). A Weblog is essentially a Web page where all writing and editing is managed through a Web browser (Armstrong, Berry & Lamshed, 2004). The user can publish to the Web without any programming code or server software (Martindale & Wiley, 2004). Weblog content typically consists of short time-stamped entries arranged in reverse chronological order. Through a hyperlinked post structure, individual entries can be referenced by others and archived by

date. Weblog applications usually allow viewers to write comments in reply to individual entries, thereby engaging in discussion with the writer of the post and other viewers.

Despite the apparent popularity of Weblogs, there is a high rate of Weblog abandonment. Bialik (2005) revealed that only 55% of Weblogs are considered active, having at least one post in the three months leading up to July 2005. Sifry (2005) found that only 13% of all Weblogs (currently 1.8 million Weblogs) are updated at least weekly. These figures are perhaps not surprising, given the existence of numerous Weblog hosting services and the fact that many such services enable Weblogs to be created quickly, easily and often free of charge by almost anybody with Internet access.

3.2 Objectives and Protocol

Hence, Weblogs may offer a number of possibilities for student-centred learning in higher education (Theng and Lew, 2007). They extend the scope for interaction and collaboration among students beyond the physical classroom. Discussion can take place at times and places chosen by students. Interactivity also encourages self and peer assessment, a critical part of the learning process (Connell, 2004). Writing entries in Weblogs and exchanging ideas with others refine students' thinking and writing skills. Weblogs also support active learning as learning logs track the progress of knowledge construction through all iterations made, rather than simply display finished work (e.g., Armstrong, Berry & Lamshed, 2004; etc.). Syndication of Weblog content reduces information overload by aggregating content from multiple Weblogs into one location for viewing (Martindale & Wiley, 2004). Weblogs further reduce information overload (Oravec, 2003), and support content management by enabling the blogger to link to Web resources and to organize such links in Weblog entries. Weblogs also support the creation of knowledge communities, in which related posts made on disparate Weblogs can be connected with hyperlinks (Pullich, 2004).

Using a modified TAM, Study I aimed to investigate three research questions (RQs) to examine the critical factors that might affect students' perceptions of acceptance of Weblogs to support learning:

- **RQ1:** To what extent are students' perceptions of Weblog usefulness influenced by awareness of Weblog technology and Weblog capabilities, peer and tutor support, and readiness for student-centred learning?

- **RQ2:** To what extent are students' perceptions of ease of use of Weblogs influenced by feelings of Weblog self-efficacy, prior computing and IT experience and facilitating conditions?

- **RQ3:** In the context of the use of Weblogs in higher education, what is the relationship between students' perceptions of Weblog usefulness, Weblog ease of use and their intentions to use Weblogs?

Since Study I was concerned with the perceptions and intentions of tertiary students regarding Weblogs, undergraduate and postgraduate students of a local university were selected to participate in the study. The questionnaire was administered by hand or as an attachment to email messages sent to students at a local university. Responses were collected over a period of three weeks.

Figure 2 shows the modified TAM for Study I addressing the three research questions with hypotheses (see Table 1) identified, and corresponding question items indicated. External variables influencing the construct of PU include awareness of blogs (Lee et al., 2002), peer and tutor support, student-centred learning readiness (Bernard et al., 2004); and the construct of PEOU are Weblog self-efficacy (Agarwal et al., 2000), prior experience (Martins and Kellermanns, 2004) and facilitating conditions (Taylor and Todd,

1995). Details of study and findings can be found in Theng and Lew (1997).

3.3 Summary of Findings and Analyses

Of the sixty-eight students who participated in Study I, an overwhelming majority of respondents rated themselves as highly experienced in operating a personal computer (85.3%), accessing information on the Internet (89.7%), and using email (88.3%). More than half of the respondents considered themselves highly experienced with Hypertext Markup Language (HTML) and discussion threads (57.4% each). Slightly more than a third (35.3%) of respondents rated themselves highly experienced with Weblogs. A summary of findings & analyses is presented as follows:

- H1a was supported as relationship between overall Weblog awareness and PU is statistically significant ($\chi2 = 14.2$, $df = 4$, p = 0.007). In other words, students' awareness of Weblogs and their capabilities has a significant effect on the PU of Weblogs as learning tools.

- Support from persons most closely connected with the student in the educational process, namely his or her peers and tutors, has a significant effect on the student's perception of Weblog usefulness for learning purposes, supporting H1b ($\chi2 = 9.771$, $df = 4$, p = 0.044).

- The survey on the interactive aspect of student-centred learning (SCL) quizzed students on motivations to participate in interactive learning activities, such as the discussion of course topics with classmates and tutors, peer review of coursework and group work conducted online. It also queried their experience with interacting with classmates in an online written forum. Overall readiness for SCL ($\chi^2 = 5.254$,, $df = 4$, p = 0.262) was not significantly related

Figure 2. Research model for study I

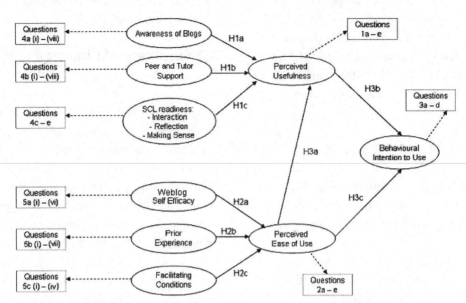

to PU of Weblogs as learning tools, hence H1c was not supported. However, the relationship between PU and a student's inclination towards interactive learning was statistically significant (χ^2 = 10.827,, df = 4, p = 0.029). The findings suggested that students who were motivated towards interactive learning and comfortable with online interaction would likely find Weblogs to be a useful for learning.

- Computer self-efficacy is defined as one's beliefs about the ability to use computers effectively (Compeau et al., 1999). Students' feelings of Weblog self-efficacy significantly influenced (χ^2 = 21.348,, df = 4, p = 0.000) their PEOU for learning purposes, supporting H2a is true as Weblogs were perceived as easier to use by students with higher levels of self-efficacy.

Table 1. Hypotheses for RQ1, RQ2 and RQ3 in Study I

Research Questions		Hypotheses
RQ1	H1a	Students' awareness of Weblogs and their capabilities have a significant effect on the PU of Weblogs as learning tools.
	H1b	Peer support and tutor support have a significant effect on PU.
	H1c	Readiness for student-centred learning has a significant effect on PU.
RQ2	H2a	Students' Weblog self-efficacy significantly affects the PEOU of Weblogs as a learning tool.
	H2b	Prior computing and IT experience has a significant effect on PEOU.
	H2c	Facilitating conditions have a significant effect on PEOU.
RQ3	H3a	PEOU has a significant effect on PU.
	H3b	PU has a significant effect on the BI to use Weblogs as a learning tool.
	H3c	PEOU has a significant effect on BI.

- Overall, prior computing and IT experience had significant influence on PEOU (χ^2 = 15.925, df = 4, p = 0.003), hence H2b is true. However, prior experience with personal computers (p = 0.081) and the Internet (p = 0.323) did not affect perceptions of Weblog ease of use. The following prior experiences gave significant results: with Weblogs (χ^2 = 20.187,, df = 4, p < 0.001); HTML (χ^2 = 13.949,, df = 4, p = 0.007), discussion threads (χ^2 = 18.778,, df = 4, p = 0.001), Wikis (χ^2 = 11.401,, df = 4, p = 0.022) and email (χ^2 = 13.737,, df = 4, p = 0.008).

- H2c was supported as facilitating conditions had a significant effect on students' PEOU for learning purposes (χ^2 = 13.184,, df = 4, p < 0.05). Thus, students were likely to consider Weblogs easy to use if the necessary infrastructure and technical support were available.

- PEOU had no significant effect on students' PU for learning purposes implying that H3a is not true. In other words, even if students found Weblogs easy to use, they might not necessarily consider Weblogs a useful learning tool.

- PU of Weblogs for learning significantly influenced overall intention to use Weblogs as a learning tool in higher education, supporting H3b (χ^2 = 30.839,, df = 4, p < 0.001).

- PEOU of Weblogs for learning had no significant influence on overall intention to use Weblogs as a learning tool in higher education and Hypothesis 3c was not supported even if the Weblogs were perceived to be easy to use.

4. STUDY II ON INSTANT MESSAGING

4.1 Background

Instant Messaging (IM) is a form of communication platform that allows 2 or more persons to have private online conversations instantaneously over the Internet using a text-based tool. IM evolved from Internet Relay Chat (IRC) and its initial use was for home internet users to communicate with family members and friend. IM is a near-synchronous computer-based, one-on-one communications (Nardi et al., 2000) whereas email is asynchronous. It is somewhat like email, but much more like a chat room where both parties are online at the same time, and they "talk" to each other by typing text and sending small pictures in instantaneous time.

IM can be categorised into three sectors, namely public networks, private or enterprise network and integrated networks (Farmer, 2005). Public network, which are free clients includes IM Clients like MSN Messenger, Yahoo! Messenger and Skype Messenger which have been the main contributor of the growth of IM. These public network instant messaging systems are usually not interoperable. The private / enterprise networks are domain specific IM systems like Lotus Sametime which are available only to users of the same domain. Integrated networks are enterprise software, which integrates IM as part of the system such as Horizon Wimba.

IM has since gained wide acceptance in recent years as a communication device both in the social networking area and slowly gaining popularity in the office workspace. Research articles estimated that IM usage at home (Irvine, 2006) has increased 28% from 42 million in September 2000 to 53.8 million in September 2001 (Perera, 2001) while IM usage at the workplace has been growing at about 20% annually (Shukla, 2003). Microsoft's MSN Messenger alone had more than 75 million people using it by Feb 2003 (Yudkowsky, 2003). Research firm International Data Corporation (IDC) claims that there are now over 300 million IM users (Mingail, 2001).

In a study by Isaacs et al. (2002), IM is frequently used at the workplace as a tool for informal communication as compared to email where it is used formally. According to a 2004 Workplace

E-Mail and Instant Messaging Survey sponsored by American Management Association (AMA) and the ePolicy Institute on 840 US companies, there is a tremendous growth in the use of IM in the workplace. In another report by the Pew Internet & American Life survey, the findings show that more than four in ten online Americans use instant messaging (IM) (Shiu et al., 2004). About 11 million of them use IM at work and they are becoming fond of its capacity to encourage productivity and interoffice cooperation.

One reason for IM being popular is that instant messengers utilize IM not only as a way to expand and remain connected to their social circle, but it is also as a form of self-expression. Toda (1991) highlighted that short-lived communication is important in establishing and maintaining social networks. In another study conducted on a Korean company, results suggested that its employees used IM to maintain their working relationships with co-workers within and across various organizational boundaries, and perceived that their relationships both inside and outside of the company had improved after adopting IM in their work (Cho et al., 2005).

Comparing IM to email, studies have also shown that IM's gaining popularity as compared to email could be due to its human conversation type experience (Nardi et al., 2000). While email is more like exchanges of digital letters, IM has a close resemblance to a human's conversation where instant, short responses are experienced. Concurring with these findings, Nardi et al. (2000) describe instant messages as typically casual, informal, and friendly thus aiding communication. This informality helps to foster a warm or friendly and informal atmosphere that is found lacking in emails and other forms of communications.

4.2 Objectives and Protocol

Research into the use of IM at work highlights the positive vibes of IM users such as increased productivity, teamwork, time saving as well as some relief from daily grind. The question asked in Study II is whether IM could facilitate learning. Similar to Study I, in Study II, we were interested to investigate the factors that influence tertiary students' perceptions on acceptance of IM for learning using the modified TAM.

The structural paths of the research model represent the hypotheses generated to address the research questions (see Figure 3). Table 2 tabulates the hypothesized relationships, to be tested using the revised TAM. External variables influencing the construct of PU include technology utility (Farmer, 2003), network externality (Rohlfs, 1974), media influences (Bhattacherjee, 2000); and the construct of PEOU include self-efficacy (Burkhardt & Brass, 1990), affection (Raafat & Kira, 2006) and anxiety (Spielberger, 1972). Details of study and findings are found in Theng, Leong & Yeow (2008).

The data for Study II was collected by means of a survey conducted in a local university and to encourage more students' participation, a small gift was given out for each completed survey. Responses were collected over a period of two weeks. We targeted respondents with some working experiences, and they were mostly IT savvy and potential early adopters of technology due to their nature of work, thus, they would have used IM as a tool for communication for social networking or work-related stuff.

4.3 Summary of Findings and Analyses

A total of 104 students (30% females and 70% males) from a local university participated in the survey. More than 90% of the respondents had at least one IM account. The respondents used IM for the following 3 reasons in the order of importance: (i) keeping in touch with friends and family (46%); (ii) using for work-related tasks (29.2%); and (iii) using for academic project work (20%). The popular IM tools used by respondents include: MSN Messenger (43.5%), followed by

Figure 3. Research model for study II

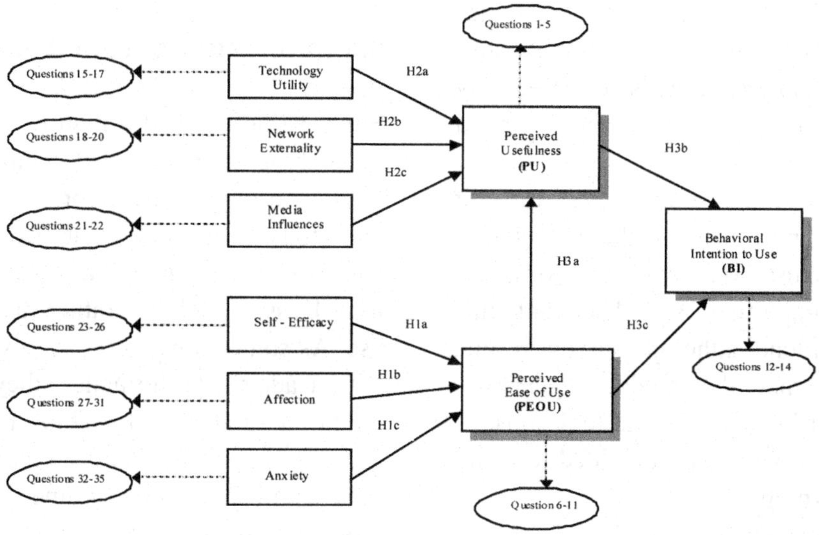

Yahoo Messenger (23.2%) and Skype (20.3%). A summary of findings & analyses is presented as follows:

- Congruent to findings from other studies in which self-efficacy is an antecedent of PEOU in TAM (Venkatesh & Davis, 1996), our findings also suggest that together with affection ($\chi2 = 51.842$, $df = 4$, $p = 0.00001$), computer self-efficacy ($\chi2 = 26.970$, $df = 4$, $p = 0.00002$) has significant influence on students' perception of IM's ease of use, hence supporting Hypotheses H1a and H1b. However, anxiety does not have a significant influence on PEOU, and Hypothesis H1c is not supported.

- Findings show that the three external variables: technology utility, network externality and media influences influence students' perceptions of IM for learning, supporting Hypotheses 2a ($\chi2 = 22.313$, $df = 4$, $p = 0.00017$), 2b ($\chi2 = 25.257$, $df = 4$, $p = 0.00004$) and 2c ($\chi2 = 19.417$, $df = 4$, $p = 0.00065$).

Table 2. Hypotheses for RQ1, RQ2 and RQ3 in study II

	Hypotheses
H1a	Students' self-efficacy of IM significantly affects the PEOU of IM as a learning tool.
H1b	Technology affection on students has a significant effect on PEOU.
H1c	Technology anxiety on student has a significant effect on PEOU.
H2a	Technology utility has a significant effect on the PU.
H2b	Network externality has a significant effect on PU.
H2c	Media influences have a significant effect on PU.
H3a	There will be a positive relationship between PEOU and PU, meaning PEOU has a significant effect on PU.
H3b	There will be a positive relationship between PU and BI, meaning PU has a significant effect on BI to use IM as a tool to help them in learning.
H3c	There will be a positive relationship between PEOU and BI, meaning PEOU has a significant effect on BI.

- PEOU significantly affects PU, hence supporting H3a. Congruent to other studies (e.g. Landry, 2006; etc.), this finding supports the claim that if IM is perceived easy to use by students, it will also be perceived useful.

- Contrary to other studies, PU was not significant in influencing the behavioural intention to use IM as an enabler for learning, not supporting H3b. Analyzing further, we found although survey results suggested that the students generally agreed that IM was a useful tool, most of the students were not committed to using IM for learning.

- The relationship between PEOU and BI was positively correlated with a result of 0.004, supporting H3c and suggesting that PEOU would influence students to use IM as enabler for learning.

Figure 4 illustrates the relationships among the study variables. A straight line indicates supported hypothesis while a dotted line is unsupported hypothesis.

5. DISCUSSION AND CONCLUSION

5.1 Implications from Study I

Study I findings had a number of implications for Weblog use in university courses. First, they seemed to suggest that in order to persuade students to take up courses that incorporate Weblog use, it would be more important to stress the usefulness of Weblogs rather than their ease of use. As students would generally be concerned with academic performance, they would likely require assurance that Weblog use has the potential to improve grades, increase productivity in accomplishing tasks or otherwise make them more effective learners.

Second, the findings seemed to suggest that to increase usefulness perceptions, students should be made aware of how Weblog use is compatible with learning activities. To prepare students for Weblogs use in education, tutors might consider starting their own class Weblogs and using them for announcements and dissemination of course materials. Students might also be encouraged to communicate with the tutor and each other on the

Figure 4. Study II: Relationships among the study variables

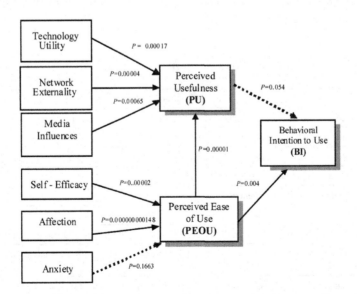

Weblog. This could help both tutor and students ascertain the value of Weblog use. Ferdig and Trammell (2004) suggested that Weblog awareness can also be increased by visiting existing Weblogs in use by other classes and other schools.

Third, since tutor support played an important part in encouraging favourable perceptions of Weblogs in education, it would be important for tutors to take an active part in communications across student Weblogs. Due to the public nature of Weblog entries, Weblog communications could be discussed in the physical classroom as well as online. Tutors could also show their support for Weblog use by stipulating the specific outcomes and uses for blogging as well as clear rules for blogging such as frequency, length of posts, number of hyperlinks, staying on topic and the use of references and citations when quoting the work of others (Ferdig & Trammell, 2004). These rules could be created together with students. Developing house rules regarding Weblogs would be useful in demonstrating to students the tutor's commitment to ensuring that Weblogs would used effectively to further the learning process.

Fourth, a student's motivation to learn by interaction affected perceptions of Weblog usefulness. Weblog use is not itself passive in nature. A user must communicate effectively with others and accept peer review with good grace. In order for Weblogs use to be effective and poor attendance at online discussions to be avoided, tutors should inform students wishing to enroll in courses that incorporate blogging that they should be prepared to engage in online discussion as part of the learning process and to make their written work publicly available to their peers.

Fifth, the study showed that perceptions of the ease of use of Weblogs did not significantly affect intentions to use them for learning purposes. As Weblogs are relatively user-friendly in comparison to most Web publishing tools, extensive in-class training would likely be unnecessary. It should be noted, however, the findings were confined to a survey population with high levels of Weblog self-efficacy and confidence that they had the resources and knowledge required to blog for learning purposes. For students less skilled in IT, some degree of technical support would increase perceptions of use. The provision of contact information for technical assistance or optional Weblog or Web programming tutorials would help such students accept Weblog use for learning purposes.

5.2 Implications from Study II

Study II findings seemed consistent with the research by The Pew Internet & America and Life surveys where some 21% of IM users, or approximately 11 million American adults, use instant messaging at work (Shiu et al., 2004). In a study by Mock (2001) on the use of IM in education on 35 students, only 35% used IM software for class materials. Despite the low usage, the students rated IM positively and indicated the willingness to use IM. In another study at Mount Saint Vincent University, about 88% of its students used IM and a trial experiment indicated majority of students used IM for social networking with one another (Farmer, 2005). Promising as it maybe, IM does have some issues to address if implemented, and the two major issues are:

- **Lack of Protocols:** There are standard protocols for emails but not for IM. Currently, IM is developed by different vendors like AOL, Microsoft Yahoo. The lack of IM standards as mentioned by Mock (2001) means that potential interoperability could deter the uptake of such technology by students. Network externality as measured in Study II could have an impact.
- **IM's Security:** IM has its own issues with menaces such as viruses and unsolicited messages. But IM viruses discovered so far are relatively harmless compared with virulent e-mail-borne infections, and email is still the easiest way to get virus (Hu,

2001). However, the trend of IM viruses seems to be looking upwards. There were over 60 vulnerabilities that have already been mapped to IM and the list is growing (Stone et al., 2004).

5.3 Concluding Remarks

Findings from the two studies have shown that factors influencing the acceptance of social tools such as Weblogs and IM for the purpose of learning are dependent on students' perceptions of usefulness, followed by usability of the social tools.

Hence, to design usable and useful learning digital environments supporting socially constructed and collective learning, perhaps appropriate social tools enhancing collaboration and competition of communities of learners should be encouraged. To tap upon the socially constructed, collective intelligence (that is, shared or group intelligence) in this participatory culture, Jenkins et al (2006) postulate that there must be a strong support for creating and sharing what users create with others as well, in other words, the most experienced members pass along knowledge, skills and norms to novices; members feel that their contributions matter; and members feel some degree of social connection with each other at least to the degree to which they care about what they have created.

This is preliminary work. Certainly, more can be done for future studies: using a larger sample, preferably consisting of respondents with more diversified backgrounds, experiences and levels of access to computing and Internet resources; and more objective usage measures (e.g. frequency and length of Weblog entries, the average number of hyperlinks used in an entry or appearing in the blogroll, etc.). Further research could be done on a larger and more diverse student population, as the two studies focused on tertiary, technology-literate students.

ACKNOWLEDGMENT

I would like to thank Elaine Lew, Ding Hong Yan, Jimmy Chong Jeah Leong & Stanley See Boon Yeo who carried Study I and Study II, and the subjects who took part in the two studies.

REFERENCES

Abrami, P. (1996). Computer supported collaborative learning and distance education. *American Journal of Distance Education, 10*(3), 37–41. doi:10.1080/08923649609526920

Agarwal, R., Sambamurthy, V., & Stair, R. M. (2000). Research report: the evolving relationship between general and specific computer self-efficacy - An empirical assessment. *Information Systems Research, 11*, 418–430. doi:10.1287/isre.11.4.418.11876

Armstrong, L., Berry, M., & Lamshed, R. (2004). Blogs as electronic learning journals. *e-Journal of Instructional Science and Technology, 7*(1).

Benkler, Y. (2006). *The wealth of networks: How social production transforms markets and freedom.* Yale University Press.

Bernard, R. M., Brauer, A., Abrami, P. C., & Surkes, M. (2004). The development of a questionnaire for predicting online learning achievement. *Distance Education, 25*(1), 31–47. doi:10.1080/0158791042000212440

Bhattacherjee, A. (2000). Acceptance of e-commerce services: the case of electronic brokerages. *Systems, Man and Cybernetics, Part A, IEEE Transactions, 30*(4), 411-420.

Bialik, C. (2005, May 26). Measuring the impact of blogs requires more than counting. *Retrieved August 3rd, 2005,* from The Wall Street Journal Online at http://online.wsj.com/public/article/0,SB111685593903640572,00.html?mod=2_1125_1.

Boyd, S. (2003). *Are you ready for social software?* Retrieved July 3, 2004, from http://www.darwinmag.com/read/050103/social.html.

Bures, E. (2000). Student motivation to learn via computer conferencing. *Research in Higher Education, 41*(5), 593–621. doi:10.1023/A:1007071415363

Burkhardt, M. E., & Brass, D. J. (1990). Changing patterns or patterns of change: The effects of a change in technology on social network structure and power. *Administrative Science Quarterly, 35,* 104–127. doi:10.2307/2393552

Burton-Jones, A., & Hubona, G. S. (2005). Individual differences and usage behavior: Revisiting a technology acceptance model assumption. *The Data Base for Advances in Information Systems, 36*(2), 58.

Cheung, W., & Huang, W. (2005). Proposing a framework to assess Internet usage in university education: an empirical investigation from a students' perspective. *British Journal of Educational Technology, 36*(2), 237–253. doi:10.1111/j.1467-8535.2005.00455.x

Cho, H.-K. (2005). The use of instant messaging in working relationship development: A case study. *Journal of Computer-Mediated Communication, 10*(4).

Connell, S. (2004). *Uses for social software in education: A literature review.* Retrieved August 20th, 2005, from http://soozzone.com/690review.htm.

Davis, F. D., Bagozzi, R. P., & Warshaw, P. R. (1989). User acceptance of computer technology: A comparison of two theoretical models. *Management Science, 35*(8), 982–1003. doi:10.1287/mnsc.35.8.982

Farmer, R. (2005). Instant messaging: IM online! RU? *EDUCAUSE Review, 40*(6).

Ferdig, R. E., & Trammell, K. D. (2004, February). *Content delivery in the blogosphere.* Retrieved November 7th, 2005, from T.H.E Journal Online at http://www.thejournal.com/magazine/vault/A4677.cfm

Hong, W., Thong, J. Y. L., Wong, W.-M., & Tam, K.-Y. (2002). Determinants of user acceptance of digital libraries: an empirical examination of individual differences and system characteristics. *Journal of Management Information Systems, 18*(3), 97–124.

Hoschka, P. (1998). *The social web research program: Linking people through virtual environments.* Retrieved on June 8, 2007, from http://www.fit.fhg.de/~hoschka/Social%20Web.htm.

Hu, J. (2001). *CNET news: Viruses wiggle into IM chats.* Retrieved August 31, 2006, from http://www.library.ucsb.edu/untangle/langston.html

Hubona, G. S., & Kennick, E. (1996). The influence of external variables on information technology usage behavior. In J.F. Nunamaker & R.H. Sprague (Eds.), *Proceedings of the 29th Annual Hawaii International Conference on Systems Sciences,* Maui (pp.166-76).

Igbaria, M., Guimaraes, T., & Davis, G. B. (1995). Testing the determinants of microcom-puter usage via a structural model. *Journal of Management Information Systems, 11*(4), 87–114.

Irani, T. (1998). Communication potential, information richness and attitude. *ALN Magazine, 2.*

Irvine, M. (2006). *E-mail losing ground to IM, text messaging, Young people driving switch to instant gratification communication.* Retrieved September 3, 2006, from http://msnbc.msn.com/id/13921601/wid/11915829

Isaacs, E., et al. (2002). *The character, functions, and styles of instant messaging in the workplace.* Paper presented at the Proceedings of the 2002 ACM conference on Computer supported cooperative work New Orleans, Louisiana, USA

Jenkins., et al. (2006). *Confronting the challenges of the participatory culture.* Retrieved on March 19, 2007, http://incsub.org/awards/2006/nominations-for-best-research-paper-2006/

Kaplan-Leiserson, E. (2003). We-learning: Social software and e-learning. Retrieved July 2, 2004, from http://www.learningcircuits.org/2003/dec2003/kaplan.htm

Karahanna, E., & Straub, D. (1999). The psychological origins of perceived usefulness and ease-of-use. *Information & Management, 35*(4), 237–250. doi:10.1016/S0378-7206(98)00096-2

Landry, B. et al. (2006). Measuring Student perceptions of blackboard using the technology acceptance model. *Decision Sciences Journal of Innovative Education, V41N1.*

Lavonen, J. (2000). Using computers in science and technology education. *SIGCSE Bulletin, 33*(v), 127–135. doi:10.1145/571922.571966

Lee, J., Ng, L. H., & Ng, L. L. (2002). An analysis of students' preparation for the virtual learning environment. *The Internet and Higher Education, 4,* 231–242. doi:10.1016/S1096-7516(01)00063-X

Levy, D., & Marshall, C. (1994). What color was George Washington's white horse? A look at the assumptions underlying digital libraries. In *Proceedings of Digital Libraries, 94,* 163–169.

Lou, H., Luo, W., & Strong, D. (2000). Perceived critical mass effect on groupware accep-tance. *European Journal of Information Systems, 9*(2), 91–103. doi:10.1057/palgrave/ejis/3000358

Martin, P. T. (1996). *Email and the Internet as a teaching tool: A critical perspective.* Paper presented at the Proceedings of the ASEE/IEEE Frontiers in Education Conference, Salt Lake City, USA

Martindale, T., & Wiley, D. A. (2004). Using Weblogs in scholarship and teaching. *TechTrends, 49*(2), 55–61. doi:10.1007/BF02773972

Martins, L. L., & Kellermanns, F. W. (2004). A model of business school students' acceptance of a Web-based course management system. *Academy of Management Learning & Education, 3*(1), 7–26.

Mingail, E. (2001). Instant messaging: Next best thing since e-mail. *Canada Law Book Inc. publication:* Retrieved August 30, 2006, from http://www.canadalawbook.com/headlines/headline128_arc.html

Mock, K. (2001). The use of Internet tools to supplement communication in the classroom. *The Journal for Computing in Small Colleges, 17*(2).

Muir-Herzig, R. (2004). Technology and its impact in the classroom. *ComputersandEducation, 42,* 111–131.

Nardi, B. A., et al. (2000). Interaction and outeraction: Instant messaging in action. *Proc. CSCW 2000* (pp. 79-88).

Nardi, B. A., Schiano, D. J., & Gumbrecht, M. (2004). Blogging as social activity, or, would you let 900 million people read your diary? In *Proceedings of 2004 ACM on Computer-Supported Cooperative Work,* 222-231.

Oravec, J. A. (2003). Blended by Blogging: Weblogs in blended learning initiatives. *Journal of Educational Media, 28*(2-3), 225–233. doi:10.1080/1358165032000165671

Perera, R. (2001). *Study: Instant messaging at work up 110 percent.* Retrieved September 4,2006, from http://www.cnn.com/2001/TECH/internet/11/16/workplace.IM.idg/

Pullich, L. (2004, September 30). *Usage of Weblogs in Festum - A distance education program for teachers.* Paper presented at the ICL Conference, Villach, Austria. Retrieved November 7, 2005, from http://bt-mac2.fernuni-hagen.de/peter/gems/lpWeblogsinfestum.pdf

Raafat, G. S., & Kira, D. (2006). The emotional state of technology acceptance. *Issues in Informing Science and Information Technology, 3.*

Rohlfs, J. (1974). A Theory of Interdependent Demand for a Communications Service Bell. *Journal of Economics and Management Science, 5*(1), 16–37.

Rouibah, K., et al. (2006, Mar 2006). *Does instant messaging usage impact students' performance in Kuwait?* Paper presented at the IASTED International Conference Networks and Communication Systems, Chiang Mai, Thailand.

Selim, H. M. (2003). An empirical investigation of student acceptance of course Websites. *Computers & Education, 40*, 343–360. doi:10.1016/S0360-1315(02)00142-2

Shaw, F. S., & Giacquinta, J. B. (2000). *A survey of graduate students as end users of computer technology.*

Shiu, E., et al. (2004). *Pew Internet & American life surveys how Americans use instant messaging.* Retrieved September 1, 2006, from http://www.pewinternet.org/PPF/r/133/report_display.asp

Shukla, U. (2003). *The future of enterprise instant messaging.* Retrieved September 3, 2006, from http://www.expresscomputeronline.com/20030505/tech1.shtml

Sifry, D. (2005, August 2). *State of the blogosphere.* Retrieved August 4, 2005, from The Technorati Weblog at http://www.technorati.com/Weblog/2005/08/34.html

Spielberger, C. D. (1972). Conceptual and methodological issues in anxiety research. *Anxiety: Current Trends in Theory and Research, 2*, 481-494. New York: Academic Press.

Stoel, L., & Lee, K. H. (2003). Modeling the effect of experience on student acceptance of Web-based courseware. *Internet Research: Electronic Networking Applications and Policy, 13*(5), 364–374. doi:10.1108/10662240310501649

Stone, J. (2004). Instant messaging or instant headache? *ACM Queue; Tomorrow's Computing Today, 2*(2). doi:10.1145/988392.988410

Straub, D. (1994). The effect of culture on IT diffusion e-mail and FAX in Japan and the U.S. *Information Systems Research, 5*(1), 23–47. doi:10.1287/isre.5.1.23

Taylor, S., & Todd, P. A. (1995). Understanding information technology usage: a test of competing models. *Information Systems Research, 6*(2), 144–178. doi:10.1287/isre.6.2.144

Theng, Y. L. J., Leong, J., & Yeow, S. (2008). An empirical study investigating instant messaging as an enabling tool for education. *Accepted to ICA 2008*, Montreal, Canada.

Theng, Y. L., & Lew, Y. W. (2007). Perceived usefulness and usability of Weblogs for collaborative learning. Full paper. *HCI International 2007 (HCII2007)*, Beijing, China.

Theng, Y. L., Mohd-Nasir, N., Buchanan, G., Fields, B., Thimbleby, H., & Cassidy, N. (2001). Dynamic digital libraries for children. *First ACM and IEEE Joint Conference in Digital Libraries*, Ronaoke, Virginia (pp. 406–415).

Toda, M. (1991). *Common sense, emotion, and chatting, and their roles in interpersonal interactions*, Chukyo University.

Venkatesh, V. (2000). Determinants of perceived ease of use: integrating control, intrinsic motivation and emotion into the Technology Acceptance Model. *Information Systems Research, 11*(4), 342–365. doi:10.1287/isre.11.4.342.11872

Venkatesh, V., & Davis, F. D. (1996). A model of the antecedents of perceived ease of use: development and test. *Decision Sciences, 27*(3), 451–481. doi:10.1111/j.1540-5915.1996.tb01822.x

Wrede, O. (2003, May 23-24). *Weblogs and discourse.* Paper presented at the Blogtalk Conference, Vienna.

Yudkowsky, C. (2003). *IM in a corporate environment: Is instant messaging a nuisance or an untapped tool?* Retrieved September 3, 2006, from http://accounting.smartpros.com/x37078.xml

This work was previously published in International Journal of Organizational and Collective Intelligence, Volume 1, Issue 1, edited by Hideyasu Sasaki, pp. 76-90, copyright 2010 by IGI Publishing (an imprint of IGI Global).

Chapter 6
CSMA:
Context–Based, Service–Oriented Modeling and Analysis Method for Modern Enterprise Applications

Khouloud Boukadi
Ecole des Mines, Saint-Etienne, France

Chirine Ghedira
University Lyon 1, France

Lucien Vincent
Ecole des Mines, Saint-Etienne, France

Zakaria Maamar
Zayed University, UAE

ABSTRACT

Since the beginning of the Service-Oriented Architecture (SOA) paradigm, with its various implementation technologies such as Web services, the focus of industrial communities has been on providing tools that would allow seamless and flexible application integration within and across enterprises' boundaries. In this paper, the authors present a Context-based, Service-oriented Modeling and Analysis (CSMA) method that guides service engineers in their choices of identifying, defining, and analyzing adaptable business services. The proposed method is business centric and comprises a set of structured steps grouped in two phases. Besides, the CSMA embraces Model-Driven Architecture (MDA) principles to model and refine adaptable business services models in the PIM level. The results from a pilot validation of CSMA for SOA enablement of a realistic enterprise training solutions are also presented.

INTRODUCTION

Service-Oriented Architecture (SOA) paradigm has a major role to play in the development of modern enterprise application systems. Other design paradigms like object-oriented and component-based have tied up such systems to some architectural solutions. By doing so, the capacity of these systems to smoothly accommodate changes in business requirements and regulations has seriously been limited (Nuffel, 2007). SOA promotes system flexibility using independent, reusable automated business services. Each service can through the "possible" help of other peers implement complex business processes and system functions as well. Business services are, also, defined as units of work that are performed in response to some consumers'

DOI: 10.4018/978-1-4666-1577-9.ch006

needs satisfaction (Erl, 2005). This paradigm shift in enterprise architectural solutions from traditional single entity to service collaboration is fueling intense debates among IT practitioners. Despite the benefits of this shift such as business process reusability and spreadability cross organizational boundaries, enterprises are still reluctant to abandon the traditional ways of designing business processes in order to embrace an entirely new paradigm based on services. Several SOA-related limitations undermine these benefits. Industry definitions for service principles and standardized frameworks for modeling business services are still in progress and several proposals and thoughts are still unsettled (Arsanjani, 2004; Heuvel, Hasselbring, & Papazoglou, 2000; Erradi, Anand, & Kulkarni, 2006a). A comprehensive framework that would set guidelines for service-oriented modeling and analysis is required. Many enterprises in their early use of SOA simply thought of wrapping their existing components in compliance with services' standards. Deploying large-scale, modern SOA-based applications goes beyond component wrapping. An effective approach for identifying, modeling, and analyzing services is crucial to achieve SOA benefits (Papazoglou & Heuvel, 2006). Our extensive literature review reveals that a few methods exist and lessons learnt from previous experiences along with best practices are almost inexistent. Works like (Arsanjani, 2004) and (Papazoglou & Heuvel, 2006) propose methods for designing and modeling services in enterprise. However, these methods are very aligned to the particular technology of Web services. In addition, critical issues (e.g., non-functional-requirements, context-aware, etc.) that concern delivering high-quality services are barely touched. A method that promotes the use of SOA at a high level of abstraction and specifically tackles the issue of service adaptability to context changes during the design stage is still missing.

In this paper, we propose a method that guides service engineers in their choices of identifying, defining, and analyzing adaptable business services. Our method called Context-based, Service-oriented Modeling and Analysis (CSMA) is adaptable-business-service centric and provides appropriate guidance for SOA analysis and modeling. In CSMA, business services are designed in a way that their behavior is fine tuned according to today's markets' needs. Issues such as reusability, customizability, manageability, and context-awareness of service development need to be considered early in service-system development. Moreover, CSMA describes the service-oriented development process at a high level of abstraction regardless of implementation details. To this end, CSMA embraces Model-Driven Architecture (MDA) principles to facilitate and improve SOA development (Lopez-Sanz, Cuesta, & Marcos, 2008). Within MDA, models are used as core class elements during system design and implementation. MDA separates a system development process into three abstraction levels known as Computational Independent Model (CIM), Platform Independent Model (PIM), and Platform Specific Model (PSM) (OMG, 2003). Our contributions are twofold: business service description at a higher level of abstraction by using UML profiles so that concerns of high-quality and context-aware services are captured and then, tackled; and the CSMA method that eases SOA adoption in enterprises. The remainder of this paper is organized as follows. In Section 2, the Model Driven Architecture (MDA), the context and the service oriented architecture are outlined. Section 3 details some related work. The CSMA meta-model as well as our UML profiles defined to support the representation of adaptable business SOA concepts are presented in section 4. Section 5 details the CSMA key phases validated with the enterprise training solutions case study. Finally, a conclusion and possible further research is discussed.

BACKGROUND

Model Driven Architecture

According to the Object Management Group, MDA is *"a new way of writing specifications, based on a platform-independent model. A complete MDA specification consists of a definitive platform-independent base UML model, plus one or more platform-specific models and interface definition sets, each describing how the base model is implemented on a different middleware platform"* (OMG, 2003). MDA is basically a controlled process of a series of model transformation from one level to another. This process models business logic with PIMs that are afterwards transformed later into PSMs. This transformation complies with pre-defined guidelines. The main advantage of MDA is the ability to transform a PIM into several PSMs, one per type of platform or technology upon which the final system is expected to run. MDA can potentially reduce the life cycle of software development and promote system modules reuse (OMG, 2003); it is not necessary to redesign a new system with similar functions from scratch when a new implementation/technology becomes available.

Context

Context stems out of the American pragmatist philosopher Charles Sanders Peirce's observation that all human inquiries occur within contexts (Pavel & Alain, 2003). Context has been studied in various fields for quite a long time. Different definitions and uses of context are reported in the literature. In some disciplines, context is treated as "meta-information" that characterizes the situation of an entity, or as a construct that facilitates reasoning services (Benslimane et al., 2006). Schilit and Theimer associate context with location, identities of nearby people, objects, and changes in these objects (Schilit & Theimer, 1994). Dey et al. (2001) define context as "any

information that can be used to characterize the situation of an entity. An entity is a person, place or object that is considered relevant to the interaction between a user and an application, including the user and the application themselves" *(Dey, Abowd & Salber, 2001). Another definition by Coutaz et al. (2003) suggests that context "... is* not simply the state of a predefined environment with a fixed set of interaction resources. It is part of a process of interacting with an ever-changing environment composed of reconfigurable, migratory, and multi-scale resource"*(Coutaz, Crowley, Dobson & Garlan, 2003).*

Service-Oriented Architecture

Several definitions of SOA exist, which in fact does not help reach a consensus on what SOA should be or mean. However, the IT community agrees that SOA is not a product but rather a new way of thinking system architectures. Thomas Erl defines SOA as *"an open, agile extensible, federated, composable architecture comprised of autonomous, capable, vendor diverse, interoperable, discoverable and potentially reusable services. SOA can establish an abstraction of business logic and technology, resulting in a loose coupling between domains"* (Erl, 2005). Another definition with a business flavor is given in (Marks & Bell, 2006) where SOA *"... is a conceptual business architecture where business functionality, or application logic, is made available to SOA users as shared, reusable services on an IT network. Services in an SOA are modules of business or application functionality with exposed interfaces, and are invoked by messages"*. The W3C defines SOA as *"a set of components which can be invoked, and whose interface descriptions can be published and discovered "* (W3C, 2004).

The aforementioned definitions permit to look at SOA from different perspectives. The definitions in (Erl, 2005) and (Marks & Bell, 2006) offer a wider perspective of SOA than (W3C, 2004) by focusing on architectural features that could maximize service compliance. The definition in (Marks & Bell, 2006) has a very strong business focus. Finally, the W3C provides a very technical definition of what can be done with a service, but neither refers to the architecture nor gives information on how a service should be designed or configured.

RELATED WORK

Several methods for the design and development of SOA-based enterprise applications are reported in the literature (Erl, 2005), (W3C, 2004), (Erradi, An & Kulkarni, 2006b), (OASIS, 2006),(M. P. Papazoglou & W.-J. Heuvel, 2006). Our literature review exercise studied some methods, benchmarked them according to a set of existing criteria (Arsanjani, 2004), (Ramollari, Dranidis & Simons, 2007), and finally suggested some features that a method for the design and development of SOA-based enterprise applications should have.

IBM modeling method known as Service-Oriented Modeling and Architecture (SOMA) consists of three phases (Arsanjani, 2004): service identification, specification, and realization. The service identification phase includes three steps: (i) top-down application domain decomposition, (ii) bottom-up analysis of existing (sometimes legacy) systems, and (iii) middle-out service modeling according to the goal of the future SOA-based enterprise application. The specification phase presents the different services that result out of the first phase. Finally, the realization phase guides the development of the identified services using the Web service technology. Despite the impressive number of steps that SOMA includes, its details are not available to the public making its analysis difficult.

Thomas Erl suggests a service-oriented analysis and design method that comprises twelve steps to describe a service analysis and design process (Erl, 2005). In this method, the analysis phase is a top-down business-centric view that decomposes

business process logic into a series of granular steps that represent candidate service operations. Afterwards these operations are grouped into logical contexts that represent services. These services serve as input for the service design phase, where they are specified in detail and later realized according to a specific implementation technology such as Web services.

OASIS proposes a method for a systematic Web services development (OASIS, 2006). This method consists of six phases ranging from analysis to deployment of Web services. Each phase involves activities and the corresponding roles (i.e. business analyst, software engineers, etc.) and produced artifacts (i.e. document, model, etc.). OASIS method supports the development of Web services only, while the management of business processes and integration of legacy systems into Web services are completely neglected. In addition the method is biased towards Web services, which reduces its applicability in other exercises of analyzing and designing SAO-based enterprise applications.

Papazoglou et al. present a SOA modeling method for the development of enterprise services (Papazoglou & Heuvel, 2006) that is based on the Rational Unified Process (RUP), the Component-Oriented Development (COD), and the Business Process Modeling (BPM). This method applies an iterative and incremental process that comprises one preparatory and eight distinct main phases. These phases propose activities revolving around service provisioning, deployment, execution and monitoring. Nevertheless, Papazoglou et al.'s work is based on the Web services principles. Besides, the authors consider that the success of SOA development is based on the modeling and the development of meaningful Web services.

Erradi et al. propose a Service-Oriented Architecture Framework (SOAF) consisting of five main phases (Erradi, et al., 2006b): information elicitation, service identification, service definition, service realization, and roadmap and planning. The SOAF adopts a top-down approach to describe the required business processes, and a bottom-up approach to describe current business processes as they are implemented by the existing applications.

Our literature review exercise continued by comparing and evaluating the aforementioned methods using criteria established in the SOA field (Arsanjani, 2004), (Ramollari, et al., 2007).

- **Development approach:** three approaches support the development of SOA-based enterprise applications depending on the front-end analysis of the business domain and the handling of existing legacy systems. First, the top-down approach decomposes the business logic of existing processes into services. Second, the bottom-up approach analyses legacy systems in order to identify the different services of the existing IT system. Finally the meet-in-the-middle approach incorporates a parallel top-down and a bottom-up approach.

- **Degree of clarity and description:** As usually known a method is a set of guidelines that transform an initial state in a field to a target state. These guidelines can be structured hierarchically in phases, activities, tasks, or steps. For each activity, executing roles should be specified. Activities produce results, but may also use existing results as inputs. This criterion measures

the quality of a method in terms of clarity and description. The clarity of a method depends heavily on the detailed description of its activities, corresponding roles, and produced results.

- **Process flexibility:** a number of methods consider flexibility as an important element in the design and development of services so that changes in business processes are taken into account. Yet, other methods do not address the issue of flexibility at all. A quantitative scale (1-5) is used to measure the flexibility of the process (i.e. 1 means that the proposed method is not flexible).

- **Used techniques and notations:** a large number of existing methods for service oriented development adopt technologies that are approved in the world of software development such as Object Oriented Application Development (OOAD), Component Based Development (CBD), and Business Process Modeling (BPM). However some others are closely allied to the Web service technology and thus do not propose a generic SOA.

Table 1 is a summary of the different SOA-based methods along the criteria of development strategy, degree of clarity and description, process flexibility, and used techniques and notations.

Table 1. Comparison of SOA methods

Criterion	Method				
	SOMA	Service oriented analysis and design method	OASIS method	Papazoglou et al. method	SOAF
Development approach	Meet-in the Middle	Top-Down	Top-Down	Meet-in the Middle	Meet-in the Middle
The degree of clarity and description	Lack of detailed description	Detailed description	Detailed description	Detailed description	Lack of detailed description
Process flexibility	1	1	2	3	3
Used techniques and notations	Not mentioned	BPM	Web service technology	BPM, CBD, Web service technology	BPM, Web service technology

Despite the research efforts presented in these SOA methods, some methods are closely related to Web services. Hence, the scope in which SOA can be used is constrained since it cannot be generalized to other execution platforms apart from the ones that follow the Web service technology. Describing SOA-based enterprise applications at a high level of abstraction and without any biases towards a certain implementation technology such as Web services are still missing. Furthermore, some methods' details are not available to the public, which makes difficult their analysis. In addition, flexibility issues of these enterprise applications are not properly handled in detail in these methods, and thus left to random decisions. Flexibility is an important concern when an enterprise decides to embrace SOA. A flexible method should take into account, the context-related information when identifying and modeling enterprise services. Context-related information deals with changes in the enterprise environment, such as availability of business partners or unexpected changes in business goals. This information must be managed effectively and promptly to address challenges and opportunities, and to maximize profits of an enterprise. However, most of the previous methods so far focus on defining processes for developing business process and services without considering contextual information in details.

In conclusion of our literature review exercise, we outline that a detailed SOA adoption roadmap should help derive suitable business services for enterprises based on high-level business requirements and business process models. These services should (1) support the required business functionalities and business processes, (2) align the IT implementation with first, the business processes and later, the business functionalities, and (3) adhere to architectural goals such as performance, scalability, and security.

Within SOA, services should be the blueprint for an enterprise architecture's future state by supporting current business goals and providing

capabilities for future growth (Zimmermann, Krogdahl & Gee, 2004). This blueprint should provide "traceability" between IT and business functionalities/capabilities of the enterprise. Consequently, the key questions that raise when embracing SOA concern service definition with respect to enterprise architectural goals as well as enterprise business drivers (e.g., emerging business opportunities). These questions are part of the service-oriented analysis and design exercise (Erl, 2005), (Zimmermann et al., 2004) that should take into account the following considerations:

1. Serving as enterprise foundations, services must be aligned with the enterprise current and future functionality, performance, scalability, and security.
2. Making an enterprise respond to context changes, services must be more than functions to trigger from the Web but should have the capacity to accommodate the requirements and needs of the current situation.
3. Creating loosely-coupled, cross-enterprise business applications, services should be composable.

THE CONTEXT-AWARE, SERVICE-ORIENTED MODELING AND ANALYSIS METHOD

This section consists of two parts. The first part introduces the meta-model upon which CSMA is built, and the second part illustrates how CSMA complies with MDA principles through the definition of UML profiles. These profiles introduce new concepts that permit to represent adaptable business SOA.

CSMA Meta-Model

Section 3 has shown the lack of methods to model and analyze SOA-based enterprise applications. For this purpose, we came up with the CSMA

Figure 1. Meta-model of CSMA method

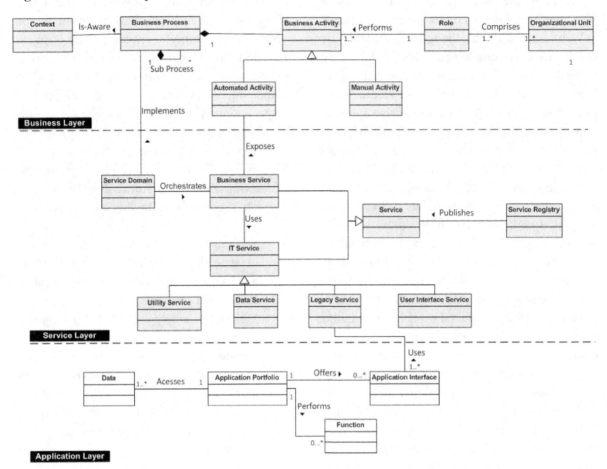

method. It is vendor-independent, explicitly states business architecture goals, and provides a systematic approach to guide the design and development of SOA-based enterprise applications. Figure 1 depicts a meta-model for CSMA, which is the result of applying two kinds of SOA practices (Arsanjani, 2004) (Nuffel, 2007): IT SOA and Adaptable Business SOA. On the one hand, IT SOA promotes the use of traditional methods like SAP NetWeaver and IBM WebSphere to identify IT services. On the other hand, adaptable business SOA offers user-friendly and high quality business services that help achieve an enterprise's mission. This mission is identified from the enterprise's business processes. Our meta-model consists of business, service, and application layers and identifies several services that

correspond to enterprise business processes such as delivery process, customer order management process, etc. Each layer has specific architectural characteristics and addresses particular concerns.

• **The business layer** describes the business logic that underpins an enterprise's business models and business processes. A business process is a set of activities that are initiated by an event, transform data, and produce outputs. In a previous work (Boukadi, Chaabane, & Vincent, 2009), we enhanced each business process model with situational circumstances that may impact the design and execution of this process. We refer to these circumstances as business process *context*. Each set of activities in a process is the responsibility of a business role that belongs to an enterprise organizational unit. These activities could be automated using services.

- **The service layer** contains services of two types: business and IT. On the one hand, business services express the business logics that are related to end-users' functionalities. Usually business services can be discovered from business models and possibly choreographed into intra or inter-business processes. On the other hand, IT services provide reusable functions that are related to processing data within legacy applications. IT services can fall into different categories such as utility service, application service, data service, etc.
- **The application layer** describes the existing applications that implement the functionalities of an enterprise. These applications could be legacy systems and can potentially be used in automated business activities such as computing order cost, checking customer credit-rate, etc. Each application has a structure, databases, accesses system resources, etc.

MDA and CSMA

The compliance of CSMA with MDA principles is essential. In the following, we show how we map the CSMA layers onto the MDA three models.

- The CIM in CSMA describes the business logic that is associated with an enterprise's business models and business processes. These models and processes are extremely important for business services identification and modeling. Examples of models that belong to the CIM level include business motivation models, business process models, and enterprise architecture.

- The PIM in CSMA describes business service models in a way that is technology independent and includes hence, a PIM for Adaptable Business SOA. These models are created by refining the business models identified at the CIM level. Each model defines new modeling elements in terms of UML profiles that permit to extend the UML meta-model (OMG, 2004)[1]. The business services models are completed by designing and analyzing service *variability* with respect to different service clients and contexts. The aim of looking into service variability is to design business services that are more than a simple functionality to provide through the Web. Business services should adapt in response to changes in the environment and customize its basic functions according to customer's context or preferences. The use of Aspect-Oriented Programming (AOP) provides abstraction and encapsulation mechanisms that guarantees separation of concerns (AOP, 2007). This separation is applied to the service modeling process proposed in the CSMA method. In the PIM for Adaptable Business SOA, aspects help identify and model crosscutting concerns like security and separate them from service functions during the service modeling process. In the rest of this paper, we refer to these aspects as "Conceptual Aspects" because of the conceptual level of PIM.

- The PSM in CSMA includes models related to a certain implementation technology for instance Web services. Business services models identified at the PIM level should be implemented using a technology. Example of these models in the PSM could be BPEL, Jboss aspect models, and Web service model. Note: the PSM in CSMA is beyond the scope of this paper.

UML Profiles for Adaptable Business SOA

To comply with MDA principles, we propose a set of UML profiles to use in the definition of the adaptable business SOA at the PIM level. An UML profile extends (or specializes) the standard UML elements (e.g., class and association) in order to describe specific domain or application concepts (OMG, 2004). We describe hereafter the proposed UML profiles in the PIM for Adaptable Business SOA, the concepts used in the business service profile, and the concepts used in the Conceptual Aspect profile. Our Adaptable Business SOA UML profiles consist of:

- *Business Service profile* that describes how to model a service including its description and interactions.
- *Conceptual Aspect profile* that extends the business service profile and describes how to model context-aware business services.

Concepts Involved in the Business Service Profile

When dealing with a business SOA, four concepts are associated with a service: business service, service description, interactions, and adaptability. Figure 2 presents an UML-based business SOA meta-model.

- **Business Service:** is treated as a core class modeling entity in our business SOA meta-model. Business services in CSMA method play different roles. They can be classified according to their atomicity and scope. Business services can be either atomic called functional or composite called service domains. Functional services are fine grained, expose a set of business activities, and are identified when analyzing enterprise business processes. Business activities within a process can be identified as

belonging to the logic that a functional service should encapsulate. Examples of functional services can be *price computing* or *merchandise delivery*. A service domain logically defines a combination of related functional services as a single service. A service domain is published as a composite service in order to reduce the complexity of publishing, selecting, and combining fine grained functional services. This composite structure is used as a major building block when implementing on-demand enterprise collaboration.

- **Service Description:** business services have a set of operations (serviceOperations) that fulfill goals (Goal). A goal is an "optative" statement (Rolland, Prakash & Benjamen, 1999), in fact an intention that expresses what is wanted. A goal can be expressed at different levels of abstraction in terms of strategy, tactic, and operation. Functional services relate to operational goals, i.e., goals that are achieved with a service tasks. Service domains correspond to high level goals (tactical) that need to be decomposed into lower levels until operational goals are identified. For example, *take customer order* service domain fulfils an enterprise tactical goal which is "use the Web to expose enterprise products", whereas a computing delivery price, which is a functional service, achieves "manage customer invoice" goal. This is an operational goal, which can be fulfilled by service operations. Operations and goals constitute the service description at the PIM level.

- **Interactions:** business services interact with each other through contracts. Within SOA, a contract establishes engagement terms among the different architecture components. Different contracts can be established between services depending on the entities taking part in a communication

Figure 2. Adaptable business SOA meta-model

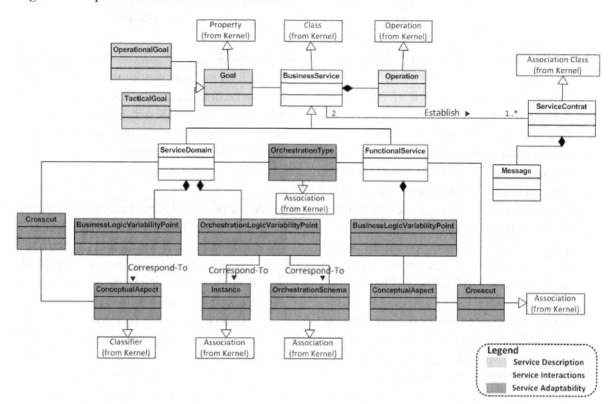

session for example customer and service. In this paper, we explore service-to-service contracts only and refer to them as service contracts. Interactions include service contract and message flow between services.

∘ **Service Contracts:** are established between services and must identify the participant services in the contract, the roles played, and other properties such as purpose, constraints, or expiration time. Some authors like (Krafzig, Banke & Slama, 2004) treat service contract as part of the service description itself. Even though the way to interact with a service depends generally on the operations reported in this service interface, we propose to make a service contract independent so that the characteristics of each contract are maintained separately.

For example, a delivery service can establish diverse contracts with different merchandise verification services belonging to independent enterprises. Each contract includes specific obligations and restrictions.

∘ **Messages:** messages in SOA represent the communication exchanged between services. Each message is related to a service contract and has meaning to both the service and consumer. Some authors in the literature consider that message at the PIM level should include references to the ontology model or semantic constraints (Lopez-Sanza, Acuna, Cuesta & Marcos, 2008). Others suggest that the message format and its addresses such as HTTP or SMTP should be included in the model (Amir & Zeid,

2004). We agree that the format of a message is an implementation concern and thus, should be addressed in the corresponding PSM-level models.

- **Adaptability:** to ensure that an enterprise can easily adapt to context changes, business services must alter their behavior to accommodate these changes. To meet this objective, service engineers should model services with "points" that mark where a service can be customized depending on the context. We call these, variability points, similar to those variability used in the software product line engineering (Mietzner, 2008). Depending on the business service itself (service domain or functional service), we identify two types of variability points. A functional service has a set of variability points, which concern essentially its business logic, whereas a service domain has variability points concerning its business logic as well as its orchestration logic. At the design phase, variability points that concern the orchestration logic, deal with the creation of a set of orchestration schemas for a single service domain. When a service domain receives a request, it communicates with the orchestration registry in order to select a suitable schema and identify the best functional service instances to fulfill this request. The selection of the orchestration schema and functional service instances, takes into account the context of the request. The variability of orchestration logic was the object of our research project in (Boukadi, Ghedira, & Vincent, 2008), so further details are provided there. In our current work, the variability points concerning the business logic, which are handled through Conceptual Aspects, are examined. They are explained in the next section.

Concepts Involved in the Conceptual Aspect Profile

We define Conceptual Aspect as a domain-specific concern for a business service which groups non functional requirements or designates a business rule or addresses an adaptability action in response to context changes. We distinguish three types of Conceptual Aspects: non-functional, business rule and context enabler aspects.

- *Non-Functional Aspect* classifies the quality attributes of a service such as security, performance, and availability. It provides a behavioral guideline for a service or its element, as well as means to control one or several services. For example, a non-functional aspect for security enforces the access control to services.
- *Business Rule Aspect* defines or constrains some concerns of the business. It is intended to control the behavior of the business. As its name suggests, this aspect encapsulates a rule that can be: constraint, action enabler, computation, or inference. These rules are written in natural language and are not executable. For example a business rule could define the list of preferred suppliers and supply schedules.
- *Context Enabler Aspect* personalizes the basic functions of services according to customer's context or preference. The primary goal of Context Enabler aspect is to satisfy customer preferences and improve convenience by altering the messages or operations in a service.

Conceptual aspects need to be explicitly and coherently modeled. In addition their design should not be scattered throughout the business service model. To this end, we use AOP along with its notions of *join points*, *pointcuts* and *advice* (AOP, 2007). These notions have to be explicitly distinguished from basic business services. Figure

Figure 3. Conceptual Aspect meta-model

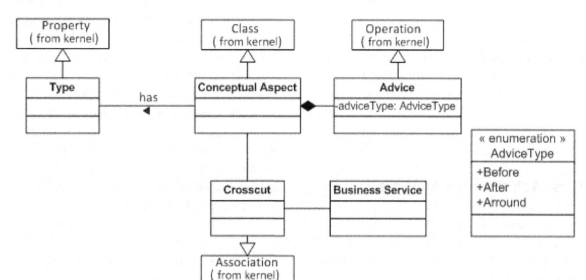

3 presents the meta-model of a Conceptual Aspect, which extends the one presented in Figure 2. The advice is represented by the advice stereotype that can be applied to operation. Advice is linked to a business service by the <<crosscut>> association. Each sort of advice has a type which specifies that the advised action will be executed before, after or around the intercepted operation of a given business service.

Scenario of the Case Study

Enterprise Training Solutions (ETS) is a company that offers training courses to different bodies such as public and private organizations. ETS is well-known for its reliable session planning and project execution as well as for the quality of resources it deploys to cater for large scale training sessions' needs. ETS hires highly qualified staff with different backgrounds like IT, knowledge management, etc. ETS has rapidly grown during the last years in terms of number of employees and training volume. However, most of the business is still handled via phone calls and excel sheets. As a result, ETS has more and more problems keeping track of all its commitments, which will

over time worsen and then, impact its image and credibility. The ETS Information System Management Group (ISMG) argues that improving ETS information system would help address the current problems. ISMG considers that the enterprise processes should be more flexible so that on-demand or last-minute training requests are handled. Although ETS has to react promptly and efficiently, it wants to adopt a well defined approach to assure that future applications will support the improved business processes. In the rest of this paper we present the key phases of CSMA with some illustrative examples taken from the ETS case study.

CSMA KEY PHASES

According to the SOA delivery life cycle (Papazoglou & Georgakopoulos, 2003), CSMA targets modeling and analyzing services. CSMA combines business and IT concerns to provide a coherent roadmap for the development of enterprise applications. In addition, CSMA is deployed in a step-by-step way by combining top-down (Adaptable Business SOA) and bottom-up (IT

SOA) approaches for domain decomposition and application portfolio analysis, respectively. In this paper, we focus on adaptable business SOA building, only. IT concerns are addressed in our previous work (Boukadi, Vincent, & Burlat, 2009). CSMA includes a set of phases, each containing several steps. A step is specified in terms of executing roles, input and output artifacts, and supporting tools and notation.

Phase 1: Enterprise Analysis

The outcome of this phase is to study the feasibility of adopting service solutions in the context of an enterprise and restricting the scope of these solutions. A crucial task for any enterprise is to identify the constraints and business drivers that motivate the migration towards SOA. The steps in the enterprise analysis phase comprise: building business motivations models, and conceptualizing the As-is and To-be Business Process Model. All these steps are performed by a business analyst.

Step 1: Building Business Motivation Models

A Business Motivation Model (BMM) is created according to the OMG specification (OMG, 2006a). It provides a structure to develop, communicate, and manage business plan in an organized manner. The idea is to develop a business model that outlines the business plans towards adopting SOA before launching any detailed business modeling. Hence, the business plans become the foundation for connecting system solutions firmly to their business intent. Specifically, a BMM identifies factors that motivate the establishing of business plan and indicates how all these factors inter-relate. BMM basic concepts are ends and means. The first encompass the vision, goals, and objectives, while the latter suggest the mission, strategies, and tactics. The *vision* is an overall image of what the organization wants to be or become, regardless of how it will be achieved. A

Goal is a state or condition of the enterprise to be brought to or sustained through appropriate *Means*. A *Goal* tends to be longer term, qualitative, general, and ongoing, whereas an objective is attainable, time-targeted, and measurable that the enterprise seeks to meet in order to achieve its Goals. Concerning the mission, it describes the ongoing operational activities of the company. This makes the vision a reality. The mission is projected through strategies that represent the actions needed to achieve the goals. Strategies are implemented through tactics.

The BMMs are basically considered as the master plan for the CSMA method; a comprehensive view of how to build, use, and evolve all business services. When considering the business requirements and interviewing ETS managers, a BMM can be built. Figure 4 depicts the ETS's BMM, which shows the factors that motivate service-oriented system development.

Step 2: Conceptualizing the As-Is and To-Be Business Process Model

Industrial experience has demonstrated that strategic transformation of an enterprise system is more effective and efficient if it is based on an agreed "enterprise-wide architecture". An architecture is defined as a coherent whole of principles, methods, and models that are used in the design and development of an enterprise's organizational structure, business processes, information systems, and infrastructure. Enterprise architecture captures the essentials of the business, IT, and its evolution.

The most important characteristic in an enterprise architecture is to provide a holistic view of the enterprise. It is an indispensable instrument to control the complexity of an enterprise systems and processes. A well-defined architecture is an important asset in positioning the service-oriented solution within the context of existing processes, IT systems, and other assets of an organization. Thus, good architectural practices help a company innovate and change

Figure 4. The business motivation model for the ETS

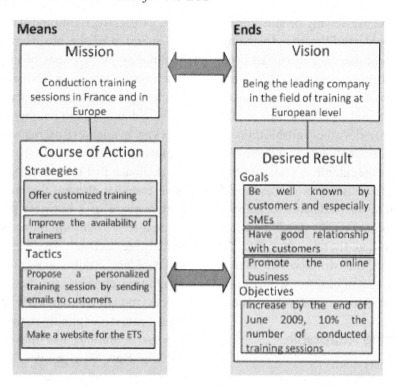

by providing both stability and flexibility. The insights provided by an enterprise architecture are needed on the one hand to determine the needs and priorities for change, when migrating to a service solution, and on the other hand to assess how a company may benefit from a service-oriented solution. Within an enterprise architecture, business analysts should define an "as-is" process model to let the stakeholders be aware of the available business processes. The process model should list and categorize the available business processes into 4 categories:

- Operational processes: directly bound to the realization of a product or service;
- Management processes: guide the company towards the given objectives and control that the decisions made are in line with these objectives;
- Measurement processes: assess results to identify the corrective actions;

- And, support processes: contribute to the good functioning of other processes.

Then, the flows between these types of processes are listed. This leads to process cartography that provides a general view and synthetic scheme of the enterprise's processes and interactions between them. Based on this cartography, business analysts can simulate and analyze potential changes to the current application portfolio before they commit to any changes to business processes. This analysis concludes to the development of the "to-be" process model that an SOA solution is expected to implement.

When dealing with ETS business process models, we recognize that the enterprise has not a process management culture. Besides, little efforts have been put into formalizing or designing the proposed functionalities. Hence, conducting interviews should result in identifying business process cartography. Some processes are extracted from applications already working; others are taken directly when interviewing people. For illustration purposes, order fulfillment and planning training sessions processes are discussed. The former is a manual process performed through phone calls between the customer management service and the customer. The latter uses an old software planning to retrieve the available trainers and access to their information from a database.

To better support the enterprise's mission and goals, the two identified business processes should be analyzed and improved. The analysis concludes that the customer order process should be automated and the order should be taken from the ETS Web site. In addition, the two processes should be implemented by a set of business services that facilitate the on-demand enterprise collaboration.

Phase 2: Building Adaptable Business SOA

The key outcome of this phase is to define the context-aware business process models so that adaptable business services are identified and modeled. The building adaptable business SOA phase consists of five steps: context-aware business process modeling, business service identification, business service modeling, Conceptual Aspects identification, and Conceptual Aspects modeling and orchestration model creation.

Step 1: Context-Aware Business Process Modeling

Based on the business motivation models, business processes required to support an enterprise's strategies can be identified. The context-aware business process modeling step includes reviewing the business processes that are already in place and the new processes that will be introduced and implemented according to the new business goals and objectives.

Business process modeling is to capture processes and highlight significant organizational

and operational aspects of the business (BPMI, 2002). Recently, a new field of research has drawn the attention of the business process research community that consists of integrating contextual information into a business process model. Context-aware business process modeling is a new field and a small number of research references are available (Rosemann & Recker, 2006), (Saidani & Nurcan, 2007). In our previous work, we demonstrated that "contextual information" is an essential element that must be part of the design phase of a business process. By using context-related information, business process models are "active", flexible, and aligned with stakeholders' requirements. The importance of integrating context into the field of business process modeling is backed with two arguments. First, context is explicitly stated in some business process definitions like the one suggested by the Workflow Management Coalition that says: "Business process is a set of one or more linked procedures or activities which collectively realize a business objective or policy goal, within the context of an organizational structure defining functional roles and relationships". Second, when a service-oriented solution is adopted, identifying contextual information that affect a business process leads to more flexible business service solutions. We propose to categorize context into *functional, non-functional,* and *environmental. Functional context* includes information that is directly connected to a business process in terms of *role-based*, *business rules*, and *business goals (strategic goal). Non-functional context* captures elements that are not directly related to a process and most of the time beyond the control of the process itself. *Environmental context* specifies the environment in which a business process is expected to run. Further details on this specific context are given in Boukadi, Chaabane, et al. (2009). The modeling notation supported by CSMA is the Business Process Modeling Notation (BPMN) (OMG, 2006b), which we enhance with contextual information.

To better illustrate the context-aware business process modeling, we give a brief overview of ETS order fulfillment process. Then, we identify the contextual information related to this process before we proceed to its modeling. The order fulfillment process is triggered upon receipt of an online customer order. This order includes details like customer's identity, location, training dates, number of trainees, etc. First, the order information is verified and then, submitted to the financial department to control the customer's payment history. The personal management department retrieves the list of available trainers who could run the requested training. If the availability hours of trainers are greater than or equal to the number of training hours requested by the customer, the order is accepted. Otherwise, a message is sent to both customer and training manager to inform them about the rejection decision owing trainer unavailability. In case of positive response, the finance department calculates the total cost of training, which depends on the training topic and trainers' daily expenses. If the customer is abroad, travel expenses are also anticipated.

The order fulfillment process runs smoothly in regular business circumstances. However, some parts of the process are subject to changes in response to different cases. Hence, contextual information that may affect this process should be defined.

- *Environmental-related context* depicts that a process is triggered upon customer order receipt during ETS working hours. Outside these hours, the process should not be activated.
- *Functional-related context* includes business rules, which are context-dependant, role-based context, and strategic goals. ETS business analysts introduce a role-based context, which states that only the financial analyst can check the customer's payment history and decide whether orders should be accepted or not. Besides, the process

can have a business rule, which defines that a customer order with training hours that exceed 100 hours can be accepted even if the customer has some financial problems. Concerning the third sub-category of functional context, namely strategic goals, they are discovered from the business motivation model. We recall that each business process must support at least one strategic goal. According to its nature and purpose, the process of taking customer order aims to achieve the strategic goal SG_1, which is "achieve on-demand training session".

- *Non-functional related context* includes quality and security that may influence the behavior of a process. Business stakeholders of the ETS express security constraints that concern some business activities. These constraints require a mechanism to secure access to data such as customer data, or data related to trainers (only authorized users can access to these information).

Figure 5 depicts the customer orders process modeled using BPMN formalism enhanced with a set of contextual annotations.

Step 2: Business Service Identification

Once an enterprise business processes (current and target) are modeled and analyzed, services that support these processes can be discovered. The activities in this step are performed jointly by a business analyst and a software architect. In CSMA method, business service identification is critical. Identifying appropriate services with the right level of granularity can have a major influence on the whole system. We agree that all business services should be identified to meet an enterprise business goal. Goals can be formulated at different levels of abstraction, ranging from high-level and strategic to low-level and operational. Analyzing enterprise goals can be a baseline to find proper business services. This

Figure 5. Order fulfillment process

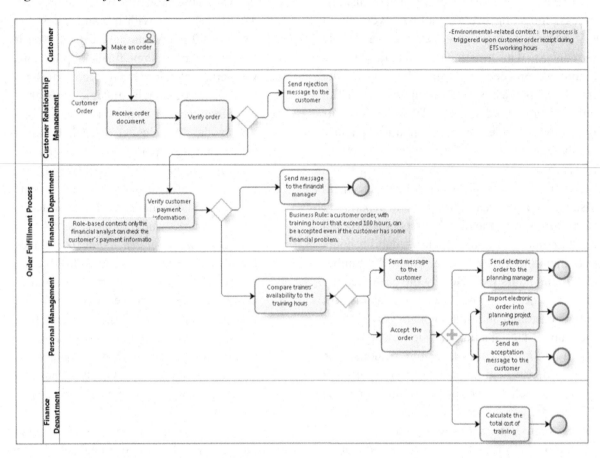

is based on two arguments. The first is that the notion of goal explicitly appears in the definition of business service, which is "a functional unit to achieve business goals". Second, we comply with the Sawyer's vision that the elicitation of the necessary services cannot be disconnected from their goal and usage, i.e., the business process they serve (Sawyer, Hutchison, Walkerdine & Sommerville, 2005). The core idea in a business service identification is that business goals can be good candidates for identifying business services. We recall that functional services relate to operational goals (i.e., goals that are fulfilled by functionalities provided by the service). Service domains correspond to high-level goals (tactical goals) that need to be decomposed into lower level goals till operational goals are found.

To identify business services from business goals, we suggest the following guidelines.

- **Guideline 1 - decompose business goals:** for each business process, a strategic goal is identified and analyzed. This strategic goal must be decomposed into tactical goals. To do so, we adopt graph decomposition of goals reported in the AI field. The satisfaction of a strategic goal requires the fulfillment of one or more tactical goals, which themselves are decomposed into operational goals.

For example, order fulfillment process aims to accomplish "achieve on-demand training session" strategic goal. Taking customer orders from

Figure 6. The goal decomposition tree of the order fulfillment process

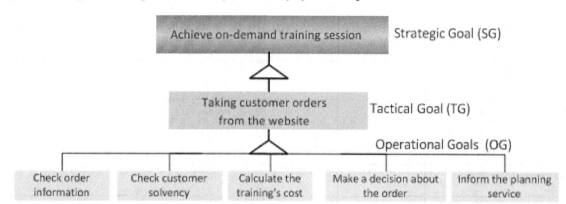

a Web site reveals a company's mission, which is to make easier for customers to do business with ETS. Thus, ETS stakeholders intend to provide a trusted and valued service to the clients they serve thanks to their Web site. The decomposition of the strategic goal is depicted in Figure 6.

- **Guideline 2 - identify service domains:** service domains are identified by analyzing the tactical goals that a business process is expected to achieve. Service domains implement business processes and are used as major building block for implementing on-demand enterprise collaboration. This justifies their identification based on tactical goals. Thus, we propose that each tactical goal defined in the goal tree of a business process is fulfilled by one and only one service domain.

For example, "achieve on-demand training session" strategic goal needs to be accomplished by the order fulfillment process (Figure 6). This goal is decomposed into "take customers orders from the website" TG_1. Thus, the service domain that will implement this process should meet TG_1. This service is called "Order Fulfillment Service".

- **Guideline 3 - Identify functional services:** functional services encapsulate busi-

ness activities. Hence, we propose to group highly-coupled business activities within the same functional service. The purpose is to examine the operational goal that each activity has to achieve. Business activities fulfilling the same operational goal should belong to the same functional service. It is important to notice that the number of business activities that belong to a service candidate is not important in the business service identification step as the primary purpose here is to establish the required set of service candidates. The mapping between Business Activities (BA) and Operational Goals (OG) of the order fulfillment process is illustrated in Table 2.

Some business activities meet the same operational goals. Thus, they are candidates that could be grouped into the same functional service. Hence, 5 services could be identified: The Checking Order Service, Managing Trainers Service, Verification of Customer Information Service, Import Electronic Order Service, Compute Training Price Service and Managing Order Service.

Step 3: Business Service Modeling

In CSMA method, business services modeling complies with the MDA principles. Figure2

Table 2. Mapping between the business activities and operational goals of the order fulfillment process

OG \ BA	Check order information	Check customer solvency	Make a decision about the order	Calculate the training's cost	Inform the planning service
Receive order document	×				
Verify order	×				
Send rejection message to the customer	×				
Verify customer payment information		×			
Send message to the financial manager		×			
Compare trainers' availability with the training hours			×		
Send an acceptation message to the customer			×		
Accept the order			×		
Compute travel expenses				×	
Compute the training cost				×	
Import electronic order into planning project system					×
Send electronic order to the planning manager					×

shows the models that we suggest to carry out this modeling. Basically these models illustrate the behavioral aspect of business services using UML 2.0 behavior diagram. Each model defines new elements that extend the UML meta-model.

- **The Business Activity Model** provides a microscopic view of the business activities that a functional service encapsulates. This model extends UML use-cases. Each business activity can be decomposed into one or several tasks based on the description of business processes and the operational goal that needs to be reached. Some business activities are fine grained and thus, cannot be decomposed into tasks. A business activity is represented by a use case named *BusinessActivity*, and a task is represented by a use case called *Task*. In comparison to UML use cases, a business activity model contains *include* and *extends* relationships, only. Table 3 depicts the stereotypes introduced in a business activity model.

For illustration purposes, *Verification of Customer Information* service is considered. It consists of two basic activities that will be modeled as two use-cases stereotyped with *<<BusiAct>>*. We decompose "verify customer payment information" activity into "get customer information" task. The purpose of this task is to verify payment information based on customer information that is collected from the ETS database. Finally, we identify *include* and *extend* relationships between business activities and tasks. In this example, verify customer payment information includes get customer information task and at the same time is extended by send message to the financial manager. Figure 7 shows the business activity model for Checking Customer Information Service.

Table 3. Stereotypes of business activity model

BusinessActivity	
UML meta-class	Extend the UML meta-class 'use case'
Meaning	Denote a business activity encapsulated by a functional service.
Notation	<< BusiAct >>
Task	
UML meta-class	Extend the UML meta-class 'use case'
Meaning	Describe in detail the functions supported by a business activity
Notation	<< Task>>

- **The Functional Service Model** focuses on the description of a functional service in terms of operations to implement. This model, also, extends UML use-cases. Each task reported in a business activity model is transformed into a service operation. In a functional service model, we identify two types of service operation: *BasicOperation (BO)* and *DataOperation (DO)*. BOs achieve a service business logic and DOs allow accessing data repositories. Table 4 depicts the stereotypes introduced in a functional service model.

To develop a functional service model for *Verification of Customer Information* service, we start by mapping each <<*BusiAct*>> or <<*Task*>> identified into a business activity model onto <<*BO*>> or <<*DO*>>. This mapping is a semi-automatic that requires analyzing service operations so that, data and basic operations are distin-

guished. *Get customer information* is an operation that retrieves customer information from a customer database. Therefore, it will be stereotyped as <<DO>>. S*end message to the financial manager* is a basic operation that will be stereotyped as <<BO>>. Figure 8 shows the functional service model for *Checking Customer Information Service*.

- **The Functional Service Specification Model** is represented with an UML activity diagram and represents the execution flow of the different service operations. This model introduces a new concept called *ServiceActivityOperation*. Each basic service operation is represented as a special kind of *ActivityNodes* called *ServiceActivityBasicOperation*. Similarly, each data service operation is represented as a special kind of ActivityNodes called *ServiceActivityDataOperation*. The new

Figure 7. The Business Activity Model for Checking Customer Information Service

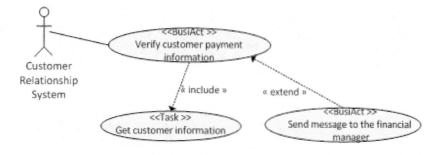

Table 4. Stereotypes of functional service model

BasicOperation	
UML meta-class	Extend the UML meta-class 'use case'
Meaning	Denote an operation responsible for achieving business logic of the functional service
Notation	<<BO>>
DataOperation	
UML meta-class	Extend the UML meta-class 'use case'
Meaning	Denote an operation responsible for accessing to data repositories to retrieve some necessary information
Notation	<<DO>>

elements of this model are described in Table 5. In comparison to UML activity model, a functional service specification model includes *ServiceActivityOperation, ActivityEdge* and *ControlNode* elements, only.

In CSMA method, modeling business services includes the development of the business activity, functional service, and functional service specification models. We support moving from one model to another through a set of mapping rules that offer a great compliance with MDA principles (Castro, Marcos, & Sanz, 2006; Miller & Mukerji, 2003). These rules are reported in Table 6 using structured English. Some rules can be fully automated (A) while others require modeler decisions (P).

For example, to develop the functional service specification model of Verification of Customer Information, we consider the elements identified

in the functional service model (Figure 8) and then apply the following mapping rules:

- R_2: to transform the two service operations into two activities,
- R_3: the "include" association between Verify customer payment information and Get customer information use cases in the Functional Service Model is transformed into two activities. The Activity corresponding to the source of the include association (Verify customer payment information) must be subsequent to the activity corresponding to the target of the include association (Get customer information).
- *R4:* the *ext*end association identified in the Functional Service Model between Verify customer payment information and Send message to the financial manager uses cases is represented by a flow of type "Fork". The activity that corresponds to the target

Figure 8. The Functional Service Model for Checking Customer Information Service

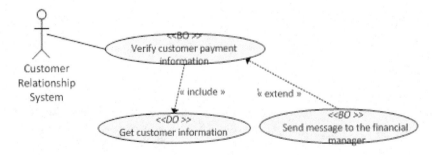

Table 5. Stereotypes of functional service specification model

ServiceActivityBasicOperation	
UML meta-class	Extend the UML meta-class 'Activity'
Meaning	Describe the behavior of an operation responsible for achieving business logic of the functional service
Notation	<<SABO>>
ServiceActivityDataOperation	
UML meta-class	Extend the UML meta-class 'Activity'
Meaning	Describe the behavior of an operation responsible for accessing to data repositories to retrieve some necessary information
Notation	<<SADO>>

use case (Verify customer payment information) is triggered before the activity that corresponds to the source use case (Send message to the financial manager). Thereafter, the "Fork" presents the activity (Send message to the financial manager) as an alternative to another flow with no activities. Later, both flows will meet thanks to a join flow.

Figure 9 depicts the Functional Service Specification Model of Checking Customer Information Service.

Step 4: Adding Conceptual Aspects

Business services should evolve according to the rapid changing e-service market trends and demands. Even a fully functional service has to

Table 6. Mapping rules between models of the Business service modeling

Source Model	Target Model	Mapping Rule	Automation Grade
Business Activity Model	Functional Service Model	R_1: for each << *BusiAct* >> or << *Task*>> found in the Business Activity Model, there will be a service operation in the Functional Service Model (<<*BO*>> or <<*DO*>>).	P
Functional Service Model	Functional Service Specification Model	R_2: for each <<*BO*>> or <<*DO*>>, there will be an activity in the Functional Service Specification Model	A
		R_3: the *include* association identified in the Conceptual Aspect Model and relating two uses cases (<<BO>> or <<OD>>)will be represented by two activities (<<SABO>> or <<SADO>>). The activity corresponding to the source use case of the include association must be subsequent to the activity corresponding to the target use case of the include association.	A
		$R_{3.1}$: if the *include* association has several targets use cases, the modeler must decide the right sequence for the different <<SABO>> or <<SADO>>.	P
		R_4: Each extend association identified in the Functional Service Model will be represented in the Functional Service Specification Model by a fork. The activity <<SABO>> or <<SADO>> corresponding to the source <<*BO*>> or <<*DO*>> of the extend association must be previous to the activity corresponding to the target <<*BO*>> or <<*DO*>> of the extend association. - If the extend association has only one source, the fork will present the <<SABO>> or <<SADO>> as an alternative to another flow with no activities. Later, a join can be used to meet these flows. - If the extend association has several sources, the fork will present the different <<SABO>> or <<SADO>> as alternatives to another flow with no activities. Later, a join can be used to meet these flows.	A

Figure 9. Functional Service Specification Model

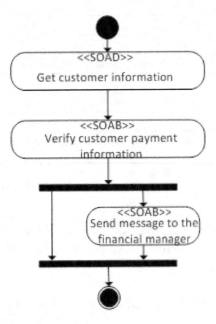

be adapted in order to support a wide spectrum of customers. This requires not only an agile development of services, but also supports different versions of a service for a service provider to satisfy various context and preferences of customers. We use AOP to define Conceptual Aspects. These aspects could be non-functional, business rules, and context enablers. Identifying conceptual aspects means seeking the assistance of business experts in order to analyze the contextual parameters of the business processes that are now associated with business services. Contextual annotations of a business process must be taken into account for adaptability requirements. For example, a Context Enabler Aspect (C_1) is assigned to Compute Training Price Service. This service is aware of runtime context changes that correspond to changes in the number of people who participate in training, once the project is planned. When there are changes, extra fees must be added to the total price.

Step 5: Conceptual Aspect Modeling

Similarly to business service modeling, Conceptual Aspect modeling belongs to the PIM level of the MDA and more exactly to PIM-2-PIM transformation. This modeling involves two new models that outline the behavioral facets responsible for delivery the following crosscutting concerns namely quality and context-aware services. These models extend the UML behavioral diagram, which are use case and activity diagrams, by adding new stereotypes. Each model has specific architectural characteristics and studies some particular concerns:

- **The Conceptual Aspect Model** describes the Conceptual Aspects using a use case diagram. In this model, the core concept is *AspectAdvice* which depicts a feature offered by an aspect. This concept is represented by a special kind of use case stereotyped with << *AspectAdv*>>. Each *AspectAdvice* can be decomposed into fine grained actions named *AdviceAction*. The different stereotypes listed are described in Table 7.

For example, the Conceptual Aspect Model for the Context Enabler Aspect (C_1) describes the Compute Training Price Service awareness to runtime context changes corresponding to changes in the number of people who participate in a training session. When there are changes, extra fees must be added to the total training price. Hence, the Conceptual Aspect proposes two actions called "Identify number of added person" and "Identify cost per person". These two actions constitute the baseline for calculating additional costs stereotyped with <<aspectAdv>> (see Figure 10).

- **The Conceptual Aspect Specification Model** completes the behavioral description of the Conceptual Aspect by adding the execution flow among the various ac-

Table 7. Stereotypes of conceptual aspect model

AspectAdvice	
UML meta-class	Extend the UML meta-class 'use case'
Meaning	Describe in detail a function supported by a Conceptual Aspect
Notation	<<AspectAdv>>
AdviceAction	
UML meta-class	Extend the UML meta-class 'use case'
Meaning	Denote an action proposed by an AspectAdvice
Notation	<<AdviceAct>>
Constraint	- the only actor in this model is the system

tions belonging to the aspect. It extends the UML activity diagram. Activity in the Conceptual Aspect Specification Model is represented as a special node called *AspectActivity*. This represents the *AdviceAction* already defined in the previous model. The Conceptual Aspect Specification Model can only contain *AspectActivity*, *ActivityEdge* and *ControlNode* elements.

The mapping rules between the two models are depicted in Table 9.

The process for the Conceptual Aspect modeling includes the two new models defined previously and takes as input the identified Conceptual Aspect from the step 3. The output of this process is the Conceptual Aspect Specification Model from that can be mapped to any aspect oriented programming languages or technology.

Step 6: Orchestration Model creation

The aim of this step is to identify the most common orchestration scenarios that can take place within the boundaries of the business process. This gives us a good idea as to how appropriate the grouping of the business activities is. Besides, it demonstrates the potential relationships between service domain and functional services.

After the services are defined, the processes have to be prepared by creating the orchestration model per service domain. As aforementioned, the service domain orchestrates a set of functional services. Thus, the orchestration model contains functional services as well as the execution flow between them. This model follows the meta-model proposed in section 4 (see Figure 2). Thus the purpose is to identify different patterns of the service domain responsible for implementing the business process. Besides, this model can be completed with all Conceptual Aspects relating to the business services.

Figure 10. The Conceptual Aspect Model for C₁

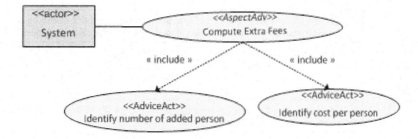

Table 8. Stereotype of conceptual aspect specification model

AspectActivity	
UML meta-class	Extend the UML meta-class 'Activity'
Meaning	Describe a behavior of an action proposed by an *AspectAdvice*
Notation	<<AspectActiv>>

For example, the resulting orchestration model responsible for implementing the order fulfillment process is depicted in Figure 11. This model contains the identified business services as well as the allocated Conceptual Aspects. As we can notice the *Order Fulfilment Service*, which is a service domain, does not contain any operation. This simply means that this service is dedicated to orchestrating a set of functional services.

CONCLUSION

The service oriented architecture presents a promising integration approach to deliver maximum reusability, agility and flexibility to change. However, its implementation in a real enterprise context is more challenging and requires a particular attention, a comprehensive guiding method and strong engineering principles. In this paper, we have proposed a Context-based, Service-oriented Modeling and Analysis (CSMA) method that guides service engineers in their choices of identifying, defining, and analyzing adaptable business services. In contrast to traditional SOA development methods, the CSMA introduced in this paper emphasizes activities revolving around identification, modeling and design of adaptable business services. We believe that integrating and modeling the service adaptability to context changes at the design phase is increasingly important in the world of business services as it contributes in the delivering of high-quality business services. These services can continually morph themselves to respond to environmental demands and changes.

To success in the service modeling and design exercise, our method highlights the importance of the application of the MDA principles to the service-oriented development process. Hence, UML profiles for the design of PIM-level adaptable business SOA as well as its corresponding meta-models are proposed. These profiles cover all concerns required for delivering high-quality and context-aware services. Based on the proposed meta-models and profiles, the CSMA key phases are described and tested in a realistic enterprise training solutions case study.

Table 9. Mapping rules between models of the conceptual aspect modeling

Source Model	Target Model	Mapping Rule	Automation Grade
Conceptual Aspect Model	Conceptual Aspect Specification Model	R_1: for every use case identified in the Conceptual Aspect Model (*AspectAdv* ou *AdviceAct*), will be generated an activity in the Conceptual Aspect Specification Model.	A
		R_2: the *include* association identified in the Conceptual Aspect Model and relating two uses cases, will be represented by two activities. The activity corresponding to the source use case (*AspectAdv*) of the include association must be subsequent to the activity corresponding to the target use case of the include association (*AdviceAct*).	A
		R_{21}: if the *include* association has several targets use cases, the modeler must decide the right sequence for the different *AdviceAct*.	P

Figure 11. The Orchestration Model for the Order Fulfillment Service Domain

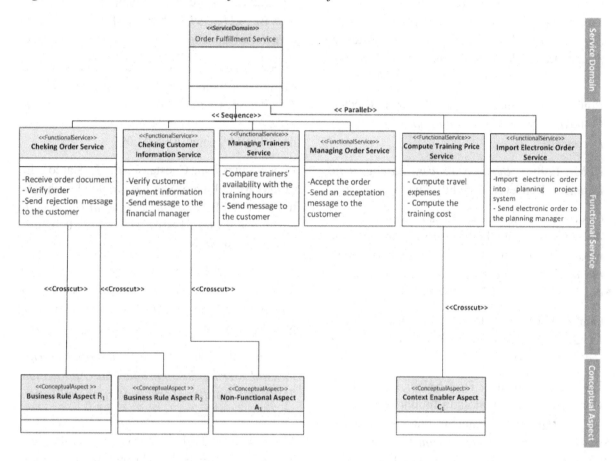

For future endeavor, we intend to further strengthen and refine the approach by conducting several real-life case studies in different domains, from which experience will be gained and more design concerns may be derived. Furthermore, we plan to develop an integrated tool support for CSMA.

REFERENCES

W3C. (2004). Web Services Glossary: Retrieved from http://www.w3.org/TR/ws-gloss.

Amir, R., & Zeid, A. (2004). *An UML Profile for Service Oriented Architectures.* Paper presented at the Companion to the 19th Annual ACM SIGPLAN Conference on Object-Oriented Programming, Systems, Languages, and Applications, OOPSLA 2004.

AOP. (2007). *Aspect-Oriented Software Development.* Retrieved from http://www.aosd.net

Arsanjani, A. (2004). Service-oriented modeling and architecture. Retrieved from http://www.ibm.com/developerworks/library/ws-soa-design1/

Benslimane, D., Arara, A., Falquet, G., Maamar, Z., Thiran, P., & Gargouri, F. (2006, October 18-20). *Contextual Ontologies: Motivations, Challenges, and Solutions.* Paper presented at the 4th Biennial International Conference on Advances in Information Systems, Izmir, Turkey.

Boukadi, K., Chaabane, A., & Vincent, L. (2009, May 13-15). *A Framework for Context-Aware Business Processes Modelling.* Paper presented at the In the International Conference on Industrial Engineering and Systems Management, IESM, Montreal, Canada.

Boukadi, K., Ghedira, C., & Vincent, L. (2008). *An Aspect Oriented Approach for Context-Aware Service Domain Adapted to E-Business.* Paper presented at the 20th International Conference on Advanced Information Systems Engineering, Montpellier, France.

Boukadi, K., Vincent, L., & Burlat, P. (2009). *Contextual Service Oriented and Analysis: the IT concerns.*

BPMI. (2002). *Business Process Management Initiative.* Retrieved from http://www.bpmi.org.

Castro, V. d., Marcos, E., & Sanz, M. L. (2006). A model driven method for service composition modelling: a case study. *International Journal of Web Engineering and Technology, 2*(4). doi:10.1504/IJWET.2006.010419

Coutaz, J., Crowley, J. L., Dobson, S., & Garlan, D. (2003). Context is key. *Communications of the ACM, 48*(3).

Dey, A. K., Abowd, G. D., & Salber, D. (2001). A Conceptual Framework and a Toolkit for Supporting the Rapid Prototyping of Context-Aware Applications. *Human-Computer Interaction, 16*(2), 97–166. doi:10.1207/S15327051HCI16234_02

Erl, T. (2005). *Service-Oriented Architecture (SOA): Concepts, Technology, and Design.* Upper Saddle River, NJ: Prentice Hall.

Erradi, A., Anand, S., & Kulkarni, N. (2006a). *SOAF: An Architectural Framework for Service Definition and Realization.* Paper presented at the IEEE International Conference on Services Computing.

Erradi, A., Anand, S., & Kulkarni, N. (2006b, September 18-22). *SOAF: An Architectural Framework for Service Definition and Realization.* Paper presented at the IEEE International Conference on Services Computing (SCC'06), Chicago.

Heuvel, W.-J. v. d., Hasselbring, W., & Papazoglou, M. (2000). Top-Down Enterprise Application Integration with Reference Models. *Australian Journal of Information Systems.*

Krafzig, D., Banke, K., & Slama, D. (2004). *Enterprise SOA Service Oriented Architecture Best Practices.* Upper Saddle River: Prentice Hall PTR.

Lopez-Sanza, M., Acuna, C. J., Cuesta, C. E., & Marcos, E. (2008). Modelling of Service-Oriented Architectures with UML. *Electronic Notes in Theoretical Computer Science, 194*(4), 23–37. doi:10.1016/j.entcs.2008.03.097

Lopez-Sanza, M., Cuesta, C. E., & Marcos, E. (2008). Modelling of Service-Oriented Architectures with UML. *Electronic Notes in Theoretical Computer Science, 194*(4), 23–37. doi:10.1016/j.entcs.2008.03.097

Marks, E. A., & Bell, M. (2006). *Service-Oriented Architecture: A Planning and Implementation Guide for Business and Technology* (1st ed.). New York: Wiley.

Mietzner, R. (2008). *Using Variability Descriptors to Describe Customizable SaaS Application Templates. Institute of Architecture of Application Systems.* IAAS.

Miller, J., & Mukerji, J. (2003). *MDA Guide Version 1.0.1.* Retrieved from http://www.omg.com/mda/03-06-01.pdf

Nuffel, D. V. (2007). Towards a Service-Oriented Methodology: Business-Driven Guidelines for Service Identification. In S. B. Heidelberg (Ed.), *On the Move to Meaningful Internet Systems 2007: (OTM 2007) Workshops 4805* (pp. 294-303).

OASIS. (2006). Reference Model for Service Oriented Architecture 1.0: retrieved from http://www.oasis-open.org/committees/download.php/19679/soa-rm-cs.pdf.

OMG. (2003). *MDA guide version 1.0.1.*

OMG. (2004). *Object Management Group, UML2.0 Super Structure Specification.*

OMG. (2006a). *Business Motivation Model (BMM) Specification.* Retrieved April 20, 2007, from http://www.omg.org/cgi-bin/doc?dtc/2006-08-03

OMG. (2006b). *Business Process Modeling Notation Specification.* Retrieved June 6, 2006, from http://www.omg.org/cgi-bin/doc?dtc/2006-02-01

Papazoglou, M. P., & Georgakopoulos, D. (2003). Service oriented computing. *Communications of the ACM, 46*(10), 24–28. doi:10.1145/944217.944233

Papazoglou, M. P., & Heuvel, W.-J. (2006). Service-Oriented Design and Development Methodology. *International Journal of Web Engineering and Technology, 2*(4), 412–442. doi:10.1504/IJWET.2006.010423

Papazoglou, M. P., & Heuvel, W.-J. d. (2006). Service-oriented design and development methodology. *International Journal of Web Engineering and Technology, 2*(4), 412–442. doi:10.1504/IJWET.2006.010423

Pavel, B., & Alain, W. (2003). Context Based Reasoning in Business Process Models. In *Proceedings of the 2003 IEEE International Conference on Information Reuse and Integration.* IRI.

Ramollari, E., Dranidis, D., & Simons, A. J. H. (2007, June 11-12). *A Survey of Service Oriented Development Methodologies.* Paper presented at the 2nd European Young Researchers Workshop on Service Oriented Computing, University of Leicester, UK

Rolland, C., Prakash, N., & Benjamen, A. (1999). A multi-Model View of Process Modelling. *Requirements Engineering, 4*(4), 169–187. doi:10.1007/s007660050018

Rosemann, M., & Recker, J. C. (2006). *Context-aware Process Design: Exploring the Extrinsic Drivers for Process Flexibility.* Paper presented at the 18th International Conference on Advanced Information Systems Enginnering, Workshops and Doctoral Consortium.

Saidani, O., & Nurcan, S. (2007, June). *Towards Context Aware Business Process Modelling.* Paper presented at the Workshop on Business Process Modelling, Development, and Support (BPMDS), 19th International Conference on Advanced Information Systems Engineering (CAiSE'07), Trondheim, Norway.

Sawyer, P., Hutchison, J., Walkerdine, J., & Sommerville, I. (2005, August). *Faceted Service Specification.* Paper presented at the Workshop on Service-Oriented Computing Requirements (SOCCER), Paris.

Schilit, B. N., & Theimer, M. M. (1994). Disseminating active map information to mobile hosts. *IEEE Network, 8*(5), 22–32. doi:10.1109/65.313011

Zimmermann, O., Krogdahl, P., & Gee, C. (2004). *Elements of Service-Oriented Analysis and Design.* Retrieved from http://www.ibm.com/developerworks/library/ws-soad1/

ENDNOTE

[1] The process describing the tasks associated with the generation of each business service model as well as the mapping rules between them will be described later.

This work was previously published in International Journal of Organizational and Collective Intelligence, Volume 1, Issue 2, edited by Hideyasu Sasaki, pp. 1-28, copyright 2010 by IGI Publishing (an imprint of IGI Global).

Chapter 7
Towards a Trust Management Enabled Identity Metasystem

Weiliang Zhao
Macquarie University, Australia

Jian Yang
Macquarie University, Australia

ABSTRACT

Existing identity metasystems provide enabling tools to manage, select, and control of digital identities but they have not provided the support of trust management that should cover how trust requirements associated with digital identities are modeled, how runtime conditions for trust are evaluated, and how the results of trust evaluation are consumed by systems/applications. In this paper, the authors propose an approach toward a trust management enabled identity metasystem that covers the analysis of trust requirements and the development of trust management system in a consistent manner. The proposed trust management architecture extends the existing identity metasystems by introducing computing components for carrying out typical trust management tasks associated with digital identities. The computing components in proposed architecture provide intelligent services for these tasks. The proposed high level architecture targets the automation of the development of the trust management layer for digital identities.

1. INTRODUCTION

More and more economic and social activities are carried out on the Internet. The Internet was originally built without a way to know who and what users are connecting to. Digital identities are widely employed for providing enable solutions

DOI: 10.4018/978-1-4666-1577-9.ch007

to address the above "unknown" issue in different information systems and applications on the Internet. Service-oriented computing has become a well adopted technology and it has reshaped a vast number of business models and processes. Digital identities have been widely employed as crucial components for weaving a world of cooperating Web services where application components are assembled to support dynamic business processes that span multiple enterprizes, organizations, and computing platforms.

In the "The laws of identity" (Cameron, 2005), a digital identity is defined as a set of claims made by one digital subject about itself or another digital subject. The digital subject is a person or thing represented or existing in the digital realm which is being described or dealt with and a claim is an assertion of the truth of something. There are different management tasks for the processes of representing, recognizing, and usage controlling of digital identities. The identity management in the digital world normally relates to the behavior of corresponding entities of digital subjects in their real world activities (Claub & Kohntopp, 2001). Digital identities normally convey sensitive information of their subjects. The employment of digital identities will normally bring in many critical security and privacy issues such as identity phishing, pharming, and privacy protection for sensitive information embedded in digital identities. The disclosure of digital identities must be under the control based on the satisfaction of related trust requirements (Josang, Fabre, Hay, Dalziel, & Pope, 2005). The existing identity systems including CardSpace (Bertocci, Serack, & Baker, 2007), Sxip (Sxip, 2009), Higgins (Eclipse-Foundation, 2009), and OpenID (OpenID-Foundation, 2009) have provided different functions for users to manage, select, and control digital identities. However, these identity systems have not provided further support for the modeling of trust requirements associated with digital identities, evaluation of runtime status for trust, and a range of mechanisms of trust consumption related with digital identities. The privacy and security are still a hindrance for digital identities to support wide range of e-commerce, governmental and social activities.

When digital identities are used on the Internet, their usages normally cross business boundaries and security domains. Identity 2.0 (stemming from Web 2.0) brings in a digital revolution of identity verification on the Internet. It employs user-centric technologies such as Information Cards (Bhargavan, Fournet, Gordon, & Swamy, 2008) and OpenID (OpenID-Foundation, 2009) for providing a simple and open method to employ digital identities in supporting transactions as corresponding physical identities in the physical world. These information cards and OpenID are the employed digital identities. There are two categories of identity management. The first category includes those domain-centric approaches such as the Liberty Alliance (The Liberty Alliance Project, 2009) which are actually based on federation protocols. These approaches have the limitation for supporting grander structures beyond federated domains on Internet. The second category includes user-centric approaches such as Microsoft's CardSpace (Bertocci et al., 2007), Sxip (Sxip, 2009), and Higgins (Eclipse-Foundation, 2009). These approaches leverage Internet and Web protocols with different ways for storing identity attributes and using digital identities for securing associated transaction and/or interactions. The approaches in the second category have the issue of interoperability. The currently existing identity management approaches in both categories only target providing facilities to enable users to have convenience and control over their digital identities by defining how to generate, select, and verify them. The further trust management concerns about how to define trust mechanisms, evaluate runtime status, manage various ways of trust consumption are not included in these approaches. The trust management for digital identities is always related with a range of trust relationships which can be specified based on users, relying parties, required digital identities, and context specific requirements. It is highly desirable to have a formal model of trust relationship that can be used as a solid foundation for the analysis and modeling of trust requirements and the development of sub system of trust management for digital identities to be used on the Internet. The specification/modeling of trust relationships and the development of trust management systems should be considered in a consistent manner.

This paper proposes a specific solution of trust management for digital identities including the guidelines for the analysis/modeling of trust relationships and architecture of a trust management system for digital identities. With the help of the proposed trust management approach for digital identities, the development of trust management system can be automated to a substantially high level. This research provides a solid foundation towards a trust management enabled identity metasystem that can handle modeling of trust requirements, trust-related data storage, trust request, trust evaluation, and trust consuming about digital identities in a consistent manner.

The remainder of this paper is organized as follows. Section 2 provides a brief review of identity metasystem. Section 3 discusses the requirements and challenges for the trust management enabled identity metasystem. Section 4 describes the proposed trust management approach for digital identities. Typical trust relationships related with digital identities are discussed. The architecture for trust management approach is proposed. Discussion about the proposed trust management architecture is provided. Section 5 provides a scenario example for the development of trust management extension of CardSpace by employing the proposed architecture. Section 6 discusses some related work. Section 7 concludes this paper.

2. IDENTITY METASYSTEM

In the Cyberspace, there are a wide variety of digital identities that simulate the real world's identities and there are some digital identities without corresponding entities in the real world. Different digital identities are associated with different information and are expressed in different ways. A set of principles, referred to as "Laws of Identity" (Cameron, 2005), has been proposed and refined for key concerns about an identity metasystem. The identity metasystem is an interoperable architecture for digital identities that enables users to use and manage a collection of digital identities based on a range of underlying technologies, implementations, and providers. It provides a consistent user interface for different Internet identity systems to work together in a secure manner.

In any digital identity system, there are three generic entities, namely the subject, identity provider, and relying party. A subject is an entity that is associated with the digital identity about which claims are made. Examples of subjects include people, companies, applications, and machines. An identity provider issues digital identities associated with the subjects. Digital identities issued by different identity providers carry different information for the claimed identity. A relying party is an entity that requests digital identities. Normally, a relying party is an application that frequently uses digital identities for authentication and authorization. A typical example of a relying party is a web service of an online bookstore that accepts digital credit cards for payment. The Figure 1 (from Microsoft' Web Site) shows the fundamental interactions among the subject, identity provider, and relying party.

The well-known identity metasystems are embodied in Microsoft's CardSpace (Bertocci et al., 2007) and Higgins' open source identity framework (Eclipse-Foundation, 2009).

CardSpace (Microsoft-Corporation, 2005; Chappell et al., 2006; McLaughlin, 2006; Alrodhan & Mitchell, 2007), formerly known as InfoCard, is the firstly developed identity metasystem. CardSpace uses a consistent way to deal with the portfolio of digital identities. It targets a standards-based solution for storing and delivering diverse digital identities for the Internet. Microsoft claims that CardSpace can provide the support for any digital identity system, consistent user control of digital identity, replacement of password based web login, and improved user confidence in the identity of remote applications. In the CardSpace identity selection screen (Chappell et al., 2006); a digital identity is displayed as an information

Figure 1. Interactions among user, identity provider, and relying party

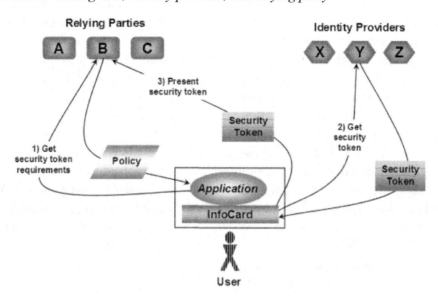

card that can potentially present to a relying party. Information cards are selected and sent to relying parties, while the technical complexity of information cards is hidden. CardSpace has graphic user interfaces and functions to require every user to approve the use of every identity provider and relying party that he or she wishes to access. CardSpace allows replacing password-based web login with information cards. Relying parties use information cards for authentication and authorization rather than authenticating users with passwords.

Microsoft has developed its next generation identity and access management platform as Card-Space "Geneva" (Microsoft, 2009) which is built on active directory service. The "Geneva" is designed to be used in any web application or web service that uses the .NET Framework version 3.5 or after. It targets claims-aware applications in which users present their identities to applications as a set of claims. "Geneva" works with Information Cards that "Geneva" Server and other identity providers generate. "Geneva" has the flexibility to be configured by domain administrators to enable a Kerberos-like sign-in experience across domain boundaries. The "Geneva" is based on industry standard protocols

including WS-* (Alonso, Casati, Kuno, & Machiraju, 2004) and SAML 2.0 for interoperability.

Higgins is an open source identity framework that supports all platforms. It has the full compatibility with Microsoft's CardSpace. It enables users and applications on a broad range of platforms to have the capability for integrating identities, profiles, and relationship information by exploiting different kinds of protocols. The Higgins has three categories of computing components as Higgins Selector, Identity Services (i.e. Identity Provider and Relying Party code), and the Higgins Identity Data Service. Higgins provides the software infrastructure for supporting consistent user experience for digital identities and it works with protocols including WS-Trust, OpenID, SAML, XDI, LDAP, and so on.

3. REQUIREMENTS AND CHALLENGES

Identity metasystems such as CardSpace or Higgins provide utilities for users/applications to provide digital identities to relying parties. All existing identity metasystems have not addressed the issue about how the users judge the trustworthiness of relying parties. The trustworthiness of relying parties from the view point of users/applications is a critical security concern which may be related with complicated and complex trust mechanisms. In identity metasystems, there are different trust requirements associated with digital identities, users of digital identities, and relying parties to be considered in their specific situations. The users are normally the subjects of digital identities but there can be some exceptions. For example, a user of a digital identity is a proxy of the subject of the digital identity who can make the decision on the usage of the digital identity.

Identity metasystems allows users to manage their digital identities from different identity providers, and employ them in their specific contexts to access online services. It is necessary to define different kinds of trust relationships for covering a wide range of situations for the usage of digital identities. A range of trust mechanisms including credentials and reputation should be included under a unified umbrella. As a further step, a sub trust management system for digital identities is anticipated to look after all the trust management tasks in those complicated and complex systems that employ digital identities through identity metasystem.

In identity metasystems, the nature of distributed environments in which digital identities are employed brings in a set of common characteristics of trust management tasks. They are listed as the following:

- **Multiple Trust Mechanisms:** It may be necessary to establish trust relationships between users/applications and relying parties based on multiple trust mechanisms. Beyond the broadly used credentials in distributed authentication/authorization, the users /applications may use specific knowledge (both local and acquired from remote nodes or resources) to make trust decisions. In more complex cases, multiple

trust mechanisms, such as credentials and reputation, can be required to work together for a single trust decision.

- **Open Nature:** Digital identities are normally used in open environments such as the Internet. The relying parties may have various levels of familiarity from frequent customers to strangers. It is highly possible to use different trust requirements for involved parties in different situations to access data and resources. When digital identities are employed, the open nature of applications and systems makes the trust management of digital identities a crucial part of the systems.

- **Multiple Domains:** Digital identities may be used across several networks and there may be multiple administrative or organizational boundaries. The applications and systems that use digital identities may be composed of many interconnected heterogeneous resources that belong to multiple domains, and the relationship between these domains can be peer to peer or hierarchical, or a combination thereof. There may be some complicated and complex trust requirements associated with digital identities.

- **Real Time Trust:** In many information systems using digital identities, trust relationships must be evaluated and established in real time. Situations related with trust are not static and they are continuously changing. The dynamic properties of trust must be included and related evidences must be collected in real time for trust evaluation. The valid period of the result of trust evaluation is also time relevant (for example, it can only be used in a fixed time period).

- **Complexity:** Information systems using digital identities can be very complicated with complex business functions and employing multiple advanced technologies.

The complicated business requirements and complex technologies employed in applications and systems can bring in challenging trust management tasks.

The above observed common characteristics provide a position for the proposed trust management solution for digital identities. When an identity metasystem is implemented and employed in applications and systems, it is highly desirable to build a trust management layer for digital identities as an extension of the employed identity metasystem. The trust management tasks are dealt in the trust management layer which provides support the needs of particular functions/applications in systems. Following the basic idea of M. Blaze et al (Blaze et al., 1996), the trust management layer of digital identities is separated from applications and systems. The trust management layer will deal with trust request, trust evaluation, and trust consuming in a comprehensive and consistent manner. The trust management extension of an identity metasystem will be composed of computing components that carry out the trust management tasks associated with the usages of digital identities and associated trust requirements. In next section, we will provide details about our trust management approach.

4. TRUST MANAGEMENT SOLUTION

The trust management solution for digital identities covers both the analysis and modeling of trust and the development of trust management system. In this section, the analysis and modeling of trust relationships and trust management architecture will be discussed in separate sub sections. In first sub section, the digital identities are considered as same type of objects with common characteristics from the view point of identity metasystems. The set of trust relationships related with the usage of digital identities will be analyzed and modeled based the formal model of trust relationship defined in (Zhao et al., 2004). This sub section provides the guidelines for capturing the trust requirements about digital identities with the help of a formal model. In second sub section, generic trust management architecture is proposed to facilitate the development of trust management system for digital identities. The trust management architecture targets a standard, high level design for the trust management extension of identity metasystems. This architecture can be used as an auxiliary tool in the whole life cycle of the development of trust management components, including specifications of requirements, preliminary design, active deployment, and maintenance. The architecture will provide a foundation for dependency and consistency analysis for trust management of digital identities.

4.1 Analysis and Modeling of Trust Relationships

The formal model of trust relationship (Zhao et al., 2004) will be employed as the foundation for understanding of trust requirements and the analysis/modeling of involved trust relationships. A trust relationship is formally defined as:

A trust relationship is a four-tuple $T = < R; E; C; P >$ where:

- R is the set of trustors. It cannot be empty.
- E is the set of trustees. It cannot be empty.
- C is the set of conditions. It contains all conditions (requirements) for the current trust relationship. Normally, a trust relationship has some specified conditions. If there is no condition, the condition set is empty.
- P is the set of properties. The property set describes the actions or attributes of the trustees. It cannot be empty. The property set can be divided into two sub sets:

- ◦ Action Set: the set of actions which trustors trust that trustees will/can perform.
- ◦ Attribute Set: the set of attributes which trustors trust that trustees have.

A trust relationship T expresses that under the condition set C, trustor set R trust that trustee set E have property set P. This model has a strong expressive power that can cover commonly used trust notations. The formal model has four tuples and each tuple is a set as a security label. The trustor set and trustee set are both included in the formal model. They have the similar meaning of roles in classic role models. The condition set and property set are used to define the specific context of the trust relationship. The condition set defines the associated on-time requirements of the trust relationship. The condition set indicates a set of checking functions to be defined in trust management system for processing the corresponding trust relationship. In next sub section, components of evaluating trust provide processing support for defined conditions. This formal model can be regressed to the role model when trustor set is "system" and condition set is empty.

A series of definitions, propositions, and operations have been defined in (Zhao et al., 2004) as enabling tools for the analysis and modeling of trust relationships. Related with the usage of digital identities supported by identity metasystems, the analysis and modeling of trust relationships should include the following specific concerns:

- The trustor set is normally modeled as a set of users or applications.
- The trustee set includes a group of relying parties.
- The condition set may include the trust mechanisms such as credentials, reputation, data storage, and environment parameters. For an instance, when relying parties are web services, security tokens in SOAP messages defined in WS-Trust (OASIS, 2007) provide evidences for some conditions in the condition set and it is possible to have conditions that require other trust mechanisms such as reputation.
- The property set normally includes a group of digital identities.

The system of university library may have multiple trust relationships to be defined. The following is a scenario example of a trust relationship. We assume the employed digital identity is digital credit cards and the identity metasystem is CardSpace. There is a service of a university library that can facilitate the purchase of books for departments and individual staff from online bookstores. The service of the library uses digital credit cards for all involved payments. The digital identities are the digital credit cards that belong to academic departments or some individual staff and the relying parties are web services of online bookstores. CardSpace can provide an intuitive interface for selecting digital credit cards and sending them to relying parties as the online bookstores. It is necessary to specify trust requirements and check their satisfaction before digital credit cards are released. The associated trust relationship is modeled as: purchasers as academic departments trust Web services of online bookstores if they can provide their business licences and have good reputation that the web services of online bookstores can have purchasers' digital credit cards. Following the formal model, the trust relationship noted by T1 is expressed as:

The trust relationship $T1 = < R1; E1; C1; P1 >$. R1 is a specific set of academic departments; E1 is a specific set of Web services of online bookstores; C1 includes business licence and reputation level; P1 includes the release permission of digital credit cards.

The whole set of trust relationships will capture trust requirements about employed digital identities in applications and systems supported by identity metasystems. A trust management layer will be built for processing and managing these modeled trust relationships and associated trust data. The trust management layer should be separated from applications and systems for administration and management tasks related with trust. The trust management layer will be composed of various computing components for handling trust-related data storage, trust request from applications, trust evaluation, and trust consumption. In the next subsection, we will propose a trust management architecture which can provide infrastructure and guidelines for the development of trust management enabled digital metasystems.

4.2 Trust Management Architecture

This subsection proposes a trust management architecture that targets the automation of the development of trust management enabled identity metasystems. The architecture describes scribes the high level design of trust management computing components and their interrelationships. The trust management architecture covers the frequently used trust mechanisms for the evaluation of trust relationships and a range of ways of trust consumption related with digital identities.

In the following part of this paper, we refer to the architecture for the trust management extension of an identity metasystem as TrustExtArch. TrustExtArch considers the specific characteristics of trust management enabled identity metasystems and inherits the major characteristics of the general trust management architecture in distributed information systems (Zhao et al, 2006).

TrustExtArch holds all trust management components about digital identities. TrustExtArch addresses applications' trust requests like a database query engine. TrustExtArch accepts a requested trust relationship, or a set of inputs, that could be used to determine the requested trust relationship. An example of the inputs includes a user/application (trustor), a relying party (trustee), and a set of required digital identities. TrustExtArch locates the trust relationship requested by applications/systems, handles trust context in

terms of employed WS-* protocols and associated messages, evaluates the trust relationship by checking the required conditions, and manages the consumption of the evaluation result with the capability to link the trust relationship to associated applications/systems in different ways. Trust relationships should be defined and loaded into the TrustExtArch before they are processed at runtime.

In TrustExtArch, there is a persistent data storage mechanism that provides data support for other components. In TrustExtArch, trust relationships are processed by exploiting various trust management components. These trust management components are grouped into different component packages for finding of trust relationships based on requests, handling of trust context, evaluation of trust relationships, and managing trust consumption. TrustExtArch has TrustDatabase for the storage of trust related data. TrustExtArch includes component packages: TrustControl, LocatingTrust, TrustContext, EvaluatingTrust, and ConsumingTrust. In TrustExtArch, some components are the implementation of corresponding generic components of general trust management architecture for distributed information systems (Zhao et al., 2006) with some specific concerns about the characteristics of the digital metasystem and relying parties and other components are specific for trust management extension of identity metasystems. The architecture of TrustExtArch is expressed in Figure 2.

TrustDatabase provides a persistent storage mechanism for storing and retrieving trust related information including trust relationships and trust related data. These trust related data will only be used by computing components of TrustExtArch. TrustDatabase can be implemented by a relational database or data profiles. Trust relationships and trust parameters should be loaded into the TrustDatabase before they are involved at runtime.

TrustControl is the computing component performing the overall management and control of TrustExtArch at run time. TrustControl links

Figure 2. The architecture for trust management extension of identity metasystems

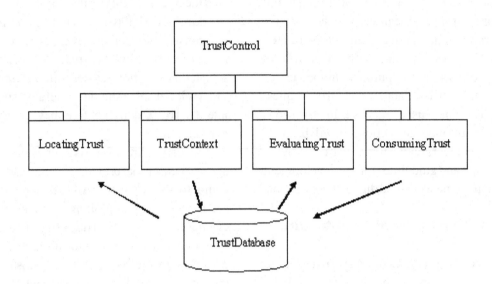

applications and functional packages of Trust-ExtArch including LocatingTrust, TrustContext, EvaluatingTrust, and ConsumingTrust. It is the trust management controller at the top level.

LocatingTrust is the package for finding the trust relationship based on the request. There are three components in this package that are referred to as "Locating Trust Controller", "Trust Relationship Locator", and "Authentication Controller". "Locating Trust Controller" is the management component that receives the request from applications and it assigns tasks to "Trust Relationship Locator" and "Authentication Controller". "Trust Relationship Locator" is the component that finds the requested trust relationship from the TrustDatabase. "Authentication Controller" is the component that deals with authentication of a relying party that requests a digital identity; normally it employs existing authentication services in the system to perform the tasks. The components of LocatingTrust are shown in Figure 3.

TrustContext contains the computing components for the management and processing of contextual information related with trust manage-

ment of digital identities. On the Internet, identity metasystems are normally integrated with technologies that support WS-* protocols such as WS-Security, WS-Trust, WS-MetadataExchange and WS-SecurityPolicy. In particular, WS-Trust provides a mechanism for an incoming message to prove a set of claims (e.g., name, key, permission, capability, etc.) that are important for establishing trust. WS-Trust works at the messaging level. It is necessary to have a computing component to facilitate the integration of WS-Trust with trust management of digital identities. It is necessary for users/applications and relying parties to communicate with each other for exchanging contextual information in order to establish trust for the usage of digital identities. It needs a computing component to handle trust-relevant contextual information.

TrustContext has computing components as "TrustContextController", "WS-Trust Message Handler" and "ContextInformation Handler". "TrustContext Controller" is the manager of this package that assigns tasks to "WS-Trust MessageHandler" and "Context Information Handler".

Figure 3. Components of LocatingTrust

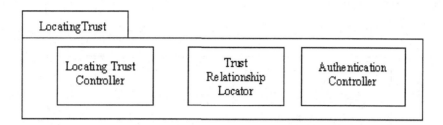

"WS-TrustMessage Handler" adapts the incoming WS-Trust SOAP messages and generates the outgoing WS-Trust SOAP messages. "Context Information Handler" looks after the management of trust-relevant contextual information for trust evaluation and trust consuming in a defined processing scope such as a transaction or a session. The components of TrustContext are shown in Figure 4.

EvaluatingTrust contains computing components required for the evaluation of trust relationships. The evaluation of a trust relationship involves checking whether the conditions of a trust relationship can be satisfied or not. The conditions of trust relationships are set up against the risks from the evil actions of relying parties, online attacks, and unstable environments. One trust relationship can have multiple conditions and the checking for each of them is related a specific trust mechanism such as that is based on credential or reputation. Multiple trust mechanisms can be involved in the evaluation of a single trust relationship. The EvaluatingTrust provides an integration place for these trust mechanisms to cooperate with each other. Any existing system or mechanism for checking or evaluating the evidence of trust can be included in the EvaluatingTrust package. For instance, the existing reputation-based systems and credential based systems can be employed for providing required information for trust evaluation.

In EvaluatingTrust, "Trust Evaluation Controller" is the computing component that assigns the evaluation tasks to other functional components in this package. EvaluatingTrust has functional components for specific evaluating tasks, namely "Credential Evaluation", "Reputation Evaluation", "Stored Data Evaluation", and "Environment Evaluation". The components of EvaluatingTrust are shown in Figure 5.

Figure 4. Components of TrustContext

Figure 5. Components of EvaluatingTrust

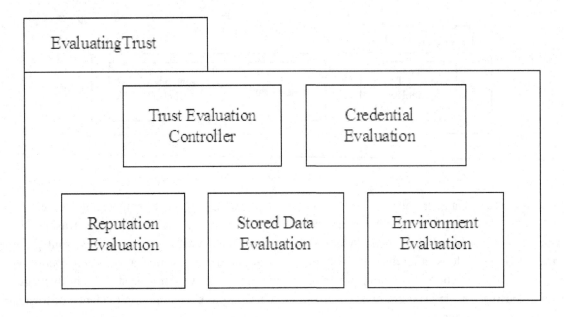

ConsumingTrust contains the computing components for the control and management of trust consuming. Consuming trust deals with how to use the output of the evaluation of a trust relationship by applications and systems. Rather than the immediate consumption by requesting users/applications, the evaluation result of a trust relationship can be stored and/or distributed in different ways. It is possible to generate credentials based on the evaluation result of a trust relationship for further distribution and usage. The evaluation result of a trust relationship can also be stored in database that can be retrieved in the future. It is also possible for the evaluation result to be consumed by the trust management system itself or by an auditing system. In ConsumingTrust, "Consuming Controller" is the manager of trust consuming. It receives the result of trust evaluation and assigns consuming tasks to "Direct Trust Consuming Controller", "Credential Generator Consuming", and "Data Storage Consuming", and "System Consuming". The components of ConsumingTrust are shown in Figure 6.

4.3 Discussion about Trust Management Architecture

TrustExtArch is the architecture with specific concerns about trust management extension of identity metasystems. It is assumed that identity metasystems are used on the Internet and Web services protocols are exploited in associated applications and information systems. The goal of TrustExtArch is to provide a solid foundation upon which the system's functions may evolve for trust management tasks related with digital identities in identity metasystems. Comparing to existing trust management systems, TrustExtArch has the following characteristics:

- **Unified Framework of Trust Mechanisms**: Most of existing trust management systems only focus on one kind of trust mechanisms. For example, PolicyMaker, KeyNote, REFEREE, and IBM Trust Establishment employ credentials as the only kind of mechanism for trust management. TrustExtArch

Figure 6. Components of ConsumingTrust

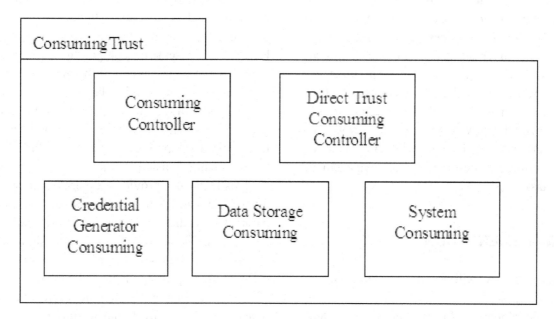

supports multiple trust mechanisms and they can work together under the same framework.

- **Multiple Ways of Trust Consumption**: Most of the existing trust management systems assume a straightforward way of trust consumption, where the application requesting the trust evaluation will consume the trust evaluation results directly. Different to existing trust management systems, TrustExtArch provides computing components that support multiple ways of trust consumption. These ways of trust consumption are controlled and managed by the trust management system as well.

- **Embracement of Established Standards**: The proposed TrustExtArch has the ability to embrace established standards or existing systems for trust management tasks. All the existing standards or systems for trust management can be employed by TrustExtArch to perform some specific tasks. For example, in reputation evaluation, the reputation could be calculated by

existing utility in the system. Established standards and existing systems can be easily integrated in TrustExtArch.

- **Trust Relationships Oriented**: Most of existing trust management systems separate mechanisms from application-specific policies directly. It is always necessary to define a policy language to express and interpret trust policies. TrustExtArch is based on trust relationships rather than trust policies. A trust relationship has a strict structure and can be accurately interpreted both in TrustExtArch and requested applications. The analysis/modelling of trust relationships about digital identities and the development of trust management extension of identity metasystems are considered in a comprehensive and consistent manner.

- **High Extensibility**: TrustExtArch is module-based. Its implementation is highly extensible. When a new trust mechanism is introduced, the corresponding computing component for this trust mechanism can be easily added into the target trust management system. There is minimal or no affect on the other computing components.

- **Intelligent Services:** computing components in TrustExtArch provide intelligent services for trust management tasks associated with digital identities. Most of components in TrustExtArch can be implemented with Web services and they will intelligently collaborate with each other for performing customized trust management tasks.

5. IMPLEMENTATION

In this section, we will provide an implementation example to show how TrustExtArch is helpful in the development of trust management extension of CardSpace in the real world. We use the same scenario example described in last section. The service of a university library facilitates the purchase of books for academic departments and individual staff from online bookstores. The university library has the CardSpace installed. The CardSpace has an interface for selecting digital credit cards and sending them to online bookstores. However, the CardSpace can not provide further support related with the trust issues about digital identities. In Section 4, trust relationship T1 has been defined for capturing trust requirements about the usages of digital credit cards by CardSpace. We assume that business licences are expressed as digital credentials. The good reputation of an online bookstore is decided based on it has enough successful transactions with the library or not.

This section provides details about how to develop the trust management extension of CardSpace by exploiting TrustExtArch. The target trust management sub system has the capability to process trust relationship at different phases in terms of locatingtrust, trustcontext, evaluatingtrust, and consumingtrust. The TrustExtArch is employed for providing a high level architecture for an extension of CardSpace that focus on trust management

tasks of digital identities. The computing components in TrustExtArch are customized based the requirements of related trust management tasks. Here we only discuss the computing components related with the processing of the modeled trust relationship T1 for buying books from online bookstores with digital credit cards. In the following, we provide some brief description about the required computing components in the trust management extension of CardSpace:

TrustDatabase provides a permanent storage mechanism for trust relationships and trust parameters such as the transactions with online bookstores. The modelled trust relationships are stored in TrustDatabase before they are used by other computing components in TrustExtArch.

TrustControl provides runtime control of trust management layer of digital identities. It links LocatingTrust, TrustContext, EvaluatingTrust, and ConsumingTrust. Its implementation is straightforward for the processing of the modelled trust relationship.

LocatingTrust has computing components as "Locating Trust Controller", "Trust Relationship Locator", and "Authentication Controller". Before sending a digital credit card to an online bookstore, the "Locating Trust Controller" assigns tasks to "Trust Relationship Locator" to find the request trust relationship for buying books from online bookstores, and "Authentication Controller" to authenticate the online bookstore. In our example, it is a straight forward task to find the trust relationship because we only model one in the system. In the real system, there may be multiple trust relationships and some finding mechanism could be involved (such assignment of trustor set, trustee set, and requested property set).

TrustContext has the computing components for the management and processing of contextual information. Here we use "WS-Trust Message Handler" to request and receive the business licences of online bookstores. The "Context Information Handler" is used to maintain the status of trust evaluation and trust consuming for buying multiple books in one online session. The "TrustContext Controller" is the runtime manager of this package and it links with computing components in other packages. EvaluatingTrust has computing components for the evaluation of trust relationships. For the scenario example in this section, the "Trust Evaluation Controller" assigns evaluation tasks to "Credential Evaluation", and "Reputation Evaluation" should be included. The "Credential Evaluation" checks the credentials (business licences of online bookstores) that are received by "WS-Trust Message Handler" and the "Reputation Evaluation" checks the reputation of the involved online bookstore. The evaluation result will be returned to "TrustControl".

ConsumingTrust has the computing components as "Consuming Controller", "Direct Trust Consuming Controller", "Credential Generator Consuming", and "System Consuming". The "Consuming Controller" is the manager of the ConsumingTrust package that assigns consuming tasks to other components in this package. "Direct Trust Consuming Controller" looks after the consuming of evaluation result of the trust relationship and CardSpace can send the involved digital credit card to the online bookstore immediately. Here we assume that "Credential Generator Consuming" can generate a credential including the evaluation result of the trust relationship and deliver it the original requestor (an academic department or individual staff who is the requestor and the owner of the digital credit card). "System Consuming" records the evaluation result of the trust relationship for auditing purpose or future usage by the trust management layer of digital identities.

The computing components discussed above can cover trust management tasks for processing the modelled trust relationship related with buying books from online bookstores using digital credit cards. The other trust relationships may require more computing components than above ones. We hope that the above scenario example can give readers a rough idea about the implementation of proposed TrustExtArch for building trust management extension of CardSpace in the real world.

6. RELATED WORK

In this section, we will discuss some related research about digital identities and general trust management in distributed information systems.

Digital identity and related management have been studied by researchers from different aspects. Quite a few research results have been published focusing on the nature of digital identity and its required elements (Camp, 2004; Cameron, 2005; Cavoukian, 2006).

From the view point of identity providing and verifying, the existing identity management models can be classified into isolated model, federated model, and centralized model. The isolated model lets service provider act as both digital identity provider and identity verifier to their clients (McQuaide, 2003). A user has credentials such as passwords associated with user's identities for verification. The simplicity of this model is obvious and the client and service provider only need to trust with each other for specific purposes. However, it becomes impractical if there are huge amount of web services and the users need memorizing multiple credentials (passwords). The federated identity management model addresses the limitation of the isolated model by defining a set of standards for users to be recognized by service providers with a federated domain. This model is practical when a user want to manage only one set of identifiers and credentials (Morgan, 2006). Gomi et al have proposed a federated identity management framework to enable users to manage their privileges and service providers to control access of entities based on delegated privileges (Gomi et al., 2005). The centralized model has a single identifier and credential providers which are employed by all service providers (Simon, 2004). The centralized model can be implemented in different ways such as a single certificate authority (Voltage Security, 2006) or single log-on (Pashalidis & Mitchell, 2004).

In the real world, there are a broad range of digital identities which may belong to different identity management models. Windley (2005) defined identity management architecture as "'…a coherent set of standards, policies, certifications and management activities…aimed at providing a context for implementing a digital identity infrastructure that meets the current goals and objectives of the business". Several identity management architectures (Koch & Worndl, 2001; Claub & Kohntopp, 2001; Hansen et al., 2004) have been proposed. These architectures only focus on one or multiple individual aspects of identity management such as the storage of user profile, maintenance of privacy, and/or secure authentication (White, 2008).

In the section "Identity Metasystem", we have reviewed basic concepts of identity metasystem and several well-known identity metasystems. The existing identity metasystems (Bertocci, Serack, & Baker, 2007; Sxip, 2009; Eclipse-Foundation, 2009; OpenID-Foundation, 2009) can only provide support for users to generate, select, and verify digital identities and communicate with relying parties. Trust relationships and trust mechanisms are not included in these identity metasystems.

Trust and trust management (Blaze, Feigenbaum, & Lacy, 1996; Grandison & Sloman, 2000; Reith, Niu, & Winsborough, 2007) have been extensively investigated. Research about the credibility relationship management in a web service integration environment has been reported in (Chan et al, 2005). Chiu et al (Chiu et al., 2009) have provided their latest research progress about trust and reputation on the making of service recommendations. The trust management approach for digital identities presented in this paper is developed based on the general trust management research (Zhao, Varadharajan, & Bryan, 2004, 2006) for distributed information systems. In Zhao et al. (2004), a formal model of trust was defined for capturing a range of common notions of trust in distributed information systems. A unified framework for trust management (Zhao et al., 2006) was developed that can cover a broad variety of trust mechanisms including reputations, credentials, local data, and environment

parameters. This framework provides a high level architecture and guidelines for the development of general trust management systems. The above formal model and the unified framework work together for dealing with analysis/modeling of trust relationships and development of the trust management system.

7. CONCLUSION

This paper provides a trust management solution for the digital identities when they are used on the Internet. It starts from analysis and modeling of trust relationships based on a formal model for capturing trust requirements associated with the usage of digital identities on the Internet. Then it proposes the architecture for building up the trust management layer as an extension of employed identity metasystem. The architecture provides a high level design for building up a real world trust management system for digital identities and it will be customized and implemented based on specific trust requirements in associated applications and systems. The proposed solution covers both the formally analysis and modeling of trust relationships and the development of trust management system supported by a generic architecture when identity metasystems are employed.

In the proposed architecture, trust request, trust context management, trust evaluation, and trust consumption are handled in a comprehensive and consistent manner. At runtime, computing components in proposed architecture provide intelligent services for trust management tasks associated with digital identities. A variety of trust mechanisms including credentials, reputation, stored data, and environment are covered under the same framework. The architecture includes multiple ways of trust consumption that provides a high flexibility for the target trust management system to be used on the Internet, in particular in service-oriented systems. The proposed architecture has a high capability to embrace existing trust standards and computing facilities. The web technologies, particularly the SOAP based WS-*protocols, can be easily integrated with the proposed architecture. It is hoped that the research results in this paper can provide a solid starting point and useful high level tools for the development of trust management enabled identity metasystems in the real world.

REFERENCES

Alonso, G., Casati, F., Kuno, H., & Machiraju, V. (2004). *Web services: concepts, architectures and applications*. New York: Springer Verlag.

Alrodhan, W. A., & Mitchell, C. J. (2007). Addressing privacy issues in cardspace. In *Proceedings of the Third International Symposium on Information Assurance and Security* (pp. 285-291).

Bertocci, V., Serack, G., & Baker, C. (2007). *Understanding windows cardspace: an introduction to the concepts and challenges of digital identities*. Reading, MA: Addison-Wesley.

Bhargavan, K., Fournet, C., Gordon, A. D., & Swamy, N. (2008). Verified implementations of the information card federated identity-management protocol. In *Asiaccs '08: Proceedings of the 2008 ACM Symposium on Information, Computer and Communications Security* (pp. 123-135). New York: ACM.

Blaze, M., Feigenbaum, J., & Lacy, J. (1996). Decentralized trust management. In *Proceedings of IEEE Symposium on Security and Privacy* (pp. 164-173).

Cameron, K. (2005). The laws of identity: Retrieved from http://msdn2.microsoft.com/en-us/library/ms996456.aspx

Camp, J. L. (2004). Digital identity. *IEEE Technology and Society Magazine, 23*, 34–41. doi:10.1109/MTAS.2004.1337889

Cavoukian, A. (2006). *7 laws of identity: the case for privacy-embedded laws of identity in the digital age.*

Chan, H. S., Chiu, D. K. W., Hung, P. C. K., & Leung, H. F. (2005). *Credibility Relationship Management in a Web Service Integration Environment*. Paper presented at the 4th ICIS Workshop on e-Business, Las Vegas, USA.

Chappell, D., et al. (2006). Introducing windows cardspace, Microsoft Whitepaper: Retrieved from http://msdn2.microsoft.com/en-us/library/aa480189.aspx

Chiu, D. K. W., Leung, H. F., & Lam, K. M. (2009). On the making of service recommendations: an action theory based on utility, reputation, and risk attitude. *Expert Systems with Applications, 36*(2), 3293–3301. doi:10.1016/j.eswa.2008.01.055

Claub, S., & Kohntopp, M. (2001). Identity management and its support of multilateral security. *Computer Networks, 37*, 205–219. doi:10.1016/S1389-1286(01)00217-1

Eclipse-Foundation. (2009). Higgins open source framework: Retrieved from http://www.eclipse.org/higgins/higgins-charter.php

Gomi, H., Hatakeyama, M., Hosono, S., & Fujita, S. (2005). *A delegation framework for federated identity management*. Proc. of the ACM workshop on Digital identity management (pp. 94-103).

Grandison, T., & Sloman, M. (2000). *A survey of trust in internet applications. IEEE Communications Surveys*. Fourth Quarter.

Hansen, M., Berlich, P., Camenisch, J., Claub, S., Pfitzmann, A., & Waidner, M. (2004). Privacy-enhancing identity management. *Information Security Technical Report, 9*, 35–44. doi:10.1016/S1363-4127(04)00014-7

Josang, A., Fabre, J., Hay, B., Dalziel, J., & Pope, S. (2005). Trust requirements in identity management. In Acsw frontiers '05: In *Proceedings of the 2005 Australasian Workshop on Grid Computing and E-Research*, Darlinghurst, Australia (pp. 99–108). Darlinghurst, Australia: Australian Computer Society, Inc.

Koch, M., & Worndl, W. (2001). *Community support and identity management*. Paper presented at the Seventh European Conference on Computer-Supported Cooperative Work, Bonn, Germany.

Liberty Alliance. (2009). *The liberty alliance project*. Retrieved from http://projectliberty.org/liberty/specifications 1

McLaughlin, L. (2006). What Microsoft's identity metasystem means to developers. *IEEE Software*, *23*(1), 108–111. doi:10.1109/MS.2006.18

McQuaide, B. (2003). Identity and access management, transforming E-security into a catalyst for competitive advantage.

Microsoft. (2005). *Microsoft's vision for an identity metasystem*. Retrieved from http://msdn2.microsoft.com/en-us/library/ms996422.aspx

Microsoft. (2009). *Microsoft code name "geneva"*. Retrieved from http://www.microsoft.com/forefront/geneva/en/us/overview.aspx

Morgan, R. (2006). *Federated identity management components*. University of Washington.

OASIS. (2007). *Oasis standard ws-trust 1.3*. Retrieved from http://docs.oasisopen. org/ws-sx/ws-trust/200512/ws-trust-1.3-os.html

Open, I. D-Foundation. (2009*). Openid authentication*. Retrieved from http://openid.net/developers/specs/

Pashalidis, A., & Mitchell, C. J. (2004). A single sign-on system for use from untrusted devices. In *Proceedings of the IEEE Global Telecommunications Conference* (pp. 5057-5059).

Reith, M., & Niu, J. & Winsborough, W. H. (2007*). Engineering trust management into software models. In *Proceedings of the International Workshop on Modeling in Software Engineering*, Washington, DC (pp. 9-15). Washington, DC: IEEE Computer Society.

Simon, H. (2004). *SAML - The secret to centralized identity management*.

SXIP. (2009). *Skipper*. Retrieved from http://www.sxip.com/

Voltage Security. (2006). *Public key infrastructure*.

White, P. (2008). Identity management architecture: a new direction. In *Proceedings of the 8th IEEE International Conference on Computer and information Technology* (pp. 408-413).

Windley, P. (2005). *Digital identity*. Sebastopol, CA: O'Reilly Media Inc.

Zhao, W., Varadharajan, V., & Bryan, G. (2004). Modelling trust relationships in distributed environments. In *Proceedings of the international conference on trust and privacy in digital business* (pp. 40-49), Zaragoza, Spain: Springer.

Zhao, W., Varadharajan, V., & Bryan, G. (2006). A unified framework for trust management. In *Proceedings of the securecomm and workshops* (pp.1-8).

This work was previously published in International Journal of Organizational and Collective Intelligence, Volume 1, Issue 2, edited by Hideyasu Sasaki, pp. 29-45, copyright 2010 by IGI Publishing (an imprint of IGI Global).

Chapter 8
Access Control on Semantic Web Data Using Query Rewriting

Jian Li
Hong Kong Baptist University, China

William K. Cheung
Hong Kong Baptist University, China

ABSTRACT

Semantic Web technologies allow on-line resources to be semantically annotated to support more effective and intelligent online services. However, ontologies sometimes may contain sensitive information. Providing access to them requires proper control to ensure the data protection requirement. Yet, the protection should not be too restrictive to make the access management inflexible. While there has been recent work on policy-based access control, in this paper, the authors present a policy representation specifically for access control on ontology-based data and explain how issues like policy propagation and policy conflict resolution are addressed. The authors present bucket-based query rewriting algorithms for realizing the access control policies to avoid sensitive resources leakage in the context of the Semantic Web. The authors validate the correctness of the proposed mechanisms by going through some illustrative examples in detail.

1 INTRODUCTION

The recent proliferation of the Semantic Web technologies has resulted in an increasing amount of on-line resources being semantically annotated to support more effective and intelligent

online services, including customized search, autonomous information integration, etc. We here call such kind of semantically annotations of resources *semantic web data*, where domain ontologies are needed as some background knowledge for support semantic interpretation of various types. In the literature, projects on developing semantic web data management

DOI: 10.4018/978-1-4666-1577-9.ch008

systems are abundant (Broekstra, et al., 2002; Wilkinson, et al., 2003; Heflin, et al., 1999) and related software tools have been available in the market for quite a while. By specifying the user retrieval requirements on the data as some semantic web queries which involve entities defined in some domain ontologies, relevant data can readily be retrieved. However, allowing better search on such distributed on-line resources also implies that more complicated access control is needed, especially for applications where data containing sensitive and private information (e.g., business, healthcare, national defense, etc.) could be found in the query results. In addition, if the queries are for supporting intelligent on-line services, the on-demand requirement will require the access control system to be not only secure but also flexible, or it will not be operationally viable. The conventional role-based access control model does allow some form of access control to be enforced, but rather restricted (e.g., context specific access control mechanisms are hard to be supported). In recent years, enforcing access control based on some declarative policies is gaining attention (Kagal, et al., 2003), and has been considered to be especially suitable for the dynamic characteristic of semantic web data (Bonatti, et al., 2006). One intuitive idea to implement the policy-based approach is to rewrite queries by adding some restrictions on them so that the rewritten queries will result only the data which can be accessed according to the access control policies. In this paper, we argue that proper use of ontology can allow more flexible access control on semantic web data to be supported. Also, we present a particular policy-based approach to demonstrate the viability of controlling query-based access to the semantic web data.

The main contributions of this paper include (1) an in-depth study of an ontological approach to specify access control policies as permission or forbiddance to access resources; and (2) algorithms for automatically rewriting queries which is

made possible due to the unambiguous semantics of the proposed access control policies. For the latter, in particular, we propose algorithms that, given an ontology-based conjunctive query for web resources, can a) select the policies which are relevant to the query, b) extract the restrictions expression from the policies, and c) rewrite the queries accordingly.

2 A BRIEF OVERVIEW ON SEMANTIC WEB

The vision of the Semantic Web (Berners-Lee, et al., 2001) is to have on-line resources expressed in a machine understandable format so that they can be interpreted and used by software agents. The ultimate goal is to enable Web users to find, share, integrate and thus reason on distributed information or knowledge more effectively. In the Semantic Web, ontology is one of the key concepts where entities and relationships intended to be modeled within some domains are described or posited as a form of knowledge. "Concept" and "role" are the two common terms used to refer to the two modeling elements in ontologies. Concepts (also called classes) refer to the abstract definitions of entities within the domain, whereas roles express the relationships between entities. On-line resources annotated with the labels of concepts are generally termed as *instances* of these concepts. Figure 1 shows a simple ontology about the domain of weapons, where concepts (e.g., "Weapon" and "Missile") are annotated using ellipses, "subclass" roles and other user defined roles (e.g., "HasRange") are annotated using dashed and solid lines respectively, and individual values are annotated using rectangles (e.g., "Liquid Fuel" and "Solid Fuel"). Resources about missiles can then be described accordingly using instances of concepts defined in this ontology.

Several markup languages, e.g., Resource Description Framework - RDF (Brickley & Guha,

Figure 1. An ontology for the domain of weapon

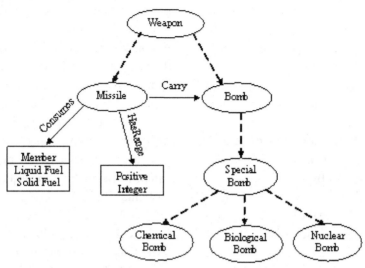

2004) and Web Ontology Language - OWL (Mc-Guinness & van Harmelen, 2004), have been proposed for describing ontologies and semantic web data. To retrieve semantic web data described in RDF and OWL, SPARQL (Prud'hommeaux & Seaborne, 2008) and SPARQL-DL (Sirin & Parsia, 2007) are two examples of the query language proposed for that. In general, a retrieval requirement should first be expressed as a query Q using terms defined in some ontologies. For example, applying the query "$Q(x) \leftarrow Missile(x)$" to the semantic data described using the ontology in Figure 1 will result in all the instance resources under the concept of "Missile".

3 ACCESS CONTROL MODELS FOR SEMANTIC WEB

In this paper, we study how access control models can be applied to safeguard semantic web data when being queried. We propose the use of access authorization policies which specifies the rights of different subjects (e.g., users or other on-line services which can initiate access requests) to gain access to the data.

3.1 Policies for Access Control

Here we first give the formal definition of access control model for semantic web data and the corresponding policies being adopted in this paper.

Definition 1. An access control model for semantic web data can be defined as a tuple $<O, R, S, P>$, where O is an ontology of the concerned domain; R is the set of instance resources annotated using entities in O; S is the set of subjects which can be entities like on-line services requesting to gain access to resources, which can be defined in O as well; and P is the set of policies specifying when some s in S can gain access to some r in R.

Definition 2. Given an access control model $<O, R, S, P>$, a policy p ($p \in P$) is denoted as $<s, v, sign>$, where

$s \in S$ is a subject requesting to gain access to some resources,

v is a **view** that defines a set of tuples with instance resources relevant to p, given as

$$v(x_1, \ldots, x_n) \leftarrow c_i(x_i), \ldots, c_j(x_j), r_k(x_{k1}, x_{k2}), \ldots, r_m(x_{m1}, x_{m2}), aps$$

with commas between predicates denoting conjunctive relationships, $c_1,...,c_j$ and $r_k,...,r_m$ denoting some concepts and roles in O, $c_i(x_i)$ referring to concept c_i's instances to be bound with variable x_i, $r_k(x_{k1}, x_{k2})$ referring to relation r_k between variables x_{k1} and x_{k2}, and *aps* denoting a conjunctive expression that consists of additional predicates such as "=", "<", ">", and

sign $\in \{+,-\}$ defines an authorization that grants (for "+") or deny (for "-") subject s access right to the resources as defined by v.

In addition, we define "$c_i(x_i),...,c_j(x_j),r_k(x_{k1}, x_{k2}),...,r_m(x_{m1}, x_{m2}), aps$" to be the body expression of v, denoted as *body(v)*, and the variables $\{x_1,..., x_n\}$ appearing in v's head as *head_variable(v)*. The variables $\{x_1,...,x_n\}$ in the head of v indicate the particular resources allowed for viewing per turple. The body of v governs the set of tuples which can be accessed. In particular, $c_i(x_i)$ implies that x_i is restricted to match with only instances of concept c_i and $r_k(x_{k1}, x_{k2})$, with x_i being either x_{k1} or x_{k2}, posts an additional restriction on x_i that it needs to satisfy as well the relation r_k with some other instances which in turn can be restricted as well. Also, the range of x_i can also be constrainted if specified in *aps*. We call v a safe view if the variables in *head_variable(v)* also appear in *body(v)*. There also exist cases where a subject is only granted access to some of the variables defined in *body(v)*. By allowing this variation in describing views, more flexible authorization rights can be described. To illustrate the flexibility, the following are some policy examples derived based on Definition 2 and the weapon ontology presented in Figure 1:

p_1: $<s, v_1, +>$, $v_1(x) \leftarrow$ *Missile(x), Carry(x,y), BiologicalBomb(y)*

p_2: $<s, v_2, +>$, $v_2(x,y) \leftarrow$ *Missile(x), Carry(x,y), BiologicalBomb(y)*

p_3: $<s, v_3, ->$, $v_3(x) \leftarrow$ *Missile(x), Carry(x,y), SpecialBomb(y), HasRange(x,z), z>3000*

Policy p_1 depicts the authorization which grants subject s the permission to gain access to the resources described as missiles that carry biological bombs as their warheads. Although the variable y (for binding with biological bomb instances) appears in the view's body, it does not appear in the view's head and thus the policy does not grant the permission to gain access to the resources of biological bombs. So, while the instances of missiles carrying biological bombs can be retrieved by s, the information about what particular biological bombs being carried is not accessible based p_1. Policy p_2 distinguishes from p_1 by retaining variable y in the head of its view so that instances of the biological bombs become accessible. Policy p_3 specifies the denial of subject s to gain access to the resources about missiles carrying special bombs with their range over 3000 miles.

3.2 Policy Propagation

As it is common for concepts and roles in the subject ontology and domain ontology to possess hierarchical relationships (e.g., "rdf:type" or "rdf:subClassOf" in RDF/RDFS), the authorization defined in a policy for subject s to have access to some resources could also be propagated to other subjects and/or resources accordingly (Javanmardi, et al., 2006).

Given a policy $<s,v,sign>$ and the condition that s' is an instance or subclass of s (later on denoted as $s' \leq s$), a new policy $<s',v,sign>$ should also be valid. In other words, the authorization right assigned to s as defined by v should also be propagated and applied to s'. When compared with some existing policy propagation mechanisms (Javanmardi et al., 2006), the propagation of the type of policies we proposed is more complicated as the authorizations are here associated with sets of instance resources defined via views instead of explicitly specified individual instances. In addition, one view can be a "constrained" (to be more formally defined later) version of another one. Also, we can have views containing instances in common. How to propagate policies among such "overlapping" views is non-trivial due to the potential policy conflicts and thus the need to resolve the conflicts. In the remaining part of this subsection, we define formally the notion of constrained views. In the next section, we describe how the detection and resolution of conflicting policies caused by "overlapping" views can be handled.

Definition 3. Given views v and v', v' is a constrained view of v, denoted as $v' \preceq v$, if and only if the set of tuples defined by v'

(1) is equivalent to that defined by v, or
(2) is a subset of that defined by v, and/or the element set of each tuple in v' is a subset of the counterpart in v.

Lemma 1. Given views v and v', $v' \preceq v$ if one of the following holds:

(1) $body(v') = body(v)$ and $head\_variable(v') \subseteq head\_variable(v)$
(2) $head\_variable(v') = head\_variable(v)$, all members in $body(v)$ also appear in $body(v')$, and $body(v')$ contains additional constraint expressions which do not appear in $body(v)$.
(3) $head\_variable(v')=head\_variable(v)$, members in $body(v')$ and $body(v)$ are equivalent except that there exists either (1) one concept $c'(x)$ in $body(v')$ which is a subclass of its counterpart in $body(v)$, or (2) one role $r'(x,y)$ in $body(v')$ which is a subproperty of its counterpart in $body(v)$.

Proof. Let R be the set of tuples defined by v. For condition (1) where $body(v') = body(v)$ and $head\_variable(v') \subseteq head\_variable(v)$, the set of tuples defined by view v' will become $R' =\pi_{head\_variable(v')}(R)$ where π denotes a project operation. Then, it is easy to show that the element set of tuples in

R' is a subset of that in R, and thus $v' \preceq v$ (by definition). For condition (2) where $body(v')$ contains more constraints than $body(v)$, R' will be a subset of R and thus $v' \preceq v$ (by definition). For condition (3) with $body(v')$ containing $c'(x) \subseteq c(x)$ or $r'(x,y) \subseteq r(x,y)$, again R' will be a subset of R which completes the proof. ∎

Lemma 2. "$\preceq$" is a transitive relation, i.e., $v'' \preceq v$ if $v' \preceq v$ and $v'' \preceq v'$ hold.

Proof. Let the sets of tuples defined by v, v' and v'' be R, R' and R'' respectively. If $v' \preceq v$ and $v'' \preceq v'$ hold, one can derive that $R'=\pi\sigma(R)$ and $R''=\pi'\sigma'(R')$ where π and π' correspond to some project operations and σ, σ' corresponding to some select operations. Then, it can easily be shown that $R'' =\pi'\sigma'(\pi\sigma(R)) =\pi''\sigma''(R)$ for some π'' and σ'', which completes the proof. ∎

As the resources associated with view v' are always associated with view v if $v' \preceq v$, the authority of subject s on view v can be propagated to s as its authority on view v'. So the authority propagation for our policies can be refined as: Given a policy $<s,v,sign>$, a new policy $<s,v',sign>$ can be derived if $v' \preceq v$.

The followings are some view examples derived based on the weapon ontology as depicted in Figure 1:

$v_4(x) \leftarrow Missile(x), Carry(x,y), SpecialBomb(y)$

$v_5(x,y) \leftarrow Missile(x), Carry(x,y), SpecialBomb(y)$

$v_6(x,y) \leftarrow Missile(x), Carry(x,y), BiologicalBomb(y)$

$v_7(x,y) \leftarrow Missile(x), Carry(x,y), Biological-Bomb(y), HasRange(x,z), z>3000$

Figure 2. Policy conflicts are caused when a positively and negatively authorized policies overlap

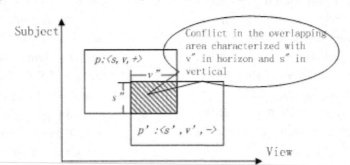

Based on Lemma 1, one can easily derive that $v_4 \preceq v_5$, $v_6 \preceq v_5$ and $v_7 \preceq v_6$. Also, one can also derive that $v_7 \preceq v_5$ based on Lemma 2. In addition, given a policy $<s,v_5,sign>$, new policies $<s,v_4,sign>$, $<s,v_6,sign>$ and $<s,v_7,sign>$ can be derived. The only difference between v_4 and v_5 is the absence of variable y in the head of v_4. As $<s,v_5,sign>$ grants/denies subject s the permission to both instance variables x and y in v_5, same authorization rights should be granted to s for variable x in v_4 too.

3.3 Policy Conflict Resolution

Policy conflicts arise when there are policies which assert conflicting authorizations (permission and denial) for a subject to have access to identical resources at the same time.

Definition 4. Two policies are conflicting if one grants and the other denies permission for a subject s to have access to some resource u.

Lemma 3. Policies $p\,(<s,v,+>)$ and $p\,'\,(<s',v',->)$ are conflicting if there exist subject $s\,''$ and non-empty view $v\,''$ such that $s\,'' \leq s$, $v\,'' \preceq v$ and $s\,'' \leq s'$, $v\,'' \preceq v'$. (see Figure 2 for an illustration)

Proof. If $s\,'' \leq s$, $v\,'' \preceq v$, all instances of $s\,''$ are also instances of s and the tuple set defined by $v\,''$ is the subset defined by v. So, policy p $(<s,v,+>)$ should be propagated to $s\,''$ for granting it access to resources of $v\,''$. By the

same argument, $p\,'(<s',v',->)$ will deny subject $s\,''$ to gain access to resource of $v\,''$. So, two policies $p(<s,v,+>)$ and $p\,'(<s',v',->)$ are conflicting.

For instance, according to the previously described example, policy p_2 grants subject s the permission to gain access to resources about missiles carrying biological bombs. Meanwhile, policy p_3 denies subject s to have access to resources about missiles carrying special bombs with their range over 3000 miles. Via propagation of p_3, subject s should be denied to have access to resources about the missiles carrying biological bombs (a subclass of special bombs) with their range over 3000 miles.

To resolve policy conflicts, some meta-policy rules based on priority or additional knowledge are normally required so as to determine which one prevails in the overlapped area. Then, the prevailing policy is reserved for the authority definition of the overlapped area, and the non-overlapping areas should be "split" and covered by several new policies revised from the originally conflicting ones. Consider the two aforementioned conflicting policies p_2 and p_3. If p_2 is chosen to grant subject s permission to gain access to the resources about missiles carrying biological bombs with their range over 3000 miles, p_3 should be revised and split into two policies with the help of policy propagation as follows:

p_3': $<s, v_3, ->, v_3(x) \leftarrow$ *Missile(x), Carry(x,y),*
ChemicalBomb(y), HasRange(x,z), z>3000

p_3'': $<s, v_3, ->, v_3(x) \leftarrow$ *Missile(x), Carry(x,y),*
NuclearBomb(y), HasRange(x,z), z>3000

Policies p_3' and p_3'' cover the range of policy p_3 except the overlapping range of p_2 and p_3 as the concept "Special Bomb" in Figure 1 is a union of the concepts "Chemical Bomb", "Biological Bomb" and "Nuclear Bomb". Alternatively, if p_3 is chosen to deny subject *s* to have access to the overlapping area, policy p_2 should be revised to a new policy p_2', given as:

p_2': $<s, v_2, +>, v_2(x,y) \leftarrow$ *Missile(x), Carry(x,y),*
BiologicalBomb(y), HasRange(x,z), z≤3000.

It restricts the permission of subject *s* to have access to resources about missiles whose ranges are *within* 3000 miles to avoid conflicts with policy p_3.

3.4 Access Decision for Policies

Even after we have propagated policy authorizations and resolved policy conflicts, there still exists the possibility that access rights of some subjects on some resources are neither declared as permitted nor denied according to the policies. Jajodia et al. (2001) mentioned two well-known decision mechanisms called "Open" and "Close". Regarding whether subject *s* can gain access to resource *u*, we consider a policy $<s',v,\pm>$ to be *applicable* if *u* is included in the resources that can be found in view *v* and $s \leq s'$. *Open and close decisions* can then be defined as follow:

Open Decision: The access of subject *s* to resource *u* is denied only if a negatively authorized policy $<s',v,->$ is applicable, or allowed otherwise.

Close Decision: The access of subject *s* to resource *u* is allowed only if a positively

authorized policy $<s',v,+>$ is applicable, or denied otherwise.

Without any policy conflict, the difference between Open and Close decision mechanisms lies on the access rights of subject *s* to resource *u* which is neither allowed nor denied by any positive or negative authorization policies. For Open (Close) decision, all the unspecified will be granted (denied) access. In other words, positive (negative) authorization policies need not be taken into consideration for access control under Open (Close) decision mechanism as shown in Figure 3. The access is denied (allowed) only when a negative (positive) authorization policy can be applied.

Different from open decision and close decision, there also exist some possibilities for making access decisions where both positively authorized policies and negatively authorized policies are considered together. For example, we can have:

Access Priority Decision: If a positively authorized policy $<s',v,+>$ is applicable **then** the access of subject *s* to resource *u* is allowed, **else if** a negatively authorized policy $<s',v,->$ is applicable **then** this access is denied, **else** this access is allowed.

Deny Priority Decision: If a negatively authorized policy $<s',v,->$ is applicable **then** the access of subject *s* to resource *u* is denied, **else if** a positively authorized policy $<s',v,+>$ is applicable **then** this access is allowed, **else** this access is denied.

As the access is allowed by default for access priority decision when there exist no policies applicable, it can be derived that access priority decision will become the same as open decision. By a similar argument, deny priority decision will become equivalent to close decision. This, however, is only true if there exist no conflicts among the policies. If the policy conflicts are

Figure 3. The scopes of access permitted or denied under different decision mechanisms. The access requests falling in the shaded areas are permitted, or denied otherwise.

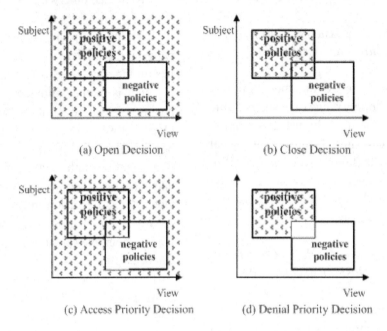

(a) Open Decision

(b) Close Decision

(c) Access Priority Decision

(d) Denial Priority Decision

not resolved and the access falls onto the area of policy conflicts, the positively authorized policy prevails to allow it under access priority decision while it is denied under open decision; and the negatively authorized policy prevails to deny it under deny priority decision while it is allowed in close decision.

4 QUERY REWRITING FOR ACCESS CONTROL

Based on the declarative access control policies introduced in the previous section, we propose algorithms for rewriting queries on semantic web data so that sensitive information can be protected from unauthorized access via online services.

Definition 5. A semantic web data query Q for retrieving some targeted instance resources takes a similar form as a view (defined in Definition 2), and is defined as:

$$Q(x_1, \ldots, x_n) \leftarrow c_i(x_i), \ldots, c_j(x_j), r_k(x_{k1}, x_{k2}), \ldots, r_m(x_{m1}, x_{m2}), aps$$

where $c_i, \ldots, c_j$ and $r_k, \ldots, r_m$ are some concepts and roles defined in the underlying ontology, $c_i(x_i)$ restricts variable x_i to be assigned with only instances of concept c_i, and $r_k(x_{k1}, x_{k2})$ restricts that there should exist an r_k relation between instances of the variables x_{k1}, x_{k2}, and aps is a conjunction expression consists of additional predicates such as "=", "<", ">".

The retrieval results based on a query take the form of an n-tuple, and each of the tuples contains instances which satisfies the relationships specified in the body (i.e., the right hand side of the arrow sign) of the query. Figure 4 illustrates w tuples returned (indicated using a box with solid line borders) given a query Q, where each tuple contains n instances corresponding to the variables $x_1, \ldots, x_n$ in the head of Q. If access to the tuples t_1, t_2 and t_w in this result set should be denied except for those indicated using the box with dashed line, say, according to some policy(ies), Q is then

Figure 4. An illustration of some rewritten queries

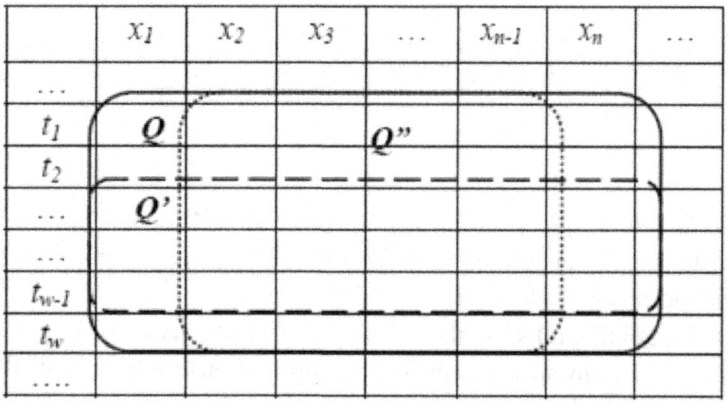

expected to be rewritten to a new Q' so as to reflect that. As previously described, the proposed policy representation also allows restriction to be imposed on variables. According to Figure 4, if x_1 and x_2 are restricted according to some policies, the resulting set of tuples will be shrunk as the box with pointed line and Q is then expected to be rewritten as Q'' to reflect that.

Definition 6. A query Q_1 is said to be **contained** by a query Q_2, denoted by $Q_1 \trianglelefteq Q_2$, if, for all resources, the tuples computed for Q_1 are tuples or reduced tuples (without some members) contained in those for Q_2. "$\trianglelefteq$" **is a** transitive relation.

It can be derived from this definition that $Q_1 \cup Q_2$ are also contained by query Q denoted by $Q_1 \cup Q_2 \trianglelefteq Q$ if $Q_1 \trianglelefteq Q$ and $Q_2 \trianglelefteq Q$.

The query rewriting algorithms to be discussed in the following are to rewrite query Q' of query Q such that the retrieval results respect but only

the query but also the access control policies, and thus the relationship $Q' \trianglelefteq Q$ should be hold.

4.1 Query Rewriting Algorithm under Close Decision

Under the close decision mechanism, only positive authorization policies are needed to be considered for access control.

As the decision for access control is close, it can be deduced from the policy e_{11} that subject s only has access to the resources about missiles whose ranges are within 3000 miles. Thus, only part of Q_1's results that meets policy e_{11} are allowed to be returned to s. One obvious solution is to add the expression "HasRange(x,z), z<3000" to Q_1's body to form Q'_1:

$$Q'_1(x) \leftarrow \text{Missile}(x), \text{HasRange}(x,z), z<3000,$$

where $Q'_1 \trianglelefteq Q_1$, meaning that Q'_1 will return a subset of Q_1's result.

Box 1. Example 1

Example 1 (Access Control: Close Decision)
Query from s: $Q_1(x) \leftarrow Missile(x)$
Policies: e_{11}: $<s, v_1, +>$, $v_1(x) \leftarrow Missile(x), HasRange(x,z), z<3000$

Box 2. Example 2

Example 2 (Access Control: Close Decision)
Query from s: $Q_2(x,y) \leftarrow$ *Missile(x), Carry(x,y), SpecialBomb(y)*
Policies: e_{21}: $<s,v_2+>$, $v_2(x) \leftarrow$ *Missile(x), HasRange(x,z), z<3000*

Compared with Example 1, query Q_2 is for (i) retrieving missile instances which are equipped with special bombs as well as (ii) retrieving the associated special bombs. As there is no policy allowing access to any special bomb (and thus nothing can be matched to the variable y), the result of Q_2 is an empty set. If we change $Q_2(x,y)$ to $Q_2(x)$, policy e_{21} becomes applicable and the variable x can be matched with the values such that "HasRange(x,z), z<3000" as that in Example 1:

$Q'_2(x) \leftarrow$ Missile(x),Carry(x,y),SpecialBomb (y), HasRange(x,z), z<3000

This kind of variable reduction is useful when one only wants to hide the value of some sensitive variables.

Query Q_3 in Example 3 is to retrieve missile instances which are equipped with "Special-Bomb". There are two positive authorization policies e_{31} and e_{32} governing the query. Policy e_{31} allows only missiles with their ranges within 3000 miles to be accessed (allowed instances for x). Policy e_{32} allows only information related to biological bombs to be accessed (allowed instances for y). With both variables x and y governed by their corresponding positive authorization policies, the query Q_3 can thus be rewritten as:

$Q'_3(x,y) \leftarrow$ Missile(x),Carry(x,y),BiologicalBo mb(y), HasRange(x,z), z<3000.

If the subject s is further restricted to access information associated with the variable x or y, Q_3 could also be rewritten as Q'_{31} and Q'_{32}, given as:

$Q'_{31}(x) \leftarrow$ Missile(x),Carry(x,y),SpecialBomb (y), HasRange(x,z), z<3000

$Q'_{32}(y) \leftarrow$ Missile(x),Carry(x,y),BiologicalBom b(y).

Example 4 gives another illustration with a query being governed by four positive authorization policies. Applicable policies include e_{41}, e_{42} and e_{44}. Policy e_{43} is not applicable as it conflicts with Q_4 in the sense that it is only related to missiles consuming "Solid Fuel" which is disjointed with "Liquid Fuel" as put in the body of Q_4. The query can thus be rewritten as the union of the following two:

$Q'_{41}(x,y) \leftarrow$ Missile(x), Consume(x,z), Carry(x,y), NuclearBomb(y), HasRange(x,w), z =Liquid Fuel, w<3000;

$Q'_{42}(x,y) \leftarrow$ Missile(x), Consume(x,z), Carry(x,y), ChemicalBomb(y), HasRange(x,w), z =Liquid Fuel, w<3000;

Box 3. Example 3

Example 3 (Access Control: Close Decision)
Query from s: $Q_3(x,y) \leftarrow$ *Missile(x),Carry(x,y),SpecialBomb(y)*
Policies: e_{31}: $<s,v_{31}+>$, $v_{31}(x) \leftarrow$ *Missile(x),HasRange(x,z), z<3000*
e_{32}: $<s,v_{32}+>$, $v_{32}(y) \leftarrow$ *BiologicalBomb(y)*

Box 4. Example 4

Example 4 (Access Control: Close Decision)
Query from s: $Q_4(x,y) \leftarrow Missile(x), Consume(x,z), Carry(x,y), SpecialBomb(y), z=Liquid\ Fuel;$
Policies:
e_{41}: $<s, v_{41}, +>$, $v_{41}(x,y) \leftarrow Missile(x), HasRange(x,w), Carry(x,y), NuclearBomb(y), w<3000;$
e_{42}: $<s, v_{42}, +>$, $v_{42}(x) \leftarrow Missile(x), Consume(x,z), HasRange(x,w), w<3000, z = Liquid\ Fuel;$
e_{43}: $<s, v_{43}, +>$, $v_{43}(x) \leftarrow Missile(x), Consume(x,z), z = Solid\ Fuel;$
e_{44}: $<s, v_{44}, +>$, $v_{44}(y) \leftarrow ChemicalBomb(y);$

$Q'_{41}(x,y)$ is derived by adding the restrictions described in policy e_{41} to Q. In particular, policy e_{41} restricts variable y to match with not all the instances of "SpecialBomb" but only those of its sub-concept "NuclearBomb", and at the same time with the additional restriction "HasRange(x,w), w<3000" satisfied. Similarly, $Q'_{42}(x,y)$ is derived by adding the restrictions in policies e_{42} and e_{44} to Q. In particular, the concept "SpecialBomb" is restricted to "ChemicalBomb" and additional restriction "HasRange(x,w), w<3000" is added.

The query rewriting process illustrated can be computationally formulated. Three main steps are needed for the rewriting. First, policies which are applicable to the query have to be identified. Then, for each applicable policy, their restriction expressions to be added to the query are computed by comparing the policy's view bodies and the query body. Lastly, different combinations of the restriction expressions are computed (with details to be provided afterwards) so that all the variables in Q's head can be covered and the query can be rewritten accordingly.

The detailed query rewriting algorithm based on the close decision mechanism is presented as follows:

```
Input
Query form s:  Q(x₁,…,xₙ)←cᵢ(xᵢ),…
,cⱼ(xⱼ),rₖ(xₖ₁, xₖ₂),…,rₘ(xₘ₁, xₘ₂),aps ;
Policy set: P
Ontology: O
Output
```

```
Rewritten query:  Q'(x₁,…,xₙ)←cᵢ(xᵢ),…
,cⱼ(xⱼ),rₖ(xₖ₁, xₖ₂),…,rₘ(xₘ₁,
xₘ₂),aps' ;
```

Process

1. Create buckets for storing restrictions of applicable policies to the query.
   For each variable in Q's head, create a bucket for storing (1) the concepts in the body of the query that the variables are associated, and (2) the restriction expressions of the applicable policies' views.[1]

2. Identify applicable policies with respect to Q.
   For each variable x in Q's head, identify its associate concepts by either locating the concept $c(x)$ directly in Q's body or locating x in one of the roles $r(x_{k1}, x_{k2})$ from which the concept of x can be deduced based on the ontological description in O. Also, apply the same concept identification step to the variables defined in the view's head of each positive authorization policy p ($<s'$, v, $+>$) in P where $s \leq s'$. Then, try to establish a semantic match between each variable, say x, in Q and those in v, and replace the label of the corresponding variable in v by x. Let this kind of semantic match between variables be Θ. In addition, ensure that there is no conflict found between the bodies of Q and the view of p so that p is identified as an applicable policy for Q; or p will be not applicable and can be ignored. With all the previous checking passed, add v to the "Views" slot of x's bucket created in Step 1 to

prepare for restriction expression extraction. In the sequel, the view's body after the variable replacement is denoted as $\Theta(body(v)))$.

3. Derive restriction expressions from the applicable policies and fill up the corresponding buckets.

   For each applicable policy identified in Step 2, compare $\Theta(body(v))$ with Q's body to derive the following two types of restrictions on Q and then add the restriction expressions to its corresponding buckets:

   a. Subsumption Restriction: The scope of each c_i (r_k) in Q should be further restricted if some sub-concept $c_{i'}$ (sub-role $r_{k'}$) is found to appear in $\Theta(body(v))$. Once identified, add the annotation "$c_i{\rightarrow}c_{i'}$"(or "$r_k{\rightarrow}r_{k'}$") in "Subsumption Restriction" column of the bucket(s) of v.

   b. Additional Restriction: After the subsumption restrictions are handled, locate the remaining expressions in $\Theta(body(v))$ that have not been matched and add them to the "Additional Restriction" column of the bucket(s) of v.

4. Collect appropriate restriction expressions from the buckets and rewrite the query by adding them to the query body.

   In the buckets, find a minimal set of views $\{v_1,...,v_u\}$ such that all variables in Q's head are covered[2]. If there exists any conflict among the restrictions covered by the minimal view, the view should be ignored and the next minimal set of views will be checked again until it is conflict-free. Then, extract all subsumption restrictions and additional restrictions from these views' buckets and rewrite Q as follow:

   a. Replace c_i or r_k in Q's body with the greatest lower bound[3] of c_i or r_k among all subsumption restrictions "$c_i{\rightarrow}c_{i'}$" or "$r_k{\rightarrow}r_{k'}$" in the buckets of the minimal view set.

   b. Add all the "Additional Restriction" expressions in the buckets of this view set to Q's body to give Q'.

   Repeat this step with different minimal sets of views to get all possible Q', and return $Q' =\cup Q'$ as the output.

5. If Step 4 fails, check if Q can be rewritten with a reduced variable set so that some results can still be obtained.

   If it is impossible to find a view set that can cover all variables in Q's head according to the buckets created, the query rewriting will not be possible. There is an option that the query system can be designed to identify some rewritten version of Q with some column(s) of the returned tuple removed. Assume that $\{x_1,...,x_w\}$ is a maximal subset of variables in Q's head where a minimal view set $\{v_1,...,v_u\}$ can be found to cover them, try to construct the body of rewriting query Q' for reduced variable set $\{x_1,...,x_w\}$ in Q's head as in Step 4.

   Repeat this step to find all such Q', and return $Q' =\cup Q'$ as the output.

6. If Step 5 still fails after all the variables being removed from Q's head, return Φ.

   According to Example 4, Q_4's head contains two variables x and y. v_{41}, v_{42} and v_{43} are related to the variable x indicating that the resources to match with are under the concept of "Missile", and v_{41} and v_{44} are related to the variable y indicating the resources to match with are under the concept of "SpecialBomb" (as shown in the second column of Table 1). v_{41} is then added to variable x's bucket with the subsumption restriction "SpecialBomb $\rightarrow$ NuclearBomb" and the additional restriction "HasRange(x,w), $w<3000$" inserted. There is no need to add v_{43} as "$z =$ Solid Fuel" in v_{43} and "$z =$ Liquid Fuel" in Q_2 conflicts with each other. View v_{41} covers also the variable y and is inserted to its buckets. In a similar manner, as v_{42} covers x and v_{44} covers y, the subsumption

Table 1. The buckets created for rewriting Q_4 in Example 4

	Concept	Views		
			Subsumption Restriction	Additional Restriction
x	Missile	v_{41}	SpecialBomb → NuclearBomb	HasRange(x,w), w<3000
		v_{42}		HasRange(x,w), w<3000
y	SpecialBomb	v_{41}	SpecialBomb → NuclearBomb	HasRange(x,w), w<3000
		v_{44}	SpecialBomb → ChemicalBomb	

and additional restrictions are added to the corresponding buckets, as shown in Table 1. For this example, there are two minimal sets of views, including $\{v_{41}\}$ and $\{v_{42}, v_{44}\}$. Rewriting Q_4 according to the restrictions from corresponding buckets of the two minimal sets of views gives Q'_{41} and Q'_{42} respectively as previously presented. The query $Q_4' = Q'_{41} \cup Q'_{42}$ is then the final output.

It is to be noticed that the idea of this algorithm comes from the bucket algorithm in the area of answering queries with views for databases surveyed by Halevy, (2001). Different from the bucket algorithm, the rewriting queries are not composed of authorized views but are obtained by adding some restrictions to the original ones according to the policies. Also, ontology specific features which are different from those of database schema, such as the "is-a" relation between concepts, are required to be considered in our algorithm.

4.2 Query Rewriting under Open Decision

In contrary to close decision, only negative authorization policies are needed to be considered for access control with open decision mechanism adopted. Query rewriting with negative authorization policies is different from that with positively authorized policies. To illustrate the differences, two more examples are shown as follow:

In Example 5, policy e_{51} denies subject s to have access to missiles with their ranges over 3000 miles. Access to the missiles with their ranges within 3000 miles is thus permitted under open decision mechanism. So, Q_5 should be rewritten as follow:

$Q'_5(x) \leftarrow$ *Missile(x), HasRange(x,z), z<3000*

In Example 6, all policies e_{61}, e_{62} and e_{63} are applicable and should be considered in rewriting Q_6. Based on policy e_{61}, information related to missiles carrying special bombs and consuming "Liquid Fuel" is NOT ALLOWED for access.

Box 5. Example 5

Example 5. (Access Control: Open Decision)
Query from *s*: $Q_5(x) \leftarrow$ *Missile(x)*
Policies: e_{51}: <*s,v_{51},->*, $v_{51}(x) \leftarrow$ *Missile(x), HasRange(x,z), z>=3000*

Box 6. Example 6

Example 6. (Access Control: Open Decision)
Query from s: $Q_6(x,y) \leftarrow Missile(x)$, $Carry(x,y)$, $SpecialBomb(y)$;
Policies: e_{61}: $<s,v_{61},->$, $v_{61}(x,y) \leftarrow Missile(x)$, $Consume(x,z)$, $Carry(x,y)$, $SpecialBomb(y)$, $z = Liquid\ Fuel$;
e_{62}: $<s,v_{62},->$, $v_{62}(x) \leftarrow Missile(x)$, $HasRange(x,w)$, $w>3000$;
e_{63}: $<s,v_{63},->$, $v_{63}(y) \leftarrow NuclearBomb(y)$;

Based on policy e_{62}, information related to missiles with their range larger than 3000 miles are NOT ALLOWED for access. Also, based on policy e_{63}, missiles carrying nuclear bombs are NOT ALLOWED. The overall set of instances whose access is NOT ALLOWED can be specified by the disjunction of the three "NOT ALLOWED" conditions. For providing access control to the query, the constraints to be directly added should be specifying the *allowable* range of instances. For this open decision case, the allowable range is formed by taking the conjunction of the negation of the restrictions derived from the negative policies. Referring to Example 6, the restriction expressions to be added to the query should be the conjunction of "missiles carrying special bombs and NOT consuming Liquid Fuel", "missiles with their range within 3000 miles", and "missiles carrying special bombs which are NOT nuclear bombs".

As "NOT nuclear bombs" can result in either "BiologicalBomb" or "ChemicalBomb" based on the ontology O, Q_6 can thus be rewritten as the union of the following:

$Q'_{61}(x,y) \leftarrow Missile(x)$, $Carry(x,y)$, $Consume(x,z)$, $HasRange(x,w)$, $BiologicalBomb(y)$, $z \neq Liquid\ fuel$; $w \leq 3000$;

$Q'_{62}(x,y) \leftarrow Missile(x)$, $Carry(x,y)$, $Consume(x,z)$, $HasRange(x,w)$, $ChemicalBomb(y)$, $z \neq Liquid\ fuel$; $w \leq 3000$;

In case no results can be obtained by the union of $Q'_{61}(x,y)$ and $Q'_{62}(x,y)$, the query can be rewritten with further restriction on the variable set in Q_6's head as follow:

$Q'_{63}(x) \leftarrow Missile(x)$, $Carry(x,y)$, $Consume(x,z)$, $HasRange(x,w)$, $SpecialBomb(y)$, $z \neq Liquid\ Fuel$; $w \leq 3000$;

$Q'_{64}(y) \leftarrow Missile(x)$, $Carry(x,y)$, $BiologicalBomb(y)$;

$Q'_{65}(y) \leftarrow Missile(x)$, $Carry(x,y)$, $ChemicalBomb(y)$;

To summarize, the query rewriting process involves three main steps for the rewriting. First, policies which are applicable to the query have to be identified. Then, for each applicable policy, compare the policies' view bodies and the query body and extract the policies' their restriction expressions which match with the query. Compute the conjunction of the negations of the restrictions, obtained based on O, for rewriting the query.

```
Input
Query form s: Q(x1,…,xn) ← ci(xi),…
,cj(xj),rk(xk1, xk2),…,rm(xm1,
xm2),aps ;
Policy set: P
Ontology: O
Output
Rewritten query Q'(x1,…
,xn')←ci'(xi'),…,cj'(xj'),rk'(xk1',
xk2'),…,rm'(xm1', xm2'),aps';
```

Process
1. Identify applicable policies and create buckets to store the corresponding restrictions. For each negative authorization policy ($<s'$, v, $->$) in P that $s \leq s'$ and for each variable x in its view's head, check if it is

semantically related to some variables in Q's head so as to identify all the applicable policies for the query Q. For each applicable policy, create a bucket to be used for storing restrictions related to its view v. Also, add the variables in Q's head being "governed" by the policy to its "Related Variables" column.

2. Match applicable policies' view bodies with the query body.

    Establish a match Θ between the view v of each applicable policy and the query Q as those in Algorithm 1.

3. *Derive restriction expressions from the applicable policies and fill up the corresponding buckets.*

    Compare $\Theta(body(v))$ with Q's body. If all concepts in $\Theta(body(v))$ are found to subsume their matched counterparts in Q's body, the policy will for sure deny all the access to instances matched to the variables in Q, and thus add "Null" to v's bucket; or else, derive the following two kinds of restrictions from $\Theta(body(v))$:

    a. Subsumption Restriction: For each c_i (or r_k) in Q with some sub-concept $c_{i'}$ (or sub-role $r_{k'}$) identified in $\Theta(body(v))$, compute based on O a set of concepts $\{c'\}$ which are subsumed by c_i and disjointed with $c_{i'}$ as its negation. For each element in $\{c'\}$, if Q's body contains c_i, add "$c_i \rightarrow c'$" to the "Restricted Concepts" column of v's bucket; or else add or "$+ c'(x)$".

    b. Additional Restriction: After the subsumption restrictions are handled, locate the remaining expressions and compute their negations based on O. Then add them to the column "Restricted Expression" of v's bucket.

4. Extract appropriate restrictions from buckets and rewrite the query accordingly

    If no "Null" exists in any bucket, rewrite Q as follow:

For each row of the buckets, choose one restriction from its "Restricted Concepts" or "Restricted Expression" columns and add it to the column "Restricted Concepts" or "Restricted Expression" in the total bucket accordingly (see Table 2). Repeat that for all the rows. Then, rewrite query Q' according to annotations as "$c \rightarrow c'$" or "$+c'(x)$" in the column "Restricted Concepts" of the total bucket by replacing c with c' or adding "$c'(x)$" in Q's body. Then, add all expressions in the column "Restricted Expression" of the total bucket to Q's body.

Repeat this step for all the possible choices of extracting the restrictions from the buckets to rewrite Q', and return $Q' = \cup Q'$ as the final rewritten query. Note that this step tries to compute an approximate of the maximally rewritten query.

5. If Step 4 fails, check if Q can be rewritten with a reduced variable set so that some results can still be obtained.

    If it fails to rewrite the query Q with all the variables in Q's head considered, find a rewritten version of Q with a reduced set of variables. In particular, remove all the variables with "Null" in their buckets, and then obtain the rewritten query Q' as Step 4 according to the buckets of the reduced variable set.

    Repeat this step to find all such Q', and return $Q' = \cup Q'$ as the output.

6. If it fails to find a rewritten query Q' when all variables are removed from Q's head, return Φ.

The buckets created for query Q_6 are shown in Table 2. As the restricted expressions resulted from applying e_{61} and e_{62} to Q_6's body are "Consume(x,z), z = Liquid fuel" and "HasRange(x,w), $w>3000$", we add their negated versions "Consume(x,z), $z \neq$ Liquid Fuel" and "HasRange(x,w), $w \leq 3000$" to v_{61} and v_{62}'s bucket respectively. As the concept "NuclearBomb" in v_{63}'s body conflicts with

Table 2. The buckets created for rewriting Q_6 in Example 6

View's Buckets			
Views	Related Variables	Restricted Concepts	Restricted Expression
e_{61}:v_{61}	x, y		Consume(x,z), $z \neq$ Liquid Fuel
e_{62}:v_{62}	x		HasRange(x,w), $w \leq 3000$
e_{63}:v_{63}	y	SpecialBomb $\rightarrow$ BiologicalBomb	
		SpecialBomb $\rightarrow$ ChemicalBomb	

Total Bucket		
	Restricted Concepts	Restricted Expression
	SpecialBomb $\rightarrow$ BiologicalBomb or SpecialBomb $\rightarrow$ ChemicalBomb	Consume(x,z),$z \neq$ Liquid Fuel HasRange(x,w), $w \leq 3000$

its super-concept "SpecialBomb" in Q_6's body, we reduce the concept "SpecialBomb" to the disjunction of "BiologicalBomb" and "ChemicalBomb" which is disjointed with "NuclearBomb" and add them to v_{63}'s bucket. The restricted expressions in v_{41} and are added to the total bucket as there exists no restriction annotation in their "Restricted Concepts" columns. Also, one of the restrictions "SpecialBomb$\rightarrow$ BiologicalBomb" and "SpecialBomb$\rightarrow$ ChemicalBomb" in v_{63}'s bucket can be added to the total bucket. The union of the two obtained rewritten queries Q'_{61} and Q'_{62} should be the final output.

Note that one crucial step for this algorithm is to compute the negation of the restrictive expressions described in the policy. To compute that using the domain ontology O, the domain experts together with the system administrator with semantic web knowledge have to work together to come up with the definition explicitly. In general, the problem of handling negation of ontology-based expression automatically in general is still open and is out of the scope of this paper.

4.3 Query Rewriting under Access Priority and Deny Priority Decisions

Access priority decision grants access if the access is allowed under either open or close decision. For deny priority decision, it grants access if the access is allowed under both open and close decisions. So, both positively authorized and negatively authorized policies should be taken into consideration, and involved in the corresponding querying rewriting algorithms.

Referring to Example 7, the rewritten query under close decision (only positive authorization policies involved) is given as:

$Q'_{71}(x,y) \leftarrow$ Missile(x),Carry(x,y),SpecialBomb (y), HasRange(x,w),$w<3000$,

and those under open decision (only negative authorization policies involved) are given as:

$Q'_{72}(x,y) \leftarrow$ Missile(x),Carry(x,y),BiologicalBomb(y), Consume(x,z), $z =$ Solid Fuel;

$Q'_{73}(x,y) \leftarrow$ Missile(x),Carry(x,y),ChemicalBomb(y), Consume(x,z), $z =$ Solid Fuel;

Box 7. Example 7

Example 7. (Access Control: Open Decision / Deny Priority Decision)
Query from *s*:
$Q_7(x,y) \leftarrow$ Missile(x), Carry(x,y), SpecialBomb(y);
Policies:
e_{71}: <*s,v,+*>, $v_{71}(x,y) \leftarrow$ Missile(x), HasRange(x,w), Carry(x,y), SpecialBomb(y), w<3000;
e_{72}: <*s,v,-*>, $v_{72}(x) \leftarrow$ Missile(x), Consume(x,z), z = Liquid Fuel;
e_{73}: <*s,v,-*>, $v_{73}(y) \leftarrow$ NuclearBomb(y);

As all of their results will be granted access under access priority decision, the rewritten query is the disjunction of them: $Q'=Q'_{71} \cup (Q'_{72} \cup Q'_{73})$. However, under deny priority decision, only the results coming from Q'_{71} and $Q'_{72} \cup Q'_{73}$ are allowed for access. So the rewriting query should be a conjunction of them: $Q'_{71} \cap (Q'_{72} \cup Q'_{73})$. The restrictions due to Q'_{71} in fact can be added into the queries Q'_{72} and Q'_{73} so that they can be rewritten as:

$Q''_{72}(x,y) \leftarrow$ Missile(x),Carry(x,y), BiologicalBomb(y), Consume(x,z), z = Solid Fuel, HasRange(x,w),w<3000;

$Q''_{73}(x,y) \leftarrow$ Missile(x),Carry(x,y), ChemicalBomb(y), Consume(x,z), z = Solid Fuel, HasRange(x,w),w<3000;

The rewritten query of Q under deny priority decision can then be obtained as $Q'= Q''_{72} \cup Q''_{73}$.

The detailed query rewriting algorithms under access/deny priority decision are provided as follow:

```
Input
Query: Q(x₁,…,xₙ) ← cᵢ(xᵢ),…
,cⱼ(xⱼ),rₖ(xₖ₁, xₖ₂),…,rₘ(xₘ₁, xₘ₂),aps ;
Policy set: P
Ontology: O
Output
Rewritten Query Q' of Q on resources
of O according to P:
Q'(x₁,…,xₙ,) ← cᵢ,(xᵢ,),…
,cⱼ,(xⱼ,),rₖ,(xₖ₁,, xₖ₂,),…,rₘ,(xₘ₁,,
xₘ₂,),aps' ;
```

Process

1. Apply the query rewriting algorithm under open decision to Q according to policy set P and obtain the rewritten query Q'_1.
2. Apply the query rewriting algorithm under close decision to Q according to policy set P and obtain the rewriting query Q'_2.
3. Output $Q' = Q'_1 \cup Q'_2$ as the result.

```
Input
Query: Q(x₁,…,xₙ) ← cᵢ(xᵢ),…
,cⱼ(xⱼ),rₖ(xₖ₁, xₖ₂),…,rₘ(xₘ₁, xₘ₂),aps ;
Policy set: P
Ontology: O
Output
Rewritten Query Q' of Q on resources
of O according to P:
Q'(x₁,…,xₙ,) ← cᵢ,(xᵢ,),…
,cⱼ,(xⱼ,),rₖ,(xₖ₁,, xₖ₂,),…,rₘ,(xₘ₁,,
xₘ₂,),aps' ;
```

Process

1. Apply the query rewriting algorithm under open decision to Q according to policy set P and obtain the rewritten query Q'_1.
2. For each Q'_{1i} in the rewritten query Q'_1 where $Q'_1 = \cup Q'_{1i}$, apply the query rewriting algorithm under close decision to the query Q'_{1i} according to policy set P and obtain the rewritten query Q'_{2i}.
3. Output $Q' = \cup Q'_{2i}$ as the result.

5. A CONCEPTUAL SYSTEM ARCHITECTURE FOR SUPPORTING POLICY-BASED ACCESS CONTROL IN THE SEMANTIC WEB

The policy-based query rewriting mechanisms described so far leverage on the Semantic Web technologies so that more flexible access control can be applied to on-line services. Figure 5 shows a conceptual system architecture illustrating how the proposed mechanisms can be deployed. Users first submit their retrieval requests to the Personal Agent service which translates the requests to queries taking the form as described in Definition 5. Before submitting the query to the Semantic Web data store, the queries should be rewritten by the Query Rewriter service which relies on the policies stored in a separate policy system which implements the query rewriting algorithms. The rewritten queries are then sent to the query agent to get the information of the resources to be retrieved, with the guarantee that all the access control polices once specified in the policy system will automatically be respected.

In order for the conceptual architecture to work, we make a few assumptions. First, we assume the ontologies which define the user concerned domain have been established, where domain experts are normally needed. Also, ontology learning methods also exist and can be integrated with Web spider to support semi-automatic ontology creation. Given the well-defined ontologies, the instance resources found in the Web can be annotated accordingly. Besides, we also assume that the access control requirements for the online resources are managed by some policy editors who have the expertise of specifying rule-based policies as what being described in this paper and should know clearly the implication of those policies. This is especially important in service-oriented environments as the deployment in principle can take effect in real time and the policies, if mis-specified, will affect all the systems which are consuming the controlled services. In general, intelligent software tools for helping the ontology and policy editors to validate their work before deployment should be of great help.

6 RELATED WORK

Policies are often used to define the authorities to access for security requirements in access control.

Figure 5. A conceptual system architecture for supporting the proposed access control model

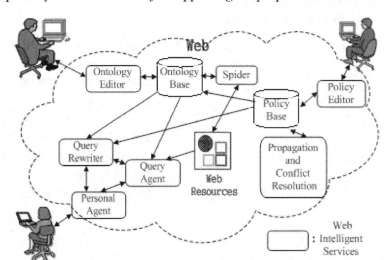

There are roughly two types of policy languages, namely role-based and rule-based.

Role-base polices are intuitive as they endow or deprive subjects of the role with the rights to access objects. For example, the policies for access control in (Jajodia, et al., 2001) are in the form of $<o,s,\pm a>$ stating whether an authorization subject s can (for "$+a$") or cannot (for "$-a$") execute an action a on an authorization object o. As the subjects and objects are organized hierarchically according to the "is-a" relation between them, the policies can be propagated among them.

Rule-based policies use rules to define the authorization under certain conditions. Rei (Kagal, et al., 2003) is one of the representative ones where a policy language based on OWL-Lite was adopted for trust and security management in a pervasive computing environment. Based on the language, access control policies for allowable actions on particular resources can be expressed as rule-like constraints. In contrast with the rule-based policies as Rei (Kagal, et al., 2003), views on instance resources are newly introduced in this work to enhance the flexibility of the access control model. To support the introduction of views, a number of policy management issues have been carefully reconsidered in this paper.

For research work related to privacy in the Semantic Web, the use of policies languages for access control has been advocated in the literature. Bonatti, et al., (2006) discussed the requirements and research issues for semantic web policies. Also, Duma, et al., (2007) compared six prominent policy languages, namely Protune, Rei, Ponder, Trust-X, KeyNote and P3P-APPEL with respect to the needs to protect sensitive data in the context of the Semantic Web, and made some observations that aspects like trust and cooperation need further advancement. Damiani, et al., (2004) extended the XACML language with RDF statements for semantic web data, with an architecture called OntoPassport proposed.

Instead of studying merely access control policies languages, there also exists work study-ing ways to control access to ontologies for the Semantic Web. For instance, Li and Atluri (2003) proposed a policy-based concept-level access control model, in which the control is for access to concept-level entities, such as classes in ontologies. Jain et al. (2006) presented an access control model of secure RDF for protecting the RDF data. Policy propagation and conflict resolution are also addressed in their paper. Jeong et al. (2007) proposed the use of databases to store the OWL ontologies and users can be controlled to have access to only part of ontologies (also called ontology views). Kaushik et al. (2005) proposed a method, in which part of the ontology was suggested to be removed, hidden or modified to protect them from illegal access. Different from security control on ontologies themselves, our work addresses the security issue of resources which are specified using ontologies. Javanmardi et al. (2006) studied policy-based protection of concepts and instances in ontologies. Our work is different by the fact that we use the notion of views to specify the objects to be protected.

Query writing with views is an effective way for implementing access control in relational databases. Halevy (2001) presented a survey on techniques for answering queries using views, in which the bucket algorithm is described. Rizvi et al. (2004) proposed techniques to rewrite SQL queries according to authorized views. Lakshmanan et al. (2006) studied query answering using views for tree pattern queries. Cautis et al. (2007) presented an XML query rewriting approach for distributed access control, in which queries are modified when they are delivered between agents. Abel et al. (2007) proposed an algorithm for rewriting *SeRQL* queries with policies. It gets all restrictions for the triples in the from-clause of the queries and adds them to the where-clause of the original queries to obtain the rewritten queries. Compared with these methods, our queries are rule-based, and our algorithm considers views covering the required on-line resources.

7 CONCLUSION AND FUTURE WORK

In this paper, we explained the importance of providing the more flexible policy-based access control in a service-oriented environment to safe-guard sensitive information embedded in Semantic Web data not to be disclosed via ontology-based query services. In particular, we presented an access control model, in which authorizations for accessing the resources are defined using rule-based policies. The notion of views on instance resources is adopted in defining policies and the corresponding policy propagation and conflict resolution issues are both addressed in this paper. For controlling sensitive information from leaking via answers to users' queries, a query rewriting approach based on the access control policies is then proposed. Queries rewritten using the proposed algorithms can have their returned results free from policy violated resources information. For future work, we will implement a prototype based on the proposed query rewriting algorithms.

ACKNOWLEDGMENT

This work is partially supported by HKBU Faculty Research Grant (FRG/07-08/II-75).

REFERENCES

Abel, F., Coi, J., Henze, N., Koesling, A. W., Krause, D., & Olmedilla, D. (2007). Enabling advanced and context-dependent access control in RDF Stores. In *Proceedings of the Sixth International Semantic Web Conference* (pp. 1-14).

Beeri, C., Levy, Y. A., & Rousset, M.-C. (1997): Rewriting queries using views in description logics. Symposium on Principles of Database Systems. In A. Mendelzon & Z. M. Özsoyoglu (Eds.), In *Proceedings of the sixteenth ACM SIGACT-SIGMOD-SIGART symposium on Principles of database systems* (pp. 99-108). New York: ACM Press.

Bertino, E., Buccafurri, F., Ferrari, E., & Rullo, P. (1999): A Logical Framework for Reasoning on Data Access Control Policies. In B. Werner (Ed.), In *Proceedings of the 12th IEEE Computer Security Foundations Workshop (CSFW-12)* (pp. 175-189). Los Alamitos, CA: IEEE Computer Society Press.

Bonatti, P. A., Duma, C., Fuchs, N., Nejdl, W., Olmedilla, D., Peer, J., et al. (2006). Semantic Web policies - A discussion of requirements and research issues. In Y. Sure, & J. Domingue (Eds.), In *Proceedings of the European Semantic Web Conference* (pp. 712-724).

Brickley, D., & Guha, R. V. (2004). *RDF Vocabulary Description Language 1.0: RDF Schema*. Retrieved from http://www.w3.org/TR/rdf-schema/

Broekstra, J., Kampman, A., & van Harmelen, F. (2002). Sesame: A generic architecture for storing and querying RDF and RDF Schema. In I. Horrocks, & J. Hendler (Eds.), *Proceedings of the First International Semantic Web Conference* (pp. 54-68). Sardinia, Italy: Springer Verlag.

Cautis, B. (2007). Distributed access control: A privacy-conscious approach. In *Proceedings of the Twelfth ACM Symposium on Access Control Models and Technologies* (pp. 61-70). New York: ACM Press.

Damiani, E., De Capitani di Vimercati, S., Fugazza, C., & Samarati, P. (2004). Extending policy languages to the Semantic Web. In *Proceedings of the International Conference on Web Engineering* (pp. 330-343).

Duma, C., Herzog, A., & Shahmehri, N. (2007). Privacy in the semantic web: What policy languages have to offer. In *Proceedings of the Eighth IEEE International Workshop on Policies for Distributed Systems and Networks* (pp. 109-118).

Halevy, A. Y. (2001). Answering queries using views: A survey. *The VLDB Journal, 10*(4), 270–294. doi:10.1007/s007780100054

Heflin, J., Hendler, J., & Luke, S. (1999). *SHOE: A knowledge representation language for internet applications.* (Tech. Rep. No. 99-71). College Park, MD: University of Maryland, Dept. of Computer Science.

Jain, A., & Farkas, C. (2006). Secure resource description framework: An access control model. In *Proceedings of the Eleventh ACM Symposium on Access Control Models and Technologies* (pp. 121-129).

Jajodia, S., Samarati, P., Sapino, M. L., & Subrahmaninan, V. S. (2001). Flexible support for multiple access control policies. *ACM Transactions on Database Systems, 26*(2), 214–260. doi:10.1145/383891.383894

Javanmardi, S., Amini, M., & Jalili, R. (2006). An access control model for protecting Semantic Web resources. In *Proceedings of the Second International Semantic Web Policy Workshop.*

Jeong, D., Jing, Y., & Baik, D.-K. (2007). Access control model based on RDB security policy for OWL ontology. In Y. Shi, et al. (Eds.), In *Proceedings of the Seventh International Conference on Computational Science* (pp. 720-727).

Kagal, L., Finin, T., & Joshi, A. (2003). A policy based approach to security for the Semantic Web. In *Proceedings of the Second International Semantic Web Conference* (pp. 402-418). New York: ACM Press.

Kaushik, S., Wijesekera, D., & Ammann, P. (2005). Policy-based dissemination of partial web-ontologies. In *Proceedings of the 2005 Workshop on Secure Web Services* (pp. 43-52).

Lakshmanan, V. S. L., Wang, H., & Zhao, Z. (2006). Answering tree pattern queries using views. In *Proceedings of the Thirty Second International Conference on Very Large Databases* (pp. 571-582).

Li, Q., & Atluri, V. (2003). Concept-level access control for the Semantic Web. In *Proceedings of the 2003 ACM Workshop on XML Security* (pp. 94-103). New York: ACM Press.

McGuinness, D. L., & van Harmelen, F. (2004). *OWL Web Ontology Language Overview.* Retrieved from http://www.w3.org/TR/owl-features/

Prud'hommeaux, E., & Seaborne, A. (2008). *SPARQL Query Language for RDF.* Retrieved from http://www.w3.org/TR/rdf-sparql-query/

Rizvi, S., Mendelzon, A., Sudarshan, S., & Roy, P. (2004). Extending query rewriting techniques for fine-grained access control. In *Proceedings of 2004 ACM SIGMOD International Conference on Management of Data* (pp. 551-562). New York: ACM Press.

Sirin, E., & Parsia, B. (2007). SPARQL-DL: SPARQL Query for OWL-DL. In *Proceedings 3rd OWL Experiences and Directions Workshop (OWLED-2007).*

Tim Berners-Lee, T., Hendler, J., & Lassila, O. (2001). The Semantic Web. *Scientific American, May.*

Wilkinson, K., Sayers, C., Kuno, H., & Reynolds, D. (2003). Efficient RDF storage and retrieval in Jena2. In *Proceeding of the First International Workshop on Semantic Web and Databases* (pp. 35-43).

ENDNOTES

[1] See Table 1 for an illustration where each row corresponds to the bucket of a variable, and the concepts and the restriction expressions are stored in two separate main columns.

2   A set of views $\{v_1,\ldots,v_u\}$ cover the variable x if x appears in the head of any view v_i in this set. The minimal set of views for covering all variables is the view set that can't cover all variables any more if any view is removed from this view set. We can use a greedy algorithm to find the minimal set of views to cover all variables. It repeats the process that adding more view to current view set if the new view set covers more variables compared to the old one until the view set covers all variables.

3   The greatest lower bound of two concepts is considered as the most general sub-concept which is subsumed by both of them, e.g., "Special Bomb" is the greatest lower bound of the concepts "Bomb" and "Special Bomb" according to the ontology shown in Figure 1.

Chapter 9
Insurance–Based Business Web Services Composition

An Liu
University of Science & Technology of China, China

Liusheng Huang
University of Science & Technology of China, China

Liu Wenyin
City University of Hong Kong, China

Qing Li
City University of Hong Kong, China

Mingjun Xiao
University of Science & Technology of China, China

ABSTRACT

As more web services that implement core functions of business are delivered to customers with service charges, an open and competitive business web services market must be established. However, the qualities of these business web services are unknown without real experiences and users are unable to make decisions on service selection. To address this problem, the authors adopt insurance into business web services composition. In this paper, the authors propose three insurance models for business web services. Based on the insurance models, the authors propose an approach to compute the expected profit of composite business web services, which can be used as a criterion for business web services composition. The insurance of business web services and the criterion for business web services composition will help service competition and boost the development of more business web services and the software industry.

INTRODUCTION

As the latest distributed computing technology and the most suitable technology for realization of service-oriented-architecture (SOA), web services have gained a lot of attention in the past few years. A web service is actually a kind of software that

DOI: 10.4018/978-1-4666-1577-9.ch009

can be described, discovered, and accessed by some XML-based specifications that include Web Service Description Language (WSDL), Universal Description, Discovery, and Integration (UDDI), and Simple Object Access Protocol (SOAP) (Curbera et al., 2002). Web services fulfill user requests in an on-demand manner and therefore can be used to realize software-as-a-service (SaaS) which is a model of software deployment whereby a provider licenses an application to customers for use as a service on demand. Gartner (2009) says that the market of SaaS will reach $9.6 billion in 2009, a 21.9 percent increase from 2008 revenue of $6.6 billion, and will show consistent growth through 2013 when worldwide SaaS revenue will total $16 billion for the enterprise application markets. Meanwhile, more and more web services that implement core functions of business will be delivered to customers with service charge and we refer to this kind of web services as business web services. For example, Amazon Simple Storage Service (Amazon S3) charges customers in United States $0.01 per 10,000 GET requests (Amazon, 2009). In the remaining parts of this paper, we also mean "business web services" when we talk about "web services", if it is not clearly specified.

It can be expected that, with the facilities of advanced web services technologies, more and more web services of various functions will be developed, deployed, published on the web and users will have more opportunities to choose among these services. The factors that may affect a user's decision on service selection include service price and quality (or quality of service, QoS). QoS is a broad concept that includes a number of non-functional properties (Sullivan et al., 2002; Menasce, 2002; Ran, 2003; Maximilien & Singh, 2004). In terms of web services, QoS may include response time, reliability, security, etc. Just like other kind of services, people have to make tradeoffs between price and quality. Some services with the same functions or qualities may ask for different prices, which may not be worthy of (or matching) their qualities. It is quite hard for a user to choose a service provider and its service from available ones (of the same or similar kinds). Actually, users may require different levels of QoS for different purposes of businesses and different QoS should deserve different prices. For those critical businesses, users usually are willing to pay a higher price for a more reliable service, and for non-critical businesses, a moderate quality with a lower price is more preferable.

To fulfill SOA promise, basic services need to be composed into new larger services which could be further composed until the composite services can accomplish the whole business requirements. From the outside world, a composite service looks like any other basic service. From the inside perspective, a composite service is a collection of tasks, each of which is carried out by a service that is either basic or composite. Generally, a number of services can be used to perform the same task, but they may have different QoS. Therefore, one important objective of service composition is to maximize (or minimize) a user-defined utility function while satisfying all QoS constraints. This actually is an NP-hard problem (Bonatti & Festa, 2005) and quite a few algorithms have been proposed to solve it (Zeng et al., 2004; Canfora et al., 2005; Berbner et al., 2006; Ardagna & Pernici, 2007; Yu et al., 2007; Alrifai & Risse, 2009).

In terms of business web services, the objective of service composition becomes more straightforward: to maximize the profit of composite services while satisfying all QoS constraints (Cheng et al., 2007). Ideally, this problem can be solved using the aforementioned service selection algorithms by assigning appropriate weights to different QoS attributes in the utility function. This is however problematic in practice due to the following reasons. First, these algorithms assume that the advertised QoS is trusty. Unfortunately, this is not the case. In fact, users are usually unable to know the qualities of services in detail before really using them. They usually get to know these services and their qualities from their providers' own reports or advertisements. No objective, third-party, independent report is currently available. Secondly, these algorithms neglect the economic losses caused by QoS degradation or buggy services. Sometimes, QoS is more critical in the success of a business since potential loss due to QoS is risky (Kokash & D'Andrea, 2007). Losses caused by services can be huge, depending on the role of services in the entire business. Similar to hardware devices and equipments, services also cannot be guaranteed technically and completely to function as expected all the time. Hence, the customers of these services are suffering some critical losses while benefiting from their functionalities. Due to the impossibility of complete testing (Liu, Jia, & Au, 2002), no matter how many time spent on service testing, we cannot test all inputs or all combinations of inputs. This even does not include the case of potential problems of the complicated Internet environment, which makes the testing more difficult. Hence, the situation of QoS degradation or buggy services is very likely to stay for a long period.

To help build trust in the market of web services and further provide support for business web services composition, we adopt insurance, a business-oriented solution, in this new computing paradigm. More specifically, we propose three insurance models for business web services. Based on the insurance model, we propose an approach to compute the expected profit of composite services, which can be used as a criterion for business web services composition.

The remainder of the paper is organized as follows. We first review some related work on QoS-aware web services composition and software insurance. Then, we present three insurance models for business web services. After that, we formally define business web services and their composition. Based on the insurance model and business service model, we detail our approach to compute expected profit of business web services composition. Finally, we draw conclusions and make some suggestions for future work.

RELATED WORK

QoS-aware web services composition has been a hot research issue recently. Various algorithms have been proposed to select services with different qualities into composition to maximize a utility function while keeping QoS constraints satisfied.

Zeng et al. (2004) consider the service selection as an integer programming (IP) problem in which the utility function is defined as a linear composition of multiple QoS attributes, including time, cost, availability, reliability, and reputation. Users have to set exact weights for these attributes and global QoS constraints according to their preferences and requirements. Ardagna and Pernici (2007) also adopt IP technique but they have a different method to eliminate loop constructs in the process of composite services.

Though IP can find the optimal solution, its time complexity is very high, so it cannot be used to solve larger problems. To overcome this shortcoming, Berbner et al. (2006) first relax the IP formulation by allowing the variable representing whether a service is selected to take any real values between 0 and 1 (in standard IP formulation, the value of the variable is either 0 or 1), then consider the real values as the possibility that a service is selected in the optimal solution, and finally use backtracking algorithm to construct a near-optimal service selection. In addition, Ye and Mounla (2008) point out that the existing solutions can be used to speed up the selection process. Specifically, if a service request is totally new, they use IP technique to get the optimal solution; otherwise, they adopt case-based reasoning (CBR) to select one from existing solutions.

Besides high time complexity, IP cannot be applied when the objective function is not a linear function. Therefore, some common optimization techniques in natural computing (Kari & Rozenberg, 2008) are introduced into QoS-aware service selection. Canfora et al. (2005) adopt genetic algorithm (GA) for service selection. They use one dimension coding schema, that is, a chromosome is represented as a one-dimension array. Their experiments show that GA has a better performance than IP especially when a composite service has a small number of tasks, each of which has a large number of candidate services. Though one dimension coding schema is simple and straightforward, it cannot effectively represent loops and alternative paths in composite services. Ma and Zhang (2008) propose a relation matrix coding schema as well as an enhanced initial population policy and an evolution policy to improve the performance of GA. Recently, Xu and Reiff-Marganiec (2008) apply immune algorithm into QoS-aware service selection. They propose some heuristic rules to accelerate the convergence. However, they do not compare their approach with existing ones. Their experiments show that their approach is better than pure IP, but they do not compare their approach with other methods such as GA.

Yu et al. (2007) propose two models for QoS-aware service selection: a combinatorial model and a graph model. The combinatorial model considers service selection as a multi-dimension multi-choice 0-1 knapsack problem. The graph model considers service selection as a multi-constraint optimal path problem. They propose a polynomial heuristic algorithm for the combinatorial model and an exponential heuristic algorithm for the graph model. Li et al. (2007) make use of the correlations among component services to prune the search space and therefore improve the selection efficiency. Alrifai and Risse (2009) propose a novel approach for QoS-aware service selection. The key idea is to decompose global QoS constraints into an optimal set of local QoS constraints by using IP technique. The satisfaction of local constraints guarantees the satisfaction of global constraints. By decomposition of global constraints, it is only necessary to conduct several local selections simultaneously, which significantly improves the performance of selection process.

However, the above algorithms cannot be applied directly into business web services composition. The reason is that the utility function is a simple combination of multiple QoS attributes and cannot reflect service providers' interests from a business viewpoint. In addition, these algorithms assume that the advertised QoS are trusty which is actually missing in the open and competitive service market. Therefore, some mechanisms are needed in the composition to take into account the losses caused by QoS degradation or buggy services.

Our solution is based on insurance. The insurance industry began in the middle of 19th century as the engineering insurance emerged with the advent of steam power (Daley, 1999). After that, it took more than one hundred years for the insurance industry to get full development. In the last half century, especially, in the last 20 years, insurance has been expanded to many new areas, e.g., medical insurance and liability insurance, and has become more and more popular in our daily lives and works. However, software, as either products or services, has constantly been out of from the policy coverage of insurance companies. As Voas (1999) pointed out, the reason is that the insurers do not have enough time to collect sufficient historical data for actuaries to estimate premium before a software product becomes obsolete. Another reason is that the intrinsic software quality is usually not guaranteed. For example, it was estimated that the well-known Y2K problem might have needed 300~600 billion dollars for the massive repair effort, which might be beyond the capability of the entire insurance industry. The high risk of software mishap has kept insurers away from this area. Only in recent years, several companies (SpamEater.Net, 2009; Voas, 1999) began to offer insurance on certain types of software/ service hazards, such as security breach. A general framework for insurance for such cyber-risks has been discussed by Gordon et al. (Gordon et al., 2003). However, the compensation is usually in fixed amounts and the coverage is too limited. Users can hardly benefit from such insurance.

Chiu et al. (2009) propose a formal quantitative model for recommendations based on utility, reputation, impression, trustworthiness, risk attitude, and persuasiveness. The model is useful for single service selection, but needs further investigation in the context of service composition as some key parameters of the model, such as the gain and loss of a composite service, cannot be obtained directly. Our work aims at establishing a quantitative model for business web services composition and therefore complements their work.

INSURANCE MODELS

Figure 1 is the working model of web services. In such a model, a web service is registered in a web service directory and its client searches from the directory, and requests the service and binds (calls) it within itself. Currently, this working model is supported by the following three core technologies: WSDL, UDDI, and SOAP. WSDL is a language that programmers can use to describe the programmatic interfaces of web services. UDDI lets web services register their characteristics with a registry so that other applications can look them up. SOAP provides the means for communication between web services and client applications.

We propose three insurance models for business web services: service provider insurance model, service user insurance model, and service agent insurance model. Figure 2 shows the relationship among stakeholders in the service provider insurance model. In this model, the service provider requests insurance for his service in total from the insurance company. Once a service user/client claims for compensation, the provider first claims and obtains the compensation from the insurance company and then pays to the service

user/client. In this case, the service charge includes the premium paid to the insurance company.

Figure 3 depicts the relationship among stakeholders in the service user insurance model. In this model, the service user/client requests insurance for this service as individual from the insurance company. The service user should claims for compensation from the insurance company directly once a loss happens. In this case, the service charge requested by the service provider can be lower since it should not include the premium. But the insurance company might need to estimate the insurance premium for each individual case of the applications of this web service.

Figure 4 illustrates the relationship among the stakeholders in the service agent insurance model. In this model, a new party, web service agent, is introduced. Unlike the above two models, web service user and web service provider do not communicate directly in the service agent model but through a web service agent. This is based on the observation that the web service user may not be familiar with the provider. When a user decides to purchase a web service, the information obtained by searching the web service directory is not enough. He would probably need to pay a lot of effort to investigate the details of the service provider and compare between different vendors. In this situation, a delegated web service agent is useful. The web service agent is supposed to be familiar with the web service market and know the advantage and disadvantage

Figure 1. The working model of web services

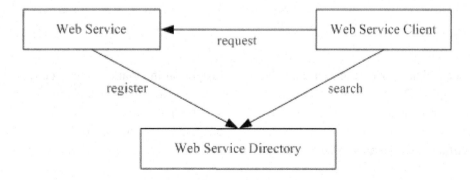

Figure 2. The service provider insurance model

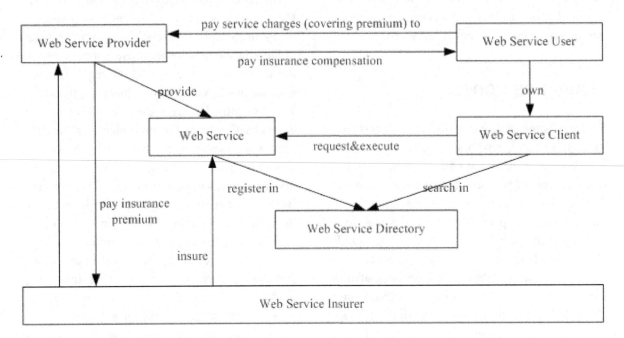

Figure 3. The service user insurance model

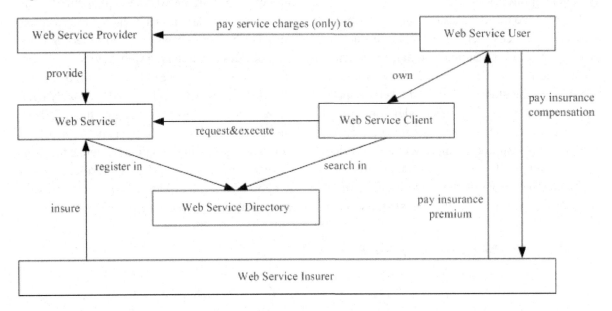

of each provider. Hence, when the user raises his requirements, the web service agent is able to provide the user with a good suggestion and specific training for the user to consume the web service. Since the web service agent has a profound insight on the market, it can better estimate the risk of using specific web service and buy the suitable insurance accordingly for the user. The process is transparent to the user. The user just needs to provide his requirements, pay the service

Figure 4. The service agent insurance model

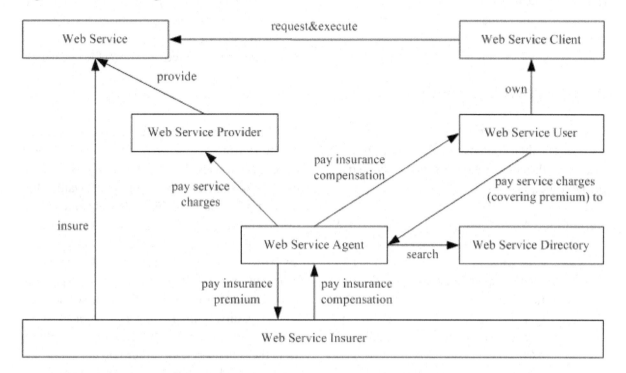

charges (which includes the premium, and service charge of web service and agent), and receive compensation from the agent if any problem occurs. In other words, the web service agent plays a role similar to the retailer between the factory and the user, and the consulting firm between the market and the client.

Each model may be suitable for certain types of services. The service provider insurance model is more suitable for those services focusing on calculation and generation of data in a core business solution. The providers of such services are responsible for the correctness, speed, and other internally responsible qualities of these services. Hence, it is the liability of service providers to buy insurance on such services. For example, a service provider can buy insurance on his security service, such as a 128-bit encryption scheme, which will need billions of years to test all the keys to break the code. Although it can also be very lucky to find the key on the first attempt, this possibility is very low (e.g., a billionth

per year in this case), and the insurance company can estimate on the premium based on this possibility

The service user insurance model is more suitable for those services focusing on communication, delivery of data, and other externally dependent functionalities. The quality of such services can hardly be controlled by the providers, e.g., the delivery of data can be delayed due to network congestion. Since the data channel is public and involves more factors and can hardly be guaranteed by few providers, users can buy insurance on such services for themselves.

The service agent model is more suitable for those large services which have plenteous budget and require high quality. Generally, in large software projects, investigation to the market to choose a suitable middleware may be crucial to the final quality and cost of the whole project. By delegating this as well as the insurance affair to a professional agent, the web service user can focus on his own affair. Furthermore, as a third party, the web service agent can provide an objective to the web service quality, which has strong influence on how much insurance that the user should buy in his optimal case.

BUSINESS WEB SERVICES

In this section, we formally define business web services and their composition in order to provide a basis for the composition criterion discussed in the next section.

Definition 1. A basic business web service *BBWS* is defined as a tuple (*F, Q, C, M, L*) where:
- ○ $F = \{op_1, op_2, ..., op_{|F|}\}$ is a set of WSDL operations that describe the function of *BBWS*.
- ○ $Q = \{q_1, q_2, ..., q_{|Q|}\}$ is a set of QoS values that describe the quality of *BBWS*.
- ○ *C* is the service charge of *BBWS*.
- ○ *M* is the premium of *BBWS*.
- ○ $L = \{l_0, l_1, ..., l_{|L|}\}$ is a set of insurance policies that stipulate the insurance compensation of *BBWS*. In particular, l_k ($0 \leq k \leq |L|$) is a tuple (e_k, p_k, c_k) specifying that the probability of event e_k is p_k and the service should pay insurance compensation c_k to users when e_k occurs.

The quality of *BBWS* contains a number of QoS attributes. Here, we introduce four representative attributes related to business web services:

- Availability (q_{av}) is the probability that a service is available.
- Reliability (q_{re}) is the probability that a service functions correctly and consistently and provides the same service quality despite system and network failures.
- Average response time (q_t) is the average delay between the time a request is sent and the time the result is received.

- Cancellation fee (q_{ca}) is the fee that a user needs to pay when he wants to abort a running service.
- Compensation fee (q_{co}) is the fee that a user needs to pay when he wants to undo the effect of a completed service.

The above two kinds of fees can be regarded as a method to improve service quality. For example, a user pays service charge to invoke a service for a complex scientific computation. While waiting for the computation result, he finds that some errors have occurred (say, the input data is wrong and the result becomes trivial), and therefore wants to abort the service execution. If the service supports cancellation and charges him only a small portion of the original price, he may think the service has a good quality. Similarly, if a user is not satisfied with the reserved goods but he can get a refund from the seller service by returning the goods, he may also think the quality of the service is good.

The insurance policy set *L* specifies lots of orthogonal events and their corresponding insurance compensation. By orthogonal, we mean that one and only one event will take place at a time. We distinguish four types of events: successful service (denoted as e_0), unavailable service (denoted as e_1), failed service (denoted as e_2), and QoS degradation (denoted as e_i ($3 \leq i \leq |L|$)). For a service user, he may observe the second type of event when he invokes the service, and the other three types of events when the service completes. Every event will take place at a certain probability, and $\sum_{i=0}^{|L|} p_i = 1$. In particular, the probabilities of e_1 and e_2 can be computed through availability and reliability, respectively. That is, we have $p_1 = 1 - q_{av}$ and $p_2 = 1 - q_{re}$. Moreover, p_i ($3 \leq i \leq |L|$) can be obtained according to service execution history. As q_{av} and q_{re} are domain-independent QoS, e_1 and e_2 are domain-independent events. On the contrary, e_i ($3 \leq i \leq |L|$) is domain-specific event, so p_i ($3 \leq i \leq |L|$) can be seen as a domain-specific QoS if necessary.

Composite services differ from basic services in internal logic. In a composite service, multiple services are invoked according to a pre-defined workflow that is typically specified by an XML-based language such as WS-BPEL. It is therefore natural to represent the workflow by a tree. Formally, we have following definitions.

Definition 2. A service composition tree *SCT* is a multi-way tree. In an *SCT*:

○   There are two types of nodes: service node (*SN*) and route node (*RN*). *SN* is always a leaf node while *RN* is always an internal node.

○   *SN* represents a web service that performs a task.

○   *RN* specifies the execution dependency among its children. Currently, four types of *RN* are considered: RN_s, RN_f, RN_c, and RN_w. For RN_s, its children are executed sequentially. For RN_f, its children can be executed simultaneously. For RN_c, only one of its children can be executed at a time. For RN_w, its children are executed repeatedly until its condition evaluates to false.

We have decided to describe the workflow only by four types of route nodes for three reasons. The first reason is because these route nodes are supported by the WS-BPEL. Specifically, RN_s, RN_f, RN_c, and RN_w correspond to the structured activities sequence, flow, switch, and while in WS-BPEL, respectively. The second reason is that these route nodes can be nested in any level to describe quite complex workflows. The last reason is that these route nodes are simple, making it easy to understand the basic idea of business web services composition

Definition 3. A service composition binary tree *SCBT* is a binary tree derived from *SCT*. Let

$\{n_1,...,n_k\}$ be the nodes of *SCT*. Let $\{n_1',...,n_k'\}$ be the nodes of the corresponding *SCBT*, where node n_k corresponds to n_k'. We have:

○   The root of *SCBT* is the root of *SCT*.

○   If n_1 is the leftmost child of n_k, n_1' is the left child of n_k'. (If n_k has no children, n_k' has no left child.)

○   If n_s is the next (immediately right) sibling of n_k, n_s' is the right child of n_k'.

It is straightforward to transform an *SCT* to an *SCBT* based on their definitions. Figure 5 shows an example *SCT* and its corresponding *SCBT*.

Definition 4. An atomic *SCBT* is a special *SCBT* that only contains two types of route nodes: RN_s and RN_f. If an *SCBT* contains RN_c or RN_w, it is non-atomic.

A remarkable property of atomic SCBT is that every service node in the tree will be executed once, and only once. This property is useful when assessing profit of composition, so we need to transform a non-atomic SCBT into several atomic SCBTs by removing the route nodes RNc and RNw in the non-atomic SCBT. Such removes need the operational profiles of route nodes, in particular, the execution probability of each child of RNc and the average (or maximal) repeating times of RNw. Generally, the operational profiles can be collected over an adequate number of different invocations of a composite service. In case operational profiles cannot be obtained due to insufficient service invocations, a human expert must provide estimated values. The transformation algorithm is shown in Figure 6. First, function RemoveRNw removes route node RNw by cloning the sub tree rooted with RNw multiple times. Then, function RemoveRNc removes route node RNc by constructing a tree for each execution possibility

Figure 5. An example SCT (a) and its corresponding SCBT (b)

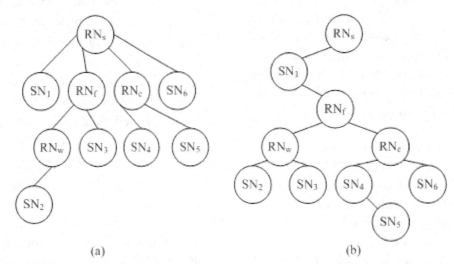

(a)   (b)

of the non-atomic SCBT. Finally, the algorithm generates more than one atomic SCBT. Consider the non-atomic SCBT in Figure 5 as an example. Suppose the average repeating times of RNw is two and the execution probability of the left child of RNc is 0.8. By applying the transformation algorithm to the tree, we can obtain two atomic SCBTs, as showed in Figure 7. Note that each atomic SCBT is associated with an execution probability, which can be computed directly from the operational profiles of route node RNc. In the above example, the left atomic SCBT and the right atomic SCBT have an execution probability of 0.8 and 0.2, respectively.

Based on the above definitions, we define composite business web services as follows:

Definition 5. A composite business web service *CBWS* is defined as a tuple (*F, Q, C, M, L, T*) where:
- ◦ *F* is a set of WSDL operations.
- ◦ *Q* is a set of QoS values.
- ◦ *C* is the service charge of *CBWS*.
- ◦ *M* is the premium of *CBWS*.
- ◦ *L* is a set of insurance policies.
- ◦ *T* is an *SCBT* that describes the workflow of *CBWS*.

PROFIT-DRIVEN BUSINESS WEB SERVICES COMPOSITION

The objective of business web services composition is to maximize the profit of composite services while satisfying all QoS constraints, Note that a composite service plays two roles in the web services market. First, it is a service consumed by some users. Meanwhile, it is a user invoking multiple services to fulfill its function. Ideally, its (expected) profit (*PR*) equals to the price being paid by users minus the total charge it has to pay the services it invokes:

$$PR = C - \sum_i C_i \qquad (1)$$

where C_i is the service charge of component services s_i.

The above formula does not consider insurance and potential losses. To overcome this shortcoming, we propose in this section an approach to compute the expected profit in order to provide a reasonable criterion for business web services composition. The details of profit computation depend on the applied insurance models, but the basic idea is similar. Therefore, we choose the

Figure 6. Tree transformation algorithm

```
GenerateBasicSCBT() {
   Queue tmpTrees, Set BasicSCBTs;
   RemoveRNw(root);
   RemoveRNc(root);
}

RemoveRNw(Node cn) {
   inOrderRRNw(cn);
}

InOrderRRNw(Node cn) {
   if (cn != null) {
      InOrderRRNw(cn.lchild);
      if (cn is RNw) {
         // For RNw, its left child is either a service node or  a route node, and its right child is always null
         p0 = cn.lchild;
         replace cn with a new node q that is RNs;
         q.lchild = p0;
         for (i = 1; i < cn.repeatTimes; i++) {
            pi = new Node(p);
            pi-1.rchild = pi ;
         }
      }
      InOrderRRNw(cn.rchild);
   }
}

RemoveRNc() {
   tmpTrees.add(root);
   while (tmpTrees is not empty) {
      Node cn = tmpTrees.remove();
      if (inOrderRRNc(cn) == true) then BasicSCBTs.add(cn);
   }
}

boolean InOrderRRNc(Node cn) {
   if (cn != null) {
      if (InOrderRRNc(cn.lchild) == false) then return false;
      else {
         if (cn is RNc) {
            // ch is the child of cn in the corresponding SCBT
            for each child ch of cn do
               construct a new tree T by replacing cn with ch;
               tmpTrees.add(T);
            endfor
            return false;
         }
         return InOrderRRNc(cn.rchild);
      }
   }
   return true;
}
```

Figure 7. Atomic SCBTs

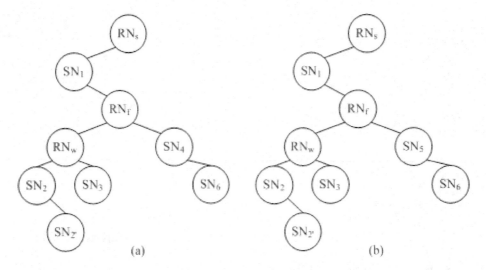

(a)   (b)

service provider insurance model to present the computation approach.

The insurance policy set of every service has defined four types of events. For a composite service, its event may be triggered by the event of its component services. Specifically, the unavailable service and failed service events of a component service will lead to the failed service event of the composite service. This is because the composite service cannot fulfill its advertised function. In addition, the QoS degradation event of a component service will not necessarily trigger the same event of the composite service. The reason is that the effect of QoS degradation of one component service may be balanced by the QoS improvement of another component service.

We first compute the expected profit of a composite service whose workflow is an atomic *SCBT*. According to the possible events, the expected profit of a composite service can be divided into four parts:

- PR_0: the expected profit that it will make when it completes with guaranteed QoS.

- PR_1: the expected profit that it will make when it is unavailable.
- PR_2: the expected profit that it will make when it fails.
- PR_3: the expected profit that it will make when it completes with degraded QoS.

Obviously, the expected profit equals to the sum of the above four parts:

$$PR = \sum_{i=0}^{3} PR_i \qquad (2)$$

We first consider PR_0. In this case, all component services are available and complete. Hence, the composite service should obtain service charge from users and pay premium to service insurers. For a component service, if it completes with guaranteed QoS, the composite service should pay service charges to it. If it completes with degraded QoS, it should pay insurance compensation to the composite service. Hence, we have:

$$PR_0 = p_0(C - M - \sum_{j}(p_{j0}C_j - \sum_{k=3}^{|L_j|} p_{jk}c_{jk})) \qquad (3)$$

We then consider PR_1. The probability that the composite service is unavailable is given by p_1. In this case, the composite service should pay premium to and obtain insurance compensation from service insurers and pay insurance compensation to users. Hence, we have:

$$PR_1 = p_1(c_{I1} - c_1) \tag{4}$$

Next, we consider PR_3. In this case, the composite service should pay premium to and obtain insurance compensation from service insurers and pay insurance compensation to users. In addition, if a component service completes with guaranteed QoS, the composite service should pay service charges to it. If it completes with degraded QoS, it should pay insurance compensation to the composite service. Hence, we have:

$$PR_3 = \sum_{i=3}^{|L|} (p_i(c_{Ii} - c_i - \sum_j (p_{j0}C_j + \sum_{k=3}^{|L_j|} p_{jk}c_{jk}))) \tag{5}$$

Finally, we consider PR_2. In this case, some component services are unavailable and some fail. To compute PR_2, we need to predict when these events will take place. In a workflow, every component service has its start time and finish time, which can be computed according to the workflow structure and the average response time of component services. As mentioned in the last section, the unavailable service event and failed service event of a component service occur at its start time and finish time, respectively. Therefore, the problem of predicting when the two types of events will occur equals to the problem of computing the start time and finish time of component services. Figure 8 shows an algorithm to compute these times on an atomic *SCBT*.

At each time t, component services may have different execution states (e.g., some services are being executed while some others have already completed). Based on the execution state, component services can be divided into five groups

- G_1: services that have not yet started at time t.
- G_2: services that start at time t.
- G_3: services that are being executed at time t.
- G_4: services that complete at time t.
- G_5: services that have been completed at time t.

We first compute the probability that unavailable service event and failed service event do not occur before time t. Clearly, services in G_3 and G_4 should be available and services in G_5 should complete. Thus, we have:

$$p(0,t) = \prod_{s_i \in G_3 \cup G_4} (1 - p_{i1}) \prod_{s_j \in G_5} (1 - p_{j1})(1 - p_{j2}) \tag{6}$$

We also compute the probability that unavailable service event and failed service event do not occur at time t. This means that services in G2 are available and services in G4 complete. Hence, we have:

$$\mathrm{Pr}_s(t) = \prod_{s_i \in G_2} (1 - p_{i1}) \prod_{s_j \in G_4} (1 - p_{j2}) \tag{7}$$

PR_2 can be divided into a set of sub parts (denoted as $PR_2(t)$) according to time t. Each sub part can be further divided into several parts (denoted as $PR_2(t, G_j)$) according to the groups. To facilitate simpler discussion, the composite service user and the composite service insurer are also considered as a special group and denoted as G_0. Following this principle, we have:

$$PR_2 = (1 - p_1) \sum_t \mathrm{Pr}_s(0,t) PR_2(t) \tag{8}$$

Figure 8. Time computation algorithm

```
TimeComputation() {
    InOrderTC(root, 0, null);
}

Time InOrderTC(Node cn, Time st, Node lrn) {
    if (cn != null) { //ST: start time; FT: finish time
        cn.ST = st;
        if (cn is SN) then cn.FT = cn.ST + q_cd(cn);
        else {
            lchDuration = InOrderTC(cn.lchild, st, cn);
            cn.FT = cn.ST + lchDuration;
        }
        if (lrn is RN_s) then rchst = cn.FT;
        else rchst = st;
        rchDuration = InOrderTC(cn.rchild, rchst, lrn);
        if (lrn is RN_s) then return cn.FT - cn.ST + rchDuration;
        else return max {cn.FT - cn.ST, rchDuration};
    }
    else return 0;
}
```

$$PR_2(t) = \sum_{i=0}^{5} PR_2(t, G_i) \qquad (9)$$

As the composite service should pay premium to and obtain insurance compensation from service insurers and should pay insurance compensation to its user when it fails, we have:

$$PR_2(t, G_0) = (c_{12} - M - c_2)(1 - \Pr_s(t)) \qquad (10)$$

As services in G_1 have not yet started at time t, no payment should be carried out, i.e.:

$$PR_2(t, G_1) = 0 \qquad (11)$$

To decrease cost spent on component services, the composite service will always try to cancel services in G_3 and G_5. Hence, we have:

$$PR_2(t, G_3) = -1 \sum_{s_i \in G_3} q_{ca}^{s_i} (1 - \Pr_s(t)) \qquad (12)$$

$$PR_2(t, G_5) = -1 \sum_{s_i \in G_5} q_{co}^{s_i} (1 - \Pr_s(t)) \qquad (13)$$

The estimation of $PR_2(t,G_2)$ and $PR_2(t,G_4)$ becomes more complex.. As the probability that two or more services are unavailable or fail simultaneously is very small, we assume that only one service will be unavailable or fail at a time. For a service in G_2, if it is unavailable, it should pay insurance compensation to the composite service. Otherwise, the composite service should pay cancellation fee to it. For a service in G_4, if it fails or completes with degraded QoS, it should pay insurance compensation to the composite service. Otherwise, the composite service should pay compensation fee to it. Therefore, we have:

$$PR_2(t, G_2) = \sum_{s_i \in G_2} p_{i1} \prod_{s_j \in G_2 - s_i} (1 - p_{j1}) \prod_{s_k \in G_4} (1 - p_{k2})(c_{i1} - \sum_{s_j \in G_2 - s_i} q_{ca}^{s_j} - \sum_{s_k \in G_4} (p_{k0} q_{co}^{s_k} - \sum_{m=3}^{|L_k|} p_{km} c_{km}))$$

$$(14)$$

$$PR_2(t, G_4) = \sum_{s_i \in G_4} p_{i2} \prod_{s_j \in G_4 - s_i} (1 - p_{j2}) \prod_{s_k \in G_2} (1 - p_{k1})(c_{i2} - \sum_{s_j \in G_4 - s_i} (p_{j0}q_{eo}^{x_j} - \sum_{m=3}^{|L_2|} p_{jm}c_{jm}) - \sum_{s_k \in G_2} q_{ea}^{x_k})$$

$$(15)$$

Up to now, we have solved the problem of computing the expected profit of a composite service whose workflow is an atomic *SCBT*. If the workflow is a non-atomic *SCBT*, we can always obtain a set of atomic *SCBTs* by applying the transformation algorithm in Figure 6. Each atomic *SCBT* can be seen as a runtime instance of the original non-atomic *SCBT*, and is associated with an execution probability α. We first compute the expect profit on each atomic *SCBT*, and then scale them using execution probability, and finally sum up them to obtain the whole expect profit:

$$PR = \sum_n \alpha_n PR_n \qquad (16)$$

CONCLUSION

In this paper, we have studied the problem of business web services composition. We have proposed three insurance models for business web services—service provider insurance, service user insurance and service agent insurance—to help build trust in the open and competitive market-place of business web services and reduce the economic losses caused by degraded QoS or buggy services. Based on the insurance models, we have proposed an approach to compute the expected profit of composite business web services, which provides a reasonable criterion for business web services composition. We believe that the insurance of business web services will help service competition and hence boost the development of more and more business web services, and the software industry at large.

From the computation process, we can learn that the expected profit is a complicated function of multiple QoS attributes which is more complex than the traditional utility function considered in existing works. Therefore, one of future directions

is to design efficient algorithms for business web services composition. Another interesting issue is to estimate premium which is assumed to be known in our current work. Actually, insurers need some mechanisms to automatically or semi-automatically set or adjust the premium so that both insurers and service providers can benefit from the business solution. Moreover, we advocate the impact of governments and legislatures on web services insurance and web service qualities. The governments' attitudes to the Y2K problem have successfully helped the world pass that time smoothly. We hope they can help again in the insurance of business web services.

ACKNOWLEDGMENT

This work is supported by the National Basic Research Fund of China ("973" Program) under Grant Nos. 2006CB303006, the Major Research Plan of the National Natural Science Foundation of China under Grant No. 90818005, the National Natural Science Foundation of China under Grant No. 60803009, the China Postdoctoral Science Foundation funded project under Grant No. 20090460732, and a Strategic Research Grant from City University of Hong Kong (Project No. 7002212).

REFERENCES

Alrifai, M., & Risse, T. (2009). Combining global optimization with local selection for efficient QoS-aware service composition. In *Proceedings of International Conference on World Wide Web (WWW)* (pp. 881-890).

Amazon. (2009). *Amazon simple storage service (Amazon S3)*. Retrieved August 1, 2009, from http://aws.amazon.com/s3/

Ardagna, D., & Pernici, B. (2007). Adaptive service composition in flexible processes. *IEEE Transactions on Software Engineering, 33*(6), 369–384. doi:10.1109/TSE.2007.1011

Berbner, R., Spahn, M., Repp, N., Heckmann, O., & Steinmetz, R. (2006). Heuristics for QoS-aware web service composition. In *Proceedings of International Conference on Web Services* (pp. 72-82).

Bonatti, P. A., & Festa, P. (2005). On optimal service selection. In *Proceedings of International Conference on World Wide Web (WWW)* (pp. 530-538).

Canfora, G., Penta, M. D., Esposito, R., & Villani, M. L. (2006). An approach for QoS-aware service composition based on genetic algorithms. In *Proceedings of International Conference on Genetic and Evolutionary Computation (GECCO)* (pp. 1069-1075).

Chan, H.-S., Chiu, D. K. W., Hung, P. C. K., & Leung, H. F. (2005). Credibility relationship management in a web service integration environment. In *Proceedings of ICIS Workshop on e-Business*.

Cheng, S., Chang, C. K., Zhang, L.-J., & Kim, T.-H. (2007). Towards competitive web services market. In *Proceedings of IEEE International Workshop on Future Trends of Distributed Computing Systems (FTDCS)* (pp. 213-219).

Chiu, D. K. W., Leung, H.-F., & Lam, K.-M. (2009). On the making of service recommendations: An action theory based on utility, reputation, and risk attitude. *Expert Systems with Applications, 36*(2), 3293–3301. doi:10.1016/j.eswa.2008.01.055

Curbera, F., Duftler, M. J., Khalaf, R., Nagy, W., Mukhi, N., & Weerawarana, S. (2002). Unraveling the web services web: an introduction to SOAP, WSDL, and UDDI. *IEEE Internet Computing, 6*(2), 86–93. doi:10.1109/4236.991449

Daley, A. (1999). Towards safer electrical installations: The insurer's view. In *Proceedings of IEEE Colloquium on toward safer electrical installations - learning the lessons* (pp. 1-6).

Gartner. (2009). *Gartner says worldwide SaaS revenue to grow 22 percent in 2009.* Retrieved August 1, 2009, from http://www.gartner.com/it/page.jsp?id=968412

Gordon, L. A., Loeb, M. P., & Sohail, T. (2003). A framework for insurance for cyber-risk management. *Communications of the ACM, 46*(3), 81–85. doi:10.1145/636772.636774

Jordan, D., & Evdemon, J. (2007). *Web services business process execution language version 2.0.* Retrieved May 31, 2009, from http://docs.oasis-open.org/wsbpel/2.0/OS/wsbpel-v2.0-OS.html

Kari, L., & Rozenberg, G. (2008). The many facets of natural computing. *Communications of the ACM, 51*(10), 72–83. doi:10.1145/1400181.1400200

Kokash, N., & D'Andrea, V. (2007). Evaluating quality of web services: a risk-driven approach. In *Proceedings of International Conference on Business Information Systems (BIS)* (pp. 180-194).

Li, L., Wei, J., & Huang, T. (2007). High performance approach for Multi-QoS constrained web services selection. In *Proceedings of International Conference on Service Oriented Computing (IC-SOC)* (pp. 283-294).

Liu, W., Jia, W., & Au, P. O. (2002). Add exception notification mechanism to web services. In *Proceedings of International Conference on Algorithms & Architectures for Parallel Processing (ICA3PP)* (pp. 483-488).

Ma, Y., & Zhang, C. (2008). Quick convergence of genetic algorithm for QoS-Driven web service selection. *Computer Networks, 52*(5), 1093–1104. doi:10.1016/j.comnet.2007.12.003

Maximilien, E. M., & Singh, M. P. (2004). A framework and ontology for dynamic web services selection. *IEEE Internet Computing, 8*(5), 84–93. doi:10.1109/MIC.2004.27

Menasce, D. A. (2002). QoS issues in web services. *IEEE Internet Computing, 6*(6), 72–75. doi:10.1109/MIC.2002.1067740

O'Sullivan, J., Edmond, D., & Hofstede, A. T. (2002). What's in a service? Towards accurate description of non-functional service properties. *Distributed and Parallel Databases, 12,* 117–133. doi:10.1023/A:1016547000822

Ran, S. (2003). A model for web services discovery with QoS. *ACM SIGecom Exchanges, 4*(1), 1–10. doi:10.1145/844357.844360

SpamEater. Net. (2009). *Home.* Retrieved August 1, 2009, from http://www.spameater.net

Voas, J. (1999). The cold realities of software insurance. *IT Professional, 1*(1), 71–72. doi:10.1109/6294.774795

Xu, J., & Reiff-Marganiec, S. (2008). Towards heuristic web services composition using immune algorithm. In *Proceedings of IEEE International Conference on Web Services (ICWS)* (pp. 238-245).

Ye, X., & Mounla, R. (2008). A hybrid approach to QoS-aware service composition. In *Proceedings of IEEE International Conference on Web Services (ICWS)* (pp. 62-69).

Yu, T., Zhang, Y., & Lin, K.-J. (2007). Efficient algorithms for web services selection with end-to-end QoS constraints. *ACM Transactions on Web, 1*(1), 1–26.

Zeng, L., Benatallah, B., Ngu, A. H. H., Dumas, M., Kalagnanam, J., & Chang, H. (2004). QoS-Aware middleware for web services composition. *IEEE Transactions on Software Engineering, 30*(5), 311–327. doi:10.1109/TSE.2004.11

This work was previously published in International Journal of Organizational and Collective Intelligence, Volume 1, Issue 2, edited by Hideyasu Sasaki, pp. 67-82, copyright 2010 by IGI Publishing (an imprint of IGI Global).

174

Chapter 10
A Social Bookmarking-Based People Search Service:
Building Communities of Practice with Collective Intelligence

Jeff J.S. Huang
National Central University, Taiwan

Jeng C.C Chen
National Central University, Taiwan

Stephen J.H. Yang
National Central University, Taiwan

Irene Y.S. Li
National Central University, Taiwan

Indy Y.T. Hsiao
National Central University, Taiwan

ABSTRACT

The emergence of Web 2.0 has brought along the trend of community. It is also the trend that contributes to socialization of the Internet. The essence of Web 2.0 is creation and sharing which give rise to social networking communities such as Blog, Wikipedia and Facebook. Through Wikipedia, Blogs, Facebook and other kinds of social networking websites, interactive relationship and bridge of knowledge sharing have been built up successfully. This paper attempts to propose an effective way to locate people with shared interests. By using Internet resources bookmarked by the users, the similarity of interests between them can be analyzed. Based on this relationship, people could build communities. Also, through community activities, the innovation and exchange of collective intelligence are accomplished.

INTRODUCTION

The emergence of Web 2.0 not only accelerates the development of diverse communities but also promotes socialization of the Internet. Lots of social software is created along with Web 2.0.

DOI: 10.4018/978-1-4666-1577-9.ch010

The socialization of the Internet has become powerful and trendy. It inspires social networking websites such as Blog, Facebook, etc. The mechanism of socialized internet improves close interpersonal relationship and provides nonverbal communication media such as multimedia audio-visual objects, images, pictures, and other diverse media. By communicating and sharing with others through the resourceful media, the interpersonal interaction becomes closer.

Furthermore, through the services of Social Software such as Blog, Wiki, Facebook, Del.icio.us, Flickr, etc., Social Networking between users is established. This social networking helps users locate people with shared interests and form CoP(Communities of Practice). Through these social platforms, collective intelligence is realized. Afterwards, people can bring different CoPs together to form CoIs (Communities of interest) which can provide unique opportunities to bring social creativity alive by transcending individual perspectives (Fischer, 2001). Accordingly, some researchers assert that Social Network mainly emphasizes building various CoP so that users can share and exchange information with each other based on their similar interests (Rachel, 2008).

Indeed, products of knowledge sharing and creating by users are mostly on a certain social platform. For example, Flicker allows users to share pictures or images and Del.icio.us allows users to share bookmarks. These products are the aggregate of collective intelligence. However, real collective intelligence should not be limited to the sharing and creating products. The most significant resources are producers of these products. As Diederich & Iofciu (2006) pointed out, "using tag-based profile can give more recommendations than standard object-based user profiles." It means that producers play an important part in forming collective intelligence. If users can find those who share the same interests with them and interact with each other, innovation of knowledge and new world would be inspired by collective intelligence. Therefore, this paper mainly focuses on finding out people of shared interests by analyzing collaborative tags. By doing so, new knowledge communities are established. On the other hand, the use of similarity algorithm and Tag Cloud inspires the power of Web 2.0 collective intelligence, leads to communities of collective intelligence, and promotes innovative thinking and creativity.

WEB SEARCH SERVICE IN PEOPLE SEARCH AND RESOURCE SEARCH

The various social networking websites can be roughly categorized into two types (Guo & Zhao, 2008). One is human-centered which refers to the websites such as MySpace, FaceBook, etc. These websites emphasize online connection between people. The so-called "connection" here refers to the interaction such as "Electronic Mail", "Chat", "Blog", etc. These kinds of interaction will leave some records. By analyzing these records, researchers will have the information that shows the interrelationship between people. Early in 1993, Schwartz et al. had made use of the interactive records of interpersonal electronic mails along with Heuristic Graph Algorithms to explore people with shared interests or other relevant resources(Schwartz & Wood. 1993). Furthermore, Adamic & Adar (2005) pointed that interpersonal relationships can be analyzed by investigating the interactive process of electronic mail. Besides, Ali-Hasan and Adamic (2007) also indicated that the interests and specialties shared among people could be identified by analyzing the interactive records between bloggers and readers.

The other type is object-centered. The representative websites are Del.icio.us, YouTube, Flickr, etc. These websites put emphasis on sharing object. Several articles have been devoted to the studies of object-centered websites. For example, Heymann et al (2008) conducted research on Del.icio.us to discuss whether social bookmarking improves web search (Heymann et al., 2008, Yanbe et al., 2007). Kato et al. (2008) also conducted research on Del.icio.us to discuss whether social tagging improves web image (Kato et al., 2008, Bustos et al., 2005). However, the studies mentioned above do not focus on the interaction between people. Thus, we attempt to analyze objects shared by people in the object-centered websites and find out the interrelationship between people. We take Del.

icio.us as our experimental object. The data extracted from Del.icio.us are analyzed to locate people with shared interests. Through this mechanism, communities of collective intelligence are established. In 2007, some relevant research conducting by well-known researchers such as Vu et al. analyzed and search people who have similar specialties by calculating similarity between documents they use on the Internet(Vu et al., 2007). Guo et al. (2005) and Sripanidkulchai (2003) investigated people's interests from peer-to-peer web resources sharing and saving. They found the interests shared by people by analyzing documents uploaded and downloaded by the users.

PEOPLE SEARCH SERVICE WITH COLLECTIVE INTELLIGENCE

"Human" is a set of knowledge or content producer. However, current search techniques are all fixed on "objects" such as the files, resources, and the specific information and knowledge documents located by Google Search. However, this search technique ignores the producers behind these resources - "human." Therefore, in this paper, "human" is considered as "intelligence resources" and the "objects" shared by these people on Del.icio.us, namely bookmarking resources, are considered as "knowledge resources." However, how can "intelligence resources" and "knowledge resources" be identified through the platforms of networking websites? Undoubtedly, this is what this paper discusses and centers on, especially the "intelligence resources." Therefore, the Internet resources tagged by collaborative tags are used as the medium to analyze the similarities between each other's interests. From this relationship, "intelligence resources" that include similar interests are located. Furthermore, through further interaction, communities of practice are established. Through community activities in these communities, in-

novation and sharing of collective intelligence are realized. On the other hand, people can find relevant "knowledge resources" they need through collaborative tags.

Moreover, there is research that centers on "human." Artiles et al. (2005) used "people name" to locate people. In this way, they solved problems of naming ambiguity and same name. They designed WePS(Web People Search)as a test platform. Users input "people names" and search relevant people rank as results on the list. Although searching by people names is helpful to find people, it is possible to lose people similar to the users. Accordingly, research of locating people of similar field by analyzing documents is conducted. Wan et al. proposed a method to search relevant "people" from relevant people-document and conducted resolution of people names to find out people of relevant field (Wan, Gao, Li, & Ding, 2005). Diederich and Iofciu (2006) proposed another method to locate people in the website. They used tag-based profiles to find people with similar interests. In terms of this, if people of similar fields can be located in social network and gather them to form CoP, through community activities, collective intelligence is realized. It will highlight the efforts of people search service. Other researchers such as Mori et al. (2008) proposed an important finding. They discovered that finding relevant people in certain fields is important to Collaborative System. Thus, they recommend a people search interface and tool which requires users to input information about those who are searched for before people search. In this way, search results of the target people can be more accurate. According to the forth mentioned relevant research, the research of using "human" as a resource in the era of Web 2.0 becomes significant. In this paper, the research emphasizes searching "human" and forming CoP.

BUILDING COP FROM COLLABORATIVE SOCIAL TAGGING

Social Interesting Sharing in Collaborative Social Tagging

Social Tagging is also known as Free tagging or Collaborative Tagging. It allows users to place tags which has the function of classification on web resources. Therefore, Harry, Valentin, & Hana (2007) claimed that "Tagging systems allow much greater malleability and adaptability in organizing information than do formal classification systems." In addition, with the rise of Web 2.0, the Threshold of classification transforms from specialist classification into direct classification by general users. This method of direct classification has been more approachable, socialized, and popularized for common users. Therefore, the Vander (2005) first coined the new term "Folksonomy" which is the combination of "Folks"and "Taxonomy." Folksonomy, a bottom-up classification, means that members in the society all participate in the classification, which could also be interpreted as "popularized classification" (Stefan, 2007).

Besides, due to the trend of Web 2.0 which drives the Internet ecology of virtual communities, the focus on the knowledge within the corporation itself was gradually shifted to emphasis on exterior resources and human resources in a way of global thinking. Thus, the interior professionals in corporations have been transferred into exterior global human resources. This global thinking contributes to the space for collective cooperation. For instance, Wikipedia is one of the successful models in collective cooperation; it not only gathers people who share the same interests or professionals from various fields to create collectively but also brings the intelligence and power of the Internet crowd into full play through social networking platforms. Therefore, the trend of interdisciplinary cooperation with collective intelligence is inspired. Moreover,

the tagging techniques of Web 2.0 have brought distinct effect on the application of collective collaboration. The techniques help people classify the sharing. For example, the social bookmarking, a kind of tagging techniques, has a distinct effect on improving searching quality. (Heymann et al., 2007) The social bookmarking provided by Del.icio.us is a good model of collective collaboration. Del.icio.us used tagging techniques to classify social bookmarkings shared by users. This mechanism provides an important foundation in connecting "learning new things" with "new members".

We especially take Del.icio.us as our study material. Del.icio.us not only provides the function for users to collect their favorite resource pages but also provides the mechanism for users to share their resource pages. For example, it provides resource pages which are more popular and are posted recently for users to refer to and collect. Besides, it provides the mechanism for users to build up personal People Network manually. Users can add people with shared interests to their People Network. However, Del.icio.us does not provide the function for users to find people with shared interests. Furthermore, Del.icio.us provides lists which are the most popular and recent resource pages. Although the lists are preferred by most people, it does not mean that everyone prefers the most popular and recent resources. There are differences in users' preference. Therefore, it is too arbitrary to conclude that the most popular resources are preferred by every user.

Building CoP Based on People Search Service

The term "Community of Practice" was first proposed by Etienne C. Wenger in 1998. He thought that community of practice was an informal group in the corporation. He also claimed that it was not an organization aiming at completing specific tasks and missions. Thus, it was different from the organized units of formal task-oriented missions. Instead, it belonged to spontaneous informal groups formed by sharing specialized knowledge and emotions. Through the social interaction and exchanges in this group, members could learn social skills, share knowledge and the process of problem-solving, and even develop innovative thinking. In this way, collective intelligence was realized.

Furthermore, Wenger made a simple definition to CoP (Communities of Practice). He said, "Communities of Practice are groups of people who share a passion for something they do and who interact regularly to learn how to do it better." (Wenger,2000). Wenger further said, "A CoP is a group of professionals who share a common interest for a domain or a specific topic." (Wenger,1998; Wenger, McDermott, & Snyder, 2002). That is, the passion of sharing and the interests of people are the driving force of CoP. Based on the passion of sharing and the interests of people, this paper used the global website of social sharing, Del.icio. us, as the experimental data set. By analyzing the resources users were interested in and the tags people placed on the resources, we could get the similarity degree between users and then formed CoP. CoP bridged their relationship through the same interest, provided motivation to one another, and developed the interactive model of new innovative collaborations.

In terms of Wenger's viewpoints, this paper tries to analyze the degree of similarity between users from the sharing mechanism of social tagging. Thus, Del.icio.us is used as the data set of this experiment. After calculating by the revised algorithm, people with similar interests are analyzed and located. The experimental platform is presented in Figure 1. Users input key words or phrases in section A for analysis of tags, resources and people. The results of analysis are displayed by names in section D. After searching and comparison, the relevant resources are listed in section B. When users click on the names listed in section D, the system will display all the information about the target group in section C.

Through this mechanism, the original static sharing is replaced by interactive sharing of dynamic communication. It realizes community ecology of collective intelligence. Owing to the communities, passive users are inspired to share actively.

SOCIAL BOOKMARKING-BASED PEOPLE SEARCH SERVICE

Applying VSM to Find Similar Interest People

Vector Space Model (VSM), first proposed by Salton in 1984(Salton et al., 1984), was originally used to categorize documents. Firstly, the related characteristic of the content of the documents was asserted, and then the representative characteristic items were extracted from each document. After that, Vector Space was transformed by these characteristic items, and used to calculate similarity. Finally, these documents were categorized by the degree of similarity. However, similarity-based method was used not only in verbal texts but also in nonverbal fields (You & Chen, 2006). As long as characteristic points related to objects were identified, and transformed into digital vector space model, similarity measurement could be conducted, such as measuring similarity between graphs (Xifeng, Philip, Jiawei, 2005), Web Page (Hou & Zhang, 2003) and so on.

The research and application of similarity have been generally adopted in many fields as a mean of computing similarity between objects. Cosine similarity-based method was first used in this field to measure similarities between contents (Salton, 1989). Through the measurement, documents could be categorized. On the other hand, some researchers used similarity-based method in searching documents. They computed the similarity between key words and the content of the documents, ordered it based on the degree of

Figure 1. Building CoP based on People Search Service

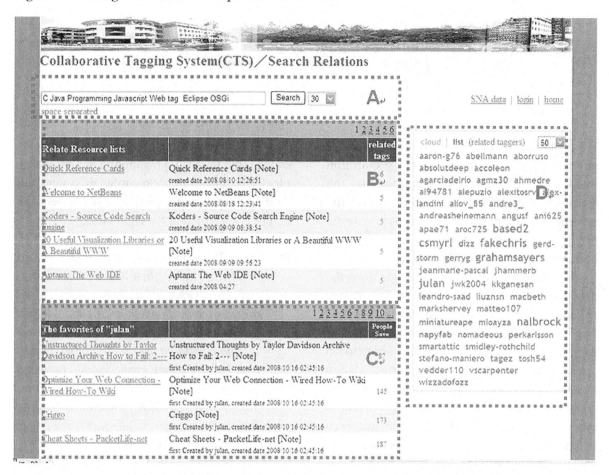

similarity, and displayed the results to the users (Yencken et al., 2008).

Cosine similarity utilizes the distance between two identical sets of base and dimension vectors to measure the angle between two context vectors (You & Chen, 2006). The value is among 0 to 1. When the angle between two vectors is smaller, the cosine value is smaller and close to 1 which means that the similarity between the two vectors is considerable. On the contrary, the similarity between the two vectors is low when the value is close to 0. For example, the assumptions in the two n-dimensional vector space, namely a and b, respectively, the vector [a1, a2, ..., an] and [b1, b2, ..., bn], then a and b cosine similarity degree in mathematics as follows:

$$Sim(a,b) = \cos ine\theta = \frac{a \bullet b}{|a||b|} = \frac{\sum_{i=1}^{n} a_i * b_i}{\sqrt{\sum_{i=1}^{n} a_i^2} * \sqrt{\sum_{j=1}^{n} b_j^2}}$$

Basically, users are interested in the topic of tag made by the users. If a user use a tag to note the number of network resources several times that means the users are interested in the topic. On the other hand, they note few times that means the users are less interested in the topic. For example, an user, Jeff, places thirty tags of e-learning on Del.icio.us website and three tags of Java. Therefore, there is a possibility that Jeff is interested in e-learning.

Figure 2. Tags vector set

	T1	T2	T3
User~Base~	R1,R2	R1,R3,R5,R7,R9	R2,R4,R6,R8
User1	R1	R1,R3,R9	R2,R6
User2	0	R5,R7	0

	T1	T2	T3
User~Base~	2	5	4
User1	1	3	2
User2	0	2	0

We try to apply vector space model on social networking of delicious. Exploring common interests between people according to the historical data of the tags are used and the information of network resources by users. Finally, users who share the same interest become a community of practice.

The sample of this paper was based on the data from Del.icio.us. Thus, from the website, we collected three items of data including "people", "tag", and "resource". According to the relation of these three essential factors, the three-dimension space vector was constituted, and this relation meant some person could do the action that he could tag on the resources randomly. Therefore, everyone possessed the Tag Set that had been noted. That is, everyone possessed his own tag, namely the Resource Set. Accordingly, this paper defined two space vector set, Users Tags Vector Set and Tags Vector Set with common interesting resources were included.

Definition 1. *A user U places n tags labeled as t1, t2, …, tn to the resources R1, R2, …, Rm. This process is called Users Tags Vector Set with Resource. The formula of Tags vector set can be presented as T=(Rt1, Rt2, …, Rtn). Rti is the amount of tags ti user U places to the resources. N is the dimension of the vector space.*

For example, User 1, User 2 and User 3 use 3 tags, 2 tags and 1 tag respectively (see Figure 2). The Vector Spaces here are 3 dimensions. User 1 uses T1 to mark two different resources R1 and R2 (the [User$_1$,T$_1$] position in the left table). User

2 uses T2 to mark three different resources R4, R5 and R2 (the [User$_2$,T$_2$] position in the left table). Finally, the data which is recorded by system will be transformed into digital tags vector set. The output is presented in the right table.

Definition 2. *A reference user U$_B$ places n tags labeled as t1,t2, …, tn to resources R1, R2, …, Rm. The amount of tags placed by U$_B$ are the tags vector dimensions. R$_1$, R$_2$, …, R$_m$ are the resources that interest the reference user U$_B$ and compared user u$_i$. Under the condition that the reference user and the compared user place same tags to the same resources, Tags Vector Set with Common Interesting Resources is formed. The formula of Tags Vector Set with Common Interesting Resources can be presented as T=(T$_{1Ri}$, T$_{2Ri}$, …, T$_{nRi}$). T$_{iRi}$ represents the amount of same tags that are used by the reference user and compared user.*

User 1 and User 2, the compared users, use eight tags and two tags to mark resources respectively. No matter how many tags the compared users use, we take the tags used by the reference user as the base. For example, the reference user User$_{Base}$ uses three tags in Figure 3. The tags vectors here are three dimensions. User 1 and User$_{Base}$ use the same tag T1 to mark resource R1 (the [User$_1$,T$_1$] position in the left table). They use tag T2 to mark resource R1, R3 and R9. (the [User$_1$,T$_2$] position in the left table). Finally, the data which is recorded by system will be transformed into digital tags vector set. The output is presented in the right table.

Figure 3. Tags vector set with common interesting resources

	T1	T2	T3
User1	R1,R2	R3,R5	R2,R4,R6,R8
User2	R1	R4,R5,R6	0
User3	0	R2	0

	T1	T2	T3
User1	2	2	4
User2	1	3	0
User2	0	1	0

People Search Service Process based on Social Bookmarking

To put Social Community into practice, this paper was based on the social platform, Del.icio. us, to collect the experimental data. In figure 4, we designed Web Crawler to collect data, and then obtain users' behavior data through analyzing and extracting mechanism. These behavior data including the three related essential factors, "people", "tags" and "resources", formed the Data Set of User Tagging Behavior Profile. Finally, the people similar to the users would be found by the formula for calculating similarity we amended, and the partners could be accommodated to the loginers. That is, once the users login into the system, the system will automatically show the people having the similar interests to the users by people clouds.

Furthermore, the system provides a community multiple dimensions of practice, and the community multiple dimensions of practice is composed of multi-interest or professional searching inputted by users. For example, when users input three key words, C++, Java, and ASP, the system will find partners concurrently satisfy these three interests, and show them to users by People Clouds.

After we collected data from Del.icio.us, we used the following algorithm to find people with similar interests. The algorithm was as follows:

Algorithm for Similar People Search
Require: User tagging behavior profile
Data set:from Del.icio.us
1:    Read the User tagging behavior profile

2:    behavior profile Convert to Users Tags vector set with resource
3:    behavior profile Convert to Tags Vector Set with Common interesting resources
4:    **for** all Users Tags vector with resource **do**
5:    Calculate *sima(Ub,Ui)*
6:    **end for**
7:    **for** all Tags Vector Set with Common interesting resources **do**
8:    Calculate *simb(Ub,Ui)*
9:    **end for**
10:   **return** Sort *sima+simb*

EXPERIMENTS AND EVALUATION

The experiment's data were retrieved from the Del.icio.us for the experiment data set. This data set contained three related elements including people, tags and resources. To find users sharing similar interests and to recommend to the loginers of the system from importing Cosine similarity algorithm. Furthermore, to find who share similar interests from verifying the algorithms that is having high accuracy. Therefore, the control group in this experiment using the FCA (formal concept analysis) algorithm to compare and verification.

The data were collected from April, 2008 to October, 2008. It took approximately half a year. In this period, the system continuously collected experimental data every two hours from Del.icio. us. The aggregated data were as follows:
˙Tagger:435,940 users ˙Resource:73,445 items ˙Tag:212,076 items

The limitation of this experiment was that the amount of tags marked by some taggers was too

Figure 4. People search service process

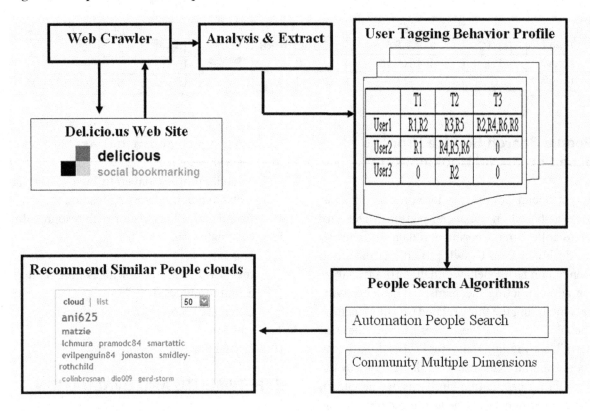

small to be taken into consideration. To make this experiment representative, we selected a tagger who marked enough tags as the "reference user" of the experiment. Then, we analyzed the data by the following steps:

1. The control group adopted the FCA algorithm to recommend people with similar interests.
2. The experimental group adopts the revised Cosine similarity algorithm to recommend people with similar interests.
3. Compare the results of step 3 and step 4, and find out the differences between the rankings listed by FCA and revised Cosine similarity algorithm.
4. Conduct the correlation analysis to the differences found in step 3, and search the database by SQL-like.

5. Use the result of step 4 as evidence. Observe and compare the results of step 1 and 2.

Quantitative Evaluation and Discuss

The experimental results are showed in figure 5. We chose Julan as the reference user. Besides, we also chose ten users whose interests were similar to Julan's as the recommended users. The users in the left table were found by the revised Cosine similarity algorithm and recommended according to the ranking. The users in the right table were found by FCA (Formal Concept Analysis) algorithm and recommended according to the ranking. When we examined the first three recommended users in these two tables, we can see that the rankings were different. We might infer that the accuracy of these two algorithms was different. In the remaining section, we will discuss the accuracy of these algorithms. We will further prove

Figure 5. Our approach and FCA algorithm for people search ranking

Our Ranking	Top 10 Taggers	Similar with Julan Score	FCA Ranking	Top 10 Taggers	Similar with Julan tags number
1.	ani625	131.078	1.	smartattic	577
2.	smartattic	103.954	2.	matzie	543
3.	matzie	90.073	3.	ani625	506
4.	lchmura	68.854	4.	agiletimes	479
5.	pramodc84	63.400	5.	pramodc84	447
6.	smidley-rothchild	53.605	6.	netsuke	430
7.	evilpenguin84	46.508	7.	tewfiq	428
8.	JonAston	42.225	8.	smidley-rothchild	425
9.	agiletimes	40.612	9.	colinbrosnan	418
10.	colinbrosnan	37.954	10.	JonAston	400

that the revised Cosine similarity algorithm is more accurate.

The FCA algorithm only uses the amount of same tags to analyze the similarity value between the reference user and the recommended users. From figure 5, we can see that smartattic and Julan have 577 identical tags while ani625 and Julan have 506 identical tags. By using FCA algorithm, smartattic is the first recommended users in the ranking and ani625 the second. The ranking of the rest recommended users are showed in the right table.

The revised Cosine similarity algorithm not only considers the amount of same tags between the reference user and the recommended user, but also considers whether the reference user and the recommended user marked the same tags to the same resources. By using the revised Cosine similarity algorithm, we can see that the similarity value of ani625 and Julan is 131.078. Therefore, the first recommended user in the ranking is ani625. The second recommended user is smartattic. The rest recommended users are showed in the left table.

In the following section, we will compare smartattic, the first recommended user by FCA

algorithm, with ani625, the first recommended user by revised Cosine similarity algorithm. For smartattic, we adopt FCA to conduct statistical analysis. As for ani625, we use revised Cosine similarity algorithm to conduct statistical analysis. The experimental result is showed in figure 6. The x-axis represents the intervals of re-used tag numbers. The y-axis shows the degree of similarity between smartattic & Julan and ani625 & Julan (in percentage). The observations and analysis are as follows:

- FCA only uses the amount of same tags to analyze the similarity value between the reference user and the recommended user. It neglects the amount of tags that are marked repeatedly. For example, ani625 places the tag *e-learning* 21 times. However, it will be counted only once by using FCA algorithm. Thus, if some tags are used repeatedly, the similarity value calculated by FCA algorithm will not be so accurate.

- Based on the above phenomena, we use the factor "the amount of tags that are used re-

Figure 6. smartattic and ani625 for Julan similar

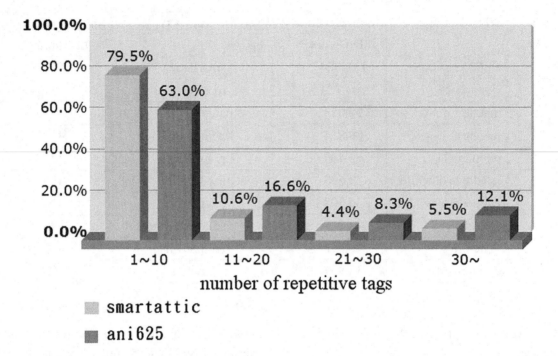

peatedly" to evaluate the accuracy of FCA and revised Cosine similarity algorithm. We divide "the amount of tags that are used repeatedly" into four intervals. The intervals are 1-10, 11-20, 21-30 and above 30.

• In figure 6, we can see clearly that by using FCA algorithm, smartattic will be the first recommended user in interval 1-10. In other words, if all of the tags are marked once and will not be used repeatedly, FCA algorithm can recommend users accurately. However, users' actual behaviors are not so limited.

• If a tag is used more than 11 times by a user, the revised Cosine similarity shows its influence on the result. The revised Cosine similarity shows higher degree of similarity than FCA. We can see from figure 6 that ani625 is the first person to be recommended in interval 11-20.

• The revised Cosine similarity has higher accuracy than FCA in interval 21-30 and interval above 30.

• We can infer from the experiment that the threshold of "tags that used repeatedly" is 11. In other words, if a user repeatedly places a tag more than 11 times, the revised Cosine similarity will have higher accuracy in recommending users.

CONCLUSION AND FUTURE WORK

This paper proposes people search algorithm to recommend people with similar interests and form a community. We analyze tags marked by users and the resources that users are interested in to find people with similar interests. People with similar interests will be the driving force to form CoP which realizes the innovation and communication of collective intelligence. Because data set of the system are extracted from Del.icio. us, there may be privacy problems. Therefore, it is hard for us to trace the subsequent interaction between users. Fortunately, we have had obvious contribution to the social networking, especially in recommending people with similar interests on the global tag-sharing data set. The platform we develop can not only find people with similar interests, but also input some interest items to find multi- profession people and form multi-dimension community. In the future, we will conduct Social knowledge mining to the community. Then, we will use Social Network Analysis to analyze the roles everyone acts, and further form the Knowledge Network.

ACKNOWLEDGMENT

This work is supported by National Science Council, Taiwan under grants NSC96-2628-S-008-008-MY3, NSC98-2511-S-008-006-MY3 and NSC98-2511-S-008-007-MY3.

REFERENCES

Adamic, L. A., & Adar, E. (2005). How to search a social network. *Social Networks*, *27*(3), 187–203. doi:10.1016/j.socnet.2005.01.007

Ali-Hasan, N., & Adamic, L. (2007). Expressing social relationships on the blog through links and comments. *In Proc. of International Conference on Weblogs and Social Media, Mar.*

Artiles, J., Gonzalo, J., & Verdejo, F. (2005). A testbed for people searching strategies in the WWW. In Proceedings of the 28th annual International ACM SIGIR conference on Research and Development in Information Retrieval (SIGIR'05), 569-570.

Bustos, B., Keim, D. A., Saupe, D., Schreck, T., & Vranic, D. V. (2005). Feature-based similarity search in 3D object databases. *ACM Computing Surveys*, 345–387. doi:10.1145/1118890.1118893

Diederich, J., & Iofciu, T. (2006). Finding communities of practice from user profiles based on folksonomies. *In Proceedings of the 1st International Workshop on Building Technology Enhanced Learning Solutions for Communities of Practice.*

Ehrlich, K., Lin, C. Y., & Griffiths-Fisher, V. (2007). Searching for experts in the enterprise: Combining text and social network analysis. *Group, 07*, 117–126.

Fischer, G. (2001). Communities of interest: Learning through the interaction of multiple knowledge systems, *The 24th IRIS Conference*, Bergen, Norway, 1-14.

Guo, L., Jiang, S., Xiao, L., & Zhang, X. (2005). Fast and low-cost search schemes by exploiting localities in p2p networks. *Journal of Parallel and Distributed Computing, 65*(6), 729–742. doi:10.1016/j.jpdc.2005.01.007

Halpin, H., Robu, V., & Shepherd, H. (2007). The complex dynamics of collaborative tagging, *in Proceedings of the 16th International Conference on World Wide Web*, 211–220, New York, USA. ACM Press.

Hasan, A. N., & Adamic, L. (2007). Expressing social relationships on the blog through links and comments. *In Proc. of International Conference on Weblogs and Social Media*, Mar.

Heymann, P., Koutrika, G., & Garcia-Molina, H. (2008). Can social bookmarking improve web search? *In Proceedings of WSDM'2008.* ACM, 195-206.

Hou, J., & Zhang, Y. (2003). Utilizing Hyperlink Transitivity to Improve Web Page Clustering, in Klaus Dieter-Schewe (ed.), Database Technologies 2003: Proceedings of the Fourteenth Australasian Database Conference. *Conferences in Research and Practice in Information Technology*, 49-57, Australian Computer Society Inc., Australia.

Mori, J., Basselin, N., Kroner, A., & Jameson, A. (2008). Find me if you can: designing interfaces for people search. *In Proceedings of IUI*. 2008, 377-380.

Rachel, P. (2008). Communities of practice: using the open web as a collaborative learning platform, *iLearning Forum 2008 Proceedings*, Paris.

Salton, G. (1989). *Automatic text processing: the transformation, analysis, and retrieval of information by computer*. Boston, MA: Addison-Wesley Longman Publishing Co., Inc.

Salton, G., & McGill, M. J. (1984). *Introduction to Modern Information Retrieval*. McGraw-Hill.

Schwartz, M. F., & Wood, D. C. M. (1993). Discovering shared interests among people using graph analysis of global electronic mail traffic. *Communications of the ACM, 36*(8), 78–89. doi:10.1145/163381.163402

Schwartz, M. F., & Wood, D. C. M. (1993). Discovering shared interests using graph analysis. *Communications of the ACM, 36*(8), 78–89. doi:10.1145/163381.163402

Sripanidkulchai, K., Maggs, B., & Zhang, H. (2003). Efficient content location using interest-based locality in peer-to-peer systems. *In Proc. of INFOCOMM*, Mar.

Vander, W. T. (2005). Explaining and showing broad and narrow folksonomies. http://www.personalinfocloud.com/2005/02/explaining_and_.html.

Vu, Q. M., Masada, T., Takasu, A., & Adachi, J. (2007). Disambiguation of people in web search using a knowledge base. *In Proceedings of International Conference on Research, Innovation & Vision for the Future Information & Communication Technologies (IEEE RIVF'07)*, 185-191.

Wan, X., Gao, J., Li, M., & Ding, B. (2005). Person resolution in person search results: Webhawk. *In CIKM '05: Proceedings of the 14th ACM international conference on Information and knowledge management*, 163-170, New York, USA, ACM Press.

Wenger, E. (1998). *Communities of practice: Learning, meaning, and identity*. Cambridge University Press.

Wenger, E. and Snyder, Williams. (2000). Communities of practice: the organizational frontier. *Harvard Business Review*, (January-February): 139–145.

Wenger, E., McDermott, R., & Snyder, W. M. (2002). *Cultivating communities of practice*. Harvard Business School Press.

Yan, X., Yu, P. S., & Han, J. (2005). Substructure similarity search in graph databases. *SIGMOD Conference 2005*, 766-777.

Yanbe, Y., Jatowt, A., Nakamura, S., & Tanaka, K. (2007) Can social bookmarking enhance search in the web? *In Proceedings of JCDL'2007*. 107-116

Yencken, L., & Baldwin, T. (2008). Orthographic similarity search for dictionary lookup of Japanese words, *In Proc. of the 22nd International Conference on Computational Linguistics* (COLING 2008), Manchester, UK.

You, J. M., & Chen, K. J. (2006). Improving context vector models by feature clustering for automatic thesaurus construction. *Proceedings of the Fifth SIGHAN Workshop on Chinese Language Processing*.

Yu, B., & Singh, M. P. (2003). Searching social networks. *AAMAS, 2003*, 65–72.

This work was previously published in International Journal of Organizational and Collective Intelligence, Volume 1, Issue 2, edited by Hideyasu Sasaki, pp. 83-95, copyright 2010 by IGI Publishing (an imprint of IGI Global).

Chapter 11
Architectures for Enabling Flexible Business Processes:
A Research Agenda

Sietse Overbeek
Delft University of Technology, The Netherlands

Yiwei Gong
Delft University of Technology, The Netherlands

Marijn Janssen
Delft University of Technology, The Netherlands

ABSTRACT

For decades, information systems have been designed for controlling and managing business processes. In the past, these systems were often monolithic in nature and not made for interacting and communicating with other systems. Today, departments and organizations must collaborate, which requires distributed Web-based systems to support the enactment of flexible business processes. In this paper, four architectures of process management systems are investigated by studying the components and the relationships with the tasks that make up the business processes. These different architectures support automation of non-repetitive, customized processes, and are compared based on dimensions of flexibility. This evaluation showed that the process orchestration architecture scored best, but still has its shortcomings. The results from the comparison are used for developing a research agenda that includes the suggestion to develop reference architecture for connecting individual architectural components.

INTRODUCTION

In the early days of computing, information systems were often build as monolithics without having the need to interact with other systems. These monolithic systems also provided limited

variety and were hard to change. Over time the need to interact with other systems and the pressure to open these systems increased. Nowadays, the creation of flexible business processes has received more and more attention by organizations to remain competitive, to satisfy customer wishes and to be able to react to the competitive environment (Aalst, Benatallah, Casati, Curbera,

DOI: 10.4018/978-1-4666-1577-9.ch011

& Verbeek, 2007). Customization developments resulted in the need for the creation of demand-driven and unique business processes tailored to the specific need of customers. These are often hard to predefine in advance, as many variations are possible.

A business process can be defined as a time-dependent sequence of activities. These activities depend on each other and these dependencies need to be coordinated. The coordination of these activities is often supported by workflow management (WFM) (Georgakopoulos, Hornick, & Sheth, 1995) or business process management (BPM) systems (van der Aalst, ter Hofstede, & Weske, 2003). These types of systems have a variety of architecture often guided by the workflow reference model which is developed by the Workflow Management Coalition (WFMC, 2004). This model aims at promoting the interoperability between different WFMS. Central in the reference model is the workflow 'enactment service' that consists of one or more workflow engines. These engines execute the workflows, start new processes, select the people or applications that have to perform a task, send the necessary documents to the right people or applications, etc.

The demand on flexibility can be viewed from two complementary perspectives, which are the organizational (internal) and customer (external) perspectives. From the organizational perspective the properties of agility, adaptivity, and being able to anticipate on varying needs are important. By breaking up an organization in modular services, a new level of flexibility and agility can be reached (Cherbakov, Galambos, Harishankar, Kalyana, & Rackham, 2005). These services need to be orchestrated into a workflow, which has become an essential capability in a service-oriented enterprise (Tewoldeberhan & Janssen, 2008). The use of IT enables and improves the efficiency of business services and at the same time there should be a specific need to process the request. Furthermore, managers want to have insight in the performance of processes over time to be able to continuously improve them and they want to have insight in the current status of processes to take appropriate actions, if necessary. For example, by allocating additional resources to a task to ensure that it is finished in time.

From the customers' perspective a service provides high value if it satisfies needs like speed and convenience and provides the right answer to a request. This often requires the bundling of individual services and the handling of these services as one request, instead that a customer needs to make multiple requests. This aspect can be represented by the notion of 'value of service'. The customization trend results in the declining 'degree of repetition' of standardized business processes. Instead of having predefined business processes, a unique business process is created for each customer by determining the next step only after the previous step is completed. Consequently, whereas in the past customers were presented with a uniform process, such an approach enables customized service provisioning. Clients expect businesses to provide high quality services in a way that minimizes complexity and maximizes the users' ability to get what they need in a timely manner. In response, businesses have to integrate the service delivery to improve both service access and service quality. Therefore, dynamic and ad hoc processes are pursued by many organizations, so that flexibility stemming from various dynamic changes has become one of the major research topics in the area of today's management of business processes (Zhou & Ye, 2006).

The quest toward non-standardized, customized business processes providing high value can be characterized by the search for new architectures. IEEE defines an architecture as: *"The fundamental organization of a system embodied in its components, their relationships to each other and to the environment and the principles guiding its design and evolution"* (Architecture_Working_Group, 2000). In this paper we will explore the architecture of process management systems by looking at the components and the relationships with the tasks that make up the business processes. Four architectures are identified and described by investigating the developments within a large insurance company. The research presented in this paper compares different architectures to automate non-repetitive processes providing flexibility and uses this as an input to derive an agenda for future research. Our aim is not to copy the workflow reference model developed by the workflow management coalition (WFMC) promoting standardization of interoperability and connectivity between the various workflow management systems (WFMS) that have arisen over the years. Our main research questions are what are the differences in performance of these architectures on the flexibility dimension and what are the shortcomings. These questions should contribute to the development of a research agenda.

This paper reviews various forms of the creation of flexibility in business processes and compares them using the various dimensions of flexibility. The rest of this paper is organized as follows. First, the background on flexibility is presented. Then, a case study of business process management in an insurance company is introduced. Next, the development of four present BPM implementations is discussed and the four different BPM implementations are compared by means of flexibility dimensions. This is followed by presenting a research agenda addressing what needs to be done to achieve a BPM implementation that provides an optimum balance between the flexibility dimensions. The paper is concluded in the final section.

WHAT IS FLEXIBILITY?

The need for creating more flexibility and gaining more efficiency at the same time in the field of business process management (BPM) has gained the attention of contemporary businesses and researchers. BPM includes methods, techniques, and tools to support the design, enactment, man-

agement, and analysis of operational business processes. It can be considered as an extension of classical workflow management (WFM) approaches (van der Aalst et al., 2003). WFM is process orientated, which refers to the time-ordered sequence of activities. A workflow shows the sequence of activities to be performed and how a particular case, normally an application, should be dealt with. Besides stating how information is operationally processed, BPM also involves the consideration of what information is offered from whom to whom. Services can be used to match supply and demand of information, which brings a possibility to align the current popular Service-Oriented Architecture (SOA) thought way. SOA is a framework for integrating business processes and supporting IT infrastructure as secure, standardized components—service—that can be reused and combined to address changing business priorities (Bieberstein, Laird, Jones, & Mitra, 2008).

The notion of *flexibility* can be defined in several different ways depending on the discipline or the nature of the research (Alter, 2004). In the information system domain, flexibility is the ability to respond to changes in the environment (Li & Zhao, 2006). According to the discussion above, two meanings are implied: workflow flexibility and information source flexibility. The former requires the information system, which is the primary implementation of business processes (Georgakopoulos et al., 1995), to allow for the modification of processes with minimal change on the system itself. The latter requires information providing in a loose-coupled way.

Flexibility is a multidimensional concept and various conceptualizations can be found in the literature (Carlsson, 1989; Gosain, Malhotra, & Sawy, 2005; Tan & Sia, 2006). These dimensions include *robustness, modifiability, new capability,* and *partnering flexibility* (Tan & Sia, 2006). For this research we extend these with *accountability and reliability as these are important requirements for business processes*. The first dimension of flexibility is *robustness*, the ability to endure variations and perturbations, withstand pressure, or tolerate external changes (Tan & Sia, 2006). This relates to situations in which an organization has the built-in capacity to address uncertainty for varying levels of demand, product mix, and resource availability (Carlsson, 1989). The second dimension, *modifiability*, is the ability of an organization to make modifications (e.g., to adjust existing product attributes or alter service composition) to cope with less foreseeable events when they occur (Tan & Sia, 2006). An example is the altering of existing business rules without major setup efforts. *New capability* is the third dimension referring to the ability to innovate in response to dramatic changes or novel situations, as a network might change and new services might be added and removed (Tan & Sia, 2006). *Service flexibility* is included as the fourth dimension, which is similar to *partnering flexibility* (Gosain et al., 2005). This is the ability to allow the transfer of services to other organizations or to be brought in house.

Broadly conceived, *accountability* implies answerability for one's actions or inactions and to be responsible for their consequences (Roberts, 2002). Accountability should ensure that managers and accountants have insight into how resources are used and decisions are made. Accountability is complicated if processes are not predefined as this makes it difficult to judge the soundness of a process beforehand. Often this results in post-accountability, which means that only after the execution it can be checked whether the right process has been followed and the right decision has been made.

Both flexibility and accountability are based on trade-offs between feasibility and desirability. Meeting high requirements will be at the expense of high costs. Costs, accountability and adaptability properties can usually be traded against each other to optimize some of the properties while relaxing others. Moreover, they might be conflicting, as research suggests that adaptation needs loosely coupled systems (Moitra & Ganesh,

2005), whereas accountability requires tight coupling (e.g., Janssen, 2007; Roberts, 2002). In the information systems domain, *reliability* can be defined as the ability of the system to perform required functions uninterrupted for a stated period of time (Strandberg & Andersson, 1982). Translated to a WFMS, this implies that the reliability of a WFMS is determined by the ability of the WFMS to fluently support the execution of business processes for a designated time period. The reliability of a distributed program in a distributed computing system is the probability that a program which runs on multiple processing elements and needs to communicate with other processing elements for remote data files will be executed successfully (Lin & Chen, 1997). Therefore, architectures that enable flexible business processes depend on the execution of distributed services and are only reliable if such services can be delivered successfully. In this paper we will compare four architectures and compare them on the dimensions of robustness, modifiability, new capability, partnering flexibility, accountability, and reliability, which are used as indicators for flexibility.

CASE STUDY: INSURANCE COMPANY

A case study has been conducted at a large insurance company in the Netherlands to explore possible forms of flexibility in process automation that can prove beneficial for the company. This insurance company is a large organization consisting of many functional departments and having a number of different insurance products. Historically, most of the insurance products have their own back office which processes customer requests. These back offices are automated using workflow systems. The company is organized in business units that operate fairly autonomous within the company's strategy. One of the disadvantages of this approach is that each business unit developed information systems without having the interoperability with other systems in mind. Moreover, similar customer information is stored at each business unit.

Over the years this fragmentation has become more apparent due to the need to have a single overview of all customers and their products (Gong, Janssen, Overbeek, & Zuurmond, 2009). This is necessary for marketing activities and because often a discount is given when persons have more than a certain number of insurance products. The company has introduced a customer relationship system (CRM) that collects information from the information stored in the systems operated by the various business units.

Another development is the unbundling of services, the concentration of these services in a business unit (often called a shared service center) and the reuse of these services in multiple business processes (Janssen, Joha, & Zuurmond, 2009). The use of shared services can have many advantages, including increased service levels and cost reduction (Janssen & Joha, 2006). Each insurance product consists of similar business processes that are customized to the specific situation. The main business processes include an offering process, order status process, insurance acceptance, insurance administration, collecting insurance contribution, and settlement and payment of claims. These business processes share similar services.

The insurance business needs to adapt frequently due to changes in the law. For this purpose, a shared service center for law expertise exists which interprets new laws and translates them into working practice. The need for adapting to new laws poses significant challenges on the flexibility of business processes.

Figure 1 shows contemporary developments to realize flexibility in business process automation within the insurance company. A monolithic architecture supports process execution by offering prescribed static workflows. The knowledge rule separates knowledge for decision-making from the

process flow. The business rule architecture goes one step beyond and offers intelligence to manage process execution by taking effective organizational rules into account. A process orchestration architecture offers support to dynamically create and manage process-specific workflows.

Still today, monolithic (legacy) systems are employed that have been encapsulated by a web service interface to interact with other systems. In the following part we will discuss four forms of flexibility in process automation which are illustrated with references to the case study.

FORMS OF FLEXIBILITY IN PROCESS AUTOMATION

The insurance company shows that there is a need for flexibility 1) to react to changes in legislation, rules, and regulations and 2) in order to create customized processes. Four BPM architectures are derived from the case study and presented in this section. In the next section they are compared with each other based on the identified flexibility dimensions. Complete details of the technical implementations of these architectures are not given to prevent a lengthy discussion, but references to technologies that can implement a part of an architecture are made if that is needed for clarification.

Monolithic Architecture

The early implementation of workflow systems was document driven, and included hardcoded business rules and tightly coupled components (Georgakopoulos et al., 1995; van der Aalst et al., 2003). It consisted of a class of information objects, e.g., forms, and defined workflow as a sequence of actions to be done on those objects. The primary organizing structure is the 'routing' of information objects among users, and the specification of automatic actions to be taken in that routing. It can be viewed like the routing

Figure 1. Historical developments in business processes

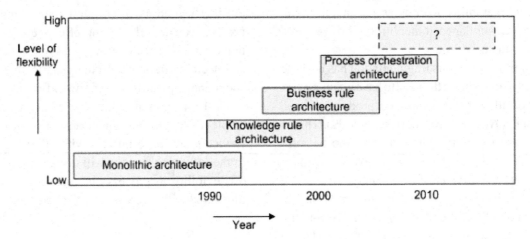

material process view, in which parts are passed along from one 'station' to another in a factory for processing, and some of the component tasks are taken over by automated machinery (Medina-Mora, Winograd, Flores, & Flores, 1992).

In Figure 2, a typical workflow for application processing in an organization is given as a static workflow example. The architecture is very simple as the systems consist of one monolithic component that handles the complete system. Often, the protocol determining the sequence of tasks is hardcoded in the system.

Such a workflow generally contains several steps like the 'apply', 'intake', and 'decision to accept' step. In the 'apply' step, the applicator is able to submit certain application documents via a portal provided by the organization. In case of the insurance company, a client can apply for an insurance product via the company's web portal. The 'apply' step is a typical starting point of a business process and can be compared to the 'offering' process step of the insurance company. The 'intake' step is to register the application inside the organization and initiate a corresponding process to deal with the application. This can be compared to the 'order status process' of the insurance company, which deals with handling the request for an insurance product.

Because a service providing organization usually provides more than one service to clients, this step includes the role of a selector and brings the application to a relevant decision maker. This can be illustrated by the application of a car insurance, which is passed to a decision maker who has knowledge of car insurances. Then, a decision is made in the 'decide to accept' step according to

Figure 2. Architecture for supporting static workflow

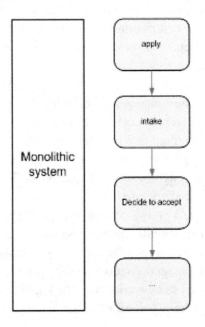

the current policy, law, regulation, or any related rule. This step can be related to the 'insurance acceptation' process at the insurance company. The step after the decision making step is about execution and can vary in different organizations. These execution steps can be illustrated by the remaining processes at the insurance company, viz. insurance administration, collecting insurance contribution, and settlement and payment of claims. In order to focus on information processing, the execution steps are not further discussed in this paper. Technically speaking, typical attempts to automate these processes are based on writing ad-hoc code to execute the flow logic and point-to-point connection between steps. This approach works for large volume processes, which do not need to be changed frequently.

Knowledge Rule Architecture

In this architecture the knowledge rules for making decisions are separated from the WFMS. An example of a simple knowledge rule in the acceptation process of car insurance is: "IF damage-free years of car owner are > 10 years THEN owner receives 50% price reduction" or there can be a rule stating that persons below a certain age cannot apply for an insurance policy. The number of years and reduction percentage in the first example can be changed regularly by the marketing department and age in the second example can be changed by law. By capturing this in a knowledge component, it is ensured that it can be easily updated and will affect all the rules in which the year, percentage, or age are used. Apart from the easiness to update, the updates are concentrated in one point affecting all relevant rules.

The WFMS can invoke the knowledge rule component using web services. The resulting knowledge rules will be used in the process to (automatically) process a task. Along with the development of software technology and wide usage of BPM systems, the IT industry did realize the problems and made efforts to solve them.

One of the main improvements is the separation of process and (decision making) rule (Müller, Greiner, & Rahm, 2004). A process defines ways for the organization to interact with its internal entities (e.g. applications, staff, and departments) and with its external entities (e.g., partners and customers). It is about how to conduct the business in organizations. A rule represents the logic and knowledge in decision making. It is about what rather than how (Faget, Marin, Patrick, Owens, & Tarin, 2003).

The consideration of this separation is that in some organizations, including the insurance industry, large sets of rules are involved. Rules may change frequently and should be managed by people other than the ones concerned with the actual business process, in our case the expertise center 'law'. It is also dubbed as 'separation of concerns' (Lienhard & Künzi, 2005). To be precise and avoid confusion with the concept of business rules, we employ the words 'knowledge rules' or 'decision rules' to denote the logic and knowledge in decision making. If we applied this approach to the typical workflow mentioned above, the technical solution is adding a repository to the step of 'decide to accept' and manage the knowledge rules of acceptance separately (see Figure 3). Each time when the application reaches this step, the decision is provided automatically as the computing result by using the corresponding rule in the repository.

Besides adding knowledge rules to process designs, the addition of business rules can further improve flexibility.

Business Rule Architecture

Knowledge rules are necessary for making decisions, whereas business rules are focused on which tasks are needed to make a decision. An example of a business rule for the insurance company can be: "IF result of the task order status is positive THEN perform accept task else start manual decision making task". Business rules concern

Figure 3. Separation of knowledge rules component from (static) process system

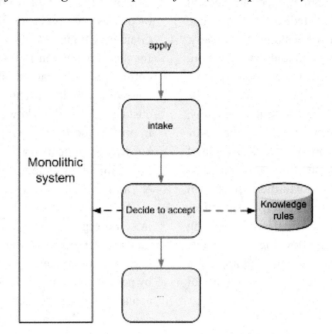

the management of subsequent tasks and the dependencies among these tasks.

Tasks are more and more accessed and invoked as web services. Web service technology is widely used in integrating steps in workflow (Zhao & Cheng, 2005). It helps to streamline business processes by creating an open, distributed system environment and promises to reduce the costs of business process management because it enables dynamic process integration without hard coding (Gottschalk, Graham, Kreger, & Snell, 2002). Corresponding web services can be selected and invoked based on a given condition. Therefore, the integration flexibility increases. This advantage has led to a further step in BPM systems development.

In business rule architecture the condition-action (CA) notion was introduced to determine the next steps in a workflow. In CA, a rule is activated or triggered when its condition becomes true, and deactivated when its condition becomes false. The underlined logic is:

IF *condition* THEN *action*.

'Condition' is a criterion for selection, while 'action' is an initiation of a certain task. An example of the implementation of a CA approach can be seen in Figure 4 (including a knowledge component positioned on the left in this Figure). The main difference between this approach and the last one is that not only the knowledge rules are managed in a separated repository, but also the business rules. A business rule is a statement that defines or constrains some aspects of the business. It is intended to assert business structure or to control or influence the behavior of the business (Morgan, 2002). When an application is submitted, the business rule engine firstly queries the criteria in a business rules repository. Then the system only selects the right task to invoke according to the business rules. The execution of further steps also depends on corresponding business rules from a corresponding repository. Since CA rules allow an application's reactive functionality to be specified and managed within a rule repository rather than being dispersed in diverse programs, the flexibility can be enhanced.

Figure 4. Business rules (condition-action)

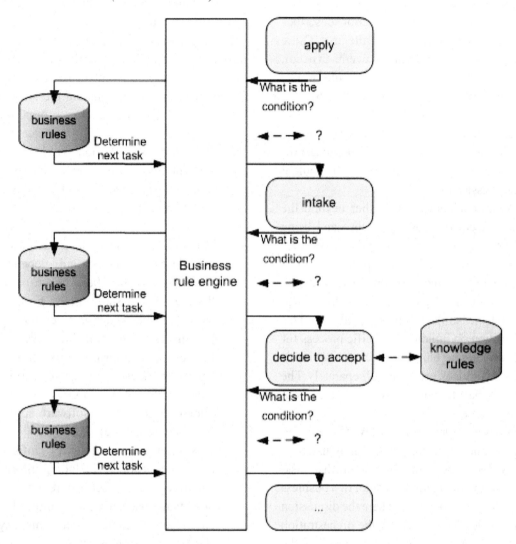

This solution does bring more flexibility as tasks are not hardcoded and the dependencies can be changed by updating the business rules.

Next, events can be introduced to provide the next level of BPM implementation.

Process Orchestration Architecture

Besides the aforementioned approaches, the concept of event-condition-action (ECA) orchestration can be found. ECA is broadly discussed in the database domain, and it is used to provide reactive functionality in many other settings, including network management, personalization, publish / subscribe technology, and workflow management (Bailey, Poulovassilis, & Wood, 2002; Goh, Koha, & Domazetb, 2001; Papamarkos, Poulovassilis, & Wood, 2006). Instead of focusing on each processing unit, ECA treats each submission as an event, and considers an event as the object of process tracking. An ECA rule has the general syntax:

ON *event* IF *condition* DO *action*.

The 'event' specifies when the rule will be triggered. The 'condition' is a query which determines if the information system is in a particular state, in which case the rule fires. The 'action' describes the actions to be performed if the rule fires. These actions may in turn cause further events to occur, which may in turn cause more ECA rules to fire (Bailey et al., 2002; Papamarkos et al., 2006). This is an effective mechanism in dealing with diverse combined submissions, as each submission can be regarded as an event, and corresponding processes can be triggered according to the content of the submission.

ECA approaches can go further beyond the limitation of current CA approaches and bring more flexibility. Instead of using business rules to describe predefined business processes, ECA gives guidelines on how to construct a process. Here, we use the word 'process rules' to distinguish it from 'business rules'. A process rule provides a specification on building a specific process for a given event. The building blocks (resources), such as web services, are managed separately. The execution of building such a process is carried out by an *orchestrator*.

Web Service Orchestration (WSO) refers to a composed business process that may use both internal and external Web services to fulfill its task. It is focused on the internal behavior of a business process (Pahl & Zhu, 2006), where the discussion is at the service level. In BPM, the orchestration concept can be used in a similar way, albeit on the process level instead of on the service level. If we are looking at the external behavior of multiple processes, such as process selection, interaction, and coordination, it is called *process orchestration*. Process orchestration provides the possibility to enable integrated service delivery. With integrated service delivery, clients perceive a cohesive bundle of services without being required to know who the service provider of each service is. Since the process is not predefined but built on the fly, ad-hoc processes and parallel processes are feasible.

Event-based structures allow for loosely-coupled processes. The basic promise is that a combination of events, rules, agents, and services create a flexible and service-oriented infrastructure for cross-agency integrated service delivery. Agreements and Service Level Agreement's (SLA's) allow for coordination of the processes behind the cross-agency service. Events can notify of a change in information, but not contain the information itself. This allows for autonomic organizations to maintain own systems and architectures. At the same time, orchestration provides capability of the automated arrangement, coordination, and management of processes. For this purpose a number of repositories are needed:

- **Process rules:** provide guidelines about the necessary tasks and dependencies among the tasks to build processes on the fly, e.g., which steps should be involved, and what is the order of execution.
- **Resources of information:** awareness of the source of information, such as which agent provides the wanted service, or whether the information is provided by human input or by a software application (e.g., a web service).
- **Customer data:** includes information about the customer, including information submitted in the service request. Please note that this can contain multiple databases like a document management system (DMS), a customer relationship management system (CRM), and so on.
- **Process control data:** this data involves status of the process, past lead time, expected lead time and other information necessary for process control and management.

In the center of this pattern is a process orchestration engine, which collects and integrates the information from those components and composes executable business processes (Figure 5). In this way, the process logics, the source of information, and the run-time workflow are managed separately. At the same time, processes can be controlled and monitored.

Figure 5. Event-condition-action orchestration

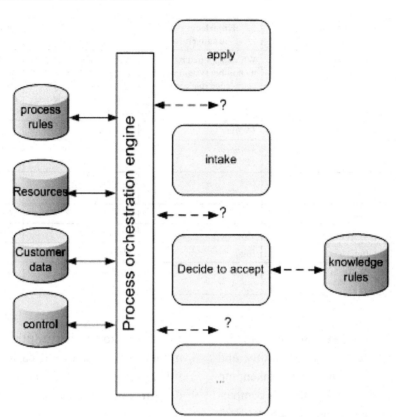

The basic assumption of flexible process orchestration is that a change of this system can be accommodated by a change of the information stored in one or more of the four repositories. In the ideal situation, a change would not require any change in the process engine or other software components. Although this is not proven yet, the idea is that the need to adapt to changes in business processes becomes much easier in that way and new processes can be implemented faster with less cost.

COMPARING PROCESS AUTOMATION APPROACHES ON FLEXIBILITY DIMENSIONS

Table 1 shows the high-level comparison of the previous approaches based on the dimensions related to flexibility.

The table shows that the robustness of all four architectures is problematic and therefore an important research issue. A future architecture for enabling flexible business processes should have improved robustness when compared to the four discussed ones. Modifiability of knowledge rules is higher for the architectures that support the ability to use knowledge rule repositories. The modifiability of the business processes themselves will increase if architectures support more flexibility in process redesign. This counts most for the condition-action and the event-condition-action approaches. Obviously, flexibility to respond to new capabilities is highest for the event-condition-action architecture. Partnering flexibility is also best supported by this kind of architecture. However, the more static WFMS are highly accountable and reliable when compared to the most flexible ones. The motivation for the results will be discussed next.

Table 1. Comparison of process automation approaches

	Monolithic architecture	Knowledge rule architecture	Business rule architecture	Process orchestration architecture
(Brief) description	WFM supported by a monolithic system	WFM supported by monolithic system with knowledge rule repository	WFM supported by distributed Web services that are invoked by using business rule repositories	WFM supported by process orchestration engine with many repositories
Robustness	*Medium*	*Medium*	*Medium*	*Low*
Modifiability of knowledge rules	*Low*	*Medium*	*Medium*	*Medium*
Modifiability of processes	*Low*	*Low*	*Medium*	*High*
New capability	*Low*	*Low*	*Medium*	*High*
Partnering flexibility	*Low*	*Medium*	*Medium*	*High*
Accountability	*High*	*High*	*Medium*	*Low*
Reliability	*High*	*High*	*Medium*	*Dependent on use of (proven) technology*

Other requirements like ease-of-use, maintainability, performance, testability, portability, and so on might play roles which were not taken into account in these comparisons. Besides comparing the architecture approaches on several flexibility dimensions, it is possible to compare the architectures on more properties like the ones mentioned. Inspiration for possible architecture properties can be found in existing literature that give indications for comparison based on possible properties. Examples of what can be found in literature are safety, liveness and completeness properties (Barber, Graser, & Holt, 2003), and extensibility, effectiveness and scalability (Boer & van Vliet, 2009). Future research will include further selection and inclusion of such properties to make an even better architecture selection for supporting design and enactment of flexible business processes. The high-level comparison of the four architectures based on the flexibility dimensions can be explained as follows.

Flexibility of Monolithic Architecture

If a static workflow needs to be changed, the process implementation needs to be modified by hand, which implies that it requires manual software modifications in the monolithic system. If services are insourced, process designs need to be changed to realize supply of these services. As these changes require manual intervention in the hardcoded process implementations, this requires a substantial development effort. If services are outsourced, it needs to be clear which service providers supply which services during process execution. In the static approach, this information is not dynamically tracked and therefore requires human attention every time. The WFMS is required to be open in order to connect to the service provider. The hardcoded and point-to-point connection makes such a requirement very hard to fulfill. Because all information related to process execution is stored in one system, it is an easy task to find out who did what in a process or who is responsible for the fulfillment of a process step, which has a positive effect on the accountability. A WFMS based on the monolithic architecture is highly reliable, because the entire process execution in organizations is supported by a single system.

Flexibility of Knowledge Rule Architecture

The knowledge rule approach is as robust as the static workflow approach. The necessity to add new knowledge rules to the repository will be less time consuming if the knowledge repository has a flexible design that is loosely coupled and has a high cohesion. When compared to the static approach, the modifiability of the knowledge rule approach is improved when the decisions to accept an intake are changed. In the knowledge approach, some additional knowledge rules need to be added to the rule repository only. The introduction of new processes also includes the introduction of new knowledge rules to the repository. Partnering flexibility is also improved if insourcing and outsourcing of services affect the 'decide to accept' step. For example, if a service is outsourced to another company, that other company may also have the ability to decide to accept an intake that is related to the supply of the outsourced service. Except for an additional knowledge rule repository, all information related to process execution is stored in one system leading to a high accountability.

Flexibility of Business Rule Architecture

The main difference between this approach and the previous one is that not only the knowledge rules are managed in a separate repository, but also the business rules. The WFMS now doesn't consist of one system anymore but consists of distributed systems, including several business rule repositories. This means that the robustness depends on the vulnerability to changes that impact these distributed systems. The way of separating business rules from processes at each step implies that this approach focuses on the modifiability of processing units (workflow steps). Therefore, the modifiability of processes is higher when compared to the previous two architectures. Because of the distributed nature of

the business rule architecture, changes to business rules and knowledge rules can be implemented easily and don't have to affect the whole WFMS. Business and knowledge rules can both be modified if that is necessary for partnering flexibility. Accountability becomes more difficult because a WFMS based on this architecture is of a distributed nature, which requires more effort to track the execution of a process. When compared to monolithic architectures, it is more difficult to track down disturbances or flaws in the WFMS, because there are dependencies with other distributed components.

Flexibility of Process Orchestration Architecture

The process orchestration architecture goes further beyond the limitation of architectures based on business rules and knowledge rules. A WFMS based on the process orchestration architecture has many dependencies with distributed components. Changes in the processes may easily affect a component which requires a modification. Therefore, robustness is lower than the previous three architectures. Numerous parts that make up a process design are split into loosely coupled components, which make it easy to implement changes to (parts of) the distributed system. If the supply of new services requires new processes to be introduced in an organization, the separate and independent components in the WFMS can be updated when necessary. Because of its distributed and loosely coupled design, the process orchestration architecture is also highly flexible to cope with insourcing and outsourcing of services. However, an advanced tracking and monitoring system is needed to cope with responsibilities during execution of processes. Reliability will be good if proven technologies and standards are used.

Next, a research agenda is introduced based on the findings that are the result from comparing the architectures on flexibility.

RESEARCH AGENDA

The research agenda consists of two main parts. First, several research recommendations can be made for the development of new architecture components that needs to tackle the flexibility issues shown in Table 1. Second, a proposal for reference architecture is made which can be used for the assembly of individual components to support a dynamic workflow.

Development of New Architecture Components

Flexibility is based on tradeoffs between feasibility and desirability. Meeting high requirements will be at the expense of high costs and complex systems. According to Table 1, robustness, accountability, and reliability need the most attention when improving flexibility of the current architectures. Robustness can be improved if a reference architecture is used that allows easy and even automated configuration of a WFMS by connecting and disconnecting individual components necessary for the support of process execution. These components can be deduced from the four introduced approaches to support flexible process automation and include a business rule repository, a knowledge rule repository, a process rule repository, a process control component, and a tracking and monitoring component. This implies that all these components can be used in a WFMS if very tight monitoring and control of business processes is necessary. Eventually, this will create a BPM environment that enables an organization that can learn from process execution, and to make process comparisons and evaluations leading to process optimization. Less components can be selected for more loose process monitoring and control.

Accountability mechanisms are still rather unexplored but gain more attention due to the financial crisis to be able to understand who made which decisions (Janssen, 2007). Accountability can be improved by adding an advanced tracking and monitoring component to a distributed WFMS. This component can be realized by introducing event-driven interactions in a WFMS. An event is a service request by an individual or business, an indication of a state change, or an annual trigger (Scheer, 2000). An example of an event in the insurance company case is "awaiting client's approval of insurance policy". If the client accepts the policy, the next step in the insurance acceptation process can be made. Therefore, events reflect what is going on during process execution and when implemented as a Simple Object Access Protocol (SOAP)-aware message queing infrastructure they can be used for process tracking and monitoring purposes. The tracking and monitoring component should keep track of responsibilities, security, quality of process performance and process results, and process execution status. Reliability can be improved when proven technologies and standards are used for the components that make up a WFMS. This includes, of course, known standards from the information systems engineering domain such as Asynchronous JavaScript And XML (AJAX), Unified Modeling Language (UML), eXtensible Markup Language (XML), but also standards for the description and modeling of web services like the Web Service Modeling Ontology (WSMO) and the Web Service Modeling Language (WSML) (Roman et al., 2005). Future research will include further selection and inclusion of architecture properties to make an even better architecture selection for supporting design and enactment of flexible business processes.

Changes in regulations and laws might result in adaptation of current services or brings new services. New laws influence often multiple business processes, therefore BPM mechanisms are needed to ensure that not only single business processes are updated, but all business processes are updated. Old processes may get lost due to these frequent changes to processes, which leads to the need to store these old processes. Further research needs to be carried out to determine what is needed to store processes to prevent them from getting lost. In this research we've already identified rule repositories, but we've not yet identified the detailed data that is needed for process storage. Partner organizations might also provide new services or adapt existing services for some reason like optimization (both at organization level and IT system level), new technology employment, or service improvement. All these changes are hardly dealt with by just updating the rules in the repository. Although the SOA provides a loosely coupled connection for service interaction, the traditional manual configuring is not flexible enough in such a dynamic environment. This fuels the need to derive generic process components that can be reused in many processes, but can be maintained as if they are one.

Typical implementation of a (decision-support) business rules repository employs a decision tree or a decision matrix, which both contain algorithms to provide decision making (Rosca, Greenspan, & Wild, 2002). Its function is limited in decision making based on certain input and given precondition as context. If one submission contains two applications, application split is required so that two (or more) different processes should be initiated. This can be exemplified by a submission that contains both an application for car insurance and an application for a house insurance. Although it is not necessary to be the case, the final results of co-submitted applications should be returned to the client together on many occasions. From the client's perspective, it is an integrated service. For example, a collection of housing-related services can be offered to a house buyer. The insurance company can offer services to apply for house insurances together with a bank that can offer a service to apply for a mortgage and a real estate agent that can offer a service to mediate in the acquisition of a property. Because all the submissions are judged by being mapped with predefined conditions, combined submissions are only able to be mapped with predefined combined conditions. Current condition-action

approaches hardly provide an integrated service delivery when combined submissions are diverse and unpredictable. Even when co-submitted applications are split, the integrated result is difficult to achieve without an appropriate control and monitoring. Therefore, it is desirable to introduce process control and monitoring components that are integrated by reference architecture.

Reference Architecture for Connecting Individual Components

Figure 6 shows a draft of a reference architecture that should be able to connect and disconnect individual components before, during or after execution of processes.

Dependent of a specific workflow, the process orchestrator can connect selected components. Executable processes are built by the orchestrator and it arranges those components that are wanted to manage workflows. The Business Process Execution Language (BPEL) can be used to define processes that can be executed on the orchestration engine. Such an engine can be implemented by using NetBeans Enterprise Pack or Microsoft BizTalk Server for example. Decisions on which components to connect are made by interpreting the process rules, because process rules provide a specification on building a specific process for a given event. A possible event from the insurance company case can be: 'determining if client fulfils requirements to apply for a car insurance'. Process rules related to this event can provide a specification for a process to find out if a specific client indeed satisfies all requirements to conclude a car insurance. This specification should then include all steps that an employee of the insurance company should perform to determine whether the application is valid.

If, for instance, the insurance company wants to study the executions of the 'settlement and payment of insurance claims' process because management wants to determine how many claims are successfully settled it is desirable to connect a

Figure 6. Draft of a reference architecture for connecting individual components, based on (Klievink, Derks, & Janssen, 2008)

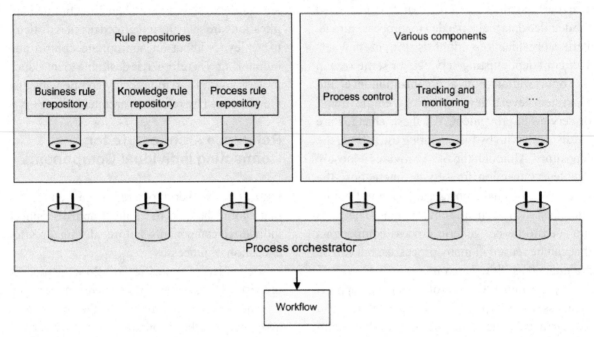

tracking and monitoring component to the orchestrator. This implies that the orchestration engine should have knowledge on which components should be connected in order to comply with the process rules. These dependencies should be made clear when designing the reference architecture. As Figure 6 already shows, several component libraries are imaginable such as a library with all sorts of rule repositories or a library with a variety of tracking and monitoring components that can be selected. More research should be carried out to discover and introduce available component libraries. A limitation of the proposed approach is that no computer-based support is provided for the decision making process to determine which components need to be connected for which process based on process rules. After realizing the proposed reference architecture, it is desirable to introduce a decision support system that can determine which components should be selected and connected to the process orchestrator for a given process based on the interpretation of pro-

cess rules. Such a decision support system can lead to complete automation of the component selection procedure.

Apart from using process rule repositories as a basis for selecting BPM components, process management algorithms can be used (Dijkman, Dumas, & García-Bañuelos, 2009). These algorithms can be used to compare similarities in business process specifications. Three types of algorithms for business process similarity can be distinguished: text similarity, structural similarity and behavioral similarity. Text similarity is based on a comparison of the labels that appears in process models, which can be task labels and event labels for instance. Structural similarity algorithms can measure similarity based on the structure of process models in terms of graphs. Behavioral similarity is based on the execution semantics of process models. The idea is that the process orchestrator can select the same set of BPM components for similar business processes.

CONCLUSION

Four architectures supporting flexibility were derived from an insurance case study and compared and evaluated based on flexibility dimensions. These architectures comprised a monolithic architecture, a 'knowledge rule' architecture, a 'business rule' architecture, and a 'process orchestration' architecture. All architectures scored poor on the level of robustness and the more flexibility is created the less accountable were the processes. This shows the tradeoff between feasibility and desirability. More research is needed in accomplishing these requirements at the same time. There are many forms of flexibility and various architectures support different forms of flexibility while performing differently. Further research suggests selecting the best architecture parts to develop a new architecture based on those parts that meets all requirements posed. Nevertheless, utilization of a selected architecture implies that tradeoffs are made and if other requirements are prioritized other architectures might be preferred. Eventually, a draft of a reference architecture is introduced so that individual components can be connected and disconnected to suit various situations for which business processes need to be flexible and which call for different forms of architectural support.

ACKNOWLEDGMENT

This work was supported in part by the AGILE project (acronym for Advanced Governance of Information services through Legal Engineering, http://www.jacquard.nl/?m=426). AGILE is a Jacquard project funded by the Netherlands Organisation for Scientific Research (NWO).

REFERENCES

Alter, M. J. (2004). *Science of Flexibility*. Champaign, IL: Human Kinetics.

Architecture_Working_Group. (2000). *IEEE Std 1471-2000 Recommended Practice Architectural Description of Software-Intensive Systems*. Washington, DC: IEEE Software Engineering Standards Committee.

Bailey, J., Poulovassilis, A., & Wood, P. T. (2002). Analysis and optimisation of event-condition-action rules on XML. *Computer Networks*, *39*, 239–259. doi:10.1016/S1389-1286(02)00208-6

Barber, S. K., Graser, T., & Holt, J. (2003). Evaluating dynamic correctness properties of domain reference architectures. *Journal of Systems and Software*, *68*(3), 217–231. doi:10.1016/S0164-1212(03)00064-5

Bieberstein, N., Laird, R. G., Jones, K., & Mitra, T. (2008). *Executing SOA: A Practical Guide for the Service-Oriented Architect*. Boston: Addison-Wesley.

Boer, R. C., & van Vliet, H. (2009). On the similarity between requirements and architecture. *Journal of Systems and Software*, *82*(3), 544–550. doi:10.1016/j.jss.2008.11.185

Carlsson, B. (1989). Flexibility and the theory of the Firm. *International Journal of Industrial Organization*, *7*(2), 179–203. doi:10.1016/0167-7187(89)90018-0

Cherbakov, L., Galambos, G. M., Harishankar, R., Kalyana, S., & Rackham, G. (2005). Impact of service orientation at the business level. *IBM Systems Journal*, *44*(4), 653–668. doi:10.1147/sj.444.0653

Dijkman, R., Dumas, M., & García-Bañuelos, L. (2009). Graph matching algorithms for business process model similarity search. In U. Dayal, J. Eder, J. Koehler & H. A. Reijers (Eds.), *Proceedings of Business Process Management, 7th International Conference, BPM 2009*, Ulm, Germany (Vol. 5701, pp. 48-63). Berlin: Springer.

Faget, J., Marin, M., Patrick, M., Owens, V. J., & Tarin, L.-O. (2003). Business processes and business rules: business agility becomes real. In *Proceedings of Workflow Handbook, 2003*, 77–92.

Georgakopoulos, D., Hornick, M., & Sheth, A. (1995). An overview of workflow management: from process modeling to workflow automation infrastructure. *Distributed and Parallel Databases, 3*, 119–153. doi:10.1007/BF01277643

Goh, A., Koha, Y. K., & Domazetb, D. S. (2001). ECA rule-based support for workflows. *Artificial Intelligence in Engineering, 15*, 37–46. doi:10.1016/S0954-1810(00)00028-5

Gong, Y., Janssen, M., Overbeek, S. J., & Zuurmond, A. (2009, November 10-13). Enabling flexible processes by ECA orchestration architecture. In *Proceedings of the 3rd International Conference on Theory and Practice of Electronic Governance (ICEGOV 2009)*, Bogota, Columbia. New York: ACM Press.

Gosain, S., Malhotra, A., & Sawy, O. A. E. (2005). Coordinating for flexibility in e-Business supply chains. *Journal of Management Information Systems, 21*(3), 7–45.

Gottschalk, K., Graham, S., Kreger, H., & Snell, J. (2002). Introduction to web services architecture. *IBM Systems Journal, 41*, 170–177. doi:10.1147/sj.412.0170

Janssen, M. (2007, December 10-13). *Adaptability and accountability of information architectures in interorganizational networks*. Paper presented at the International Conference on Electronic Governance (ICEGOV) Macao, China.

Janssen, M., & Joha, A. (2006). Motives for establishing shared service centers in public administrations. *International Journal of Information Management, 26*(2), 102–115. doi:10.1016/j.ijinfomgt.2005.11.006

Janssen, M., Joha, A., & Zuurmond, A. (2009). Simulation and animation for adopting shared services: Evaluating and comparing alternative arrangements. *Government Information Quarterly, 26*(1), 15–24. doi:10.1016/j.giq.2008.08.004

Klievink, A. J., Derks, W., & Janssen, M. (2008). Enterprise architecture and governance challenges for orchestrating public-private cooperation. In Saha, P. (Ed.), *Advances in Government Enterprise Architecture* (pp. 263–283). Hershey, PA: IGI Global.

Li, L., & Zhao, X. (2006). Enhancing competitive edge through knowledge management in implementing ERP systems. *Systems Research and Behavioral Science, 23*(2), 129–140. doi:10.1002/sres.758

Lienhard, H., & Künzi, U.-M. (2005). Workflow and business rules: a common approach. In *Proceedings of the Workflow Handbook, 2005*, 129–140.

Lin, M.-S., & Chen, D.-J. (1997). The computational complexity of the reliability problem on distributed systems. *Information Processing Letters, 64*(3), 143–147. doi:10.1016/S0020-0190(97)00150-6

Medina-Mora, R., Winograd, T., Flores, R., & Flores, F. (1992). The action workflow approach to workflow management technology. In *Proceedings of the 1992 ACM conference on Computer-supported cooperative work* (pp. 281-288). New York: ACM.

Moitra, D., & Ganesh, J. (2005). Web services and flexible business processes: towards the adaptive enterprise. *Information & Management, 42*(7), 921–933. doi:10.1016/j.im.2004.10.003

Morgan, T. (2002). *Business Rules and Information Systems: Aligning IT with Business Goals*. Reading, MA: Addison-Wesley.

Müller, R., Greiner, U., & Rahm, E. (2004). Agent work: a workflow system supporting rule-based workflow adaptation. *Data & Knowledge Engineering*, *51*, 223–256. doi:10.1016/j.datak.2004.03.010

Pahl, C., & Zhu, Y. (2006). A semantical framework for the orchestration and choreography of web services. *Electronic Notes in Theoretical Computer Science*, *151*, 3–18. doi:10.1016/j.entcs.2005.07.033

Papamarkos, G., Poulovassilis, A., & Wood, P. T. (2006). Event-condition-action rules on RDF metadata in P2P environments. *Computer Networks*, *50*, 1513–1532. doi:10.1016/j.comnet.2005.10.022

Roberts, N. (2002). Keeping public officials accountable through dialogue: Resolving the accountability paradox. *Public Administration Review*, *62*(2), 658–669. doi:10.1111/1540-6210.00248

Roman, D., Keller, U., Lausen, H., de Bruijn, J., Lara, R., & Stollberg, M. (2005). Web service modeling ontology. *Applied Ontology*, *1*(1), 77–106.

Rosca, D., Greenspan, S., & Wild, C. (2002). Enterprise modeling and decision-support for automating the business rules lifecycle. *Automated Software Engineering*, *9*, 361–404. doi:10.1023/A:1020372710433

Scheer, A. (2000). *ARIS: Business Process Modelling*. Berlin: Springer.

Strandberg, K., & Andersson, H. (1982). On a model for software reliability performance. *Microelectronics and Reliability*, *22*(2), 227–240. doi:10.1016/0026-2714(82)90181-0

Tan, C., & Sia, S. K. (2006). Managing flexibility in outsourcing. *Journal of the Association for Information Systems*, *7*(4), 179–2006.

Tewoldeberhan, T. W., & Janssen, M. (2008). Simulation-based experimentation for designing reliable and efficient Web service orchestrations in supply chains. *Electronic Commerce Research and Applications*, *7*(1), 82–92. doi:10.1016/j.elerap.2006.11.007

van der Aalst, W. M. P., Benatallah, B., Casati, F., Curbera, F., & Verbeek, E. (2007). Business process management: Where business processes and web services meet. *Data & Knowledge Engineering*, *61*(1), 1–5. doi:10.1016/j.datak.2006.04.005

van der Aalst, W. M. P., ter Hofstede, A. H. M., & Weske, M. (2003). Business process management: a survey. *Business Process Management*, 1-12.

WFMC. (n.d.). *About the WFMC - Introduction to the Workflow Management Coalition*. Retrieved July 12, 2004, from http://www.wfmc.org/about.htm

Zhao, J. L., & Cheng, H. K. (2005). Web services and process management: a union of convenience or a new area of research? *Decision Support Systems*, *40*, 1–8. doi:10.1016/j.dss.2004.04.002

Zhou, J., & Ye, X. (2006). A flexible control strategy on workflow modeling and enacting. *Advanced Communication Technology*, *3*, 1712–1716.

This work was previously published in International Journal of Organizational and Collective Intelligence, Volume 1, Issue 3, edited by Hideyasu Sasaki, pp. 1-19, copyright 2010 by IGI Publishing (an imprint of IGI Global).

Chapter 12
Distributed Intelligence for Constructing Economic Models

Ting Yu
University of Sydney, Australia

ABSTRACT

This paper presents an integrated and distributed intelligent system being capable of automatically estimating and updating large-size economic models. The input-output model of economics uses a matrix representation of a nation's (or a region's) economy to predict the effect of changes in one industry on others and by consumers, government, and foreign suppliers on the economy (Miller & Blair, 1985). To construct the model reflecting the underlying industry structure faithfully, multiple sources of data are collected and integrated together. The system in this paper facilitates this estimation process by integrating a series of components with the purposes of data retrieval, data integration, machine learning, and quality checking. More importantly, the complexity of national economy leads to extremely large-size models to represent every detail of an economy, which requires the system to have the capacity for processing large amounts of data. This paper demonstrates that the major bottleneck is the memory allocation, and to include more memory, the machine learning component is built on a distributed platform and constructs the matrix by analyzing historical and spatial data simultaneously. This system is the first distributed matrix estimation package for such a large-size economic matrix.

INTRODUCTION

The input-output model of economics uses a matrix representation of a nation's (or a region's) economy to predict the effect of changes in one industry on others and by consumers, government, and

foreign suppliers on the economy (Miller & Blair, 1985). Because the economic constantly evolves, the input-output model needs to be updated at least annually to reflect the new circumstance. Unfortunately, in most countries such as Australia, the input-output model is only constructed every 3-4 years, because the large amount of monetary and human cost is involved to complete a survey

DOI: 10.4018/978-1-4666-1577-9.ch012

Table 1. An example of the input-output table defined by the 3-level tree and the 2-level tree

			China (1)		U
			Shoe (1)	Retail (2)	
Australia (1)	NSW (1)	Sheep (1)	X_1	X_2	$U_1 = X_1 + X_2$
		Oil (2)	X_3	X_4	$U_2 = X_3 + X_4$
	VIC (2)	Sheep (1)	X_5	$X_6 = 0.23$	$U_2 = X_3 + X_4$
		Oil (2)	X_7	X_8	$U_2 = X_3 + X_4$
V			$V_1 = \sum_{i=2n} X_i$	$V_2 = \sum_{i=2n+1} X_i$	

(ABS, 2007a). The Centre for Integrated Sustainability Analysis (ISA), University of Sydney, is developing an integrated intelligent system to estimate and update the input-output model at different level on a regular basis.

The input-output model consists of a time series of matrices (Table 1) representing the industry structure of a given year. At Table 1, each entry X_i represents the commodity flow between the industry sections of different regions. For example, the entry X_6 represents the commodity flow from the sheep industry at Victoria (VIC), a state of Australia, to the retail industry in China. In this example, the goods worth of 0.23 million dollar are sold. Often X_i is missing as it is very detailed information and hard to be surveyed. However government agents published aggregated information more frequently, such as V and U which represent the total export of a given industry in Australia (ABS, 2007b). The aggregated information is available for a rather long period, for example agriculture information from 1861 to 2007 in the database (ABS, 2007b). It is worth clarifying that the aggregated information is not limited by the sums of rows or columns as the V and U. The main purpose of this distribute intelligent system is to utilize those available aggregated information and the economic models

from previous years to populate and update current or future X_i s to build a series of this economic models for current year or coming years.

A time series of input-output models represents the evolution of industry structure within and between regions, where the region is defined as a geographic concept. Within a given time period, extra information regarding certain parts of the matrix is often available from various government agents or other public or private organizations, such as the Bureau of Statistics. However, most of this information is often incomplete and only gives a snapshot of a part of the underlying model. There are at least four sources of uncertainty in the model: 1) if the model is survey-based, then there could be classical sampling errors; 2) in the case of large surveys, an error in the inference design can arise; 3) the underlying real industry structures are not constant over the time, and in an age of structural change due to technological development, this error can be important; 4) errors in compiling the large database can affect the quality of the final model (Percoco, Hewings, & Senn, 2006). This paper does not intend to analysis the stochastic behavior of the input-output table, but presents a machine learning algorithm addressing the temporal stability or temporal patterns to account for this characteristic. Dozens of years of research has accumulated substantial amount of general knowledge of the national economy. Any researcher could utilize this public knowledge to facilitate their discovery. To utilize those structured information, the machine learning algorithm is a spatio-temporal knowledge discovery process with the help of rich domain knowledge. Including temporal dimension introduces additional complexity to the geographic knowledge discovery (Miller & Han, 2001). The novel distributed intelligence presented in this paper estimates and updates the economic matrix, and preserves the valuable temporal and spatial information. The algorithm collectively utilizes the heterogeneous information from multiple sources and is built upon a distributed platform.

In the machine learning community, major researches been done to estimate matrix for the transportation planning and network design, and discover and preserve the structure of the matrix. There are three main approaches: Linear Programming approach, Bayesian Inference techniques, and Expectation Maximization (EM) (Medina, Taft, Salamatian, Bhattacharyya, & Diot, 2002). These methods are widely employed to estimate the traffic flow matrix in the transportation planning (McNeil & Hendrickson, 1985). Those researches have significant influence on the algorithm discussed in this paper, because the nature of traffic flow is very similar to the nature of the industry flow. However the data availability and quality causes some difference between two streams of researches. There are large amount of heterogeneous data related to national economy, but the data often contains very large amount of noises. By contrast, traffic flow data is in relatively simple structures and normally collected very accurately. The algorithm proposed in this paper is closer to the linear programming method than other two methods. In the economics research community, RAS methods (Miller & Blair, 1985) is the dominant approach, due to its simplicity and transparence of the estimation

process. However this method suffers from many drawbacks: 1) when the information conflicts each other, the RAS method cannot work. Although the CRAS, a modified version of the RAS, addresses this problem, but it still suffers from its own limitation (Lenzen, Wood, & Gallego, 2006) The RAS method cannot be implemented upon the distributed system, so its performance is limited by the size of the target matrix. The advantage of the method discussed in this paper is that it is capable of including heterogeneous information and handling a large amount of data upon a distributed platform.

The following part of the paper is organized as follows: the first section introduces the whole system briefly. The second section introduces the machine learning algorithm, and the third section describes the distributed training method for the machine learning algorithm.

SYSTEM ARCHITECTURE

The integrated intelligent system consists of a series of functional components: data retrieval and integration, query, machine learning, distributed training engine, and model presentation (See Figure 1). As the first step, the data retrieval component acts as interfaces to various types of datasets including macro and micro economic data that are stored in various formats such as Excel files, databases etc. The data integration component unifies these heterogeneous datasets to a single format, integrates and restructures the data retrieved by the previous component. At the same time, users' specification of the concept hierarchy is interpreted and translated into hierarchies defining the structure of the matrix. This concept hierarchy is very similar to the data warehousing (Hobbs, Hillson, Lawande, & Smith, 2005). This hierarchy allows users to roll up and drill down the data very easily and also introduce the dynamic to the matrix. The machine learning component employs a unique

Figure 1. System architecture

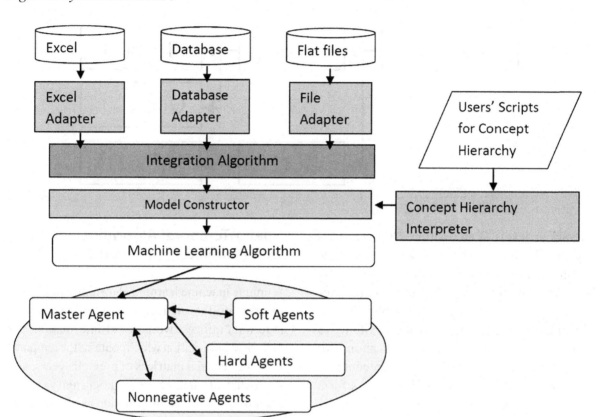

algorithm designed to estimate the matrix. In order to process extremely large amount of data, this component sits on a distributed platform to quickly converge to the optimal estimation of the unknown matrix. As the final step, the model checking and presentation components check the quality of the estimated model and present it to users in a structured format.

Model Constructor

The model constructor component communicates with other two components: the concept hierarchy interpreter and data integration algorithm. The concept hierarchy interpreter constructs the tree-like hierarchy that we will discuss in detail later, and the data integration component integrates the heterogeneous datasets. The model constructor

then 1) require the data integration component to retrieval data from various sources and integrate them, and 2) restructure and assign the meaning to the data according to the previous concept hierarchy in order to populate the following machine learning algorithm.

On the process of building a model, the first step is to construct the concept hierarchy. The hierarchy is pre-required for restructuring data from various sources. The hierarchy structure is introduced by a multi-tree structure. For example, the hierarchy representing Australia national economic can be like Figure 2. Of course, the real hierarchy is much more complex than this example.

The hierarchy brings two major benefits. First, it provides the different levels of abstraction. The flexibility of the concept hierarchy makes the users to have snapshots of the matrix

Figure 2. An example of concept hierarchy

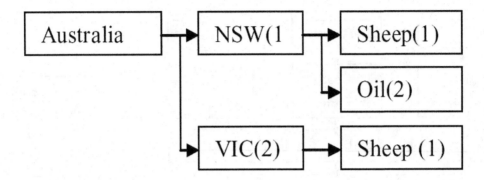

at various levels of abstraction. Users can easily drill down or roll up the matrix without redefining the matrix. Secondly, it allows the dynamic structure of the resultant matrix. Regarding the difference between applications, a dynamical hierarchy provides the flexibility to expand this system to different application with different structure of matrices. It is very common to mix two different concept hierarchies for a matrix. For example, in Table 1, a matrix is organized by one three-level hierarchy and one two-level hierarchy. The coordinate of one entry, say X_1, can be defined as by [1,1,1] at the row side and [1,1] at the column side. That means the entry, X_1, defined by a three-level concept hierarchy and a two-level concept hierarchy at the column side.

Large amounts of data collected from multiple sources are often in different formats. In order to estimate a 3000-by-3000 matrix which representing Australian national economy, more than 200,000 constraints are specified with 9 million variables. A single user has to spend a long period preparing the specification manually. The model constructor automates the data collection, integration and restructures operations. Inside the model constructor, the concept hierarchy plays a crucial role to organize data retrieved from various sources and feed them into following construct the machine learning algorithm.

Spatio-Temporal Algorithm with Conflicting Information

A unique machine learning algorithm is designed to estimate the matrix. This machine learning algorithm utilizes two types of information: the historical information which contains the temporal patterns between matrices of previous years, and the spatial information within the current year. For example, this spatial information can be the total commodity output of the given industry within the current year, or the total greenhouse emission of the given industry. The simplified version of the machine learning algorithm can be written in the format of an optimization model as following:

$$Min[\frac{dis(X - \overline{X})}{\varepsilon_1} + \sum \frac{e_i^2}{\varepsilon_{i+1}}] \quad (1)$$

$$\text{Subject to:} \quad \begin{aligned} G_1 X + E &= C_1 \\ G_2 X &= C_2 \\ X &\geq 0 \end{aligned} \quad \text{where: } X \in R^n \text{ with}$$

$n = m \times m$ is a vector presenting the target square matrix $\in R^{m \times m}$ to be estimated, $\overline{X} \in R^n$ is a vector representing the matrix of the previous year, E is a vector of the error components $[e_1, ..., e_h]^T$ where h is the number of soft constraints, *dis* is a distance metric which quantifies the difference between two matrices. As the *dis* metric has many variety, the one used in this experiment is

$\sum (x_i - \bar{x}_i)^2$. $\begin{bmatrix} G_1 & G_2 \end{bmatrix} \in R^{n \times h}$ is a coefficient matrix for h local constraints, $\begin{bmatrix} C_1 & C_2 \end{bmatrix} \in R^h$ is a vector representing the right-hand side values for the local constraints. The stochastic coefficient ε_1 and ε_{i+1} assign different weights or confidence to the datasets, and the different levels of confidence of the potentially conflicting datasets give the algorithm to compromise the impacts on the final matrix from the conflicting information.

The idea here is to minimize the difference between the target matrix and the matrix of the previous year, while the target matrix satisfies with the local regional information to some degree. For example, if the total export of the sheep industry from Australia to China is known as C_1, then $GX + E = C$ can be $[1,1]\begin{bmatrix} x_1 \\ x_2 \end{bmatrix} + e_1 = C_1$ The element e_i in E represents the difference between the real value and estimate value, for example,

$$e_1 = C_1 - [1,1]\begin{bmatrix} x_1 \\ x_2 \end{bmatrix}$$

This learning algorithm assumes the temporal stability, which assumes the industry structure of a certain region keeps constant or has very few changes within the given short time period. This assumption often required to be verified for long time period. Within the short time period, the dramatic change of the industry structure is relatively rare.

Data objects in typical machine learning algorithm often can be reduced to points in some multidimensional space without information loss. But the spatio-temporal modelling algorithm can analyze data containing two types of information simultaneously; thereby maximally utilize the available information. In our case, $dis(X - \bar{X})$ models the temporal information of the input-output models between years, and $G_1X + E = C_1$ and $G_2X = C_2$ models the spatial or other type of information of the input-output model within the current year.

The reason why the spatio-temporal modelling algorithm is suitable to this system is due to the unique characteristics of the datasets that the system aims to process. The datasets often contain the temporal patterns between years, such as the trend of the carbon emission of certain industry sections, and also much spatial information regarding the total emission within a certain region such as national total emission and state total emission. Even more, the datasets also contains the interrelationship between the industries within a given region or between regions. On the other hand, it is very common that either of datasets is not comprehensive and imperfect and even the conflicts between the datasets exist. Thereby, the modeling algorithm is required to consolidate the conflicted datasets to uncover underlying models, and at the same time, the modelling algorithm is required to incorporate the spatial information and keep the spatial relationship (such as dependency and heterogeneity (Miller, 2007)) within datasets.

Distributed Training Engine

In real world practice, the machine learning algorithm often processes matrix with dimensions over 1000-by-1000. In the foreseeable future, the size of estimated matrix will increase over 100,000-by-100,000. This requires the algorithm to have an outstanding capacity of processing large datasets. Furthermore, at Equation 1, $G_1X + E = C_1$ and $G_2X = C_2$ contains information from various sources, not only U and V which are the sums of rows and columns. In real practice, the sizes of $G_1X + E = C_1$ and $G_2X = C_2$ increase as more new information is collected. This requires the training engine to be flexible and extendable to include new aggregated information. In order to address these two problems, one distributed training algorithm is designed as the solver. The algorithm consists of a few steps:

Soft constraints handled by soft agents	Hard constraints handled by hard agents	Nonnegative constraints handled by nonnegative agents
$Min[\dfrac{(X-\overline{X})^2}{\varepsilon_1} + \sum \dfrac{e_i^2}{\varepsilon_{i+1}}]$ Subject to: $G_1X + E = C_1$	$Min[\dfrac{(X-\overline{X})^2}{\varepsilon_1}]$ Subject to: $G_2X = C_2$	$Min[\dfrac{(X-\overline{X})^2}{\varepsilon_1}]$ Subject to: $X \geq 0$

Step 1: Divide the constraint set into a few subsets of constraints within the master agent;

Step 2: Construct a set of heterogeneous slave agents according the subsets of constraints;

Step 3: Do training at each slave agent against the subset of constraints respectively;

Step 4: Combine the training results and check whether the result satisfies the stop criteria within the master agent.

At Figure 1, the distributed training engine consists of four types of agents: a master agent, hard agents, soft agents and nonnegative agents. This construct bases on a parallel optimization algorithm, in which the Equation 1 is partitioned into three sub-problems as below:

First the master agent partitions the original optimization model into three types of sub-problems (including soft constraints, hard constraints and nonnegative constraints) and then sends sub-problems to all the slave agents, including the soft agents, hard agents and nonnegative agents. After receiving the sub-problem, each slave agent solves the sub-problem and sends the result back to the master agent. At the master agent, the results from all slave agents are combined as a weighted sum which consequently acts as a start point for the next iteration. Let $(S_i)_{i \in I}$ denotes ith set of constraints among the family of constraint sets where I is the set of the indices of sets of constraints, and the solution is the joint set of the family of constraint subsets $S = \bigcap_{i \in I}(S_i)_{i \in I}$. In this section $X \in R^{n+h}$ is slightly different from the previous definition, as $X = [X, E]$ which is a vector combining the variables and errors at the previous setting. The solution of each agent is the projection of X_n at the nth iteration on three constraint subsets, $P_{S_i}(X_n)$. In this case, three constraints subsets (soft, hard and nonnegative) are linear constraints, which are convex as well. For the soft constraints, $P_{S_i}(X_n) = (Q_1 + G_1^T Q_2 G_1)^{-1}(Q_1 X_{n-1} + G_1^T Q_2(C_1 + E_{n-1}))$, for hard constraints, $P_{S_i}(X_n) = (G_2^T Q_2 G_2)^{-1}(Q_1 X_{n-1} + G_1^T Q_2 C_2)$ where Q_1 and Q_2 are matrices with diagonal ε_1 and ε_{i+1} respectively, and for nonnegative constraints, $P_{S_i}(X_n) = \begin{cases} X_{n-1}, & if X_{n-1} > 0 \\ 0, & if X_{n-1} < 0 \end{cases}$. At the master agent, the starting point of next iteration is convex combination of the projection $P_{S_i}(X_n)$ which is calculated at the slave agents. In order to get the starting point of the $(n+1)$th iteration, the projections of $P_{S_i}(X_n)$ inside the slave agent are assembled at the master agent by using a weighted sum:

$$X_{n+1} = X_n + L*[\sum w_i P_{S_i}(X_n) - X_n] \qquad (2)$$

where L is the relaxation parameter, and w_i is a weight assigned for the ith agent (normally we treat all slave agents equally) with $\sum w_i = 1$. This method can be seen as a special case of the parallel projection method (PPM) (Combettes, 2003) (Censor & Zenios, 1998). Because the objective function of this particular problem is quadratic, thereby convex and the constraints are linear thereby convex as well, the optimization process is simpler than general projection methods.

The distributed training algorithm is implemented over the Message Passing Interface (MPI). For the purpose of demonstration, a 4-agent training algorithm is tested over a dataset for a 12-by-12 matrix provided at (Cole, 1992).

According to the experiments (see Figure 3 and Figure 4), the simultaneous convergence proves the synchronization among the agents. The agents can communicate and collaborate with each other to reach an optimal solution. The major difficulty of a distributed intelligent system is to make sure all the agents work towards the same goal. The experiment shows this distributed intelligent algorithm is successful.

EXPERIMENTAL RESULTS

Here we present two methods of checking the quality of the estimated matrix: direct and indirect checking. The reason why we introduce the indirect method is that the direct evaluation of a large-size matrix is a rather difficult task. A thousand-by-thousand matrix contains up to ten million of numbers. The simple measurements such as the sum do not make too much sense, as the important deviation is submerged by the total deviation which normally is far larger than the individual ones. The key criterion here is the distribution or the interrelationship between the entries of the matrix: whether the matrix reflects the true underlying industry structure, not necessary the exactly right value, at least the right ratios.

First, we create some artificial data, a 12-by-12 matrix in order to see the performance of this approach. During the experiment, the coefficient $1/\varepsilon_1$ in the equation (1) is tuned to fit the data properly. We change $1/\varepsilon_1$ ranging from 10, 1, 0.1 to 0.01, and the result is below:

Clearly, with the decrease of value of $1/\varepsilon_1$, the resulted matrix is moving away from the matrix of previous year. While $1/\varepsilon_1$ is set smaller, the mining algorithm pushes the model toward the second part of the equation (1).

The multipliers in the input-output framework reflect the impacts of the final demand changes on the upstream industries (Miller & Blair, 1985). The information contained by the multipliers is very similar to the sensitivity analysis in the general statistics. The general formula of constructing the multipliers is:

$$M = D(I - A)^{-1} \tag{3}$$

where M is the multiplier, I is the identity matrix, A is the technique coefficients matrix each element of which $a_i = \dfrac{x_i}{x_1 + x_2 + \ldots + x_n}$, and D is the change of the final demand.

This sensitivity multiplier counts the impact of any change of outputs on the whole upstream inputs, and not only the direct inputs. Any deviation occurring in the upstream inputs from the underlying true structure will be amplified and reflected on the multipliers. Thereby, the multipliers send an indirect warning signal to imply the structural deviation occurring on the upstream inputs. As a case study, a matrix aims to calculate the total water usage of the different industries in Australia.

Here a part of the multipliers are used to measure the quality of the resulting matrix. This matrix aims to calculate the total water usage of the different industries in Australia. A part of the data is collected from the Water Account reports produced by the Australian Bureau of Statistics (ABS, 2008a).

In Table 2, the direct intensity indicates the direct usage of the water by the industry, and total multipliers indicate the all upstream water usage of the industry. The difference between the direct intensity and total multiplier indicates the upstream consumption. For example, the pig industry has total multiplier 0.273531332. That means each dollar of pork will cost 0.27 litre of water, but the direct usage of water is only 0.177 litre per dollar. The 0.1 litre water is consumed by upstream industries such as some agriculture sections which supply the food for pigs.

Figure 3. Three agents (hard, soft and nonnegative) converge to zero respectively after 50 iterations. The y-axis indicates the distance $|G_1 X + E - C_1|$ between the X vector and the soft constraints, the distance $|G_2 X - C_2|$ between the X vector and the hard constraints, and the distance between the X vector and nonnegative hyperplance (if X is negative, the distance is the $|X|$). The x-axis is the number of the iteration the distributed system takes.

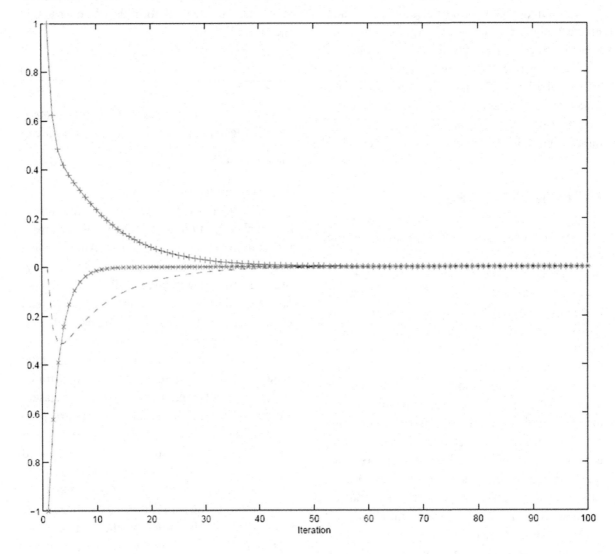

From the above plot comparing the two series of the multipliers, two series basically follow the same trend, which indicates the industry structure is estimated properly. However the estimated multipliers are more frustrated than the true underlying multipliers, which indicates the estimated multipliers amplifies the impact on the upstream. One possible reason for this phenom-

enon is the shift of the underlying industry structure. For example, "Rice plantings dropped to the lowest levels since 1927, from 20,000 hectares in 2006–07 to 3,000 hectares in 2007–08 while production was down 86% to 23,000 tones" (ABS, 2008b) corresponds the dispersion between the estimated multiplier and real multiplier of the rice industry (the 8th industry section at Figure 6). As

Figure 4. Two parts of the objective function $\dfrac{(X - \overline{X})^2}{\varepsilon_1}$ *and* $\sum \dfrac{e_i^2}{\varepsilon_{i+1}}$ *converge to constant levels after the same number of iterations as the distances of agents converge to zero.*

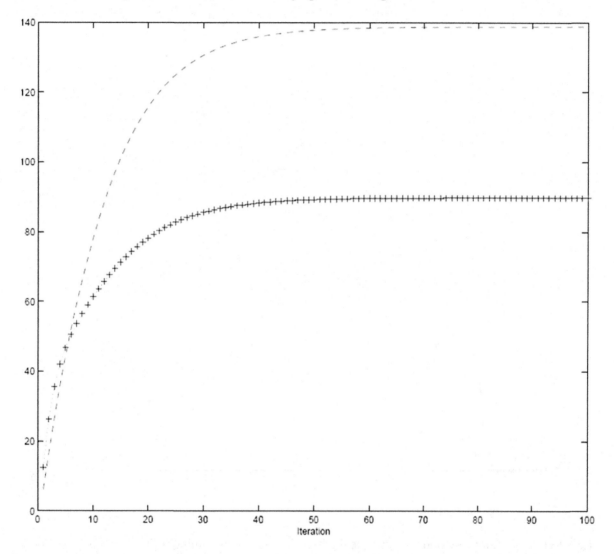

the domestic rice production drops, the water usage reduces constantly. More and more rice is imported from overseas, and the ratio of (water usage) /rice drops constantly, which causes the dispersion.

A commercial optimization package, ILOG CPLEX supplied by IBM, is employed as a benchmark to demonstrate the improvement of the memory allocation for the 3000-by-3000 matrix. In order to construct a matrix with such

a large size, the learning algorithm (see Equation 1) has 8,792,676 variables to be estimated, 333,290 constraints with 26,789,785 nonzero coefficients. This distributed machine learning algorithm takes 2,461 MB memory cross 12 CPUs, approximately 205 MB per CPU. The runtime is 14:30 (Minute:Second). For the comparison, CPLEX package with the penalty method (Bazaraa, Jarvis, & Sherali, 2005), which runs on a single CPU, takes 12,157MB memory and

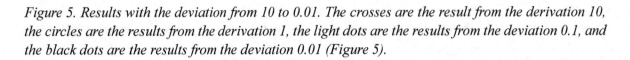

Figure 5. Results with the deviation from 10 to 0.01. The crosses are the result from the derivation 10, the circles are the results from the derivation 1, the light dots are the results from the deviation 0.1, and the black dots are the results from the deviation 0.01 (Figure 5).

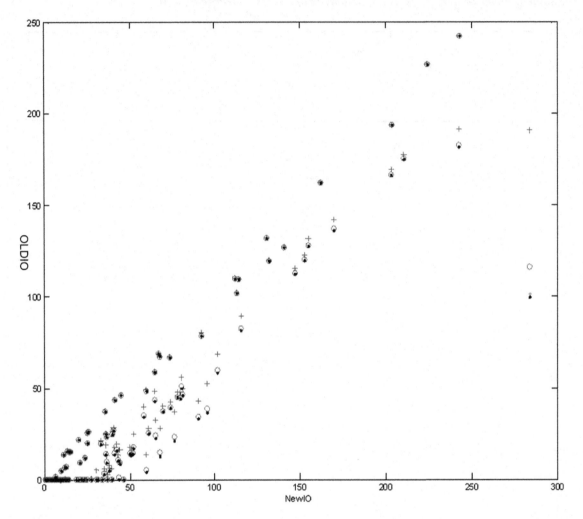

01:53:13 (Hour:Minute:Second) to complete the estimation for the same problem. The 20GB memory is current upper limit for a CPU at the National Computational Infrastructure (NCI) (Kahn, 2009). Currently, ISA is estimating an 8000-by-8000 matrix, this distributed learning algorithm provides enough power, but CPLEX package simply cannot handle the dataset with this size.

The performance of this distributed system is determined not only by the size of target matrix, but also by the setting of the system including the number of CPUs cross which the agents run. According to the experiments (see Table 3), the increase of the number of CPUs can improve the performance of the system, but the performance may be deteriorated by including too many CPUs. For example, by including 32 CPUs, the virtual memory usage increases disproportional to the size of matrix, and it is caused by the large volume of communication among the agents.

Table 2. A snapshot of the estimated total multiplier for the water usage of Australian industry sections

Industry	Direct Intensity (litre/$)	Total Multiplier (litre /$)
Sheep and lambs	0.175306192	0.229353737
Wheat	0.179059807	0.27047284
Barley	0.178962619	0.235765397
Beef cattle	0.175528219	0.265691956
Untreated milk & Dairy cattle	1.233958	1.46699422
Pigs	0.177604301	0.273531332
Poultry & Eggs	0.288054	0.47927187
Sugar cane	3.664307556	3.720540595
Vegetables & Fruit	0.262444	0.3157365
Ginned cotton	0.000836372	0.297221617
Softwoods	0.175060473	0.236982027
Hardwoods	0.175416808	0.239130312
Forestry	0.175046587	0.229861225

Figure 6. Comparison between the Serie of Real Multipliers and the Series of Estimated Multipliers. The y-axis is the values of multipliers and the x-axis is the industry sections.

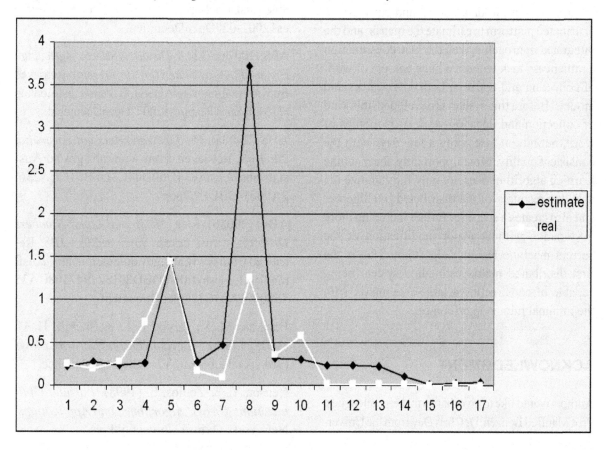

Table 3. The performances of the distributed machine learning algorithm over various datasets, the virtual memory includes the physical memory and communication overhead etc.

Target Matrix	120-by-120 matrix	460-by-460 matrix	3000-by-3000 matrix
Physics Memory(RAM)	40MB	617 MB	2313MB
Virtual Memory(RAM)	54MB	1076 MB	2461MB
Number of CPUs (or agents)	6	32	12
Elapsed Time	25 Seconds	29 Seconds	14:30 Mins

CONCLUSION

The paper demonstrates a distributed intelligent system for updating large-scale economic models. The unique characteristics of the data determine that the distributed intelligent system must be capable of dealing the temporal and spatial data simultaneously. Furthermore, the large size of the estimated matrix requires the system to process large amounts of heterogeneous data efficiently. According to the results of the experiments, the system successfully integrates multiple data source and runs over a distributed platform to estimate the matrix, and the integrated approach makes the matrix estimation a rather easy task without a huge amount of work of collecting and updating both data sources and models. Before this system is developed, this kind of collection and updating work costs months of work, but now it takes only a few days with the consistent quality. More importantly, the machine learning algorithm does not only fully unitize the abandon resource of the distributed intelligence, and also creates a space for further including more information without major modification of the current machine learning algorithm. This is the first distributed matrix estimation system being capable of constructing a large-size matrix with the minimal human interference.

ACKNOWLEDGMENT

Authors would like to give thanks to their colleagues, Prof Manfred Lenzen, Dr Chris Dey from the University of Sydney, Dr Yalcin Kaya, and A/Prof Regina Burachik from the University of South Australia and reviewers for their comments and suggestions.

REFERENCES

ABS. (2007a). *5215.0.55.001 - Australian National Accounts: Input-Output Tables (Product Details) - Electronic Publication, 2001-02.* Retrieved from www.abs.gov.au/AUSSTATS/abs@.nsf/Lookup/5215.0.55.001Main+Features12001-02?OpenDocument

ABS. (2007b). *7124.0 - Historical Selected Agriculture Commodities, by State (1861 to Present).* Retrieved from www.abs.gov.au/AUSSTATS/abs@.nsf/Lookup/7124.0Main+Features12007?OpenDocument.

ABS. (2008a). *4610.0 - Water Account, Australia, 2004-05.* Retrieved from www.abs.gov.au/Ausstats/abs@.nsf/0/34D00D44C3DFB51CCA2568A900143BDE?Open.

ABS. (2008b). *Rice, Sheep and Lamb Numbers Drop to Lowest Levels Since 1920s: ABS.* Retrieved from www.abs.gov.au/ausstats/abs@.nsf/mediareleasesbytitle/9DBD801527947508CA257500001A04C1?OpenDocument

Bazaraa, M. S., Jarvis, J. J., & Sherali, H. D. (2005). *Linear Programming and Network Flows* (3rd ed.). Hoboken, NJ: Wiley-Interscience.

Censor, Y., & Zenios, S. (1998). *Parallel Optimization: Theory, Algorithms, and Applications.* New York: Oxford University Press.

Cole, S. (1992). A note on a Lagrangian derivation of a general multi-propotional scaling algorithm. *Regional Science and Urban Economics, 22*(2), 291–297. doi:10.1016/0166-0462(92)90017-U

Combettes, P. L. (2003). A Block-iterative Surrogate Constraint Splitting Method for Quadratic Signal Recovery. *IEEE Transactions on Signal Processing, 51*(7), 1771–1782. doi:10.1109/TSP.2003.812846

Hobbs, L., Hillson, S., Lawande, S., & Smith, P. (2005). *Oracle Database 10g Data Warehousing*. Dordrecht, The Netherlands: Elsevier Digital Press.

Kahn, M. (2009). *SGI XE Cluster SGI XE Cluster System Details*. Retrieved from www.nf.nci.org.au/facilities/vayu/hardware.php

Lenzen, M., Wood, R., & Gallego, B. (2006, 26-28 July). *RAS matrix balancing under conflicting information*. Paper presented at the Intermediate Input-Output Meetings 2006 on Sustainability, Trade and Productivity, Sendai, Japan.

McNeil, S., & Hendrickson, C. (1985). A Regression Formulation of the Matrix Estimation Problem. *Transportation Science, 19*(3), 278–292. doi:10.1287/trsc.19.3.278

Medina, A., Taft, N., Salamatian, K., Bhattacharyya, S., & Diot, C. (2002). Traffic Matrix Estimation: Existing Techniques and New Directions. In *Proceedings of the ACM SIGCOMM Computer Communication Review, 2002 SIGCOMM conference, SESSION: Measuring and simulating networks* (Vol. 32, No. 4, pp. 161-174).

Miller, H. J. (2007). Geographic Data Mining and Knowledge Discovery. In Wilson, J., & Fotheringham, A. S. (Eds.), *The Handbook of Geographic Information Science*. Hoboken, NJ: Wiley-Blackwell. doi:10.1002/9780470690819.ch19

Miller, H. J., & Han, J. (2001). *Geographic Data Mining and Knowledge Discovery*. New York: CRC. doi:10.4324/9780203468029

Miller, R. E., & Blair, P. D. (1985). *Input-output Analysis, Foundations and Extensions*. Englewood Cliffs, NJ: Prentice-Hall Inc.

Percoco, M., Hewings, G., & Senn, L. (2006). Structural Change Decomposition Through a Gobal Sensitivity Analysis of Input--output Models. *Economic Systems Research, 18*(2), 115–131. doi:10.1080/09535310600652919

This work was previously published in International Journal of Organizational and Collective Intelligence, Volume 1, Issue 3, edited by Hideyasu Sasaki, pp. 20-33, copyright 2010 by IGI Publishing (an imprint of IGI Global).

Chapter 13
Analyzing Community Deliberation and Achieving Consensual Knowledge in SAM

Krissada Maleewong
Shinawatra University, Thailand

Chutiporn Anutariya
Shinawatra University, Thailand

Vilas Wuwongse
Asian Institute of Technology, Thailand

ABSTRACT

This paper presents a novel approach to harnessing collective intelligence that will allow a community to create, collaborate, and share knowledge based on the Semantic Argumentation Model (SAM). It encourages multiple users to express ideas or positions on complex issues, and to submit arguments that support or oppose the ideas of the other members. In principle, ideas considered possible solutions to an issue are those that contain high content quality and achieve great community agreement. Therefore, the authors define several useful measures to analyze the deliberation for determining the content quality, community preference, and achieving quality-assured consensual knowledge. Finally, a web-based prototype system founded on the proposed approach is developed and made available for public use. A preliminary study on the system usability shows that the system is practical and can enhance the collaborative knowledge creation and sharing process.

1. INTRODUCTION

Collective intelligence has become increasingly important for community-driven knowledge creation and sharing by enabling collaborative deliberation to society. Many collaborative knowledge management systems, especially social webs such as Wikis, blogs, discussion forums, and question-answering portals are continuing to grow with increasing number of contributors and covering a wide range of disciplines. Many are successful in encouraging people to participate actively in content creation and knowledge sharing which lead to the growth of innovative ideas

DOI: 10.4018/978-1-4666-1577-9.ch013

and a substantial number of online community knowledge bases.

In order to take advantage of collective knowledge concerning complex problems or controversial challenges, multiple users collaboratively create and share knowledge based on their skills, viewpoints, and experiences. However, the quality and reliability of such user-generated content vary greatly depending on individuals' interests and expertise. This often results in inconsistent and untrustworthy information. Moreover, a community unintentionally faces several conflicts due to the different opinions in geographically dispersed community and the lack of an effective mechanism for facilitating group collaboration and deliberation. Accordingly, the cost of content quality management and conflict resolution are unavoidable, and these problems are occasionally difficult to solve without human involvement.

To tackle such problems, this paper employs the *Semantic Argumentation Model* (*SAM*) (Maleewong, Anutariya, & Wuwongse, 2009a) to enhance collaborative knowledge creation and sharing by allowing members to raise issues on any topic and propose positions as alternative solutions. A member can submit arguments to support or oppose a particular position based on his judgment. The community deliberation are structurally and semantically captured and encoded in RDF/OWL language conforming to the *SAM Schema* (*SAMS*) (Maleewong, Anutariya, & Wuwongse, 2009a) which enables automated analysis across the community knowledge base. In order to achieve quality-assured consensual knowledge, a number of useful measures are formally defined for measuring the quality of users' generated contents and determining group preference on a certain position. A high-quality position supported by most members is considered as a potential position to solve the issue. Moreover, the proposed feedback mechanism allows members to improve the position quality and revise their submitted arguments (and

rebuttals) regarding other members' opinions for driving the community to achieve a consensus. In addition, an online collaborative knowledge creation and sharing system, namely *ciSAM*, has been developed in order to validate the practicality and usability of the proposed approach in real-world scenarios.

The organization of this paper is as follows: Section 2 describes the related work. Section 3 presents Semantic Argumentation Model. Section 4 explains community deliberation analysis. Section 5 draws discussions, conclusions, and future research direction.

2. RELATED WORK

By allowing users to easily create and edit articles, Wikipedia has grown to be the world's largest free encyclopedia. Its mechanism, however has resulted in edit war and vandalism problems (Viegas, Wattenberg, Kriss, & van Ham, 2007), which then lead to untrustworthy problems. Moreover, its history pages representing information in reverse chronological order (most recent first) also confuse its users when searching for an evolution of a specific knowledge. In order to improve information access and enable knowledge exchange across applications, *Semantic Wikipedia* (Krotzsch, Vrandecic, Volkel, & Haller, 2007) allows users to semantically annotate wiki pages. However, high technical skill is required for inexperienced users to structurally formalize their knowledge, and the several aforementioned problems caused by wiki mechanism remain unsolved.

To effectively capture the deliberation and to facilitate group collaboration, many recent researches have applied argumentation technologies in various domains as follows. *Compendium* (Shum, Selvin, Sierhuis, & Conklin, 2006) is a knowledge management environment, developed based on *graphical IBIS system* (*gIBIS*) (Conklin & Begeman, 1988), for supporting group deliberations. *Collaboratorium* (Iandoli, Klein, & Zollo, 2008) is a collaborative framework, which integrates *IBIS model* (Rittel & Kunz, 1970), *Walton's argumentation schemes* (Walton, 2006), and *Toulmin's Argument Scheme* (Toulmin, 1958) to capture discussions as argumentation networks. However, these systems do not have rich formal semantics to handle sophisticated processing of argumentative statements such as ensuring quality of argumentation and determining group agreement. With a focus on the ontology engineering domain, *DILIGENT* (Tempich, Simperl, Luczak, Studer, & Pinto, 2007) and *HCOME* (Kotis & Vouros, 2005) develop ontology engineering environments by applying the IBIS model to capture the discussion and allow members to construct an ontology in a collaborative manner. However, both systems still lack an explicit model to evaluate a community agreement, and hence require a human moderator to mediate and resolve conflicts.

With a huge number of users having different interests and skills, the community knowledge could be diverse and contain untrustworthy information. To assure the quality and reliability of created knowledge, a variety of quality metric frameworks have been proposed as follows. *ProbReview model* (Hu, Lim, Sun, & Lauw, 2007) measures a Wikipedia article's quality by considering the amount of editing and reviewing words, while the work by Wilkinson and Huberman (2007) considers the number of editions and distinct editors. On the other hand, Bian, Liu, Agichtein, and Zha (2008) have proposed a *ranking framework* to retrieve relevant and high-quality answers from Yahoo! Answer. However, its ranking process does not incorporate the quality of user-generated contents and user reputation. By combining content information (e.g., punctuation and typos, syntactic and semantic complexity, as well as grammaticality) and non-content information (e.g., users' ratings and contents-users interaction), a *classification*

framework (Agichtein, Castillo, Donato, & Gionis, 2008) has been developed for finding high quality contents. However, the need for manual supervision remains a problem.

With the aim to determine the reliability and trustworthiness of a resource (e.g., information, citation, people, and organization) in a social network, *PageRank* algorithm (Brin & Page, 1998) has been widely applied in many recent works, especially in trust and reputation systems as follows. In 2003, Kamvar, Schlosser and Garcia-Molina proposed a decentralized PageRank algorithm, namely *EigenTrust*, to compute global trust values in peer-to-peer networks. That is, peers with poor performance will receive a corresponding low trust rating. Later, Zhang, Ackerman, and Adamic (2007) developed *ExpertiseRank* algorithm for finding an expert in an online community where an individual gains expertise in PageRank fashion. In linguistic domain, Esuli, and Sebastiani (2007) also employed PageRank to automatically rank *WordNet synsets* for determining how strongly they possess a given semantic property. Moreover, to evaluate the *ISI Impact Factor*, the weighted PageRank is used for determining the prestige of the citing journals rather than counting the amount of citations (Bollen, Rodriguez, & Van, 2006).

3. SEMANTIC ARGUMENTATION MODEL

This section presents the *Semantic Argumentation Model* (*SAM*) which can respond to a set of key requirements and properties of a collaborative knowledge creation and sharing system. It facilitates community-driven knowledge creation and sharing, analyzes community deliberation, resolves conflicts and achieves a consensus. Moreover, an example of the system usage and the prototype system are discussed.

Figure 1. SAM's architecture

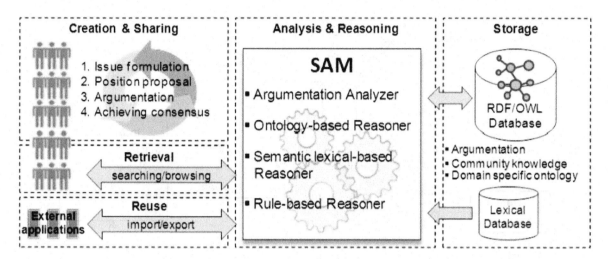

3.1 SAM's Architecture

Figure 1 depicts the architecture of SAM, which consists of the following five functionalities: (*i*) *Creation and Sharing*, (*ii*) *Analysis and Reasoning*, (*iii*) *Storage*, (*iv*) *Retrieval*, and (*v*) *Reuse*.

The **creation and sharing function** motivates members to cooperatively create and share knowledge in a collective improvement mechanism. The **analysis and reasoning function** provides sophisticated analysis across community deliberation using the *argumentation analyzer*, and enables semantic reasoning using the *ontology-based* and *semantic lexical-based reasoners*. Moreover, conflicting arguments can be detected by employing the *rule-based reasoner*. In order to allow machine-processable semantics of the collective knowledge, the **storage function** maintains a database that encodes the argumentation, community knowledge, and domain specific ontology in RDF/OWL metadata format. In addition, the **retrieval function** supports semantic search, while the **reuse function** allows information exchange across different platforms. With emphasis on analyzing community deliberation and achieving consensual knowledge, this paper focuses on knowledge creation and sharing function in cooperation with the argumentation analyzer.

3.2 Semantic Argumentation Process

To enhance collaborative works and to support community deliberation, the creation and sharing function follows the developed *semantic argumentation process*, which consists of the following activities:

- **Issue formulation:** When creating collective knowledge regarding a complex problem and controversial challenge, a community often confronts with many *issues/sub-issues* to be resolved by collaborative thinking. Thus, this activity enables members to formulate issues for community deliberation.

- **Position proposal:** For each issue, members are encouraged to express *positions* as alternative solutions, which are presented to all members for their judgments and feedbacks. New members are motivated for critical thinking in order to propose better solutions. A position can consist of several sub-positions, and can raise a new issue for further discussion. For each position, *data* represents a fact and *backing* provides information for supporting the position, while a *certainty degree* express-

Figure 2. SAMS: SAM Schema

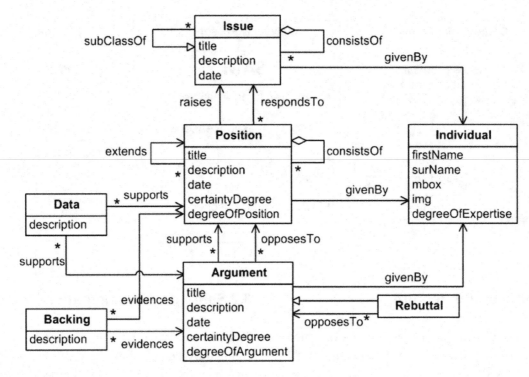

es the confidence of the member who posts the position.

- **Argumentation:** Each member can submit an *argument* to support or oppose a certain position. In general, a position supported by many arguments is considered as a potential position to solve the issue. On the other hand, a position made against by many arguments requires further revision. Similar to a position, each argument contains *data*, *backing*, and *certainty degree*. Moreover, an argument can be made against by a *rebuttal*.

- **Achieving consensus:** This activity aims to obtain the quality-assured consensual knowledge by allowing multiple users to collectively create knowledge, and revise earlier ideas according to other members' responses. However, since the complete agreement in a large-scale community deliberation is impossible, SAM employs *soft consensus* (Kacprzyk & Fedrizzi, 1988) to

evaluate group agreement, and hence allowing the *consensus level* to be identified by a specific threshold (*consensus threshold*), which determines the quality and preference of a desired position. When a position reaches the predefined threshold, such position is said to be *acceptable* and considered as a potential solution to solve the issue; otherwise, the community is encouraged for more deliberation in position proposal and argumentation activities.

Figure 2 presents *SAM Schema* (*SAMS*) for structurally and semantically capturing the community deliberation.

3.3 Example

This section presents an example scenario having multiple users participating and raising a number of issues related to the 2009 Influenza A (H1N1) topic. The community collaboratively proposes

Figure 3. An Example of Community Deliberation.

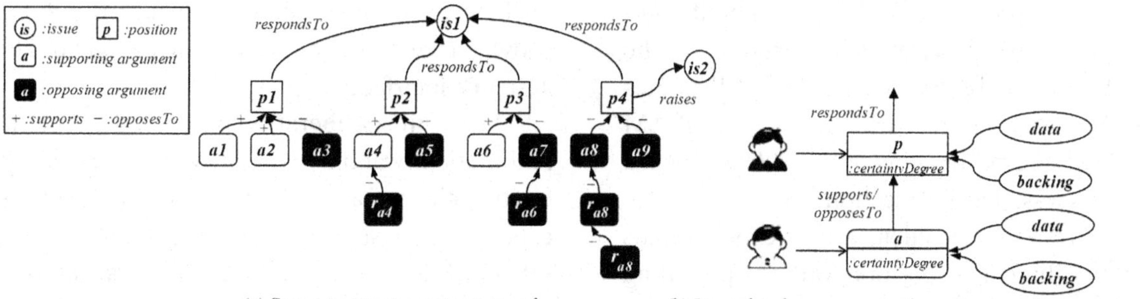

(a) Semantic argumentation network   (b) Interrelated components of position p and argument a

positions and submits arguments regarding the raised issues. An interesting issue is: *"How to distinguish ordinary flu from 2009 H1N1?"*, which has four positions proposed as follows:

Position p1: Some warning signs are concerned as H1N1 symptoms,

Position p2: No symptoms can distinguish H1N1 from regular flu,

Position p3: High fever over 100 F more than 3 days indicates H1N1 infection,

Position p4: Blood test can identify H1N1 infection.

Figure 3(*a*) summarizes the community deliberation by presenting important components and social interactions in a semantic argumentation network. The figure shows that an issue *is*1 is raised for community deliberation, and positions *p*1, *p*2, *p*3, and *p*4 are proposed as alternative solutions to solve it. The position *p*1 is supported by arguments *a*1 and *a*2, and opposed by an argument *a*3, while the position *p*2 is supported by an argument *a*4 and opposed by *a*5, and a rebuttal r_{a4} is submitted to object to the argument *a*4. The position *p*3 is supported by an argument *a*6 and opposed by *a*7, and a rebuttal r_{a7} is submitted to object to the argument *a*7. On the other hand, the position *p*4 is opposed by arguments *a*8 and *a*9. Since the position *p*4 needs further discussion, an issue *is*2 is raised.

Figure 3(*b*) shows that a member can propose a position and submit an argument by articulating his opinion in terms of *data* and providing a number of *backings* as evidence for supporting the proposed idea. Moreover, he can express a certainty degree concerning the posted position or argument.

3.4 Prototype System: ciSAM

Founded on SAM, an online collective intelligence explorer, namely *ciSAM*, has been developed as a Web-based, two-tiered application, and is available for public usage at http://research.siu.ac.th:8080/cisam. The client-side application employs ActionScript and MXML to create the interaction part embedded in HTML pages for rich graphics user interfaces, as illustrated in Figure 4. The server-side application contains a Java Server Page (JSP) and servlets which are responsible for the application and data processing. In particular, it employs *Sesame* – an open-source RDF/OWL database (Broekstra, Kampman, & Harmelen, 2002) to maintain the community knowledge and deliberation. In addition, it implements the *argumentation analyzer* in Java, and constructs the *ontology-based reasoner*, the *semantic lexical-based reasoner*, and the *rule-based reasoner* by using *OWLIM* – a semantic repository for RDF(s) and OWL, which provides a Storage and Inference Layer (SAIL) with reasoning support for the *Sesame*.

With ciSAM, users can raise issues and collaboratively propose positions and submit arguments about the issues of their interests using the simple GUIs and entry forms. Figure 4 illustrates ciSAM's user interface and shows how ciSAM facilitates the deliberation on the 2009 influenza issue discussed in Sub-section 3.3.

To propose a position, a user expresses his idea by filling in the position form and providing the title, description, data, backing, and certainty degree. Five predefined linguistic terms (*strongly confident*, *confident*, *possible*, *maybe*, and *not sure*) are available to choose to identify the user's certainty degree.

For each position, a user can give a supporting argument (represented in green), an opposing argument, or rebuttal (represented in red) using the argument form. Similar to the position form, the user describes his argument in terms of title, description, data, backing, and certainty degree.

By visualizing the deliberation in the list view with different icons and colors presenting different types of contributions (i.e., issue, position, supporting argument, opposing argument, and rebuttal), the users can easily follow every step in the collaborative argumentation process,

as depicted by Figure 4. In addition, by simply clicking on each contribution, its details will be shown in the information pane, on the right of the system's interface.

During the deliberation process, the system automatically and dynamically analyzes all the contributions for discovering and presenting a potential position to the community, while other positions remain available for traceability and further clarification. The community deliberation analysis is described in the following section.

4. COMMUNITY DELIBERATION ANALYSIS

This section analyzes community deliberation described in SAMS by formally defining important measures to determine the quality and group preference of a position and argument, and to achieve quality-assured consensual knowledge. The defined measures include: a *content quality*, a *degree of argument*, a *degree of individual preference*, a *degree of group preference*, a *degree of position*, and a *degree of expertise*.

Figure 4. User interface of ciSAM system

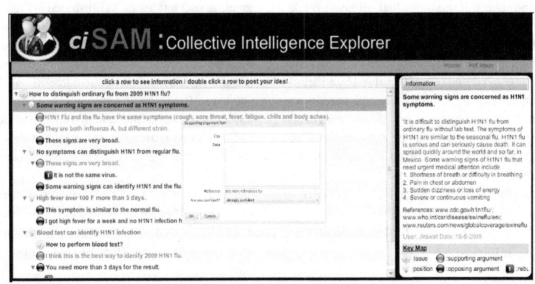

4.1 Measuring Quality of Position and Argument

The quality of a position or an argument is measured by considering its *data quality*, *backing reliability*, together with *certainty degree* and the *degree of expertise* of the proposer, as follows:

Data quality: To linguistically assess the quality of user-generated contents (i.e., positions and arguments), which are usually described in textual format, a number of intrinsic quality metrics (Stvilia, Twidale, Smith, & Gasser, 2008) are considered including *misspelling*, *grammaticality*, and *readability*. Poor quality text implies low conformance of writing skills, which is an obstacle for effective reading and understanding of a user.

Throughout this section, let P be the set of positions, A the set of arguments, and I the set of individuals. For a content (either position or argument) $c \in P \cup A$, let $data_c$ denote its data. The quality of $data_c$, denoted by $quality(data_c)$, is then measured as follows:

$$quality(data_c) = \frac{(1 - misspelling(data_c)) + grammaticality(data_c) + readability(data_c)}{3},$$

where $- misspelling(data_c) \in [0, 1]$ is the average number of spelling mistakes, typos, and out-of-vocabulary words appeared in $data_c$,

- *Grammaticality*$(data_c) \in [0, 1]$ identifies the grammar correctness of $data_c$ by applying *link grammar* (Lafferty, Sleator, & Temperley, 1992), a widely accepted English syntactic theory, and is measured by calculating the average number of sentences that contains no grammar mistake, and

- *Readability*$(data_c) \in [0, 1]$ evaluates comprehension difficulty when reading the data content $data_c$ using *Flesch Readability Score* (Flesch, 1949), the most popular readability metric applied by many US government agencies and a variety of word processing applications (e.g., Microsoft Word, OpenOffice, and Abiword), which is calculated by combining the word length and the sentence length; the content with a high score eases user readability.

Therefore, based on the proposed measure, a content with a high data quality score implies that it has less number of misspelling and grammar mistakes, and is easy to read.

Backing reliability: Due to a huge number of publicly available resources and services on the Internet, a cooperative community mostly prefers its members to provide backing information in terms of citation to online reference resources. This allows other members to validate the backings' reliability more easily and to explore for further related details. In addition, reliable backings can help encourage other members to support the proposed idea.

Here, an algorithm based on *PageRank* is proposed to measure such backing reliability. Intuitively, it determines the importance of each backing in a *PageRank* fashion. Let $backing_c$ denote the set of all backings of a content $c \in P \cup A$, and $PageRank(b) \in [0, 1]$ denote the PageRank of a backing $b \in backing_c$. The reliability of $backing_c$, denoted by $reliability(backing_c)$, could then be evaluated as follows:

$$reliability(backing_c) = \frac{\sum_{b \in backing_c} PageRank(b)}{\mid backing_c \mid},$$

Certainty degree: Frequently, a member proposes an idea or opinion with a particular certainty degree using widely different words. For example, "I am confident that…", "I strongly agree with…", or "It might be better if…". Thus, the member can use the following five linguistic terms: *strongly confident*, *confident*, *possible*, *maybe*, and *not sure* to express his certainty regarding the submitted contribution. The certainty degrees defined for these five terms are 1, 0.8, 0.6, 0.4, and 0.2, respectively. Let *certainty*$_c$ denote the corresponding certainty degree of the member when submitting a content $c \in P \cup A$.

Degree of expertise: An individual, who gains high expertise in a particular area, usually provides reliable knowledge with higher quality than a beginner. As a result, the quality of a contributing content is partly evaluated based on its contributor's expertise.

Denote an individual who articulates a content $c \in P \cup A$ by i_c. For an individual i, denote his degree of expertise by $\delta_E(i)$. Such degree has an initial value of 1, and can be dynamically updated based on the accuracy and contribution that each individual participates in proposing positions and submitting arguments. More details about the degree of expertise and its calculation are discussed in Sub-section 4.4.

Definition 1 (Quality of Position or Argument) Let δ_Q be the mapping $P \cup A \rightarrow [0, 1]$ which defines the quality of a position or an argument $c \in P \cup A$ as follows:

$$\delta_Q(c) = ((\alpha \; quality(data_c) + (1 - \alpha)$$
$$reliability(backing_c) \times certainty_c \times (\frac{\delta_E(i_c)}{\max_{i \in I}(\delta_E(i))})$$

Where:

- *Quality(data_c)* measures the linguistic quality of the content's data as defined earlier,
- *Reliability(backing_c)* evaluates how reliable the given backings of the content c are,

- *Certainty_c* denotes the certainty degree of the contributor when posting the content c,
- $\delta_E(i_c)$ denotes the degree of expertise of individual i who proposed the content c,
- The weights $\alpha \in (0, 1)$ and $(1 - \alpha)$ for *quality(data_c)* and *reliability(backing_c)* respectively define the importance of well-written data and trustworthy references.

Note that the quality of content in other formats rather than text can be measured using different metrics; for instance, a content described in ontology format can be evaluated by considering schema and instance metrics for measuring the quality and effectiveness of designed ontology (Maleewong, Anutariya, & Wuwongse, 2009b).

Example 1 Refer to the example scenario and the H1N1 issue of Sub-section 3.3. Figure 5 depicts two selected positions: $p1$ and $p2$, proposed to resolve the issue.

Suppose that the community identically defines the weights of 0.5 for both data quality (α) and backing reliability ($1 - \alpha$), and the degrees of expertise of all contributors are initialized to 1. The quality of the positions $p1$ and $p2$ are computed as follows:

$$\delta_Q(p1) = ((0.5 \times 0.85) + (0.5 \times 0.83) \times 1 \times (1/1)) = 0.84$$

$$\delta_Q(p2) = ((0.5 \times 0.58) + (0.5 \times 0.25) \times 1 \times (1/1)) = 0.42.$$

The above results demonstrate that the position $p1$ maintains high quality due to its high data quality (no misspellings and grammar mistakes, and high readability score) and reliable backings (*CDC*: *Center of Disease Control and Prevention*, *WHO*, and reuters.com with corresponding PageRank scores of 0.9, 0.9, and 0.7, respectively). On the other hand, the quality of the position $p2$ yields a small value due

Figure 5. Position p1 and p2

Title: Position p1
Data: It is difficult to distinguish H1N1 flu from ordinary flu without lab test. The symptoms of H1N1 are similar to the seasonal flu. H1N1 flu is serious and can seriously cause death. It can spread quickly around the world and so far, in Mexico. Some warning signs of H1N1 flu that need urgent medical attention include 1. Shortness of breath or difficulty in breathing 2. Pain in chest or abdomen 3. Sudden dizziness or loss of energy 4. Severe or continuous vomiting 5. Flu like symptoms, bad cough and fever
quality(data_{p1}) = ((1 − 0) + 1 + 0.56)/3 = 0.85
Backing: • www.cdc.gov/h1n1flu/ • www.who.int/csr/disease/swineflu/en/ • www.reuters.com/news/globalcoverage/swineflu
reliability(backing_{p1}) = (0.9+0.9+0.7)/3 = 0.83
Certainty degree: strongly confident

Title: Position p2
Data: There is no particular symptoms that distinguish 2009 H1N1 flu from other types of flu. Symtoms like diarhea and vomiting are also associated with 2009 flu. Those symptoms can also be caused by many other conditions, and that means that you can't know, just based on your symptoms. Diagnosis is the identification, by process of elmination, of the nature of anything. Blood test is done to identify 2009 h1n1 flu from normal flu.
quality(data_{p2}) = ((1 − 0.04) + 0.33 + 0.46)/3 = 0.58
Backing: • en.wikipedia.org/wiki/Influenza_A_virus_subtype_H1N1 • www.blogtopsites.com/post/h1n1
reliability(backing_{p2}) = (0.5+0)/2 = 0.25
Certainty degree: strongly confident

to its low data quality (caused by a number of spelling and grammar mistakes), and the use of unreliable references.

4.2 Determining Group Preference

During the deliberation, each member can present his view by submitting either supporting or opposing arguments to a particular position, and making rebuttals to other disagreeing arguments. This sub-section presents how to analyze such information and obtain the preferences (views) of all members with respect to each proposed position. These individual preferences can then be aggregated into a group preference which is used to find a potential position.

Firstly, the *degree of argument* is defined for quantifying the expressive level of each argument submitted to support or oppose a specific position. It is evaluated by considering the quality of an argument, less the summation of all degrees of rebuttals objecting to it.

Definition 2 (Degree of argument) Let δ_A be the mapping $A \to [0, 1]$ which determines the degree of an argument $a \in A$, and be defined inductively as follows:

$$\delta_A(a) = \begin{cases} \delta_Q(a) - \sum_{r_a \in R_a} \delta_A(r_a), & \text{if } \delta_Q(a) > \sum_{r_a \in R_a} \delta_A(r_a); \\ 0, & \text{otherwise} \end{cases}$$

where $-\delta_Q(a)$ determines the quality of the argument a,

- R_a is the set of rebuttals of the argument a.

Example 2 Figure 6 illustrates the set of arguments submitted to support or oppose the positions $p1$ and $p2$, and their degrees of argument.

From the figure, the position $p1$ is supported by the arguments $a1$ and $a2$ with high degrees of argument (0.74 and 0.72, respectively) owing to their high data quality, reliable backing, and high certainty degree. However, it is opposed by the argument $a3$ with a small degree of argument due to its poor data quality, missing backing, and low certainty degree. On the other hand, the position $p2$ is supported by the argument $a4$ and opposed by the argument $a5$. Although, the argument $a4$ provides high data quality (0.37), its degree of argument is decreased to 0 due to the degree of

Figure 6. Arguments submitted to support or oppose the positions p1 and p2

Position p1
⋂ Supporting argument: $a1$
Data: H1N1 Flu and the flu have the same symptoms and they are both contracted the same way. However, the above warning signs are considered as emergency symptoms that need urgent attention.
quality(data$_{a1}$) = ((1 − 0) + 1 + 0.65)/3 = 0.88
Backing: http://www.doh.wa.gov/swineflu/
reliability(backing$_{a1}$) = 0.6
Certainty degree: strongly confident
$\delta_Q(a1)$ = ((0.5x0.88)+(0.5x0.6))x1x(1/1) = 0.74
$\delta_A(a1)$ = 0.74 − 0 = 0.74
⋂ Supporting argument: $a2$
Data: They are both influenza A, but seasonal flu and H1N1 are different strains. So, there is almost no difference between H1N1 and the regular flu. But, I believe that the mentioned symptoms are risk factors of H1N1.
quality(data$_{a2}$) = ((1 − 0) + 1 + 0.66)/3 = 0.89
Backing: http://www.who.int/csr/disease/swineflu/en/index.html
reliability(backing$_{a2}$) = 0.9
Certainty degree: confident
$\delta_Q(a2)$ = ((0.5x0.89)+(0.5x0.9))x0.8x(1/1) = 0.72
$\delta_A(a2)$ = 0.72 − 0 = 0.72
⋂ Opposing argument: $a3$
Data: These signs are very broad. I think H1N1 symptom (or at least ordnary flu) are different amoung children, adults, elderly and pregnant women.
quality(data$_{a3}$) = ((1 − 0.09) + 0.5 + 0.65)/3 = 0.69
Backing: –
reliability(backing$_{a3}$) = 0
Certainty degree: maybe
$\delta_Q(a3)$ = ((0.5x0.69)+(0.5x0))x0.4x(1/1) = 0.14
$\delta_A(a3)$ = 0.14 − 0 = 0.14

Position p2
⋂ Supporting argument: a_4
Data: H1N1 is a common 'regular' flu. All the symptoms are the same, except people are scared for swine flu because there's no vaccine yet.
quality(data$_{a4}$) =((1 − 0) + 1 + 0.75)/3 = 0.91
Backing: -
reliability(backing$_{a4}$) = 0
Certainty degree: confident
$\delta_Q(a4)$ = ((0.5x0.91)+(0.5x0))x0.8x(1/1) = 0.37
$\delta_A(a4)$ = 0
⋂ Rebuttal: r_{a4}
Data: It is not the same virus. The current strain is a new variation of an H1N1 virus, which is a mix of human and animal versions.
quality(data$_{ra4}$) = ((1 − 0) + 1 + 0.65)/3 = 0.88
Backing: http://pagingdrgupta.blogs.cnn.com/category/swine-flu
reliability(backing$_{ra4}$) = 0.5
Certainty degree: strongly confident
$\delta_Q(r_{a4})$ = ((0.5x0.88)+(0.5x0.5))x1x(1/1) = 0.69
$\delta_A(r_{a4})$ = 0.69 − 0 = 0.69
⋂ Opposing argument: $a5$
Data: Although there are no distinct symptms to identify H1H1 from ordinary flu, some warning signs help you to identify 2009 flu such as fever with a rash, bluish skin color, shortness of breath, pain in the chest or persistent vomiting.
quality(data$_{a5}$) =((1 − 0.02) + 1 + 0.31)/3 = 0.76
Backing: http://www.newscientist.com/special/swine-flu
reliability(backing$_{a5}$) = 0.6
Certainty degree: confident
$\delta_Q(a5)$ = ((0.5x0.76)+(0.5x0.6))x0.8x(1/1) = 0.54
$\delta_A(a5)$ = 0.54 − 0 = 0.54

the rebuttal r_{a4} (0.69). Thus, the member who submits the argument $a4$ is motivated to revise his idea or to submit a rebuttal against r_{a4} for clarification.

Next, the *degree of individual preference* is defined to specify the preference (view) of each member with respect to each proposed position. Intuitively, it is calculated by taking the average of the degree of arguments submitted by a particular member on a particular position. A positive (+) or negative (−) sign is then assigned to indicate that such individual preference on that position is supportive or not.

Definition 3 (Degree of individual preference) Define δ_I as the mapping $I \times P \rightarrow [-1, 1]$ which denotes the preference degree of an individual i on a position p as follows:

$$\delta_I(i, p) = \begin{cases} \dfrac{\sum_{a \in A_{i,p}^+} \delta_A(a)}{|A_{i,p}^+|} & \text{if } A_{i,p}^+ \neq \varnothing, \\[3ex] \dfrac{-\sum_{a \in A_{i,p}^-} \delta_A(a)}{|A_{i,p}^-|} & \text{if } A_{i,p}^- \neq \varnothing, \\[3ex] \text{undefined} & \text{if } A_{i,p}^+ \cup A_{i,p}^- = \varnothing. \end{cases}$$

Where:

- $A_{i,p}^{+}$ is the set of supporting arguments submitted by the individual i on the position p,
- $A_{i,p}^{-}$ is the set of opposing arguments submitted by the individual i on the position p,
- $A_{i,p}^{+} \cup A_{i,p}^{-} = \varnothing$ means that the individual i submits no arguments, or in other words, his preference on the position p is undefined.

Note that a member can make several arguments to a particular position, all of which must consistently support or oppose the position. Arguments made by a member, some of which support yet some of which oppose a certain idea, are thus considered to be conflicting arguments which are automatically detected and disallowed.

Subsequently, the *degree of group preference* is defined for representing the group preference of each position. Intuitively, it is evaluated by aggregating the degrees of all individual preferences on such position. The aggregation operation is carried out by means of an *Ordered Weighted Averaging* (*OWA*) operator $\varnothing_Q$ (Yager, 2007). In brief, it provides a parameterized class of mean type aggregation operators (e.g., min, max, average, median) by giving preferences or weights to the argument values based on their ordered position. For example, the Min gives all the weights to smallest argument, while the Max gives all the weights to the largest. A variety of different aggregation operators can be obtained regarding the selected parameters, which relate to linguistic quantifiers such as "*at least half*", "*as many as possible*", or "*most*". This flexibility and parameterization makes the OWA operator suitable for modeling group preference.

By appropriately selecting a linguistic quantifier Q defined by the parameter (a, b), the weighting vector of $\varnothing_Q$, denoted by $W = (w_1, …, w_n)$, is calculated by

$$w_j = Q(j/n) - Q((j - 1)/n),$$

where $w_j \in [0, 1]$, $\sum_{j=1}^{n} w_j = 1$, and for $r \in [0, 1]$, $Q(r)$ is computed as follows:

$$Q(r) = \begin{cases} 0 & \text{if } r < a, \\ \dfrac{r - a}{b - a} & \text{if } a \leq r \leq b, \\ 1 & \text{if } r > a. \end{cases}$$

Definition 4 (Degree of group preference) Let $\delta_G : P \rightarrow [-1, 1]$ determine the degree of group preference on a position p in P, by means of the OWA operator $\varnothing_Q$. Define δ_G as follows:

$$\delta_G(p) = \varnothing_Q(\delta_I(i_1, p), …, \delta_I(i_n, p)) = \left(\sum_{j=1}^{n} w_j \times \delta_I(i_j, p)\right) \times \frac{|I_p|}{|I|},$$

where $I_p = \{i_1, …, i_n\}$ P is the ordered set of individuals who submit arguments to the position p such that $\delta_I(i_j, p) \geq \delta_I(i_k, p)$, for all $j < k$; in other words, I_p is arranged in descending order by the degree of individual preference on p, and $\delta_I(i_1, p) \geq \delta_I(i_2, p) \geq … \geq \delta_I(i_n, p)$.

Example 3 This example aggregates the degrees of individual preference on the positions $p1 - p4$ as shown in Table 1 into a corresponding group preference.

Table 1 depicts that the individuals $i1$ to $i6$ prefer the position $p1$ as a potential position to solve the issue, while they object to the positions $p2$ and $p3$. On the other hand, the individuals $i7$, $i8$, and $i9$, respectively, prefer the positions $p2$, $p4$, and $p3$. In this scenario, the position $p1$ would be immediately selected when the voting system is applied and the opinions of the individuals $i7$, $i8$, and $i9$ who strongly oppose the position $p1$ are discarded. To carefully aggregate all individual preferences, the degree of group preference is computed using the linguistic quantifier "*most*", defined by the parameter $(0.3, 0.8)$ (Yager, 1996) for representing the preference of "*most*" members

Table 1. The degrees of individual preference

$\delta_I(i, p)$	p1	p2	p3	p4
i1	0.9	-0.7	-0.6	-0.3
i2	0.5	-0.4	-0.7	0.3
i3	1.0	-0.9	-0.5	-0.2
i4	0.9	-0.3	-0.3	-0.1
i5	0.7	-0.5	-0.4	0.2
i6	0.3	-0.7	-0.1	0.1
i7	-0.9	0.7	-0.5	0.4
i8	-0.4	-0.5	-0.2	0.5
i9	-0.2	-0.8	0.4	-0.5

on each position. Therefore, the degrees of group preference on the positions p1 to p4 are calculated by means of the OWA operator with the weighting vector W = (0, 0, 0.06, 0.22, 0.23, 0.22, 0.22, 0.05, 0) as depicted in Table 2. Obviously, the position p1 obtains the highest degree of group preference, while such degrees for the positions p2 and p3 have negative values indicating that most members do not support the positions.

4.3 Achieving Quality-Assured Consensual Knowledge

With the goal of achieving quality-assured consensual knowledge, the *degree of position* is defined here for representing the acceptance level of each position and discovering potential position based on the consensus. Intuitively, it is calculated by fusing the quality and group preference of each position. If the calculated degree reaches a predefined *consensus threshold*, such position is said to have satisfactorily good quality and is acceptable by the community, while the other positions

that obtain the lesser degrees will be ordered in the collective ranking. On the other hand, if the degree has a negative value, such position is said to be rejected by the community.

Since the specified consensus threshold indicates whether to accept or reject a proposed position, it should be properly defined to reflect the properties of the positions to be accepted by the community. For example, to resolve a very sensitive issue, a consensus threshold with a high value (close to 1) should be specified in order to assure that the positions to be accepted will maintain high position quality and are supported by most members.

Definition 5 (Degree of position) Let $\delta_P: P \rightarrow [-1, 1]$ determine the degree of a position p in P, and be defined as follows:

$$\delta_P(p) = \beta\, \delta_Q(p) + (1 - \beta)\, \delta_G(p),$$

where $\beta \in [0, 1]$ denotes the weight of $\delta_Q(p)$ and $1 - \beta$ the weight of $\delta_G(p)$.

Table 2. The degrees of group preference

	p1	p2	p3	p4
$\delta_G(p)$	0.33	−0.60	−0.42	0.01

It is important to note that the weighting factor β can be assigned differently according to the applications. For example, when applying it to *Wikipedia* with two important concerns: (i) the quality of the published knowledge for maintaining trustworthy information, and (ii) the community agreement on a raised issue for avoiding editing wars, the weighting factor β could be specified with the value 0.5. On the other hand, when using it with *Yahoo! Answer*, which gives precedence to the group preference rather than the quality of each proposed answer, one could specify β with a value close to 0. In contrast, if applying the proposed approach to support collaborative ontology engineering, where the quality of the resulting ontology is the primary concern, the value of β should then be close to 1. In this case, the degree of group preference can help support ontology engineers in decision making, mediating conflicts, and achieving the community agreement.

However, when no position can achieve the specified consensus threshold and a stopping criterion is reached (e.g., maximum deliberation time or maximum numbers of positions and arguments), a *feedback mechanism* kicks in to drive the community towards a consensus. The process works as follows: Firstly, the position with the highest degree will be selected, and all members will be encouraged to participate in such position for further deliberation and revision. The member who originally submits that position will also be allowed to enrich his position quality by correcting misspelling and grammar mistakes as well as improving text readability, while other members are encouraged to make critical thinking by submitting additional arguments, withdrawing previously submitted ones, or proposing a new challenging position.

Example 4 In this example, the consensus threshold is specified at 0.7 and the weighting factor β is 0.5, which means that the community identically considers position quality and group preference. The degrees of position of $p1$ to $p4$ are computed as follows:

$$\delta_P(p1) = 0.5 \times 0.84 + 0.5 \times 0.33 = 0.58$$

$$\delta_P(p2) = 0.5 \times 0.42 + 0.5 \times (-0.60) = -0.09$$

$$\delta_P(p3) = 0.5 \times 0.75 + 0.5 \times (-0.42) = 0.17$$

$$\delta_P(p4) = 0.5 \times 0.51 + 0.5 \times 0.01 = 0.26.$$

The above result shows that $p1$ has the highest degree of position because it has a high position quality and is the most preferred position, while $p2$ gains a negative degree of position due to its poor content quality and the least preference. At this stage, however, $p1$ does not yet achieve the consensus threshold and that the maximum deliberation time is reached. Thus, *feedback mechanism* is invoked and all members are encouraged to participate in the position $p1$ for more deliberation and revision.

By allowing members to make critical thinking and clarify the existing deliberation, a new position $p5$ is proposed by extending $p1$ as depicted in Figure 7.

The position $p5$ extends the data of the position $p1$ by separating H1N1 symptoms between children and adults as suggested by the opposing argument $a3$. It also provides more information about a flu test for identifying H1N1 infection. Moreover, a reliable backing referring to CDC is added. The quality of the position $p5$ is then computed as follows:

$$\delta_Q(p5) = ((0.5 \times 0.88) + (0.5 \times 0.85) \times 1 \times (1/1)) = 0.86.$$

Although the quality of $p5$ slightly improves when compared to that of $p1$, the revised and enriched supporting information (both data and backing) can encourage all members to support the position, which leads to a higher degree of group preference, and hence increases the degree of position as summarized in Table 3.

Since the degree of position of $p5$ (0.74) can reach the consensus threshold (0.7), it is said to

Figure 7. Position p5

Title: Position p5
Data: 2009 H1N1 and ordinary flu are both influenza A, but different strains. Thus, it is difficult to distinguish H1N1 flu from ordinary flu without lab test. The symptoms of H1N1 are similar to the regular flu. H1N1 flu is serious and can seriously cause death. It can spread quickly around the world and so far, in Mexico. Some warning signs of H1N1 flu that need urgent medical attention include: *In children*: 1) Shortness of breath or difficulty in breathing, 2) Pain in chest or abdomen, 3) Sudden dizziness or loss of energy, 4) Severe or continuous vomiting, and 5) Flu like symptoms, bad cough and fever *In adults*: 1) Difficulty breathing or shortness of breath, 2) Pain or pressure in the chest or abdomen, 3) Sudden dizziness, 4) Confusion, 5) Severe or persistent vomiting, and 6) Flu-like symptoms improve but then return with fever and worse cough. Flu tests (nasal swab) at your doctor's can tell you what kind of flu you have. It might be flu A, flu B, swine flu, or one of many flu-like viruses.
quality(data$_{p1}$) = ((1 − 0) + 1 + (65.60/100))/3 = 0.88
Backing: • www.cdc.gov/h1n1flu/ • www.who.int/csr/disease/swineflu/en/ • www.reuters.com/news/globalcoverage/swineflu • www.cdc.gov/h1n1flu/identifyingpatients.htm
reliability(backing$_{p1}$) = (0.9+0.9+0.7+0.9)/4 = 0.85
Certainty degree: strongly confident

be *accepted* by the community with satisfactorily good quality and is considered as a potential position to solve the issue, while *p2* has a negative degree of position and is considered to be rejected. The collective ordered rank of all positions (from best to worst) is *p5, p1, p4, p3, p2* which can be represented to a user who searches for all proposed solutions concerning the issue.

4.4 Updating Degree of Expertise

The *degree of expertise* is defined to specify the capability to resolve an issue of each individual. Initially, the degree of expertise of all individuals is set to 1 and is dynamically updated based on the *accuracy rate* and *contribution rate* of each individual.

Intuitively, the accuracy rate of an individual *i* defines his ability to propose a potential position and to evaluate positions contributed by other members, and then correspondingly submit arguments for supporting a potential position and opposing a poor quality one. Thus, it is calculated by combining the individual's ability and accuracy rate in three aspects as follows:

- The ratio of the total degrees of positions which are accepted by the community and proposed by *i* to the number of all positions proposed by *i*,
- The ratio of the degree of arguments submitted by *i* for supporting any positions that are later accepted by the community to the number of all arguments submitted by *i*.
- The ratio of the degree of arguments submitted by *i* for opposing any positions that are later rejected by the community to the number of all arguments submitted by *i*.

Here, let P^+ be the set of positions that are accepted by the community (i.e., they all reach the consensus threshold), and P^- be the set of rejected positions (i.e., their degree of positions have negative values). For an individual $i \in I$, his accuracy rate, denoted by *accuracy_rate(i)*, could then be formally evaluated as follows:

$$accuracy\_rate(i) = \gamma \frac{\sum_{p \in P_i^+} \delta_P(p)}{|P_i|} + (1-\gamma)\left(\frac{\sum_{a \in A_{i,P^+}^+} \delta_A(a) + \sum_{a \in A_{i,P^-}^-} \delta_A(a)}{|A_i|}\right),$$

Table 3. Summary: the calculated results for Example 4

$\delta_i(i, p)$	p1	p2	p3	p4	p5
i1	0.9	-0.7	-0.6	-0.3	0.9
i2	0.5	-0.4	-0.7	0.3	0.8
i3	1.0	-0.9	-0.5	-0.2	1.0
i4	0.9	-0.3	-0.3	-0.1	0.9
i5	0.7	-0.5	-0.4	0.2	0.7
i6	0.3	-0.7	-0.1	0.1	0.6
i7	-0.9	0.7	-0.5	0.4	0.4
i8	-0.4	-0.5	-0.2	0.5	0.2
i9	-0.2	-0.8	0.4	-0.5	-0.1
$\delta_Q(p)$	0.84	0.42	0.75	0.51	0.86
$\delta_G(p)$	0.33	-0.60	-0.42	0.01	0.62
$\delta_P(p)$	0.58	-0.09	0.17	0.26	0.74

where $-P_i \subset P$ is the set of positions proposed by i,

- P_i^+ is the set of accepted positions proposed by i (i.e., $P_i^+ = P_i \cap P^+$),
- $A_i \subset A$ is the set of arguments submitted by i,
- $A_{i,P^+}^+ \subset A_i$ is the set of arguments submitted by i for supporting any accepted positions in P^+,
- $A_{i,P^-}^- \subset A_i$ is the set of arguments submitted by i for opposing any rejected positions in P^-,
- The weight $\gamma \in [0, 1]$ specifies the importance of the individual's ability in proposing accepted positions, while $(1 - \gamma)$ denotes the importance of the individual's ability in evaluating positions contributed by other members and then posting corresponding supporting or opposing arguments.

Next, consider the contribution rate of an individual, which determines his contributing experiences in a specific domain. Roughly speaking, an individual who continually and frequently participates in proposing positions and submitting arguments is considered as an experienced

member in the contributed area. Therefore, the contribution rate of an individual i, denoted by *contribution_rate(i)*, is evaluated by considering the number of all positions and arguments submitted by as shown below:

$$contribution\_rate(i) = \sigma \frac{|P_i|}{|P|} + (1-\sigma)\frac{|A_i|}{|A|},$$

where $\sigma \in [0, 1]$ and $(1 - \sigma)$ are weighting factors which define the importance of submitting positions and arguments, respectively.

Definition 6 (Degree of expertise) Let $\delta_E: I \to [1, \infty]$ denote the degree of expertise of an individual and be defined as follows:

$\delta_E(i) = 1 + (\varphi\ accuracy\_rate\ (i) + (1 - \varphi)\ contribution\_rate(i))$,

where $\varphi \in [0, 1]$ and $(1 - \varphi)$ denote the weights of *accuracy_rate* and *contribution_rate*, respectively.

Example 6 This example updates the degrees of expertise of the individuals $i1$ to $i9$ by predefining $\gamma = \sigma = 0.7$, which means that the capability of proposing a position is more important than submitting an argument, while $\varphi = 0.7$, which means that an individual's accuracy has priority over his contribution. Hence, the updated degrees of expertise of $i1$ to $i9$ are 1.14, 1.12, 1.86, 1.20, 1.30, 1.40, 1.24, 1.12, and 1.08, respectively. The individual $i3$ obtains the highest degree as a result of his accuracy in proposing the accepted position and submitting arguments to oppose the rejected position, while the individual $i9$ gains the lowest degree of expertise because he gives neither a supporting argument to the position $p5$ nor an opposing argument to the position $p2$ which means that he obtains no accuracy rate.

5. PRELIMINARY EXPERIMENTS AND RESULTS

This section conducts two preliminary experiments to evaluate the usability of SAM and ciSAM. They offer the opportunity to observe the user behaviors and responses as well as to implement several improvements.

5.1 Usability Study: Semantic Argumentation Process

The first experiment focuses on validating the practicality and usability of the proposed *semantic argumentation process* by having two groups of users participating in face-to-face deliberation in order to develop two different ontologies of the same complexity. The first group consisting of six IT students worked on an *"Expert ontology"* without following the *semantic argumentation process* support. The second group with five IT students collaboratively developed an *"IT course ontology"* by following the *semantic argumentation process*.

The resulting ontologies developed by both groups were verified by an ontology expert, and were found to meet the defined requirements with high quality. However, without deliberation guidance, the first ontology team could reach the agreed ontology in six hours (within three days). The team confronted with several conflicts,

which were difficult to be resolved without any moderator and consensus building techniques, and were inconvenient to be traced. Moreover, the deliberation was also time-consuming. For example, the issue "How to present an expertise level?" was raised, and many members proposed several different positions with various backings. Thus, it was very difficult for the team to agree on a position by considering many important aspects such as ontology design criteria, the quality of the created ontology and the expertise of the member who proposed a position. On the other hand, the second team could reach the final agreed ontology in one hour. Many issues were raised during the deliberation, and could be resolved using the *semantic argumentation process*. Moreover, the team members could quickly understand and follow the proposed process after a brief introduction.

5.2 Usability Study: ciSAM System

This subsequent experiment aims to evaluate the usability of *ciSAM* system by encouraging multiple users to participate in online community deliberation in a variety of topic categories (e.g., arts, business and finance, computer, and health). There were several groups of users consisting of university-level students, academics, ordinary users and experts in various domains. All users were introduced to the deliberation process, and learned how to use the system independently by themselves by simply reading the system's overview and instruction page available online. Based on their interests, the users collaboratively participated in creating new knowledge by raising issues, proposing positions, and submitting arguments by using the system.

To analyze the community deliberation, the weighting factors and consensus threshold were defined as follows: $\alpha = 0.5$ for maintaining high data quality and backing reliability; $\beta = 0.5$ for achieving the quality assured consensual knowledge; and consensus threshold = 0.6 for achieving preliminary results and resolving issues in various domains and categories. In addition, to determine the degree of expertise, the weights γ, σ and φ were identically specified with the value 0.7 for defining the importance of user's accuracy in proposing accepted positions, the importance of the users' contribution in submitting positions, and the importance of the accuracy rate, respectively.

Since the prototype system has been available online for only a few months, the community deliberation is still limited within a small group of users. At present (November 2009), there are 32 registered users, 24 issues categorized in 11 topics, 35 positions, and 57 arguments. A short-term usability study of *ciSAM* was performed using user-based evaluation. The questionnaire comprises nine questions, with Likert scale-based, focusing on three aspects: (i) learnability, (ii) effectiveness, and (iii) satisfaction.

In summary, the results show that most users found the system easy to learn and use (84.5%) while all of them agreed that the provided approach well supported the community deliberation (100%). The information presented by the system allowed the deliberation to be easily traced (86.7%). In addition, the system was well designed and self-descriptive (86.7%). Although the study presented satisfactory results in all aspects, a few improvements were suggested, as follows. Some add-on tools such as text editor or grammar checker should be adopted for facilitating and checking the content quality during the creation process. Communication features, such as a chatting tool and email alert, should be enabled. The complete results of the questionnaire are available at http://research.siu.ac.th:8080/sam/cisam-usabilitystudy.

6. DISCUSSION AND CONCLUSION

SAM harnesses collective intelligence in a community by encouraging multiple users to propose a position concerning a challenging issue, and to submit supporting or opposing arguments about other members' ideas. The community collectively creates knowledge by proposing innovative solutions, extending potential positions, and improving as well as revising existing ideas.

To assure the quality and reliability of a position and an argument, the *position quality* and *argument quality* are analyzed based on their data and backing information together with the certainty degree and the degree of expertise. Moreover, the *degree of argument* is defined to measure the expressive level of an argument expressed by a member to support or oppose a certain position. Such degree is used to further analyze the *preference* (view) of the member on that particular position. The *degree of group preference* is then obtained by aggregating the individual preferences of all members in the community using the OWA operator. To represent an acceptance level of each position, the *degree of position* is computed by combining its position quality and the degree of group preference. Therefore, based on the proposed measures, a position with its degree higher than a predefined *consensus threshold* implies that it has satisfactorily good quality and is accepted by the community. In other words, it is considered as a potential position to solve the issue.

To facilitate a thorough and insightful evaluation of the proposed approach in real-world scenarios, *ciSAM* has been developed and made available for public usage. The preliminary results demonstrate that the proposed *semantic argumentation process* can facilitate and speed up the community deliberation by providing a simple yet effective process with an intuitive workflow. The user-based evaluation also reveals that the tool can well support the deliberation.

For further experiments, more invitations and publicity material have been distributed with an aim to substantially increase the number of members and to obtain more deliberation and more user-generated contents in a more variety of topics. Several thoroughly conducted experiments on such large amount of data, which yield highly reliable and accurate results will then become possible. The planned experiments include comparing the effectiveness of the proposed approach with existing and widely-accepted methods by considering several important aspects such as simplicity, traceability, the quality and reliability of the collective knowledge as well as the usefulness of the proposed measures. The evaluation metrics to be employed includes several statistical metrics and user-based evaluations.

Further research plan involves an enhancement of the proposed feedback mechanism by appropriately formalizing the dispersion of the users' opinions. In addition, an extension of the current system by incorporating ontology-based and semantic lexical-based reasoners to enhance the semantic reasoning and searching capability is envisaged.

REFERENCES

Agichtein, E., Castillo, C., Donato, D., & Gionis, A. (2008). Finding High-quality Content in Social Media. In *Proceedings of the International Conference on Web Search and Web Data Mining (WSDM'08)*, Palo Alto, CA (pp. 183-193). New York: ACM.

Bian, J., Liu, Y., Agichtein, E., & Zha, H. (2008). Finding the right facts in the crowd: Factoid question answering over social media. In *Proceeding of the 17th International Conference on World Wide Web (WWW)*, Beijing, China. New York: ACM press.

Bollen, J., Rodriguez, M. A., & Van, H. (2006). Journal Status. *Scientometrics, 69*(3), 669–687. doi:10.1007/s11192-006-0176-z

Brandes, U., Kenis, P., Lerner, J., & Raaij, D. (2009). Network Analysis of Collaboration Structure in Wikipedia. In *Proceeding of the 18th International Conference on World Wide Web (WWW)* (pp. 731-740). New York: ACM press.

Brin, S., & Page, L. (1998). The Anatomy of a Large-Scale Hypertextual Web Search Engine. In *Proceeding of the 7th International World Wide Web Conference (WWW)*. New York: ACM press.

Broekstra, J., Kampman, A., & Harmelen, F. (2002). Sesame: A Generic Architecture for Storing and Querying RDF and RDF Schema. In *Proceedings of the 1st International Workshop on Practical and Scalable Semantic Systems* (pp. 54-56).

Conklin, J., & Begeman, M. L. (1988). gibis: a hypertext tool for exploratory policy discussion. In *Proceedings of the ACM Conference on Computer-supported cooperative work*. New York: ACM press.

Esuli, A., & Sebastiani, F. (2007). PageRanking WordNet synsets: An Application to Opinion-Related Properties. In *Proceedings of the 35th Meeting of the Association for Computational Linguistics*, Prague, CZ (pp. 424-431).

Flesch, R. F. (1949). *The Art of Readable Writing*. New York: Harper & Row.

Hu, M., Lim, E., Sun, A., & Lauw, W. H. (2007). Measuring Article Quality in Wikipedia: Models and Evaluation. In *Proceedings of the 16th ACM Conference on Information and Knowledge Management* (pp. 243-252). New York: ACM press.

Iandoli, L. K., Klein, M., & Zollo, G. (2008). *Can We Exploit Collective Intelligence for Collaborative Deliberation? The Case of the Climate Change Collaboratorium*. Cambridge, MA: MIT.

Kacprzyk, J., & Fedrizzi, M. (1988). A "soft" measure of consensus in the setting of partial (fuzzy) preferences. *European Journal of Operational Research, n.d.*, 316–325. doi:10.1016/0377-2217(88)90152-X

Kamvar, S. D., Schlosser, M. T., & Garcia-Molina, H. (2003). The EigenTrust Algorithm for Reputation Management in P2P Networks. In *Proceedings of the Proceedings of the 12th International World Wide Web Conference*, Budapest, Hungary.

Kotis, K., & Vouros, G. (2005). Human-centered ontology engineering: The HCOME Methodology. *Knowledge and Information Systems*, *10*(1), 109–131. doi:10.1007/s10115-005-0227-4

Krotzsch, M., Vrandecic, D., Volkel, M., & Haller, H. (2007). Semantic Wikipedia. *Journal of Web Semantics*, *5*, 251–261. doi:10.1016/j.websem.2007.09.001

Lafferty, J., Sleator, S., & Temperley, D. (1992). Grammatical trigrams: A probabilistic model of link grammar. In *Proceedings of the AAAI Fall Symposium on Probabilistic Approaches to Natural Language*.

Maleewong, K., Anutariya, C., & Wuwongse, V. (2008). A Collective Intelligence Approach to Collaborative Knowledge Creation. In *Proceeding of the 4th International Conference Semantics, Knowledge, and Grid (SKG 2008)* (pp. 64-70). Washington, DC: IEEE press.

Maleewong, K., Anutariya, C., & Wuwongse, V. (2009a). SAM: Semantic Argumentation based Model for Collaborative Knowledge Creation and Sharing System. In *Proceeding of the 1st International Conference on Computational Collective Intelligence (ICCCI'09)*, Wroclaw, Poland. New York: Springer.

Maleewong, K., Anutariya, C., & Wuwongse, V. (2009b). A Semantic Argumentation Approach to Collaborative Ontology Engineering. In *Proceeding of the 11th International Conference on Information Integration and Web-based Applications & Services (iiWAS'09)*, Kuala Lumpur, Malaysia. New York: ACM press.

Rittel, H., & Kunz, W. (1970). *Issue as elements of information systems (Tech. Rep.)*. CA: University of California, Institue of Urban and Regional Development.

Shum, S., Selvin, A., Sierhuis, M., & Conklin, J. (2006). Hypermedia Support for Argumentation-Based Rationale: 15 Years on from gIBIS and QOC. In Dutoit, A. H. (Ed.), *Rationale Management in Software Engineering* (pp. 111–132). Heidelberg, Germany: Springer. doi:10.1007/978-3-540-30998-7_5

Stvilia, B., Twidale, M., Smith, L., & Gasser, L. (2008). Information quality work organization in. *Journal of the American Society for Information Science and Technology*, *59*(6), 983–1001. doi:10.1002/asi.20813

Tempich, C., Simperl, E., Luczak, M., Studer, R., & Pinto, H. S. (2007). Argumentation-based ontology engineering. *IEEE Intelligent Systems*, *22*(6), 52–59. doi:10.1109/MIS.2007.103

Toulmin, S. (1958). *The Uses of Argument*. Cambridge, UK: Cambridge University Press.

Viegas, F., Wattenberg, M., Kriss, J., & van Ham, F. (2007). Talk before you type. In *Proceeding of the 40th Hawaii International Conference on System Sciences*, CA (p. 78). Washington, DC: IEEE press.

Walton, D. (2006). *Fundamentals of Critical Argumentation*. Cambridge, UK: Cambridge University Press.

Wilkinson, D., & Huberman, B. A. (2007). Cooperation and Quality in Wikipedia. In *Proceedings of the WikiSym*, (pp. 157-164).

Yager, R. R. (1996). Quantifier Guided Aggregation using OWA operators. *International Journal of Intelligent Systems*, *11*, 49–73. doi:10.1002/(SICI)1098-111X(199601)11:1<49::AID-INT3>3.3.CO;2-L

Yager, R. R. (2007). Centered OWA operators. *Soft Computing, 11*, 631–639. doi:10.1007/s00500-006-0125-z

Zhang, J., Ackerman, M. S., & Adamic, L. (2007). Expertise networks in online communities: structure and algorithms. In *Proceeding of the 16th International Conference on World Wide Web (WWW)* (pp. 221-230). New York: ACM Press.

This work was previously published in International Journal of Organizational and Collective Intelligence, Volume 1, Issue 3, edited by Hideyasu Sasaki, Dickson K.W. Chiu, Epaminondas Kapetanios, Patrick C.K. Hung, Frederic Andres, Ho-fung Leung, Richard Chbei, pp. 34-53, copyright 2010 by IGI Publishing (an imprint of IGI Global).

Chapter 14
Improvement of Restaurant Operation by Sharing Order and Customer Information

Takeshi Shimmura
National Institute of Advanced Industrial Science and Technology, Japan

Takeshi Takenaka
National Institute of Advanced Industrial Science and Technology, Japan

Motoyuki Akamatsu
National Institute of Advanced Industrial Science and Technology, Japan

ABSTRACT

In full-service restaurants, it is important to share customer information among staff members in real time in order to perform complicated operations. Conventional point of sale (POS) systems in restaurants was developed to improve the verification and transmission of order information passed from the dining hall to the kitchen. However, POS systems have remained insufficient to share customers' order information among many staff members in different positions. This paper introduces an information sharing system for full-service restaurants using an advanced POS system with which staff members can share order information in real time. Using this system, kitchen staff members can grasp the total number of orders and the elapsed time for preparation of each order. Moreover, service staff members can grasp the status of each customer quickly. Using this system in a large-scale restaurant, preparation processes can be made more efficient and reduce customer complaints.

INTRODUCTION

Recently, science and technology are expected to improve service industry productivity because many existing services are thought to be provided less efficiently than manufactured products (Sako,

DOI: 10.4018/978-1-4666-1577-9.ch014

2006). Service engineering is a new research field to support actual services by integrating academic disciplines such as engineering, computer sciences, human sciences, and social sciences (Kimita et al., 2008, Shimomura et al., 2008, Spohrer & Maglio, 2008, Ueda et al., 2009). For the promotion of service productivity, both streamlining service operations and enhancing values for customers are necessary. Therefore, service engineering focuses on various topics such as optimization of service provision, elucidation of customer satisfaction and value co-creation among stakeholders (Cronin et al., 2000; Moller, Rajala, & Westerlund, 2008; Shimomura, Hara, & Arai, 2008; Spohrer & Maglio, 2008; Takenaka & Ueda, 2008; Ueda et al., 2008; Voss et al., 2008).

From 2007 for instance, the Japanese Ministry of Economy, Trade and Industry started a national project promoting service engineering to improve service sector productivity (Japanese Ministry of Economy, Trade and Industry, 2007). The Japan Productivity Center also established Service Productivity and Innovation for Growth (SPRING) in 2007 (Morikawa, 2008).

Restaurant industry is one of the biggest service industries from the viewpoint of workforce in many countries. On the other hand, it has been less scientifically-studied than manufacturing industries because it includes many human factors of employees and customers. Now, the service management of a restaurant is a good research target for service engineering because both streamlining service operations and enhancing values for customers are needed to enhance the service productivity.

In Japan, the industrialization of restaurant businesses generally started in the 1970s. Up to that time, restaurant businesses were mainly family run. As the market scale of restaurant businesses increased, some restaurants started to introduce chain store systems. In addition, large restaurants were introduced to increase productivity. Consequently, the market scale of the restaurant industry in Japan increased from approximately 8,000 billion Yen (90 U.S. billion dollars) to 250,000 billion Yen (2.8 trillion U.S. dollars) during the 1970s – 1990s. In the latest report, approximately 737,000 restaurants were operating in Japan in 2006 (Japanese Ministry of Internal Affairs, and Communications, 2006). The increase of restaurant markets also brought severe competition among companies. Nowadays,

restaurants must improve service operations and to reduce costs. However, provision of services in large restaurants is more difficult than in small restaurants. As chain stores expand, it becomes more difficult to educate staff members to learn high-skill services.

In restaurant businesses, information technologies have played important roles in areas such as in inventory control (Ngai et al., 2008), supply chain management (Murphy & Smith, 2009), and knowledge-based management (Muller, 1999). In the 1980s in Japan, restaurant industries introduced point-of-sale (POS) systems that had been originally developed for retail and convenience store (CVS) businesses (Stein, 2005; Trappey & Trappey, 1998) to improve store operations. Different from the usage of POS systems in CVS, restaurants used them for management of customer orders. As a result, POS systems in restaurant businesses added ordering systems. The system obviated the need of servers to go to the kitchen after accepting orders. Moreover, check-out operations were improved because they were calculated automatically for each table. As Jensen (2007) pointed out, smooth check-out is important because it affects customer satisfaction.

Although innovative for restaurants, the restaurant POS system had persistent problems. When service staff transmitted order information using a handheld registration device, the information was carried to kitchen staff members on paper for each table, which created the need for the kitchen staff to calculate the number of dishes repeatedly. When kitchen operations were rushed, kitchen staff became unable to remember the elapsed times from receiving an order because the POS did not record the elapsed time of each order. The waiting time for dish is a crucial factor for customer satisfaction and complaints (Mittal et al., 2008).

Therefore, we need to pay more attention to the information sharing of customer information among various staffs from the viewpoint of customer satisfactions. Because the conventional POS systems mainly focused on the management of sales information, it was insufficient to grasp the each customer's situation. This problem is not limited to just restaurants; sharing the customer information is a critical issue in many fields of services such as healthcare services or public services (Han et al., 2006). For instance, in a hospital, various departments are needed to share each patient's information in real time for the smooth and safe operation (Turcu, Popa, & Ieee, 2009). For this purpose, information technologies such as web-based process modeling methods (Ahn et al., 2001) or visualization techniques (Delrieux, Dominguez, & Repetto, 2002) have been introduced to support the information sharing among various stakeholders.

In this paper, we propose a system that expands conventional POS systems in which staff members can share order information in real-time using an information system. We especially added a display function of order information to the conventional POS system for the real-time information sharing among various staffs. The next section overviews existing methods for process management in restaurants and elucidates problems underlying those conventional methods.

PROBLEMS OF INFORMATION SHARING METHODS IN RESTAURANTS

In simple terms, the service process of a restaurant consists of order receipt, preparation, and serving. An important goal is to serve dishes to customers at the right place at the right time. Staff members who cannot share accurate information cannot cook or serve dishes smoothly. Moreover, the restaurant scale depends deeply on the capacity of information sharing. In general, three methods have been used in restaurants for process managements: verbal confirmation, order sheets, and a POS system. Problems of conventional process management systems are shown as the following.

Verbal Confirmation

This method, although the oldest, is still used for service process management in small restaurants. Service staff members memorize a customer order after receiving it and then give the information to the kitchen staff verbally. Kitchen staff members prepare dishes in order or sometimes in some different sequence. Then, they call the service staff and "hand over" the prepared dish. The service staff members recall which table ordered the dish and serve it to the customer. The kitchen staff members often are unconcerned about tables. However, because the capacity of human memory is restricted, staff often mistake or forget orders, especially when a restaurant become busy. Consequently, the restaurant scale is limited to the capacity of human memory. This is one reason why many restaurants can only operate on small scale.

Order Sheet

Using this method, when servers receive orders, they write them to an order sheet with a table number, and hand them to kitchen staff. Then, the kitchen staff members prepare dishes according to the sheet information. When the dishes are prepared, they are handed off to the service staff with the sheet. Service staff members serve dishes to the table shown on the sheet.

Using this method, although staff need not memorize order information, some problems remain. When orders are rushed, staff must make a round trip, which delays order acceptance and dish service. Moreover, order sheets do not record the order-received time. Consequently, kitchen staff cannot distinguish the sequence of orders. Customers might become irate if later-ordered dishes are served to other tables faster than their own.

POS

Figure 1 portrays the structure of widely used POS systems. Originally, POS systems in restaurants

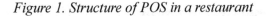

Figure 1. Structure of POS in a restaurant

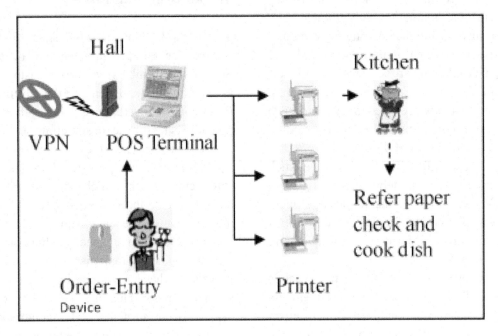

were developed to skip the handing-over processes of customer orders from servers to kitchen staff members. The POS system records and manages order information by table. When service staff members receive orders, they input information to a small order-entry device and transmit it to POS terminal. Then the POS terminal adds the order-received time to order information and sends it to the kitchen. Each order, organized by table, is printed by a printer in the kitchen. The kitchen staff member checks some sheets and starts preparations. After preparation, they pass the dishes with their sheets to a server. The POS obviates the need of servers to make a round trip to exchange order sheets by hand. They can concentrate on service and can grasp the sequence of orders from the order sheets, and serve dishes to customers properly.

Although POS improves the handing-over processes of customer orders, some problems remain. The kitchen staff members often calculate the total number of identical dishes irrespective of the table and cook them collectively because this batch method is more efficient. Although the

POS terminal provides comprehensive order information, staff members often cannot use it. It is difficult for them to grasp the elapsed time of each order. Conventional POS systems therefore present problems in their presentation of information. Moreover, they cannot support temporal management of preparation and service processes.

For the reasons explained above, we developed a new system that particularly addresses real-time process management of services by extending POS systems in restaurants.

The next section introduces concepts and functions of the proposed system.

NEW INFORMATION SHARING SYSTEM FOR RESTAURANTS

This section introduces a new information sharing system (ISS) developed by Ganko Food Service Co. Ltd. in 2008 for their full-service restaurants. As described in the *Introduction*, POS systems were originally developed for use in the CVS industry. Their main purpose is to grasp the total sales of each item periodically to optimize the stock and assortment of CVS stores. In contrast, important functions of POS in restaurants are registration of orders to avoid accounting mistakes. As Stein (2005) pointed out, the use of POS systems in restaurants is intended to improve check out functions and thereby avoid mistakes.

In addition to those basic functions, ISS especially targets temporal aspects of process management and information sharing among staff. It enables staff members to share order information not by paper but by a display to confirm processes of orders in real time.

Figure 2 presents a schematic structure of ISS in a restaurant. This system has an information terminal (ISS terminal) connected to order-entry handheld devices and displays located in kitchens and halls. The ISS terminal is connected to many other systems: accounting systems, attendance management systems, and buying control systems maintained at headquarters.

Moreover, new functions have been developed for ISS to improve operations and service through information sharing. Using conventional information systems, store managers and cooks cannot refer to situations of other positions, which prevents them from helping burdened positions. Furthermore, staff members cannot share customer's qualitative requests related to tastes, allergies, etc.

The ISS functions can be summarized as follows.

1. Order checking function by each dish at the kitchen
2. Display function of elapsed time and warning function of delay
3. Checking function of all kitchen positions' status
4. Search function and reissue for lost order sheet
5. Writing function to share customers' requirements

1. Order checking function by dish at each kitchen

When the ISS terminal receives order information from servers using the handheld devices, ISS records the receiving time of each order and recalculates the total number of dishes. Then the ISS transmits an order checking system (Figure 2) placed in each kitchen area. Figure 3 presents a sample display of the order checking system at a certain kitchen area. For instance, this kitchen area prepares coffee, cakes, and light meal items. The vertical line shows the kind of dish. The total number of orders is shown to the left of each dish in this display. When kitchen staff members start preparation, they can know the total number of each dish needed. This function can improve productivity because it facilitates batch cooking processes. Moreover, using this display system, kitchen staff members need not check order sheets. Order sheets printed at kitchens are used for servers after preparation.

2. Display functions of elapsed time and warning functions of delay

The ISS checks the order-received time of all orders and calculates the elapsed time by dish until the kitchen staff finish preparing them. The horizontal axis of Figure 3 shows the passage of time by table. The square moves to the right every 2 min and the color changes at every 10 min (blue–yellow–red). When elapsed time get over 20 min, alarm sounds to notify delay to staff. Kitchen staff members usually check and grasp condition of process. They judge the priority of orders and cook them.

When a kitchen staff completes preparation, he touches the display to issue an order sheet. At the same time, order checking displays completion. In the dining hall, servers can watch preparation processes by another order checking display. They come to the kitchen to receive dishes and

Figure 2. Structure of ISS in a restaurant

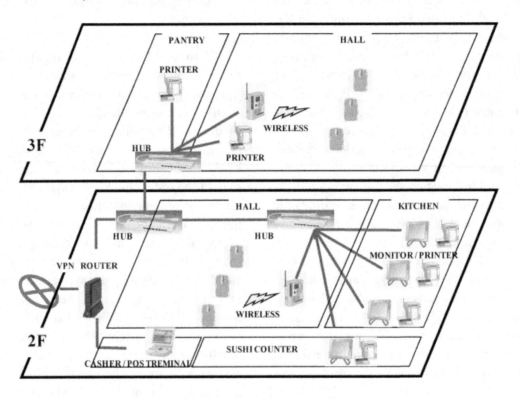

Figure 3. Layout for order checking system

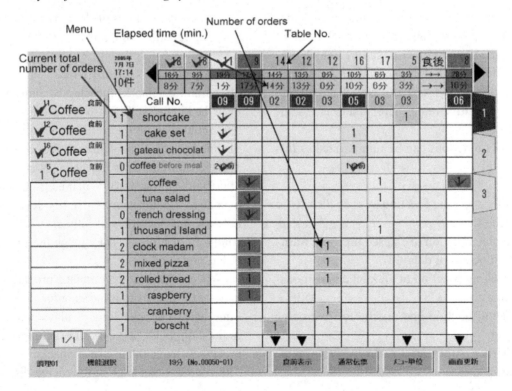

order sheets. Using this function, staff members can grasp the elapsed time easily and cope with delays of dishes.

3. Checking function of all kitchen positions' status

The order checking display can show statuses of other positions. When the chief or manager can know of a delay at a certain position, she can order other staff members to support the busy position. Using this function, they can manage the load at each position, and reduce labor costs to improve productivity by mobilization of staff positions. Especially, this function is useful for large restaurants or hotels that have plural kitchens (Sill, 1994). In such cases, but without this system, a chef in a certain kitchen would be unable grasp the situations of other kitchen areas.

4. Search function and reissue for lost order sheet

Unlike conventional POS systems in restaurants, ISS does not print order sheets when it receives orders. Instead, order sheets are printed automatically when kitchen staff members touch the dish they finish preparing on the order checking system. The order sheets are used when the service staff delivers dishes to appropriate tables.

When a server loses on order sheet, they can search for information easily using the order checking system and reprint the order sheet. Figure 4 shows using of the reissue function. If a staff lost an order sheet, the staff can easily reissue it by touching display. Using this function, staff members need not search around all tables to find customers who have ordered the dish. In other words, ISS is more robust than conventional POS systems for preventing human errors.

5. Writing Function to Share Customer's requirement

Kitchen staff sometimes must refer to customer preferences related to taste, ingredients, condition of baking. Usually, when service staff members receive customer requirements, they should memorize the requirement and inform the kitchen staff verbally because the POS cannot transmit non pre-input information. However, kitchen staff workers sometimes forget or misunderstand customer requirements and cook dishes that are not referred.

The ISS, which is equipped with a writing function, enables the service staff to write a customer's requirement directly—using a fingernail, for instance—and transmit it to kitchen. Kitchen staff members can refer to that information and prepare a dish appropriately. Figure 5 shows writing function which is load on order entry device.

INTRODUCTION OF ISS TO A RESTAURANT

To test the ISS system effectiveness, we introduced it to a restaurant named "Ganko Hankyu-Higashi Restaurant" owned by Ganko Food Service Co. Ltd. (Osaka, Japan) on September 24, 2009. This large restaurant has two dining halls on separate floors (2nd floor has 132 tables, 3rd floor has 132 tables), and two kitchens (sushi counter on 2nd floor, open kitchen on 2nd floor). This restaurant provides a menu with over 300 a la carte items, 20 lunch sets, and 50 courses. In the restaurant, it is difficult for staff members to grasp the situations of other floors and positions because they cannot see all positions simultaneously, especially those of other floors. The ISS system that was installed there comprises a single ISS terminal, 10 order entry devices for service staff, and 6 order-checking displays and printers for kitchen staff.

To grasp the operation speed and load using conventional POS, serving time of a dish from taking the order to finish preparation of it are checked at this restaurant during September 7–13, 2009. In this system, the order-received time can

Figure 4. Reissue function for lost order sheet

Figure 5. Writing function of order entry device

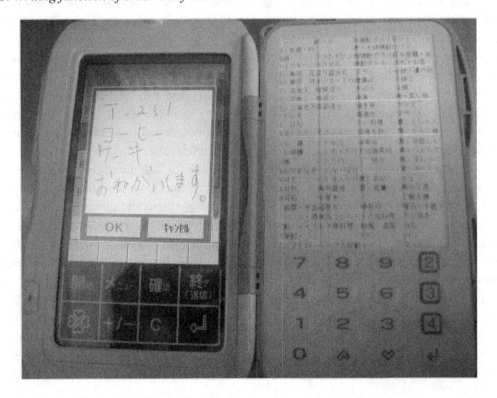

be record by POS terminal automatically, but the finish time of each dish was recorded by kitchen staff. The finish time was added to the POS data that originally include the date, order-received time, name of dish, category of dishes and customer's ID.

After introducing ISS to the same restaurant, staff members received ISS system operational training to operate it smoothly. Then, an evaluation experiment of ISS was conducted during October 12–18, 2009. As with previous measurements using conventional POS, the same indexes are recorded using ISS and by staff.

Some staff members were interviewed after the experiment to assess the qualitative efficiency for store operation and handling load of the ISS system.

RESULT OF INTRODUCTION OF ISS

This section reports results of the ISS system introduction. We acquired 1073 order data when conventional POS was used during September 7–13, 2009, and acquired 957 order data after ISS was introduced during October 12–18, 2009. We analyzed and compared those results, particularly addressing the preparation time, categories of dishes and order-received time because customer satisfaction deeply depends on waiting time (Davis & Maggard, 1990). Moreover, customers' staying time could affect total profit of a restaurant when it is busy.

The averaged serving time of all dishes from taking the order to finish preparation was significantly improved: from 8.98 min to 8.44 min ($F[1, 2028]=5.01$, $p<0.025$). This result demonstrates that ISS improved the operation speed of preparation for 32 s. Figure 6 presents the frequency distribution of serving time.

However, such improvements are not shown in all categories of dishes. Table 1 shows averaged preparation time in some categories: categories with fewer orders are excluded from the table. As

Table 1 shows, improvements are apparent especially for Sushi, Lunch set, and Sashimi (sliced raw fish) categories. Sushi and Sashimi are prepared at the Sushi counter. The order checking display near the Sushi counter helped staff members to check the number of orders and elapsed time of each order. The servers sometimes hasten the kitchen staff members to prepare dishes that are late. A significant improvement was found in the Lunch set category. Lunch sets consist of some menu items such as fried foods, grilled foods, and sashimi; they are combinations of different preparation processes. Therefore, kitchen staff members in different positions must cooperate to finish a Lunch set. In this case, they must cook in order of priority. The order checking display helped kitchen staff members in different positions to finish the same Lunch set in order of priority. In other words, they can find and relieve bottlenecks in preparation process. At lunchtime, this restaurant is very busy and has many different orders at a time. The improvement of preparation times on the second time scale presents an important problem for improvement of the seat-turnover rate.

Meanwhile, in other categories such as those of fried food, stewed (boiled) food and appetizer, we were unable to find improvements in the serving time. One simple reason is that production capacities of fried foods, stewed foods, and appetizer are limited. They cannot be helped when they have many orders at once. For seasonal reasons, orders for stewed foods increased when the ISS was introduced in October.

We interviewed 14 staffs; 1 store manager, 1 chief concierge, 4 service staffs, 1 chef, and 7 kitchen staffs (11 male, and 9 female). Two of them have worked in restaurants for over 10 years. Four of them have worked for between 5 and 10 years. Another Four of them have worked for 3 years. The other four staffs are freshmen.

Table 2 presents a summary of results of the staff member interviews. For example, some kitchen staff members reported that they concen-

Figure 6. Frequency distribution of preparation time of a dish from order-receipt to preparation finish

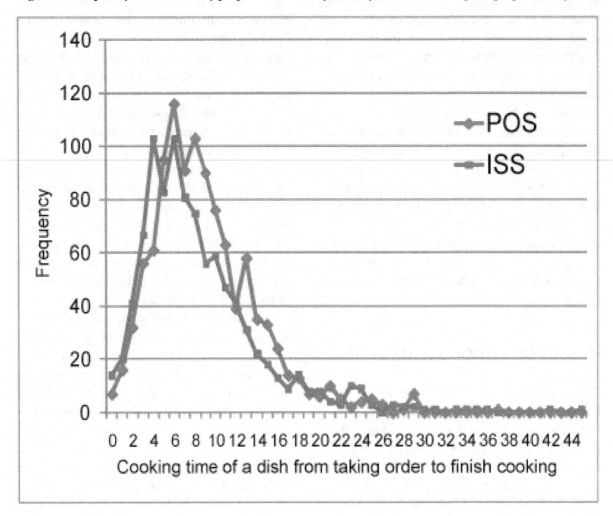

Table 1. Cooperation cooked time between POS and ISS

Category	POS		ISS	
	Average serving time (min)	Total number of orders	Average serving time (min)	Total number of orders
Sushi	11.39	1492	10.49	640
Set menu	11.14	21	10.30	20
Lunch Set	7.30	248	6.67	217
Fried food	11.13	163	12.61	173
Stewed foods	7.24	29	7.86	58
Sashimi (raw fish)	7.17	125	6.02	99
Appetizer	6.55	88	9.13	95
Salad	5.82	56	5.52	52

trated on preparation because the order checking system gives them information for preparation. On the other hand, some service staff members are pleased with the fact that they did not need to walk around tables when they lost order sheets: the ISS can easily reissue the order sheets.

We confirmed the positive effect of ISS, but the hardware system must be improved. For example, kitchen staff members are unaware of the alarm sound sometimes because of kitchen noise. The sound volume must be increased. Kitchen staff members found it difficult to view the order checking system display because of reflected light. Lighting and display must be improved.

DISCUSSION 1: ISS' FUNCTION AND IMPROVEMENT IN RESTAURANT

Based on results of interviews of kitchen staff and service staff, we analyzed improvements by introducing ISS to the restaurant. Figure 7 presents the relation among the ISS functions, benefits for staff members, and effects for customers and the restaurant.

Reduction of Complaints

The main customer complaint is delay of food service. After a customer orders a dish, they can wait for dishes for several minutes for a dish to arrive. However, the customers might get angry if a long time passes with no apologies from servers. The ISS has a function to show the elapsed time and provides a checking function for other positions. Using those functions, the service staff members were able to find delayed dishes and also were able to refer to a situation of preparation positions. When they find delayed dishes and confirm that the kitchen was busy, they visited to customer's table and apologized to customers. Thereby, the restaurant was able to prevent customers from becoming angry and complaining. In the interview, some staff members pointed out this importance

for complaint reduction. It has been discussed that it is an important problem for restaurants to design of product system to reduce the customers' waiting time (Hwang & Lambert, 2008). Some studies have examined the durations that customers will wait for service without frustration (Davis & Maggard, 1990).

Improvement of Preparation Times

Using the ISS order checking function, kitchen staff members were able to grasp the total number of dishes easily. When they finished preparation of a dish, they touched the item on the display to issue the order sheet for servers. Simultaneously, all orders on the display were updated. Moreover, by viewing the elapsed time, they were always conscious of the time that had passed after they received the order. Additionally, when time had passed beyond 20 min from when the order was received, an alarm sounded. Those functions prevented kitchen staff members from being late for preparation. Consequently, they united preparation and cooking processes of identical dishes efficiently.

As Stalk and Hout (1990) reported, it is important for restaurants to serve dishes fast because it makes a company more competitive in today's market. Muller (1999) insisted that time management is important not only in fast food outlets but also in full service restaurants.

Management of Busy Positions

When a restaurant is busy, the manager must grasp the load of preparation positions and should shift staff members from idle positions to busy positions. It is important for restaurants to optimize between customer's requests and preparation capacity. The checking function for other positions of ISS helps the manager and chef to find troubled positions without walking around; they can thereby shift staff to support the bottleneck position.

Table 2. Results of staff member interviews

Function	Comment
Order checking function	The PMS displays all orders. Therefore, I did not need to calculate the number of dishes. (Kitchen staff)
	Finished and unfinished dishes are shown in the display. It is easy to distinguish them. (Kitchen staff)
	Because operations were improved using the system, productivity increased and the load was reduced. (Kitchen staff)
	The sound of the order-received alarm is small. Staff cannot hear it when the kitchen is noisy.
Elapsed Time display function	It was easy to grasp the transition of each order, preventing preparation sequence mistakes. (Kitchen staff)
	The print function using the touch panel was awkward to use. Double-clicking sometimes occurred. (Kitchen staff)
	It is good to be conscious of time passage as represented by the alarm. (Kitchen staff)
Checking function of other positions	It is easy to know the timing of preparation in other positions and to be able to prepare dishes on time for customers. (Kitchen staff)
	We were able to shift kitchen staff to busy positions for smooth operations. (Chef)
	We were able to detect crowds at each floor, and control employee shifts and entry of customers. (Manager)
	Claims related to cooking delays were reduced about 70% because service staff refer to the display and act for customers quickly. (Manager)
	If service staff finds delayed food on the display, they can notify kitchen staff as a precaution. (Service staff)
Reissue function	It was easy to find the table—when losing order sheets—by using the search and reissue function. (Service staff)
	Because preparation and serving times were shortened, customer claims decreased drastically. (Service staff)
Writing Function	Customers do not get angry because kitchen staff does not forget to refer to customers' requirements. (Service staff)

Figure 7. Relation between ISS functions and improvement of operations

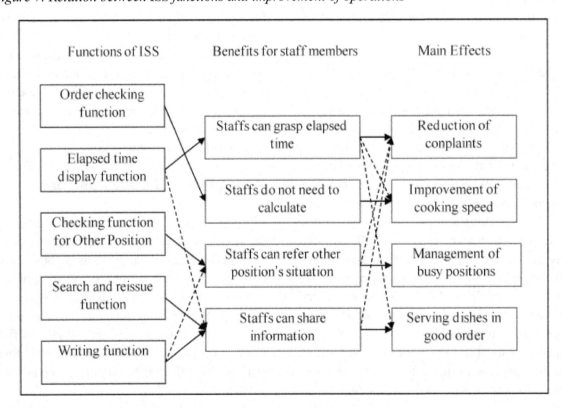

Serving Dishes in Good Sequence

The time required for preparation differs among dishes. Customer might feel dissatisfaction when another table is served earlier, even though the other table ordered later. When a customer feels that staff treats them unfairly, they react badly (Jensen & Hansen, 2007).

Using the elapsed time display function, the kitchen staff members can hand dishes to servers giving instructions of the service order of dishes. Consequently, ISS advised serving dishes in good order and enhanced information sharing between kitchen and service staff members.

Some problems still remain. ISS did not improve the operation for all categories of dishes; cooking speed of Fried food, stewed food, and appetizer were not improved. Other approach will be required to improve these categories. Furthermore, hall staffs had to walk to the display when they refer orders or other position's information. It will be more convenient for hall staffs to check the same information on their own order-entry devices.

DISCUSSION 2: DIFFERENCES IN OPERATION FOR CVS AND RESTAURANT INDUSTRIES

In this section, we discuss the manner in which ISS improves restaurant operations. Actually, CVS industries targeted to optimize merchandizing system and information loop. The value chain in CVS industry can be portrayed as shown in Figure 8. The loop of the value chain encircles the CVS shop, CVS headquarters, vendors, and distributors. The POS' information encircles around this value chain. It is important for retail operations (include CVS) to adapt to requirements of customers by supplying sufficient number and varieties of goods. At the same time that customers buy goods at a CVS store, POS transmits information to the CVS headquarters. Headquarters staff can readily grasp how many and what kind goods are bought by

a customer. Headquarters analyzes information from various perspectives, and makes orders for distributors. Using POS, for example, CVS can change the total number, kind, and stock of goods for morning, daytime, and night. Moreover, CVS can maximize sales revenue, and minimize stocks and loss. The use of POS systems promotes profit and productivity in the CVS industry.

Restaurant industries have order transmission systems using POS because they have a productive function. However, the restaurant industry retains an information loop similar to that of CVS in spite of differences of the value chain. Value chains in the restaurant industry are presented in Figure 9. The value chain circles inside of restaurant, customer, service staff kitchen, and customer. Of course, it is important for restaurant headquarters to collect and analyze information. So-called ABC analysis (grasping the total number of sales goods by goods) is important to plan menus in restaurant. However, to adapt to customers' requirements and preparation, information must circle inside of the restaurant store to be useful. As Stalk and Hout (1990) describe, up-to-date information is valuable, but when it ages, it loses value.

In a restaurant, customers, kinds, and numbers of dishes, and order-received times differ from day to day, and time by time. To serve customers' needs, restaurants must use real-time information for preparation and serving. The ISS optimizes the information loop between the value chain and information loop in restaurant. Functions of ISS enable use information not only headquarters but also restaurant staff. Kitchen staff workers refer to real-time totaled order information easily and prepare dishes simultaneously to unite overlapping processes and optimize productivity, while increasing the serving speed. Actually, ISS has a time management function. Kitchen staff workers can grasp orders of each dish regularly and prepare them in sequence. Time passage and customer satisfaction are linked deeply.

As explained before, existing results of research show that it is important to improve opera-

Figure 8. Information loop of CVS

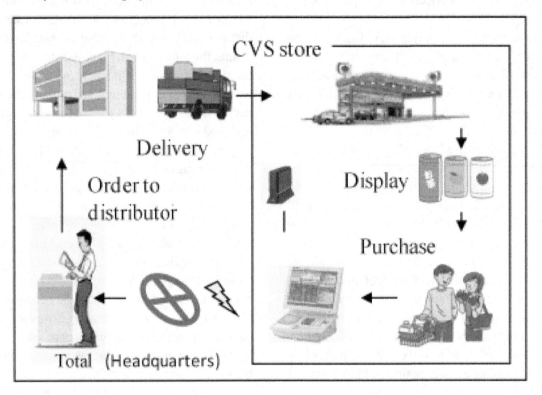

Figure 9. Information loop of a restaurant

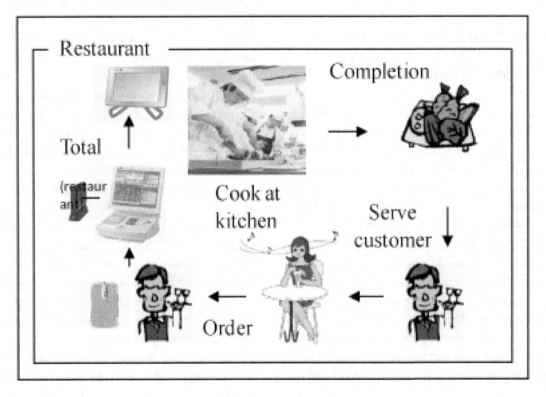

tion to heighten customer satisfaction (Hwang & Lambert, 2008; Davis & Maggard, 1990). Moreover, "time" is a critical cost, along with food cost and labor costs for customers (Muller, 1999). To reduce time (cost), restaurants can improve their value and hold a dominant position.

CONCLUSION

This paper introduced a new process management system (ISS) that augments POS systems for restaurants. In restaurant businesses, real-time management of customer orders is crucial. To that end, ISS provides an order checking function by dish and a display function of elapsed time. Moreover, the checking function of other positions' status helps managers to optimize staff assignments. By introducing this system to an actual restaurant, we confirmed that the average serving time was improved and that complaints decreased. In fact, PMS contributed to both efficiency and customer satisfaction. Those two goals do not conflict, but rather exist in the same context.

Future work will be undertaken to investigate aspects of customer satisfaction—customer preferences, motivation, and personality—more qualitatively. The opinions of loyal customers are expected to be important sources of customer satisfaction information (Hau-siu Chow et al., 2007). Moreover, development of new ISS functions will be pursued to share additional customer information such as their motivation to come or accompanying situations among staff members in real time. For example, servers' handheld devices might be improved by adding a new function for sharing information among them.

ACKNOWLEDGMENT

This study was partially supported by the project of promotion of Service Engineering from Japanese Ministry of Economy, Trade and Industry (METI) in 2009.

REFERENCES

Ahn, C., Nah, Y., Park, S., & Kim, J. (2001). An integrated medical information system using XML. In Kim, W., Ling, T. W., Lee, Y. J., & Park, S. S. (Eds.), *Human Society and the Internet, Proceedings - Internet-Related Socio-Economic Issues* (*Vol. 2105*, pp. 307–322). Berlin: Springer Verlag. doi:10.1007/3-540-47749-7_25

Chow, H.-S. I., & Lau, V. P., Wing-chun Lo, T., Sha, Z., & Yun, H. (2007). Service quality in restaurant operations in China: Decision- and experiential-oriented perspectives. *International Journal of Hospitality Management, 26*(3), 698–710. doi:10.1016/j.ijhm.2006.07.001

Cronin, J. J., Brady, M. K., & Hult, G. T. M. (2000). Assessing the effects of quality, value, and customer satisfaction on consumer behavioral intentions in service environments. *Journal of Retailing, 76*(2), 193–218. doi:10.1016/S0022-4359(00)00028-2

Davis, M. M., & Maggard, M. J. (1990). An analysis of customer satisfaction with waiting times in a two-stage service process. *Journal of Operations Management, 9*(3), 324–334. doi:10.1016/0272-6963(90)90158-A

Delrieux, C., Dominguez, J., & Repetto, A. (2002). Advanced techniques for real-time flow visualization. In Sisti, A. F., & Trevisani, D. A. (Eds.), *Enabling Technologies for Simulation Science Vi* (*Vol. 4716*, pp. 375–385). Bellingham, WA: Spie-Int Soc Optical Engineering.

Han, B. M., Song, S. J., Lee, K. M., Jang, K. S., Shin, D. R., & Icact. (2006). *Multi-Agent System based efficient healthcare service*. Seoul, South Korea: National Computerization Agency.

Hwang, J., & Lambert, C. U. (2008). The interaction of major resources and their influence on waiting times in a multi-stage restaurant. *International Journal of Hospitality Management, 27*(4), 541–551. doi:10.1016/j.ijhm.2007.08.005

Japanese Ministry of Economy. Trade and Industry. (2007). *Towards Innovation and Productivity Improvement in Service Industries*. Retrieved November 22, 2007, from http://www.meti.go.jp/english/report/data/0707SPRING.html/

Japanese Ministry of Internal Affairs, and Communications. (2006). *The number of business establishments and companies in service sectors*. Retrieved November 22, 2009, from http://www.stat.go.jp/data/jigyou/2006/kakuhou/gaiyou/02.htm

Jensen, Ø., & Hansen, K. V. (2007). Consumer values among restaurant customers. *International Journal of Hospitality Management, 26*(3), 603–622. doi:10.1016/j.ijhm.2006.05.004

Kimita, K., Yoshimitu, Y., Shimomura, Y., Arai, T., & Asme. (2008, Aug 03-06). *A customers' value model for Sustainable service design*. Paper presented at the ASME International Design Engineering Technical Conferences/Computers and Information in Engineering Conference, New York.

Mittal, V., Huppertz, J. W., & Khare, A. (2008). Customer complaining: The role of tie strength and information control. *Journal of Retailing, 84*(2), 195–204. doi:10.1016/j.jretai.2008.01.006

Morikawa, M. (2008). W*hat Do Japanese Unions Do for Productivity? An Empirical Analysis Using Firm-Level Data* (Tech. Rep. No. 08-E-027). Lazio, Italy: RIETI. Retrieved November 15, 2009, from http://www.rieti.go.jp/jp/publications/dp/08e027.pdf

Muller, C. C. (1999). The business of restaurants: 2001 and beyond. *International Journal of Hospitality Management, 18*(4), 401–413. doi:10.1016/S0278-4319(99)00045-6

Murphy, J., & Smith, S. (2009). Chefs and suppliers: An exploratory look at supply chain issues in an upscale restaurant alliance. *International Journal of Hospitality Management, 28*(2), 212–220. doi:10.1016/j.ijhm.2008.07.003

Ngai, E. W. T., Suk, F. F. C., & Lo, S. Y. Y. (2008). Development of an RFID-based sushi management system: The case of a conveyor-belt sushi restaurant. *International Journal of Production Economics, 112*(2), 630–645. doi:10.1016/j.ijpe.2007.05.011

Sako, M. (2006). Outsourcing and offshoring: Implications for productivity of business services. *Oxford Review of Economic Policy, 22*(4), 499–512. doi:10.1093/oxrep/grj029

Shimomura, Y., Hara, T., & Arai, T. (2008). A service evaluation method using mathematical methodologies. *CIRP Annals - Manufacturing Technology, 57*(1), 437-440.

Shimomura, Y., Sakao, T., Sundin, E., Lindahl, M., & Faculty of Mechanical, E. (2006, 2006). *Service Engineering: A novel engineering discipline for high added value creation*. Paper presented at the 9th International Design Conference, Dubrovnik, Croatia.

Sill, B. (1994). Operations engineering: Improving multiunit operations. *The Cornell Hotel and Restaurant Administration Quarterly, 35*(3), 64–71.

Spohrer, J., & Maglio, P. P. (2008). The emergence of service science: Toward systematic service innovations to accelerate co-creation of value. *Production and Operations Management, 17*(3), 238–246. doi:10.3401/poms.1080.0027

Stalk, G. Jr, & Hout, T. M. (1990). *Competing Against Time* (p. 88). New York: The Free Press.

Stein, K. (2005). Point-of-Sale Systems for Foodservice. *Journal of the American Dietetic Association, 105*(12), 1861–1861. doi:10.1016/j.jada.2005.10.003

Takenaka, T., & Ueda, K. (2008). An analysis of service studies toward sustainable value creation. *Int. J. Sustainable Manufacturing, 1*(1-2), 168–179.

Trappey, C. V., & Trappey, A. J. C. (1998). A chain store marketing information system: realizing Internet-based enterprise integration and electronic commerce. *Industrial Management & Data Systems, 98*(5-6), 205–213. doi:10.1108/02635579810227733

Turcu, C., Popa, V., & Ieee. (2009). *An RFID-based System for Emergency Health Care Services.* Washington, DC: IEEE.

Ueda, K., Takenaka, T., & Fujita, K. (2008). Toward value co-creation in manufacturing and servicing. *CIRP Journal of Manufacturing Science and Technology, 1*(1), 53–58. doi:10.1016/j.cirpj.2008.06.007

Ueda, K., Takenaka, T., Váncza, J., & Monostori, L. (2009). Value creation and decision-making in sustainable society. *CIRP Annals - Manufacturing Technology, 58*(2), 681-700.

Voss, C., Roth, A. V., & Chase, R. B. (2008). Experience, service operations strategy, and services as destinations: Foundations and exploratory investigation. *Production and Operations Management, 17*(3), 247–266. doi:10.3401/poms.1080.0030

This work was previously published in International Journal of Organizational and Collective Intelligence, Volume 1, Issue 3, edited by Hideyasu Sasaki, pp. 54-70, copyright 2010 by IGI Publishing (an imprint of IGI Global).

Chapter 15
The Computing of Digital Ecosystems

Gerard Briscoe
London School of Economics and Political Science, UK

Philippe De Wilde
Heriot-Watt University, UK

ABSTRACT

A primary motivation this research in digital ecosystems is the desire to exploit the self-organising properties of biological ecosystems. Ecosystems are thought to be robust, scalable architectures that can automatically solve complex and dynamic problems. However, the computing technologies that contribute to these properties have not been made explicit in digital ecosystems research. In this paper, the authors discuss how different computing technologies can contribute to providing the necessary self-organising features, including Multi-Agent Systems (MASs), Service-Oriented Architectures (SOAs), and distributed evolutionary computing (DEC). The potential for exploiting these properties in digital ecosystems is considered, suggesting how several key features of biological ecosystems can be exploited in Digital Ecosystems, and discussing how mimicking these features may assist in developing robust, scalable self-organising architectures. An example architecture, the Digital Ecosystem, is considered in detail. The Digital Ecosystem is then measured experimentally through simulations, which consider the self-organised diversity of its evolving agent populations relative to the user request behaviour.

INTRODUCTION

Digital Ecosystems are distributed adaptive open socio-technical systems, with properties of self-organisation, scalability and sustainability, inspired by natural ecosystems (Briscoe, 2009),

DOI: 10.4018/978-1-4666-1577-9.ch015

and are emerging as a novel approach to the catalysis of sustainable regional development driven by Small and Medium sized Enterprises (SMEs). Digital Ecosystems aim to help local economic actors become active players in globalisation, valorising their local culture and vocations, and enabling them to interact and create value networks at the global level (Dini et al., 2008).

We have previously considered the biological inspiration for the technical component of Digital Ecosystems (Briscoe, Sadedin, & Paperin, 2007; Briscoe & Sadedin, 2007), and we will now consider the relevant computing technologies. Based on our understanding of biological ecosystems in the context of Digital Ecosystems (Briscoe & De Wilde, 2006), we will now introduce fields from the domain of computer science relevant to the creation of Digital Ecosystems. As we are interested in the digital counterparts for the behaviour and constructs of biological ecosystems, instead of simulating or emulating such behaviour or constructs, we will consider what parallels can be drawn. We will start by considering MASs to explore the references to agents and migration (Briscoe et al., 2007; Briscoe & Sadedin, 2007); followed by evolutionary computing and SOAs for the references to evolution and self-organisation (Briscoe et al., 2007; Briscoe & Sadedin, 2007).

The value of creating parallels between biological and computer systems varies substantially depending on the behaviours or constructs being compared, and sometimes cannot be done so convincingly. For example, both have mechanisms to ensure data integrity. In computer systems, that integrity is absolute, data replication which introduces even the most minor change is considered to have failed, and is supported by mechanisms such as the Message-Digest algorithm 5 (Rivest, 1992). While in biological systems, the genetic code is transcribed with a remarkable degree of fidelity; there is, approximately, only one unforced error per one hundred bases copied (McCulloch et al., 2004). There are also elaborate proof-reading and correction systems, which in evolutionary terms are highly conserved (McCulloch et al., 2004). In this example establishing a parallel is infeasible, despite the relative similarity in function, because the operational control mechanisms in biological and computing systems are radically different, as are the aims and purposes. This is a reminder that considerable finesse is required when determining parallels, or when using existing ones.

MULTI-AGENT SYSTEMS

A software agent is a piece of software that acts, for a user in a relationship of agency, autonomously in an environment to meet its designed objectives. A MAS is a system composed of several software agents, collectively capable of reaching goals that are difficult to achieve by an individual agent or monolithic system. Conceptually, there is a strong parallel between the software agents of a MAS and the agent-based models of a biological ecosystem (Green, Klomp, Rimmington, & Sadedin, 2006), despite the lack of evolution and migration in a MAS. There is an even stronger parallel to a variant of MASs, called mobile agent systems, in which the mobility also mirrors the migration in biological ecosystems (Pham & Karmouch, 1998).

The term mobile agent contains two separate and distinct concepts: mobility and agency (Rothermel & Hohl, 1999). Hence, mobile agents are software agents capable of movement within a network (Pham & Karmouch, 1998). The mobile agent paradigm proposes to treat a network as multiple agent-friendly environments and the agents as programmatic entities that move from location to location, performing tasks for users. So, on each host they visit mobile agents need software which is responsible for their execution, providing a safe execution environment (Pham & Karmouch, 1998).

Generally, there are three types of design for mobile agent systems (Pham & Karmouch, 1998): (1) using a specialised operating system, (2) as operating system services or extensions, or (3) as application software. The third approach builds mobile agent systems as specialised application software that runs on top of an operating system, to provide for the mobile agent functionality, with such software being called an agent station (McCabe & Clark, 1994). In this last approach, each agent station hides the vendor-specific aspects of its host platform, and offers standardised services to visiting agents. Services include access to local resources and applications; for example, web servers or web services, the local exchange of information between agents via message passing, basic security services, and the creation of new agents (McCabe & Clark, 1994). Also, the third approach is the most platform-agnostic, and is visualised in Figure 1.

SERVICE-ORIENTED ARCHITECTURES

To evolve high-level software components in Digital Ecosystems, we propose taking advantage of the native method of software advancement, human developers, and the use of evolutionary computing for combinatorial optimisation of the available software services. This involves treating developer-produced software services as the functional building blocks, as the base unit in a genetic-algorithms-based process. Our approach to evolving high-level software applications requires a modular reusable paradigm to software development, such as SOAs. SOAs are the current state-of-the-art approach, being the current iteration of interface/component-based design from the 1990s, which was itself an iteration of event-oriented design from the 1980s, and before then

modular programming from the 1970s (Krafzig, Banke, & Slama, 2004). Service-oriented computing promotes assembling application components into a loosely coupled network of services, to create flexible, dynamic business processes and agile applications that span organisations and computing platforms (Papazoglou, 2003). This is achieved through a SOA, an architectural style that guides all aspects of creating and using business processes throughout their life-cycle, packaged as services. This includes defining and provisioning infrastructure that allows different applications to exchange data and participate in business processes, loosely coupled from the operating systems and programming languages underlying the applications. Hence, a SOA represents a model in which functionality is decomposed into distinct units (services), which can be distributed over a network, and can be combined and reused to create business applications (Papazoglou, 2003).

A SOA depends upon service-orientation as its fundamental design principle. In a SOA environment, independent services can be accessed without knowledge of their underlying platform implementation. Services reflect a service-oriented approach to programming that is based on composing applications by discovering and invoking

Figure 1. Mobile Agent System: Visualisation that shows mobile agents as programmes that can migrate from one host to another in a network of heterogeneous computer systems and perform a task specified by its owner

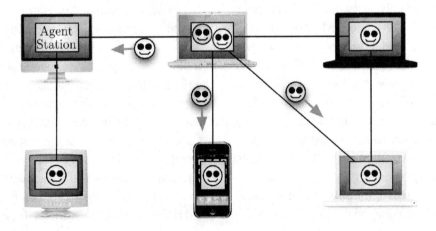

network-available services to accomplish some task. This approach is independent of specific programming languages or operating systems, because the services communicate with each other by passing data from one service to another, or by co-ordinating an activity between two or more services (Papazoglou, 2003). So, the concepts of SOAs are often seen as built upon, and the development of, the concepts of modular programming and distributed computing (Krafzig et al., 2004).

SOAs allow for an information system architecture that enables the creation of applications that are built by combining loosely coupled and interoperable services. They typically implement functionality most people would recognise as a service, such as filling out an online application for an account, or viewing an online bank statement (Krafzig et al., 2004). Services are intrinsically unassociated units of functionality, without calls to each other embedded in them. Instead of services embedding calls to each other in their source code, protocols are defined which describe how services can talk to each other, in a process known as orchestration, to meet new or existing business system requirements.

This is allowing an increasing number of third-party software companies to offer software services, such that SOA systems will come to consist of such third-party services combined with others created in-house, which has the potential to spread costs over many users and uses, and promote standardisation both in and across industries. For example, the travel industry now has a well-defined, and documented, set of both services and data, sufficient to allow any competent software engineer to create travel agency software using entirely off-the-shelf software services (Cardoso & Sheth, 2004). Other industries, such as the finance industry, are also making significant progress in this direction (Zimmermann, Milinski, Craes, & Oellermann, 2004).

The vision of SOAs assembling application components from a loosely coupled network of services, that can create dynamic business processes and agile applications that span organisations and computing platforms, is visualised in Figure 2. It will be made possible by creating compound solutions that use internal organisational software assets, including enterprise information and legacy systems, and combining these solutions with external components residing in remote networks. The great promise of SOAs is that the marginal cost of creating the n-th application is virtually zero, as all the software required already exists to satisfy the requirements of other applications. Only their combination and orchestration are required to produce a new application (Modi, 2007). The key is that the interactions between the chunks are not specified within the chunks themselves. Instead, the interaction of services (all of whom are hosted by unassociated peers) is specified by users in an ad-hoc way, with the intent driven by newly emergent business requirements (Leymann, Roller, & Schmidt, 2002).

The pinnacle of SOA interoperability is the exposing of services on the internet as web services. A web service is a specific type of service that is identified by a Uniform Resource Identifier (URI), whose service description and transport utilise open Internet standards. Interactions between web services typically occur as Simple Object Access Protocol (SOAP) calls carrying eXtensible Markup Language (XML) data content. The interface descriptions of web services are expressed using the Web Services Definition Language (WSDL) (Papazoglou & Georgakopoulos, 2003). The Universal Description Discovery and Integration (UDDI) standard defines a protocol for directory services that contain web service descriptions. UDDI enables web service clients to locate candidate services and discover their details. Service clients and service providers utilise these standards to perform the basic operations of SOAs (Papazoglou & Georgakopoulos, 2003). Service aggregators can then use the Business Process Execution Language (BPEL) to create new web services by defining corresponding compositions of the interfaces and internal

Figure 2. Service-Oriented Architectures: Abstract visualisations, with the loosely joined services as cuboids, and the service orchestration as a polyhedron

processes of existing services (Papazoglou & Georgakopoulos, 2003).

SOA services inter-operate based on a formal definition (or contract, e.g., WSDL) that is independent of the underlying platform and programming language. Service descriptions are used to advertise the service capabilities, interface, behaviour, and quality (Papazoglou & Georgakopoulos, 2003). The publication of such information about available services provides the necessary means for discovery, selection, binding, and composition of services (Papazoglou & Georgakopoulos, 2003). The (expected) behaviour of a service during its execution is described by its behavioural description (for example, as a

workflow process). Also, included is a quality of service (QoS) description, which publishes important functional and non-functional service quality attributes, such as service metering and cost, performance metrics (response time, for instance), security attributes, integrity (transactional), reliability, scalability, and availability (Papazoglou & Georgakopoulos, 2003). Service clients (end-user organisations that use some service) and service aggregators (organisations that consolidate multiple services into a new, single service offering) utilise service descriptions to achieve their objectives (Papazoglou & Georgakopoulos, 2003). One of the most important and continuing developments in SOAs is Semantic

Web Services (SWS), which make use of semantic descriptions for service discovery so that a client can discover the services semantically (Cabral, Domingue, Motta, Payne, & Hakimpour, 2004).

There are multiple standards available and still being developed for SOAs, most notably of recent being REpresentational State Transfer (REST) (Singh & Huhns, 2005). The software industry now widely implements a thin SOAP/WSDL/UDDI veneer atop existing applications or components that implement the web services paradigm, but the choice of technologies will change with time. Therefore, the fundamentals of SOAs and its services are best defined generically, because SOAs are technology agnostic and need not be tied to a specific technology (Papazoglou, 2003). Within the current and future scope of the fundamentals of SOAs, there is clearly potential to evolve complex high-level software applications from the modular services of SOAs, instead of the instruction level evolution currently prevalent in genetic programming (Koza, 1992).

DISTRIBUTED EVOLUTIONARY COMPUTING

Having previously suggested evolutionary computing (Briscoe et al., 2007; Briscoe & Sadedin, 2007), and the possibility of it occurring within a distributed environment, not unlike those found in mobile agent systems, leads us to consider a specialised form known as DEC. The fact that evolutionary computing manipulates a population of independent solutions actually makes it well suited for parallel and distributed computation architectures (Cantu-Paz, 1998). The motivation for using parallel or distributed evolutionary algorithms is twofold: first, improving the speed of evolutionary processes by conducting concurrent evaluations of individuals in a population; second, improving the problem-solving process by overcoming difficulties that face traditional evolutionary algorithms, such as maintaining diversity to avoid premature

convergence (Stender, 1993). There are several variants of distributed evolutionary computing, leading some to propose a taxonomy for their classification, with there being two main forms (Cantu-Paz, 1998; Stender, 1993):

- multiple-population/coarse-grained migration/island
- single-population/fine-grained diffusion/neighbourhood

In the coarse-grained island models (Punch & Goodman, 1994; Cantu-Paz, 1998), evolution occurs in multiple parallel sub-populations (islands), each running a local evolutionary algorithm, evolving independently with occasional migrations of highly fit individuals among sub-populations. The core parameters for the evolutionary algorithm of the island-models are as follows (Lin et al., 1994):

- number of the sub-populations: 2, 3, 4, more
- sub-population homogeneity
  - ○ size, crossover rate, mutation rate
- topology of connectivity: ring, star, fully-connected
- static or dynamic connectivity
- migration mechanisms:
  - ○ isolated/synchronous/asynchronous
  - ○ how often migrations occur
  - ○ which individuals migrate

Fine-grained diffusion models (Stender, 1993) assign one individual per processor. A local neighbourhood topology is assumed, and individuals are allowed to mate only within their neighbourhood, called a deme. The demes overlap by an amount that depends on their shape and size, and in this way create an implicit migration mechanism. Each processor runs an identical evolutionary algorithm which selects parents from the local neighbourhood, produces an offspring, and decides whether to replace the current individual with an offspring. However, even with the advent of multi-processor computers, and more recently multi-core processors, which provide the ability to execute multiple threads simultaneously, this approach would still prove impractical in supporting the number of agents necessary to create a Digital Ecosystem. Therefore, we shall further consider the island models.

An example island-model (Lin et al., 1994; Cantu-Paz, 1998) is visualised in Figure 3, in which there are different probabilities of going from island 1 to island 2, as there is of going from island 2 to island 1. This allows maximum flexibility for the migration process, and mirrors the naturally inspired quality that although two populations have the same physical separation, it may be easier to migrate in one direction than the other, i.e., fish migration is easier downstream than upstream. The migration of the island models is like the notion of migration in nature, being similar to the metapopulation models of theoretical ecology (Levins, 1969). This model has also been used successfully in the determination of investment strategies in the commercial sector, in a product known as the Galapagos toolkit (Ward,

2004). However, all the islands in this approach work on exactly the same problem, which makes it less analogous to biological ecosystems in which different locations can be environmentally different (Begon, Harper, & Townsend, 1996). We will take advantage of this property later when defining the Ecosystem-Oriented Architecture of Digital Ecosystems.

THE DIGITAL ECOSYSTEM

We will now define the architectural principles of Digital Ecosystems. We will use our understanding of theoretical biology (Briscoe & De Wilde, 2006; Briscoe, 2009), mimicking the processes and structures of life, evolution, and ecology of biological ecosystems. We will achieve this by combining elements from mobile agents systems, distributed evolutionary computing, and Service-Oriented Architectures, to create a hybrid architecture which is the digital counterpart of biological ecosystems. Combing these technologies, based on the biological inspiration, the technical component

Figure 3. Island-Model of Distributed Evolutionary Computing: There are different probabilities of going from island 1 to island 2, as there is of going from island 2 to island 1

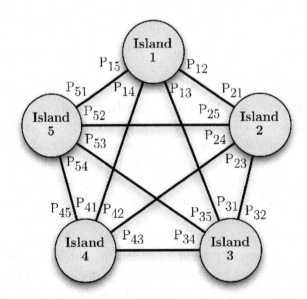

of Digital Ecosystems provide a two-level optimisation scheme inspired by natural ecosystems, in which a decentralised peer-to-peer network forms an underlying tier of distributed agents. These agents then feed a second optimisation level based on an evolutionary algorithm that operates locally on single habitats (peers), aiming to find solutions that satisfy locally relevant constraints. The local search is sped up through this twofold process, providing better local optima as the distributed optimisation provides prior sampling of the search space by making use of computations already performed in other peers with similar constraints (Briscoe, Chli, & Vidal, 2006). So, the Digital Ecosystem supports the automatic combining of numerous agents (which represent services), by their interaction in evolving populations to meet user requests for applications, in a scalable architecture of distributed interconnected habitats. The sharing of agents between habitats ensures the system is scalable, while maintaining a high evolutionary specialisation for each user. The network of interconnected habitats is equivalent to the abiotic environment of biological ecosystems (Begon et al., 1996); combined with the agents, the populations, the agent migration for distributed evolutionary computing, and the environmental selection pressures provided by the user base, then the union of the habitats creates the Digital Ecosystem, which is summarised in Figure 4. The continuous and varying user requests for applications provide a dynamic evolutionary pressure on the applications (agent aggregations), which have to evolve to better fulfil those user requests, and without which there would be no driving force to the evolutionary self-organisation of the Digital Ecosystem.

If we consider an example user base for the Digital Ecosystem, the use of SOAs in its definition means that business-to-business (B2B) interaction scenarios (Krafzig et al., 2004) lend themselves to being a potential user base for Digital Ecosystems. So, we can consider a business ecosystem of Small and Medium sized Enterprise (SME) networks (Moore, 1996), as a specific class of examples for B2B interaction

Figure 4. Digital Ecosystem: Optimisation architecture in which agents (representing services) travel along the P2P connections; in every node (habitat) local optimisation is performed through an evolutionary algorithm, where the search space is determined by the agents present at the node

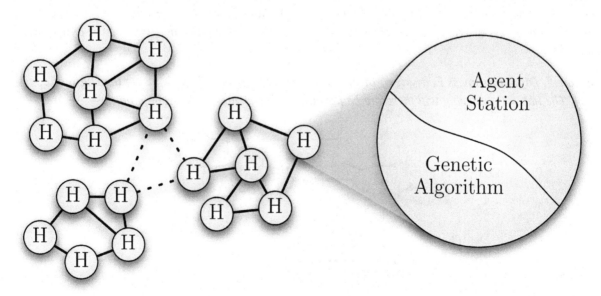

scenarios; and in which the SME users are requesting and providing software services, represented as agents in the Digital Ecosystem, to fulfil the needs of their business processes, creating a Digital Business Ecosystem as shown in Figure 5. SOAs promise to provide potentially huge numbers of services that programmers can combine, via the standardised interfaces, to create increasingly more sophisticated and distributed applications (Papazoglou & Georgakopoulos, 2003). The Digital Ecosystem extends this concept with the automatic combining of available and applicable services, represented by agents, in a scalable architecture, to meet user requests for applications. These agents will recombine and evolve over time, constantly seeking to improve their effectiveness for the user base. From the SME users' point of view the Digital Ecosystem provides a network infrastructure where connected enterprises can advertise and search for services (real-world or software only), putting a particular emphasis on the composability of loosely coupled services and their optimisation to local and regional, needs and conditions. To support these SME users the Digital Ecosystem is satisfying the companies' business requirements by finding the most suitable services or combination of services (applications) available in the network. An application (composition of services) is defined be an agent aggregation (collection) in

the habitat network that can move from one peer (company) to another, being hosted only in those where it is most useful in satisfying the SME users' business needs.

The agents consist of an executable component and an ontological description. So, the Digital Ecosystem can be considered a MAS which uses distributed evolutionary computing (Cantu-Paz, 1998; Stender, 1993) to combine suitable agents in order to meet user requests for applications.

The landscape, in energy-centric biological ecosystems, defines the connectivity between habitats (Begon et al., 1996). Connectivity of nodes in the digital world is generally not defined by geography or spatial proximity, but by information or semantic proximity. For example, connectivity in a peer-to-peer network is based primarily on bandwidth and information content, and not geography. The island-models of distributed evolutionary computing use an information-centric model for the connectivity of nodes (islands) (Lin et al., 1994). However, because it is generally defined for one-time use (to evolve a solution to one problem and then stop) it usually has a fixed connectivity between the nodes, and therefore a fixed topology (Cantu-Paz, 1998). So, supporting evolution in the Digital Ecosystem, with a multi-objective selection pressure (fitness landscape with many peaks), requires a re-configurable network topology, such that habitat connectivity can be dynamically

Figure 5. Digital Business Ecosystem: Business ecosystem, network of SMEs, using the Digital Ecosystem. The habitat clustering will therefore be parallel to the business sector communities

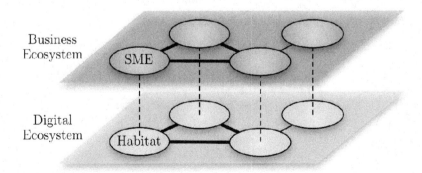

adapted based on the observed migration paths of the agents between the users within the habitat network. Based on the island-models of distributed evolutionary computing (Lin et al., 1994), each connection between the habitats is bi-directional and there is a probability associated with moving in either direction across the connection, with the connection probabilities affecting the rate of migration of the agents. However, additionally, the connection probabilities will be updated by the success or failure of agent migration using the concept of Hebbian learning: the habitats which do not successfully exchange agents will become less strongly connected, and the habitats which do successfully exchange agents will achieve stronger connections. This leads to a topology that adapts over time, resulting in a network that supports and resembles the connectivity of the user base. If we consider a business ecosystem, network of SMEs, as an example user base; such business networks are typically small-world networks (White & Houseman, 2002). They have many strongly connected clusters (communities), called sub-networks (quasi-complete graphs), with a few connections between these clusters (communities). Graphs with this topology have a very high clustering coefficient and small characteristic path lengths (Watts & Strogatz, 1998). So, the Digital Ecosystem will take on a topology similar to that of the user base, as shown in Figure 5.

The novelty of our approach comes from the evolving populations being created in response to similar requests. So whereas in the island-models of distributed evolutionary computing there are multiple evolving populations in response to one request (Lin et al., 1994), here there are multiple evolving populations in response to similar requests. In our Digital Ecosystems different requests are evaluated on separate islands (populations), and so adaptation is accelerated by the sharing of solutions between evolving populations (islands), because they are working to solve similar requests (problems).

The users will formulate queries to the Digital Ecosystem by creating a request as a semantic description, like those being used and developed in SOAs, specifying an application they desire and submitting it to their local peer (habitat). This description defines a metric for evaluating the fitness of a composition of agents, as a distance function between the semantic description of the request and the agents' ontological descriptions. A population is then instantiated in the user's habitat in response to the user's request, seeded from the agents available at their habitat. This allows the evolutionary optimisation to be accelerated in the following three ways: first, the habitat network provides a subset of the agents available globally, which is localised to the specific user it represents; second, making use of applications (agent aggregations) previously evolved in response to the user's earlier requests; and third, taking advantage of relevant applications evolved elsewhere in response to similar requests by other users. The population then proceeds to evolve the optimal application (agent aggregation) that fulfils the user request, and as the agents are the base unit for evolution, it searches the available agent combination space. For an evolved agent aggregation (application) that is executed by the user, it then migrates to other peers (habitats) becoming hosted where it is useful, to combine with other agents in other populations to assist in responding to other user requests for applications.

SIMULATION AND RESULTS

We have previously compared the performance of Digital Ecosystems to traditional SOA based systems, and found that it outperforms at greater scales (Briscoe & De Wilde, 2006), and so here we focus on the self-organising behaviour which makes this possible. Self-organisation is perhaps one of the most desirable features in the systems that we design, and a primary motivation for our research in Digital Ecosystems is the desire to exploit the self-organising properties of biological ecosystems (Levin, 1998), which are thought to be robust, scalable architectures that can automatically solve complex, dynamic problems. Over time a biological ecosystem becomes increasingly self-organised through the process of ecological succession (Begon et al., 1996), driven by the evolutionary self-organisation of the populations within the ecosystem. Analogously, a Digital Ecosystem's increasing self-organisation comes from the agent populations within being evolved to meet the dynamic selection pressures created by the requests from the user base. The self-organisation of biological ecosystems is often defined in terms of the complexity, stability, and diversity (King & Pimm, 1983), which we will also apply to our Digital Ecosystems, here considering the diversity.

Self-organisation has been around since the late 1940s (Ashby, 1947), but has escaped general formalisation despite many attempts (Nicolis & Prigogine, 1977; Kohonen, 1989). There have instead been many notions and definitions of self-organisation, useful within their different contexts (Heylighen, 2002). They have come from cybernetics (Ashby, 1947; Beer, 1966; Heylighen & Joslyn, 2001), thermodynamics (Nicolis & Prigogine, 1977), mathematics (Lendaris, 1964), information theory (Shalizi, 2001), synergetics (Haken, 1977), and other domains (Lehn, 1990). The term self-organising is widely used, but there is no generally accepted meaning, as the abundance of definitions would suggest. Therefore, the philosophy of self-organisation is complicated, because organisation has different meanings to different people. So, we would argue that any definition of self-organisation is context dependent, in the same way that a choice of statistical measure is dependent on the data being analysed.

While we could measure the self-organised diversity of individual evolving agent populations, or even take a random sampling, it will be more informative to consider their collective self-organised diversity. Also, given that the Digital Ecosystem is required to support a range of user behaviour, we can consider the collective self-organised diversity of the evolving agent populations relative to the global user request behaviour. So, when varying a behavioural property of the user requests according to some distribution, we would expect the corresponding property of the evolving agent populations to follow the same distribution. We are not intending to prescribe the expected user behaviour of the Digital Ecosystem, but investigate whether the Digital Ecosystem can adapt to a range of user behaviour. So, we will consider Uniform, Gaussian (Normal) and Power Law distributions for the parameters of the user request behaviour. The Uniform distribution will provide a control, while the Normal (Gaussian) distribution will provide a reasonable assumption for the behaviour of a large group of users, and the Power Law distribution will provide a relatively extreme variation in user behaviour. So, we simulated the Digital Ecosystem, varying aspects of the user behaviour according to different distributions, and measuring the related aspects of the evolving agent populations. This consisted of a mechanism to vary the user request properties of length and modularity (number of attributes per atomic service), according to Uniform, Gaussian (normal) and Power Law distributions, and a mechanism to measure the corresponding application (agent aggregation) properties of size and number of attributes per agent. For statistical significance each scenario (experiment) will be averaged from ten thousand simulation runs. We expect it will be obvious whether the observed behaviour of the Digital Ecosystem matches the expected behaviour from the user base. Nevertheless, we will also implement a chi-squared (χ^2) test to determine if the observed behaviour (distribution) of the agent aggregation properties matches the expected behaviour (distribution) from the user request properties.

User Request Length

We started by varying the user request length according to the available distributions, expecting the size of the corresponding applications (agent aggregations) to be distributed according to the length of the user requests, i.e., the longer the user request, the larger the agent aggregation needed to fulfil it.

We first applied the Uniform distribution as a control, and graphed the results in Figure 6. The observed frequencies of the application (agent aggregation) size mostly matched the expected frequencies, which were confirmed by a χ^2 test; with a null hypothesis of no significant difference and sixteen degrees of freedom, the χ^2 value was 2.588, below the critical 0.95 χ^2 value of 7.962.

We then applied the Gaussian distribution as a reasonable assumption for the behaviour of a large group of users, and graphed the results in Figure 7. The observed frequencies of the application (agent aggregation) size matched the expected frequencies with only minor variations, which was confirmed by a χ^2 test; with a null hypothesis of no significant difference and sixteen degrees of freedom, the χ^2 value was 2.102, below the critical 0.95 χ^2 value of 7.962.

Finally, we applied the Power Law distribution to represent a relatively extreme variation in user behaviour, and graphed the results in Figure 8. The observed frequencies of the application (agent aggregation) size matched the expected frequen-

cies with some variation, which was confirmed by a χ^2 test; with a null hypothesis of no significant difference and sixteen degrees of freedom, the χ^2 value was 5.048, below the critical 0.95 χ^2 value of 7.962.

There were a couple of minor discrepancies, similar to all the experiments. First, there were a small number of individual agents at the thousandth time step, caused by the typical user behaviour of continuously creating new services (agents). Second, while the chi-squared tests confirmed that there was no significant difference between the observed and expected frequencies of the application (agent aggregation) size, there was still a bias to larger applications (solutions). Evident visually in the graphs of the experiments, and evident numerically in the chi-squared test of the Power Law distribution experiment as it favoured shorter agent-sequences. The cause of this bias was most likely some aspect of bloat not fully controlled.

USER REQUEST MODULARITY

Next, we varied the user request modularity (number of attributes per atomic service) according to the available distributions, expecting

Figure 6. Graph of Uniformly Distributed Agent-Sequence Length Frequencies: The observed frequencies of the application (agent aggregation) size mostly matched the expected frequencies

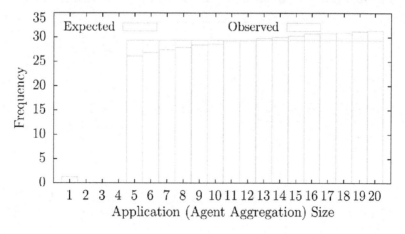

Figure 7. Graph of Gaussian Distributed Agent-Sequence Length Frequencies: The observed frequencies of the application (agent aggregation) size matched the expected frequencies with only minor variations

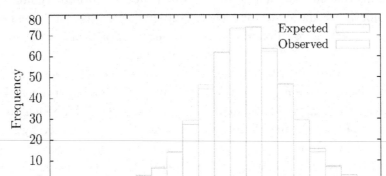

the sophistication of the agents to be distributed according to the modularity of the user requests, i.e., the more complicated (in terms of modular non-reducible tasks) the user request, the more sophisticated (in terms of the number of attributes) the agents needed to fulfil it.

We first applied the Uniform distribution as a control, and graphed the results in Figure 9. The observed frequencies for the number of agent attributes mostly matched the expected frequencies, which were confirmed by a $\chi 2$ test; with a null hypothesis of no significant difference and ten degrees of freedom, the $\chi 2$ value was 1.049, below the critical 0.95 $\chi 2$ value of 3.940.

We then applied the Gaussian distribution as a reasonable assumption for the behaviour of a large group of users, and graphed the results in Figure 10. The observed frequencies for the number of agent attributes again followed the expected frequencies, but there was variation which led to a failed $\chi 2$ test; with a null hypothesis of no significant difference and ten degrees of freedom, the $\chi 2$ value was 50.623, not below the critical 0.95 $\chi 2$ value of 3.940.

Figure 8. Graph of Power Law Distributed Agent-Sequence Length Frequencies: The observed frequencies of the application (agent aggregation) size matched the expected frequencies with some variation

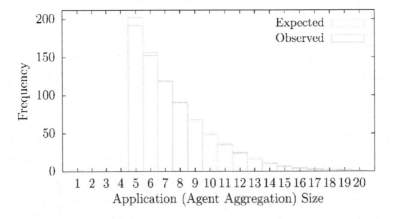

Figure 9. Graph of Uniformly Distributed Agent Attribute Frequencies: The observed frequencies for the number of agent attributes mostly matched the expected frequencies

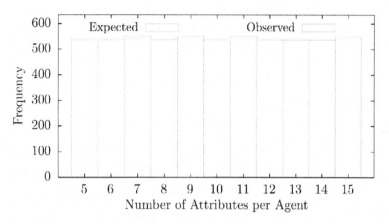

Finally, we applied the Power Law distribution to represent a relatively extreme variation in user behaviour, and graphed the results in Figure 11. The observed frequencies for the number of agent attributes also followed the expected frequencies, but there was variation which led to a failed $\chi2$ test; with a null hypothesis of no significant difference and ten degrees of freedom, the $\chi2$ value was 61.876, not below the critical 0.95 $\chi2$ value of 3.940.

In all the experiments the observed frequencies of the number of agent attributes followed the expected frequencies, with some variation in two

of the experiments. This could only be confirmed statistically, by a $\chi2$ test, for the Uniform distribution experiment. In the Gaussian and Power distribution experiments the $\chi2$ tests failed by considerable margins, most likely because the evolving agent populations were still self-organising to match the user behaviour, shown by the observed frequencies approaching the expected frequencies, but not yet sufficiently to meet $\chi2$ tests, because by the thousandth time step (user request event) each user had placed an average of only ten requests.

Figure 10. Graph of Gaussian Distributed Agent Attribute Frequencies: The observed frequencies for the number of agent attributes again followed the expected frequencies, but there was variation

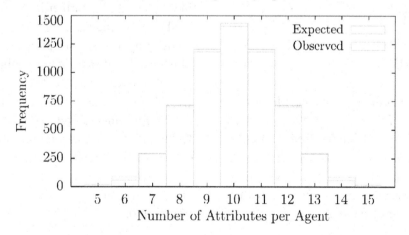

Figure 11. Graph of Power Law Distributed Agent Attribute Frequencies: The observed frequencies for the number of agent attributes also followed the expected frequencies, but there was variation

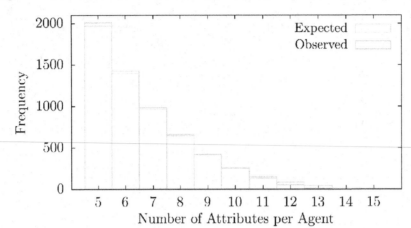

Collectively, the experimental results confirm that the self-organised diversity of the evolving agent populations is relative to the selection pressures of the user base, which was confirmed statistically for most of the experiments. So, we have determined an effective understanding and quantification for the self-organised diversity of the evolving agent populations of our Digital Ecosystem. While the minor experimental failures, in which the Digital Ecosystem responded more slowly than in the other experiments, have shown that there is potential to optimise the Digital Ecosystem, because the evolutionary self-organisation of an ecosystem is a slow process (Begon et al., 1996), even the accelerated form present in our Digital Ecosystem.

CONCLUSION

We have confirmed the fundamentals for a new class of system, Digital Ecosystems, created through combining understanding from theoretical ecology, evolutionary theory, MASs, distributed evolutionary computing, and SOAs. Digital Ecosystems, where the word ecosystem is more than just a metaphor, being the digital counterpart of biological ecosystems, and therefore having their desirable properties, such as scalability and self-organisation. It is a complex system that shows emergent behaviour, being more than the sum of its constituent parts.

With the core infrastructure of Digital Ecosystems defined, some intelligence-based augmentations have been considered for its acceleration and optimisation (Briscoe & De Wilde, 2008; Briscoe, 2009). In which the agents were endowed with memory, intelligence and the ability to share information, with the aim of optimising the ecological dynamics, through the emergent optimisation of the agent migration patterns. While not yet as sophisticated as swarm intelligence, we would argue it is a step in that direction, and we would like to investigate further in the future.

The ever-increasing challenge of software complexity in creating progressively more sophisticated and distributed applications, makes the design and maintenance of efficient and flexible systems a growing challenge (Markoff, 2007), for which current software development techniques have hit a complexity wall (Lyytinen & Yoo, 2001). In response we have created Digital Ecosystems, the digital counterparts of biological ecosystems, possessing their properties of self-organisation, scalability and sustainability (Levin,

1998); Ecosystem-Oriented Architectures that overcome the challenge by automating the search for new algorithms in a scalable architecture, through the evolution of software services in a distributed network.

REFERENCES

Ashby, W. (1947). Principles of the self-organizing dynamic system. *The Journal of General Psychology, 37*, 125–128.

Beer, S. (1966). *Decision and control: The meaning of operational research and management cybernetics*. New York: Wiley.

Begon, M., Harper, J., & Townsend, C. (1996). *Ecology: Individuals, populations and communities*. Oxford, UK: Blackwell Publishing.

Briscoe, G. (2009). *Digital ecosystems*. Unpublished doctoral dissertation, Imperial College London, London.

Briscoe, G., Chli, M., & Vidal, M. (2006). Creating a Digital Ecosystem: Service-oriented architectures with distributed evolutionary computing (BOF-0759). In *Proceedings of the Javaone conference*. Sun Microsystems. Retrieved from http://arxiv.org/0712.4159

Briscoe, G., & De Wilde, P. (2006). *Digital Ecosystems: Evolving service-oriented architectures. In Conference on bio inspired models of network, information and computing systems*. Washington, DC: IEEE Press. Retrieved from http://arxiv.org/abs/0712.4102

Briscoe, G., & De Wilde, P. (2008). Digital Ecosystems: Optimisation by a distributed intelligence. In *Proceedings of the Digital ecosystems and technologies conference*. Washington, DC: IEEE Press. Retrieved from http://arxiv.org/abs/0712.4099

Briscoe, G., & Sadedin, S. (2007). Digital Business Ecosystems: Natural science paradigms. In Nachira, F., Nicolai, A., Dini, P., Le Louarn, M., & Rivera Le'on, L. (Eds.), *Digital Business Ecosystems* (pp. 48–55). European Commission.

Briscoe, G., Sadedin, S., & Paperin, G. (2007). *Biology of applied digital ecosystems. In Digital ecosystems and technologies conference* (pp. 458-463). Washington, DC: IEEE Press. Retrieved from http://arxiv.org/abs/0712.4153

Cabral, L., Domingue, J., Motta, E., Payne, T., & Hakimpour, F. (2004). Approaches to semantic web services: an overview and comparisons. In *The semantic web: Research and applications* (pp. 225–239). New York: Springer.

Cantu-Paz, E. (1998). A survey of parallel genetic algorithms. *R'eseaux et syst'emes r'epartis, Calculateurs Parall'eles, 10*, 141-171.

Cardoso, J., & Sheth, A. (2004). Introduction to semantic web services and web process composition. In Cardoso, J., & Sheth, A. (Eds.), *Semantic web services and web process composition* (pp. 1–13). New York: Springer.

Dini, P., Lombardo, G., Mansell, R., Razavi, A., Moschoyiannis, S., & Krause, P. (2008). Beyond interoperability to digital ecosystems: regional innovation and socio-economic development led by SMEs. *International Journal of Technological Learning. Innovation and Development, 1*, 410–426.

Green, D., Klomp, N., Rimmington, G., & Sadedin, S. (2006). *Complexity in landscape ecology*. New York: Springer.

Haken, H. (1977). *Synergetics: an introduction: non-equilibrium phase transitions and self-organization in physics, chemistry, and biology*. New York: Springer.

Heylighen, F. (2002). The science of self-organization and adaptivity. *The Encyclopedia of Life Support Systems*, 253-280.

Heylighen, F., & Joslyn, C. (2001). Cybernetics and second order cybernetics. *Encyclopedia of Physical Science & Technology, 4*, 155-170.

King, A., & Pimm, S. (1983). Complexity, diversity, and stability: A reconciliation of theoretical and empirical results. *American Naturalist, 122*, 229–239.

Kohonen, T. (1989). *Self-organization and associative memory*. New York: Springer.

Koza, J. (1992). Overview of genetic programming. In *Genetic programming: On the programming of computers by means of natural selection* (pp. 73–78). Cambridge, MA: MIT.

Krafzig, D., Banke, K., & Slama, D. (2004). *Enterprise soa: Service-oriented architecture best practices*. Upper Saddle River, NJ: Prentice Hall.

Lehn, J. (1990). Perspectives in supramolecular chemistry—from molecular recognition towards molecular information processing and self-organization. *Angewandte Chemie International Edition in English, 29*, 1304–1319.

Lendaris, G. (1964). On the definition of self-organizing systems. In W. Banzhaf (Ed.), *Proceedings of the European conference on advances in artificial life* (pp. 324-325). Washington, DC: IEEE Press.

Levin, S. (1998). Ecosystems and the biosphere as complex adaptive systems. *Ecosystems (New York, N.Y.), 1*, 431–436.

Levins, R. (1969). Some demographic and genetic consequences of environmental heterogeneity for biological control. *Bulletin of the Entomological Society of America, 15*, 237–240.

Leymann, F., Roller, D., & Schmidt, M. (2002). Web services and business process management. *IBM Systems Journal, 41*, 198–211.

Lin, S., Punch, W., III, & Goodman, E. (1994). Coarse-grain parallel genetic algorithms: categorization and new approach. In *Proceedings of the Symposium on parallel and distributed processing* (pp. 28-37). Washington, DC: IEEE Press.

Lyytinen, K., & Yoo, Y. (2001). The next wave of nomadic computing: A research agenda for information systems research. *Sprouts, 1*, 1–20.

Markoff, J. (2007). Faster chips are leaving programmers in their dust (Tech. Rep.). *New York Times*. Retrieved from http://www.nytimes.com/2007/12/17/technology/17chip.html

McCabe, F., & Clark, K. (1994). April-agent process interaction language. In M. Wooldridge & N. Jennings (Eds.), *Intelligent agents: Workshop on agent theories, architectures, and languages* (pp. 324-340). New York: Springer.

McCulloch, S., Kokoska, R., Chilkova, O., Welch, C., Johansson, E., & Burgers, P. (2004). Enzymatic switching for efficient and accurate translesion DNA replication. *Nucleic Acids Research, 32*, 4665–4675.

Modi, G. (2007). *Service oriented architecture & web 2.0* (Tech. Rep.). Guru Tegh Bahadur Institute of Technology. Retrieved from http://www.gsmodi.com/files/SOAWeb2 Report.pdf

Moore, J. (1996). *The death of competition: Leadership and strategy in the age of business ecosystems*. Boston: Harvard Business School Press.

Nicolis, G., & Prigogine, I. (1977). *Self-organization in nonequilibrium systems: From dissipative structures to order through fluctuations*. New York: Wiley.

Papazoglou, M. (2003). Service-oriented computing: concepts, characteristics and directions. In T. Catarci, M. Mecella, J. Mylopoulos, & M. Orlowska (Eds.), *International conference on web information systems engineering* (pp. 3-12). Washington, DC: IEEE Press.

Papazoglou, M., & Georgakopoulos, D. (2003). Service-oriented computing. *Communications of the ACM, 46*, 25–28.

Pham, V., & Karmouch, A. (1998). Mobile software agents: an overview. *IEEE Communications Magazine, 36*, 26–37.

Rivest, R. (1992). *The MD5 message-digest algorithm* (Tech. Rep.). Cambridge, MA: MIT. Retrieved from http://people.csail.mit.edu/rivest/Rivest-MD5.txt

Rothermel, K., & Hohl, F. (1999). Mobile agents. In Kent, A., & Williams, J. (Eds.), *Encyclopedia for computer science and technology* (*Vol. 40*, pp. 155–176). Boca Raton, FL: CRC Press.

Shalizi, C. (2001). *Causal architecture, complexity and self-organization in time series and cellular automata*. Unpublished doctoral dissertation, University of Wisconsin-Madison, WI.

Singh, M., & Huhns, M. (2005). *Service-oriented computing: Semantics, processes, agents*. New York: Wiley.

Stender, J. (1993). *Parallel genetic algorithms: Theory and applications*. New York: IOS Press.

Ward, M. (2004). *Life offers lessons for business*. Retrieved from http://news.bbc.co.uk/1/hi/technology/3752725.stm

Watts, D., & Strogatz, S. (1998). Collective dynamics of 'small-world' networks. *Nature, 393*, 440–442.

White, D., & Houseman, M. (2002). The navigability of strong ties: Small worlds, tie strength, and network topology. *Complexity, 8*, 72–81.

Zimmermann, O., Milinski, S., Craes, M., & Oellermann, F. (2004). Second generation web services-oriented architecture in production in the finance industry. In J. Vlissides & D. Schmidt (Eds.), *Proceedings of the Conference on object-oriented programming, systems, languages, and applications* (pp. 283-289). New York: ACM Press.

This work was previously published in International Journal of Organizational and Collective Intelligence, Volume 1, Issue 4, edited by Hideyasu Sasaki, pp. 1-17, copyright 2010 by IGI Publishing (an imprint of IGI Global).

Chapter 16

An Autonomous Agent Approach to Query Optimization in Stream Grids

Saikat Mukherjee
International Institute of Information Technology, India

Srinath Srinivasa
International Institute of Information Technology, India

Krithi Ramamritham
Indian Institute of Technology, India

ABSTRACT

Stream grids are wide-area grid computing environments that are fed by a set of stream data sources, and Queries arrive at the grid from users and applications external to the system. The kind of queries considered in this work is long-running continuous (LRC) queries, which are neither short-lived nor infinitely long lived. The queries are "open" from the grid perspective as the grid cannot control or predict the arrival of a query with time, location, required data and query revocations. Query optimization in such an environment has two major challenges, i.e., optimizing in a multi-query environment and continuous optimization, due to new query arrivals and revocations. As generating a globally optimal query plan is an intractable problem, this work explores the idea of emergent optimization where globally optimal query plans emerge as a result of local autonomous decisions taken by the grid nodes. Drawing concepts from evolutionary game theory, grid nodes are modeled as autonomous agents that seek to maximize a self-interest function using one of a set of different strategies. Grid nodes change strategies in response to variations in query arrival and revocation patterns, which is also autonomously decided by each grid node.

DOI: 10.4018/978-1-4666-1577-9.ch016

INTRODUCTION

Stream grids are grid computing environments that are fed with streaming data sources from instrumentation devices like cameras, RFID (radio-frequency identification) sensors, network monitoring or other applications. Queries by users or applications seek to tap into one or more such streams. The main costs for such queries include bandwidth costs and bookkeeping costs at each grid node. In such scenarios, there are conflicting optimization requirements. While end-users prefer reduced latency, individual grid nodes prefer reduced book-keeping costs and the grid as a whole seeks to minimize bandwidth consumption.

Queries in such grids may originate on any node and seek data from any stream or a set of streams. Such queries are typically long lived, but not necessarily infinitely long lived.

Traditionally, query optimization has been addressed for two classes of queries: transient or "one-shot" queries, and infinite or "standing" queries (Cormode & Garofalakis, 2007). One-shot queries are transient in nature and have very short life spans. In such environments, the speed of query processing takes precedence over computing the globally optimal execution plan. On the other hand, for standing queries whose lifetimes are practically infinitely long, it is desirable to invest time and resources to obtain optimal execution plans. Queries on stream grids however, are of a third interim type that we call long-running continuous (LRC) queries or "open-world" queries. These queries are "open" in the sense that, the system does not have control on when and where a query appears, seeking which stream, and when it is revoked. Since queries are typically long lived, ignoring query plan optimization would not be a good idea; at the same time optimizing query execution for the best possible plan is also undesirable, since queries may terminate or new queries may enter the system at any time.

An example of the kind of challenges faced in LRC queries is illustrated in Figure 1 (a).

Grid node SN1 is a stream data source and the three other nodes CN1, CN2 and CN3 are nodes responsible for answering user queries. There is also a distance function d(x; y) defined between pairs of nodes that calculates the latency in shipping a data stream between pairs of nodes. Each query has to be answered with as little latency as possible. Assume that the nodes are arranged such that d(CN1;CN2) > d(CN2;CN3). Now if a query for S1 arrives at CN1 at time t1, it is optimal for CN1 to request for the stream at the source node SN1 (Figure 1 (a)). Suppose a second query and third query for SN1 arrive at time t2 and time t3 on compute nodes CN3 and CN2 respectively. When a query appears on a node, it is apparent that latency can be minimized by fetching the required data from the nearest available source. Given this, the routing of the data streams would be as shown in Figure 1 (b). It is immediately apparent that the routing of the data streams as shown in Figure 1 (b) is not optimal from the global (grid-wide) perspective. The optimal strategy would be as shown in Figure 1 (c). Now, if the query at node CN3 is revoked as shown in Figure 1 (d), the routing of the data streams would remain the same, as node CN3 is still active given the need to serve node CN2. This again is sub-optimal. It is clear that arrival and revocation of queries create a need for re-optimization. However determining the globally optimal query plan on every new query arrival or revocation, and enforcing it over the entire grid is infeasible.

In this paper, we explore the notion of *emergent* optimization where grid nodes act as self-interested autonomous agents and optimize on local properties. Local optimization is facilitated by a set of *strategies* using which nodes connect to other nodes. However, the choice made by each node affects not only its own optimality, but also the global optimality of the grid. In order to reconcile mismatches between local and global optimality, the choice of strategy is changed in an evolutionary fashion. The evolutionary dynamics are derived from Axelrod's now classic model of

Figure 1. Impact of query arrivals and revocations in LRC query optimization

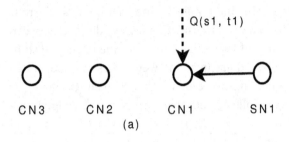

(a)

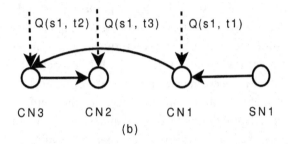

(b)

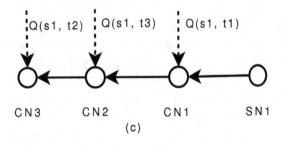

(c)

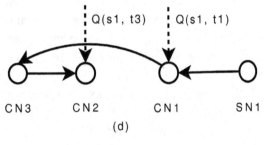

(d)

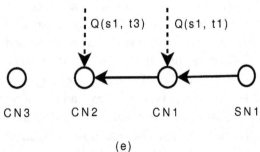

(e)

evolutionary games (Axelrod, 1984) and are shown to be effective in managing open-world dynamics, i.e., unexpected changes in query patterns.

RELATED WORK

In an earlier work (Mukherjee, Srinivasa, & Patil, 2007), we had explained the need for query plan re-optimization at the time of query revocations and considered an economic model to optimize query plans. However, the efficiency and load distribution measures used were unable to accurately model the optimization goals. Secondly, the strategies proposed for optimization were able to optimize only a single optimization parameter at any point of time and hence are not able to optimize in the presence of varying query patterns. The StreamGlobe project (Stegmaier, Kuntschke, & Kemper, 2004; Kuntschke, Stegmaier, Kemper, & Reiser, 2005) uses in-network query processing and multi-query optimization techniques to efficiently process queries. However, StreamGlobe does not model autonomous behavior of the grid nodes. Once a query plan is formulated by some node, other nodes that are contained as part of the plan will adopt the plan. As a result, unexpected query revocations are expected to result in suboptimal dynamics.

The TelegraphCQ project (Chandrasekaran et al., 2003) builds on initial implementations of CACQ (Madden, Shah, Hellerstein, & Raman, 2002) and PSoup (Chandrasekaran & Franklin, 2002) to support an adaptive dataflow architecture using SteM (Raman, Deshpande, & Hellerstein, 2003) and Eddies (Avnur & Hellerstein, 2000) for continuous re-optimizations on a query. Eddies can also be shared across multiple queries. However, the eddies re-optimize based on the performance (tuple rates) of query modules (pipelines, non-blocking versions of standard relational operators). In contrast, the primary focus of our work is on reducing network usage. TelegraphCQ uses Flux (Shah, Hellerstein, Chandrasekharan, & Franklin,

2003) to load-balance and provide fault-tolerance. Data is exchanged between various modules using non-blocking queues provided by Fjords (Madden & Franklin, 2002). Borealis (Abadi et al., 2005) is a distributed stream processing engine. The query processing is similar to the TelegraphCQ project. The operators in the query model can be distributed and optimization is done with respect to the placement of networks of operators that run continuously and interact with each other. The Borealis stream processing engine inherits its stream processing functionality from Aurora (Carney, 2002) and its distribution functionality from Medusa (Zdonik, 2003). STREAM (Arasu et al., 2003) is data stream management system (DSMS) where all data streams and queries arrive. STREAM processes queries by generating query plans for new queries and if possible merging it with existing query plans. The TinyDB (Madden, Franklin, Hellerstein, & Hong, 2003), Cougar (Yao & Gehrke, 2002) and related projects focus primarily on in-network aggregation and algorithms to reduce power consumption in sensors.

Open Grid Service Architecture- Distributed Query Processing (OGSA -DQP) (Alpdemir et al., 2003) is a service based distributed query processing engine for grids. OGSA-DQP supports evaluation of queries using one or more database services provided on the grid. OGSA-DQP uses the now standard GDSs (Grid Discovery Services) to get access to grid metadata and the databases on the grid. It uses techniques adapted from parallel databases to efficiently process queries (Smith et al., 2003). In dynamic data dissemination (Shah, Ramamritham, & Shenoy, 2004), repositories cooperate with each other and the sources to distribute dynamic data with coherence preservation, but do not consider query revocations.

Multi-query optimization (Sellis, 1988; Gupta, Sudarshan, & Viswanathan, 2001; Roy, Seshadri, Sudarshan, & Bhobhe, 2000; Gorman, Agarwal, & Abbadi, 2002) is done using scheduling, pipelining and caching techniques, which assume complete knowledge of the set of queries over which the optimization needs to be done and is primarily meant for centralized implementations. Network aware query processing techniques (Ahmad, Cetintemel, Jannotti, Zgolinski, & Zdonik, 2005; Pietzuch et al., 2006) focus on the correct placement of operators in the network. A novel spring relaxation technique (Pietzuch et al., 2006) is also used to place operators in the network. It however does not consider replicated operators for distributing load, instead the load distribution algorithm provided tries to place the single operator on a suitable grid node. This would lead to overloading of the grid node if there a large number of queries on the grid requiring data from the same operator.

MODELLING THE GRID

The stream grid is modeled as: $G = (X, d)$, where X represents all the grid nodes. A subset of the grid nodes, $S \subseteq X$ are also stream sources. $d : X \times X \to \Re^+$ is a distance function encapsulating latency between nodes. The distance function is assumed to have the following characteristics:

- $\forall x \in X, d(x, x) = 0$, and

- Triangle inequality:

$$\forall x, y, z \in X, x \neq y \neq z, d(x, z) \leq d(x, y) + d(y, z)$$

It is important to note that the distance function d represents the latency incurred by the *best path* between pairs of nodes. In this sense, even though the triangle inequality doesn't hold for packet routing on the Internet (Anderson, 2001), it still holds for the distance function. The space described is a logical space, which need not directly correspond to any geography and/or network topology. The grid model used here is similar to the notion of cost space in stream-based overlay networks (Pietzuch et al., 2006). Stream data is considered to be in the form of tuples, with each tuple representing a row in an infinitely long table. Queries may arrive on any node in the grid requesting for one or more streams. Queries are represented as relational algebra expressions over the data streams. For the purposes of grid-level optimization, this work considers three basic relational operations: projections ($q = \pi_{s_{i1}...s_{ik}}(S_i)$), selections ($q = \sigma_{(condition)} S_i$) and joins ($q = S_i \bowtie S_j$).

At any given grid node $x \in X$ a subset of one or more streams may be available as part of current query execution plan. These streams can be reused to serve other queries in the vicinity without them having to go all the way to the required stream sources.

OPTIMIZATION OBJECTIVE

From the grid node perspective, the key optimization goal is to ensure reduced response times or latency, while from the system perspective, the key objective is to reduce the required bandwidth. These two objectives conflict with one another as, to ensure minimal response times, each query would need to be satisfied with a direct connection to the required source (minimum d) which would lead to multiple connections to the source increasing the bandwidth usage. If the data were to be routed sequentially through all the nodes requiring it, the bandwidth required would be lesser albeit at the cost of higher latency. A bandwidth-delay product combines both requirements and is termed as *network usage* in this work. The optimization objective is to minimize network usage.

The other parameter which influences response time is load on a node. Nodes with heavy loads would be a bottleneck increasing the overall response time of queries. The load on a node is a combination of communication and computational load. Assuming that the computational load on a node is due to processing of incoming and outgoing data, the load on a node is proportional to the communication load itself. A simple measure used to represent the communication load on a node, as used in this work, is the number of incoming and outgoing data links from a node. Hence, the second optimization objective in this work is to balance load distribution. Although stream optimization is a continuous process, except when referring to unfolding behavior, we shall not be concerned with the time variable while formally defining optimization objectives in the next subsections.

Network Usage

A given query q at any node $x \in X$ is ultimately answered by returning a set of *stream links* $L(q) = \{l_1, l_1, l_2, ..., l_n\}$. For instance in Figure 2, a query on node CN_1 requesting for $s_1 \bowtie s_2 \bowtie s_3$ can be answered by forming the stream link set $\{l_1, l_2, l_3\}$. A link is a directed edge, represented as an ordered pair, $l_p = (x_p, y_p)$. Data flows from data source y_p to destination x_p , to satisfy in part or completely, a query at x_p . In Figure 2, the link l_1 would be represented as (CN_1, SN_1) .

For a link $l_i = (x_i, y_i)$, its *network usage* is given as,

$$u(l_i) = Bandwidth(l_i) \cdot d(l_i) \qquad (1.1)$$

where, $Bandwidth(l_i)$ is the data rate of the stream l_i , and $d(l_i) = d(x_i, y_i)$ as described earlier, is the latency of the data stream.

Let Q be the set of all queries incident on the grid G at any instance of time. Let L denote the set of all links that have been returned in response to queries in Q . We refer to L as the ``Estuary graph'' or the ``link graph'' of the grid G for the present time. The Estuary graph is formally defined as:

$$L = \bigcup_{q \in Q} L(q) \qquad (1.2)$$

The global optimization objective on network usage is to obtain an Estuary graph such that the overall network usage is minimized. This is stated as:

$$\arg\min_L \sum_{l_i \in L} u(l_i) \qquad (1.3)$$

Load Distribution

For a given link $l_p = (x_p, y_p)$, two functions $source(l_p)$ and $sink(l_p)$ are defined such that, $source(l_p) = y_p$ and $sink(l_p) = x_p$. Given a grid G, let L be the Estuary graph at a given instance of time. For any grid node x the set of incoming links $I_{\{x,L\}}$ and the set of outgoing links $O_{\{x,L\}}$ are given by,

$$I_{\{x,L\}} = \{l_p \in L : sink(l_p) = x\} \qquad (1.4)$$

$$O_{\{x,L\}} = \{l_p \in L : source(l_p) = x\} \qquad (1.5)$$

The set of links $L_{\{x,L\}}$ contributing to the load, on grid node x is given by,

$$L_{\{x,L\}} = I_{\{x,L\}} \cup O_{\{x,L\}} - (I_{\{x,L\}} \cap O_{\{x,L\}}) \qquad (1.6)$$

where, $I_{\{x,L\}} \cap O_{\{x,L\}}$ represents the set of *self loops* in L. A self loop is a link l_p where $source(l_p) = sink(l_p)$. For instance, link l_6 in Figure 2 is a self loop. As the source and destination for the data is the same node, self loops are not considered for load calculation. Self loops represent situations where the stream being queried for on a grid node x is already available on x. Self loops do not

add to the load or network usage, although they are required for completeness of the representation.

In Figure 2, node CN_2 answers the query s_1 by creating link l_4 and the subsequent query for $s_1 \bowtie s_3$ by reusing the s_1 data already available (local link l_6) and fetching data from secondary source CN_1 using link l_5. At time t_3 the set of links answering all queries in the grid shown in Figure 2 is given as $L = \{l_1, l_2, l_3, l_4, l_5, l_6\}$. The incoming link set for node CN_2 at time t_3 is $I_{\{CN_2,L\}} = \{l_4, l_5, l_6\}$ and the outgoing link set is $O_{\{CN_2,L\}} = \{l_6\}$. Since link l_6 is local to node CN_2, it is not considered as a loading factor, resulting in the set of links contributing to load as $L_{\{CN_2,L\}} = \{l_4, l_5\}$.

Let Q_x be the set of all queries incident on grid node x at any given instance of time. The *instantaneous load* on x is given by:

$$w_{\{x,L\}} = | L_{\{x,L\}} | + | Q_x | \qquad (1.7)$$

The global optimization objective is to minimize the skew in load distribution at any given instance of time, and is referred to as the *instantaneous load distribution*. Skew in load distribution is calculated by the variance in instantaneous load across all the grid nodes. Optimization for load distribution is hence to build an Estuary graph that minimizes the variance in load distribution at any given instance. This is defined as:

$$\arg\min_L \sum_{x \in X} (w_{\{x,L\}} - \overline{w_{\{x,L\}}})^2 \qquad (1.8)$$

Here, $\overline{w_{\{x,L\}}}$ is the mean value of the instantaneous load across all nodes.

Figure 2. Query result generation using streams links

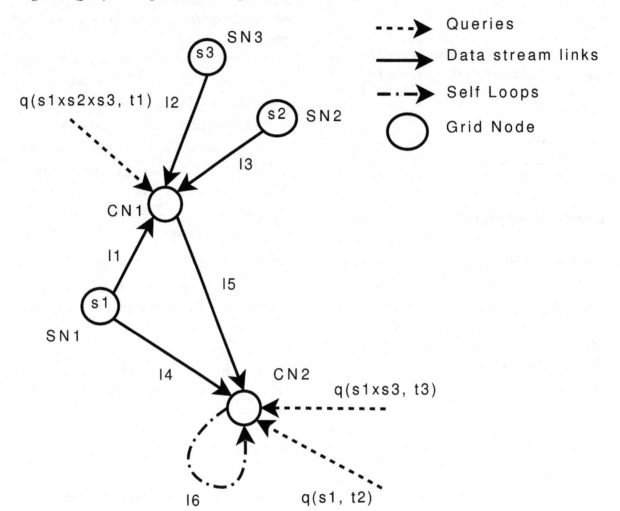

EMERGENT OPTIMIZATION

To enable long running, continuous query optimization in a grid, the notion of *emergent optimization* is proposed in this work. Grid nodes act as self-interested autonomous agents optimizing on some local property. In order to achieve local optimization, grid nodes utilize one of several *strategies* to connect to one another. These strategies enable a node to select the set of source nodes from which data is fetched to answer a query and are hence also called as "source selection strategies."

Variations in query patterns require nodes to evaluate its strategy for its effectiveness on a continuous basis. In this regard, a "fitness function" is used to determine the feasibility of a particular strategy given the grid environment. Although the fitness function works at a system-wide level, we ensure that it is simple enough to be computed by each node in a distributed fashion.

Fitness is based on a "payoff function" which determines the payoff each node receives on answering a query. The payoff would depend on: (1) the query requirements, (2) the strategy used by the node and, (3) the grid conditions.

By selecting a payoff function which operates at the grid nodes, the system designer can control intrinsic characteristics of the grid like its innate preference towards one optimization objective over the other. The entire process of emergent optimization is shown in Figure 3.

Based on the payoff and fitness functions defined, some nodes may switch to a different strategy, thus altering the distribution of the different strategies in the grid. We call this the *grid demographics*. Strategy switch happens after every pre-defined interval called a *generation*. This process continues until the demographics stabilize and the resulting demographics is said to be the emergent property which represents the best response characteristics of the grid given the open nature of the LRC queries. A more detailed explanation of the entire process follows.

Agents and Strategies

For emergent optimization, a stream grid is modeled as $G = (X, d, \chi)$, where X is a set of agents representing grid nodes, d is the distance function as defined earlier and χ is a pool of *source selection strategies* from which agents pick a given strategy in order to make decisions regarding connecting to other agents.

At any given instance of time t, the *state* of any agent $x \in X$ is given by the following attributes: $x^t = (Q_x^t, \chi_x^t)$. Here, Q_x^t is the set of queries incident on node x at time t and $\chi_x^t \in \chi$ is the source selection strategy chosen by node x at time t. As earlier, most of the operations are defined for a given instance of time, and we shall drop the reference to time when the context is clear.

Each source selection strategy χ_x is of the form $\chi_x : Q_x \times X \to [0,1]$, where $\sum_X \chi_x = 1$. In other words, given a query, a strategy returns a probability vector over the set of all agents, using which connections are made with other agents.

The unfolding behavior of an agent over time is defined as follows. For any grid node or agent $x \in X$, if $Q_x^t \neq Q_x^{t-1}$ that is, if an event (arrival of a new query or revocation of an existing query) has happened at time t, the agent performs one or both of the following tasks:

- Answer one or more queries in Q_x^t by connecting to other nodes based on χ_x^t and creating a set of *incoming* streams denoted as: $I^t(\chi_x)$
- Provide one or more data streams to other nodes in the grid (by accepting connection requests from them) and creating a set of outgoing streams denoted as: $O^t(\chi_x)$.

We shall use the term $L^t(\chi_x)$ to mean $I^t(\chi_x) \cup O^t(\chi_x)$ representing the set of all streams incident on x at time t. The term L^t is used to represent the Estuary graph of the grid at time t. While Q_x^t represents user queries and are not under the control of the system, $I^t(\chi_x)$ and $O^t(\chi_x)$ are dependent on (1) the state of the grid (its Estuary graph) at time $t-1$ or L^{t-1}, (2) the set of queries at the node x: Q_x^t, and, (3) the strategy adopted by the node: χ_x^t.

The temporal unfolding of an agent's behavior can be seen as closed-loop control system (Figure 3), where the actions taken by an agent impacts grid characteristics, which in turn impacts further actions taken by the agent.

Payoffs, Generations and Demographics

Once an agent x chooses a source selection strategy $\chi_x \in \chi$, it retains this strategy for a pre-specified time period called a ``generation.'' Strategies are changed for an agent only across generations. The first time a strategy is chosen, this choice is made with a uniform or a pre-de-

Figure 3. Overview of the emergent optimization process

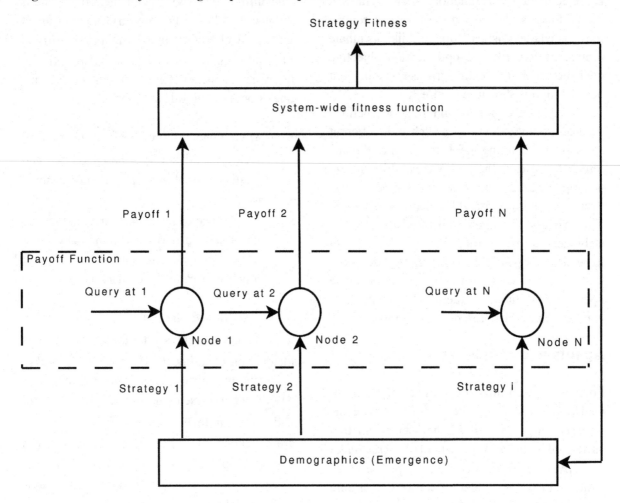

termined probability distribution across all the strategies in χ. The ``demographics'' of the grid is the distribution of different source selection strategies adopted by the agents. The set of nodes adopting source selection strategy χ_i is given by,

$$D(\chi_i) = \{x : x \in X \wedge \chi(x) = \chi_i\}$$

where $\chi(x)$ represents the strategy adopted at node x.

A payoff function ρ provides a payoff for each node at every time step, based on the amount of queries it has answered and/or its connections with other nodes. Agents accumulate payoffs till the end of a generation after which the agent possibly changes its source selection strategy. A new generation then begins with all agents having a payoff of 0.

Let $\bar{P}_x$ be the average payoff per query accumulated by agent x at the end of a generation with strategy χ_x. From the grid perspective, the average payoff per grid node obtained by any given strategy χ_i is computed as

$$\hat{P}_{\chi_i} = \frac{\sum_{x \in X, \chi(x)=\chi_i} \bar{P}_x}{\mid D(\chi_i) \mid} \tag{1.9}$$

The ``fitness'' of any given strategy χ_i at the end of a generation is given by

$$\Phi(\chi_i) = \frac{\widehat{P}_{\chi_i}}{\sum_{\chi_i \in \chi} \widehat{P}_{\chi_i}} \qquad (1.10)$$

At the end of a generation, agents re-evaluate their current strategies and possibly change to another strategy. The probability that a given strategy χ_i is chosen is given by $\Phi(\chi_i)$.

Source Selection Strategies

The set of source selection strategies χ is a critical element of emergent optimization. Each agent initially chooses a strategy at random from this pool. Each strategy returns a probability vector that guides the agent in making connections with other agents. The strategy itself takes the present query as input and optionally depends upon other information obtained from the grid.

A strategy may seek to optimize a single optimization parameter like network usage or load distribution in isolation or consider both parameters together. As a rule, the greater the amount of information that a strategy requires from the grid, the greater is the sophistication possible. However, the more the information requirement for a strategy, the greater the overhead in obtaining this information and computing the probability vector.

Figure 4 depicts this schematically. It shows a hierarchy of strategies and their corresponding information requirements.

In this work, we consider some simple strategies whose information requirements are small and that seek to optimize on only a single optimization parameter. Such strategies are also termed as singleton strategies. The three singleton strategies evaluated in the work are:

1. **Distance ordering (DO):** Fetch data from nearest source having the data
2. **Random ordering (RO):** Fetch data from a random node having the required data
3. **Load ordering (LO):** Fetch data from the least loaded node having the data

Of the above, DO and LO are strategies where the probability of connecting to a given node is either 1 or 0 while in RO, given a choice of k nodes that are stream sources, the probability of connecting to any one of them is $\frac{1}{k}$. The three strategies also have different information requirements from the grid. Table 1 lists the information requirements for these strategies.

EXPERIMENTAL RESULTS

For experimental verification, a grid is simulated with 64 nodes arranged in a 8×8 square. 12 source nodes are distributed around the center of the grid along the periphery of a smaller square resulting in the possibility of 4095 unique queries. 10000 queries arrive uniformly on the grid nodes at a rate of one query every unit of time. Queries seek data or a subset of the data available at the source nodes. Each query remains in the grid for a certain random amount of time and is then terminated.

In the experiments we first evaluate the effectiveness of emergent optimization using the DO strategy in reducing network usage when compared with globally optimal query plans generated by taking snapshots of the grid with every new query arrival and query revocation. We then confirm the ability of the LO strategy in distributing load evenly. We also demonstrate the ability of the grid nodes to identify the correct strategy for (1) a given global optimization objective and (2) for varying query patterns. The payoff function used in the experiments and its rationale is described in the next section.

Figure 4. Strategy hierarchy: sophistication of strategies with information

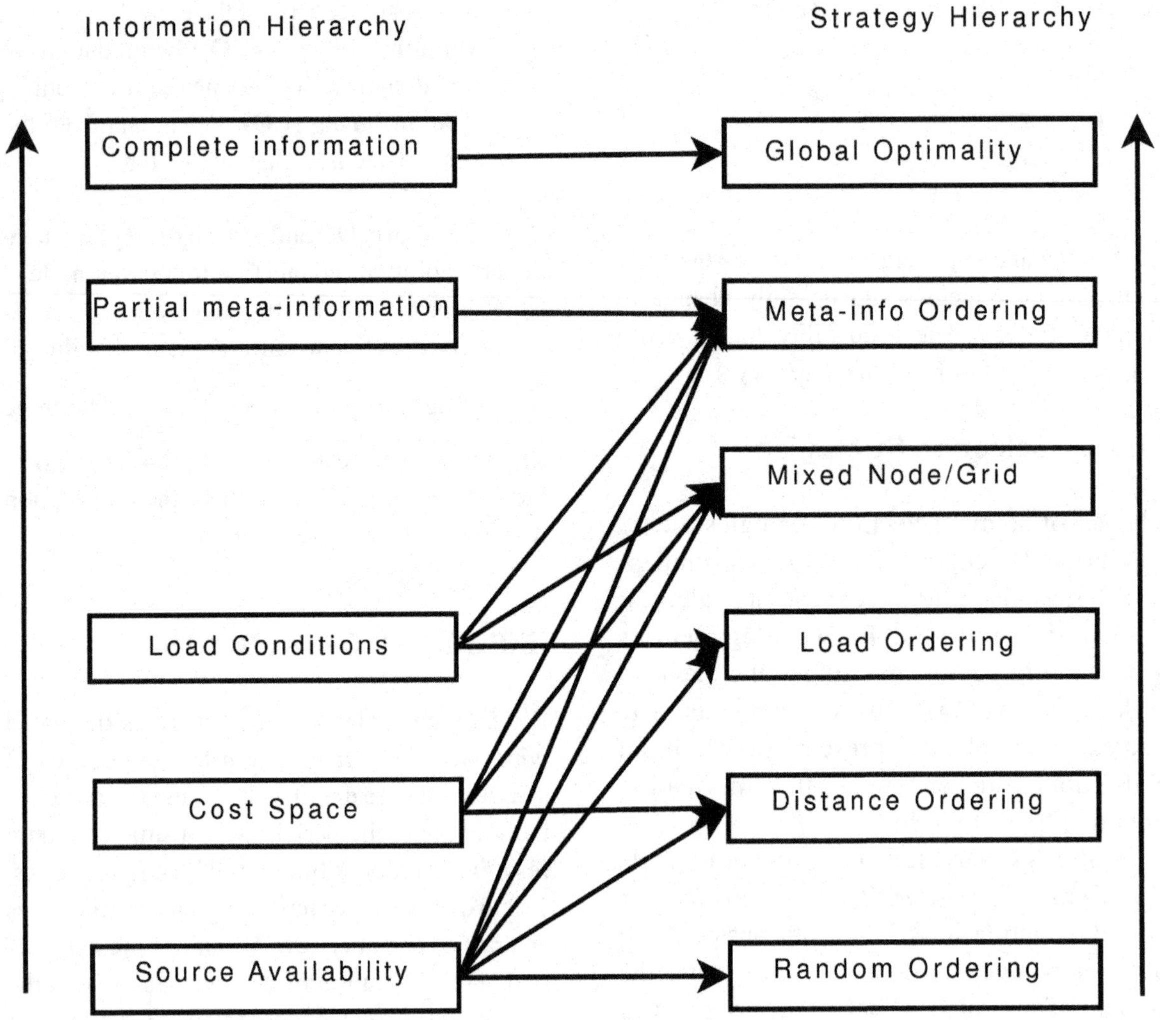

Payoff Function

For the experiments we use payoff function that has two payoff components, one of which is based on network usage and the other on the resulting load on data sources. We choose a payoff function that results in, (1) higher payoffs for a node if its source selection leads to reduced network usage and, (2) reduction in payoffs, with the reduction proportional to the load on the data sources selected.

Any query q_i on node i is thought of bringing with it a certain amount of virtual currency or income, $I(q_i)$ which is equal to the network usage if the query were to be answered directly from the source nodes. The payoff function ρ is modeled on the savings incurred over the virtual currency. If $L(q_i)$ is the set of links using which q_i is answered, the network usage part of ρ called ρ_U, is the ratio of unused virtual currency to the income:

$$\rho_U = \frac{1}{I(q_i)} \cdot [I(q_i) - \sum_{l_i \in L(q_i)} u(l_i)] \qquad (1.11)$$

Table 1. Information Required for Single Strategies:

Strategy	Information Required	History Dependent
Random Ordering	Source availability	No
Distance Ordering	Source availability and cost space	Yes
Load Ordering	Source availability and load conditions	Yes

while the load distribution part of ρ called ρ_W, is measured as the average load ratio over all the links required to answer a query and is given by,

$$\rho_W = \frac{1}{|L(q_i)|} \sum_{l_i \in L(q_i)} \frac{w_{\{source(l_i),L\}}}{MAXLOAD(source(l_i))} \quad (1.12)$$

where $MAXLOAD(source(l_i))$ is the maximum number of links node $source(l_i)$ can handle. The overall payoff ρ for the query is evaluated as,

$$\rho = \alpha \cdot \rho_U - (1-\alpha) \cdot \rho_W \quad (1.13)$$

where, $\alpha \in [0,1]$ is a configurable parameter that determines the intrinsic importance to be given by the grid to network usage or load distribution. Since ρ_U and ρ_W are both ratios, they can be added together in a single equation. However, they may not have the same characteristics and the impact of α on ρ_U and ρ_W need not be the same. In our grid scenario, a value of 0.2 for α was empirically seen to provide equal importance to network usage and load distribution.

In prior work, (Stegmaier et al., 2004; Kuntschke et al., 2005), the value of α needs to be set by the grid administrator to reflect the preference for optimizing either on network usage or load distribution. However, it should be noted here that in StreamGlobe, α cannot be a static parameter fixed to optimize under all possible conditions in the grid. Consider a small set of queries incident on the grid and therefore do not

load the nodes in the grid. Under such circumstances, it does not make sense to consider load distribution. Similarly, if there are a lot of queries and the nodes in the grid are heavily loaded, then it does not make sense to consider network usage during optimization. Hence α needs to be adjusted according to the varying query patterns incident on the grid. This would entail that the grid be monitored continuously and α adjusted to meet the varying query patterns. Finally, it would also be difficult for the administrator to predict the exact value of α which would result in the required global optimization objectives being met.

In contrast, in our work, the emergent nature of the optimization ensures that the grid itself adjusts to the varying query patterns incident on the grid and the administrator needs to set α just once during the initial setup based on the grid characteristics.

Results

To evaluate the performance of the DO strategy, we compare network usage at any given time, with the network usage resulting from the globally optimal query plan. The globally optimal query plan is computed with a centralized query processor which has access to information including the entire set of queries, the location of the queries and individual node information. The globally optimal query plan is re-computed on the arrival of a new query and on query revocations to ensure the optimality of the global query plan. We evaluate the LO strategy in a similar manner. Since we are interested in measuring the performance of the various strategies and the ability of the grid to correctly select the correct strategy for a given optimization objective, we switch α between two extremes: 1 (payoff only for optimizing network usage) and 0 (payoff only for optimizing load distribution) to indicate the optimization objective. The grid nodes are provided with the set of three strategies: DO, RO and LO. At the start of the experiment, nodes select a strategy with equal probability.

Instantaneous Network Usage:

Figure 5 compares network usage across time, between the globally optimal plan and with two varieties of emergent optimization: (a). when the objective is to optimize solely on network usage ($\alpha = 1$), and (b). when the objective is to optimize solely on load distribution ($\alpha = 0$).

In these experiments, a generation comprised 250 time steps. We can see that emergent optimization comes very close to the globally optimal network usage when $\alpha = 1$ within a few generations. The network usage starts off with a high value given the random nature in which strategies are chosen initially. However, the demographics stabilize very quickly and the network usage drops very close to the optimal usage (with a difference of 11%). When $\alpha = 0$ however, network usage is continually high, since the emphasis is on load distribution. This confirms the effectiveness of the emergent strategy using DO strategy for reducing network usage.

Instantaneous Load Distribution:

Figure 6 compares load distribution characteristics across time, when the global optimization objective is to optimize on network usage ($\alpha = 1$) and when the objective is to optimize on load distribution ($\alpha = 0$). The standard distribution of load is around 4 when the objective is to optimize network usage and around 2 when the objective is optimize load distribution, thereby indicating

that the LO strategy is better at balancing load compared to the DO strategy.

Figure 7 and Figure 8 plots demographic change of each of the strategies (DO, RO and LO) change across generations when $\alpha = 1$ and when $\alpha = 0$ respectively. When $\alpha = 1$, we observe that the all nodes converge to the DO strategy while the LO and RO strategy becomes non-existent in the grid. Similarly, when $\alpha = 0$, we observe that all the nodes converge to the LO strategy. This demonstrates the ability of emergent optimization to select the correct strategy for a given optimization objective. It should be noted here that when α is 0 or 1, nodes do not select the RO strategy. This essentially shows that strategies which do not perform well for a given objective will be rooted out of the system.

Generational Dynamics

As seen in Figure 7 and Figure 8, the convergence towards a particular strategy is quick and leads to one of either the distance ordering or load ordering strategies surviving. Since the strategy selection is based on payoffs for a particular strategy, if the number of grid nodes adopting a particular strategy drops to zero, the grid will never be able to consider that strategy further on. This might lead to the grid being unable to adjust the varying conditions of the grid and query characteristics.

To mitigate this issue, grid nodes perform a strategy reset after some specified time "random interval" and select strategies at random, instead of computing the strategy fitness function. In a real implementation, we envisage a distributed snapshot algorithm like (Chandy & Lamport, 1985) being used by the grid nodes to synchronize the strategy reset's. To simulate responses of the grid to fluctuating query patterns, the grid is subjected to three different query sets as shown in Figure 9 with varying average query loads. All the query sets have an increase in query load between time interval 4000 and 6000 to simulate changing query patterns. The distribution of

Figure 5. Instantaneous network usage

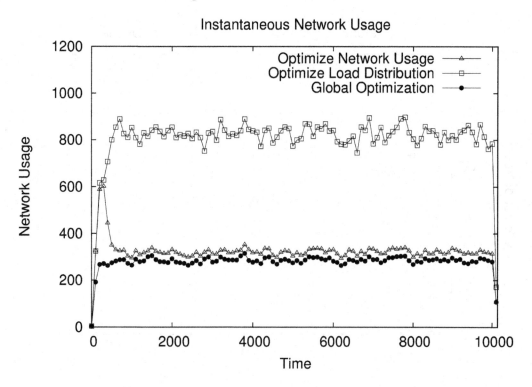

Figure 6. Instantaneous load distribution

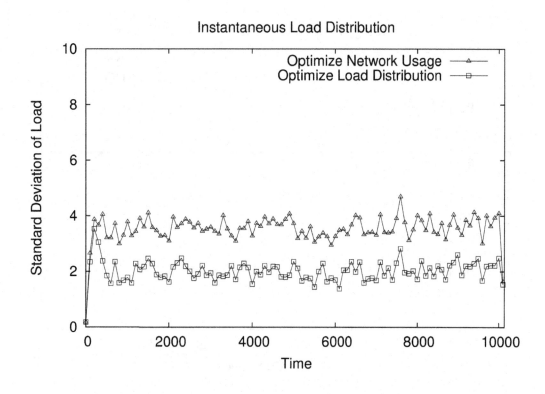

Figure 7. Strategy distribution (Alpha=1)

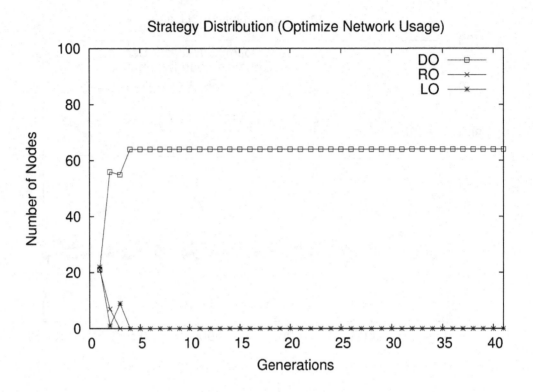

Figure 8. Strategy distribution (Alpha=0)

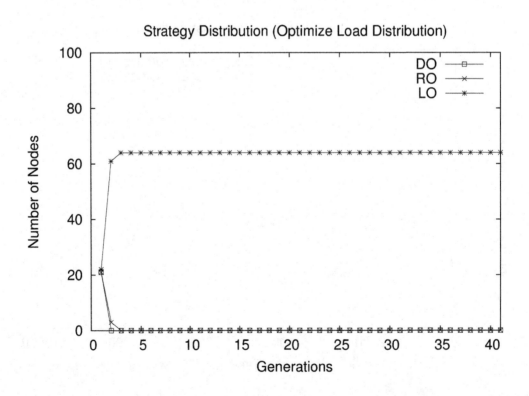

strategies in the grid nodes for the three different query sets is shown in Figure 10, Figure 11, and Figure 12. We use bezier curves to smooth out the disruptions caused by the strategy resets which occur at instances as indicated by the vertical lines in the graphs. The value of α was set to 0:2 for all the experiments depicting equal importance to network usage and load distribution.

Query set 1 (Figure 9) has very little average load and the fluctuation in load is not significant enough for the grid nodes to change their strategy and hence and as seen in Figure 10 all the nodes select the DO strategy throughout the experiment and optimize on network usage. When the grid is subjected to query set 2, the nodes select the DO strategy initially when the average load is around 200 and switch to the LO strategy to balance the load when the average load increases to 500. Once the average load decreases to 200, the grid nodes switch back to the DO strategy and continue to optimize network usage (Figure 11). This clearly shows that emergent optimization is able to identify and adapt to the changing grid conditions without any manual intervention.

The *MAXLOAD* parameter for each grid node in this experiment was 25 links per node. In query set 3, the initial grid load is around 500 and each node is loaded close to its *MAXLOAD*. Hence the nodes adopt the LO strategy to balance the load. The nodes continue to use the LO strategy for the entire duration of the experiment (Figure 12) as the load on the grid is remains high.

This set of experiments indicates that the principle of emergent optimization is able to select the best strategy among the set of strategies it is provided with and is also able to address the varying query patterns incident on the grid by switching from one strategy to another without any intervention.

ANALYTICAL MODELING

While experimental results indicate that emergent optimization comes close to globally optimal solutions, it would be interesting to understand the individual strategies analytically. Unfortunately, for all but the simplest of strategies, analytical modeling involves modeling the behavior of closed-loop feedback systems, making it very complex. The focus of this section is in constructing an analytical framework forming the basis over which richer models can be built to explain more complex strategies. The model described here makes the following assumptions.

Assumptions

The grid is modeled as $G = (X, d)$, where X represents all the grid nodes and $d : X \times X \rightarrow \Re^+$ is a distance function encapsulating latency between nodes. The grid is also assumed to have the following properties,

- $\forall x \in X, d(x, x) = 0$

- Triangle inequality holds for a multi-dimensional grid: $\forall x, y, z \in X, x \neq y \neq z, d(x, z) \leq d(x, y) + d(y, z)$

- The grid is divided into discrete regions with the distance between consecutive regions being 1.

The following assumptions are expected to hold over the grid nodes which make up the grid,

- There is a single node present in each region of the grid
- The probability of nodes being a sensor node is equal
- Nodes receiving data from a source can behave as secondary sources.

Figure 9. Query Sets

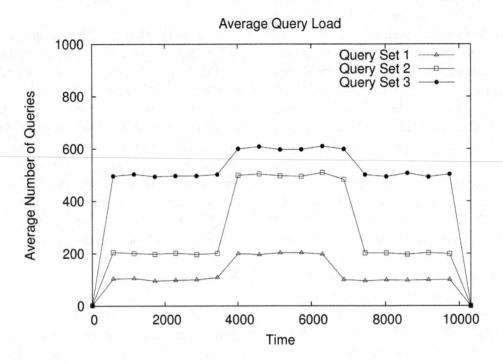

Figure 10. Strategy distribution for query set 1

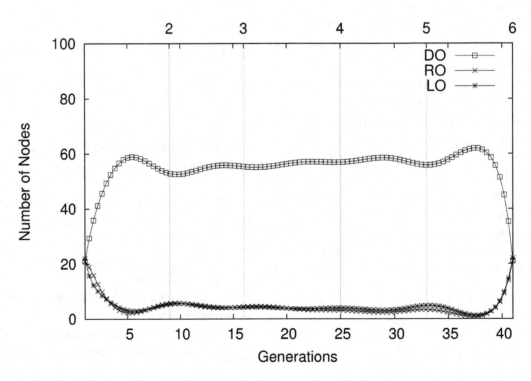

Figure 11. Strategy distribution for query set 2

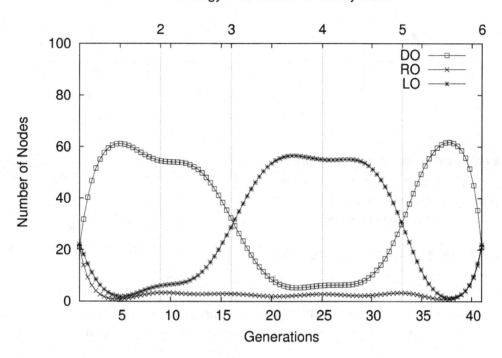

Figure 12. Strategy distribution for query set 3

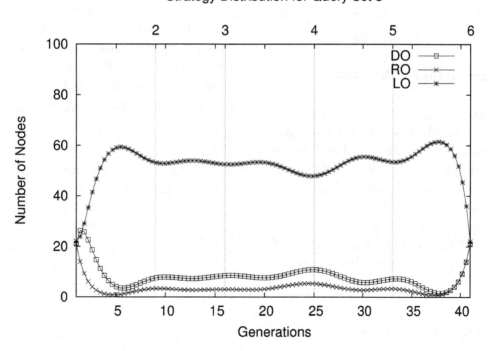

Figure 13. Straight line grid

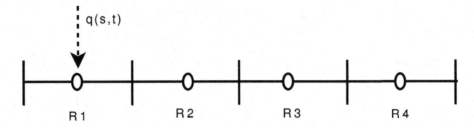

- The effective number of sources $E(q)$ for a query q is defined as the sum of number of primary and secondary sources having the required data to answer query q.

The queries which arrive at the grid node have the following properties,

- Queries are either project or select queries
- Queries arrive on the nodes with equal probability
- Queries are selected from a query set Q containing all the possible simple queries
- Queries are selected with uniform probability from Q. This would also mean that the $E(q_i) = E(q_j)$ for all $q_i, q_j \in Q$.

Hence $E(q_i)$ is the same for a given grid.

Single Dimensional Modeling

Given the above assumptions, a grid on a single dimension where all the nodes are placed along a straight line would be represented as shown in Figure 13. The grid shown in Figure 13 has four nodes in a straight line and each node in a discrete region R1 to R4 with the distance between any two consecutive regions being 1.

If the effective number of sources for a grid having N nodes is E, the number of possible source locations is given by $\binom{N}{E}$. In the grid shown in Figure 13 if $E = 2$ then, the number of possible locations for sources is $\binom{4}{2}$ and the possible source locations are, $\{\{R1,R2\},\{R1,R3\},\{R1,R4\},\{R2,R3\},\{R2,R4\},\{R3,R4\}$.

A query arriving on the node in region selects a single node from the set of nodes in $\binom{N}{E}$ possibilities based on the source selection strategy adopted by the node. For the grid in Figure 13, a query arriving on the node in region R1, using strategy DO would select a node as given in Table 2 from the set of $\binom{4}{2}$ source location possibilities.

$p(Rx, Ry)$ denotes probability of a node Ry being selected to answer a query incident on node Rx and is dependent on the source selection strategy. Assuming each of the source location possibilities to be equally probable, the selections described in Table 2 would lead to $p(R1, R1) = \frac{1}{2}$,

Table 2. Source Selection using DO Strategy for a query on Region R1

Source Location Possibilities	Selected Node
{R1,R2}	R1
{R1,R3}	R1
{R1,R4}	R1
{R2,R3}	R2
{R2,R4}	R2
{R3,R4}	R3

$p(R1, R2) = \dfrac{1}{3}$ and $p(R1, R3) = \dfrac{1}{6}$ at any given time.

The expected network usage $E[u(Rx)]$ of answering a query at node Rx in a grid of N nodes is given as,

$$E[u(Rx)] = \sum_{i=1}^{N} p(Rx, Ri) \cdot d(Rx, Ri) \qquad (1.14)$$

From Table 2, it can be seen that the probability of a query on R1 being answered by R1 is $p(R1, R1)$ or $\dfrac{1}{3}$. Similarly, when a query is on node R2, the probability that node R1 answers the query is given by $p(R2, R1)$. If there are a total of N queries in the system, given that all the queries are uniformly distributed on the grid nodes, the total load on node R1 is $\sum_{i=1}^{N} p(Ri, R1)$.

Generalizing, the expected load $E[L(Rx)]$, on node Rx for answering queries is given as,

$$E(L(Rx)) = \sum_{i=1}^{N} p(Ri, Rx) \qquad (1.15)$$

For a set of N queries incident on the grid in Figure 13, Figure 14 shows the expected network usage and Figure 15 shows the expected load distribution characteristics when the grid nodes adopt the DO strategy and the RO strategy. It can be seen from Figure 14 that the expected network usage for the distance ordering strategy is lesser than that of the random ordering strategy. This is because when nodes use the random ordering strategy, the source selected for answering a particular query may not be the nearest one available. However it is because of this random behavior that the expected load is evenly distributed between the nodes as seen in Figure 15. When the grid nodes adopt the distance ordering strategy, the expected load on the grid nodes towards the center of the grid are seen to be loaded more than the fringe nodes. This is because the average

distance from any node to the centrally located nodes is less compared to the nodes located at the fringe of the grid. While analytical modeling of RO strategy is simple, DO and LO strategies are history dependent. By assuming the probability of source location possibilities as uniform, it is possible to model the DO strategy. However, assuming that all the nodes have uniform load to model the LO strategy does not provide any additional information. Hence, the LO strategy is not modeled in this work.

Single Dimensional Modeling

The single dimensional model explained in the previous section can be extended to two dimensions by considering a grid on a plane instead of a line. The equations for calculating the expected network usage and load remain the same. For a grid with 16 nodes in a two dimensional plane, arranged in a 4 × 4 matrix, the comparative expected network usage when the grid nodes adopt the DO and RO strategy is shown in Figure 16. As seen from Figure 16, the expected network usage is higher when the grid nodes use the RO strategy compared to when the grid nodes use the DO strategy.

The expected load distribution in the grid when the nodes adopt the DO and RO strategy is as shown in Figure 17. As with a single dimensional grid, the expected load is even when the grid nodes use the RO strategy and skewed when the nodes use the DO strategy. The reason for the nodes towards the center of the grid having a higher expected load compared to the fringe nodes is the same as in the single dimensional grid.

Modeling the distance ordering and random ordering strategy provides insights into the network usage and load distribution characteristics of these two strategies. Although the load ordering strategy is not modeled, it is expected to provide better load distribution compared to both distance and random ordering as neither of these two strategies consider the load on a grid node while selecting source node.

Figure 14. Expected network usage

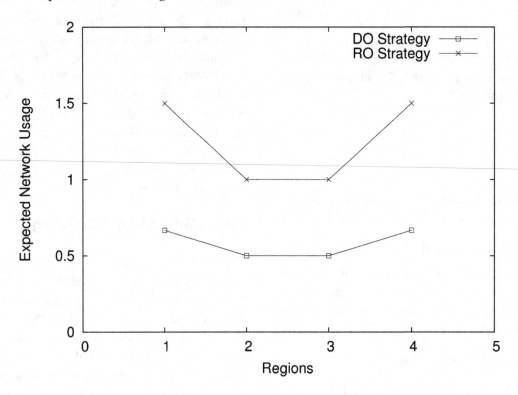

Figure 15. Expected load distribution

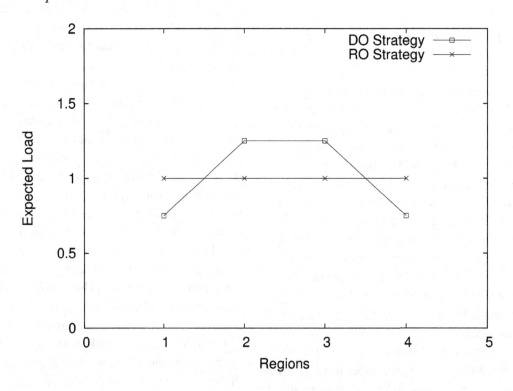

Figure 16. Expected network usage

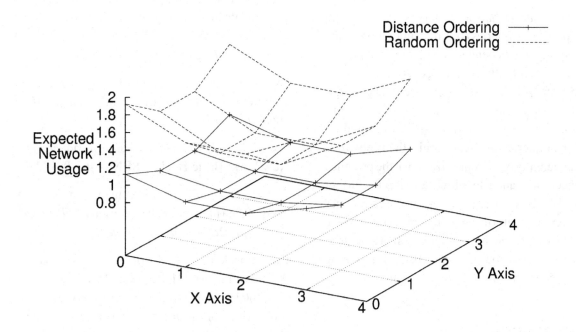

Figure 17. Expected load distribution

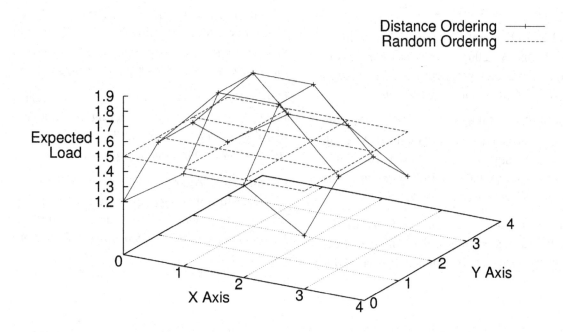

CONCLUSION AND FUTURE WORK

This work shows that the primary issue in optimizing open-world queries is the dynamic nature of the queries and the dependency of the optimal query plan on the currently executing queries in the grid. Emergent optimization in such a scenario provides an efficient alternative to optimizing such systems. Although this work provides insights into optimizing open queries in stream grids, the problem is fundamentally one of optimization in the presence of uncertainty and a lot of scope exists for further work. We also envisage a variety of more strategies of different levels of sophistication than the basic ones considered in this work. It remains to be seen if there are specific principles behind designing strategies for handling open-world queries.

REFERENCES

Abadi, D. Ahmad., Y., Balazinska., M., Etintemel, U. C., Cherniack, M., Hwang, J., et al. (2005). The design of the borealis stream processing engine. In *Proceedings of the conference on innovative data systems research* (pp. 277-289).

Ahmad, Y., Cetintemel, U., Jannotti, J., Zgolinski, A., & Zdonik, S. (2005). Network awareness in internet-scale stream processing. In *Proceedings of the IEEE data engineering bulletin*.

Alpdemir, M., Mukherjee, A., Paton, N. W., Watson, P., Fernandes, A. A., Gounaris, A., et al. (2003). Ogsa-dqp: A service-based distributed query processor for the grid. In *Proceedings of uk e-science all hands meeting Nottingham*.

Anderson, D. (2001). *Resilient overlay networks*. Unpublished master's thesis, department of electrical engineering and computer science, MIT, Cambridge, MA.

Arasu, A., Babcock, B., Babu, S., Datar, M., Ito, K., & Motwani, R. (2003). Stream: The stanford stream data manager. *A Quarterly Bulletin of the Computer Society of the IEEE Technical Committee on Data Engineering*, 19–26.

Avnur, R., & Hellerstein, J. (2000). Eddies: Continously adaptive query processing. *ACM sigmod record*.

Axelrod, R. (1984). *The evolution of cooperation*. New York: Basic Books. ISBN 0-465-02122-2

Carney, D. (2002). Monitoring streams - a new class of data management operations. In *Proceedings of the 28th VLDB conference*.

Chandrasekaran, S., Cooper, O., Deshpande, A., Franklin, M., Hellerstein, J., Hong, W., et al. (2003). Telegraphcq: Continuous dataflow processing for an uncertain world. In *Proceedings of the conference on innovative data systems research*.

Chandrasekaran, S., & Franklin, M. J. (2002). Streaming queries over streaming data. In *Proceedings of the 28th VLDB conference*.

Chandy, K. M., & Lamport, L. (1985). Distributed snapshots: determining global states of distributed systems. In *Proceedings of the ACM transactions on computer systems (TOCS)* (pp. 63-75).

Cormode, G., & Garofalakis, M. (2007). Streaming in a connected world:quering and tracking distributed data streams. In *Proceedings of the International conf. in data engineering*.

Gorman, K., Agarwal, D., & Abbadi, A. E. (2002). Multiple query optimization by cache-aware middleware using query teamwork. In *Proceedings of the 18th intl conf. on data engineering*.

Gupta, A., Sudarshan, S., & Viswanathan, S. (2001). Query scheduling in multi query optimization. In *Proceedings of the intl. symposium on database engineering and applications* (pp. 11-19).

Kuntschke, R., Stegmaier, B., Kemper, A., & Reiser, A. (2005). Streamglobe: Processing and sharing data streams in grid-based p2p infrastructures. In *Proceedings of the 31st vldb conference* (pp. 1259-1262).

Madden, S., & Franklin, M. (2002). Fjording the stream: An architecture for queries over streaming sensor data. In *Proceedings of the intl conf on data engineering*.

Madden, S., Franklin, M. J., Hellerstein, J. M., & Hong, W. (2003). *The design of an acquisitional query processor for sensor networks*. Sigmod.

Madden, S., Shah, M., Hellerstein, J., & Raman, V. (2002). Continuously adaptive continuous queries over streams. In *Proceedings of the acm sigmod intl. conf on management of data* (pp. 49-60).

Mukherjee, S., Srinivasa, S., & Patil, S. (2007). Emergent (re)optimization for stream queries in grids. In *Proceedings of the IEEE congress on evolutionary computation* (pp. 729-735).

Pietzuch, P., Ledlie, J., Shneidman, J., Roussopoulos, M., Welsh, M., & Seltzer, M. (2006). Network-aware operator placement for stream-processing systems. In *Proceedings of the International conference on data engineering*.

Raman, V., Deshpande, A., & Hellerstein, J. (2003). Using state modules for adaptive query processing. In *Proceedings of the intl. conf. on data engineering*.

Roy, P., Seshadri, A., Sudarshan, A., & Bhobhe, S. (2000). Efficient and extensible algorithms for multi query optimization. In *Proceedings of the ACM sigmod conf. on management of data* (pp. 249-260).

Sellis, T. (1988). Multiple-query optimization. In *Proceedings of the ACM trans. on database systems* (pp. 23-52).

Shah, M., Hellerstein, J., Chandrasekharan, S., & Franklin, M. (2003). Flux: An adaptive repartitioning operator for continuous query systems. In *Proceedings of the intl. conf. on data engineering*.

Shah, S., Ramamritham, K., & Shenoy, P. (2004). Resilient and coherence preserving dissemination of dynamic data using cooperating peers. In *IEEE transactions on knowledge and data engineering*.

Smith, J., Watson, P., Gounaris, A., Paton, N. W., Fernandes, A., & Sakellariou, R. (2003). Distributed query processing on the grid. *International Journal of High Performance Computing Applications, 353–367*. doi:10.1177/10943420030174002

Stegmaier, B., Kuntschke, R., & Kemper, A. (2004). Streamglobe: Adaptive query processing and optimization in streaming p2p environments. In *Proceedings of the Intl. workshop on data management for sensor networks* (pp. 88-97).

Yao, Y., & Gehrke, J. (2002). The cougar approach to in-network query processing in sensor networks. *SIGMOD Record, 31*(3), 9–18. doi:10.1145/601858.601861

Zdonik, S. (2003). The aurora and medusa projects. *IEEE data engineering bulletin*.

This work was previously published in International Journal of Organizational and Collective Intelligence, Volume 1, Issue 4, edited by Hideyasu Sasaki, pp. 18-39, copyright 2010 by IGI Publishing (an imprint of IGI Global).

Chapter 17
Managing Collective Intelligence in Semantic Communities of Interest

Stefano Montanelli
Università degli Studi di Milano, Italy

Silvana Castano
Università degli Studi di Milano, Italy

Alfio Ferrara
Università degli Studi di Milano, Italy

Gaia Varese
Università degli Studi di Milano, Italy

ABSTRACT

In this paper, the authors present a reference P2P architecture based on autonomous, self-emerging semantic communities of interest (CoIs) for collective intelligence creation and management. An approach for enabling knowledge organization and management at the level of a single peer is presented in the paper, as well as techniques for supporting a peer to participate to the construction of a shared community vocabulary, according to the terminological preferences automatically extracted from its personal knowledge. Furthermore, an application example in the e-health domain is presented in the framework of the iCoord system for P2P semantic coordination to show the use of a manifesto-based collective intelligence for enforcing effective collaboration in a real case study.

INTRODUCTION

In a modern vision, P2P systems are seen as effective collaboration platforms where data and knowledge belonging to a possibly large set of peers can be shared in an effective way

DOI: 10.4018/978-1-4666-1577-9.ch017

(Androutsellis-Theotokis & Spinellis, 2004). In this context, the traditional approaches based on peer-to-peer knowledge discovery and data exchange are being replaced by more articulated architectures where the notion of *semantic community of interest (CoI)* is introduced to explicitly give shape to the *collective intelligence* of a group of peers with similar expertise/resources

(Avrithis, Kompatsiaris, Staab, & Vakali, 2008). Semantic CoIs allow to shift from a network of units to a network of coalitions where the community itself (and not the peers on their own) has the role to support queries and specific collaboration needs that can rise in a given moment. Creation and maintenance of a community-level collective intelligence push a novel attention to the critical aspects of distributed knowledge management in the P2P environment, where the goal of establishing a shared agreement among a set of peers conflicts with the intrinsic P2P nature that pursues peer autonomy, communication scalability, and rapid change propagation. In this direction, recent approaches based on P2P communities show interesting solutions to improve the efficiency of query distribution and to increase data availability, apart from the accessibility of the single peers (Aiello & Alessi, 2007; Das, Nandi, & Ganguly, 2009). However, methods and techniques for collaboratively building and negotiating any form of P2P community intelligence are still at a basic level of development and only preliminary results are currently available (Aleman-Meza, Halaschek-Wiener, & Arpinar, 2005; Ren, Anumba, & Ugwu, 2002).

In this paper, we propose a reference P2P architecture for collective intelligence creation and management based on autonomous, self-emerging semantic CoIs. In our architecture, a semantic CoI emerges from the P2P network by aggregating those peers that autonomously agree to contribute with their own data and knowledge to the construction of a collective intelligence about a certain topic of interest. The collective intelligence of a semantic CoI is made explicit in the form of a *community manifesto*, containing both an ontological description of the community interests and a shared community vocabulary. An approach for enabling knowledge organization and management at the level of a single peer is presented in the paper, as well as techniques for supporting a peer to participate to the construction of a shared community vocabulary, according

to the terminological preferences automatically extracted from its personal knowledge. As far as we know, the capability of enabling a group of independent peers to autonomously define a shared community vocabulary without relying on any centralized authority is an original contribution per sé. Furthermore, an application example in the e-health domain is presented in the framework of the iCoord system for P2P semantic coordination, to show the use of a manifesto-based collective intelligence for enforcing effective collaboration in a real case study. For the sake of clarity, an appendix is finally provided to summarize the notations adopted in the overall paper.

REFERENCE P2P ARCHITECTURE AND KNOWLEDGE MODEL

In the field of P2P systems, the notion of community refers to the capability of the network to autonomously recognize and aggregate groups of peers with common interests and similar resources to share (Castano & Montanelli, 2005; Gu & Wei, 2006). We borrow this notion of P2P community and we define a *semantic community of interest*, from now on simply called *CoI*, as a community of peers where the term "semantic" denotes that the peers participating to the community agree on the "meaning" of the resources to share, and such a meaning is formalized through an ontology-based manifesto. The manifesto gives shape to the *collective intelligence* of a CoI, which is gradually set up in a collaborative way through progressive enrichments performed by all the community members.

For creation and management of a collective intelligence in a CoI, we propose the reference P2P architecture shown in Figure 1, where the upper layer, namely the *Collective Knowledge space*, is in charge of managing CoI formation and management, and the lower layer, namely the *Peer Knowledge space*, is in charge of ensuring

Figure 1. A reference P2P architecture for collective intelligence creation and management

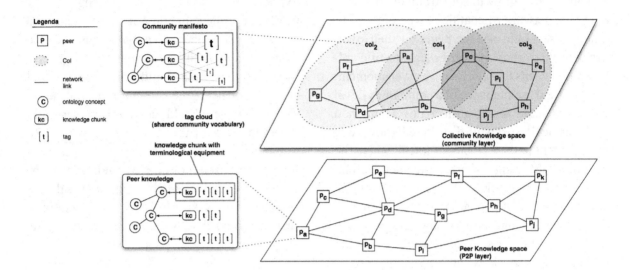

connectivity and standard communication among the overall network peers.

Formation of a CoI. The formation of a community in a P2P network is typically characterized by the adoption of a *supervised approach* where the peer promoting the community (i.e., the *community founder*) controls the formation process by leading the phases of member identification and community commitment. In other words, the supervised approach is characterized by an explicit phase of negotiation where the approval/rejection of a new peer is determined by the choice of the community founder and the list of community members is "network-aware" (Bloehdorn, Haase, Hefke, Sure, & Tempich, 2005). In our reference P2P architecture, for CoI formation and management, we define a Collective Knowledge space characterized by the use of an *unsupervised approach*, thus exhibiting the following key features.

- **Implicit negotiation:** The choice of joining the community is autonomously taken by each peer according to its level of interest in the topic(s) addressed in the community. No coordination authority (e.g., community

founder, superpeer) is expected to manage approval/rejection of the potential members.

- **Soft membership:** The complete list of community members is not made explicit within the community. This means that, at a given moment, the community members are not aware of the other peers currently joining the community.

A CoI is created by a founding peer by defining an initial community manifesto. The community manifesto is the repository of collective intelligence within a CoI and it is continuously circulating throughout the network for advertising the community existence and for enabling all the members to progressively contribute to its enrichment. A peer receiving a community manifesto can autonomously decide to join the community and to become a community member according to its level of interest in the CoI interests.

Network connectivity. A number of solutions can be adopted to enforce effective communications within a P2P network, spanning from classical approaches based on message flooding, like Gnutella (The Gnutella Protocol, 2001), up to modern strategies based on gossiping and periodic exchange of peer neighborhood, like Shuffling (Voulgaris, Gavidia, & Van Steen, 2005). Most of the available solutions in this field are different in terms of generated network traffic and accuracy of the discovery procedures, and a comparative analysis can be found in Androutsellis-Theotokis and Spinellis (2004) and in Hose, Roth, Zeitz, Sattler, and Naumann (2008). In our reference P2P architecture, to enforce network connectivity and to support CoI formation, we define a Peer Knowledge space characterized by the use of a gossiping approach. In particular, through gossiping, all the messages exchanged by peers, like for example query/answer messages and community advertisements, can be effectively propagated throughout the network, thus enforcing the phase of implicit negotiation of the unsupervised approach described above. This is due to the fact that, in a gossiping-based P2P network, a peer is connected to a small set of randomly-chosen nodes that are continuously updated through periodic exchange of neighborhood with other nodes. This way, a message (e.g., a query, an answer, a community advertisement) that needs to be propagated is piggybacked on ordinary gossiping operations and it epidemically reaches all the peers without causing traffic overhead.

Modeling Knowledge at the Peer Level

Each peer is considered as a single agent having view only of its personal knowledge, namely the *peer ontology*, describing its own contents/resources. Given a peer P_i, the peer ontology $PO(P_i)$ is a semantic-web resource like a RDF(S) repository or an OWL ontology, where N is the set of element names, P is the set of property/relation names, and L is the set of datatypes and literal values in the signature of $PO(P_i)$, respectively. The elements of the peer ontology $PO(P_i)$, either concepts and instances, are formalized as a set of knowledge chunks $KC(P_i)$.

Given an element $e \in PO(P_i)$ (concept or instance), a *knowledge chunk kc(e)* $\in KC(P_i)$ provides a synthetic representation of the constituent axioms/assertions of e, both explicitly and implicitly defined in $PO(P_i)$. A knowledge chunk $kc(e)$ is defined as a set of axioms $kc(e) = \{a_1, a_2, ..., a_n\}$ constituting the specification of the corresponding element e. An axiom $a_i(kc(e))$ with $i \in [1,n]$ has the form $a_i(kc(e)) = <n(kc), r(a_i), v(a_i)>$, where:

- $n(kc) \in N$ is the name of the knowledge chunk $kc(e)$, that is the name of e;
- $r(a_i) \in P \cup \{\equiv, \subseteq\}$ is a semantic relation contained in the definition of e;
- $v(a_i) \in N \cup L$ is the value of the corresponding relation $r(a_i)$.

Moreover, a knowledge chunk $kc(e)$ is associated with a terminological equipment $E(kc(e))$ and a change-log timestamp $TS(kc(e))$.

The *terminological equipment* $E(kc(e))$ denotes the set of tags (i.e., terms) featuring e in $PO(P_i)$. For a given knowledge chunk $kc(e)$, the corresponding terminological equipment $E(kc(e))$ is computed by considering the tags describing the element e, that is, the terms appearing in the set of all axioms in $PO(P_i)$ containing a reference to e (i.e., concept names, property names, annotation labels, and comments). Before insertion in $E(kc(e))$, a tag is submitted to a normalization/tokenization procedure. In this phase, various terminology-related procedures are executed, like for example a procedure to split compound tags and a procedure to derive lemmas/synonyms from a terminological thesaurus (e.g., WordNet). A detailed description of how to derive knowledge chunks and associated terminological equipments from OWL ontology specifications is provided in Castano, Ferrara, and Montanelli (2009).

The *change-log timestamp TS(kc(e))* denotes the timestamp of the last update involving the specification of $kc(e)$. Each time the peer P_i performs an update to an element $e \in PO(P_i)$, the corresponding knowledge chunk *kc(e)*, the terminological equipment *E(kc(e))* and the change-log timestamp *TS(kc(e))* are updated accordingly.

Example 1. As an example of peer knowledge, we consider a peer P_a with a portion of a peer ontology $PO(P_a)$ in the e-health domain. Given the following OWL-DL axioms:

Drug ⊆ Pharmaceutical_Preparation
Drug ⊆ ∃hasIngredient.Active_Ingredient
Therapeutic_Procedure ⊆ ∃uses.Drug
Therapeutic_Procedure ⊆ ∃treats.Disease

the knowledge chunks kc(Drug) and kc(Therapeutic_Procedure) are inserted in the set $KC(P_a)$ (Table 1).

According to the specification in $PO(P_a)$, the terminological equipments associated with the knowledge chunks of $KC(P_a)$ are:

E(kc(Drug)) = {active, chemical, drug, ingredient, pharmaceutical, preparation}
E(kc(Therapeutic_Procedure)) = {disease, drug, procedure, use, therapeutic, treat}

We note that verbs are inserted in the terminological equipments in their basic form (e.g., treats → treat), compound tags are tokenized (e.g., Therapeutic_Procedure → therapeutic, procedure), and auxiliary verbs are not considered (e.g., hasIngredient → ingredient). Finally, the change-log timestamp t_0 is set for both the knowledge chunks kc(Drug) and kc(Therapeutic_Procedure),

that is TS(kc(Drug)) = TS(kc(Therapeutic_Procedure)) = t_0.

Modeling Knowledge at the CoI Level

The consensus reached in a CoI around a topic/concept of interest is called collective intelligence and it is expressed in the form of a *community manifesto*. For a community *coi*, a community manifesto *m(coi)* is defined as a 4-tuple of the form: *m(coi) = <KC(coi), E(KC(coi)), TC(coi), CP(coi)>*, where:

- *KC(coi)* denotes the set of knowledge chunks describing the concepts of the focused ontology featuring the interests of *coi*;
- *E(KC(coi)) = {E(kc) | kc ∈ KC(coi)}* denotes the set of terminological equipments associated with the knowledge chunks in *KC(coi)*;
- *TC(coi) = {<t_i, k>}* denotes a tag cloud representing the shared vocabulary of *coi*, where $t_i \in E(kc)$ *(E(kc) ∈ E(KC(coi)))* is a tag, and $k \in N$ denotes the frequency counter of t_i, namely the number of peers using the tag t_i;
- *CP(coi) = {<ID(P_j), TS(P_j)>}* is the list of contributing peers, namely the peers that have worked on *m(coi)*, where *ID(P_j)* is the identifier of the peer P_j, and *TS(P_j)* is the timestamp of the last update applied by P_j to the manifesto.

Table 1. Knowledge Chunks of the Peer a

KC(P_a) – Set of knowledge chunks of the peer P_a		
Knowledge chunk (*n(kc)*)	**Semantic relation (*r(a_j)*)**	**Relation value (*v(a_j)*)**
Drug	rdf:subClassOf	Pharmaceutical_Preparation
Drug	hasIngredient	Chemical
Drug	hasIngredient	Active_Ingredient
Therapeutic_Procedure	uses	Drug
Therapeutic_Procedure	treats	Disease

The founder of the community *coi* has the role to define the initial focused ontology *KC(coi)*. This set remains unchanged during the overall community life-cycle and it is used by the peers receiving the manifesto *m(coi)* to assess their level of interest in *coi*. On the opposite, the set *E(KC(coi))* initially coincides with the terminological equipments associated with the knowledge chunks in *KC(coi)* of the founder, and it is progressively enriched by the community members according to the terminology used for describing their own resources. The tags in *E(KC(coi))* are used to feed the tag cloud *TC(coi)* where they are stored together with the associated frequency counters expressing their popularity in the community. The cloud *TC(coi)* enables each community member to become aware of the terminology used by other peers with similar interests and to enforce consolidation and standardization of a shared community vocabulary.

Due to the progressive enrichment of the manifesto *m(coi)* performed by the community members, a number of different versions of *m(coi)* are generated during the overall life-cycle of the community *coi*. We denote as $v_1(m(coi))$ the initial version of the community manifesto *m(coi)* created by the founder of the community, while the jth version of the manifesto *m(coi)* is denoted as $v_j(m(coi))$.

Example 2. As an example of community manifesto, we consider a community coi_1 about medical drugs founded by the peer P_a with an initial manifesto $v_1(m(coi_1))$ defined in Table 2.

$E(KC(coi_1)) = E(kc(Drug)) = \{$active, chemical, drug, ingredient, pharmaceutical, preparation$\}$

$TC(coi_1) = \{$(active,1), (chemical,1), (drug,1), (ingredient,1), (pharmaceutical,1), (preparation,1)$\}$

$CP(coi_1) = \{<P_a, t_1>\}$

The community manifesto $v_1(m(coi_1))$ is defined by the peer P_a by specifying $KC(coi_1) = \{kc(Drug)\}$ with $kc(Drug) \in KC(P_a)$. The tag cloud $TC(coi_1)$ initially coincides with the terminological equipment $E(kc(Drug))$ and the popularity of each tag is set by default to 1. Finally, the set $CP(coi_1)$ initially contains only the community founder P_a and the timestamp t_1.

CONSTRUCTION OF THE COLLECTIVE INTELLIGENCE

In the Peer Knowledge space, the gossiping mechanism enforces the advertisement of the existing CoIs by disseminating the associated community manifestos. When a peer P_i receives from the network the manifesto $v_j(m(coi))$, the following tasks are executed.

1. The peer P_i evaluates its level of interest in the community *coi* (*matching task*).
2. If the community is joined, the peer P_i contributes to the collective intelligence of the community *coi* by enriching the manifesto $v_j(m(coi))$ with its terminological preferences (*contribution task*). The

Table 2. Knowledge chunks of community manifesto

KC(coi_1) – Set of knowledge chunks of the community manifesto of coi_1		
Knowledge chunk (*n(kc)*)	Semantic relation (*r(a_j)*)	Relation value (*v(a_j)*)
Drug	rdf:subClassOf	Pharmaceutical_Preparation
Drug	hasIngredient	Chemical
Drug	hasIngredient	Active_Ingredient

updated version $v_{j+1}(m(coi))$ of the community manifesto is generated by the peer P_i.

3. This updated version of the community manifesto is propagated throughout the P2P network to advertise the other community members of the changes (*propagation task*).

Matching task. The goal of the matching task is to determine whether the peer P_i is interested in the incoming manifesto $v_j(m(coi))$, and thus in the community *coi*. The criterion adopted in our approach is featured by an affinity-based interest, which means that a peer is interested in a CoI if its knowledge "has to do" with the topics described by the manifesto. Thus, the knowledge in the peer ontology of P_i is matched against the focused ontology of the CoI. To this end, we employ our ontology matching engine HMatch 2.0 which has been specifically conceived to match semantic web ontologies in open distributed systems, like P2P systems. HMatch 2.0 has been successfully tested and evaluated over the 2006, 2007, and 2009 benchmarks of the Ontology Alignment Evaluation Initiative (OAEI)[1], and over real datasets in the framework of the BOEMIE research project[2].

HMatch 2.0 takes as input two ontologies and returns as output the mappings between pairs of concepts with the same or the closest intended meaning in the two ontologies. HMatch 2.0 measures the semantic affinity of two concepts by exploiting the information of their corresponding knowledge chunk representations. Given two knowledge chunks kc' and kc'', the function $SA(kc',kc'') \rightarrow [0,1]$ calculates their semantic affinity value as the linear combination of a linguistic affinity value $LA(kc',kc'')$ and a contextual affinity value $CA(kc',kc'')$. In particular, $LA(kc',kc'')$ is calculated by comparing the name of kc' and kc''. For evaluating $LA()$, HMatch 2.0 relies on a thesaurus of terms and terminological relationships automatically extracted from the WordNet lexical system. The contextual affinity function of HMatch 2.0 provides a measure of similarity between two knowledge chunks by taking into account the number of their matching axioms as follows:

$$CA(kc',kc'') = \frac{2 \cdot |\{matching\ axioms\ of\ kc'\ and\ kc''\}|}{|kc'| + |kc''|}$$

where $|kc'|$, $|kc''|$, and $|\{matching\ axioms\ of\ kc'\ and\ kc''\}|$ denote the number of axioms of kc', the number of axioms of kc'', and the number of matching axioms between kc' and kc'', respectively.

Conditions for considering a pair of axioms (a_i, a_j) as matching axioms depend on the kind of involved semantic relations $r(a_i)$ and $r(a_j)$ and on their corresponding values $v(a_i)$ and $v(a_j)$, respectively (see Table 3).

In particular, three different cases can occur.

- $r(a_i)$ and $r(a_j)$ are both object properties. In this case, the corresponding values $v(a_i)$ and $v(a_j)$ are concept names. Thus, a_i and a_j are considered as matching axioms iff the linguistic affinity of $r(a_i)$ and $r(a_j)$ is greater than or equal to a given threshold th_1 and the linguistic affinity of $v(a_i)$ and $v(a_j)$ is greater than or equal to a given threshold th_2.

- $r(a_i)$ and $r(a_j)$ are both datatype properties. In this case, the values $v(a_i)$ and $v(a_j)$ are the corresponding datatype ranges. Two datatype ranges are considered as matching ranges when they are compatible. For example, a range xsd:numeric is compatible with other numeric datatypes like xsd:float or xsd:integer. A set of compatibility rules has been defined in HMatch 2.0 to code the main range-type compatibilities featuring OWL ontologies.

- $r(a_i)$ is a datatype property and $r(a_j)$ is an object property (or vice versa). In this case, the corresponding values $v(a_i)$ and $v(a_j)$ are incomparable. Thus, we assume that the axioms a_i and a_j match when the linguistic affinity of $r(a_i)$ and $r(a_j)$ is greater than or equal to a given threshold th_1.

Table 3. Conditions for matching axioms

Kind of semantic relations	Conditions for matching axioms
$r(a_i)$ and $r(a_j)$ are object properties	$LA(r(a_i),r(a_j)) \geq th_1$ AND $LA(v(a_i),v(a_j)) \geq th_2$
$r(a_i)$ and $r(a_j)$ are datatype properties	$LA(r(a_i),r(a_j)) \geq th_1$ AND $v(a_i)$, $v(a_j)$ are compatible ranges
$r(a_i)$ is a datatype property and $r(a_j)$ is an object property	$LA(r(a_i),r(a_j)) \geq th_1$

A comprehensive Semantic Affinity value of *kc'* and *kc''* is calculated as follows:

$$SA(kc',kc'') = W_{LA} \cdot LA(kc',kc'') + (1 - W_{LA}) \cdot CA(kc',kc'')$$

where $W_{LA} \in [0,1]$, is a weight expressing the relevance assigned to the Linguistic Affinity in the overall computation of *SA(kc',kc'')*. The use of the weight W_{LA} in *SA(kc',kc'')* is motivated by the need of enabling a peer P_i to support a flexible matching process. In some circumstances, the Semantic Affinity value can be calculated on the basis of the Linguistic Affinity only, thus excluding the computation of the Contextual Affinity (i.e., $W_{LA} = 1$). This is suggested, for example, when poor computational resources are available on a peer P_i, and a fast matching execution is required. Instead, a balanced use of the weight W_{LA} is suggested when a more accurate semantic affinity evaluation is requested by the peer P_i and both Linguistic and Contextual Affinity need to be calculated (i.e., $W_{LA} = 0.5$). In the examples of this paper, we work with a default value $W_{LA} = 0.5$. For the selection of such a default value of W_{LA}, we chose the value that provided more satisfactorily results in the ontology matching experiments performed over the OAEI benchmarks and the BOEMIE datasets. A more detailed description of HMatch 2.0 and related ontology matching models and techniques is provided in Castano, Ferrara, and Montanelli (2006).

The result of the matching task is a mapping set $MAP(P_i, coi) = \{<kc',kc''>\}$ composed by the pairs of matching knowledge chunks $kc' \in KC(P_i)$ and $kc'' \in KC(coi)$, respectively. Each peer

defines its own set of *join constraints* which are used to configure HMatch 2.0 and to specify the minimal matching conditions that are required in order to join a community. For example, the join constraints used by a peer P_i can be based on the set cardinality $k = |MAP(P_i, coi)|$, namely on the number of matching knowledge chunks discovered by HMatch 2.0 between the peer knowledge and the community knowledge. The peer P_i tuncs its "willingness" to join a CoI by setting appropriate constraints on the value of the cardinality k. If a peer P_i aims at participating to a high number of CoIs a low value of k is set (e.g., $k = 1$), while a more selective community participation is determined by a high value of k (e.g., $k > 1$). When the join constraints are satisfied, the peer enters the community and the manifesto $v_j(m(coi))$ is locally stored, otherwise the manifesto $v_j(m(coi))$ is discarded.

We note that, for a given semantic community *coi*, the peer P_i executes the matching task only at the arrival of the first manifesto *m(coi)*, disregarding the number of the received version. Subsequent arrivals of any version of *m(coi)* are not submitted to matching since the knowledge chunks *KC(coi)* are unchanged and the mapping set *MAP(P_i, coi)* is already calculated.

Contribution task. The goal of the contribution task is to enable the peer P_i to enrich the manifesto $v_j(m(coi))$ with its own terminological preferences. The key point of this task is that, due to the gossiping mechanism, multiple and different versions of a manifesto *m(coi)* can coexist in the network at a certain moment and can be received by a peer P_i. Thus, P_i has the need to detect whether an incoming manifesto $v_j(m(coi))$

has been already received in the past and which are the tags in its peer ontology that have to be considered for insertion in the tag cloud $TC(coi)$ $\in v_j(m(coi))$. For this reason, the contribution task is implemented through timestamp-based techniques, similarly to what is done for transaction management in distributed database systems (Ozsu & Valduriez, 1999). When a manifesto $v_j(m(coi))$ is received, the list of contributing peers $CP(coi)$ $\in v_j(m(coi))$ is exploited by the peer P_i. The following scenarios can occur.

A. **$ID(P_i) \notin CP(coi)$**. This means that $v_j(m(coi))$ is the manifesto of a new CoI at its first arrival. In this case, given the mapping set $MAP(P_i, coi) = \{<kc', kc''>\}$ calculated in the matching task, the terminological equipment $E(kc')$ of a matching knowledge chunk $kc' \in KC(P_i)$ is added to the terminological equipment $E(kc'')$ of the corresponding matching knowledge chunk $kc'' \in KC(coi)$, namely $E(kc'') = E(kc'') \cup E(kc')$.

Moreover, the tags of the terminological equipment $E_{kc'}$ are added to the community tag cloud $TC(coi)$. Given a tag $t_i \in E(kc')$, the pair $<t_i, 1>$ is inserted in $TC(coi)$ if the tag t_i is missing in the tag cloud, otherwise the pair $<t_i, k> \in TC(coi)$ is updated to $<t_i, k+1>$. Finally, the identifier $ID(P_i)$ is added to $CP(coi)$ with an updated timestamp $TS(P_i)$.

B. **$ID(P_i) \in CP(coi)$**. This means that another version of $v_j(m(coi))$ was already received in the past and processed by the peer P_i. In this case, P_i has to update the manifesto by considering only the changes that occurred to its own knowledge (chunks) after the execution of the last contribution task. To this end, given the mapping set $MAP(P_i, coi)$, the peer P_i calculates the set of tags $T_{new}(coi)$ as $T_{new}(coi) = \{t_j \mid t_j \in E(kc'), TS(kc') > TS(P_i)\}$, where $kc' \in KC(P_i)$, $<kc', kc''> \in MAP(P_i, coi)$, $TS(kc')$ is the timestamp of the

last change-log on kc', and $TS(P_i) \in CP(coi)$ is the timestamp of the last contribution task performed by P_i on $v_j(m(coi))$. For each $t_j \in T_{new}(coi)$, both $E(kc'')$ and $TC(coi)$ are updated by including t_j in $E(kc'')$ and by increasing the frequency counter of t_j in $TC(coi)$. Finally, the timestamp $TS(P_i)$ is updated in $CP(coi)$. A updated version $v_{j+1}(m(coi))$ of the community manifesto is then generated

Propagation task. The goal of the propagation task is to propagate the version v_{j+1} of the manifesto $m(coi)$ over the Peer Knowledge layer. After the execution of the contribution task, $v_{j+1}(m(coi))$ is passed to the gossiping mechanism and it is forwarded to the neighboring peers of P_i for advertisement.

Example 3. We consider three peers, namely P_a, P_b, and P_c where the peer P_a is the founder of the community coi_1 introduced in Example 2, whose knowledge chunks $KC(P_a)$ are shown in Example 1. Assume that the following knowledge chunks are stored by P_b and P_c in their respective peer knowledge (Table 4, Table 5).

E(kc(Malaria)) = {anemia, disease, fever, intermittent, malaria, parasitic, symptom}
E(kc(Antimalarial_Drug)) = {antimalarial, drug, malaria, medicine, treat}
TS(kc(Malaria))=TS(kc(Antimalarial_Drug))=t_0

E(kc(Drug)) = {drug, chemical, ingredient, malaria, treat}
E(kc(Halfan)) = {drug, halfan}
E(kc(Quinine)) = {drug, quinine}
E(kc(Vibravenos)) = {drug, vibravenos}
TS(kc(Drug))=TS(kc(Halfan))=TS(kc(Quinine)) = TS(kc(Vibravenos)) = t_0

Through gossiping, the initial version of the community manifesto $v_1(m(coi_1))$ produced by the peer P_a is propagated to P_b and P_c. In Figure 2, we

Table 4. Knowledge Chunks of the Peer b

KC(P_b) – Set of knowledge chunks of the peer P_b		
Knowledge chunk (*n(kc)*)	Semantic relation (*r(a_j)*)	Relation value (*v(a_j)*)
Malaria	rdf:subClassOf	Parasitic_Disease
Malaria	hasSymptom	Intermittent_Fever
Malaria	hasSymptom	Anemia
Antimalarial_Drug	rdf:subClassOf	Medicine
Antimalarial_Drug	Treats	Malaria

Table 5. Knowledge Chunks of the Peer c

KC(P_c) – Set of knowledge chunks of the peer P_c		
Knowledge chunk (*n(kc)*)	Semantic relation (*r(a_j)*)	Relation value (*v(a_j)*)
Drug	hasIngredient	Chemical
Drug	treats	Malaria
Halfan	rdf:subClassOf	Drug
Quinine	rdf:subClassOf	Drug
Vibravenos	rdf:subClassOf	Drug

show the process of convergence of the community manifesto of coi_1. To highlight the results of the contribution task, for each version of the community manifesto produced by the various peers during convergence, in Figure 2, we only report the content of the tag cloud $TC(coi_1)$.

Receiving $v_1(m(coi_1))$, the peer P_b matches its knowledge chunks $KC(P_b)$ against the knowledge chunks $KC(coi_1)$, discovering that SA(Antimalarial_Drug,Drug) = 0.6; thus the mapping set $MAP(P_b,coi_1)$ = {<kc(Antimalarial_Drug), kc(Drug)>} is produced by HMatch 2.0. Assuming that at least one matching knowledge chunk is required to join a CoI ($|MAP(P_b,coi_1)| \geq 1$), P_b joins the community coi_1 and it stores the manifesto $v_1(m(coi_1))$. Moreover, in the contribution task, the peer P_b enriches E(kc(Drug)) $\in$ E(KC(coi_1)) and TC(coi_1) by inserting the terminological equipment E(kc(Antimalarial_Drug)). This originates the following version $v_2(m(coi_1))$ of the community manifesto (Table 6).

$E(KC(coi_1))$ = E(kc(Drug)) = {active, antimalarial, chemical, drug, ingredient, malaria, medicine, pharmaceutical, preparation, treat}

$TC(coi_1)$ = {(active,1), (antimalarial,1), (chemical,1), (drug,2), (ingredient,1), (malaria,1), (medicine,1), (pharmaceutical,1), (preparation,1), (treat,1)}

$CP(coi_1)$ = {<P_a, t_1>, <P_b, t_2>}

At the same time, receiving $v_1(m(coi_1))$, the peer P_c joins the community coi_1 due to the mapping set $MAP(P_c,coi_1)$ = {<kc(Drug), kc(Drug)>} produced by HMatch 2.0, since SA(Drug,Drug) = 0.7. A version $v_3(m(coi_1))$ of the community manifesto is produced by P_c and it is propagated over the Peer Knowledge layer through gossiping. When P_b receives the version $v_3(m(coi_1))$, the contribution task is executed to include the terminological equipment E(kc(Antimalarial_Drug)) also in $v_3(m(coi_1))$. A version $v_4(m(coi_1))$ is then produced and propagated. Similarly, a version

Figure 2. Example of manifesto convergence from v_1 to v_5

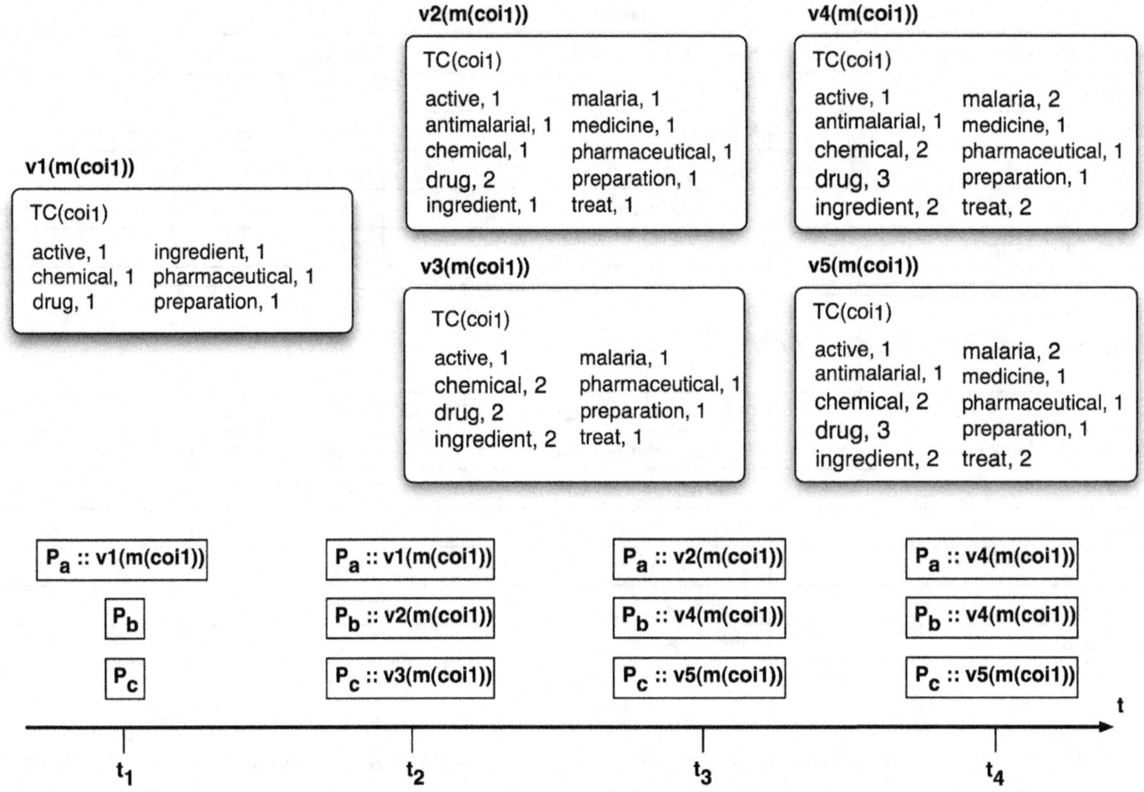

Table 6. Knowledge Chunks of the Community Manifesto

KC(coi$_1$) – Set of knowledge chunks of the community manifesto of coi$_1$		
Knowledge chunk (*n(kc)*)	**Semantic relation (*r(a$_j$)*)**	**Relation value (*v(a$_j$)*)**
Drug	rdf:subClassOf	Pharmaceutical_Preparation
Drug	hasIngredient	Chemical
Drug	hasIngredient	Active_Ingredient

$v_5(m(coi_1))$ is produced by P_c when it receives $v_2(m(coi_1))$. In Figure 2, it is simple to note that the versions v_4 and v_5 are identical and each of them represents the final community manifesto of coi$_1$ as follows (Table 7).

$E(KC(coi_1)) = E(kc(Drug)) = \{$active, antimalarial, chemical, drug, ingredient, malaria, medicine, pharmaceutical, preparation, treat$\}$

$TC(coi_1) = \{$(active,1), (antimalarial,1), (chemical,2), (drug,3), (ingredient,2), (malaria,2), (medicine,1), (pharmaceutical,1), (preparation,1), (treat,2)$\}$

$CP(coi_1) = \{<P_a, t_1>, <P_b, t_2>, <P_c, t_3>\}$

This version of the manifesto is progressively received and stored by all the community members. Further updates to the community manifesto are not required until changes to the peer ontology of the community members will occur.

Table 7. Knowledge Chunks of the Community Manifesto

KC(coi$_i$) – Set of knowledge chunks of the community manifesto of coi$_i$		
Knowledge chunk (*n(kc)*)	Semantic relation (*r(a$_j$)*)	Relation value (*v(a$_j$)*)
Drug	rdf:subClassOf	Pharmaceutical_Preparation
Drug	hasIngredient	Chemical
Drug	hasIngredient	Active_Ingredient

Considerations and Contributions

To better remark the contribution of our work, we give some considerations on the P2P convergence of a community manifesto and on the relationships between our work about CoIs and the state-of-the-art solutions about ontology-based Communities of Practice (CoPs).

Propagation and convergence of a community manifesto. The path followed by a community manifesto during propagation throughout the network cannot be predicted in advance due to the random exchange of peer neighborhoods adopted by the gossiping mechanism. This means that a certain manifesto $v_j(m(coi))$ can be received multiple times by a peer P_i, and two versions $v_j(m(coi))$ and $v_l(m(coi))$ of a manifesto can be received in a different order by two community members P_i and P_k. Thus, at a given moment for the same community *coi*, two members P_i and P_k can store two different versions of the *coi* manifesto $v_j(m(coi))$ and $v_l(m(coi))$, respectively. The manifestos v_j and v_l have the same set of knowledge chunks *KC(coi)* (i.e., those defined by the founder), but they can differ in the terminological equipments *E(KC(coi))*, or in the tag cloud *TC(coi)*, or in the list of contributing peers *CP(coi)*. For this reason, a member of *coi* storing a certain version v_j of the manifesto *m(coi)* can not be sure that this version is fully representative of the actual terminological preferences of all the community members. However, the various manifesto versions tend to converge towards a unique and comprehensive community manifesto under the (reasonable) assumption that the changes to the peer ontology of the community members are non-frequent events. In this case, the time required for reaching the manifesto convergence depends on the size of the network, on the number of community members, and on the configuration of the gossiping mechanism for what concerns the frequency of the neighbor-exchange operations.

CoIs vs. CoPs. The considered problem of collective intelligence creation within a CoI has a number of analogies with the problem of knowledge management within a Community of Practice (CoP). A CoP is a group of people within (or sometimes across) organizations who share a common set of information, needs or problems (Seely-Brown & Duguid, 1991). Knowledge management issues for CoPs are widely discussed in the literature due to the need to explicitly and formally capture the common conventions, languages, tool usage, and standards that characterize the community. Usually, ontologies are employed to specify the CoP knowledge, both at the level of a single member, where an ontology provides a semantic representation of the knowledge shared by a given community member; and at the level of an overall community, where an ontology formalizes the shared practices of the entire set of community member s (Alani, Dasmahapatra, O'Hara, & Shadbolt, 2003; Davies, Duke, & Sure, 2004). Moreover, ontology mediation techniques are sometimes proposed to discover possible points of convergence between different community members (Spaniol & Klamma, 2004). As far as we know, the existing approaches to CoP knowledge management consider web-based infrastructures where a centralized repository is used to store the shared community knowledge and a coordinating authority has the role to resolve possible conflicts between members. The focus of the approach we propose in this paper places the accent more on the problem of how to coordinate a collective intelligence that is autonomously emerging in an open distributed system, like a P2P network, rather than on the problem of how to model the different kinds of knowledge (e.g., an interest, a practice) that can be shared by a group of members. In a P2P network, a central knowledge repository as well as a coordination authority is almost missing or difficult to maintain during time. For this reason, we propose to describe the collective intelligence of a CoI through a community manifesto that is continuously circulating throughout the P2P network for enabling the community members to contribute to the progressive enrichment of the collective intelligence.

Adaptation of our approach to CoPs. In our P2P approach, the correct evolution of the collective intelligence of a CoI is guaranteed by the contribution task that is periodically executed by the community member and by the subsequent propagation task that enables to advertise the updates applied to the manifesto. We stress that the P2P approach we propose can be suitably adopted also in the case of a web-based CoP by storing the community manifesto in a centralized repository. The formalism of knowledge chunks enables a community member to model its practices and the matching task is exploited to discover similarities between the knowledge of a specific community member and the centrally-stored manifesto. The contribution task is executed by a community member when a change occurs in its local knowledge and the propagation task is no more required since any community member can acquire the up-to-date manifesto by accessing the centralized repository.

APPLICATION TO THE E-HEALTH DOMAIN

The proposed architecture based on the notion of CoI and collective intelligence has been implemented within the iCoord system for P2P semantic coordination (The iCoord System, 2008). In iCoord, coordination means the capability of each single peer to automatically retrieve and effectively share the data of interest by also dealing with the need of evolving its own knowledge over time to correctly assimilate the new external knowledge acquired from outside partners during collaboration/interaction (Castano, Ferrara, Lorusso, & Montanelli, 2008). Key features of iCoord are i) the adoption of a shuffling-based approach to enforce peer-to-peer communications in the Peer Knowledge space (Voulgaris et al., 2005), and ii) the development of advanced techniques to enable semantic query answering and tool-assisted knowledge design capable of exploiting the collective intelligence of specialized CoIs available in the network, as will be described in the following.

As application example, we consider a case study in the e-health domain, based on a P2P network of medical structures (i.e., hospitals and specialized research labs) that need to cooperate for knowledge and data sharing. Each peer of the network represents a medical structure and it is equipped with a software toolkit for accessing the functionalities of the iCoord system. In the example, we consider the community coi_1 about medical drugs, and the community members P_a, P_b, and P_c presented in Example 3.

Exploiting CoIs for Query Answering

The joined CoIs are exploited by a peer to retrieve from the network the available matching knowledge chunks about a certain concept of its own interest. Data/resource search is performed by a requesting peer P_i by formulating a *probe query pq* with an ontological specification of a target concept of interest expressed in the form of one or more knowledge chunks. For a given query *pq*, a matching-based routing mechanism, called *routing-by-community*, is provided in iCoord to choose the most appropriate recipients of *pq*, namely those CoIs whose members are most likely capable of providing relevant results for the query target. In this respect, for a community *coi*, the set *KC(coi)* in the manifesto *m(coi)* is exploited to evaluate the relevance of *coi* for the query *pq*. In particular, the HMatch 2.0 system is invoked by the requesting peer P_i to match *pq* against the manifestos of the joined communities. A community *coi* is considered as a candidate recipient for the query *pq* when at least one matching knowledge chunk $kc \in KC(coi)$ is found for *pq* by HMatch 2.0. The communities with the most relevant matching results are finally selected as query recipients by the routing-by-community mechanism. Queries are propagated throughout the network with shuffling and, given the community *coi* as query recipient, the peer members of *coi* can filter all the incoming queries by considering for processing only the requests sent to *coi*. A detailed description of the routing-by-community mechanism and related query propagation techniques are provided in Montanelli & Castano (2008).

Receiving *pq*, a peer P_k invokes HMatch 2.0 to compare the incoming probe query against its knowledge chunks $KC(P_k)$ and to identify possible semantic affinities. In particular, *SA(pq, kc)* is calculated by the peer P_k for each knowledge chunk $kc \in KC(P_k)$. A (possibly empty) list of matching knowledge chunks is returned by HMatch 2.0. If a non-empty result is produced, these matching knowledge chunks are used to compose an answer to *pq* that is returned to the requesting peer P_i. Collecting all the query answers, the peer P_i evaluates all the returned matching concepts and decides whether to further peer-to-peer interact with one or more answering peers for effective data acquisition.

Example 4. The peer P_a is interested in discovering network nodes that are capable of providing relevant knowledge about malaria and possible drugs for treating this disease. A probe query pq_1 is formulated by P_a containing the following knowledge chunks (Table 8).

By matching pq_1 against $KC(coi_1)$ with HMatch 2.0, the peer P_a obtains SA(Medicine,Drug) = 0.5. The community coi_1 is then selected as query recipient by the routing-by-community mechanism and pq_1 is submitted to the network for propagation to the coi_1 members P_b and P_c. In the peer P_b, HMatch 2.0 is invoked to compare pq_1 against the knowledge chunks $KC(P_b)$ and the semantic affinities SA(Medicine,Antimalarial_Drug) = 0.73 and SA(Malaria,Malaria) = 0.75 are returned as a result. Thus, a query answer containing the knowledge chunk kc(Antimalarial_Drug) and kc(Malaria) are sent by the peer P_b to the requesting peer P_a as a reply. At the same time, in the peer P_c, the following semantic affinities are returned by HMatch 2.0 as matching results between the query pq_1 and the knowledge chunks $KC(P_c)$:

A query answer containing the knowledge chunks kc(Drug), kc(Halfan), kc(Quinine), and kc(Vibravenos) are sent by the peer P_c to the requesting peer P_a as a reply. By exploiting the received replies, P_a recognizes that the peer P_b

Table 8. Knowledge Chunks Featuring Probe Query

pq_1 – Set of knowledge chunks featuring the probe query		
Knowledge chunk (*n(kc)*)	**Semantic relation (*r(a_j)*)**	**Relation value (*v(a_j)*)**
Malaria	rdf:subClassOf	Disease
Medicine	Treats	Malaria

Table 9.

SA(Medicine, Drug) = 0.83
SA(Medicine, Halfan) = 0.4
SA(Medicine, Quinine) = 0.4
SA(Medicine, Vibravenos) = 0.4

provides a symptomatical description of malaria and antimalarial drugs, while the peer P_c stores knowledge about drugs to treat malaria. Since the peer P_a is interested in retrieving data about drugs for malaria, the peer P_c is selected as a partner for the subsequent data acquisition phase. State-of-the-art techniques can be exploited to acquire data from matching peers (see for instance Halevy et al. (2004) for further details).

Exploiting Collective Intelligence for Knowledge Design and Evolution

The collective intelligence of the joined CoIs is exploited by a peer when it needs to update its own knowledge for specifying new ontology concepts as well as for changing/enriching the specification of existing ones. To this end, a tool-assisted environment for knowledge design, called NLE, is provided in iCoord, based on grammar-controlled syntax and natural-language descriptions of the edited concepts (Ferrara, Montanelli, Varese, & Castano, 2009). In the NLE tool environment, editing is performed on a *concept draft* which can be manually specified "from scratch" by the expert user in case of insertion of a new concept, or can be derived from a concept currently stored in the peer ontology in case of enrichment of an existing concept. In both cases, the specification of a concept axiom is performed by providing a natural-language sentence, whose structure is controlled by a formal grammar capable of supporting the *intuitive* definition of a correct OWL axiom, by hiding most of the technical details generally required to use an ontology language.

During editing of a concept draft with the NLE tool, the role of the collective intelligence is twofold. On one side, the knowledge chunks $KC(coi_i)$ of a joined community coi_i are exploited to provide possible suggestions for reuse. The idea is that a knowledge chunk specified in the manifesto of a CoI can be used as a template during the manual specification of a concept using the NLE tool. This approach to knowledge design allows to enforce the reuse of existing knowledge within a CoI and to promote the diffusion of common design patterns among the members of a given community. The HMatch 2.0 system is invoked to match the concept draft under definition against the set $KC(coi_i)$ of each joined CoI, with the aim to discover the best matching knowledge chunks that can be provided as relevant suggestions. An initial set of matching knowledge chunks is provided in the editor at the beginning of the editing session, but new chunks are continuously retrieved on the fly as long as new assertions are specified in the editor and the matching operation becomes more precise. On the other side, the tag cloud $TC(coi_i)$ of a joined community coi_i is exploited to provide terminological hints during typing of name/structural definitions of the concept axiom under definition. The idea is that the popularity of a tag within a community of peers having similar interests/expertise can provide relevant suggestions in order to choose the most suitable terms in the specification of a given concept axiom. The linguistic affinity techniques of HMatch 2.0 are employed to evaluate the level of match between a given term t in the concept draft under definition and the tags in the tag cloud $TC(coi_i)$ of each joined community. A set of tag suggestions $T_{hint} = \{t' \mid t' \in TC(coi_i) \wedge LA(t,t') > th\}$ is produced by HMatch 2.0 as a result, where coi_i is a joined community and th is a threshold setting the minimum level of semantic affinity required for considering a tag $t' \in TC(coi_i)$ as a relevant suggestion for the considered concept draft. The tags in the set T_{hint} are ranked according to their frequency (i.e., popularity) and they are provided as suggestions of alternative tags for *t* in the axiom specification. Tag reuse and terminology sharing allow peers to consolidate a shared vocabulary within a community, thus eliciting the effectiveness of the knowledge sharing functionalities.

Once that the editing phase is completed, the concept draft is assimilated in the peer ontology. The NLE tool automatically translates the natural-language specification of the draft into a corresponding OWL specification. During translation, validation is performed with the Pellet DL reasoner[3] to detect possible inconsistencies. Furthermore, after assimilation of the concept draft *c*, the corresponding knowledge chunk *kc(c)* is updated in the peer knowledge as well as the terminological equipment *E(kc(c))* and the timestamp *TS(kc(c))*.

Example 5. The peer P_b has the need to enrich the specification of its concept Antimalarial Drug, whose knowledge chunk kc(Antimalarial_Drug) is shown in Example 3.

In iCoord, the expert user of the peer P_b can visualize the list of concepts stored in its peer ontology (left panel of Figure 3) and it can start the editing phase by dragging the concept Antimalarial Drug, namely the concept draft, into the editing area (central panel of Figure 3). A matching knowledge chunk kc(Drug) $\in$ KC(coi$_1$) is discovered by HMatch 2.0 and it is shown in the suggestion area (right panel of Figure 3). In iCoord, the specifications of both concepts and suggestions are shown through the natural language descriptions produced by the NLE tool. The expert user can decide to reuse the suggestion of kc(Drug) by dragging this knowledge chunk into the editing area. In this case, the axioms of kc(drug) are appended to the axioms of the concept draft Antimalarial Drug and the expert user can choose to partially reuse the suggestion by removing those axioms that are considered as inappropriate and by modifying those terms that are considered as non-satisfactory. In particular, the axioms Drug is something that hasIngredient a Chemical and Drug is something that hasIngredient a Active

Ingredient are reused, while the axiom Drug is a Pharmaceutical Preparation is dropped. Moreover, the term Drug is manually replace by the tag Antimalarial Drug. Thus, the concept draft is finally composed by the following axioms:

Antimalarial Drug is a Medicine
Antimalarial Drug is something that treats a Malaria
Antimalarial Drug is something that hasIngredient a Chemical
Antimalarial Drug is something that hasIngredient a Active Ingredient

At the same time, the linguistic matching techniques of HMatch 2.0 are invoked to compare the terms in the concept draft against the tags of the tag cloud TC(coi$_1$). Since the term Medicine matches the tag Drug $\in$ TC(coi$_1$) and since Drug has a high popularity in coi$_1$ (i.e., frequency = 3), the replacement of the term Medicine with the tag Drug in proposed in the editing area (see the terminological suggestions in Figure 3). Such a suggestion can be accepted or rejected by the expert user according to its terminological preferences and to the frequency of the proposed tags.

RELATED WORK

In the field of open distributed systems, like P2P and Grid, work related to CoI formation and management is mainly concerned with semantics-based P2P systems, with particular focus on those systems where the notion of peer community is explicitly supported. In this context, some interesting approaches have been emerging in the recent years. For example, in Khambatti, Ryu, and Dasgupta (2002), *escalation techniques* are employed to advertise within the network the peer interests expressed through attributes (i.e., keywords) and to allow the receiving nodes to detect the existence of common interest and thus communities. A similar approach is proposed in

Figure 3. The knowledge design environment of iCoord

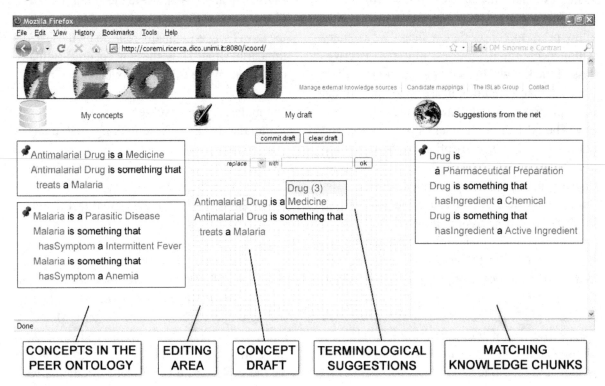

Das et al. (2009) where the advertisement phase of peer interests is used by the network nodes to build routing indexes that are subsequently exploited in the search phase to improve the efficiency of query propagation.

In Liu, Bhaduri, Das, Nguyen, and Kargupta (2006), a statistical mechanism based on the *quantile* measure is used to evaluate the similarity among the advertised peer interests. In the proposed approach, a peer can decide to promote the formation of a new community according to the level of similarity between its own interests and the received advertisements. An invitation procedure is then enforced by the community creator to initiate and supervise the concrete formation of the group. Peer interests can be inferred through mining techniques as proposed in Gu and Wei (2006). In that work, each community is defined as a vector of topics and it is assigned to a community manager which has the role of periodically

advertising the community topics. The main limit of this kind of approaches is the traffic overhead due to community advertisement.

To overcome such a restriction, the use of a shared and centralized taxonomy of community topics is usually enforced. The list of communities is thus prefixed and a peer can choose one or more preferred communities to join by simply matching its interests with the centralized topics taxonomy. In Crespo and Garcia-Molina (2004), communities are clusters of similar peers whose contents are classified according to a predefined classification hierarchy (i.e., a tree of concepts). Keyword-based matching techniques are used by peers to determine the clusters to join. In most of these examples, both peer interests and community topics are expressed as keywords and basic string matching techniques are exploited in the community formation process to enable peers to choose the most interesting communities to join.

The use of Semantic Web technologies (i.e., ontologies and ontology-based matching techniques) has being recently exploited to provide a semantically rich representation of peer interests and/or community descriptions and to support similarity-based query/answer mechanisms. In Bloehdorn et al. (2005), ontologies are used for representing both the shared conceptualization of the allowed community topics and the expertise of each system node. The use of a shared ontology is enforced also in Wang and Vassileva (2004) where the notions of team, coalition, and congregation are proposed to distinguish among three different levels of cohesion when creating a peer community. However, methods and techniques for enabling peers to perform a coordinated exploitation of the collective knowledge/intelligence of a community are only marginally considered in the current literature.

In Aiello and Alessi (2007), the notion of collective knowledge is introduced to denote the knowledge fragments about a certain concept of interest that are interlinked across different nodes. In other approaches like Sigurbjörnsson and van Zwol (2008), collective knowledge is defined to support recommendation systems for multimedia resource annotation. The idea is that the system suggests the tags to use for annotation by analyzing statistics on tag co-occurrence derived from the experience of other users. As a general remark, we observe that all the considered systems deal (at different levels) with the notion of collective semantics, and they propose their own idea of "Social Network Analysis" aimed at enforcing effective knowledge retrieval (Avrithis et al., 2008).

Original contribution. The goal of our approach is to go beyond the existing state-of-the-art solutions for P2P community formation and management by adopting an unsupervised approach where the choice of joining/leaving a community is autonomously taken by each interested peer according to its own preferences. Moreover, the use of Semantic Web technologies

like ontologies and ontology-based matching techniques allows to enforce a semantically rich approach to community and peer content description thus overcoming the need of a centralized/shared taxonomy. Furthermore, the collective construction of a community manifesto with a shared, preference-based vocabulary within a CoI represents a concrete attempt to combine the benefits of recently emerging social-based approaches with more consolidated P2P and Semantic Web technologies (Gruber, 2008).

CONCLUSION

In this paper, we presented a reference P2P architecture based on autonomous, self-emerging semantic communities of interest (CoIs) for collective intelligence creation and management. Techniques for enabling a group of independent peers to autonomously define their shared community vocabulary have been also discussed. We believe that the collective intelligence of a CoI expressed in the form of an ontology-based community manifesto can play an important role for the development of more effective P2P collaboration platforms. The iCoord system and the e-health example presented in the paper provide a significant result in this direction.

Currently, a prototype version of iCoord has been developed and it is available online as a web application (The iCoord System, 2008). Furthermore, experiments to evaluate the size of a community manifesto and associated vocabulary in real collaboration scenarios are being implemented. In particular, tests on the convergence issues of the community manifestos are being considered. In future work, we plan to investigate semantic clustering techniques based on the linguistic matching techniques of HMatch 2.0 for improving the organization of the vocabulary of a CoI by grouping tags that are semantically related.

REFERENCES

Aiello, G., & Alessi, M. (2007). DNK-WSD: a Distributed Approach for Knowledge Discovery in Peer to Peer Networks. In *Proceedings of the 15th EUROMICRO International Conference on Parallel, Distributed and Network-Based Processing (PDP '07)*, Naples, Italy (pp. 325-332).

Alani, H., Dasmahapatra, S., O'Hara, K., & Shadbolt, N. (2003). Identifying Communities of Practice through Ontology Network Analysis. *IEEE Intelligent Systems*, *18*(2), 18–25. doi:10.1109/MIS.2003.1193653

Aleman-Meza, B., Halaschek-Wiener, C., & Arpinar, I. B. (2005). Collective Knowledge Composition in a P2P Network. In L. C. Rivero, J. H. Doorn, & V. E. Ferraggine (Eds.), *Encyclopedia of Database Technologies and Applications* (pp. 74-77). Hershey, PA: IGI Global.

Androutsellis-Theotokis, S., & Spinellis, D. (2004). A Survey of Peer-to-Peer Content Distribution Technologies. *ACM Computing Surveys*, *36*(4), 335–371. doi:10.1145/1041680.1041681

Avrithis, Y., Kompatsiaris, Y., Staab, S., & Vakali, A. (Eds.). (2008). *Proceedings of the CISWeb (Collective Semantics: Collective Intelligence and the Semantic Web) Workshop, located at the 5th European Semantic Web Conference (ESWC 2008)*, Tenerife, Spain.

Bloehdorn, S., Haase, P., Hefke, M., Sure, Y., & Tempich, C. (2005). Intelligent Community Lifecycle Support. In *Proceedings of the 5th International Conference on Knowledge Management (I-KNOW 05)*, Graz, Austria.

Castano, S., Ferrara, A., Lorusso, D., & Montanelli, S. (2008). Ontology Coordination: The iCoord Project Demonstration. In *Proceedings of the 27th International Conference on Conceptual Modeling (ER 2008)*, Barcelona, Spain (pp. 512-513).

Castano, S., Ferrara, A., & Montanelli, S. (2006). Matching Ontologies in Open Networked Systems: Techniques and Applications. *Journal on Data Semantics*, *5*, 25–63. doi:10.1007/11617808_2

Castano, S., Ferrara, A., & Montanelli, S. (2009). The iCoord Knowledge Model for P2P Semantic Coordination. In *Proceedings of the 6th Conference of the Italian Chapter of AIS*, Costa Smeralda (Nu), Italy.

Castano, S., & Montanelli, S. (2005). Semantic Self-Formation of Communities of Peers. In *Proceedings of the ESWC Workshop on Ontologies in Peer-to-Peer Communities*, Heraklion, Greece.

Crespo, A., & Garcia-Molina, H. (2004). Semantic Overlay Networks for P2P Systems. In *Proceedings of the 3rd International Workshop on Agents and Peer-to-Peer Computing (P2PC 2004)*, New York (pp. 1-13).

Das, T., Nandi, S., & Ganguly, N. (2009). Community Formation and Search in P2P: A Robust and Self-Adjusting Algorithm. In *Proceedings of the 3rd Workshop on Intelligent Networks: Adaptation, Communication & Reconfiguration (IAMCOM 2009)*, Bangalore, India.

Davies, J., Duke, A., & Sure, Y. (2004). OntoShare - An Ontology-based Knowledge Sharing System for virtual Communities of Practice. *The Journal of Universal Computer Science*, *10*(3), 262–283.

Ferrara, A., Montanelli, S., Varese, G., & Castano, S. (2009). *Natural Language Ontology Authoring in iCoord. International Journal of Information Technology and Database Systems*. IJITDAS.

Gruber, T. (2008). Collective Knowledge Systems: where the Social Web meets the Semantic Web. *Journal of Web Semantics*, *6*(1), 4–13.

Gu, W., & Wei, W. (2006). Automatic Community Discovery in Peer-to-Peer Systems. In *Proceedings of the 5th International Conference on Grid and Cooperative Computing Workshops (GCC 2006)*, Changsha, Hunan, China (pp. 110-116).

Halevy, A., Ives, Z., Madhavan, J., Mork, P., Suciu, D., & Tatarinov, I. (2004). The Piazza Peer Data Management System. *IEEE Transactions on Knowledge and Data Engineering, 16*(7), 787–798. doi:10.1109/TKDE.2004.1318562

Hose, K., Roth, A., Zeitz, A., Sattler, K.-U., & Naumann, F. (2008). A Research Agenda for Query Processing in Large-Scale Peer Data Management Systems. *Information Systems, 33*(7-8), 597–610. doi:10.1016/j.is.2008.01.012

Khambatti, M., Ryu, K. D., & Dasgupta, P. (2002). Efficient Discovery of Implicitly Formed Peer-to-Peer Communities. *International Journal of Parallel and Distributed Systems and Networks, 5*(4), 155–164.

Liu, K., Bhaduri, K., Das, K., Nguyen, P., & Kargupta, H. (2006). Client-side Web Mining for Community Formation in Peer-to-Peer Environments. *SIGKDD Explorations, 8*(2), 11–20. doi:10.1145/1233321.1233323

Montanelli, S., & Castano, S. (2008). Semantically Routing Queries in Peer-based Systems: the H-Link Approach. *The Knowledge Engineering Review, 23*(1), 51–72. doi:10.1017/S0269888907001257

Ozsu, M. T., & Valduriez, P. (1999). *Principles of Distributed Database Systems* (2nd ed.). Upper Saddle River, NJ: Prentice Hall.

Ren, Z., Anumba, C. J., & Ugwu, O. O. (2002). Negotiation in a Multi-Agent System for Construction Claims Negotiation. *Applied Artificial Intelligence, 16*(5), 359–394. doi:10.1080/08839510290030273

Seely-Brown, J., & Duguid, P. (1991). Organisational Learning and Communities of Practice. *Organization Science, 2*(1).

Sigurbjörnsson, B., & Van Zwol, R. (2008). Flickr Tag Recommendation based on Collective Knowledge. In *Proceedings of the 17th International Conference on World Wide Web (WWW 2008)*, Beijing, China (pp. 327-336).

Spaniol, M., & Klamma, R. (2004). Mediating Ontologies for Communities of Practice. In *Proceedings of the 5th International Conference on Practical Aspects of Knowledge Management (PAKM 2004)*, Vienna, Austria (pp. 330-342).

The Gnutella Protocol. (2001). *The Gnutella Protocol Specification v0.4*. Retrieved from http://www9.limewire.com/developer/gnutella_protocol_0.4.pdf

The iCoord System. (2008). *The ISLab Knowledge Coordination Platform*. Retrieved from http://islab.dico.unimi.it/icoord/

Voulgaris, S., Gavidia, D., & Van Steen, M. (2005). CYCLON: Inexpensive Membership Management for Unstructured P2P Overlays. *Journal of Network and Systems Management, 13*(2), 197–217. doi:10.1007/s10922-005-4441-x

Wang, Y., & Vassileva, J. (2004). Trust-Based Community Formation in Peer-to-Peer File Sharing Networks. In *Proceedings of the IEEE/WIC/ACM International Conference on Web Intelligence (WI'04)*, Beijing, China (pp. 341-348).

ENDNOTES

[1]   http://islab.dico.unimi.it/content/oaei2009/
[2]   http://www.boemie.org
[3]   http://pellet.owldl.com

APPENDIX

A summary table of the notations adopted in the paper is provided in Table 10.

Notation	Description
coi	Semantic Community of Interest
P_i	i[th] peer of the network
$PO(P_i)$	Peer ontology of the peer P_i
N	Set of element names in $PO(P_i)$
P	Set of property/relation names in $PO(P_i)$
L	Set of datatypes and literal values in $PO(P_i)$
$KC(P_i)$	Set of knowledge chunks of the peer P_i
e	Element (concept or instance) of $PO(P_i)$
$kc(e)$	Knowledge chunk of the element e
a_i	i[th] axiom of a knowledge chunk
$n(kc)$	Name of the knowledge chunk kc
$r(a_i)$	Semantic relation of the axiom a_i
$v(a_i)$	Relation value of the axiom a_i
$E(kc(e))$	Terminological equipment of $kc(e)$
$TS(kc(e))$	Timestamp of the last change-log on $kc(e)$
$m(coi)$	Manifesto of the community *coi*
$KC(coi)$	Set of knowledge chunks of the community *coi*
$E(KC(coi))$	Set of terminological equipments of the community *coi*
$TC(coi)$	Tag cloud of the community *coi*
$CP(coi)$	Peers contributing to the manifesto of the community *coi*
t_i	i[th] tag in a tag cloud
$ID(P_i)$	Identifier of the peer P_i
$TS(P_i)$	Timestamp of the last update on a community manifesto performed by the peer P_i
$v_i(m(coi))$	i[th] version of the community manifesto for the community *coi*
$LA(kc',kc'')$	Linguistic Affinity value between kc' *and* kc''
$CA(kc',kc'')$	Contextual Affinity value between kc' *and* kc''
$SA(kc',kc'')$	Semantic Affinity value between kc' *and* kc''
W_{LA}	Weight of the linguistic affinity in the computation of $SA(kc',kc'')$
$MAP(P_i,coi)$	Set of similarity mappings between the knowledge chunks in $KC(P_i)$ and the knowledge chunks in $KC(coi)$
$T_{new}(coi)$	Set of new tags to insert in the tag cloud of the community *coi*
pq	Probe query
$T_{hint}(coi)$	Set of tags belonging to the tag cloud of the community *coi* that are exploited as suggestions during editing of a concept draft

Table 2. Notation summary

This work was previously published in International Journal of Organizational and Collective Intelligence, Volume 1, Issue 4, edited by Hideyasu Sasaki, pp. 40-60, copyright 2010 by IGI Publishing (an imprint of IGI Global).

Chapter 18
3D Real-Time Reconstruction Approach for Multimedia Sensor Networks

Ahmed Mostefaoui
University of Franche-Comte (LIFC), France

Benoit Piranda
LASELDI, France

ABSTRACT

Multimedia sensor networks have emerged due to the tremendous technological advances in multimedia hardware miniaturization and the application potential they present. However, the time sensitive nature of multimedia data makes them very problematic to handle, especially within constrained environments. In this paper, the authors present a novel approach based on continuous 3D real time reconstruction of the monitored area dedicated for video surveillance applications. Real-time 3D reconstruction allows an important network bandwidth reduction in context to sensor nodes sending descriptive information to the fusion server instead heavy video streams. Each node has to support additional processing in order to extract this descriptive information in real-time, which results in video sensors capturing tasks, data analysis, and extraction of features needed for 3D reconstruction. In this paper, the authors focus on the design and implementation of such sensor node and validate their approach through real experimentations conducted on a real video sensor.

INTRODUCTION

Nowadays, Wireless Sensor Networks (WSN) have emerged as one of the most promising technologies (Akyildiz, Su, Sankarasubramniam, & Cayirci, 2002) by reason of the huge potential

DOI: 10.4018/978-1-4666-1577-9.ch018

they represent in several real-world applications, ranging from health care applications to military (surveillance) applications. In fact, recent advances mainly in miniaturised hardware components, radio frequency communication technologies and low power embedded computing devises have made large scale networks of small devises a reality. In such networks, each node is able to collect information from physical environment (such as temperature, humidity, etc.), to perform simple processing tasks on the collected data (averaging for instance) and finally to transmit it, through multi-hop radio communications, to a remote base station (sink) for data fusion. Nevertheless, managing sensor networks poses a number of new challenging research issues especially because of their restricted capabilities (computing, storage, etc.) on one hand and their limited lifetime, as nodes are driven by batteries on the other hand. In addition, nodes are usually subject to frequent failures. Even though these limitations, wireless sensor networks are nowadays present in several applications that are delay tolerant and have low bandwidth requirements.

More recently, the availability of new miniaturized multimedia hardware (CMOS cameras and microphones for instance) at reasonable prices has encouraged the emergence of Wireless Multimedia Sensor Networks (WMSN (Akyildiz, Melodia, & Chowdhury, 2007)) for a large number of real applications (home automation, assistance to senior people, etc.). What differs WSMN from classical sensor network is their ability to collect multimedia content (video and audio streams, still images, etc.) in addition to scalar data.

It is obvious that the management of multimedia data (storing, retrieving, processing in real-time, fusing and correlating, etc.) within limited environments as those of sensor networks poses new issues at all levels of the applications because of the huge volume of the produced data (the size of videos or images is far away much more important than the one of scalar data) on one hand and on the other hand of the "continuous constraint", also called real-time constraint, related to multimedia data i.e., their delivery is time sensitive. It is obvious that the management and the delivery of multimedia data require much more resources in terms of processing power as well as network resources, mainly bandwidth. Furthermore, the process of multimedia data correlation and fusion differs fundamentally from that of scalar data in

the sense that the latter is primarily concerned with average computing while the first is much more complex: what does the fusion of two images or two videos mean? To the best of our knowledge, no general approach is actually available but only some specific approaches tailored for specific contexts as the one reported in Zhang (2007).

In this paper, we develop a new approach to handle the huge and voluminous multimedia sensor data generated in a video surveillance context. The key idea behind our proposition is to "continuously" construct a 3D representation of the monitored area, in which video streams originating from the video sensors are fused. In other words, the "views" of the sensor nodes are merged in the 3D scene of the monitored region. This approach presents many interesting advantages, in particular for resources limited environments like those of sensor networks.

The first important advantage of using 3D representation is its flexibility in the sense that it allows a comprehensive representation of the observed scene. In fact, it is commonly known that exploiting directly raw video data is very hard or even not possible if it is not pre-processed or annotated by experts/annotators (Mostefaoui, 2006). Moreover, it is not obvious to get comprehensive information from tens or hundreds of simultaneously delivered streams, unless focusing only on one or two streams at once. On the opposite, the 3D scene can deliver more comprehensive information to the observer, in particular if the concern is the surveillance purposes. Also, it is easier to track "objects" in 3D environment than on tens or hundreds of monitors!

Another advantage of 3D reconstruction is its ability to answer some spatio-temporal requests that are very hard to handle with raw video data. To illustrate, let's consider the example of supermarkets in which managers are interested to know the impact of some new department dispositions on the behaviour of customers i.e., measuring the average waiting time of customers at the fish department for example. Unless "manually" measuring customers waiting times through using traditional video surveillance system, no automatic approach is conceivable to answer such queries. However, it is relatively easier to handle such queries in a system based on 3D reconstruction even though its precision is approximate (the application does not require person recognition). Moreover 3D reconstruction allows some "angles of views" of the monitored scene that raw data sensor cannot offer (see our practical example presented in Figure 9).

In our 3D reconstruction system, each node performs two main tasks: (a) data extraction (processing phase) during which the node analyses the captured stream and extracts the required information necessary for the 3D reconstruction. (b) Instead of sending captured stream, the node sends only the extracted information to the fusion server which in turn reconstructs the 3D view of the monitored area. By doing so, an important network bandwidth reduction is achieved, which constitutes an important requirement for the system scalability. It has to be noted that in our approach, it is possible, upon the request from the observer/manager, that one node sends the entire video stream in case that complementary information is needed.

Nevertheless, the 3D reconstruction process poses some challenges and requirements that are not easy to handle. Among those requirements, we cite scene calibration. Its main objective is to associate a referential to the captured scene in a way that it will be possible to extrapolate 3D information from 2D data, sent by the video sensors. To this end, a manual calibration, through a software tool that we developed is needed after sensors deployment. At first sight, this manual intervention could be seen as a limitation for the use of our system. But we recall that our target applications are video surveillance as mentioned earlier. Hence, calibrating at once all the video sensors during the initialization phase, which is anyway necessary, will not, in our opinion, constitute a real limitation compared to other multimedia

features like mobility (changing of angle of view) or zooming. Likewise, the availability of a priori the 3D model of the observed area (in general a building) could also be seen as a constrained requirement. But, nowadays, this information is almost available since the majority of building architects make use of 3D technology. Then, we just have to deal with format compatibility.

Our main concern in this paper is to answer the following questions: first what kind of data extraction the node has to perform in order to ensure 3D real-time reconstruction by the fusion server? And more importantly is the sensor node able to handle such processing tasks? We focus on the development of such a sensor node by adopting real configuration and measuring its performance.

The rest of the paper is organised as follow: related work is presented along with details of our proposed architecture. Next, we present the processing tasks that the sensor node has to perform. Finally, we summarize our preliminary experimental results followed by a conclusion.

RELATED WORKS

As an emerging research domain, wireless multimedia sensor networks present interesting research challenges, especially due to the several constraints that they impose. In Rahimi et al. (2005) and Gay et al. (2003), the authors present the Cyclops image capturing and inference module. The latter has been designed for light-weight imaging and can be easily interfaced with other sensor nodes like Crossbow MICA2 Mote Specification (n.d.). Other research works tackled the problem of developing multimedia capturing devices with the associated processing tasks (Downes, Rad, & Aghajan, 2006). They pointed out that using 32 bits processors is more convenient for this purpose than 8 bits processors. This conclusion has also been confirmed in terms of energy consummation by the work presented in Canny (1983).

On the other hand, other research works focused on the development of compression schemes, especially tailored for WMSN (Chiasserini & Magli, 2002; Feng, Code, Kaiser, Shea, & Feng, 2003; Gerla & Xu, 2003; Magli, Mancin, & Merello, 2003; Pekhteryev, Sahinoglu, Orlik, & Bhatti, 2005). The common point between those works is that they are founded on JPEG 2000 compression scheme. In those works, instead of sending an entire video stream, they just send periodically images telling the fusion server what changes have been occurred in the observed area. Hence an important network bandwidth reduction is achieved.

Other works have addressed the network delivery issue with the associated quality of service requirement. Propositions have been made at the MAC level (Adamou, Lee, & Shin, 2002; Rajendran, Obraczka, & Garcia-Luna-Aceves, 2003) and at the network level (Akkaya & Younis, 2003; Deb, Bhatnagar, & Nath, 2003; Felemban, Lee, Ekici, Boder, & Vural, 2005; He, Stankovic, Chenyang, & Abdelzaher, 2003). The objective remains to guarantee a certain quality of service by respecting the "real-time" constraint of the continuous data.

Experimental experiences have also been conducted, mainly in the development of video sensor networks (Chu, Reich, & Zhao, 2004; Kulkarni, Ganesan, Shenoy, & Lu, 2005; Feng, Code, Kaiser, Shea, & Feng, 2003). For instance, in *Panoptes* (Feng, Code, Kaiser, Shea, & Feng, 2003) platform, PDAs with 64 MB of RAM equipped with video capture device have been used. The platform also includes spatial compression technique (but no temporal compression has been used) combined with distributed filters and video streams priority management.

Based on these works, we have in our approach right away made use of a 32 bits processor. We also note that we have not excluded the fact that the sensors could, in particular cases, send video data on demand to the fusion server instead of processing them. For instance, a trigger could be set in order to send native video stream when an object (generally a person) is located near or in front of or in a specified area. The objective is to get more detail on the moving person. In those cases, previously mentioned works, especially on compression schemes and delivery quality of service, could be integrated in our approach.

SYSTEM ARCHITECTURE

Figure 1 presents an overview of the proposed architecture. It is composed of three main elements named: the capture device, the fusion server and the end-user server. We detail the features of each component in the following sections.

The Capture Device

The capture device allows capturing and processing images in order to extract featuring data needed for real-time 3D reconstruction. We note that the number of sensors as well as their locations has a direct impact on the overall performance of the surveillance system.

The module « capture device » combines a digital camera with embedded software. The digital camera captures images that are processed by the program in order to "extract" featuring data (i.e., bounding boxes used later on for 3D reconstruction). These data describe under a compact form, the differences between the camera images and a referential image that corresponds to a "free" place, without moving objects (persons for instance). The goal of the pipeline of image processing tasks consists in sending only descriptive data instead of the captured images to the fusion server over the wireless network. The size of the generated data is very small compared to the size of the original digital image. Then in the "free" case where the captured image is similar to the referential image, no data are sent by the device. More precisely, when the program detects an object in the captured image, only a set of points representing the borders coordinates of the object, is sent. These data admit a small size compared to the original image size.

In order to compare the two approaches, in terms of reduction of the size of transmitted data, we present the following example: A video camera (640x480 pixels) sends a reference image which is compressed using the JPEG algorithm with 50% quality level, and has a size of 30 KB after compression. The same image is processed in order to extract the border as 38 segments. Each segment is stored in memory in 4 short integers (2 for each point of the segment), the total size is then 304 bytes! We hence obtain a ratio of about 1/100, which represents a substantial gain. But, we must remind that the price for this gain is the necessity of processing the video images at the sensor level (see next section).

The Fusion Server

The main functionality of the fusion server consists in merging information sent by the capture device in order to place the objects detected into the 3D environment.

The fusion server receives the bounding boxes coordinates extracted from all the sensors, these bounding boxes give the position of the main detected areas in the scene. This simple information seems to be insufficient to place objects in the 3D scene, but combining these 2D data with precise knowledge about the position and the direction of the sensors (early computed and recorded), allows the deduction of a probable position of the viewed object. Some simple geometrical rules may be applied to construct the extrapolation of 3D information from 2D segments data. For example, if we consider the simple hypothesis that a person viewed by the camera is standing on the floor, we can easily estimate its 3D position (cf., Figure 2).

However, it is possible to realize this processing only if the system associates a referential to the scene captured for each sensor. These referential may be computed once and for all by a

pseudo-automatic algorithm (cf., Figure 3) of camera calibration. The goal of this process is to precisely place the camera in the viewed scene by cliquing in well-known areas on the image. In the example shown in Figure 3, the colored circles represent the points placed by the user on the image. The coordinates of these points must be well-known on the scene. In our case, we use the corner of the walls as the origin of our referential and the axes defined by the intersections of walls and the floor as main axes. Moreover it is important to know the real distance between the points.

In the following calculations, we consider the digital camera as a perfect sensor. In practice, we apply a geometrical correction to the captured image in order to reduce the deformations produced by the lens.

The position of the 3D referential is obtained using a method similar to the one proposed by Hirokazu Kato and Mark Billinghurst (1999) for the placement of square marks. Considering O as the optical origin of the camera and that the rectangle ABCD (lengths l_{AB} and l_{AD} are known) is projected on the camera image, the points A' B' C' D' are the projected of ABCD (cf., Figure 4).

Considering that the two vectors AB and DC are equal, we can deduce:

$$V_1 = OB' \wedge OA', \; V_2 = OD' \wedge OC',$$
$$AB = DC = l_{AB} \frac{V_1 \wedge V_2}{\left\| V_1 \wedge V_2 \right\|} \tag{1}$$

Vector AD is obtained by the same way, and then we obtain the Z direction of our referential by:

$$Z = \frac{AB \wedge AD}{\left\| AB \wedge AD \right\|}$$

Now, we have to place one of the points of the ABCD rectangle in the 3D scene. To do that, we must calculate the distance between a point of the rectangle and the origin of the camera. We

Figure 1. System architecture

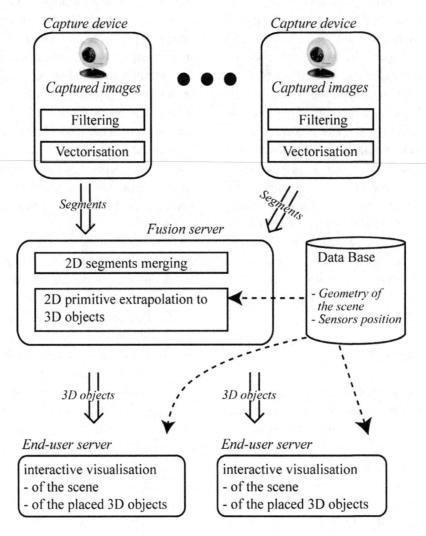

need complementary information as the angle (α) representing the camera's field of view:

$$d = \frac{1}{2\tan\left(\alpha/2\right)}$$

The following classic equation expresses the position of the projected A' of the point A in the camera referential. Figure 5 shows the principle of the projective camera i.e. the projection of a point A on the screen.

$$A' = \begin{pmatrix} d\,\dfrac{A_x}{A_z} \\ d\,\dfrac{A_x}{A_z} \\ d \end{pmatrix} \text{ and then } \begin{pmatrix} A_x = \dfrac{A'_x \times A_z}{d} \\ A_y = \dfrac{A'_z \times A_z}{d} \end{pmatrix} \quad (2)$$

The depth Z_A is calculated using that B' is both the projected of B and the projected of A+AB (AB obtained by equation 1):

Figure 2. Automatic placement of an object in the 3D scene

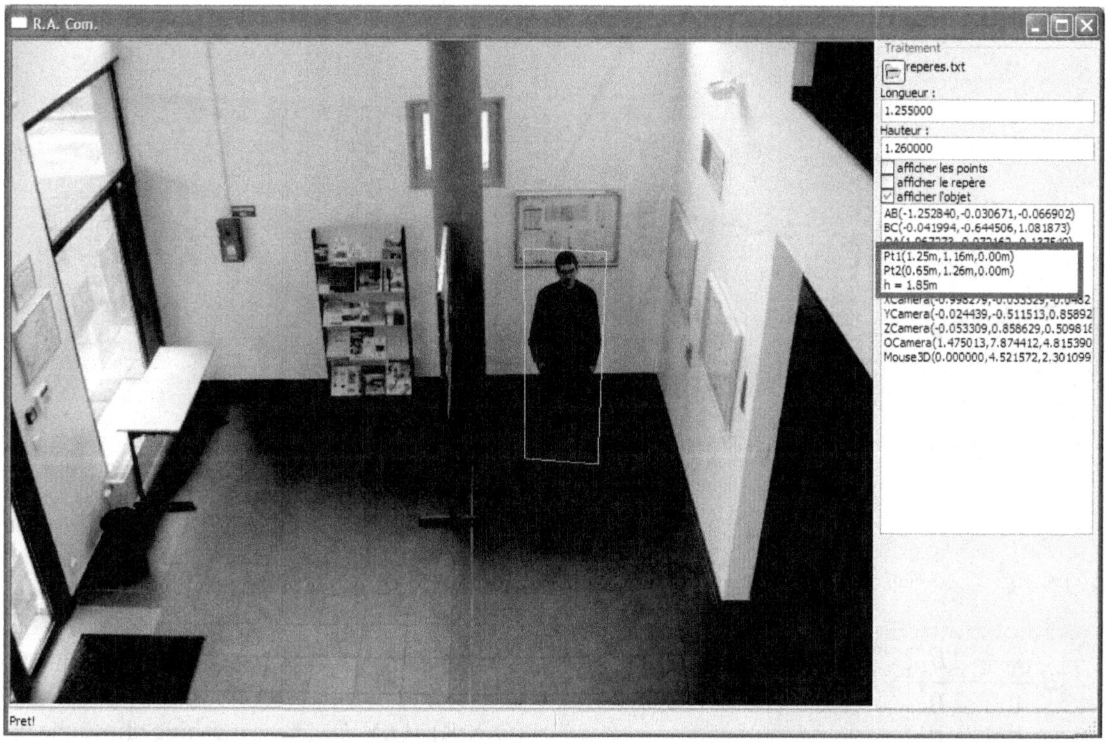

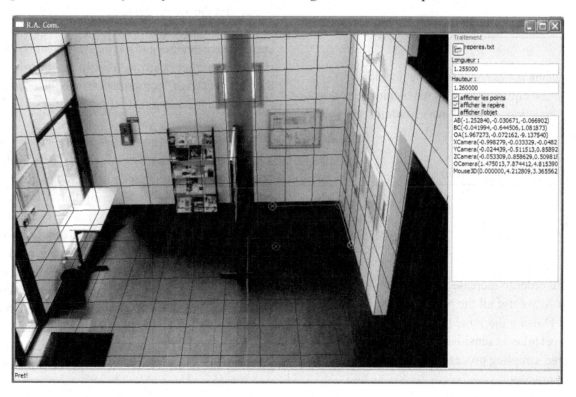

Figure 3. Placement of the referential in the scene using some well-known points

Figure 4. Projection schema

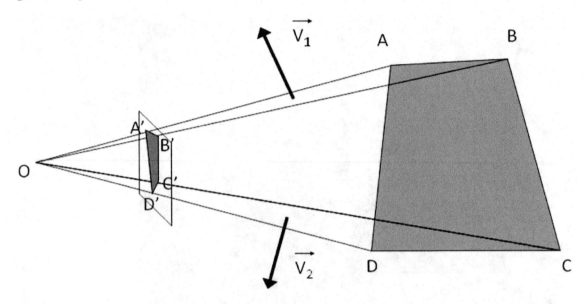

$$B' = \left| \begin{array}{c} d\,\dfrac{A_x + AB_x}{A_z + AB_z} \\[2ex] d\,\dfrac{A_y + AB_y}{A_z + AB_z} \\[2ex] d \end{array} \right| \qquad (3)$$

Using the expression of the position of A (eq. 2) in the equation (eq. 3), we obtain the following equations system, which admits only one unknown A_z:

$$\begin{cases} B_x = \dfrac{A'_x\,A_z + d \times AB_x}{A_z + AB_z} \\[3ex] B_z = \dfrac{A'_y\,A_z + d \times AB_y}{A_z + AB_z} \end{cases}$$

In order to increase the precision of the position A, we use all the projected points of A,B,C and D using the same method. The precision of the calculus is sensitive to the errors due to the image sampling process and the camera calibration process.

In Figure 3, we use the placement of the referential to show a meshing over each plane (O,X,Y), (O,X,Z), (O,Y,Z). These meshing allow checking the calibration quality.

When the geometric links between the captured image and the 3D model is defined, it is possible to compute the position of the 2D vectors sent by each capture devices and merge these positions to obtain an average position. It is exactly the role of the "fusion server" component which then sends the result of this merging to the "end-user server" as 3D primitives.

More precisely, when the fusion server receives a bounding box or a set of bounding boxes from one of the capture devices it calculates its 3D position in the scene considering that it lays on the floor as shown in Figure 6. For this end, we consider that the point of contact between the floor and the detected person corresponds to the middle of the box (point P' in Figure 6). The objective is then to calculate the corresponding 3D position P of the detected person within the 3D scene. As explained bellow, we calculate the intersection between a ray [OP') and the floor of the scene given by the plane (A,AB,AC). The viewing ray

Figure 5. Principle of projective camera

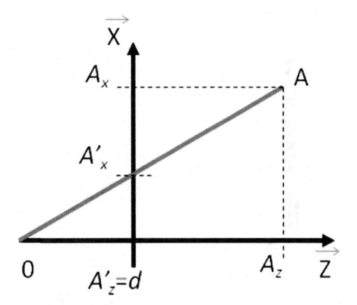

[OP') crosses the point of view O of the camera and the point P' in the image of the camera.

The point P is obtained by solving the following equations system:

$$\begin{cases} OP = kOP' \\ OP = OA + \lambda_1 AB + \lambda_2 AC \end{cases}$$

The coefficients k, λ_1, λ_2 are given by:

$$\begin{pmatrix} k \\ \lambda_1 \\ \lambda_2 \end{pmatrix} = \begin{pmatrix} OP' & AB & AC \end{pmatrix}^{-1} \times \begin{pmatrix} OA \end{pmatrix}$$

Then we obtain a 3D position of the detected person for every capture device. These positions are sent to the end-user server to associate an avatar.

Figure 7: 3D Reconstitutions of the scene by two different capture devices. Figure 7 shows an example of 3D placement of a person (shown in Figure 2) detected by two different capture devices. We can observe in the synthesis image the posi-

tion of the avatar represented by the colored axes placed on the scene by each capture device. Then we can notice the proximity of the localization by the two sensors, the small visible differences are mainly due to the captured images sampling. This difference could easily be handled by the end-user server.

The End-User Server

The end-user server proposes an interface representing in 3D the geometrical model of the filmed scene and the set of complementary data associated to the detected elements. To realize this interface, we used well known virtual reality software (e.g., Dassault System Virtools (3DS, n.d.)). The use of such software allows easy interactions in the 3D space in order to visualize the 3D model populated by the detected elements (images of people moving in the building for instance) placed in appropriate positions in the 3D map.

Figure 8 shows the same scene captured by the camera and computed in 3D under many points of view. The two first reconstructions (b) and (d) are shown with the corresponding real image (a) and

Figure 6. Intersection between a ray [OP') and the floor (A,AB,AC)

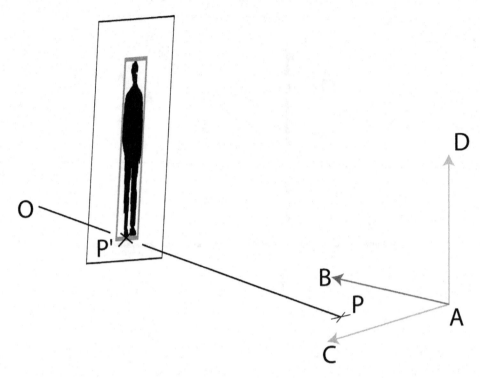

(c) captured by the camera to localize the person in the scene. These couples of images enable to verify the calculated position of the person for each source.

Figure 9 shows the 3D reconstruction proposed by the end-user server from two free positions of the camera chosen by the user.

Figure 10 shows recent works consisting in placing 3D avatars representing detected people in the scene. The server receives information about the position and the size of the detected person, so it places a generic avatar in the same place in the reconstructed environment and the size of the avatar is modulated by the detected size of the person.

3D CAPTURE DEVICE

In this section, we first detail the image processing tasks devolved to the sensor and then we discuss implementation problems over the platform.

Processing Tasks

The processing tasks running on the sensor have to extract geometrical primitives from the captured image. In this first version of the software, the primitives are only linear segments that allow the identification of all the linear part of the shapes in the image. The image treatment presented here has the merits to easily test our pipeline but lacks robustness, especially for light variation conditions. In order to reduce the processing time and the data sent by the sensor to the fusion server, the sensor now determines a box containing a set of 8-connex detected points. Many methods for primitive extraction from an image are available,

Figure 7. 3D Reconstitutions of the scene by two different capture devices

Figure 8. Real and 3D reconstruction version of the scene from the point of view of sensors

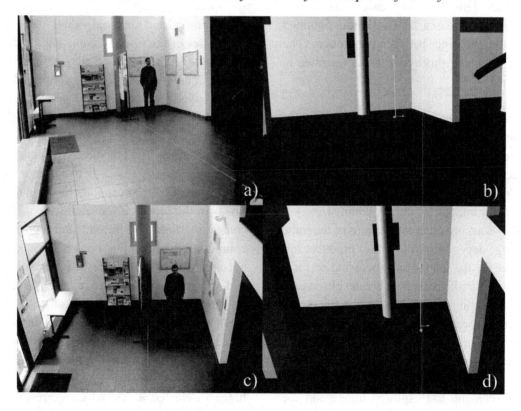

Figure 9. 3D Reconstitutions of the scene from a free point of view

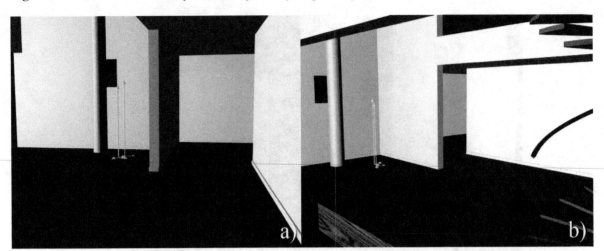

mainly using the detection of interest points, like Canny edge operator (Canny, 1983) or Harris corners detection (Harris & Stephens, 1998). These methods are very efficient and strong but not suitable in our real time case because of their complexity.

We study here a particular case of the vectorization in real time of a 2D area border obtained through the difference between two images. The pipeline of image processing tasks operates in three steps:

- The digital sensor which manages the capture of images as a matrix of pixels produces sampled data at about 30 images per second. These sensors may be remotely configured using many parameters (B&W or color images, saturation, contrast, etc.). It allows asking different versions of the same image depending if the sensor produces images for the automatic processing or for a visual identification by a human observer.
- The filtering module, applied on the sensor image, uses a pipeline of image processing tasks in order to extract the borders of detected elements. The first step (cf., Figure 11 a) consists in computing the difference between the last captured image and the

reference one. More precisely this resulting image is compared to a threshold in order to produce an image only composed of white pixels (value 1) representing the detected objet over a black background (value 0).

- The next step consists in calculating the minimal and maximal values of the coordinates of the pixels composing the detected area. So the proposed algorithm is an adaptation of the classical algorithm of flood fill applied to a 4-connected pixels area. Here after, we present this algorithm:

The complexity of the first step (consisting in computing the difference between two images) is $O(n)$ where n corresponds to the number of pixels of the image. It represents the more CPU consuming task. The second step (consisting in computing the bounding box) is linear on $O(n)$, but only read data in memory (the color of pixels), and only m pixels color are rewritten where m is the number of white pixels ($m \ll n$).

In order to delete the very small areas generated by the difference step, we count the number of white pixels contained in the area, during the computation of the bounding box. Then only the biggest detected areas, which correspond to a

Figure 10. Placing 3D avatar of the detected person in the scene

true existing object in the scene, are sent to the fusion server. This treatment is calibrated in order to delete the isolated points or very small details but keeps the small areas like the mask of the feet in Figure 11 b.

The coordinates of the bounding boxes are sent to the fusion-server. In the most general case, a detected person is represented by only one set of connected pixels, but lighting and color context may produce many separated areas for one person as shown in Figure 11 for disconnected legs for instance. In this case, the fusion server detects that all the three boxes belong to the same object (person). Actually we have used a straightforward approach that groups small boxes with the biggest ones. We recognize the limit of such naïve approach and this important issue requires much deep investigation that we plan to conduct in future works.

Current Material Configuration

In Downes et al. (2006) present a study about image sensors developments. They show that using a 32 bits processor is more recommended than 8 bits processor for image processing tasks. For example, the time processing for an image convolution task is 16 times longer using a 8 bits processor (ATMEL ATmega128, at 4 Mhz) than using 32 bits processor (ARM7, at 48Mhz), while the energetic consumption is only 6 times higher.

In our experimentations, presented in the following section, we use a small Fox Board card (small computer: 66x72mm, 37gr) from ACME Systems (Acmesystems, n.d.). The main feature of this card is that it includes open source codes and allows many hardware interfaces with other multimedia devices *via* USB ports. Moreover the performance/price rate is very attractive (about 180€ for the entire capture module).

The Fox Board card is an embedded system, with an ETRAX 100LX processor (100MIPS, 32 bit, RISC, 100 MHz) and 16/32 MB of RAM

Algorithm 1.

1. Find the first white pixel.
2. If a white pixel A exists then push (A).
3. Init(xmin,ymin,xmax,ymax)
4. While (! Stack empty)
5. { pop(A0);
6. Update(ymin,ymax);
7. A= right pixel(A0);
8. while (Pixel($A_{x,y}$) is white)
9. { update (xmax);
10. if (Pixel($A_{x,y-1}$) is white and Pixel($A_{x+1,y-1}$) is black) then push($A_{x,y-1}$)
11. if (Pixel($A_{x,y+1}$) is white and Pixel($A_{x+1,y+1}$) is black) then push($A_{x,y+1}$)
12. Set A as grey
13. A = right pixel(A)
14. }
15. A= left pixel(A0);
16. while (Pixel($A_{x,y}$) is white)
17. { update (xmin);
18. if (Pixel($A_{x,y-1}$) is white and Pixel($A_{x+1,y-1}$) is black) then push($A_{x,y-1}$)
19. if (Pixel($A_{x,y+1}$) is white and Pixel($A_{x+1,y+1}$) is black) then push($A_{x,y+1}$)
20. Set A as grey
21. A = left pixel(A)
22. }
23. }
24. Send(xmin,ymin,xmax,ymax)

Figure 11. pipeline of the image processing

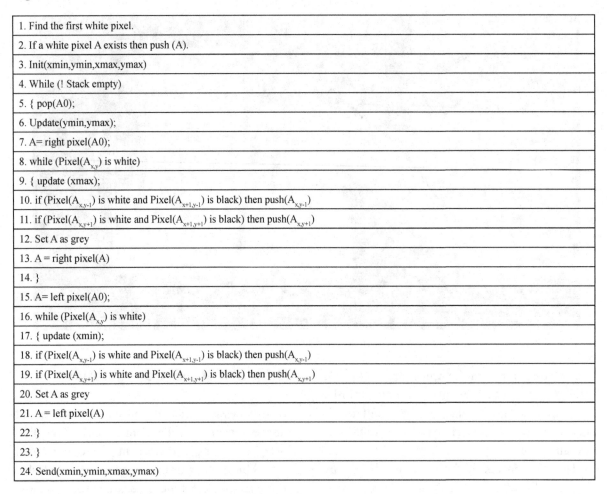

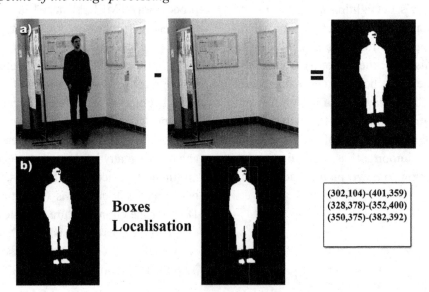

(cf. Figure 12). A native web server running on the card allows an easy integration of it in our network. Our FoxBoard card is connected to a Labtec Pro webcam and a WIFI adapter via the two USB 1.1 connectors. We develop our real time code in C under Linux.

PRELIMINARY EXPERIMENTAL RESULTS

In our experiments, we mainly focused on the performance of our capture device. More specifically, we were interested in answering the following question: is the material configuration we adopted able to support both data acquisition and features extraction for 3D real-time reconstruction?

We characterized the performance of the capture device by varying the size of the captured images and measuring the processing time accordingly. The same couple of images (presented in Figure 2 and Figure 3) are used at different resolutions. The program returns 3 pertinent bounding boxes for these examples at each resolution.

We evaluated our program on a recent Fox Board with 32MB of flash memory. The results are plotted in Figure 13.

As expected, we observed that the processing time increases proportionally to the size of the captured images. Hence, for low resolution videos (320x240), we have obtained 27 processed images per second which means that the processing time has no negative effects on the produced streams. However, with higher resolutions the capture device was not able to satisfy the real-time constraint (e.g., 25 images/s). For example, the sensor node was able to process 2 images per second when their size was 640x480. This result

Figure 12. our Fox Board capture device

Figure 13. Capture device performances on a Fox Board card with 32 MB flash memory

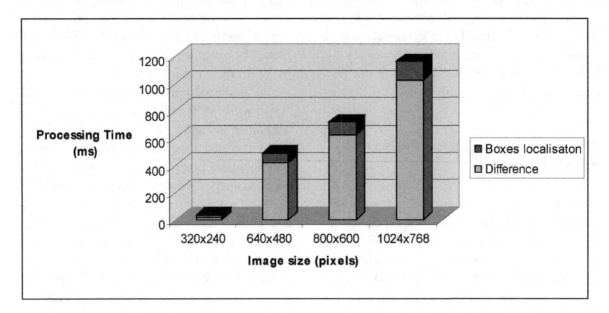

has to be interpreted in the context of a video surveillance application where the main objective is to report the movement of persons in the 3D animated scene. We believe that 2 updated values per second on their position are sufficient.

We also plotted in Figure 13 the processing time of each task. We observed, as expected, that the difference is the greedily task by reason of its intensive memory access. However, memory access is very "expensive" in terms of access time on the used Fox Board because it uses flash memory. Hence, memory access time overlaps the processing time. This is not the case for boxes localization task since it does not require much memory access. To verify this point, we have used instead of the Fox board an Asus EeePC 901, equipped with Intel Atom processor (1,6 GHz) and 1 GB of memory. The obtained results are plotted in Figure 12. These results confirmed the expected difference between "Difference task" and "boxes localization task". The latter remains the less time processing consumption task but the ratio is not the same as previously with the Fox Board. We also noted that the capture devise could

easily handle the real-time constraint since it can support the processing of 52 images/second for images of 1024x768 (Figure 14).

With regard to these obtained results, we can deduce that the overall performances of the capture device can easily fulfill the target application requirements, namely video surveillance. Furthermore, as presented in the introduction section, we have also designed our architecture to handle some special situations in which more precision is needed (for instance to get details about an event). For this purpose, we have included a service that could be requested from any video sensor to deliver the captured video stream to the server instead of sending only extracted features. By doing so, our architecture is able to respond efficiently to some emergency situations (intrusion for example).

Finally, we believe that our approach presents an acceptable compromise between system resources optimization, mainly network bandwidth and the target application requirements (precision).

Figure 14. Capture device performances on a EeePC

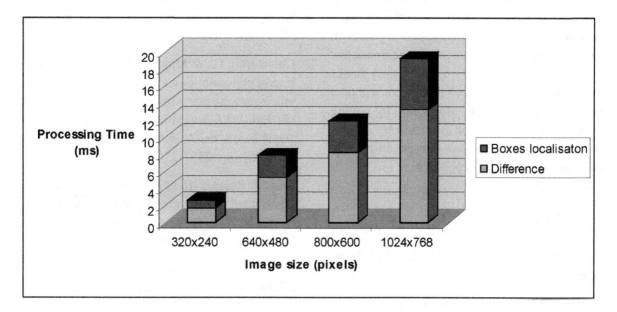

CONCLUSION AND FUTURE WORKS

Wireless multimedia sensor network is an emerging domain that poses a number of challenges, all the more multimedia data are resources consuming. In this paper, we presented the design and the preliminary performance of our system, especially tailored for video surveillance application. The main concerns that have guided our proposal are system resources optimization, particularly network bandwidth and allowing comprehensive video data fusion/exploitation. Our founding idea was real-time 3D reconstruction of the observed scene. While this architecture presents several advantages (as noted previously), it requires however that sensor nodes perform some additional tasks in addition to the capturing tasks.

In this paper, we particularly focused on this point by implementing and testing a real capture device. The latter uses two versions of the Fox Board card (66x72mm, 37gr, 16MB/32MB) interfaced with a webcam and a wifi USB key. The experiments we conducted show that the proposed capture device can easily fulfill the target appli-

cation requirements provided that low/medium resolution videos are used.

This important result stimulates us to continue our work into two main directions: (a) first, we plan to use another material (e.g., Stargate Board (Xbow, n.d.) equipped with PXA-255 XScale 400 MHZ RISC processor) to implement our capture device. We expect better performances than Fox Board. (b) Second, we plan to validate our proposal by deeply studying the fusion server and the end-user server from two points of views: performance point of view in order to support the important workload generated by an important number of sensor nodes and exploitation point of view throughout the development of intuitive and interactive tools dedicated to data exploitation.

Another important issue we want to address in future work concerns the study of new spatio-temporal data models in order to efficiently exploit the huge data volume produced over time in our system. More precisely, we want to integrate other information sources such as badges in a building or RFID identification to enhance person identification as we are concerned by video surveillance system. For example, if the system detects the presence of a person in the building without "knowing" his/her identity. If after a while, this detected person makes use of his/her badge or passes in front of an automatic face recognition camera, his/her identity is then known by the system thanks to this new "sensors". Then the system will then be able to integrate this information by putting backwards this identity on the "itinerary" of this person. The challenge here consists in making this step as automatic as possible.

REFERENCES

Acmesystems. (n.d.). Retrieved from http://www.acmesystems.it

Adamou, M., Lee, I., & Shin, I. (2002, September). An energy efficient real-time medium access control protocol for wireless ad-hoc networks. In *Proceedings of the Work in Progress Session of Eighth IEEE Real-Time and Embedded Technology and Applications Symposium*.

Akkaya, K., & Younis, M. (2003, May). An energy-aware QoS routing protocol for wireless sensor network. In *Proceedings of the Workshops in the 23rd International Conference on Distributed Computing Systems* (pp. 710-715).

Akyildiz, A.-F., Melodia, T., & Chowdhury, K.-R. (2007, March). A survey on wireless multimedia sensor networks. *Computer Networks*, *51*(4), 921–960. doi:10.1016/j.comnet.2006.10.002

Akyildiz, I., Su, W., Sankarasubramniam, Y., & Cayirci, E. (2002). A survey on sensor networks. *IEEE Communications Magazine, n.d.*, 102–114. doi:10.1109/MCOM.2002.1024422

Canny, J.-F. (1983). *Finding Edges and Lines in Images* (Tech. Rep. No. AI-TR-720). Cambridge, MA: MIT.

Chen, J. S., Huertas, A., & Medioni, G. (1987). Fast Convolution with Laplacian of Gaussian Masc. *IEEE Trans. PAMI*, *9*, 584–590.

Chiasserini, C., & Magli, E. (2002, September). Energy consumption and image quality in wireless video-surveillance networks. In *Proceedings of the 13th IEEE International Symposium on Personal, Indoor and Mobile Radio Communications (PIMRC)* (pp. 2357-2361).

Chu, M., Reich, J.-E., & Zhao, F. (2004, February). Distributed attention for large video sensor networks. In *Proceedings of the Institute of Defence and Strategic Studies (IDSS)*, London.

Crossbow MICA2 Mote Specification. (n.d.). Retrieved from http://www.xbow.com

Deb, B., Bhatnagar, S., & Nath, B. (2003, October). ReInForM: Reliable information forwarding using multiple paths in sensor networks. In *Proceedings of 28th Annual IEEE International Conference on Local Computer Networks*, Bonn, Germany (pp. 406-415).

Downes, I., Rad, L. B., & Aghajan, H. (2006, March). Development of a mote for wireless image sensor networks. In *Proceedings of the COGnitive systems with Interactive Sensors*, Paris.

3DS (n.d.). Retrieved from http://www.3ds.com/products/3dvia/3dvia-virtools

Felemban, E., Lee, C.-G., Ekici, E., Boder, R., & Vural, S. (2005, March). Probabilistic QoS guarantee in reliability and timeliness domains in wireless sensor networks. In *Proceedings of 24th Annual Joint Conference of the IEEE Computer and Communications* (pp. 2646-2657).

Feng, W., Code, B., Kaiser, E., Shea, M., & Feng, W. (2003, November). Panoptes: Scalable low-power video sensor networking technologies. In *Proceedings of the eleventh ACM international conference on Multimedia* (pp. 90-91).

Gay, D., Levis, P., von Behren, R., Welsh, M., Brewer, E., & Culler, D. (2003, June). The nesC language: a holistic approach to network embedded systems. In *Proceedings of the ACM SIGPLAN 2003 Conf. on Programming Language Design and Implementation (PLDI)*, San Diego, CA.

Gerla, M., & Xu, K. (2003, December). Multimedia streaming in large-scale sensor networks with mobile swarms. *SIGMOD Record, 32*(4), 72–76. doi:10.1145/959060.959073

Harris, C., & Stephens, M. (1998). Combined Corner and Edge Detector. *Alvey, 88*, 147–152.

He, T., Stankovic, J., Chenyang, L., & Abdelzaher, T. (2003, May). SPEED: A stateless protocol for real-time communication in sensor networks. In *Proceedings of the 23rd International Conference on Distributed Computing Systems* (pp. 46-55).

Kato, H., & Billinghurst, M. (1999, October). Marker Tracking and HMD Calibration for a video-based Augmented Reality Conferencing System. In *Proceedings of the 2nd International Workshop on Augmented Reality (IWAR)*, San Francisco, CA.

Kulkarni, P., Ganesan, D., Shenoy, P., & Lu, Q. (2005, November). SensEye: a multi-tier camera sensor network. In *Proceedings of the ACM Multimedia*, Singapore.

Magli, E., Mancin, M., & Merello, L. (2003, July). Low complexity video compression for wireless sensor networks. In *Proceedings of the 2003 International Conference on Multimedia and Expo* (pp. 585-588).

McIntire. (n.d.). Energy Benefits of 32-bit Microprocessor Wireless Sensing Systems. *Sensoria Corporation.*

Mostefaoui, A. (2006, July). A Modular and Adaptive Framework for Large Scale Video Indexing and Content-Based Retrieval: The SIRSALE System. *Software: Practice and Experience Journal, 36*(8), 871–890. doi:10.1002/spe.722

Pekhteryev, G., Sahinoglu, Z., Orlik, P., & Bhatti, G. (2005, May). Image transmission over IEEE 802.15.4 and zigbee networks. In *Proceedings of the IEEE International Symposium on Circuits and Systems (ISCAS)* (pp. 23-26).

Rahimi, M., Baer, R., Iroezi, O., Garcia, J., Warrior, J., Estrin, D., & Srivastava, M. (2005, November). Cyclops: in situ image sensing and interpretation in wireless sensor networks. In *Proceedings of the ACM Conf. on Embedded Networked Sensor Systems (SenSys)*, San Diego, CA.

Rajendran, V., Obraczka, K., & Garcia-Luna-Aceves, J.-J. (2003, November). Energy-efficient collision-free medium access control for wireless sensor networks. In *Proceedings of the 1st international conference on Embedded networked sensor systems (SenSys)*, New York (pp. 181-192).

Soro, S., & Heinzelman, W. B. (2005, October). On the coverage problem in video-based wireless sensor networks. In *Proceedings of the IEEE Intl. Conf. on Broadband Communications, Networks, and Systems (BroadNets)*, Boston.

Xbow. (n.d.). Retrieved from http://www.xbow.com/Products/Product_pdf_files/Wireless_pdf/Stargate_Datasheet.pdf

Zhang, Y. (2007, August). Adaptive region-based image fusion using energy evaluation model for fusion decision. *Signal. Image and Video Processing, 1*(3), 215–223. doi:10.1007/s11760-007-0015-6

This work was previously published in International Journal of Organizational and Collective Intelligence, Volume 1, Issue 4, edited by Hideyasu Sasaki, pp. 61-77, copyright 2010 by IGI Publishing (an imprint of IGI Global).

Chapter 19

An Experimental Performance Comparison for Indexing Mobile Objects on the Plane

S. Sioutas
Ionian University, Greece

G. Papaloukopoulos
University of Patras, Greece

K. Tsichlas
Aristotle University of Thessaloniki, Greece

Y. Manolopoulos
Aristotle University of Thessaloniki, Greece

ABSTRACT

In this paper, the authors present a time-efficient approach to index objects moving on the plane in order to answer range queries about their future positions. Each object is moving with non small velocity u, meaning that the velocity value distribution is skewed (Zipf) towards u_{min} in some range $[u_{min}, u_{max}]$, where u_{min} is a positive lower threshold. This algorithm enhances a previously described solution (Sioutas, Tsakalidis, Tsichlas, Makris, & Manolopoulos, 2007) by accommodating the ISB-tree access method as presented in Kaporis et al. (2005). Experimental evaluation shows the improved performance, scalability, and efficiency of the new algorithm.

INTRODUCTION

This paper focuses on the problem of indexing mobile objects in two dimensions and efficiently answering range queries over the objects' future locations. This problem is motivated by a set of

DOI: 10.4018/978-1-4666-1577-9.ch019

real-life applications such as intelligent transportation systems, cellular communications, and meteorology monitoring. The basic approach uses discrete movements, where the problem of dealing with a set of moving objects can be considered as equivalent to a sequence of database snapshots of the object positions/extents taken at time instants $t_1 < t_2 < \ldots$, with each time instant denoting the moment where a change took place. From this point of view, the indexing problems in such environments can be dealt with by suitably extending indexing techniques from the area of spatio-temporal databases (Gaede & Gunther, 1998; Salzberg & Tsotras, 1999). In (Manolopoulos, Theodoridis, & Tsotras, 2000) it is exposed how these indexing techniques can be generalized to handle efficiently queries in a discrete spatio-temporal environment.

The common thrust behind these indexing structures lies in the idea of abstracting each object's position as a continuous function of time, $f(t)$, and updating the database whenever the function parameters change. Accordingly an object is modelled as a pair consisting of its extent at a reference time (design parameter) and of its motion vector. One categorization of the aforementioned structures is according to the family of the underlying access method used. In particular, there are approaches based either on R-trees or on Quadtrees as explained in (Raptopoulou, Vassilakopoulos, & Manolopoulos, 2004, 2006). On the other hand, these structures can be also partitioned into those that: (a) are based on geometric duality and represent the stored objects in the dual space (Agarwal, Arge, & Erickson, 2000; Kollios, Gunopulos, & Tsotras, 1999; Patel, Chen, & Chakka, 2004), and (b) leave the original representation intact by indexing data in their native dimensional space (Beckmann, Begel, Schneider, & Seeger, 1990; Papadopoulos, Kollios, Gunopulos, & Tsotras, 2002; Saltenis, Jensen, Leutenegger, & Lopez, 2000; Saltenis et al., 2001; Tao, Papadias, & Sun, 2003). The *geometric duality transformation* is a tool extensively used in the Computational Geometry literature, which maps hyper-planes in R^d to points and vice-versa. In this paper we present and experimentally evaluate techniques using the duality transform as in (Kollios et al., 1999; Papadopoulos et al., 2002) to efficiently index future locations of moving points on the plane.

In the next section, we present a brief overview of the most basic practical methods. We then give a formal description of the problem. Next, we introduce the duality transform methods and then briefly present our main contribution, followed by the ISBs access method that compares favourably with the solutions of (Kollios et al., 1999; Papadopoulos et al., 2002), the TPR* index (Tao et al., 2003), the STRIPES index (Patel et al., 2004) and the LBTs index (Sioutas et al., 2007) as well. In simple words, the new solution is the most efficient in terms of update I/O performance. Moreover, with respect to the query I/O performance, solution of ISBs is 4 or 5 faster than LBTs method and outperforms STRIPES (state of the art as of now) in many settings. Finally, we present a thorough experimental evaluation, followed by a conclusion.

A BRIEF OVERVIEW OF THE RELEVANT METHODS

The TPR tree (Saltenis et al., 2000) in essence is an R*-tree generalization to store and access linearly moving objects. The leaves of the structure store pairs with the position of the moving point and the moving point id, whereas internal nodes store pointers to subtrees with associated rectangles that minimally bound all moving points or other rectangles in the subtree. The difference with respect to the classical R*-tree lies in the fact that the bounding rectangles are time parameterized (their coordinates are functions of time). It is considered that a time parameterized rectangle bounds all enclosed points or rectangles at all times not earlier than current time. Search and update algorithms in the TPR tree are straightforward generalizations of the respective algorithms in the R*-tree; moreover, the various kinds of spatiotemporal queries can be handled uniformly in 1-, 2-, and 3-dimensional spaces.

The TPR-tree served as the base structure for further developments in the area (Saltenis et al.,

2001). *TPR*-tree*, an extension of the TPR-tree, improves the latter in update operations (Tao et al., 2003). The main improvement lies in the fact that local optimization criteria (at each tree node) may degrade seriously the performance of the structure and more particularly in the use of update rules that are based on global optimization criteria. Thus, the authors of (Tao et al., 2003) proposed a novel probabilistic cost model to validate the performance of a spatiotemporal index and analyse with this model the optimal performance for any data-partition index.

The STRIPES index (Patel et al., 2004) is based on the application of the duality transformation and employs disjoint regular space partitions (disk based quadtrees (Gaede & Gunther, 1998)). Through the use of a series of implementations, the authors claim that STRIPES outperforms TPR*-trees for both update and query operations.

Finally, the LBTs index (Sioutas et al., 2007) has the most efficient update performance in all cases. Regarding the query performance, LBTs method prevails as long as the query rectangle length remains in realistic levels (by far superiority in comparison to opponent methods). If the query rectangle length becomes huge in relation to the whole terrain, then STRIPES is the best solution, however, only to a small margin in comparison to LBTs method.

DEFINITIONS AND PROBLEM DESCRIPTION

We consider a database that records the position of moving objects in two dimensions on a finite terrain. We assume that objects move with a constant velocity vector starting from a specific location at a specific time instant. Thus, we can calculate the future object position, provided that its motion characteristics remain the same. Velocities are bounded by $[u_{min}, u_{max}]$. Objects update their motion information, when their speed or direction changes. The system is dynamic, i.e.

objects may be deleted or new objects may be inserted.

Let $P_z(t_0) = [x_0, y_0]$ be the initial position at time t_0 of object z. If object z starts moving at time $t > t_0$, its position will be $P_z(t) = [x(t), y(t)] = [x_0 + u_x(t - t_0), y_0 + u_y(t - t_0)]$, where $U = (u_x, u_y)$ is its velocity vector.

We would like to answer queries of the form: "Report the objects located inside the rectangle $[x_{1_q}, x_{2_q}] \times [y_{1_q}, y_{2_q}]$ at the time instants between t_{1_q} and t_{2_q} (where $t_{now} \leq t_{1_q} \leq t_{2_q}$), given the current motion information of all objects."

INDEXING MOBILE OBJECTS USING DUALITY TRANSFORMATIONS

In general, the duality transform maps a hyper-plane h from R^d to a point in R^d and vice-versa. One duality transform for mapping the line with equation $y(t)=ut+a$ to a point in R^2 is by using the dual plane, where one axis represents the slope u of an object's trajectory (i.e., velocity), whereas the other axis represents its intercept a. Thus we get the dual point (u,a) (this is the so-called *Hough-X transform* (Kollios et al., 1999; Papadopoulos et al., 2002)). By rewriting the equation $y=ut+a$ as $t = \dfrac{1}{u} y - \dfrac{a}{u}$, we arrive to a different dual representation (the so called *Hough-Y transform* in (Kollios et al., 1999; Papadopoulos et al., 2002)). The point in the dual plane has coordinates (b,w), where $b = -\dfrac{a}{u}$ and $w = \dfrac{1}{u}$.

In (Kollios et al., 1999; Papadopoulos et al., 2002), motions with small velocities in the Hough-Y approach are mapped into dual points (b,w) having large w coordinates ($w=1/u$). Thus, since few objects can have small velocities, by storing the Hough-Y dual points in an index such as an R*-tree, Maximum Bounded Rectangles (MBRs) with large extents are introduced, and the index performance is severely affected. On the other hand, by using a Hough-X for the small velocities' partition, this effect is eliminated, since the Hough-X dual transform maps an object's motion to the (u,a) dual point. The query area in Hough-X plane is enlarged by the area E, which is easily computed as $E_{Hough-X} = (E1_{hough-X} + E2_{hough-X})$. By $Q_{Hough-X}$ we denote the actual area of the simplex query. Similarly, on the dual Hough-Y plane, $Q_{Hough-Y}$ denotes the actual area of the query, and $E_{Hough-Y}$ denotes the enlargement. According to these observations the solution in (Kollios et al., 1999; Papadopoulos et al., 2002) proposes the choice of that transformation which minimizes the criterion: $c = \dfrac{E_{Hough-X}}{Q_{Hough-X}} + \dfrac{E_{Hough-Y}}{Q_{Hough-Y}}$.

In order to build the index, we first decompose the 2-d motion into two 1-d motions on the (t,x) and (t,y) planes and then we build the corresponding index for each projection. Then we have to partition the objects according to their velocity: Objects with small velocity are stored using the Hough-X dual transform, whereas the rest are stored using the Hough-Y dual transform. Motion information about the other projection is also included.

To answer the exact 2-d query we decompose the query into two 1-d queries, for the (t,x) and (t,y) projection. Then, for each projection, we get the dual-simplex query and calculate the criterion c and choose the one (say p) that minimizes it. We search in projection p the Hough-X or Hough-Y partition and finally we perform a refinement or filtering step "on the fly", by using the whole motion information. Thus, the result set contains only the objects satisfying the query.

OUR CONTRIBUTION

We consider the case, where the objects are moving with non small velocities u, meaning that the velocity value distribution is skewed (Zipf) towards

u_{min} in some range $[u_{min}, u_{max}]$ and as a consequence the $Q_{Hough-Y}$ transformation is used (denote that u_{min} is a positive lower threshold). In (Kollios et al., 1999, Papadopoulos et al., 2002) and (Sioutas et al., 2007), $Q_{Hough-Y}$ is computed by querying a B⁺-tree and LBTs (Lazy B-trees) respectively, each of which indexes the b parameters. Our construction is based on the use of the ISB-tree (Kaporis et al., 2005) instead of the B⁺-tree or Lazy B-trees, achieving optimal update performance and near-optimal query performance. Next we describe the main characteristics of the ISB-tree.

THE ISB-TREE

In the following, we give some basic definitions, we describe the interpolation method of searching, we describe the Interpolation Search Tree as the basic main memory structure and finally we give the required technical details of the external memory Interpolation Search B-Tree (ISB-tree) presented in (Kaporis et al., 2005).

Basic Definitions: Regular and Smooth Input Distributions

According to Willard (Willard, 1985), a probability density μ is regular if there are constants b_1, b_2, b_3, b_4 such that $\mu(x) = 0$ for $x < b_1$ or $x > b_2$, and $\mu(x) \geq b_3 > 0$ and $|\mu'(x)| \leq b_4$ for $b_1 \leq x \leq b_2$. This has been further pursued by Mehlhorn and Tsakalidis (Mehlhorn & Tsakalidis, 1993), who introduced the *smooth* input distributions, a notion that was further generalized and refined in (Andersson & Mattsson, 1993). Given two functions f_1 and f_2, a density function $\mu = \mu[a,b](x)$ is (f_1, f_2)-*smooth* (Andersson & Mattsson, 1993) if there exists a constant β, such that for all c_1, c_2, c_3 where $a \leq c_1 < c_2 < c_3 \leq b$, and all integers n, it holds that

$$\int_{c_2 - \frac{c_3 - c_1}{f_1(n)}}^{c_2} \mu[c_1, c_3](x)dx \leq \frac{\beta \cdot f_2(n)}{n}$$

where $\mu[c_1, c_3](x) = 0$ for $x < c_1$ or $x > c_3$, and $\mu[c_1, c_3](x) = \mu(x)/p$ for $c_1 \leq x \leq c_3$ where $p = \int_{c_1}^{c_3} \mu(x)dx$.

Intuitively, function f_1 partitions an arbitrary subinterval $[c_1, c_3] \subseteq [a, b]$ into f_1 equal parts, each of length $\frac{c_3 - c_1}{f_1} = O(\frac{1}{f_1})$; that is, f_1 measures how fine is the partitioning of an arbitrary subinterval. Function f_2 guarantees that no part, of the f_1 possible, gets more probability mass than $\frac{\beta \cdot f_2}{n}$; that is, f_2 measures the sparseness of any subinterval $[c_2 - \frac{c_3 - c_1}{f_1}, c_2] \subseteq [c_1, c_3]$. The class of (f_1, f_2)-smooth distributions (for appropriate choices of f_1 and f_2) is a superset of both regular and uniform classes of distributions, as well as of several non-uniform classes (Andersson & Mattsson, 1993; Kaporis et al., 2003). Actually, *any* probability distribution is $(f_1, \Theta(n))$-smooth, for a suitable choice of β.

Searching algorithms and Interpolation Method

Let $S = \{X_i, 1 \leq i \leq n\}$ an ordered set of n elements. The basic routine of a searching operation is described by Algorithm 1 as follows:

If $next \leftarrow left + 1$ the routine above is a linear searching routine and the worst-case time is $O(n)$. If $next \leftarrow \left\lfloor \frac{right + left}{2} \right\rfloor$ we refer to a binary searching routine with $O(\log n)$ worst-case time. If $next \leftarrow \left\lfloor \frac{x - S[left]}{S[right] - S[left]}(right - left) \right\rfloor + left$

Algorithm 1.

Algorithm 1 Search(x, S)
1: *left* ← 1
2: *right* ← n
3: *next* ← $k \in [left, right]$
4: **while** $x <> S[next]$ **and** *left* < *right* **do**
5: **if** $x \leq S[next]$ **then**
6: *right* ← *next* − 1
7: **else**
8: *left* ← *next* + 1
9: **end if**
10: *next* ← $k \in [left, right]$
11: **end while**
12: **if** $x = S[next]$ **then**
13: *print*('Success')
14: **else**
15: *print*('Fail')
16: **end if**

we refer to an interpolation searching routine for which time improvements can be obtained if certain classes of input distributions are considered. In particular, for random data generated according to the uniform distribution, the interpolation searching routine achieves $\Theta(\log \log n)$ expected time. Willard (Willard, 1985) showed that this time bound holds for an extended class of regular distributions, as defined previously. A natural extension is to adapt interpolation search into dynamic data structures, that is, data structures which support insertion and deletion of elements in addition to interpolation search. Thus, the first step was to develop a static tree-like structure, which adapts the method above (the so-called **Static Interpolation Search Tree**) and the second and final step the dynamization of this tree.

The Interpolation Search Tree

The *static interpolation search tree* has been presented in (Kaporis et al., 2003). Consider a random file $S = \{X_1, ..., X_n\}$, where each key

$X_i \in [a,b] \subset \Re$, $1 \leq i \leq n$, obeys an unknown distribution μ. Let $P = \{X_{(1)}, \ldots, X_{(n)}\}$ be an increasing ordering of S. The goal is to find the largest key $X_{(j)} \in P$ that precedes a *target* element x.

A static interpolation search tree (SIST) corresponding to P can be fully characterized by three non-decreasing functions $H(n)$, $R(n)$ and $I(n)$, which are non-decreasing and invertible with a second derivative less than or equal to zero. $H(n)$ denotes the tree height, $R(n)$ denotes the root fan-out, whereas $I(n)$ denotes how fine is the partition of the set of elements. Achieving a height of $H(n)$ dictates that $R(n) = n / H^{-1}(H(n) - 1)$. Moreover, $H(n)$ should be $o(\log n)$ and not $O(1)$, and $H^{-1}(i) \neq 0$, for $1 \leq i \leq H(n) - 1$. To handle an as large as possible class of distributions μ, the approximation of the sample density should be as fine as possible, implying that $I(n)$ should be as large as possible. Since $I(n)$ $I(n)$ affects space, it is chosen as $I(n) = n \cdot g(H(n))$, where $\sum_{i=1}^{\infty} g(i) = \Theta(1)$, so that the space of SIST remains linear.

The aforementioned choice of functions $H(n)$, $R(n)$ and $I(n)$ ensures that a SIST on n elements, drawn from a $(n \cdot g(H(n)), H^{-1}(H(n) - 1))$-smooth distribution μ, can be built in $O(n)$ time and space (Kaporis et al., 2003).

The root node of SIST corresponds to the ordered file P of size n. Each child corresponds to a part of P of size $\frac{n}{R(n)}$, i.e., the subtree rooted at each child of the root has $n'=n/R(n)$ leaves and height $H(n')=H(n)-1$. The fan-out of each child is $R(n') = \Theta(H^{-1}(H(n) - 1) / H^{-1}(H(n) - 2))$, while $I(n')=n' \cdot g(H(n'))$. In general, consider an internal node v at depth i and assume that n_i leaves (elements of P) are stored in the subtree rooted at v, whose keys take values in $[\ell, u]$. Then,

we have that $R(n_i) = \Theta(H^{-1}(H(n) - i + 1) / H^{-1}(H(n) - i))$, and $I(n_i) = n_i \cdot g(H(n) - i)$.

Each internal tree node v at depth i is associated with an array $\text{REP}[1 R(n_i)]$ of sample elements, containing one sample element for each of its subtrees, and an array $\text{ID}[1 I(n_i)]$ that stores a set of sample elements approximating the inverse distribution function. The role of the ID array is to partition the interval $[\ell, u]$ into $I(n_i)$ equal parts, each of length $\frac{u - \ell}{I(n_i)}$. The role of the REP array is to partition its associated ordered sub-file of P into $R(n_i)$ equal subfiles, each of size $\frac{n_i}{R(n_i)}$. By using the ID array, we can interpolate the REP array to determine the subtree in which the search procedure will continue. In particular, for the $\text{ID}[1 I(n_i)]$ array associated with node v, it holds that $\text{ID}[i]=j$ iff $\text{REP}[j] < \ell + i(u - \ell) / I(n_i) \leq \text{REP}[j+1]$. Let x be the element we seek. To interpolate REP, compute the index $j = \text{ID}[\lfloor (I(n_i)(x - \ell) / (u - \ell)) \rfloor]$, and then search the REP array from $\text{REP}[j+1]$ until the appropriate subtree is located. For each node we explicitly maintain parent and child pointers. The required pointer information can be easily incorporated in the construction of the static interpolation search tree.

The ISB-tree: a Dynamic Interpolation Search Tree in External Memory

The ISB-tree is a two-level data structure (see Figure 1). The upper level is a non-straightforward externalization of the Static Interpolation Search Tree (SIST).

The lower level of the ISB-tree is a forest of buckets, each one implemented by a new variant

Figure 1. The ISB-tree Index

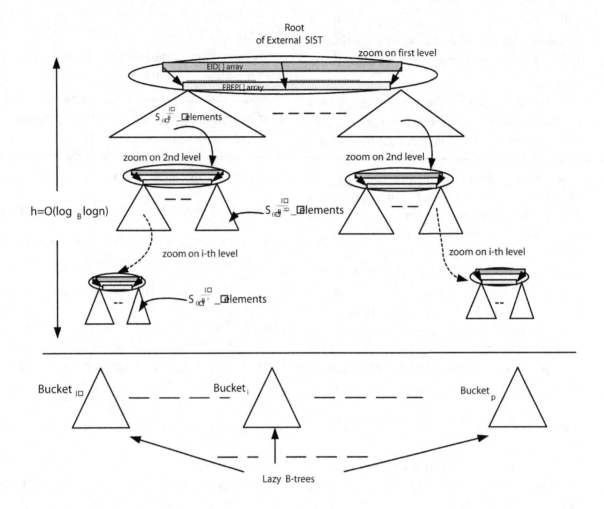

of the classical B-tree, the *Lazy B-tree*, introduced in (Kaporis et al., 2005) and used in (Sioutas et al., 2007). Each bucket contains a subset of the stored elements and is represented by a unique representative. The representatives of the buckets as well as some additional elements are stored in the upper level structure. The following theorem provides the complexities of the Lazy B-tree:

Theorem 1. The Lazy B-Tree supports the search operation in $O(\log_B N)$ worst-case block transfers and update operations in $O(1)$ worst-case block transfers, provided that the update position is given.

Proof. See (Kaporis et al., 2005; Sioutas et al., 2007).

The upper level data structure is an external version T of the static interpolation search tree (SIST) (Kaporis et al., 2003), with parameters $R(s) = s^{\delta}$, $I(s) = s / (\log \log s)^{1+\epsilon}$, where $\epsilon > 0$, $\delta = 1 - \dfrac{1}{B}$, and s is the number of stored elements in the tree. The specific choice of δ guarantees the desirable $O(\log_B \log s)$ height of the upper level structure. For each node that stores more than $B^{1+\frac{1}{B-1}}$ elements in its subtree, we represent its REP and ID arrays as static external sorted arrays; otherwise, we store all the elements in a constant number of disk blocks. In particular, let v be a node and n_v be the number of stored elements in its subtree, with $n_v \geq B^{1+\frac{1}{B-1}}$. Node v v is associated with two external arrays $EREP_v$ and EID_v that represent the REP_v and ID_v arrays of the original SIST structure. The EID_v array uses $O\left(\frac{I(n_v)}{B}\right)$ contiguous blocks, the $EREP_v$ array uses $O\left(\frac{R(n_v)}{B}\right)$ contiguous blocks, while an arbitrary element of the arrays can be accessed with $O(1)$ block transfers, given its index.

Moreover, the choice of the parameter $B^{1+\frac{1}{B-1}}$ guarantees that each of the $EREP_v$ and EID_v arrays contains at least B elements, and hence we do not waste space (in terms of underfull blocks) in the external memory representation.

To insert/delete an element, given the position (block) of the update, we simply have to insert/delete the element to/from the Lazy B-tree storing the elements of the corresponding bucket. Note that the external SIST is not affected by these updates. Each time the number of updates exceeds cn_0, where c is a predefined constant, the whole data structure is reconstructed.

The search procedure for locating a query element x can be decomposed into two phases: (i) the traversal of internal nodes of the external SIST to locate a bucket B_i, and (ii) the search for x in the Lazy B-tree storing the elements of B_i. For more technical details see (Kaporis et al., 2005). Algorithms 2-5 provide the description of ISB-tree's basic operations in pseudocode.

Lemma 2: The traversal of internal nodes of the external SIST requires $O(\log_B \log n)$ expected block transfers with high probability.

Proof: See (Kaporis et al., 2005).

The insertions and deletions of elements into the ISB-tree were simulated by a combinatorial game of balls and bins described in (Kaporis et al., 2003) for an internal finger-search data structure. In particular, balls correspond to elements and bins to buckets. Insertions of elements into the ISB-tree were simulated by the insertion of balls into bins according to an unknown smooth probability density μ. Similarly, the deletion of an element from the ISB-tree was simulated by the deletion of an element from a bin uniformly at random. For this process the following has been proven in (Kaporis et al., 2003).

Theorem 2: Consider the combinatorial game of balls and bins described in (A. Kaporis et al., 2003). Then, the expected number of balls in a bin is $O(\log n)$ with high probability.

The following lemma establishes the searching bound within a bucket of the ISB-tree.

Lemma 3: Searching for an element in a bucket of the ISB-tree takes $O(\log_B \log n)$ expected block transfers with high probability.
Proof: This is an immediate result from Theorem 1 and the size of each bucket, which is determined by Theorem 2.

The main theorem presented in (A. C. Kaporis et al., 2005) follows and holds for the very broad class of $(n / (\log \log n)^{1+\epsilon}, n^{1-\delta})$-smooth densities, where $\delta = 1 - \frac{1}{B}$ and includes the uniform, regular, bounded as well as several non-uniform distributions.

Theorem 3: Suppose that the upper level of the ISB-tree is an external static interpolation

Algorithm 2.

Algorithm 2 Sist_Search(*x*, *SIST*)
1: $v \leftarrow root(SIST)$
2: **while**($v <> leaf$) **do**
3: $i = \left\lfloor \dfrac{x - l_v}{u_v - l_v} R(n_v) \right\rfloor$ {Let v be a node on the search path for x, n_v the number of leaves in its subtree,l_v and u_v the minimum and maximum element respectively, stored in T_v}
4: Retrieve the $\left\lceil \dfrac{i}{B} \right\rceil$ -th block of the EID_v array
5: $j = EID_v[i]$
6: $l = \left\lceil \dfrac{j}{B} \right\rceil$
7: **repeat**
8: $l \leftarrow l + 1$
9: **until** $EREP_v[l] \le x < EREP_v[l + 1]$
10: **end while**
11: follow the pointer from leaf v{Let Bin_l the corresponding bin which is organized as a Lazy B-tree}

Algorithm 3.

Algorithm 3 ISB_Search(*x*, ISB-tree)
1: SistSearch(*x*, *SIST*){Let Bin_l the corresponding Bin of the static interpolation search tree SIST}
2: LazyTree_Search(*x*, Bin_l){search in the lazy B-tree was implemented in (Sioutas et al., 2007)}

Algorithm 4.

Algorithm 4 ISB_Insert(*x*, ISB-tree)
1: Sist_Search(*x*,*SIST*){Let Bin_l the corresponding Bin}
2: LazyTree_Insert(*x*,Bin_l){Bin_l is a lazy B-tree and its insert operation was implemented in(Sioutas et al.,2007)}
3: *numberofupdates* ← *numberofupdates* + 1
4: **if** *numberofupdates* = cn_0 **then**
5: Rebuild(*SIST*){n_0 is the total number of elements stored in the initial ISB-tree}
6: **end if**

Algorithm 5.

Algorithm 5 ISB_Delete(*x*, ISB-tree)
7: Sist_Search(*x*,*SIST*){Let *Bin$_i$* the corresponding Bin}
8: LazyTree_Delete(*x*,*Bin$_i$*){*Bin$_i$* is a lazy B-tree and its delete operation was implemented in(Sioutas et al.,2007)}
9: *numberofupdates*←*numberofupdates* + 1
10: **if** *numberofupdates* = *cn$_0$* **then**
11: Rebuild(*SIST*){*n$_0$* is the total number of elements stored in the initial ISB-tree}
12: **end if**

search tree with parameters $R(s_0) = s_0^\delta$, $I(s_0) = s_0 / (\log\log s_0)^{1+\epsilon}$, where $\epsilon > 0$, $\delta = 1 - \frac{1}{B}$, $s_0 = n_0$, n_0 is the number of elements in the latest reconstruction, and that the lower level is implemented as a forest of Lazy B-trees. Then, the ISB-tree supports search operations in $O(\log_B \log n)$ expected block transfers with high probability, where n denotes the current number of elements, and update operations in $O(1)$ worst-case block transfers, if the update position is given. The worst-case update bound is $O(\log_B n)$ block transfers, and the structure occupies $O(n/B)$ blocks.

Proof [1]: From Lemmas 2 and 3, the searching operation takes $O(\log_B \log n)$ expected number of block transfers with high probability. Considering the update bound, between reconstructions the block transfers for an update are clearly $O(1)$, since we only have to update the appropriate Lazy B-tree which can be done in $O(1)$ block transfers (see Theorem 1). The reconstructions can be easily handled by using the technique of global rebuilding (Levcopoulos & Overmars, 1988). With this technique the linear work spent during a global reconstruction of the upper level structure may be spread out on the updates in such a way that a rebuilding cost of $O(1)$ block transfers is spent at each update.

EXPERIMENTAL EVALUATION

This section compares the query/update performance of our solution with STRIPES as well as with those ones that use B$^+$-trees, Lazy B-trees (LBTs) and TPR*-tree, as well. We deploy spatio-temporal data that contain insertions at a single timestamp 0. In particular, objects' MBRs are taken from the LA spatial dataset[2]. We want to simulate a situation where all objects move in a space with dimensions 100x100 kilometers. For this purpose each axis of the space is normalized to [0,100000]. For the TPR*-tree, each object is associated with a VBR (Velocity Bounded Rectangle) such that (a) the object does not change spatial extents during its movement, and (b) the velocity value distribution is skewed (Zipf) towards 30 in the range [30,50], and (c) the velocity can be either positive or negative with equal probability.

We will use a page size of 1 Kbyte so that the number of index nodes simulates realistic situations. Also, for all experiments, the key length is 8 bytes, whereas the pointer length is 4 bytes. Thus, the maximum number of entries (<*x*> or <*y*>, respectively) in both Lazy B-trees and B$^+$-trees is 1024/(8+4)=85. In the same way, the maximum number of entries (2-d rectangles or <*x*1,*y*1,*x*2,*y*2> tuples) in TPR*-tree is 1024/(4*8+4)=27. On the other hand, the STRIPES index maps predicted positions to points in a dual transformed space and indexes this space using a disjoint regular partitioning of space. Each of the two dual planes, are equally partitioned into four quads. This partitioning results in a total of $4^2 = 16$ partitions, which we call *grids*. Thus, the fan-out of each internal node is 16. The ISB-tree[3] has an exponentially decreased fan-out and 2 levels at most.

For each dataset, all indexes except for STRIPES and ISBs have similar sizes. Specifically, for LA, each tree has 4 levels and around 6700 leaves with the exception of: (a) the STRIPES index which has a maximum height of seven and consumes about 2.4 times larger disk space, and (b) the ISB index which has a maximum height of 2. Each query q has three parameters: $q_R len$, $q_V len$, and $q_T len$, such that: (a) its MBR q_R is a square, with length $q_R len$, uniformly generated in the data space, (b) its VBR is $q_V = -q_V len / 2, q_V len / 2, -q_V len / 2, q_V len / 2$, and (c) its query interval is $q_T = [0, q_T len]$. The query cost is measured as the average number of node accesses in executing a workload of 200 queries with the same parameters. Implementations were carried out in C++ including particular libraries from SECONDARY LEDA v4.1.

Query Cost Comparison

We measure the performance of our technique described previously (in particular one ISB-tree for each projection, plus the query processing between the two answers), in comparison to that of the LBTs method (Sioutas et al., 2007), the traditional technique presented in (Kollios et al., 1999; Papadopoulos et al., 2002), the TPR*-tree (Tao et al., 2003) and the STRIPES method (Patel et al., 2004), using the same query workload, after every 10000 updates. Figures 2, Figure 3, Figure 4, Figure 5, and Figure 6 show the query cost (for datasets generated from LA as described above) as a function of the number of updates, using workloads with different parameters. In these figures our solution is almost 4-5 times more efficient (in terms of the number of I/Os) than the solution using LBTs and B+-trees. This fact is an immediate result

of the sublogarithmic I/O searching complexity of ISB-tree in comparison to the logarithmic I/O searching complexities of both structures B+-tree and Lazy B-tree. In particular, we have to index the appropriate b parameters in each projection and then to combine the two answers by detecting and filtering all pair permutations. As a consequence, the ISBs method is significantly faster than LBTs and traditional B+-trees methods.

Figure 2 and Figure 3 depict the efficiency of our solution in comparison to that of the TPR*-tree and STRIPES. In figure 2, where the length of the query rectangle is 100 and as a consequence the query's surface is equal to $10000m^2$ or 1 hectare (the surface of the whole spatial terrain is 10^6 hectares) the ISBs method is consistently about 53 times faster than the STRIPES method, 212 times faster than the TPR*-tree, 7.5 times faster than the B+-trees method and 2 times faster than the LBTs method. The superiority of our solution decreases as the query rectangle length grows from 100 to 1000. Thus, in figure 3, where the spatial query's surface is equal to 100 hectares, again our method is faster about 2.2 times with respect to the STRIPES method, 8.3 times wrt the TPR*-tree, 1.25 times wrt the B+-trees methods and 1.05 times wrt the LBTs method.

In real GIS applications, for a vast spatial terrain of 10^6 hectares, e.g., the road network of a big town where each road square covers no more than 1 hectare (or $10.000m^2$) the most frequent queries consider spatial query's surface no more than 100 road squares (or 100 hectares) and future time interval no larger than 100 seconds. However, to test the methods' performance in extreme cases we conducted the following experiment. When the query rectangle length or equivalently the query surface becomes extremely large (e.g., 2000, or equivalently 400 hectares), then the STRIPES index shows better performance as depicted in Figure 4. In particular, our method is still 1.9 times faster than the TPR*-tree, however, the STRIPES method is twice faster than

Figure 2. $q_V len = 5, q_T len = 50, q_R len = 100$

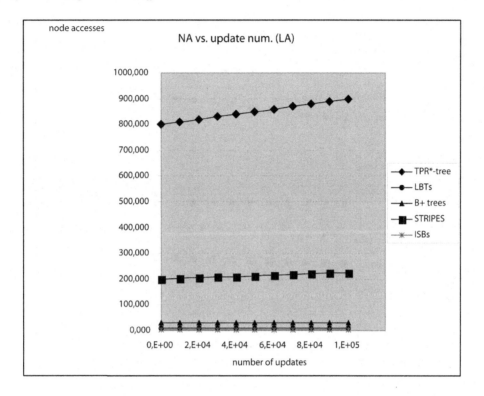

Figure 3. $q_V len = 5, q_T len = 50, q_R len = 1000$

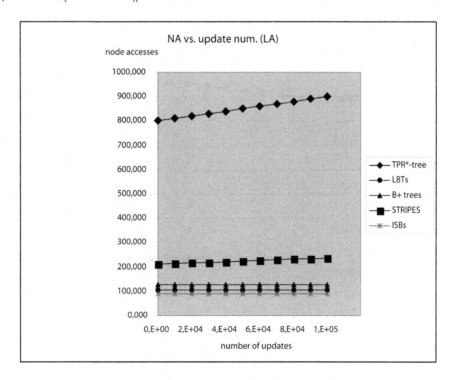

Figure 4. $q_R len = 2000, q_V len = 5, q_T len = 50$

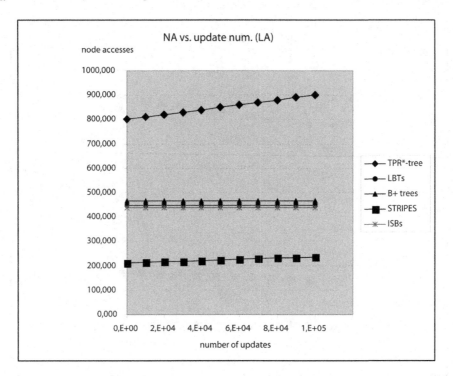

Figure 5. $q_V len = 10, q_T len = 50, q_R len = 400$

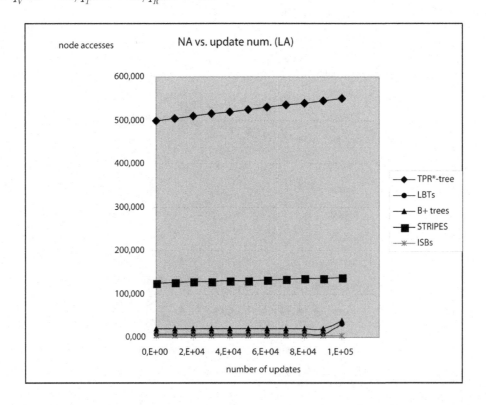

Figure 6. $q_V len = 10, q_T len = 50, q_R len = 1000$

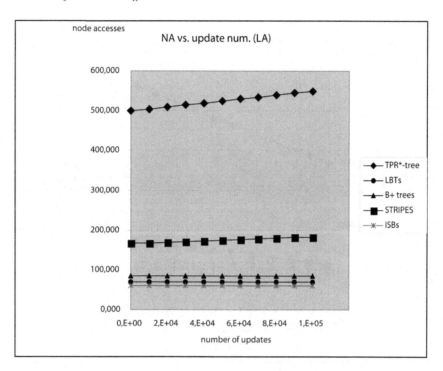

our one. The apparent explanation is that as the surface of the query rectangle grows, the answer size in each projection grows as well, thus the performance of the ISBs method that combines and filters the two answers becomes less attractive. However, we do not consider such extreme case as *realistic* scenarios. Figure 5 and Figure 6 depict the performance of all methods for a growing velocity vector. In particular, in Figure 5 the ISBs method consistently prevails about 33 times in comparison to the STRIPES method, 137 times in comparison to the TPR*-tree, 5 times in comparison to the B$^+$-trees and 2 times in comparison to the LBTs method. The superiority of our solution becomes less strong as the query rectangle length grows from 400 (16 hectares of query surface) to 1000 (100 hectares of query surface). However, notably even in the latter case (see Figure 6), our method is about 2.7 times faster with respect to the STRIPES method, 8.3 times wrt the TPR*-tree, 1.3 times wrt the B$^+$-trees and

1.06 times wrt the LBTs method. Obviously, the velocity factor is very important for TPR-like solutions, but not for the other methods, for LBTs and ISBs in particular, which depend exclusively on the query surface. Figure 7 and Figure 8 depict the performance of all methods when the time interval length approaches the 1 value. However, notably even in this case (see Figure 7), the ISBs method is about 1.6 times faster with respect to the STRIPES method, 4.6 times faster wrt the TPR*-tree, 1.3 times faster wrt the B$^+$-trees and 1.2 times faster wrt the LBTs method. As query rectangle length grows from 400 to 1000, the ISBs method advantage decreases; from the bottom figure, we remark that STRIPES is about 3 times faster, whereas our method is 1.03 times faster than the TPR*-tree, 1.07 times faster than the B$^+$-trees and 1.03 times faster than the LBTs method. Figure 9 depicts the efficiency of our solution in comparison to that of TPR*-trees and STRIPES when the time interval length reaches

Figure 7. $q_V len = 5$, $q_T len = 1$, $q_R len = 400$

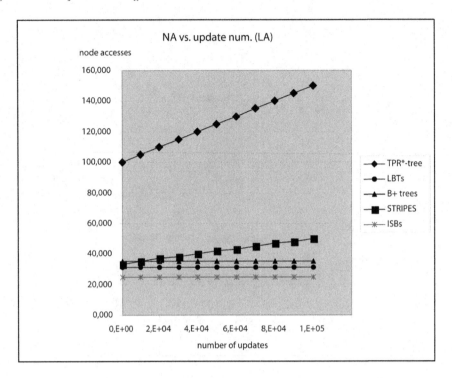

Figure 8. $q_V len = 5$, $q_T len = 1$, $q_R len = 1000$

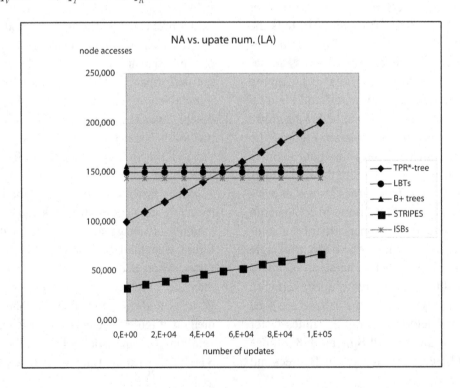

Figure 9. $q_R len = 400$, $q_V len = 5$, $q_T len = 100$

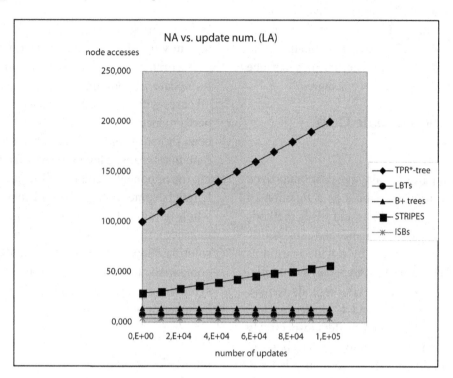

Figure 10. Update Cost Comparison

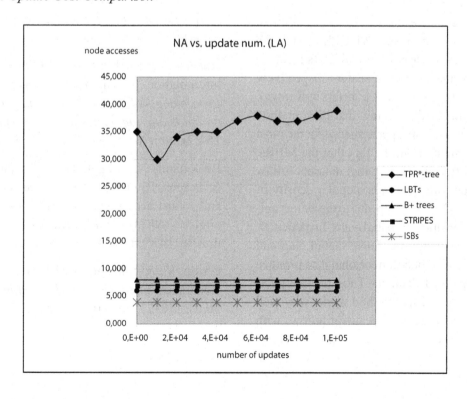

the value of 100. In particular, the ISBs method is consistently about 10 times faster than STRIPES, 37 times faster than TPR*-tree, 3.5 times faster than the B+-trees and 2 times faster than the LBTs method. As required in practice, the query surface remains in *realistic* levels (16 hectares).

Scalability and Update Cost Comparison

Figure 10 compares the average cost (amortized over insertions and deletions) as a function of the number of updates. ISBs and LBTs methods have optimal update performance and consistently outperform the TPR*-tree by a wide margin as well as the STRIPES index by a narrow margin. In particular, ISBs and LBTs methods require a constant number of 4 and 6 block transfers respectively(3 and 2 block transfers respectively for each projection, for details see (Kaporis et al., 2005)) and this update performance is independent of the dataset size. On the other hand, the other 3 solutions do not have constant update performance; instead their performance depends on the dataset size even if as in the experiment of Figure 10 B+-trees and STRIPES reach the optimal performance of ISBs and LBTs methods requiring 8 and 7 block transfers respectively (TPR*-tree requires 35 block transfers in average). The experiments above show that ISBs method achieves a near optimal performance for the most cases. This stems from the fact that the MBRs' projections from the LA spatial datasets follow an almost uniform (the most popular density of smooth family) distribution, due to the almost uniform decomposition of spatial maps. In particular, LA dataset constitutes a dense spatial map and hence the derived one-dimensional data produce densely populated elements. Thus, the interpolation technique of ISBs method works very well and its expected excellent behavior follows with high probability.

CONCLUSION

We have used a new access method for indexing moving objects on the plane to efficiently answer range queries about their future location. Its update performance is the most efficient in all cases with no exception. Regarding the query performance, the superiority of our structure has been shown as long as the query rectangle length remains in realistic levels, thus by far outperforming the opponent methods. If the query rectangle length becomes extremely huge in relation to the whole terrain (which apparently is a non-practical instance), then the STRIPES method is the best solution, however, only to a small margin in comparison to our method. We anticipate that for synthetic gigantic datasets the ISBs method will be superior in any case.

REFERENCES

Agarwal, P. K., Arge, L., & Erickson, J. (2000). Indexing moving points. In *Proceedings of 19th symposium on principles of database systems* (pp. 175-186). New York: ACM.

Andersson, A., & Mattsson, C. (1993). Dynamic interpolation search in o(log log n) time. In *Proceedings of 20th international colloquium on automata, languages and programming* (pp. 15-27). New York: Springer.

Beckmann, N., Begel, H. P., Schneider, R., & Seeger, B. (1990). The r*-tree: an efficient and robust access method for points and rectangles. *SIGMOD Record, 19*(2), 322–331. doi:10.1145/93605.98741

Gaede, V., & Gunther, O. (1998). Multidimensional access methods. *ACM Computing Surveys, 30*(2), 170–231. doi:10.1145/280277.280279

Kaporis, A., Makris, C., Sioutas, S., Tsakalidis, A., Tsichlas, K., & Zaroliagis, C. (2003). Improved bounds for finger search on a ram. In *Proceedings of 12th annual european symposium on algorithms* (pp. 325-336). New York: Springer.

Kaporis, A. C., Makris, C., Mavritsakis, G., Sioutas, S., Tsakalidis, A. K., & Tsichlas, K. (2005). Isb-tree: A new indexing scheme with efficient expected behaviour. In *Proceedings of 13th international symposium on algorithms and computation* (pp. 318-327). New York: Springer.

Kollios, G., Gunopulos, D., & Tsotras, V. J. (1999). On indexing mobile objects. In *Proceedings of 18th symposium on principles of database systems* (pp. 261-272). New York: ACM.

Levcopoulos, C., & Overmars, M. H. (1988). A balanced search tree with o(1) worst case update time. *Acta Inf., 26*(3), 269–277. doi:10.1007/BF00299635

Manolopoulos, Y., Theodoridis, Y., & Tsotras, V. J. (2000). *Advanced database indexing*. Dordrecht, The Netherlands: Kluwer Academic Publishers.

Mehlhorn, K., & Tsakalidis, A. K. (1993). Dynamic interpolation search. *Journal of the ACM, 40*(3), 621–634. doi:10.1145/174130.174139

Papadopoulos, D., Kollios, G., Gunopulos, D., & Tsotras, V. J. (2002). Indexing mobile objects on the plane. In *Proceedings of 13th international workshop on database and expert systems applications* (pp. 693-697). Washington, DC: IEEE Computer Society.

Patel, J. M., Chen, Y., & Chakka, V. P. (2004). Stripes: An efficient index for predicted trajectories. In *Proceedings of the 2004 acm sigmod international conference on management of data* (pp. 637-646). New York: ACM.

Raptopoulou, K., Vassilakopoulos, M., & Manolopoulos, Y. (2004). Towards quadtree-based moving objects databases. In *Proceedings of 8th east-european conference on advanced databases and information systems* (pp. 230-245). New York: Springer.

Raptopoulou, K., Vassilakopoulos, M., & Manolopoulos, Y. (2006). On past-time indexing of moving objects. *Journal of Systems and Software, 79*(8), 1079–1091. doi:10.1016/j.jss.2005.10.020

Saltenis, S., Jensen, C. S., Leutenegger, S. T., & Lopez, M. A. (2000). Indexing the positions of continuously moving objects. *SIGMOD Record, 29*(2), 331–342. doi:10.1145/335191.335427

Saltenis, S., Jensen, C. S. J., Bohlen, M. H., Gregersen, H., & Pfoser, D. (2001). Indexing of moving objects for location-based services. In *Proceedings of 18th ieee international conference on data engineering* (pp. 463-472). Washington, DC: IEEE Computer Society.

Salzberg, B., & Tsotras, V. J. (1999). Comparison of access methods for time-evolving data. *ACM Computing Surveys, 31*(2), 158–221. doi:10.1145/319806.319816

Sioutas, S., Tsakalidis, K., Tsichlas, K., Makris, C., & Manolopoulos, Y. (2007). Indexing mobile objects on the plane revisited. In *Proceedings of 11th east european conference on advances in databases and information systems* (pp. 189-204). New York: Springer.

Tao, Y., Papadias, D., & Sun, J. (2003). The tpr*-tree: an optimized spatio-temporal access method for predictive queries. In *Proceedings of 29th international conference on very large data bases* (pp. 790-801). VLDB Endowment.

Willard, D. E. (1985). Searching unindexed and nonuniformly generated files in log log n time. *SIAM Journal on Computing, 14*(4), 1013–1029. doi:10.1137/0214071

ENDNOTES

[1] We quote a brief description of the proof presented in (Kaporis et al., 2005)

[2] Downloaded 128.971 MBRs from http://www.census.gov/geo/www/tiger/

[3] source code of ISB-tree access method is available at http://www.ionio.gr/${\sim}$~sioutas/New-Software.htmf

This work was previously published in International Journal of Organizational and Collective Intelligence, Volume 1, Issue 4, edited by Hideyasu Sasaki, pp. 78-96, copyright 2010 by IGI Publishing (an imprint of IGI Global).

Compilation of References

3 *DS* (n.d.). Retrieved from http://www.3ds.com/products/3dvia/3dvia-virtools

Aalst, W. M. P., Benatallah, B., Casati, F., Curbera, F., & Verbeek, E. (2007). Business process management: Where business processes and web services meet. *Data & Knowledge Engineering, 61*(1), 1–5. doi:10.1016/j.datak.2006.04.005

Abadi, D. Ahmad., Y., Balazinska., M., Etintemel, U. C., Cherniack, M., Hwang, J., et al. (2005). The design of the borealis stream processing engine. In *Proceedings of the conference on innovative data systems research* (pp. 277-289).

Abe, A. (2002). Computational generation of affective phrase. In *Proceedings of the World Multi Conference on Systemics, Cybernetics and Informatics,* (SCI 2002, Vol. 16, pp. 261-266). Orlando, FL: International Institute of Informatics and Systemics.

Abe, A. (2000). Abductive analogical reasoning. *Systems and Computers in Japan, 31*(1), 11–19. doi:10.1002/(SICI)1520-684X(200001)31:1<11::AID-SCJ2>3.0.CO;2-E

Abel, F., Coi, J., Henze, N., Koesling, A. W., Krause, D., & Olmedilla, D. (2007). Enabling advanced and context-dependent access control in RDF Stores. In *Proceedings of the Sixth International Semantic Web Conference* (pp. 1-14).

Abrami, P. (1996). Computer supported collaborative learning and distance education. *American Journal of Distance Education, 10*(3), 37–41. doi:10.1080/08923649609526920

ABS. (2007a). *5215.0.55.001 - Australian National Accounts: Input-Output Tables (Product Details) - Electronic Publication, 2001-02*. Retrieved from www.abs.gov.au/AUSSTATS/abs@.nsf/Lookup/5215.0.55.001Main+Features12001-02?OpenDocument

ABS. (2007b). *7124.0 - Historical Selected Agriculture Commodities, by State (1861 to Present)*. Retrieved from www.abs.gov.au/AUSSTATS/abs@.nsf/Lookup/7124.0Main+Features12007?OpenDocument.

ABS. (2008a). *4610.0 - Water Account, Australia, 2004-05*. Retrieved from www.abs.gov.au/Ausstats/abs@.nsf/0/34D00D44C3DFB51CCA2568A900143BDE?Open.

ABS. (2008b). *Rice, Sheep and Lamb Numbers Drop to Lowest Levels Since 1920s: ABS*. Retrieved from www.abs.gov.au/ausstats/abs@.nsf/mediareleasesbytitle/9DBD801527947508CA257500001A04C1?OpenDocument

Acmesystems. (n.d.). Retrieved from http://www.acmesystems.it

Adamic, L. A., & Adar, E. (2005). How to search a social network. *Social Networks, 27*(3), 187–203. doi:10.1016/j.socnet.2005.01.007

Adamou, M., Lee, I., & Shin, I. (2002, Septebmer). An energy efficient real-time medium access control protocol for wireless ad-hoc networks. In *Proceedings of the Work in Progress Session of Eighth IEEE Real-Time and Embedded Technology and Applications Symposium.*

Agarwal, P. K., Arge, L., & Erickson, J. (2000). Indexing moving points. In *Proceedings of 19th symposium on principles of database systems* (pp. 175-186). New York: ACM.

Agarwal, R., Sambamurthy, V., & Stair, R. M. (2000). Research report: the evolving relationship between general and specific computer self-efficacy - An empirical assessment. *Information Systems Research, 11*, 418–430. doi:10.1287/isre.11.4.418.11876

Agichtein, E., Castillo, C., Donato, D., & Gionis, A. (2008). Finding High-quality Content in Social Media. In *Proceedings of the International Conference on Web Search and Web Data Mining (WSDM'08)*, Palo Alto, CA (pp. 183-193). New York: ACM.

Ahmad, Y., Cetintemel, U., Jannotti, J., Zgolinski, A., & Zdonik, S. (2005). Network awareness in internet-scale stream processing. In *Proceedings of the IEEE data engineering bulletin.*

Ahn, C., Nah, Y., Park, S., & Kim, J. (2001). An integrated medical information system using XML. In Kim, W., Ling, T. W., Lee, Y. J., & Park, S. S. (Eds.), *Human Society and the Internet, Proceedings - Internet-Related Socio-Economic Issues* (Vol. 2105, pp. 307–322). Berlin: Springer Verlag. doi:10.1007/3-540-47749-7_25

Aiello, G., & Alessi, M. (2007). DNK-WSD: a Distributed Approach for Knowledge Discovery in Peer to Peer Networks. In *Proceedings of the 15th EUROMICRO International Conference on Parallel, Distributed and Network-Based Processing (PDP'07)*, Naples, Italy (pp. 325-332).

Akaike, H. (1974). A new look at the statistical model identification. *IEEE Transactions on Automatic Control*, *19*(6), 716–723. doi:10.1109/TAC.1974.1100705

Akkaya, K., & Younis, M. (2003, May). An energy-aware QoS routing protocol for wireless sensor network. In *Proceedings of the Workshops in the 23rd International Conference on Distributed Computing Systems* (pp. 710-715).

Akyildiz, A.-F., Melodia, T., & Chowdhury, K.-R. (2007, March). A survey on wireless multimedia sensor networks. *Computer Networks*, *51*(4), 921–960. doi:10.1016/j.comnet.2006.10.002

Akyildiz, I., Su, W., Sankarasubramniam, Y., & Cayirci, E. (2002). A survey on sensor networks. *IEEE Communications Magazine*, *n.d.*, 102–114. doi:10.1109/MCOM.2002.1024422

Alani, H., Dasmahapatra, S., O'Hara, K., & Shadbolt, N. (2003). Identifying Communities of Practice through Ontology Network Analysis. *IEEE Intelligent Systems*, *18*(2), 18–25. doi:10.1109/MIS.2003.1193653

Aleman-Meza, B., Halaschek-Wiener, C., & Arpinar, I. B. (2005). Collective Knowledge Composition in a P2P Network. In L. C. Rivero, J. H. Doorn, & V. E. Ferraggine (Eds.), *Encyclopedia of Database Technologies and Applications* (pp. 74-77). Hershey, PA: IGI Global.

Ali-Hasan, N., & Adamic, L. (2007). Expressing social relationships on the blog through links and comments. In *Proc. of International Conference on Weblogs and Social Media, Mar.*

Allan, J. (2003). Challenges in information retrieval and language modeling. Report of a workshop held at the Center for Intelligent information retrieval. *ACM SIGIR Forum*, *37*(1), 31–47. doi:10.1145/945546.945549

Alonso, G., Casati, F., Kuno, H., & Machiraju, V. (2004). *Web services: concepts, architectures and applications*. New York: Springer Verlag.

Alpdemir, M., Mukherjee, A., Paton, N. W., Watson, P., Fernandes, A. A., Gounaris, A., et al. (2003). Ogsa-dqp: A service-based distributed query processor for the grid. In *Proceedings of uk e-science all hands meeting Nottingham.*

Alrifai, M., & Risse, T. (2009). Combining global optimization with local selection for efficient QoS-aware service composition. In *Proceedings of International Conference on World Wide Web (WWW)* (pp. 881-890).

Alrodhan, W. A., & Mitchell, C. J. (2007). Addressing privacy issues in cardspace. In *Proceedings of the Third International Symposium on Information Assurance and Security* (pp. 285-291).

Alter, M. J. (2004). *Science of Flexibility*. Champaign, IL: Human Kinetics.

Amazon. (2009). *Amazon simple storage service (Amazon S3)*. Retrieved August 1, 2009, from http://aws.amazon.com/s3/

Amir, R., & Zeid, A. (2004). *An UML Profile for Service Oriented Architectures*. Paper presented at the Companion to the 19th Annual ACM SIGPLAN Conference on Object-Oriented Programming, Systems, Languages, and Applications, OOPSLA 2004.

Anderson, D. (2001). *Resilient overlay networks*. Unpublished master's thesis, department of electrical engineering and computer science, MIT, Cambridge, MA.

Andersson, A., & Mattsson, C. (1993). Dynamic interpolation search in o(log log n) time. In *Proceedings of 20th international colloquium on automata, languages and programming* (pp. 15-27). New York: Springer.

Androutsellis-Theotokis, S., & Spinellis, D. (2004). A Survey of Peer-to-Peer Content Distribution Technologies. *ACM Computing Surveys*, *36*(4), 335–371. doi:10.1145/1041680.1041681

Angelov, S., & Grefen, P. (2008). An e-contracting reference architecture. *Journal of Systems and Software*, *81*(11), 1816–1844. doi:10.1016/j.jss.2008.02.023

AOP. (2007). *Aspect-Oriented Software Development*. Retrieved from http://www.aosd.net

Arasu, A., Babcock, B., Babu, S., Datar, M., Ito, K., & Motwani, R. (2003). Stream: The stanford stream data manager. *A Quarterly Bulletin of the Computer Society of the IEEE Technical Committee on Data Engineering*, 19–26.

Architecture_Working_Group. (2000). *IEEE Std 1471-2000 Recommended Practice Architectural Description of Software-Intensive Systems*. Washington, DC: IEEE Software Engineering Standards Committee.

Ardagna, D., & Pernici, B. (2007). Adaptive service composition in flexible processes. *IEEE Transactions on Software Engineering*, *33*(6), 369–384. doi:10.1109/TSE.2007.1011

Armstrong, L., Berry, M., & Lamshed, R. (2004). Blogs as electronic learning journals. *e-Journal of Instructional Science and Technology*, *7*(1).

Arsanjani, A. (2004). Service-oriented modeling and architecture. Retrieved from http://www.ibm.com/developerworks/library/ws-soa-design1/

Artiles, J., Gonzalo, J., & Verdejo, F. (2005). A testbed for people searching strategies in the WWW. In Proceedings of the 28th annual International ACM SIGIR conference on Research and Development in Information Retrieval (SIGIR'05), 569-570.

Ashby, W. (1947). Principles of the self-organizing dynamic system. *The Journal of General Psychology*, *37*, 125–128.

Auer, S., Dietzold, S., & Riechert, T. (2006). *OntoWiki - A tool for social, semantic collaboration*. (. *Lecture Notes in Computer Science*, *4273*, 736–749. doi:10.1007/11926078_53

Avnur, R., & Hellerstein, J. (2000). Eddies: Continously adaptive query processing. *ACM sigmod record*.

Avrithis, Y., Kompatsiaris, Y., Staab, S., & Vakali, A. (Eds.). (2008). *Proceedings of the CISWeb (Collective Semantics: Collective Intelligence and the Semantic Web) Workshop, located at the 5th European Semantic Web Conference (ESWC 2008)*, Tenerife, Spain.

Axelrod, R. (1984). *The evolution of cooperation*. New York: Basic Books. ISBN 0-465-02122-2

Bailey, J., Poulovassilis, A., & Wood, P. T. (2002). Analysis and optimisation of event-condition-action rules on XML. *Computer Networks*, *39*, 239–259. doi:10.1016/S1389-1286(02)00208-6

Bao, J., Hu, Z., Caragea, D., Reecy, J., & Honavar, V. G. (2006). A tool for collaborative construction of large biological ontologies, In *Proceedings of the 17ᵗʰ International Conference on Database and Expert Systems Applications.*

Barber, S. K., Graser, T., & Holt, J. (2003). Evaluating dynamic correctness properties of domain reference architectures. *Journal of Systems and Software*, *68*(3), 217–231. doi:10.1016/S0164-1212(03)00064-5

Bazaraa, M. S., Jarvis, J. J., & Sherali, H. D. (2005). *Linear Programming and Network Flows* (3rd ed.). Hoboken, NJ: Wiley-Interscience.

Beckmann, N., Begel, H. P., Schneider, R., & Seeger, B. (1990). The r*-tree: an efficient and robust access method for points and rectangles. *SIGMOD Record*, *19*(2), 322–331. doi:10.1145/93605.98741

Beck, R., Beimborn, D., Weitzel, T., & Konig, W. (2008). Network effects as drivers of individual technology adoption: Analyzing adoption and diffusion of mobile communication services. *Information Systems Frontiers*, *10*(4), 415–429. doi:10.1007/s10796-008-9100-9

Beeri, C., Levy, Y. A., & Rousset, M.-C. (1997): Rewriting queries using views in description logics. Symposium on Principles of Database Systems. In A. Mendelzon & Z. M. Özsoyoglu (Eds.), In *Proceedings of the sixteenth ACM SIGACT-SIGMOD-SIGART symposium on Principles of database systems* (pp. 99-108). New York: ACM Press.

Beer, S. (1966). *Decision and control: The meaning of operational research and management cybernetics*. New York: Wiley.

Begelman, G., Keller, P., & Smadja, F. (2006). Automated tag clustering: Improving search and exploration in the tag space. *In WWW 2006*, Edinburgh, UK.

Begon, M., Harper, J., & Townsend, C. (1996). *Ecology: Individuals, populations and communities*. Oxford, UK: Blackwell Publishing.

Beni, G., & Wang, J. (1989). Swarm intelligence in cellular robotic systems. In *Proceedings of NATO Advanced Workshop on Robots and Biological Systems*, Tuscany, Italy.

Benkler, Y. (2006). *The wealth of networks: How social production transforms markets and freedom*. Yale University Press.

Benslimane, D., Arara, A., Falquet, G., Maamar, Z., Thiran, P., & Gargouri, F. (2006, October 18-20). *Contextual Ontologies: Motivations, Challenges, and Solutions*. Paper presented at the 4th Biennial International Conference on Advances in Information Systems, Izmir, Turkey.

Berbner, R., Spahn, M., Repp, N., Heckmann, O., & Steinmetz, R. (2006). Heuristics for QoS-aware web service composition. In *Proceedings of International Conference on Web Services* (pp. 72-82).

Bernard, R. M., Brauer, A., Abrami, P. C., & Surkes, M. (2004). The development of a questionnaire for predicting online learning achievement. *Distance Education, 25*(1), 31–47. doi:10.1080/0158791042000212440

Bertino, E., Buccafurri, F., Ferrari, E., & Rullo, P. (1999): A Logical Framework for Reasoning on Data Access Control Policies. In B. Werner (Ed.), In *Proceedings of the 12th IEEE Computer Security Foundations Workshop (CSFW-12)* (pp. 175-189). Los Alamitos, CA: IEEE Computer Society Press.

Bertocci, V., Serack, G., & Baker, C. (2007). *Understanding windows cardspace: an introduction to the concepts and challenges of digital identities*. Reading, MA: Addison-Wesley.

Bhargavan, K., Fournet, C., Gordon, A. D., & Swamy, N. (2008). Verified implementations of the information card federated identity-management protocol. In *Asiaccs '08: Proceedings of the 2008 ACM Symposium on Information, Computer and Communications Security* (pp. 123-135). New York: ACM.

Bhattacherjee, A. (2000). Acceptance of e-commerce services: the case of electronic brokerages. *Systems, Man and Cybernetics, Part A, IEEE Transactions, 30*(4), 411-420.

Bialik, C. (2005, May 26). Measuring the impact of blogs requires more than counting. *Retrieved August 3rd, 2005, from* The Wall Street Journal Online at http://online.wsj.com/public/article/0,SB111685593903640572,00.html?mod=2_1125_1.

Bian, J., Liu, Y., Agichtein, E., & Zha, H. (2008). Finding the right facts in the crowd: Factoid question answering over social media. In *Proceeding of the 17th International Conference on World Wide Web (WWW)*, Beijing, China. New York: ACM press.

Bieberstein, N., Laird, R. G., Jones, K., & Mitra, T. (2008). *Executing SOA: A Practical Guide for the Service-Oriented Architect*. Boston: Addison-Wesley.

Bishop, C. M. (2006). *Pattern recognition and machine learning*. London: Springer.

Blaze, M., Feigenbaum, J., & Lacy, J. (1996). Decentralized trust management. In *Proceedings of IEEE Symposium on Security and Privacy* (pp. 164-173).

Bloehdorn, S., Haase, P., Hefke, M., Sure, Y., & Tempich, C. (2005). Intelligent Community Lifecycle Support. In *Proceedings of the 5th International Conference on Knowledge Management (I-KNOW 05)*, Graz, Austria.

Boer, R. C., & van Vliet, H. (2009). On the similarity between requirements and architecture. *Journal of Systems and Software, 82*(3), 544–550. doi:10.1016/j.jss.2008.11.185

Bollen, J., Rodriguez, M. A., & Van, H. (2006). Journal Status. *Scientometrics, 69*(3), 669–687. doi:10.1007/s11192-006-0176-z

Bonabeau, E., Dorigo, M., & Theraulaz, G. (1999). *Swarm intelligence: From natural to artificial system*. UK: Oxford University Press.

Bonatti, P. A., & Festa, P. (2005). On optimal service selection. In *Proceedings of International Conference on World Wide Web (WWW)* (pp. 530-538).

Bonatti, P. A., Duma, C., Fuchs, N., Nejdl, W., Olmedilla, D., Peer, J., et al. (2006). Semantic Web policies - A discussion of requirements and research issues. In Y. Sure, & J. Domingue (Eds.), In *Proceedings of the European Semantic Web Conference* (pp. 712-724).

Boukadi, K., Chaabane, A., & Vincent, L. (2009, May 13-15). *A Framework for Context-Aware Business Processes Modelling.* Paper presented at the In the International Conference on Industrial Engineering and Systems Management, IESM, Montreal, Canada.

Boukadi, K., Ghedira, C., & Vincent, L. (2008). *An Aspect Oriented Approach for Context-Aware Service Domain Adapted to E-Business.* Paper presented at the 20th International Conference on Advanced Information Systems Engineering, Montpellier, France.

Boukadi, K., Vincent, L., & Burlat, P. (2009). *Contextual Service Oriented and Analysis: the IT concerns.*

Boyd, S. (2003). *Are you ready for social software?* Retrieved July 3, 2004, from http://www.darwinmag.com/read/050103/social.html.

BPMI. (2002). *Business Process Management Initiative.* Retrieved from http://www.bpmi.org.

Brandes, U., Kenis, P., Lerner, J., & Raaij, D. (2009). Network Analysis of Collaboration Structure in Wikipedia. In *Proceeding of the 18th International Conference on World Wide Web (WWW)* (pp. 731-740). New York: ACM press.

Brickley, D., & Guha, R. V. (2004). *RDF Vocabulary Description Language 1.0: RDF Schema.* Retrieved from http://www.w3.org/TR/rdf-schema/

Brin, S., & Page, L. (1998). The Anatomy of a Large-Scale Hypertextual Web Search Engine. In *Proceeding of the 7th International World Wide Web Conference (WWW).* New York: ACM press.

Briscoe, G. (2009). *Digital ecosystems.* Unpublished doctoral dissertation, Imperial College London, London.

Briscoe, G., & De Wilde, P. (2006). *Digital Ecosystems: Evolving service-oriented architectures. In Conference on bio inspired models of network, information and computing systems.* Washington, DC: IEEE Press. Retrieved from http://arxiv.org/abs/0712.4102

Briscoe, G., & De Wilde, P. (2008). Digital Ecosystems: Optimisation by a distributed intelligence. In *Proceedings of the Digital ecosystems and technologies conference.* Washington, DC: IEEE Press. Retrieved from http://arxiv.org/abs/0712.4099

Briscoe, G., Chli, M., & Vidal, M. (2006). Creating a Digital Ecosystem: Service-oriented architectures with distributed evolutionary computing (BOF-0759). In *Proceedings of the Javaone conference.* Sun Microsystems. Retrieved from http://arxiv.org/0712.4159

Briscoe, G., Sadedin, S., & Paperin, G. (2007). *Biology of applied digital ecosystems. In Digital ecosystems and technologies conference* (pp. 458-463). Washington, DC: IEEE Press. Retrieved from http://arxiv.org/abs/0712.4153

Briscoe, G., & Sadedin, S. (2007). Digital Business Ecosystems: Natural science paradigms. In Nachira, F., Nicolai, A., Dini, P., Le Louarn, M., & Rivera Le'on, L. (Eds.), *Digital Business Ecosystems* (pp. 48–55). European Commission.

Broekstra, J., Kampman, A., & van Harmelen, F. (2002). Sesame: A generic architecture for storing and querying RDF and RDF Schema. In I. Horrocks, & J. Hendler (Eds.), *Proceedings of the First International Semantic Web Conference* (pp. 54-68). Sardinia, Italy: Springer Verlag.

Bures, E. (2000). Student motivation to learn via computer conferencing. *Research in Higher Education, 41*(5), 593–621. doi:10.1023/A:1007071415363

Burkhardt, M. E., & Brass, D. J. (1990). Changing patterns or patterns of change: The effects of a change in technology on social network structure and power. *Administrative Science Quarterly, 35*, 104–127. doi:10.2307/2393552

Burton-Jones, A., & Hubona, G. S. (2005). Individual differences and usage behavior: Revisiting a technology acceptance model assumption. *The Data Base for Advances in Information Systems, 36*(2), 58.

Bustos, B., Keim, D. A., Saupe, D., Schreck, T., & Vranic, D. V. (2005). Feature-based similarity search in 3D object databases. *ACM Computing Surveys*, 345–387. doi:10.1145/1118890.1118893

Buzan, T. (1996). *The mind map book.* London: Penguin Books.

Cabral, L., Domingue, J., Motta, E., Payne, T., & Hakimpour, F. (2004). Approaches to semantic web services: an overview and comparisons. In *The semantic web: Research and applications* (pp. 225–239). New York: Springer.

Cameron, K. (2005). The laws of identity: Retrieved from http://msdn2.microsoft.com/en-us/library/ms996456.aspx

Camp, J. L. (2004). Digital identity. *IEEE Technology and Society Magazine*, *23*, 34–41. doi:10.1109/MTAS.2004.1337889

Canfora, G., Penta, M. D., Esposito, R., & Villani, M. L. (2006). An approach for QoS-aware service composition based on genetic algorithms. In *Proceedings of International Conference on Genetic and Evolutionary Computation (GECCO)* (pp. 1069-1075).

Canny, J.-F. (1983). *Finding Edges and Lines in Images* (Tech. Rep. No. AI-TR-720). Cambridge, MA: MIT.

Cantu-Paz, E. (1998). A survey of parallel genetic algorithms. *R´eseaux et syst`emes r´epartis, Calculateurs Parall`eles*, *10*, 141-171.

Cardoso, J., & Sheth, A. (2004). Introduction to semantic web services and web process composition. In Cardoso, J., & Sheth, A. (Eds.), *Semantic web services and web process composition* (pp. 1–13). New York: Springer.

Carlsson, B. (1989). Flexibility and the theory of the Firm. *International Journal of Industrial Organization*, *7*(2), 179–203. doi:10.1016/0167-7187(89)90018-0

Carney, D. (2002). Monitoring streams - a new class of data management operations. In *Proceedings of the 28th VLDB conference*.

Casati, F., Fugini, M. G., Mirbel, I., & Pernici, B. (2002). WIRES: A methodology for developing workflow applications. *Requirements Engineering*, *7*(2), 73–106. doi:10.1007/s007660200006

Casati, F., & Shan, M. C. (2001). Dynamic and adaptive composition of e-services. *Information Systems*, *26*(3), 143–163. doi:10.1016/S0306-4379(01)00014-X

Castano, S., & Montanelli, S. (2005). Semantic Self-Formation of Communities of Peers. In *Proceedings of the ESWC Workshop on Ontologies in Peer-to-Peer Communities*, Heraklion, Greece.

Castano, S., Ferrara, A., & Montanelli, S. (2009). The iCoord Knowledge Model for P2P Semantic Coordination. In *Proceedings of the 6th Conference of the Italian Chapter of AIS*, Costa Smeralda (Nu), Italy.

Castano, S., Ferrara, A., Lorusso, D., & Montanelli, S. (2008). Ontology Coordination: The iCoord Project Demonstration. In *Proceedings of the 27th International Conference on Conceptual Modeling (ER 2008)*, Barcelona, Spain (pp. 512-513).

Castano, S., Ferrara, A., & Montanelli, S. (2006). Matching Ontologies in Open Networked Systems: Techniques and Applications. *Journal on Data Semantics*, *5*, 25–63. doi:10.1007/11617808_2

Castro, V. d., Marcos, E., & Sanz, M. L. (2006). A model driven method for service composition modelling: a case study. *International Journal of Web Engineering and Technology*, *2*(4). doi:10.1504/IJWET.2006.010419

Cautis, B. (2007). Distributed access control: A privacy-conscious approach. In *Proceedings of the Twelfth ACM Symposium on Access Control Models and Technologies* (pp. 61-70). New York: ACM Press.

Cavoukian, A. (2006). *7 laws of identity: the case for privacy-embedded laws of identity in the digital age.*

Censor, Y., & Zenios, S. (1998). *Parallel Optimization: Theory, Algorithms, and Applications*. New York: Oxford University Press.

Cernuzzi, L., Cossentino, M., & Zambonell, F. (2000). Process models for agent-based development. *Journal of Engineering Applications of Artificial Intelligence*, *18*(2), 205–222. doi:10.1016/j.engappai.2004.11.015

Chan, H. S., Chiu, D. K. W., Hung, P. C. K., & Leung, H. F. (2005). *Credibility Relationship Management in a Web Service Integration Environment*. Paper presented at the 4th ICIS Workshop on e-Business, Las Vegas, USA.

Chandrasekaran, S., & Franklin, M. J. (2002). Streaming queries over streaming data. In *Proceedings of the 28th VLDB conference*.

Chandrasekaran, S., Cooper, O., Deshpande, A., Franklin, M., Hellerstein, J., Hong, W., et al. (2003). Telegraphcq: Continuous dataflow processing for an uncertain world. In *Proceedings of the conference on innovative data systems research*.

Chandy, K. M., & Lamport, L. (1985). Distributed snapshots: determining global states of distributed systems. In *Proceedings of the ACM transactions on computer systems (TOCS)* (pp. 63-75).

Chappell, D., et al. (2006). Introducing windows cardspace, Microsoft Whitepaper: Retrieved from http://msdn2.microsoft.com/en-us/library/aa480189.aspx

Chau, M., Zeng, D., Chen, H., Huang, M., & Hendriawan, D. (2003). Design and evaluation of a multi-agent collaborative Web mining system. *Decision Support Systems: Web Retrieval and Mining, 35*(1), 167–183. doi:10.1016/S0167-9236(02)00103-3

Cheng, S., Chang, C. K., Zhang, L.-J., & Kim, T.-H. (2007). Towards competitive web services market. In *Proceedings of IEEE International Workshop on Future Trends of Distributed Computing Systems (FTDCS)* (pp. 213-219).

Chen, J. S., Huertas, A., & Medioni, G. (1987). Fast Convolution with Laplacian of Gaussian Masc. *IEEE Trans. PAMI, 9*, 584–590.

Cheong, F. K. W., Chiu, D. K. W., Cheung, S. C., & Hung, P. C. K. (2007). Developing a distributed e-monitoring system for enterprise Website and Web services: An experience report with free libraries and tools. In *Proceedings of the IEEE 2007 International Conference on Web Services (ICWS 2007)*, Salt Lake City, Utah (pp. 1008-1015).

Cherbakov, L., Galambos, G. M., Harishankar, R., Kalyana, S., & Rackham, G. (2005). Impact of service orientation at the business level. *IBM Systems Journal, 44*(4), 653–668. doi:10.1147/sj.444.0653

Cheung, S. C., Chiu, D. K. W., & Till, S. (2002). A three-layer architecture for cross-organization e-contract enactment. In *Proceedings of Web Services, E-Business and Semantic Web Workshop*, Toronto, Ontario, Canada, (pp. 78-92).

Cheung, W., & Huang, W. (2005). Proposing a framework to assess Internet usage in university education: an empirical investigation from a students' perspective. *British Journal of Educational Technology, 36*(2), 237–253. doi:10.1111/j.1467-8535.2005.00455.x

Chiasserini, C., & Magli, E. (2002, September). Energy consumption and image quality in wireless video-surveillance networks. In *Proceedings of the 13th IEEE International Symposium on Personal, Indoor and Mobile Radio Communications (PIMRC)* (pp. 2357-2361).

Chiu, D. K. W., Chan, W. C. W., Lam, K. W. G., Cheung, S. C., & Luk, T. F. (2003). An event driven approach to customer relationship management in an e-brokerage environment. In *Proceedings of the 36th Hawaii International Conference on System Sciences (HICSS36)*, Big Island, Hawaii, IEEE Computer Society Press, CDROM, 10 pages.

Chiu, D. K. W., Cheung, S. C., & Till, S. (2003b) An architecture for e-contract enforcement in an e-service environment. In *Proceedings of the 36th Hawaii International Conference on System Sciences (HICSS36)*, Big Island, Hawaii, IEEE Computer Society Press, CDROM, 10 pages.

Chiu, D. K. W., Cheung, S. C., Kok, D., & Lee, A. (2003). Integrating heterogeneous Web services with WebXcript. In *Proceedings of the 27th Annual International Computer System and Applications Conference (COMPSAC 2003)*, Dallas, Texas (pp. 272-277).

Chiu, D. K. W., Cheung, S. C., Hung, P. C. K., Chiu, S. Y. Y., & Chung, A. K. K. (2005). Developing e-Negotiation support with a meta-modeling approach in a Web services environment. *Decision Support Systems, 40*(1), 51–69. doi:10.1016/j.dss.2004.04.004

Chiu, D. K. W., Cheung, S. C., Kafeza, E., & Leung, H.-F. (2003c). A three-tier view methodology for adapting m-services. *IEEE Transactions on Man, Systems and Cybernetics. Part A, 33*(6), 725–741.

Chiu, D. K. W., Kafeza, M., Cheung, S. C., Kafeza, E., & Hung, P. C. K. (2009). Alerts in healthcare applications: process and data integration. *International Journal of Healthcare Information Systems and Informatics, 4*(2), 36–56.

Chiu, D. K. W., Karlapalem, K., Li, Q., & Kafeza, E. (2002). Workflow views based e-contracts in a cross-organization e-service environment. *Distributed and Parallel Databases, 12*(2-3), 193–216. doi:10.1023/A:1016503218569

Chiu, D. K. W., Kok, D., Lee, A., & Cheung, S. C. (2005b). Integrating legacy sites into Web services with WebXcript. *International Journal of Cooperative Information Systems, 14*(1), 25–44. doi:10.1142/S0218843005001006

Chiu, D. K. W., Leung, H. F., & Lam, K. M. (2009). On the making of service recommendations: an action theory based on utility, reputation, and risk attitude. *Expert Systems with Applications, 36*(2), 3293–3301. doi:10.1016/j.eswa.2008.01.055

Chiu, D. K. W., Li, Q., & Karlapalem, K. (1999). A meta modeling approach for workflow management system supporting exception handling. *Information Systems*, *24*(2), 159–184. doi:10.1016/S0306-4379(99)00010-1

Chiu, D. K. W., Li, Q., & Karlapalem, K. (2001). Web interface-Driven cooperative exception handling in ADOME workflow management system. *Information Systems*, *26*(2), 93–120. doi:10.1016/S0306-4379(01)00012-6

Cho, H.-K. (2005). The use of instant messaging in working relationship development: A case study. *Journal of Computer-Mediated Communication, 10*(4).

Chow, H.-S. I., & Lau, V. P., Wing-chun Lo, T., Sha, Z., & Yun, H. (2007). Service quality in restaurant operations in China: Decision- and experiential-oriented perspectives. *International Journal of Hospitality Management, 26*(3), 698–710. doi:10.1016/j.ijhm.2006.07.001

Chu, M., Reich, J.-E., & Zhao, F. (2004, February). Distributed attention for large video sensor networks. In *Proceedings of the Institute of Defence and Strategic Studies (IDSS)*, London.

Clarke, E. H. (1971). Multipart pricing of public goods. *Public Choice, 11*, 17–33. doi:10.1007/BF01726210

Claub, S., & Kohntopp, M. (2001). Identity management and its support of multilateral security. *Computer Networks, 37*, 205–219. doi:10.1016/S1389-1286(01)00217-1

Cole, S. (1992). A note on a Lagrangian derivation of a general multi-propotional scaling algorithm. *Regional Science and Urban Economics, 22*(2), 291–297. doi:10.1016/0166-0462(92)90017-U

Combettes, P. L. (2003). A Block-iterative Surrogate Constraint Splitting Method for Quadratic Signal Recovery. *IEEE Transactions on Signal Processing, 51*(7), 1771–1782. doi:10.1109/TSP.2003.812846

Conklin, J., & Begeman, M. L. (1988). gibis: a hypertext tool for exploratory policy discussion. In *Proceedings of the ACM Conference on Computer-supported cooperative work*. New York: ACM press.

Connell, S. (2004). *Uses for social software in education: A literature review.* Retrieved August 20th, 2005, from http://soozzone.com/690review.htm.

Cormode, G., & Garofalakis, M. (2007). Streaming in a connected world:quering and tracking distributed data streams. In *Proceedings of the International conf. in data engineering*.

Coutaz, J., Crowley, J. L., Dobson, S., & Garlan, D. (2003). Context is key. *Communications of the ACM, 48*(3).

Crespo, A., & Garcia-Molina, H. (2004). Semantic Overlay Networks for P2P Systems. In *Proceedings of the 3rd International Workshop on Agents and Peer-to-Peer Computing (P2PC 2004)*, New York (pp. 1-13).

Cronin, J. J., Brady, M. K., & Hult, G. T. M. (2000). Assessing the effects of quality, value, and customer satisfaction on consumer behavioral intentions in service environments. *Journal of Retailing, 76*(2), 193–218. doi:10.1016/S0022-4359(00)00028-2

Crossbow MICA2 Mote Specification. (n.d). Retrieved from http://www.xbow.com

Csikszentmihalyi, M., & Sawyer, K. (1995). Creative insight: The social dimension of a solitary moment. In R. J. Sternberg & J. E. Davidson (Eds.), *The nature of insight,* (pp. 329-364). Cambridge, MA: MIT Press.

Curbera, F., Duftler, M. J., Khalaf, R., Nagy, W., Mukhi, N., & Weerawarana, S. (2002). Unraveling the web services web: an introduction to SOAP, WSDL, and UDDI. *IEEE Internet Computing, 6*(2), 86–93. doi:10.1109/4236.991449

Daley, A. (1999). Towards safer electrical installations: The insurer's view. In *Proceedings of IEEE Colloquium on toward safer electrical installations - learning the lessons* (pp. 1-6).

Damiani, E., De Capitani di Vimercati, S., Fugazza, C., & Samarati, P. (2004). Extending policy languages to the Semantic Web. In *Proceedings of the International Conference on Web Engineering* (pp. 330-343).

Das, T., Nandi, S., & Ganguly, N. (2009). Community Formation and Search in P2P: A Robust and Self-Adjusting Algorithm. In *Proceedings of the 3rd Workshop on Intelligent Networks: Adaptation, Communication & Reconfiguration (IAMCOM 2009)*, Bangalore, India.

Davies, J., Duke, A., & Sure, Y. (2004). OntoShare - An Ontology-based Knowledge Sharing System for virtual Communities of Practice. *The Journal of Universal Computer Science, 10*(3), 262–283.

Davis, F. D., Bagozzi, R. P., & Warshaw, P. R. (1989). User acceptance of computer technology: A comparison of two theoretical models. *Management Science, 35*(8), 982–1003. doi:10.1287/mnsc.35.8.982

Davis, M. M., & Maggard, M. J. (1990). An analysis of customer satisfaction with waiting times in a two-stage service process. *Journal of Operations Management, 9*(3), 324–334. doi:10.1016/0272-6963(90)90158-A

Dawkins, R. (1989). *The selfish gene* (2nd edition). UK: Oxford University Press

Dayal, U. (1988). Active database management systems. In *Proceedings of the 3rd International Conference on Data and Knowledge Bases,* (pp. 150-169).

Deb, B., Bhatnagar, S., & Nath, B. (2003, October). Re-InForM: Reliable information forwarding using multiple paths in sensor networks. In *Proceedings of 28th Annual IEEE International Conference on Local Computer Networks*, Bonn, Germany (pp. 406-415).

Dell Corp. (2007) *Dell's Online policies.* Retreived March 31, 2009 from http://www.ap.dell.com/ap/hk/en/gen/local/legal_terms.htm

Delrieux, C., Dominguez, J., & Repetto, A. (2002). Advanced techniques for real-time flow visualization. In Sisti, A. F., & Trevisani, D. A. (Eds.), *Enabling Technologies for Simulation Science Vi (Vol. 4716*, pp. 375–385). Bellingham, WA: Spie-Int Soc Optical Engineering.

Dey, A. K., Abowd, G. D., & Salber, D. (2001). A Conceptual Framework and a Toolkit for Supporting the Rapid Prototyping of Context-Aware Applications. *Human-Computer Interaction, 16*(2), 97–166. doi:10.1207/S15327051HCI16234_02

Diederich, J., & Iofciu, T. (2006). Finding communities of practice from user profiles based on folksonomies. *In Proceedings of the 1st International Workshop on Building Technology Enhanced Learning Solutions for Communities of Practice.*

Dietrich, E., Markman, A. B., Stilwell, H., & Winkley, M. (2003). The prepared mind: The role of representational change in chance discovery. In Y. Ohsawa & P. McBurney, (Eds.), *Chance discovery,* (pp. 208-230). Heidelberg, Germany: Springer.

Dijkman, R., Dumas, M., & García-Bañuelos, L. (2009). Graph matching algorithms for business process model similarity search. In U. Dayal, J. Eder, J. Koehler & H. A. Reijers (Eds.), *Proceedings of Business Process Management, 7th International Conference, BPM 2009*, Ulm, Germany (Vol. 5701, pp. 48-63). Berlin: Springer.

Dini, P., Lombardo, G., Mansell, R., Razavi, A., Moschoyiannis, S., & Krause, P. (2008). Beyond interoperability to digital ecosystems: regional innovation and socio-economic development led by SMEs. *International Journal of Technological Learning. Innovation and Development, 1*, 410–426.

Donaldson, M. (1992). *Human minds: An exploration.* London: Penguin Books.

Downes, I., Rad, L. B., & Aghajan, H. (2006, March). Development of a mote for wireless image sensor networks. In *Proceedings of the COGnitive systems with Interactive Sensors*, Paris.

Duma, C., Herzog, A., & Shahmehri, N. (2007). Privacy in the semantic web: What policy languages have to offer. In *Proceedings of the Eighth IEEE International Workshop on Policies for Distributed Systems and Networks* (pp. 109-118).

Durkheim, É. (1912). *The elementary forms of religious life.*

Eclipse-Foundation. (2009). Higgins open source framework: Retrieved from http://www.eclipse.org/higgins/higgins-charter.php

Ehrlich, K., Lin, C. Y., & Griffiths-Fisher, V. (2007). Searching for experts in the enterprise: Combining text and social network analysis. *Group, 07*, 117–126.

Elwick, J. (2003). Herbert Spencer and the disunity of the social organism. *History of Science, 41*, 35–72.

Engelbrecht, A. P. (2005). *Fundamentals of computational swarm intelligence.* Hoboken, NJ: Wiley.

Erl, T. (2006). *Service-oriented architecture: Concepts, technology, and design.* Prentice-Hall.

Erl, T. (2005). *Service-Oriented Architecture (SOA): Concepts, Technology, and Design.* Upper Saddle River, NJ: Prentice Hall.

Erradi, A., Anand, S., & Kulkarni, N. (2006b, September 18-22). *SOAF: An Architectural Framework for Service Definition and Realization.* Paper presented at the IEEE International Conference on Services Computing (SCC'06), Chicago.

Esuli, A., & Sebastiani, F. (2007). PageRanking WordNet synsets: An Application to Opinion-Related Properties. In *Proceedings of the 35th Meeting of the Association for Computational Linguistics*, Prague, CZ (pp. 424-431).

Faget, J., Marin, M., Patrick, M., Owens, V. J., & Tarin, L.-O. (2003). Business processes and business rules: business agility becomes real. In *Proceedings of Workflow Handbook, 2003*, 77–92.

Farmer, R. (2005). Instant messaging: IM online! RU? *EDUCAUSE Review, 40*(6).

Farquhar, A., Fikes, R., & Rice, J. (1997). The Ontolingua server: A tool for collaborative ontology construction. *International Journal of Human-Computer Studies, 46*(6), 707. doi:10.1006/ijhc.1996.0121

Felemban, E., Lee, C.-G., Ekici, E., Boder, R., & Vural, S. (2005, March). Probabilistic QoS guarantee in reliability and timeliness domains in wireless sensor networks. In *Proceedings of 24th Annual Joint Conference of the IEEE Computer and Communications* (pp. 2646-2657).

Feng, W., Code, B., Kaiser, E., Shea, M., & Feng, W. (2003, November). Panoptes: Scalable low-power video sensor networking technologies. In *Proceedings of the eleventh ACM international conference on Multimedia* (pp. 90-91).

Ferdig, R. E., & Trammell, K. D. (2004, February). *Content delivery in the blogosphere.* Retrieved November 7th, 2005, from T.H.E Journal Online at http://www.thejournal.com/magazine/vault/A4677.cfm

Ferrara, A., Montanelli, S., Varese, G., & Castano, S. (2009). *Natural Language Ontology Authoring in iCoord. International Journal of Information Technology and Database Systems.* IJITDAS.

Finke, R. A. (1995). Creative insight and pre-inventive forms. In R.J. Sternberg & J.E. Davidson (Eds.), *The nature of insight,* (pp. 255-280). Cambridge, MA: MIT Press.

Finke, R. A., Ward, T. B., & Smith, S. M. (1992). *Creative cognition.* Cambridge, MA: MIT Press.

Fischer, G. (2001). Communities of interest: Learning through the interaction of multiple knowledge systems, *The 24th IRIS Conference*, Bergen, Norway, 1-14.

Flesch, R. F. (1949). *The Art of Readable Writing.* New York: Harper & Row.

Flew, T. (2008). *New media: An introduction.* Melbourne, Australia: Oxford University Press

Friedman, D., & Sunder, S. (1994). *Experimental methods: A primer for economics.* UK: Cambridge University Press.

Fujita, K., Takenaka, T., & Ueda, K. (2008). *Service diffusion in the market considering consumers' subjective value.* Paper presented at the 5th International Conference on Soft Computing as Transdisciplinary Science and Technology, Pontoise, France.

Gaede, V., & Gunther, O. (1998). Multidimensional access methods. *ACM Computing Surveys, 30*(2), 170–231. doi:10.1145/280277.280279

Gale, D., & Shapley, L. S. (1962). College admissions and the stability of marriage. *The American Mathematical Monthly, 69*(1), 9–15. doi:10.2307/2312726

Gartner. (2009). *Gartner says worldwide SaaS revenue to grow 22 percent in 2009.* Retrieved August 1, 2009, from http://www.gartner.com/it/page.jsp?id=968412

Gay, D., Levis, P., von Behren, R., Welsh, M., Brewer, E., & Culler, D. (2003, June). The nesC language: a holistic approach to network embedded systems. In *Proceedings of the ACM SIGPLAN 2003 Conf. on Programming Language Design and Implementation (PLDI)*, San Diego, CA.

Gentner, D. (1989). The mechanisms of analogical learning. *Similarity and Analogical Reasoning,* (pp. 199-241). Cambridge, UK: University Press.

Gentner, D. (1983). Structure mapping: A theoretical framework for analogy. *Cognitive Science, 7*(2), 155–170.

Gentzsch, W. (2002). Grid computing: a new technology for the advanced Web. In *Proceedings of the NATO Advanced Research Workshop on Advanced Environments, Tools, and Applications for Cluster Computing,* (Lecture Notes in Computer Science, 2326, pp. 1-15).

Georgakopoulos, D., Hornick, M., & Sheth, A. (1995). An overview of workflow management: from process modeling to workflow automation infrastructure. *Distributed and Parallel Databases, 3*, 119–153. doi:10.1007/BF01277643

Gerla, M., & Xu, K. (2003, December). Multimedia streaming in large-scale sensor networks with mobile swarms. *SIGMOD Record, 32*(4), 72–76. doi:10.1145/959060.959073

Gick, M. L., & Holyoak, K. J. (1980). Analogical problem solving. *Cognitive Psychology, 12*, 306–355. doi:10.1016/0010-0285(80)90013-4

Goebel, R. (1989). A sketch of analogy as reasoning with equality hypotheses. In *Proceedings of the International Workshop Analogical and Inductive Inference, LNAI-397*, 243–253.

Goh, A., Koha, Y. K., & Domazetb, D. S. (2001). ECA rule-based support for workflows. *Artificial Intelligence in Engineering, 15*, 37–46. doi:10.1016/S0954-1810(00)00028-5

Golder, S. A., & Huberman, B. A. (2006). Usage patterns of collaborative tagging systems. *Journal of Information Science, 32*(2), 198. doi:10.1177/0165551506062337

Gomi, H., Hatakeyama, M., Hosono, S., & Fujita, S. (2005). *A delegation framework for federated identity management.* Proc. of the ACM workshop on Digital identity management (pp. 94-103).

Gong, Y., Janssen, M., Overbeek, S. J., & Zuurmond, A. (2009, November 10-13). Enabling flexible processes by ECA orchestration architecture. In *Proceedings of the 3rd International Conference on Theory and Practice of Electronic Governance (ICEGOV 2009)*, Bogota, Columbia. New York: ACM Press.

Gordon, L. A., Loeb, M. P., & Sohail, T. (2003). A framework for insurance for cyber-risk management. *Communications of the ACM, 46*(3), 81–85. doi:10.1145/636772.636774

Gorman, K., Agarwal, D., & Abbadi, A. E. (2002). Multiple query optimization by cache-aware middleware using query teamwork. In *Proceedings of the 18th intl conf. on data engineering.*

Gosain, S., Malhotra, A., & Sawy, O. A. E. (2005). Coordinating for flexibility in e-Business supply chains. *Journal of Management Information Systems, 21*(3), 7–45.

Gottschalk, K., Graham, S., Kreger, H., & Snell, J. (2002). Introduction to web services architecture. *IBM Systems Journal, 41*, 170–177. doi:10.1147/sj.412.0170

Grandison, T., & Sloman, M. (2000). *A survey of trust in internet applications. IEEE Communications Surveys.* Fourth Quarter.

Greenacre, M. J. (2007). *Correspondence analysis in practice (Interdisciplinary statistics).* London: Chapman & Hall.

Green, D., Klomp, N., Rimmington, G., & Sadedin, S. (2006). *Complexity in landscape ecology.* New York: Springer.

Grefen, P., Aberer, K., Hoffner, Y., & Ludwig, H. (2000). CrossFlow: Cross-organizational workflow management in dynamic virtual enterprises. *International Journal of Computer Systems Science & Engineering, 15*(5), 277–290.

Groves, T. (1973). Incentives in teams. *Econometrica, 41*, 617–631. doi:10.2307/1914085

Gruber, T. (2008). Collective Knowledge Systems: where the Social Web meets the Semantic Web. *Journal of Web Semantics, 6*(1), 4–13.

Gu, W., & Wei, W. (2006). Automatic Community Discovery in Peer-to-Peer Systems. In *Proceedings of the 5th International Conference on Grid and Cooperative Computing Workshops (GCC 2006)*, Changsha, Hunan, China (pp. 110-116).

Guo, L., Jiang, S., Xiao, L., & Zhang, X. (2005). Fast and low-cost search schemes by exploiting localities in p2p networks. *Journal of Parallel and Distributed Computing, 65*(6), 729–742. doi:10.1016/j.jpdc.2005.01.007

Gupta, A., Sudarshan, S., & Viswanathan, S. (2001). Query scheduling in multi query optimization. In *Proceedings of the intl. symposium on database engineering and applications* (pp. 11-19).

Haken, H. (1977). *Synergetics: an introduction: nonequilibrium phase transitions and self-organization in physics, chemistry, and biology.* New York: Springer.

Halevy, A. Y. (2001). Answering queries using views: A survey. *The VLDB Journal, 10*(4), 270–294. doi:10.1007/s007780100054

Halevy, A., Ives, Z., Madhavan, J., Mork, P., Suciu, D., & Tatarinov, I. (2004). The Piazza Peer Data Management System. *IEEE Transactions on Knowledge and Data Engineering, 16*(7), 787–798. doi:10.1109/TKDE.2004.1318562

Halpin, H., Robu, V., & Shepherd, H. (2007). The complex dynamics of collaborative tagging, In *Proceedings of the 16th International Conference on World Wide Web*, (pp. 211-220).

Han, B. M., Song, S. J., Lee, K. M., Jang, K. S., Shin, D. R., & Icact. (2006). *Multi-Agent System based efficient healthcare service*. Seoul, South Korea: National Computerization Agency.

Hansen, M. D. (2007) *SOA using Java(TM) Web services*. NJ: Prentice Hall PTR.

Hansen, M., Berlich, P., Camenisch, J., Claub, S., Pfitzmann, A., & Waidner, M. (2004). Privacy-enhancing identity management. *Information Security Technical Report, 9*, 35–44. doi:10.1016/S1363-4127(04)00014-7

Harman, M. (2007). The current state and future of search based software engineering. In L. Briand & A. Wolf, (Eds.), *Future of software engineering 2007*, (pp 342-357).

Harris, C., & Stephens, M. (1998). Combined Corner and Edge Detector. *Alvey, 88*, 147–152.

Hasan, A. N., & Adamic, L. (2007). Expressing social relationships on the blog through links and comments. *In Proc. of International Conference on Weblogs and Social Media*, Mar.

He, T., Stankovic, J., Chenyang, L., & Abdelzaher, T. (2003, May). SPEED: A stateless protocol for real-time communication in sensor networks. In *Proceedings of the 23rd International Conference on Distributed Computing Systems* (pp. 46-55).

Heflin, J., Hendler, J., & Luke, S. (1999). *SHOE: A knowledge representation language for internet applications*. (Tech. Rep. No. 99-71). College Park, MD: University of Maryland, Dept. of Computer Science.

Herrero, P., Bosque, J. L., Salvadores, M., & Pérez, M. S. (2008). WE-AMBLE: A workflow engine to manage awareness in collaborative grid environments. *International Journal of High Performance Computing Applications, 22*(3), 250–267. doi:10.1177/1094342007086225

Heuvel, W.-J. v. d., Hasselbring, W., & Papazoglou, M. (2000). Top-Down Enterprise Application Integration with Reference Models. *Australian Journal of Information Systems*.

Hevner, A. R., March, S. T., Park, J., & Ram, S. (2004). Design science in information systems research. *MIS Quarterly, 28*(1), 75–105.

Heylighen, F. (2002). The science of self-organization and adaptivity. *The Encyclopedia of Life Support Systems*, 253-280.

Heylighen, F., & Joslyn, C. (2001). Cybernetics and second order cybernetics. *Encyclopedia of Physical Science & Technology, 4*, 155-170.

Heymann, P., Koutrika, G., & Garcia-Molina, H. (2008). Can social bookmarking improve web search? *In Proceedings of WSDM'2008*. ACM, 195-206.

Hobbs, L., Hillson, S., Lawande, S., & Smith, P. (2005). *Oracle Database 10g Data Warehousing*. Dordrecht, The Netherlands: Elsevier Digital Press.

Holland, J. (1995). *Hidden order: How adaptation builds complexity*. Cambridge, MA: Perseus Books.

Hong, W., Thong, J. Y. L., Wong, W.-M., & Tam, K.-Y. (2002). Determinants of user acceptance of digital libraries: an empirical examination of individual differences and system characteristics. *Journal of Management Information Systems, 18*(3), 97–124.

Horie, K., & Ohsawa, Y. (2006). Product designed on scenario maps using pictorial keygraph. *WSEAS Transaction on Information Science and Application, 3*(7), 1324–1331.

Hoschka, P. (1998). *The social web research program: Linking people through virtual environments*. Retrieved on June 8, 2007, from http://www.fit.fhg.de/~hoschka/Social%20Web.htm.

Hose, K., Roth, A., Zeitz, A., Sattler, K.-U., & Naumann, F. (2008). A Research Agenda for Query Processing in Large-Scale Peer Data Management Systems. *Information Systems, 33*(7-8), 597–610. doi:10.1016/j.is.2008.01.012

Hou, J., & Zhang, Y. (2003). Utilizing Hyperlink Transitivity to Improve Web Page Clustering, in Klaus Dieter-Schewe (ed.), Database Technologies 2003: Proceedings of the Fourteenth Australasian Database Conference. *Conferences in Research and Practice in Information Technology*, 49-57, Australian Computer Society Inc., Australia.

Hu, J. (2001). *CNET news: Viruses wiggle into IM chats.* Retrieved August 31, 2006, from http://www.library.ucsb.edu/untangle/langston.html

Hu, M., Lim, E., Sun, A., & Lauw, W. H. (2007). Measuring Article Quality in Wikipedia: Models and Evaluation. In *Proceedings of the 16th ACM Conference on Information and Knowledge Management* (pp. 243-252). New York: ACM press.

Hubona, G. S., & Kennick, E. (1996). The influence of external variables on information technology usage behavior. In J.F. Nunamaker & R.H. Sprague (Eds.), *Proceedings of the 29th Annual Hawaii International Conference on Systems Sciences,* Maui (pp.166-76).

Huemer, C., Liegl, P., Schuster, R., & Zapletal, M. (2008). A 3-level e-business registry meta model. In *Proceedings of the 2008 IEEE International Conference on Services Computing,* Washington, DC, USA (pp. 441-450).

Hurley, S., & Chater, N. (2005). *Perspectives on imitation -from neuroscience to social science.* Cambridge, MA: MIT Press.

Hwang, J., & Lambert, C. U. (2008). The interaction of major resources and their influence on waiting times in a multi-stage restaurant. *International Journal of Hospitality Management, 27*(4), 541–551. doi:10.1016/j.ijhm.2007.08.005

Iandoli, L. K., Klein, M., & Zollo, G. (2008). *Can We Exploit Collective Intelligence for Collaborative Deliberation? The Case of the Climate Change Collaboratorium.* Cambridge, MA: MIT.

Igbaria, M., Guimaraes, T., & Davis, G. B. (1995). Testing the determinants of microcom-puter usage via a structural model. *Journal of Management Information Systems, 11*(4), 87–114.

Irani, T. (1998). Communication potential, information richness and attitude. *ALN Magazine, 2.*

Irvine, M. (2006). *E-mail losing ground to IM, text messaging, Young people driving switch to instant gratification communication.* Retrieved September 3, 2006, from http://msnbc.msn.com/id/13921601/wid/11915829

Isaacs, E., et al. (2002). *The character, functions, and styles of instant messaging in the workplace.* Paper presented at the Proceedings of the 2002 ACM conference on Computer supported cooperative work New Orleans, Louisiana, USA

Ishigaki, T., & Motomura, T. Dohi, Masako, & Mochimaru, M. (2009, June 17-19). *Analysis of continuous use by a Bayesian network modeling based on a questionnaire data.* Paper presented at the Annual Conference of JSAI, Kagawa, Japan.

Jager, W. (2007). The four P's in social simulation, A perspective on how marketing could benefit from the use of social simulation. *Journal of Business Research, 60*(8), 868–875. doi:10.1016/j.jbusres.2007.02.003

Jain, A., & Farkas, C. (2006). Secure resource description framework: An access control model. In *Proceedings of the Eleventh ACM Symposium on Access Control Models and Technologies* (pp. 121-129).

Jajodia, S., Samarati, P., Sapino, M. L., & Subrahmaninan, V. S. (2001). Flexible support for multiple access control policies. *ACM Transactions on Database Systems, 26*(2), 214–260. doi:10.1145/383891.383894

Janssen, M. (2007, December 10-13). *Adaptability and accountability of information architectures in interorganizational networks.* Paper presented at the International Conference on Electronic Governance (ICEGOV) Macao, China.

Janssen, M. A., & Jager, W. (2003). Simulating market dynamics: Interactions between consumer psychology and social networks. *Artificial Life, 9*(4), 343–356. doi:10.1162/106454603322694807

Janssen, M., & Joha, A. (2006). Motives for establishing shared service centers in public administrations. *International Journal of Information Management, 26*(2), 102–115. doi:10.1016/j.ijinfomgt.2005.11.006

Janssen, M., Joha, A., & Zuurmond, A. (2009). Simulation and animation for adopting shared services: Evaluating and comparing alternative arrangements. *Government Information Quarterly, 26*(1), 15–24. doi:10.1016/j.giq.2008.08.004

Japanese Ministry of Economy. Trade and Industry (2007). *Towards innovation and productivity, improvement in service industries.* Retrieved March 27, 2009, from http://www.meti.go.jp/english/report/downloadfiles/0707ServiceIndustries.pdf

Japanese Ministry of Internal Affairs, and Communications. (2006). *The number of business establishments and companies in service sectors.* Retrieved November 22, 2009, from http://www.stat.go.jp/data/jigyou/2006/kakuhou/gaiyou/02.htm

Javanmardi, S., Amini, M., & Jalili, R. (2006). An access control model for protecting Semantic Web resources. In *Proceedings of the Second International Semantic Web Policy Workshop.*

Jenkins., et al. (2006). *Confronting the challenges of the participatory culture.* Retrieved on March 19, 2007, http://incsub.org/awards/2006/nominations-for-best-research-paper-2006/

Jensen, Ø., & Hansen, K. V. (2007). Consumer values among restaurant customers. *International Journal of Hospitality Management, 26*(3), 603–622. doi:10.1016/j.ijhm.2006.05.004

Jeong, D., Jing, Y., & Baik, D.-K. (2007). Access control model based on RDB security policy for OWL ontology. In Y. Shi, et al. (Eds.), In *Proceedings of the Seventh International Conference on Computational Science* (pp. 720-727).

Jordan, D., & Evdemon, J. (2007). *Web services business process execution language version 2.0.* Retrieved May 31, 2009, from http://docs.oasis-open.org/wsbpel/2.0/OS/wsbpel-v2.0-OS.html

Josang, A., Fabre, J., Hay, B., Dalziel, J., & Pope, S. (2005). Trust requirements in identity management. In Acsw frontiers '05: In *Proceedings of the 2005 Australasian Workshop on Grid Computing and E-Research*, Darlinghurst, Australia (pp. 99–108). Darlinghurst, Australia: Australian Computer Society, Inc.

Kacprzyk, J., & Fedrizzi, M. (1988). A "soft" measure of consensus in the setting of partial (fuzzy) preferences. *European Journal of Operational Research, n.d.*, 316–325. doi:10.1016/0377-2217(88)90152-X

Kagal, L., Finin, T., & Joshi, A. (2003). A policy based approach to security for the Semantic Web. In *Proceedings of the Second International Semantic Web Conference* (pp. 402-418). New York: ACM Press.

Kahn, M. (2009). *SGI XE Cluster SGI XE Cluster System Details.* Retrieved from www.nf.nci.org.au/facilities/vayu/hardware.php

Kamvar, S. D., Schlosser, M. T., & Garcia-Molina, H. (2003). The EigenTrust Algorithm for Reputation Management in P2P Networks. In *Proceedings of the Proceedings of the 12th International World Wide Web Conference*, Budapest, Hungary.

Kaplan-Leiserson, E. (2003). We-learning: Social software and e-learning. Retrieved July 2, 2004, from http://www.learningcircuits.org/2003/dec2003/kaplan.htm

Kaporis, A. C., Makris, C., Mavritsakis, G., Sioutas, S., Tsakalidis, A. K., & Tsichlas, K. (2005). Isb-tree: A new indexing scheme with efficient expected behaviour. In *Proceedings of 13th international symposium on algorithms and computation* (pp. 318-327). New York: Springer.

Kaporis, A., Makris, C., Sioutas, S., Tsakalidis, A., Tsichlas, K., & Zaroliagis, C. (2003). Improved bounds for finger search on a ram. In *Proceedings of 12th annual european symposium on algorithms* (pp. 325-336). New York: Springer.

Karahanna, E., & Straub, D. (1999). The psychological origins of perceived usefulness and ease-of-use. *Information & Management, 35*(4), 237–250. doi:10.1016/S0378-7206(98)00096-2

Kari, L., & Rozenberg, G. (2008). The many facets of natural computing. *Communications of the ACM, 51*(10), 72–83. doi:10.1145/1400181.1400200

Kasahara, K., et al. (1996). Viewpoint-based measurement of semantic similarity between words. In *Proceedings of the 5th Workshop on Artificial Intelligence & Statistics,* (LNS112, pp. 433-442). New York: Springer.

Kato, H., & Billinghurst, M. (1999, October). Marker Tracking and HMD Calibration for a video-based Augmented Reality Conferencing System. In *Proceedings of the 2nd International Workshop on Augmented Reality (IWAR)*, San Francisco, CA.

Katz, M. L., & Shapiro, C. (1992). Network effects, software provision, and standardization. *The Journal of Industrial Economics, 40*(1), 85–103. doi:10.2307/2950627

Kaushik, S., Wijesekera, D., & Ammann, P. (2005). Policy-based dissemination of partial web-ontologies. In *Proceedings of the 2005 Workshop on Secure Web Services* (pp. 43-52).

Khambatti, M., Ryu, K. D., & Dasgupta, P. (2002). Efficient Discovery of Implicitly Formed Peer-to-Peer Communities. *International Journal of Parallel and Distributed Systems and Networks, 5*(4), 155–164.

Kimita, K., Yoshimitu, Y., Shimomura, Y., Arai, T., & Asme. (2008, Aug 03-06). *A customers' value model for Sustainable service design.* Paper presented at the ASME International Design Engineering Technical Conferences/ Computers and Information in Engineering Conference, New York.

King, A., & Pimm, S. (1983). Complexity, diversity, and stability: A reconciliation of theoretical and empirical results. *American Naturalist, 122,* 229–239.

Klievink, A. J., Derks, W., & Janssen, M. (2008). Enterprise architecture and governance challenges for orchestrating public-private cooperation. In Saha, P. (Ed.), *Advances in Government Enterprise Architecture* (pp. 263–283). Hershey, PA: IGI Global.

Koch, M., & Worndl, W. (2001). *Community support and identity management.* Paper presented at the Seventh European Conference on Computer-Supported Cooperative Work, Bonn, Germany.

Kohonen, T. (1989). *Self-organization and associative memory.* New York: Springer.

Kokash, N., & D'Andrea, V. (2007). Evaluating quality of web services: a risk-driven approach. In *Proceedings of International Conference on Business Information Systems (BIS)* (pp. 180-194).

Kollios, G., Gunopulos, D., & Tsotras, V. J. (1999). On indexing mobile objects. In *Proceedings of 18th symposium on principles of database systems* (pp. 261-272). New York: ACM.

Korb, K. B., & Nicholson, A. E. (2004). *Bayesian artificial intelligence.* Boca Raton, FL: Chapman & Hall/CRC.

Kotis, K., & Vouros, G. (2005). Human-centered ontology engineering: The HCOME Methodology. *Knowledge and Information Systems, 10*(1), 109–131. doi:10.1007/s10115-005-0227-4

Koza, J. (1992). Overview of genetic programming. In *Genetic programming: On the programming of computers by means of natural selection* (pp. 73–78). Cambridge, MA: MIT.

Krafzig, D., Banke, K., & Slama, D. (2004). *Enterprise soa: Service-oriented architecture best practices.* Upper Saddle River, NJ: Prentice Hall.

Krishna, P. R., Karlapalem, K., Dani, A. R., & Chiu, D. K. W. (2004). An ER^EC framework for e-contract modeling, enactment and monitoring. *Data & Knowledge Engineering, 51*(1), 31–58. doi:10.1016/j.datak.2004.03.006

Krotzsch, M., Vrandecic, D., Volkel, M., & Haller, H. (2007). Semantic Wikipedia. *Journal of Web Semantics, 5,* 251–261. doi:10.1016/j.websem.2007.09.001

Kulkarni, P., Ganesan, D., Shenoy, P., & Lu, Q. (2005, November). SensEye: a multi-tier camera sensor network. In *Proceedings of the ACM Multimedia,* Singapore.

Kuntschke, R., Stegmaier, B., Kemper, A., & Reiser, A. (2005). Streamglobe: Processing and sharing data streams in grid-based p2p infrastructures. In *Proceedings of the 31st vldb conference* (pp. 1259-1262).

Kuo, Y. S., Tseng, L., Hu, H., & Shih, N. C. (2006). An XML interaction service for workflow applications. In *Proceedings of the 2006 ACM Symposium on Document Engineering,* (pp. 53-55). New York.

Kwok, K., & Chiu, D. K. W. (2004). An integrated Web services architecture for financial content management. In *Proceedings of the 37th Hawaii International Conference on System Sciences (HICSS37),* Big Island, Hawaii, Jan 2004, IEEE Computer Society Press, CDROM, 10 pages

Lafferty, J., Sleator, S., & Temperley, D. (1992). Grammatical trigrams: A probabilistic model of link grammar. In *Proceedings of the AAAI Fall Symposium on Probabilistic Approaches to Natural Language.*

Lakshmanan, V. S. L., Wang, H., & Zhao, Z. (2006). Answering tree pattern queries using views. In *Proceedings of the Thirty Second International Conference on Very Large Databases* (pp. 571-582).

Lam, A. C. Y., & Chiu, D. K. W. (2006). Cooperative brokerage integration for transaction capacity sharing: A case study in Hong Kong. In *Proceedings of the 39th Hawaii International Conference on System Sciences (HICSS39),* IEEE Press, CDROM.

Landry, B. et al. (2006). Measuring Student perceptions of blackboard using the technology acceptance model. *Decision Sciences Journal of Innovative Education, V4N1.*

Lau, G. K. T., Chiu, D. K. W., & Hung, P. C. K. (2006). Web-service based information integration for decision support: A case study on e-mortgage contract matchmaking service. In *Proceedings of the 39th Hawaii International Conference on System Sciences (HICSS39)*, IEEE Press, CDROM.

Lavonen, J. (2000). Using computers in science and technology education. *SIGCSE Bulletin, 33*(v), 127–135. doi:10.1145/571922.571966

Leadbeater, C. (2008). *We-think: The power of mass creativity*. London: Profile.

Lee, J., Ng, L. H., & Ng, L. L. (2002). An analysis of students' preparation for the virtual learning environment. *The Internet and Higher Education, 4*, 231–242. doi:10.1016/S1096-7516(01)00063-X

Lehn, J. (1990). Perspectives in supramolecular chemistry—from molecular recognition towards molecular information processing and self-organization. *Angewandte Chemie International Edition in English, 29*, 1304–1319.

Lendaris, G. (1964). On the definition of self-organizing systems. In W. Banzhaf (Ed.), *Proceedings of the European conference on advances in artificial life* (pp. 324-325). Washington, DC: IEEE Press.

Lenzen, M., Wood, R., & Gallego, B. (2006, 26-28 July). *RAS matrix balancing under conflicting information.* Paper presented at the Intermediate Input-Output Meetings 2006 on Sustainability, Trade and Productivity, Sendai, Japan.

Levcopoulos, C., & Overmars, M. H. (1988). A balanced search tree with o(1) worst case update time. *Acta Inf., 26*(3), 269–277. doi:10.1007/BF00299635

Levin, S. (1998). Ecosystems and the biosphere as complex adaptive systems. *Ecosystems (New York, N.Y.), 1*, 431–436.

Levins, R. (1969). Some demographic and genetic consequences of environmental heterogeneity for biological control. *Bulletin of the Entomological Society of America, 15*, 237–240.

Levy, P. (1999). *Collective intelligence: Mankind's emerging world in cyberspace*. Cambridge, MA: Basic Books

Levy, D., & Marshall, C. (1994). What color was George Washington's white horse? A look at the assumptions underlying digital libraries. In *Proceedings of Digital Libraries, 94*, 163–169.

Leymann, F., Roller, D., & Schmidt, M. (2002). Web services and business process management. *IBM Systems Journal, 41*, 198–211.

Li, L., Wei, J., & Huang, T. (2007). High performance approach for Multi-QoS constrained web services selection. In *Proceedings of International Conference on Service Oriented Computing (ICSOC)* (pp. 283-294).

Li, Q., & Atluri, V. (2003). Concept-level access control for the Semantic Web. In *Proceedings of the 2003 ACM Workshop on XML Security* (pp. 94-103). New York: ACM Press.

Li, Y. S., Shen, J. P., Shi, J. S., Shen, W. M., Huang, Y., & Xu, Y. X. (2006, May 03-05). *Multi-model driven collaborative development platform for service-oriented e-business systems.* Paper presented at the 10th International Conference on Computer Supported Cooperative Work in Design, Nanjing, PRC.

Liberty Alliance. (2009). *The liberty alliance project.* Retrieved from http://projectliberty.org/liberty/specifications 1

Lienhard, H., & Künzi, U.-M. (2005). Workflow and business rules: a common approach. In *Proceedings of the Workflow Handbook, 2005*, 129–140.

Li, L., & Zhao, X. (2006). Enhancing competitive edge through knowledge management in implementing ERP systems. *Systems Research and Behavioral Science, 23*(2), 129–140. doi:10.1002/sres.758

Lin, S., Punch, W., III, & Goodman, E. (1994). Coarse-grain parallel genetic algorithms: categorization and new approach. In *Proceedings of the Symposium on parallel and distributed processing* (pp. 28-37). Washington, DC: IEEE Press.

Lin, M.-S., & Chen, D.-J. (1997). The computational complexity of the reliability problem on distributed systems. *Information Processing Letters, 64*(3), 143–147. doi:10.1016/S0020-0190(97)00150-6

Liu, W., Jia, W., & Au, P. O. (2002). Add exception notification mechanism to web services. In *Proceedings of International Conference on Algorithms & Architectures for Parallel Processing (ICA3PP)* (pp. 483-488).

Liu, K., Bhaduri, K., Das, K., Nguyen, P., & Kargupta, H. (2006). Client-side Web Mining for Community Formation in Peer-to-Peer Environments. *SIGKDD Explorations, 8*(2), 11–20. doi:10.1145/1233321.1233323

Lopez-Sanza, M., Acuna, C. J., Cuesta, C. E., & Marcos, E. (2008). Modelling of Service-Oriented Architectures with UML. *Electronic Notes in Theoretical Computer Science, 194*(4), 23–37. doi:10.1016/j.entcs.2008.03.097

Lou, H., Luo, W., & Strong, D. (2000). Perceived critical mass effect on groupware accep-tance. *European Journal of Information Systems, 9*(2), 91–103. doi:10.1057/palgrave/ejis/3000358

Lovelock, J. (2000). *Gaia: A new look at life on Earth* (3rd edition). Oxford University Press

Lunn, K. (2002). *Software development with UML.* Houndmills, Basingstoke, Hampshire: Palgrave Macmillan. ISBN 0-333-98595-8.

Lyytinen, K., & Yoo, Y. (2001). The next wave of nomadic computing: A research agenda for information systems research. *Sprouts, 1*, 1–20.

Madden, S., & Franklin, M. (2002). Fjording the stream: An architecture for queries over streaming sensor data. In *Proceedings of the intl conf on data engineering.*

Madden, S., Shah, M., Hellerstein, J., & Raman, V. (2002). Continuously adaptive continuous queries over streams. In *Proceedings of the acm sigmod intl. conf on management of data* (pp. 49-60).

Madden, S., Franklin, M. J., Hellerstein, J. M., & Hong, W. (2003). *The design of an acquisitional query processor for sensor networks.* Sigmod.

Maeno, Y., & Ohsawa, Y. (2007). Human-computer interactive annealing for discovering invisible dark events. *IEEE Transactions on Industrial Electronics, 54*(2), 1184–1192. doi:10.1109/TIE.2007.891661

Magli, E., Mancin, M., & Merello, L. (2003, July). Low complexity video compression for wireless sensor networks. In *Proceedings of the 2003 International Conference on Multimedia and Expo* (pp. 585-588).

Maleewong, K., Anutariya, C., & Wuwongse, V. (2008). A Collective Intelligence Approach to Collaborative Knowledge Creation. In *Proceeding of the 4th International Conference Semantics, Knowledge, and Grid (SKG 2008)* (pp. 64-70). Washington, DC: IEEE press.

Maleewong, K., Anutariya, C., & Wuwongse, V. (2009a). SAM: Semantic Argumentation based Model for Collaborative Knowledge Creation and Sharing System. In *Proceeding of the 1st International Conference on Computational Collective Intelligence (ICCCI'09)*, Wroclaw, Poland. New York: Springer.

Maleewong, K., Anutariya, C., & Wuwongse, V. (2009b). A Semantic Argumentation Approach to Collaborative Ontology Engineering. In *Proceeding of the 11th International Conference on Information Integration and Web-based Applications & Services (iiWAS'09)*, Kuala Lumpur, Malaysia. New York: ACM press.

Manolopoulos, Y., Theodoridis, Y., & Tsotras, V. J. (2000). *Advanced database indexing.* Dordrecht, The Netherlands: Kluwer Academic Publishers.

Marjanovic, O., & Milosevic, Z. (2001). Towards formal modeling of e-contracts. In *Proceedings of the 5th IEEE International Enterprise Distributed Object Computing Conference* (pp. 59-68).

Markoff, J. (2007). Faster chips are leaving programmers in their dust (Tech. Rep.). *New York Times*. Retrieved from http://www.nytimes.com/2007/12/17/technology/17chip.html

Marks, E. A., & Bell, M. (2006). *Service-Oriented Architecture: A Planning and Implementation Guide for Business and Technology* (1st ed.). New York: Wiley.

Martin, P. T. (1996). *Email and the Internet as a teaching tool: A critical perspective.* Paper presented at the Proceedings of the ASEE/IEEE Frontiers in Education Conference, Salt Lake City, USA

Martindale, T., & Wiley, D. A. (2004). Using Weblogs in scholarship and teaching. *TechTrends, 49*(2), 55–61. doi:10.1007/BF02773972

Martins, L. L., & Kellermanns, F. W. (2004). A model of business school students' acceptance of a Web-based course management system. *Academy of Management Learning & Education, 3*(1), 7–26.

Maximilien, E. M., & Singh, M. P. (2004). A framework and ontology for dynamic web services selection. *IEEE Internet Computing, 8*(5), 84–93. doi:10.1109/MIC.2004.27

Ma, Y., & Zhang, C. (2008). Quick convergence of genetic algorithm for QoS-Driven web service selection. *Computer Networks, 52*(5), 1093–1104. doi:10.1016/j.comnet.2007.12.003

McCabe, F., & Clark, K. (1994). April-agent process interaction language. In M. Wooldridge & N. Jennings (Eds.), *Intelligent agents: Workshop on agent theories, architectures, and languages* (pp. 324-340). New York: Springer.

McCulloch, S., Kokoska, R., Chilkova, O., Welch, C., Johansson, E., & Burgers, P. (2004). Enzymatic switching for efficient and accurate translesion DNA replication. *Nucleic Acids Research, 32*, 4665–4675.

McGuinness, D. L., & van Harmelen, F. (2004). *OWL Web Ontology Language Overview.* Retrieved from http://www.w3.org/TR/owl-features/

McIntire. (n.d.). Energy Benefits of 32-bit Microprocessor Wireless Sensing Systems. *Sensoria Corporation.*

McLaughlin, L. (2006). What Microsoft's identity metasystem means to developers. *IEEE Software, 23*(1), 108–111. doi:10.1109/MS.2006.18

McNeil, S., & Hendrickson, C. (1985). A Regression Formulation of the Matrix Estimation Problem. *Transportation Science, 19*(3), 278–292. doi:10.1287/trsc.19.3.278

McQuaide, B. (2003). Identity and access management, transforming E-security into a catalyst for competitive advantage.

Mead, G. H. (1934). *Mind, self, and society.* IL: University of Chicago Press.

Medina, A., Taft, N., Salamatian, K., Bhattacharyya, S., & Diot, C. (2002). Traffic Matrix Estimation: Existing Techniques and New Directions. In *Proceedings of the ACM SIGCOMM Computer Communication Review, 2002 SIGCOMM conference, SESSION: Measuring and simulating networks* (Vol. 32, No. 4, pp. 161-174).

Medina-Mora, R., Winograd, T., Flores, R., & Flores, F. (1992). The action workflow approach to workflow management technology. In *Proceedings of the 1992 ACM conference on Computer-supported cooperative work* (pp. 281-288). New York: ACM.

Mehlhorn, K., & Tsakalidis, A. K. (1993). Dynamic interpolation search. *Journal of the ACM, 40*(3), 621–634. doi:10.1145/174130.174139

Menasce, D. A. (2002). QoS issues in web services. *IEEE Internet Computing, 6*(6), 72–75. doi:10.1109/MIC.2002.1067740

Mendling, J., & Hafner, M. (2005). From inter-organizational workflows to process execution: Generating BPEL from WS-CDL. In *Proceedings of the On the Move to Meaningful Internet Systems: OTM Workshops* (pp. 506-515).

Microsoft. (2005). *Microsoft's vision for an identity metasystem.* Retrieved from http://msdn2.microsoft.com/en-us/library/ms996422.aspx

Microsoft. (2009). *Microsoft code name "geneva".* Retrieved from http://www.microsoft.com/forefront/geneva/en/us/overview.aspx

Mietzner, R. (2008). *Using Variability Descriptors to Describe Customizable SaaS Application Templates. Institute of Architecture of Application Systems.* IAAS.

Miller, J., & Mukerji, J. (2003). *MDA Guide Version 1.0.1.* Retrieved from http://www.omg.com/mda/03-06-01.pdf

Miller, H. J. (2007). Geographic Data Mining and Knowledge Discovery. In Wilson, J., & Fotheringham, A. S. (Eds.), *The Handbook of Geographic Information Science.* Hoboken, NJ: Wiley-Blackwell. doi:10.1002/9780470690819.ch19

Miller, H. J., & Han, J. (2001). *Geographic Data Mining and Knowledge Discovery.* New York: CRC. doi:10.4324/9780203468029

Miller, R. E., & Blair, P. D. (1985). *Input-output Analysis, Foundations and Extensions.* Englewood Cliffs, NJ: Prentice-Hall Inc.

Mingail, E. (2001). Instant messaging: Next best thing since e-mail. *Canada Law Book Inc. publication:* Retrieved August 30, 2006, from http://www.canadalawbook.com/headlines/headline128_arc.html

Mittal, V., Huppertz, J. W., & Khare, A. (2008). Customer complaining: The role of tie strength and information control. *Journal of Retailing, 84*(2), 195–204. doi:10.1016/j.jretai.2008.01.006

Mock, K. (2001). The use of Internet tools to supplement communication in the classroom. *The Journal for Computing in Small Colleges, 17*(2).

Modi, G. (2007). *Service oriented architecture & web 2.0* (Tech. Rep.). Guru Tegh Bahadur Institute of Technology. Retrieved from http://www.gsmodi.com/files/SOAWeb2 Report.pdf

Moitra, D., & Ganesh, J. (2005). Web services and flexible business processes: towards the adaptive enterprise. *Information & Management, 42*(7), 921–933. doi:10.1016/j.im.2004.10.003

Mondada, G., Pettinaro, A., Guignard, I., Kwee, D., Floreano, J.-L., & Deneubourg, S. (2004). Swarm-bot: A new distributed robotic concept. *Autonomous Robots, 17*(2-3), 193–221. doi:10.1023/B:AURO.0000033972.50769.1c

Montanelli, S., & Castano, S. (2008). Semantically Routing Queries in Peer-based Systems: the H-Link Approach. *The Knowledge Engineering Review, 23*(1), 51–72. doi:10.1017/S0269888907001257

Moore, J. (1996). *The death of competition: Leadership and strategy in the age of business ecosystems.* Boston: Harvard Business School Press.

Morgan, R. (2006). *Federated identity management components.* University of Washington.

Morgan, T. (2002). *Business Rules and Information Systems: Aligning IT with Business Goals.* Reading, MA: Addison-Wesley.

Mori, J., Basselin, N., Kroner, A., & Jameson, A. (2008). Find me if you can: designing interfaces for people search. *In Proceedings of IUI.* 2008, 377-380.

Morikawa, M. (2008). *What Do Japanese Unions Do for Productivity? An Empirical Analysis Using Firm-Level Data* (Tech. Rep. No. 08-E-027). Lazio, Italy: RIETI. Retrieved November 15, 2009, from http://www.rieti.go.jp/jp/publications/dp/08e027.pdf

Morimoto, S. (2008, June 23-25). *A survey of formal verification for business process modeling.* Paper presented at the 8th International Conference on Computational Science, Cracow, Poland.

Mostefaoui, A. (2006, July). A Modular and Adaptive Framework for Large Scale Video Indexing and Content-Based Retrieval: The SIRSALE System. *Software: Practice and Experience Journal, 36*(8), 871–890. doi:10.1002/spe.722

Muir-Herzig, R. (2004). Technology and its impact in the classroom. *Computers and Education, 42,* 111–131.

Mukherjee, S., Srinivasa, S., & Patil, S. (2007). Emergent (re)optimization for stream queries in grids. In *Proceedings of the IEEE congress on evolutionary computation* (pp. 729-735).

Muller, C. C. (1999). The business of restaurants: 2001 and beyond. *International Journal of Hospitality Management, 18*(4), 401–413. doi:10.1016/S0278-4319(99)00045-6

Müller, R., Greiner, U., & Rahm, E. (2004). Agent work: a workflow system supporting rule-based workflow adaptation. *Data & Knowledge Engineering, 51,* 223–256. doi:10.1016/j.datak.2004.03.010

Murphy, K., Weiss, Y., & Jordan, M. I. (1999, July 30 – August 1). *Loopy belief propagation for approximate inference: An empirical study.* Paper presented at Uncertainty in Artificial Intelligence, London, UK.

Murphy, J., & Smith, S. (2009). Chefs and suppliers: An exploratory look at supply chain issues in an upscale restaurant alliance. *International Journal of Hospitality Management, 28*(2), 212–220. doi:10.1016/j.ijhm.2008.07.003

Namatame, A. (2006). Collective intelligence and evolution. *ERCIM News, 64.*

Nardi, B. A., et al. (2000). Interaction and outeraction: Instant messaging in action. *Proc. CSCW 2000* (pp. 79-88).

Nardi, B. A., Schiano, D. J., & Gumbrecht, M. (2004). Blogging as social activity, or, would you let 900 million people read your diary? In *Proceedings of 2004 ACM on Computer-Supported Cooperative Work,* 222-231.

Ng, N. L. L., Chiu, D. K. W., & Hung, P. C. K. (2007). Tendering process model (TPM) implementation for B2B integration in a Web services environment. In *Proceedings of the 40th Hawaii International Conference on System Sciences (HICSS39)*, CDROM, IEEE Press.

Ngai, E. W. T., Suk, F. F. C., & Lo, S. Y. Y. (2008). Development of an RFID-based sushi management system: The case of a conveyor-belt sushi restaurant. *International Journal of Production Economics*, *112*(2), 630–645. doi:10.1016/j.ijpe.2007.05.011

Nicolis, G., & Prigogine, I. (1977). *Self-organization in nonequilibrium systems: From dissipative structures to order through fluctuations*. New York: Wiley.

Nuffel, D. V. (2007). Towards a Service-Oriented Methodology: Business-Driven Guidelines for Service Identification. In S. B. Heidelberg (Ed.), *On the Move to Meaningful Internet Systems 2007: (OTM 2007) Workshops 4805* (pp. 294-303).

O'Sullivan, J., Edmond, D., & Hofstede, A. T. (2002). What's in a service? Towards accurate description of nonfunctional service properties. *Distributed and Parallel Databases*, *12*, 117–133. doi:10.1023/A:1016547000822

OASIS. (2006). Reference Model for Service Oriented Architecture 1.0: retrieved from http://www.oasis-open.org/committees/download.php/19679/soa-rm-cs.pdf.

OASIS. (2007). *Oasis standard ws-trust 1.3*. Retrieved from http://docs.oasisopen. org/ws-sx/ws-trust/200512/ws-trust-1.3-os.html

Ohsawa, Y., & Usui, M. (2006). Creative marketing as application of chance discovery. In Y. Ohsawa & S. Tsumoto (Eds.), *Chance discoveries in real world decision making* (pp. 253-272). Heidelberg, Germany: Springer

Ohsawa, Y., Benson, N. E., & Yachida, M. (1998). Key-Graph: Automatic indexing by co-occurrence graph based on building construction metaphor. In *Proceedings of the Advanced Digital Library Conference* (pp. 12-18). Los Alamitos, CA: IEEE Press.

Ohsawa, Y. (2005). Data crystallization: Chance discovery extended for dealing with unobservable events. *New Mathematics and Natural Computation*, *1*(3), 373–392. doi:10.1142/S1793005705000226

Ohsawa, Y., & Nara, Y. (2003). Understanding Internet users on double helical model of chance-discovery process. *New Generation Computing*, *21*(2), 109–122. doi:10.1007/BF03037629

OMG. (2003). *MDA guide version 1.0.1.*

OMG. (2004). *Object Management Group, UML2.0 Super Structure Specification.*

OMG. (2006a). *Business Motivation Model (BMM) Specification.* Retrieved April 20, 2007, from http://www.omg.org/cgi-bin/doc?dtc/2006-08-03

OMG. (2006b). *Business Process Modeling Notation Specification.* Retrieved June 6, 2006, from http://www.omg.org/cgi-bin/doc?dtc/2006-02-01

Open, I. D-Foundation. (2009*). Openid authentication.* Retrieved from http://openid.net/developers/specs/

Oravec, J. A. (2003). Blended by Blogging: Weblogs in blended learning initiatives. *Journal of Educational Media*, *28*(2-3), 225–233. doi:10.1080/1358165032000165671

Ozsu, M. T., & Valduriez, P. (1999). *Principles of Distributed Database Systems* (2nd ed.). Upper Saddle River, NJ: Prentice Hall.

Pahl, C., & Zhu, Y. (2006). A semantical framework for the orchestration and choreography of web services. *Electronic Notes in Theoretical Computer Science*, *151*, 3–18. doi:10.1016/j.entcs.2005.07.033

Papadopoulos, D., Kollios, G., Gunopulos, D., & Tsotras, V. J. (2002). Indexing mobile objects on the plane. In *Proceedings of 13th international workshop on database and expert systems applications* (pp. 693-697). Washington, DC: IEEE Computer Society.

Papamarkos, G., Poulovassilis, A., & Wood, P. T. (2006). Event-condition-action rules on RDF metadata in P2P environments. *Computer Networks*, *50*, 1513–1532. doi:10.1016/j.comnet.2005.10.022

Papazoglou, M. (2003). Service-oriented computing: concepts, characteristics and directions. In T. Catarci, M. Mecella, J. Mylopoulos, & M. Orlowska (Eds.), *International conference on web information systems engineering* (pp. 3-12). Washington, DC: IEEE Press.

Papazoglou, M. P., & Georgakopoulos, D. (2003). Service oriented computing. *Communications of the ACM*, *46*(10), 24–28. doi:10.1145/944217.944233

Papazoglou, M. P., & Heuvel, W.-J. (2006). Service-Oriented Design and Development Methodology. *International Journal of Web Engineering and Technology*, *2*(4), 412–442. doi:10.1504/IJWET.2006.010423

Papazoglou, M. P., & Heuvel, W.-J. d. (2007). Service-oriented computing: concepts, characteristics and directions. *The VLDB Journal, 16*(3), 389–415. doi:10.1007/s00778-007-0044-3

Papazoglou, M., & Georgakopoulos, D. (2003). Service-oriented computing. *Communications of the ACM, 46,* 25–28.

Parker, G. H. (1938). Biographical memoir of William Morton Wheeler, 1865-1937. *National Academy of Sciences Biographical Memoirs, 19,* 201–241.

Parsopoulos, K. E., & Vrahatis, M. N. (2002). recent approaches to global optimization problems through particle swarm optimization. *Natural Computing, 1*(2-3), 235–306. doi:10.1023/A:1016568309421

Pashalidis, A., & Mitchell, C. J. (2004). A single sign-on system for use from untrusted devices. In *Proceedings of the IEEE Global Telecommunications Conference* (pp. 5057-5059).

Patel, J. M., Chen, Y., & Chakka, V. P. (2004). Stripes: An efficient index for predicted trajectories. In *Proceedings of the 2004 acm sigmod international conference on management of data* (pp. 637-646). New York: ACM.

Pattabhiraman, R., Unmehopa, M., & Vemuri, K. (2007). Enhanced active phone book services: Blended lifestyle services made real! *Bell Labs Technical Journal, 11*(4), 315–326. doi:10.1002/bltj.20211

Pavel, B., & Alain, W. (2003). Context Based Reasoning in Business Process Models. In *Proceedings of the 2003 IEEE International Conference on Information Reuse and Integration.* IRI.

Pekhteryev, G., Sahinoglu, Z., Orlik, P., & Bhatti, G. (2005, May). Image transmission over IEEE 802.15.4 and zigbee networks. In *Proceedings of the IEEE International Symposium on Circuits and Systems (ISCAS)* (pp. 23-26).

Percoco, M., Hewings, G., & Senn, L. (2006). Structural Change Decomposition Through a Gobal Sensitivity Analysis of Input--output Models. *Economic Systems Research, 18*(2), 115–131. doi:10.1080/09535310600652919

Perera, R. (2001). *Study: Instant messaging at work up 110 percent.* Retrieved September 4, 2006, from http://www.cnn.com/2001/TECH/internet/11/16/workplace.IM.idg/

Pham, V., & Karmouch, A. (1998). Mobile software agents: an overview. *IEEE Communications Magazine, 36,* 26–37.

Pietzuch, P., Ledlie, J., Shneidman, J., Roussopoulos, M., Welsh, M., & Seltzer, M. (2006). Network-aware operator placement for stream-processing systems. In *Proceedings of the International conference on data engineering.*

Poole, D., Goebel, R., & Aleliunas, R. (1987). Theorist: A logical reasoning system for defaults and diagnosis. In N. J. Cercone & G. McCalla (Eds.), *The knowledge frontier: Essays in the representation of knowledge* (pp. 331-352). Heidelberg, Germany: Springer.

Prud'hommeaux, E., & Seaborne, A. (2008). *SPARQL Query Language for RDF.* Retrieved from http://www.w3.org/TR/rdf-sparql-query/

Pullich, L. (2004, September 30). *Usage of Weblogs in Festum - A distance education program for teachers.* Paper presented at the ICL Conference, Villach, Austria. Retrieved November 7, 2005, from http://bt-mac2.fernuni-hagen.de/peter/gems/lpWeblogsinfestum.pdf

Quinlan, J. R. (1993). *C4.5: Programs for machine learning.* San Mateo, CA: Morgan Kaufmann.

Raafat, G. S., & Kira, D. (2006). The emotional state of technology acceptance. *Issues in Informing Science and Information Technology, 3.*

Rachel, P. (2008). Communities of practice: using the open web as a collaborative learning platform, *iLearning Forum 2008 Proceedings,* Paris.

Rahimi, M., Baer, R., Iroezi, O., Garcia, J., Warrior, J., Estrin, D., & Srivastava, M. (2005, November). Cyclops: in situ image sensing and interpretation in wireless sensor networks. In *Proceedings of the ACM Conf. on Embedded Networked Sensor Systems (SenSys),* San Diego, CA.

Rahmandad, H., & Sterman, J. (2008). Heterogeneity and network structure in the dynamics of diffusion: Comparing agent-based and differential equation models. *Management Science, 54*(5), 998–1014. doi:10.1287/mnsc.1070.0787

Rajendran, V., Obraczka, K., & Garcia-Luna-Aceves, J.-J. (2003, November). Energy-efficient collision-free medium access control for wireless sensor networks. In *Proceedings of the 1st international conference on Embedded networked sensor systems (SenSys),* New York (pp. 181-192).

Raman, V., Deshpande, A., & Hellerstein, J. (2003). Using state modules for adaptive query processing. In *Proceedings of the intl. conf. on data engineering.*

Ramollari, E., Dranidis, D., & Simons, A. J. H. (2007, June 11-12). *A Survey of Service Oriented Development Methodologies.* Paper presented at the 2nd European Young Researchers Workshop on Service Oriented Computing, University of Leicester, UK

Ran, S. (2003). A model for web services discovery with QoS. *ACM SIGecom Exchanges, 4*(1), 1–10. doi:10.1145/844357.844360

Raptopoulou, K., Vassilakopoulos, M., & Manolopoulos, Y. (2004). Towards quadtree-based moving objects databases. In *Proceedings of 8th east-european conference on advanced databases and information systems* (pp. 230-245). New York: Springer.

Raptopoulou, K., Vassilakopoulos, M., & Manolopoulos, Y. (2006). On past-time indexing of moving objects. *Journal of Systems and Software, 79*(8), 1079–1091. doi:10.1016/j.jss.2005.10.020

Reith, M., & Niu, J. & Winsborough, W. H. (2007*).* Engineering trust management into software models. In *Proceedings of the International Workshop on Modeling in Software Engineering,* Washington, DC (pp. 9-15). Washington, DC: IEEE Computer Society.

Ren, Z., Anumba, C. J., & Ugwu, O. O. (2002). Negotiation in a Multi-Agent System for Construction Claims Negotiation. *Applied Artificial Intelligence, 16*(5), 359–394. doi:10.1080/08839510290030273

Rittel, H., & Kunz, W. (1970). *Issue as elements of information systems (Tech. Rep.).* CA: University of California, Institue of Urban and Regional Development.

Rivest, R. (1992). *The MD5 message-digest algorithm* (Tech. Rep.). Cambridge, MA: MIT. Retrieved from http://people.csail.mit.edu/rivest/Rivest-MD5.txt

Rizvi, S., Mendelzon, A., Sudarshan, S., & Roy, P. (2004). Extending query rewriting techniques for fine-grained access control. In *Proceedings of 2004 ACM SIGMOD International Conference on Management of Data* (pp. 551-562). New York: ACM Press.

Roberts, N. (2002). Keeping public officials accountable through dialogue: Resolving the accountability paradox. *Public Administration Review, 62*(2), 658–669. doi:10.1111/1540-6210.00248

Rohlfs, J. (1974). A Theory of Interdependent Demand for a Communications Service Bell. *Journal of Economics and Management Science, 5*(1), 16–37.

Rolland, C., Prakash, N., & Benjamen, A. (1999). A multi-Model View of Process Modelling. *Requirements Engineering, 4*(4), 169–187. doi:10.1007/s007660050018

Roman, D., Keller, U., Lausen, H., de Bruijn, J., Lara, R., & Stollberg, M. (2005). Web service modeling ontology. *Applied Ontology, 1*(1), 77–106.

Romano, N. C., & Fjermestad, J. (2002). Electronic commerce customer relationship management: an assessment of the research. *International Journal of Electronic Commerce, 6*(2), 61–113.

Rosca, D., Greenspan, S., & Wild, C. (2002). Enterprise modeling and decision-support for automating the business rules lifecycle. *Automated Software Engineering, 9,* 361–404. doi:10.1023/A:1020372710433

Rosemann, M., & Recker, J. C. (2006). *Context-aware Process Design: Exploring the Extrinsic Drivers for Process Flexibility.* Paper presented at the 18th International Conference on Advanced Information Systems Enginnering, Workshops and Doctoral Consortium.

Rothermel, K., & Hohl, F. (1999). Mobile agents. In Kent, A., & Williams, J. (Eds.), *Encyclopedia for computer science and technology* (*Vol. 40*, pp. 155–176). Boca Raton, FL: CRC Press.

Rouibah, K., et al. (2006, Mar 2006). *Does instant messaging usage impact students' performance in Kuwait?* Paper presented at the IASTED International Conference Networks and Communication Systems, Chiang Mai, Thailand.

Roy, P., Seshadri, A., Sudarshan, A., & Bhobhe, S. (2000). Efficient and extensible algorithms for multi query optimization. In *Proceedings of the ACM sigmod conf. on management of data* (pp. 249-260).

Russell, S. J. (1988). *The use of knowledge in analogy and induction.* London: Pitman.

Saidani, O., & Nurcan, S. (2007, June). *Towards Context Aware Business Process Modelling.* Paper presented at the Workshop on Business Process Modelling, Development, and Support (BPMDS), 19th International Conference on Advanced Information Systems Engineering (CAiSE'07), Trondheim, Norway.

Sako, M. (2006). Outsourcing and offshoring: Implications for productivity of business services. *Oxford Review of Economic Policy, 22*(4), 499–512. doi:10.1093/oxrep/grj029

Saltenis, S., Jensen, C. S. J., Bohlen, M. H., Gregersen, H., & Pfoser, D. (2001). Indexing of moving objects for location-based services. In *Proceedings of 18th ieee international conference on data engineering* (pp. 463-472). Washington, DC: IEEE Computer Society.

Saltenis, S., Jensen, C. S., Leutenegger, S. T., & Lopez, M. A. (2000). Indexing the positions of continuously moving objects. *SIGMOD Record, 29*(2), 331–342. doi:10.1145/335191.335427

Salton, G. (1989). *Automatic text processing: the transformation, analysis, and retrieval of information by computer.* Boston, MA: Addison-Wesley Longman Publishing Co., Inc.

Salton, G., & McGill, M. J. (1984). *Introduction to Modern Information Retrieval.* McGraw-Hill.

Salzberg, B., & Tsotras, V. J. (1999). Comparison of access methods for time-evolving data. *ACM Computing Surveys, 31*(2), 158–221. doi:10.1145/319806.319816

Sawyer, P., Hutchison, J., Walkerdine, J., & Sommerville, I. (2005, August). *Faceted Service Specification.* Paper presented at the Workshop on Service-Oriented Computing Requirements (SOCCER), Paris.

Scheer, A. (2000). *ARIS: Business Process Modelling.* Berlin: Springer.

Schilit, B. N., & Theimer, M. M. (1994). Disseminating active map information to mobile hosts. *IEEE Network, 8*(5), 22–32. doi:10.1109/65.313011

Schwartz, M. F., & Wood, D. C. M. (1993). Discovering shared interests among people using graph analysis of global electronic mail traffic. *Communications of the ACM, 36*(8), 78–89. doi:10.1145/163381.163402

Seely-Brown, J., & Duguid, P. (1991). Organisational Learning and Communities of Practice. *Organization Science, 2*(1).

Selim, H. M. (2003). An empirical investigation of student acceptance of course Websites. *Computers & Education, 40,* 343–360. doi:10.1016/S0360-1315(02)00142-2

Sellis, T. (1988). Multiple-query optimization. In *Proceedings of the ACM trans. on database systems* (pp. 23-52).

Shah, M., Hellerstein, J., Chandrasekharan, S., & Franklin, M. (2003). Flux: An adaptive repartitioning operator for continuous query systems. In *Proceedings of the intl. conf. on data engineering.*

Shah, S., Ramamritham, K., & Shenoy, P. (2004). Resilient and coherence preserving dissemination of dynamic data using cooperating peers. In *IEEE transactions on knowledge and data engineering.*

Shalizi, C. (2001). *Causal architecture, complexity and self-organization in time series and cellular automata.* Unpublished doctoral dissertation, University of Wisconsin-Madison, WI.

Shaw, F. S., & Giacquinta, J. B. (2000). *A survey of graduate students as end users of computer technology.*

Shimomura, Y., Hara, T., & Arai, T. (2008). A service evaluation method using mathematical methodologies. *CIRP Annals - Manufacturing Technology, 57*(1), 437-440.

Shimomura, Y., Sakao, T., Sundin, E., Lindahl, M., & Faculty of Mechanical, E. (2006, 2006). *Service Engineering: A novel engineering discipline for high added value creation.* Paper presented at the 9th International Design Conference, Dubrovnik, Croatia.

Shiu, E., et al. (2004). *Pew Internet & American life surveys how Americans use instant messaging.* Retrieved September 1, 2006, from http://www.pewinternet.org/PPF/r/133/report_display.asp

Shukla, U. (2003). *The future of enterprise instant messaging.* Retrieved September 3, 2006, from http://www.expresscomputeronline.com/20030505/tech1.shtml

Shum, S., Selvin, A., Sierhuis, M., & Conklin, J. (2006). Hypermedia Support for Argumentation-Based Rationale: 15 Years on from gIBIS and QOC. In Dutoit, A. H. (Ed.), *Rationale Management in Software Engineering* (pp. 111–132). Heidelberg, Germany: Springer. doi:10.1007/978-3-540-30998-7_5

Sifry, D. (2005, August 2). *State of the blogosphere*. Retrieved August 4, 2005, from The Technorati Weblog at http://www.technorati.com/Weblog/2005/08/34.html

Sigurbjörnsson, B., & Van Zwol, R. (2008). Flickr Tag Recommendation based on Collective Knowledge. In *Proceedings of the 17th International Conference on World Wide Web (WWW 2008)*, Beijing, China (pp. 327-336).

Sill, B. (1994). Operations engineering: Improving multiunit operations. *The Cornell Hotel and Restaurant Administration Quarterly, 35*(3), 64–71.

Simon, H. (2004). *SAML - The secret to centralized identity management*.

Singh, M., & Huhns, M. (2005). *Service-oriented computing: Semantics, processes, agents*. New York: Wiley.

Sioutas, S., Tsakalidis, K., Tsichlas, K., Makris, C., & Manolopoulos, Y. (2007). Indexing mobile objects on the plane revisited. In *Proceedings of 11th east european conference on advances in databases and information systems* (pp. 189-204). New York: Springer.

Sirin, E., & Parsia, B. (2007). SPARQL-DL: SPARQL Query for OWL-DL. In *Proceedings 3rd OWL Experiences and Directions Workshop (OWLED-2007)*.

Smith, J., Watson, P., Gounaris, A., Paton, N. W., Fernandes, A., & Sakellariou, R. (2003). Distributed query processing on the grid. *International Journal of High Performance Computing Applications*, 353–367. doi:10.1177/10943420030174002

Smith, R. G. (1980). The contract net protocol: high level communication and control in a distributed problem solve. *IEEE Transactions on Computers, 12*(29), 104–1113.

Smith, V. L. (1976). Experimental economics – Induced value theory. *The American Economic Review, 66*(2), 274–279.

Soro, S., & Heinzelman, W. B. (2005, October). On the coverage problem in video-based wireless sensor networks. In *Proceedigns of the IEEE Intl. Conf. on Broadband Communications, Networks, and Systems (BroadNets)*, Boston.

Sowa, J. F., & Majumdar, A. K. (2003). Analogical reasoning. In *Proceedings of the International Conference on Conceptual Structures,* (LNAI 2746, pp.16-36). Heidelberg, Germany: Springer.

SpamEater. Net. (2009). *Home*. Retrieved August 1, 2009, from http://www.spameater.net

Spaniol, M., & Klamma, R. (2004). Mediating Ontologies for Communities of Practice. In *Proceedings of the 5th International Conference on Practical Aspects of Knowledge Management (PAKM 2004)*, Vienna, Austria (pp. 330-342).

Spielberger, C. D. (1972). Conceptual and methodological issues in anxiety research. *Anxiety: Current Trends in Theory and Research, 2*, 481-494. New York: Academic Press.

Spohrer, J., & Maglio, P. P. (2008). The emergence of service science: Toward systematic service innovations to accelerate co-creation of value. *Production and Operations Management, 17*(3), 238–246. doi:10.3401/poms.1080.0027

Sripanidkulchai, K., Maggs, B., & Zhang, H. (2003). Efficient content location using interest-based locality in peer-to-peer systems. *In Proc. of INFOCOMM*, Mar.

Stalk, G. Jr, & Hout, T. M. (1990). *Competing Against Time* (p. 88). New York: The Free Press.

Stegmaier, B., Kuntschke, R., & Kemper, A. (2004). Streamglobe: Adaptive query processing and optimization in streaming p2p environments. In *Proceedings of the Intl. workshop on data management for sensor networks* (pp. 88-97).

Stein, K. (2005). Point-of-Sale Systems for Foodservice. *Journal of the American Dietetic Association, 105*(12), 1861–1861. doi:10.1016/j.jada.2005.10.003

Stender, J. (1993). *Parallel genetic algorithms: Theory and applications*. New York: IOS Press.

Stoel, L., & Lee, K. H. (2003). Modeling the effect of experience on student acceptance of Web-based courseware. *Internet Research: Electronic Networking Applications and Policy, 13*(5), 364–374. doi:10.1108/10662240310501649

Stone, J. (2004). Instant messaging or instant headache? *ACM Queue; Tomorrow's Computing Today, 2*(2). doi:10.1145/988392.988410

Strandberg, K., & Andersson, H. (1982). On a model for software reliability performance. *Microelectronics and Reliability, 22*(2), 227–240. doi:10.1016/0026-2714(82)90181-0

Straub, D. (1994). The effect of culture on IT diffusion e-mail and FAX in Japan and the U.S. *Information Systems Research*, *5*(1), 23–47. doi:10.1287/isre.5.1.23

Stvilia, B., Twidale, M., Smith, L., & Gasser, L. (2008). Information quality work organization in. *Journal of the American Society for Information Science and Technology*, *59*(6), 983–1001. doi:10.1002/asi.20813

Surowiecki, J. (2005). *The wisdom of crowds.* New York: Anchor Books.

SXIP. (2009). *Sxipper*. Retrieved from http://www.sxip.com/

Takenaka, T., & Ueda, K. (2008). An analysis of service studies toward sustainable value creation. *International Journal of Sustainable Manufacturing*, *1*(1-2), 168–179.

Tanase, D., & Kapetanios, E. (2008). Evaluating the impact of personal dictionaries for cross-language information retrieval of socially annotated images. *iCLEF Workshop, ECDL 2008*, Aarhus, Denmark.

Tan, C., & Sia, S. K. (2006). Managing flexibility in outsourcing. *Journal of the Association for Information Systems*, *7*(4), 179–2006.

Tao, Y., Papadias, D., & Sun, J. (2003). The tpr*-tree: an optimized spatio-temporal access method for predictive queries. In *Proceedings of 29th international conference on very large data bases* (pp. 790-801). VLDB Endowment.

Taylor, S., & Todd, P. A. (1995). Understanding information technology usage: a test of competing models. *Information Systems Research*, *6*(2), 144–178. doi:10.1287/isre.6.2.144

Tempich, C., Simperl, E., Luczak, M., Studer, R., & Pinto, H. S. (2007). Argumentation-based ontology engineering. *IEEE Intelligent Systems*, *22*(6), 52–59. doi:10.1109/MIS.2007.103

Tewoldeberhan, T. W., & Janssen, M. (2008). Simulation-based experimentation for designing reliable and efficient Web service orchestrations in supply chains. *Electronic Commerce Research and Applications*, *7*(1), 82–92. doi:10.1016/j.elerap.2006.11.007

The Gnutella Protocol. (2001). *The Gnutella Protocol Specification v0.4.* Retrieved from http://www9.limewire.com/developer/gnutella_protocol_0.4.pdf

The iCoord System. (2008). *The ISLab Knowledge Coordination Platform*. Retrieved from http://islab.dico.unimi.it/icoord/

Theng, Y. L. J., Leong, J., & Yeow, S. (2008). An empirical study investigating instant messaging as an enabling tool for education. *Accepted to ICA 2008*, Montreal, Canada.

Theng, Y. L., & Lew, Y. W. (2007). Perceived usefulness and usability of Weblogs for collaborative learning. Full paper. *HCI International 2007 (HCII2007)*, Beijing, China.

Theng, Y. L., Mohd-Nasir, N., Buchanan, G., Fields, B., Thimbleby, H., & Cassidy, N. (2001). Dynamic digital libraries for children. *First ACM and IEEE Joint Conference in Digital Libraries*, Ronaoke, Virginia (pp. 406–415).

Tim Berners-Lee, T., Hendler, J., & Lassila, O. (2001). The Semantic Web. *Scientific American, May*.

Tiwana, A. (2001). *The Essential Guide to Knowledge Management – E-Business and CRM Applications.*: Prentice Hall.

Toda, M. (1991). *Common sense, emotion, and chatting, and their roles in interpersonal interactions*, Chukyo University.

Toulmin, S. (1958). *The Uses of Argument*. Cambridge, UK: Cambridge University Press.

Trappey, C. V., & Trappey, A. J. C. (1998). A chain store marketing information system: realizing Internet-based enterprise integration and electronic commerce. *Industrial Management & Data Systems*, *98*(5-6), 205–213. doi:10.1108/02635579810227733

Turcu, C., Popa, V., & Ieee. (2009). *An RFID-based System for Emergency Health Care Services*. Washington, DC: IEEE.

Turney, P. D. (2008). The latent relation mapping engine: Algorithm and experiments. *Artificial Intelligence Review*, *33*, 615–655.

Ueda, K., Takenaka, T., Váncza, J., & Monostori, L. (2009). Value creation and decision-making in sustainable society. *CIRP Annals - Manufacturing Technology*, *58*(2), 681-700.

Ueda, K., Takenaka, T., & Fujita, K. (2008). Toward value co-creation in manufacturing and servicing. *CIRP Journal of Manufacturing Science and Technology, 1*(1), 53–58. doi:10.1016/j.cirpj.2008.06.007

van der Aalst, W. M. P., ter Hofstede, A. H. M., & Weske, M. (2003). Business process management: a survey. *Business Process Management*, 1-12.

van der Aalst, W. M. P., Benatallah, B., Casati, F., Curbera, F., & Verbeek, E. (2007). Business process management: Where business processes and web services meet. *Data & Knowledge Engineering, 61*(1), 1–5. doi:10.1016/j.datak.2006.04.005

Vander, W. T. (2005). Explaining and showing broad and narrow folksonomies. http://www.personalinfocloud.com/2005/02/explaining_and_.html.

Venkatesh, V. (2000). Determinants of perceived ease of use: integrating control, intrinsic motivation and emotion into the Technology Acceptance Model. *Information Systems Research, 11*(4), 342–365. doi:10.1287/isre.11.4.342.11872

Venkatesh, V., & Davis, F. D. (1996). A model of the antecedents of perceived ease of use: development and test. *Decision Sciences, 27*(3), 451–481. doi:10.1111/j.1540-5915.1996.tb01822.x

Vickrey, W. (1961). Counterspeculation, auctions and competitive sealed tenders. *The Journal of Finance, 16*, 8–37. doi:10.2307/2977633

Viegas, F., Wattenberg, M., Kriss, J., & van Ham, F. (2007). Talk before you type. In *Proceeding of the 40th Hawaii International Conference on System Sciences*, CA (p. 78). Washington, DC: IEEE press.

Voas, J. (1999). The cold realities of software insurance. *IT Professional, 1*(1), 71–72. doi:10.1109/6294.774795

Voltage Security. (2006). *Public key infrastructure.*

Voss, C., Roth, A. V., & Chase, R. B. (2008). Experience, service operations strategy, and services as destinations: Foundations and exploratory investigation. *Production and Operations Management, 17*(3), 247–266. doi:10.3401/poms.1080.0030

Voulgaris, S., Gavidia, D., & Van Steen, M. (2005). CYCLON: Inexpensive Membership Management for Unstructured P2P Overlays. *Journal of Network and Systems Management, 13*(2), 197–217. doi:10.1007/s10922-005-4441-x

Vu, Q. M., Masada, T., Takasu, A., & Adachi, J. (2007). Disambiguation of people in web search using a knowledge base. *In Proceedings of International Conference on Research, Innovation & Vision for the Future Information & Communication Technologies (IEEE RIVF'07)*, 185-191.

W3C. (2004). Web Services Glossary: Retrieved from http://www.w3.org/TR/ws-gloss.

Walton, D. (2006). *Fundamentals of Critical Argumentation*. Cambridge, UK: Cambridge University Press.

Wan, X., Gao, J., Li, M., & Ding, B. (2005). Person resolution in person search results: Webhawk. *In CIKM '05: Proceedings of the 14th ACM international conference on Information and knowledge management*, 163-170, New York, USA, ACM Press.

Wang, Y., & Vassileva, J. (2004). Trust-Based Community Formation in Peer-to-Peer File Sharing Networks. In *Proceedings of the IEEE/WIC/ACM International Conference on Web Intelligence (WI'04)*, Beijing, China (pp. 341-348).

Ward, M. (2004). *Life offers lessons for business.* Retrieved from http://news.bbc.co.uk/1/hi/technology/3752725.stm

Watts, D., & Strogatz, S. (1998). Collective dynamics of 'small-world' networks. *Nature, 393*, 440–442.

Weerawarana, S., Curbera, F., Leymann, F., Storey, T., & Ferguson, D. F. (2005). *Web services platform architecture: SOAP, WSDL, WS-policy, WS-addressing, WS-BPEL, WS-reliable messaging, and more.* Prentice Hall.

Weinerman, E. R., Rutzen, S. R., & Pearson, D. A. (1965). Effects of medical triage in hospital emergency service. *Public Health Reports, 80*(5), 389–399.

Wenger, E. (1998). *Communities of practice: Learning, meaning, and identity*. Cambridge University Press.

Wenger, E. and Snyder, Williams. (2000). Communities of practice: the organizational frontier. *Harvard Business Review*, (January-February): 139–145.

Wenger, E., McDermott, R., & Snyder, W. M. (2002). *Cultivating communities of practice*. Harvard Business School Press.

WFMC. (n.d.). *About the WFMC - Introduction to the Workflow Management Coalition*. Retrieved July 12, 2004, from http://www.wfmc.org/about.htm

White, P. (2008). Identity management architecture: a new direction. In *Proceedings of the 8th IEEE International Conference on Computer and information Technology* (pp. 408-413).

White, D., & Houseman, M. (2002). The navigability of strong ties: Small worlds, tie strength, and network topology. *Complexity, 8*, 72–81.

Wilkinson, D., & Huberman, B. A. (2007). Cooperation and Quality in Wikipedia. In *Proceedings of the WikiSym*, (pp. 157-164).

Wilkinson, K., Sayers, C., Kuno, H., & Reynolds, D. (2003). Efficient RDF storage and retrieval in Jena2. In *Proceeding of the First International Workshop on Semantic Web and Databases* (pp. 35-43).

Willard, D. E. (1985). Searching unindexed and nonuniformly generated files in log log n time. *SIAM Journal on Computing, 14*(4), 1013–1029. doi:10.1137/0214071

Wilson, E. O. (1971). *The insect societies*. Cambridge, MA: Harvard University Press.

Windley, P. (2005). *Digital identity*. Sebastopol, CA: O'Reilly Media Inc.

Wohed, P., Aalst, W. M. P. d., Dumas, M., & Ter Hofstede, A. H. M. (2003). Analysis of Web services composition languages: The case of BPEL4WS. In *Proceedings of the 22nd International Conference on Conceptual Modeling (ER 2003)* (pp. 200-215).

Wong, D. S. F., & Chiu, D. K. W. (2007). Collaborative workflow management with alerts: An integrated retailing system for garments brands. In *Proceedings of the 2007 IEEE International Conference on e-Business Engineering (ICEBE)*, Hong Kong IEEE Press (pp. 433-438).

Wrede, O. (2003, May 23-24). *Weblogs and discourse*. Paper presented at the Blogtalk Conference, Vienna.

Wutke, D., Martin, D., & Leymann, F. (2008). Facilitating complex Web Service interactions through a tuplespace binding. In *Proceedings of the 8th IFIP WG 6.1 International Conference on Distributed Applications and Interoperable Systems*, LNCS 5053, Springer (pp. 275-280).

Xbow. (n.d.). Retrieved from http://www.xbow.com/Products/Product_pdf_files/Wireless_pdf/Stargate_Datasheet.pdf

Xu, J., & Reiff-Marganiec, S. (2008). Towards heuristic web services composition using immune algorithm. In *Proceedings of IEEE International Conference on Web Services (ICWS)* (pp. 238-245).

Yager, R. R. (1996). Quantifier Guided Aggregation using OWA operators. *International Journal of Intelligent Systems, 11*, 49–73. doi:10.1002/(SICI)1098-111X(199601)11:1<49::AID-INT3>3.3.CO;2-L

Yager, R. R. (2007). Centered OWA operators. *Soft Computing, 11*, 631–639. doi:10.1007/s00500-006-0125-z

Yamins, D. *(2007)*. A theory of local-to-global algorithms for one-dimensional spatial multi-agent systems. *Doctoral thesis, Harvard School of Engineering and Applied Sciences.*

Yan, X., Yu, P. S., & Han, J. (2005). Substructure similarity search in graph databases. *SIGMOD Conference 2005*, 766-777.

Yanbe, Y., Jatowt, A., Nakamura, S., & Tanaka, K. (2007) Can social bookmarking enhance search in the web? *In Proceedings of JCDL'2007*. 107-116

Yang, J., Papazoglou, M. P., & Heuvel, W. J. d. (2002). Tackling the challenges of service composition in e-marketplaces. In *Proceedings of the 12th International Workshop on Research Issues in Data Engineering: Engineering E-Commerce/E-Business Systems* (pp. 125-133).

Yao, Y., & Gehrke, J. (2002). The cougar approach to in-network query processing in sensor networks. *SIGMOD Record, 31*(3), 9–18. doi:10.1145/601858.601861

Ye, X., & Mounla, R. (2008). A hybrid approach to QoS-aware service composition. In *Proceedings of IEEE International Conference on Web Services (ICWS)* (pp. 62-69).

Yencken, L., & Baldwin, T. (2008). Orthographic similarity search for dictionary lookup of Japanese words, *In Proc. of the 22nd International Conference on Computational Linguistics* (COLING 2008), Manchester, UK.

You, J. M., & Chen, K. J. (2006). Improving context vector models by feature clustering for automatic thesaurus construction. *Proceedings of the Fifth SIGHAN Workshop on Chinese Language Processing.*

Yu, B., & Singh, M. P. (2003). Searching social networks. *AAMAS, 2003*, 65–72.

Yudkowsky, C. (2003). *IM in a corporate environment: Is instant messaging a nuisance or an untapped tool?* Retrieved September 3, 2006, from http://accounting. smartpros.com/x37078.xml

Yu, T., Zhang, Y., & Lin, K.-J. (2007). Efficient algorithms for web services selection with end-to-end QoS constraints. *ACM Transactions on Web, 1*(1), 1–26.

Zdonik, S. (2003). The aurora and medusa projects. *IEEE data engineering bulletin.*

Zeng, L., Benatallah, B., Ngu, A. H. H., Dumas, M., Kalagnanam, J., & Chang, H. (2004). QoS-Aware middleware for web services composition. *IEEE Transactions on Software Engineering, 30*(5), 311–327. doi:10.1109/TSE.2004.11

Zhang, J., Ackerman, M. S., & Adamic, L. (2007). Expertise networks in online communities: structure and algorithms. In *Proceeding of the 16th International Conference on World Wide Web (WWW)* (pp. 221-230). New York: ACM Press.

Zhang, Y. (2007, August). Adaptive region-based image fusion using energy evaluation model for fusion decision. *Signal. Image and Video Processing, 1*(3), 215–223. doi:10.1007/s11760-007-0015-6

Zhao, W., Varadharajan, V., & Bryan, G. (2004). Modelling trust relationships in distributed environments. In *Proceedings of the international conference on trust and privacy in digital business* (pp. 40-49), Zaragoza, Spain: Springer.

Zhao, W., Varadharajan, V., & Bryan, G. (2006). A unified framework for trust management. In *Proceedings of the securecomm and workshops* (pp.1-8).

Zhao, J. L., & Cheng, H. K. (2005). Web services and process management: a union of convenience or a new area of research? *Decision Support Systems, 40*(1), 1–8. doi:10.1016/j.dss.2004.04.002

Zhou, J., & Ye, X. (2006). A flexible control strategy on workflow modeling and enacting. *Advanced Communication Technology, 3*, 1712–1716.

Zimmermann, O., Krogdahl, P., & Gee, C. (2004). *Elements of Service-Oriented Analysis and Design.* Retrieved from http://www.ibm.com/developerworks/library/ws-soad1/

Zimmermann, O., Milinski, S., Craes, M., & Oellermann, F. (2004). Second generation web services-oriented architecture in production in the finance industry. In J. Vlissides & D. Schmidt (Eds.), *Proceedings of the Conference on object-oriented programming, systems, languages, and applications* (pp. 283-289). New York: ACM Press.

About the Contributors

Hideyasu Sasaki is the founding Editor-in-Chief of *International Journal of Organizational and Collective Intelligence* (IJOCI), IRMA, NJ, United States. He is active in several international program committees including IEEE SMC 2011 Part B Human-Machine Systems. Prof. Sasaki is a Fellow member of IARIA and has been awarded best paper awards for his presentations twice consecutively, and the 4th Annual Excellence in Research Journal Award from IRMA for his co-authored journal article in IJSSOE about a steganography technique using artificial neural networks in 2010. Dr. Sasaki has been awarded the competitive Japan Society for Science Promotion (JSPS) grants over the past six years from the very beginning of his tenured professorship. He received the Microsoft Research Grant in 2005. Dr. Sasaki is an Associate Professor of Computer Science at Ritsumeikan University in Kyoto, Japan. He has been tenured there since 2005. Prof. Sasaki received his BA, LLB from the University of Tokyo, Japan, LLM from University of Chicago Law School, MS (Hons) and PhD (Highest Hons) in Computer and Information Sciences in 1992, 1994, 1999, 2001, and 2003, respectively. In his graduate research, he won the title of Keio Engineering Society Fellow (2001). He has experience as a lawyer and in litigation as an Attorney-at-Law in New York since 1999.

Dickson K. W. Chiu received the B.Sc. (Hons.) degree in Computer Studies from the University of Hong Kong in 1987. He received the M.Sc. (1994) and the Ph.D. (2000) degrees in Computer Science from the Hong Kong University of Science and Technology (HKUST). He started his own computer company while studying part-time. He has also taught at several universities in Hong Kong. His research interest is in service computing with a cross-disciplinary approach, involving workflows, software engineering, information technologies, agents, information system management, security, and databases. The results have been widely published in over 120 papers in international journals and conference proceedings (most of them have been indexed by SCI, SCI-E, EI, and SSCI), including many practical master and undergraduate project results. He received a best paper award in the 37th Hawaii International Conference on System Sciences in 2004. He is the founding Editor-in-Chief of the *International Journal on Systems and Service-Oriented Engineering* and serves in the editorial boards of several international journals. He co-founded several international workshops and co-edited several journal special issues. He also served as a program committee member for over 70 international conferences and workshops. He is a Senior Member of both the ACM and the IEEE, and a life member of the Hong Kong Computer Society.

Epaminondas Kapetanios was born in Athens, Hellas, where he studied Statistics and Informatics at the University of Athens. Subsequently, he received his M.Sc. degree at the Technical University of Karlsruhe, Germany, Faculty of Computer Science, Institute for Program Structures and Data Organisation, while focusing on the development of Information Systems and Database Technologies. He received his Ph.D. degree at the Institute of Information Systems, Department of Computer Science, ETH-Zurich, Switzerland, where he designed and contributed in the implementation of an ontology driven, high-level query language (MDDQL). Epaminondas has published more than 60 articles in journals and conferences. He is currently holding a position as a Senior Lecturer at the School of Computer Science, University of Westminster, London, UK. He has been General Chair of the NLDB 2008 conference, Programme Committee Co-Chair of the International Conference on Management of Emergent Digital Ecosystems (MEDES) 2009, Workshop Co-Chair of ICDIM 2009.

Patrick C. K. Hung is an Associate Professor at the Faculty of Business and Information Technology in UOIT and an Adjunct Assistant Professor at the Department of Electrical and Computer Engineering in University of Waterloo. Patrick is currently collaborating with Boeing Phantom Works (Seattle, USA) and Bell Canada on security- and privacy-related research projects, and he has filed two US patent applications on "Mobile Network Dynamic Workflow Exception Handling System." In addition, Patrick is also cooperating on Web services composition research projects with Southeast University in China. Patrick has been serving as a panelist of the Small Business Innovation Research and Small Business Technology Transfer programs of the National Science Foundation (NSF) in the States since 2000. He is an executive committee member of the IEEE Computer Society's Technical Steering Committee for Services Computing, a steering member of EDOC "Enterprise Computing," and an associate editor/ editorial board member/guest editor in several international journals such as the *IEEE Transactions on Services Computing*, *International Journal of Web Services Research* (JWSR), *International journal of Business Process and Integration Management* (IJBPIM), and the *International Journal on Systems and Service-Oriented Engineering*.

Ho-Fung Leung is currently a Professor in Computer Science and Engineering, the Chinese University of Hong Kong, China. He has been active in research on intelligent agents, multi-agent systems, game theory, and semantic web, and has published more than 160 papers in these areas. Professor Leung has served on the program committees and as chair or vice chair of many conferences. Professor Leung is a senior member of ACM and the IEEE, and a chartered fellow of the BCS. He is a chartered engineer registered by the ECUK, and is awarded the designation of chartered scientist by the Science Council, UK. He is an Associate Editor of *International Journal on Systems and Service-Oriented Engineering*. Professor Leung received his B.Sc. and M.Phil. degrees in Computer Science from The Chinese University of Hong Kong, and his Ph.D. degree in Computing from Imperial College of Science, Technology and Medicine, University of London.

Richard Chbeir received his PhD in Computer Science from the University of INSA, France, in 2001, and then his accreditation to lead research (HDR) in 2010 from the University of Bourgogne, where he is currently an Associate Professor in the Computer Science Department in Dijon, France. His research interests are in the areas of multimedia information retrieval, XML and RSS similarity, access control models, multimedia document annotation. Richard Chbeir has published in international journals, books, and conferences, and has served on the program committees of several international conferences. He is currently the Chair of the French Chapter ACM SIGAPP and the Vice-Chair of ACM SIGAPP.

* * *

Akinori Abe, a Senior Researcher at ATR Knowledge Science Laboratories, received an M.E. and Doctor of Engineering (PhD) from University of Tokyo in 1988 and 1991 respectively. His PhD thesis was titled ``A Fast Hypothetical Reasoning System using Analogical Case.'' His main research interests are abduction (hypothetical reasoning), analogical reasoning, data mining, Chance Discovery and language sense processing which researches for rather emotional aspects of language processing. He worked in NTT Communication Science Laboratories from 1991 to 2000 and NTT MSC (Malaysia) from 2000 to 2002. Since 2002 he has been working in ATR. Currently, he also works as an associate professor of IREIIMS, Tokyo Women's Medical Univ. and a visiting associate professor of Kobe Univ. Graduate School (Cooperation Course).

Motoyuki Akamatsu is the director of Institute for Human Science and Biomedical Engineering and also belongs to the Service Research Center (CfSR) at the National Institute of Advanced Industrial Science and Technology (AIST), Japan. He is also a Professor of Cooperative Graduate School Program of Tsukuba University. He received his doctor's degree of Engineering from Keio University in 1984, Japan. He joined Industrial Products Research Institute at former AIST in 1986. His research field is human factors and ergonomics. He has been working mainly on measuring and modeling of human behavior in human life environment.

Chutiporn Anutariya is an Assistant Professor of Computer Science at Shinawatra University, Thailand. Her research interests include the Semantic Web, intelligent systems and knowledge representation. She received her BSc in Statistics with first class honors from Chulalongkorn University, Thailand in 1996. Later in 1998 and 2001, she received her MSc and DTechSc in Computer Science from Asian Institute of Technology, Thailand, respectively.

Khouloud Boukadi is a teaching assistant in the LIMOS laboratory (University of Blaise Pascal, Clermont-Ferrand). Her research interests include service computing, Web services, context-aware computing and agility of Information systems. She got a Ph.D. in computer science from Ecole des Mines, Saint Etienne, France. Contact her at boukadi@isima.fr.

Gerard Briscoe is a Research Officer at the Department of Media and Communications of the London School of Economics and Political Science. He gained his PhD in Electrical and Electronic Engineering from Imperial College London. Prior to which he was a Research Fellow at the MIT Media Lab Europe, following the completion of his B/MEng in Computing also from Imperial College London. His research interests include Green/Sustainable Computing, the direct and indirect impact of IT on our environment, including the development of programs, policies, and initiatives to mediate some of the challenges posed. Including emerging paradigms such as Digital Ecosystems and Cloud Computing, and the societal impact of related technologies.

Silvana Castano is full professor of Computer Science at the Università degli Studi di Milano, where she chairs the Information systems & knowledge management (ISLab) group. She received the Ph.D. degree in Computer and Automation Engineering from Politecnico di Milano. Her main research interests are in the area of databases and information systems and ontologies and Semantic Web, with focus on ontology matching and evolution, emergent semantics, knowledge discovery in open networked systems, semantic integration and interoperability. On these topics, she has been working in several national and international research projects, such as EU FP6 BOEMIE, EU FP6 INTEROP-NoE, PRIN ESTEEM, COFIN D2I, FIRB WEB-MINDS. She has been serving as PC member for several important database, information systems, and Semantic Web conferences. In 2009, she is PC co-chair of the ER 2009 conference. Since November 2008, she is the President-Elect of GRIN, the Italian association of University Professors in Informatics.

Chrong-Cheng Chen received his master degree in the Department of Computer Science and Information Engineering from National Central University in 2008. He is now a senior programmer in Industrial Technology Research Institute of Taiwan. His research interests include Web 2.0, OSGi, Cloud Computing, and people search.

Shing-Chi Cheung received the B.Sc. degree in the Electrical Engineering from the University of Hong Kong in 1984. He received the M.Sc. and Ph.D. degrees in Computing from the Imperial College London in 1988 and 1994, respectively. He is an Associate Professor of Computer Science and Associate Director of CyberSpace Center at the Hong Kong University of Science and Technology. Professor Cheung is an associate editor of the IEEE Transactions on Software Engineering, the Journal of Computer Science and Technology (JCST), and the International Journal of Patterns (IJOP). He participates actively into the program and organizing committees of many major international conferences on software engineering, distributed systems and web technologies, such as ICSE, FSE, ISSTA, ASE, ER, COMPSAC, APSEC, QSIC, EDOC, SCC and CEC. His research interests include software engineering, services computing, ubiquitous computing, and embedded software engineering. His work has been reported in more than 100 refereed articles at international journals and conferences, which include TOSEM, TSE, ASE, DSS, TR, IJCIS, ICSE, FSE, ESEC and ER. He is a Chartered Fellow of the British Computer Society and a senior member of the IEEE. He co-found the first International Workshop on Services Computing in 2005 and was the tutorials chair of ICSE 2006. He has co-edited special issues for the Computer Journal and the International Journal of Web Services Research (JWSR).

William K. Cheung is currently an Associate Professor in the Department of Computer Science, Hong Kong Baptist University. He received the BSc and MPhil degrees in electronic engineering from the Chinese University of Hong Kong and the PhD degree in computer science in 1999 from the Hong Kong University of Science and Technology. He has served as co-chairs and program committee members of a number of international workshops/conferences, as well as guest editors of journals in areas including artificial intelligence, Web intelligence, data mining, Web services, and e-commerce technologies. He is the Managing Editor of the IEEE Intelligent Informatics Bulletin since 2007. His research interests include artificial intelligence and machine learning, as well as their applications to collaborative filtering, Web mining, distributed data mining, planning under uncertainty, and Web services management.

Philippe De Wilde obtained his PhD in mathematical physics, and his MSc degree in computer science. He was a Lecturer and then Senior Lecturer in the Department of Electrical and Electronic Engineering, Imperial College London. He is currently a Professor in the Intelligent Systems Lab of the School of Mathematical and Computer Sciences, Heriot-Watt University. He develops biological and sociological principles that improve the design of decision making and of networks. Research interests:

interacting networks in the brain; decision making under uncertainty; networked populations; stability, scalability and evolution of multi-agent systems. He has published 41 journal papers and 44 conference papers and book chapters. He has published four books, including ``Neural Network Models'', Springer 1997, and ``Convergence and Knowledge-processing in Multi-agent Systems'', Springer 2009. He is a Senior Member of IEEE, Member of the IEEE Computational Intelligence Society and Systems, Man and Cybernetics Society, and the British Computer Society. Associate Editor, IEEE Transactions on Systems, Man, and Cybernetics, Part B, Cybernetics. Member of the Editorial Board, Intelligent Decision Technologies. Research Fellow, British Telecom, 1994. Laureate, Royal Academy of Sciences, Letters and Fine Arts of Belgium, 1988. Vloeberghs Chair, Free University Brussels, 2010.

Alfio Ferrara is assistant professor of Computer Science at the University of Milano, where he received his Ph.D. in Computer Science in 2005. His research interests include database and semi-structured data integration, Web-based information systems, ontology engineering, and knowledge representation and evolution. On these topics, he works in national and international research projects, including the recent EU FP6 BOEMIE project, the EU FP6 INTEROP NoE, and the ESTEEM PRIN project funded by the Italian Ministry of Education, University, and Research. He is also author of several articles and papers in international journals and conferences about ontology management and matching.

Kosuke Fujita is a graduate student of precision engineering at the University of Tokyo. He received B.E. from the University of Tokyo in 2008. He studies Co-creation Engineering at Research into Artifacts, Center for Engineering in the University of Tokyo. His current research interests include a service market modelling using multi-agent system and elucidation of consumers' lifestyle using psychological surveys and data mining. He especially investigates the cell phone market in Japan. His latest journal article appeared in CIRP Journal of Manufacturing Science and Technology in 2008.

Chirine Ghedira is an associate professor at Claude Bernard University, Lyon, France. Her research interests include web service technology, interoperabilty, distributed and heterogeneous information systems and context-aware computing. She received a PhD degree in computer science (2002), from the National Institute for Applied Sciences (INSA) of Lyon, France. Contact her at cghedira@liris.cnrs.fr.

Yiwei Gong is a PhD candidate in the Information and Communication Technology section of the Faculty of Technology, Policy, and Management at Delft University of Technology, the Netherlands. His research interests include business process management systems, agent-based simulation and information architecture. Gong received his MSc in computer science from the Delft University of Technology. Contact him at y.gong@tudelft.nl.

Indy Y.T. Hsiao studied Electric Engineering in DYIT college and graduated in 1996. He then studied Information Management in Tamkang University (TKU) after retiring from the army. His research subject was about how to filter table information to match small device users' needs. He then worked in TKU Information Processing Center right after receiving his master degree. He had worked there for almost 7 years. His major work was maintaining the Teaching Support Platform of TKU, which is the most important teaching related platform of TKU and he had learned a lot from the job. He is now a PhD student at the Department of Computer Science and Information Engineering in National Central University, Taiwan. His research interests include Web 2.0, e-Portfolio, and Second Life.

Jeff J.S. Huang received his B.S. degree in the Department of information management from Tatung University in 1997 and M.S. degree in the Department of Computer Science and Information Engineering from Tamking University in 2000. He taught at Hsing Kuo University of Management in 2001. He is now a PhD student in the Department of Computer Science and Information Engineering in National Central University. He severed as a Program Committee member of ICCE 2008 (International Conference on Computers in Education). His research interests include Web 2.0, social networking, social computing, context aware ubiquitous computing, Computer-Supported Collaborative Learning, Computer Supported Cooperative Work, e-learning, and knowledge management.

Liusheng Huang received the M.S. degree from the University of Science and Technology of China in 1988. He is currently a professor and Ph.D. supervisor at the University of Science and Technology of China. His research interests are in the areas of information security, distributed computing and high performance algorithms.

Tsukasa Ishigaki is a postdoctoral fellow of the National Institute of Advanced Industrial Science and Technology (AIST), Tokyo, Japan. He received B.E. and M.E. degrees from Hosei University, Tokyo, Japan in 2003 and 2005, respectively and his Ph.D. degree from the Graduate University for Advanced Studies at the Institute of Statistical Mathematics (ISM) in 2007. From 2007 to 2008 he served as a postdoctoral fellow for Core Research for Evolutional Science and Technology, Japan Science and Technology Agency in ISM. His current interests are service engineering, machine learning, and information fusion methods, with particular emphasis on their application to real systems.

Marijn Janssen is an associate professor in the Information and Communication Technology section of the Faculty of Technology, Policy, and Management at Delft University of Technology, the Netherlands. His research interests include business engineering, information integration, agent-based and service-oriented architectures, and designing the coordination of networked public and private organizations. He is also the director of the interdisciplinary SEPAM Master program. Janssen received his PhD in information systems from the Delft University of Technology. Contact him at m.f.w.h.a.janssen@tudelft.nl.

Professor Krithi holds a PhD. in Computer Science from the University of Utah and MTech. from the IIT-Madras. He currently holds the Vijay and Sita Vashee Chair Professor. His research explores timeliness and consistency issues in computer systems, in particular, databases, real-time systems, and distributed applications with recent work addressing these issues in the context of Dynamic Data in sensor networks, embedded systems, mobile environments and the web. During the last few years he has been working on the use of Information and Communication Technologies for creating tools aimed at socio-economic development.

Irene Y.S. Li received her M.A. degree in Graduate Institute of Foreign Languages and Literatures from National Chiao Tung University in 2009. Her research interest was neurolinguistics. She had her teaching practice in Linkou senior high school. Now, she is a research assistant. She works at Department of Computer Science and Information Engineering, National Central University, Taiwan. She assists Ph.D students in making teaching experiment. Her currently research interests include TESL, e-learning, Web 2.0.

Jian Li received the BS and MA degrees in computer science from Wuhan University in 1998 and 2001, respectively, and the PhD degree in computer science from the Institute of Software, Chinese Academy of Sciences, in 2007. He is currently a postdoctoral fellow in the Department of Computer Science at Hong Kong Baptist University. His research interests include semantic web, information integration, and artificial intelligence with applications to data mining.

Qing Li received the B.Eng. degree from Hunan University, Changsha, China, and the M.Sc. and Ph.D. degrees from the University of Southern California, Los Angeles, all in computer science. He is currently a professor at the City University of Hong Kong. His research interests include database modeling, multimedia retrieval and management, web services, and e-learning systems. He is a senior member of the IEEE.

An Liu received the Ph.D. degrees from the University of Science and Technology of China, Hefei, China, and the City University of Hong Kong, Hong Kong, China, all in computer science. He is currently a lecturer at the University of Science and Technology of China. His research interests are in the area of service-oriented computing.

Zakaria Maamar is a full professor in the College of Information Technology at Zayed University, Dubai, UAE. His research interests include Web services, social networks, and context-aware computing. He has a Ph.D. in computer science from Laval University, Quebec City, Canada. Contact him at zakaria.maamar@zu.ac.ae.

Krissada Maleewong is a PhD candidate at Shinawatra University, Thailand. He received his BSc in Agricultural Technology with honors from Thammasat University, Thailand in 1999 and MSc in Information Technology (Software Engineering) from Shinawatra University, Thailand in 2006. His research interests include collective intelligence, the Semantic Web and knowledge management.

Yannis Manolopoulos was born in Thessaloniki, Greece in 1957. He received a B.Eng. (1981) in Electrical Eng. and a Ph.D. degree (1986) in Computer Eng., both from the Aristotle Univ. of Thessaloniki. Currently, he is Professor at the Department of Informatics of the same university. He has been with the Department of Computer Science of the Univ. of Toronto, the Department of Computer Science of the Univ. of Maryland at College Park and the Univ. of Cyprus. He has published over 300 papers in journals and conference proceedings. He is co-author of the books "Advanced Database Indexing", "Advanced Signature Indexing for Multimedia and Web Applications" by Kluwer and of the books "R-Trees: Theory and Applications", "Nearest Neighbor Search: a Database Perspective" by Springer. He has co-organized several conferences (among others ADBIS'2002, SSTD'2003, SSDBM'2004, ICEIS'2006, ADBIS'2006, EANN'2007). His research interests include Databases, Data mining, Web Information Systems, Sensor Networks and Informetrics.

Stefano Montanelli has a Post Doc position in Computer Science at the University of Milano, where he received his Ph.D. in Computer Science in 2006. His main research interests include Semantic Web, ontology matching and evolution, semantic knowledge coordination, and emergent semantics in open distributed systems. On these topics, he is involved in national and international research projects, including the recent EU FP6 BOEMIE project (Bootstrapping Ontology Evolution with Multimedia Information Extraction), the EU FP6 INTEROP NoE (Interoperability Research for Networked Enterprises Applications and Software), and the ESTEEM PRIN project (Emergent Semantics and cooperaTion in multi-knowledgE EnvironMents) funded by the Italian Ministry of Education, University, and Research. He is also author of articles and papers in international journals and conferences about ontology and instance matching, P2P semantic routing and ontology-based P2P community management.

Ahmed Mostefaoui is currently an associate professor at the University of Franche Comte since 2000. He received the M.S. and Ph.D. degrees in computer science from Ecole Normale Suprieure de Lyon (France) in 1996 and 2000, respectively. His research interests are in multimedia systems and networking, in particular, distributed architectures, video streaming and wireless ad-hoc and sensor networks emphasizing both practical and theoretical issues.

Yoichi Motomura is the team leader of Large Scale Data Based Modeling Research Team, Center for Service Research (CfSR) and the senior research scientist of Digital Human Research Center (DHRC) at National Institute of Advanced Industrial Science and Technology (AIST) in Japan. He received M.Sc from the University of Electro-Communications and then joined to the Real World Computing Project in the Electrotechnical Laboratory, AIST, MITI (the ministry of international trade and industry, Japan) in 1993. His current research works are statistical learning theory, probabilistic inference algorithms on Bayesian networks, and their applications to user modeling and human behavior understanding and prediction from sensory data. He also conducts the venture company, Modellize Inc., as the chief technology officer. He received a best presentation award, research promotive award from Japanese Society of Artificial Intelligence, Docomo Mobile Science award and IPA super creator award.

Saikat Mukherjee is a doctoral student at the International Institute of Information Technology-Bangalore. His primary area of work is in query optimization over data streams. His other research interests include distributed computing and multi-agent systems. Currently he is working with Siemens Corporate Research and Technology-India.

Jun Nakamura, Ph.D.candidate at Department of Technology for Innovation, Graduate School of Engineering, The University of Tokyo, in working at BearingPoint, management and technology consulting firm as a leader of technology solution. His main research areas are cognitive science and artificial intelligence, especially an analogical thinking, to support innovative business management. An Analogy game introduced in this paper has been developed for the purpose of not only visualization of cognitive process but also searching the way of improving individual talent of value sensing, which could support various applications. He is a visiting assistant professor as well at Kanazawa Institute of technology, Graduate Program in Business Architecture. A member of Cognitive Science Society, IEEE Education, Japanese Society of Artificial Intelligence and International Academy of Strategic Management.

Lalita Narupiyakul is a post-doctoral fellow at the Faculty of Business and Information Technology in University of Ontario Institute of Technology (UOIT). She received PhD in Computer Science from Dalhousie University and PhD in Computer and Electrical Engineering from King Mongkut's University of Technology, Thailand in 2007. Her research background is in speech computing, semantic webs and web services technology areas. Currently Lalita is working on a mobile healthcare project under the supervision of Prof. Patrick Hung with the Hong Kong Red Cross, and the Chinese University of Hong Kong. She is also working on a Flash Clinical Simulation for international health care under the supervision of Prof. Jay Tashiro at the Faculty of Health Science in UOIT.

Nariaki Nishino received his B.E. and M.E. from Kobe University and Ph.D. from the University of Tokyo in 2004. He is an assistant professor of Co-creation Engineering Research Division, Research into Artifacts, Center for Engineering (RACE) at the University of Tokyo. He was a postdoctoral fellow at RACE from 2004 to 2005. He is engaged in the studies of social systems introducing the method of experimental economics and agent-based simulation. His research interests include game theories, network externalities, auction theories, and service system design. He is also active in collaborative researches on decision making problems with manufacturing and service industries in Japan.

Yukio Ohsawa, an associate professor in the School of Engineering, received M.E. and Ph.D in Communication and Information Engineering from The University of Tokyo. He worked also for School of Engineering Science in Osaka University (research associate, 1995-1999), Graduate School of Business Sciences in University of Tsukuba (associate professor, 1999-2005), and Japan Science and Technology Corporation (JST researcher, 2000-2003). He initiated the research area of Chance Discovery, and relevant series of international conference sessions and workshops. He edited the first book on "Chance Discovery" (2003) and "Chance Discoveries in Real World Decision Making" (2005) published by Springer Verlag, and special issues in international and Japanese (domestic) journals. He was in the program committee of IJCAI 2007, editorial board of a number of interdisciplinary journals, and is the TC chair of IEEE-SMC technical committee of Information Systems for Design & Marketing since 2005.

Sietse Overbeek is an assistant professor in the Information and Communication Technology section of the Faculty of Technology, Policy, and Management at Delft University of Technology, the Netherlands. His research interests include conceptual and formal modeling of information systems, ontology modeling, and service-oriented architectures. Overbeek received his PhD in computer science from the Radboud University Nijmegen, the Netherlands. He is a member of the ACM. Contact him at s.j.overbeek@tudelft.nl.

George Papaloukopoulos was born in Greece, in 1983. He graduated from the Department of Computer Engineering and Informatics, School of Engineering, University of Patras, in 2007. He received his MSc degree from the Department of Computer Engineering and Informatics, in 2010. He is now a Ph.D. Student in Computer Engineering and Informatics Department, University of Patras. His research interests include Distributed Data Management in P2P Networks, Databases and Massive Data Algorithmics. He has published 4 papers in scientific journals and refereed conferences.

Benoît Piranda has been an associate professor at the University of Franche-Comté since 2007. He received the M.S. degree in Computer Science at the University of Franche-Comte in 1994 and the Ph.D. degree at the University of Marne-La-Vallée in 1999 where he worked as an associate professor from 2000 to 2007. His research interests are Image Synthesis, Virtual Reality and Augmented Reality. He particularly focuses on real-time rendering optimization and photo-realistic image rendering.

Takeshi Shimmura, a graduate of Kinki University in 1994, received a Bachelor of Law, and a MBA from Doshisha Graduated school of Business in 2008. He is a member of the Board, Managing Director, at Ganko food service Co, ltd (Osaka, Japan), President and Chief Executive Officer at Glandscape Co, ltd (Osaka, Japan), and research adviser, at National Institute of Advanced Industrial Science and Technology. His research includes service engineering, computer sciences, ergonomics, finance, and human resource management. He is active as a committee member at human resource development program, industrial technology, Japanese Ministry of Economy, Trade and Industry, scientific and technological approach committee, Service Productivity and Innovation for Growth, He is also a research and planning committee member of Kansai Association of Corporate Executives, and an economical and financial committee member of Kansai Economic Federation.

Spyros Sioutas was born in Greece, in 1975. He graduated from the Department of Computer Engineering and Informatics, School of Engineering, University of Patras, in December 1997. He received his Ph.D. degree from the Department of Computer Engineering and Informatics, in 2002. He is now an Assistant Professor in Informatics Department of Ionian University. His research interests include Databases, Computational Geometry, GIS, Data Structures, Advanced Information Systems, P2P Networks and Web Services. He has published over 70 papers in various scientific journals and refereed conferences.

Professor Srinath holds a Ph.D. in information systems from the Berlin-Brandenburg Graduate School for Distributed Information Systems, Germany, and an MS from IIT-Madras. He works in the broad areas of web information retrieval, distributed computing, and modeling of non-linear systems. Currently, he is a member of various technical and organizational committees for international conferences, a life member of the Computer Society of India (CSI), and a member ACM. He is also the recipient of various national and international grants for his research activities.

Takeshi Takenaka is a research scientist of Large Scale Data Based Modeling Research Team, the Service Research Center (CfSR) at the National Institute of Advanced Industrial Science and Technology (AIST), Japan. He received his Ph.D. in Psychology from Kobe University in 2002, Japan. He was an associate professor at Research into Artifacts, Center for Engineering, the University of Tokyo from 2007 to 2009. His research fields are Cognitive Psychology, Service Engineering and Co-creation Engineering. His current research specifically addresses service design based on consumer's lifestyle and values. He was a member of the committee on Technology Road Map of Service Engineering hosted by Japanese Ministry of Economy, Trade and Industry (METI) in 2007 and in 2008.

Yin-Leng Theng is an Associate Professor and Associate-Chair (Research) at the Wee Kim Wee School of Communication and Information, Nanyang Technological University (Singapore). She has participated in varying capacities as principal investigator, co-investigator and collaborator in numerous research projects in the United Kingdom and Singapore since 1998. These projects involve usable and useful interfaces for hypertext systems, the Web and mobile environments; e-learning building tools and learning objects; usability evaluation techniques; and geospatial digital libraries. She has more than 90 publications and publishes widely in international journals, and conference proceedings. She has graduated two PhDs in the areas of internet ethics and cognitive user modelling, and currently supervising four PhD students in the areas of user-centred information retrieval systems, visualization of ambient information on mobile devices, value-trust models and trust propagation for social networks and social learning.

Sven Till received his master degree (Diplom Wirtschaftsinformatiker) from University of Paderborn, Germany. He has been a researcher in academia and industry in Hong Kong, Germany and the Netherlands. He has cooperated on several projects including the Pan-European project CROSSWORK which focused on Cross-Organizational Workflow formation and enactment. Besides Business Process Management and Services Computing his interests lie in Enterprise Architecture Management and Software Development Methods and their utilization in an industry context. He is currently a Senior Project Manager in an international logistics and supply chain company and works as an architect in global software projects.

Kostas Tsichlas was born in Greece, in 1976. He graduated from the Department of Computer Engineering and Informatics, School of Engineering, University of Patras, in December 1999. He received his Ph.D. degree from the Department of Computer Engineering and Informatics, in 2004. He is now a Lecturer in Informatics Department of Aristotle University. His research interests include Data Structures for Main and Secondary Memory, Design and Analysis of Algorithms, Computational Complexity, Computational Geometry, String Algorithmics (Bioinformatics — Music Analysis), Dynamic Graph Algorithms. He has published over 40 papers in various scientific journals and refereed conferences.

Gaia Varese is a Ph.D. student in Computer Science at the University of Milano, where she received her master degree in Computer Science in 2008. Her main research interests include semantic web, ontology matching, and knowledge representation and evolution. On these topics, she has been involved in the EU FP6 BOEMIE project.

Lucien Vincent is a research professor in the Ecole des Mines, Saint Etienne, France. His research interests include modelling, integration and management of Information Systems, service oriented computing and context-aware computing. Contact him at vincent@emse.fr

Liu Wenyin received his B.Engg. and M.Engg. degrees in CS from the Tsinghua University, Beijing in 1988 and 1992 respectively, and his D.Sc. from the Technion, Israel Institute of Technology in 1998. He had worked at Tsinghua as a faculty member for three years and at Microsoft Research China/Asia as a full time Researcher for another three years. He is now Asst Professor in Dept of CS at the City University of Hong Kong. Liu Wenyin played a major role in developing the MDUS system, which won First Place in the Dashed Line Recognition Contest in 1995. In 1997, he won a Third Prize in the ACM/IBM First International Java Programming Contest (ACM Quest for Java'97). In 2003, he was awarded the ICDAR Outstanding Young Researcher Award by IAPR for his significant impact in the research domain of graphics recognition, engineering drawings recognition, and performance evaluation. He is a senior member of IEEE.

Vilas Wuwongse is a Professor of Computer Science and Information Management at Asian Institute of Technology, Thailand. His research interests include information modeling, the Semantic Web and Digital Libraries. He has a BEng, MEng, and DEng from Tokyo Institute of Technology, Japan. He is a member of the IEEE Computer Society, ACM, Information Processing Society of Japan, and Japanese Society for Artificial Intelligence.

Mingjun Xiao received the Ph.D. degree from the Department of Computer Science and Technology, University of Science and Technology of China in 2004. He is currently a lecturer at the University of Science and Technology of China. His major research interests are distributed computing and information security.

Jian Yang (PhD) is an associate professor at Department of Computing, Macquarie University. She received her PhD from Australian National University in 1995. Before she joined Macquarie University, she worked as an associate professor and assistant professor at Tilburg University, Netherlands (2000-2003), a senior research scientist at the Division of Mathematical and Information Science, CSIRO, Australia (1998-2000), and as a lecturer (assistant professor) at Dept of Computer Science, Australian Defence Force Academy, University of New South Wales (1993-1998). Dr. Yang has published papers in international journals and conferences such as IEEE transactions, Information Systems, Data &Knowledge Engineering, CACM, VLDB, ICSOC, SCC, ICWS, ICDCS, CAiSE, CoopIS, CIKM, etc. Her main research interests are: e-business transaction management, web service technologies; interoperability, trust and security issues in digital libraries and e-commerce; business process modelling, query languages and query optimization; distributed query processing; social networks; materialized view design and data warehousing.

Stephen J.H. Yang received his PhD degree in Computer Science from the University of Illinois at Chicago in 1995. He is now a professor of the Department of Computer Science and Information Engineering, and is also the Associate Dean of Academic Affairs in National Central University, Taiwan. He is the co-founder and the CEO of T5 Corp, a company providing XML-based Web services. Dr. Yang has published 2 books and over 150 journal articles and conference papers. He is currently the Co-Editor-in-Chief of International Journal of Knowledge Management & E-Learning, an advisory board member of Educational Technology and Society, and an editorial board member of International Journal of Web Services Research and International Journal of Knowledge and Learning. He severed as the Program Co-Chair of IEEE MSE 2003, IEEE CAUL 2006, and IEEE W2ME 2007. His research interests include Web services, Web 2.0, software engineering, knowledge engineering, semantic Web, and context aware ubiquitous computing. He is a member of IEEE.

Ting Yu is a research fellow at the Integrated Sustainability Analysis (ISA) Group, University of Sydney. He was awarded a Ph.D in Computing Science from the University of Technology, Sydney in 2007. He received an M.sc in Distributed Multimedia System from the University of Leeds, UK, and a B.eng from the Zhejiang University, P. R. China. His research interests include Machine Learning, Data Mining, Mathematic Optimization, Parallel Computing, Applied Economic and Sustainability Analysis. Since joining the ISA, Ting Yu emphasizes on the distributed data mining and machine learning algorithms and their applications for the sustainability analysis. He is a chairman of International workshop on Machine Learning and Data Mining for Sustainable Development, and an active program committee member at the IEEE International Joint Conference on Neutral Networks.

Weiliang Zhao (PhD) is a research fellow at Department of Computing, Macquarie University. He received his PhD in information security area from University of Western Sydney in 2009, Master of Engineering from Chinese Academy of Sciences in 1991, Bachelor of Science from Peking University in 1988. Before he joined Macquarie University, he worked in Australia and New Zealand Banking Group Limited as a programmer and in Chinese Academy of Sciences as a researcher. He has published a number of research papers in international journals and conferences. His current areas of research interest include analysis and prediction for quality of services; trust management in service-oriented computing; security protocols and cryptographic techniques in E-commerce; and security for Internet applications and Web Services.

Index